PROCEEDINGS OF THE BRITISH ACADEMY · 80

# 1991 LECTURES
# and
# MEMOIRS

*Published for* THE BRITISH ACADEMY
*by* OXFORD UNIVERSITY PRESS

*Oxford University Press, Walton Street, Oxford OX2 6DP*

*Oxford New York Toronto*
*Delhi Bombay Calcutta Madras Karachi*
*Kuala Lumpur Singapore Hong Kong Tokyo*
*Nairobi Dar es Salaam Cape Town*
*Melbourne Auckland Madrid*
*and associated companies in*
*Berlin Ibadan*

*Published in the United States*
*by Oxford University Press Inc., New York*

*British Library Cataloguing in Publication Data*
*Data available*

ISBN 0–19–726124–8

*Typeset by Falcon Typographic Art Ltd, Fife, Scotland*
*Printed in Great Britain*
*on acid-fee paper*
*at the University Press, Cambridge*

# Contents

## 1991 Lectures

## Memoirs

*Proceedings of the British Academy*, **80**, 1–18

WARTON LECTURE ON ENGLISH POETRY

# Recording Angels and Answering Machines

PETER PORTER

OURS IS AN AGE dominated by brand names and logos. It's surprising therefore to discover that some of the most famous of these identity signs hark back to the very beginning of the century. On second thoughts, perhaps this isn't so strange—the nineteenth century brought nationalism out from cover, and what is a flag or a national anthem but a working logo. It has been left to our own century (on its last millenial legs, so to speak) to give such code signs an international significance once more. The multinational corporation might be considered the reincarnation of the eighteenth century's universalism, best represented by the frontier-passing style of Italian music. 'Va, pensiero' is still sung at Italian football grounds but we are far from the time when the name Verdi suggested 'Viva Emmanuele, Re d'Italia'. This is the age of Mozart, of Italia in Germania, international casts, Salzburg Americans and discs of Herbert von Karajan on special offer from Kidderminster to Kamchatka. I bring music into this since music is even more metaphorical than literature, and because the most potent signs I know are the celebrated logos owned by the great recording companies. They too date from the beginning of the century, being typical entrepreneurial oddities of a bustling new mechanical age. First there is the Dog and Trumpet, the most idiosyncratic of all, with Nipper the fox-terrier, his head in the gramophone's trumpet, listening to His Master's Voice. Then The Recording Angel, a rather Kensington Gardens putto sitting on a disc and tracing its grooves with a stylus. Finally, there are two large-scale tied semi-quavers, called Magic Notes.

Read 26 February 1991. © The British Academy 1993.

All these now belong to EMI, but they were rivals at one time, serving The Gramophone Company and the strangely-named Columbia Graphophone Company. I forbear to extend this musical signposting to other recording firms, to Decca, Deutsche Grammophon, Hyperion etc. The ones I have mentioned will suffice for my purpose, which is to help me focus on poetry in what one might describe, violin-like, as its first position.

That is, on the human voice itself. We have come a long way since poetry was the province of the bard, harp-accompanied, relating stories of war and honour. I, for one, admit to being relieved that the poetry I care most about is anchored firmly on the page. Though the paradox of oral poetry's having invented highly elaborate forms apparently *sui generis* has to be faced, I feel confident in believing that the flux of excitement in Donne, Browning and Wallace Stevens owes much to the complication permitted by unimprovisational methods and the mass-printing of the result. Nevertheless, to a greater extent than prose, poetry has not succeeded in purging itself of its shadow cabinet of voices. Much which seems objective is, in an unproveable sense, subjective.

If we concentrate for a moment on Nipper and His Master's Voice, we may approach one of the mysteries of poetry as performance. The dog is responding to a familiar tone, but being a dog he can't know what his master is saying to him unless it is something he has learned to respond to before. Although we, more than Nipper, want to learn new things from the literary voices which speak to us, we cannot do so unless they tell us what we already know and so give us a point of departure for the new. Poetry has always shown a fondness for the aphoristic mode, the parcelling-up of information and feeling in structures easily remembered and shaped by the Pleasure Principle. Where does the authority of literary utterance lie? Or, to put it another way, why are we like Nipper in not fully understanding what is being said while immediately recognizing the annunciating voice? I exaggerate, of course, but do so to stress that shock of recognition precedes enlightment by cognition. Eliot's suggestion that a poem may communicate before it is understood might be extended to proposing that it is never completely understood at all. It only becomes more familiar. Also, paradoxically, the power of the arbitrary—and I am certain that part of the authority of poetry resides in its arbitrariness—is heightened by the way it deflects expectation from the known and wanted pattern. Sonic art where all the coordinates are unfamiliar, however, would not be art but noise. What Nipper listens to are sounds, not noise—you can tell that by his concentration and the poise of his ears. At the beginning of childhood, we learn the meaning of language largely through the attractions of the rhythmic and melodic patterns which words make. I'm not suggesting that nursery rhymes for instance are just mnemonic devices; many of them were conceived for now-forgotten satirical and political purposes, and survive as attractive sequences. Time alters literary signposts and demotes even sententiousness to the minor duty of reassurance. Only the generalized satire in *Gulliver's Travels* is recognized by most modern readers, and Lilliput has become the domain of children. What is unchanged is the voice of Jonathan Swift. But children, once past the amniotic delights of words as sound patterns, go on to school and learn meanings. They usually start to read poetry some way into their formal teaching, and this means that they either wonder why it isn't straightforward ideas-carrying stuff, or they sanctify it as if it were essentially liturgical or perhaps some species of deep-thinking like philosophy. In fact, what they are hearing are their ancestral voices, not invariably prophesying war. It would be happier for all of us if we could continue to respond to poetry as Nipper did to His Master's Voice. I know I am running the risk of finding whatever I want wherever I look—as indeed Empson did when he categorized even satire as a Version of Pastoral, or Peter Conrad did later, viewing literature across five centuries as preparation for or continuation of Shandyism. But I find that there is a voice inhabiting every poem in some way or other: from the apparently 'given' tone of description or proverbial wisdom (the Voice of God perhaps) to the identifiable voice of the speaker in a Browning monologue.

Before attempting a few light clasifications of the voices which that sharp-eared Listener, Caliban, might have heard on his island wired for sound —familiar reminders stand out, 'recondita armonia' and 'Hearing Secret Harmonies'—I should like to explore my other record logo a little—the Recording Angel, and merge it with the second device in the title of this lecture. When he was anxious to reassure himself and the ghost that he was truly serious about vengeance, Hamlet announced he would wipe from his mind 'all trivial fond records', though he remained the most haunted of analysands throughout the play. When he or any of us tries to find out what the Recording Angel has filed about us, the answer may be a brush-off or an oracular message on which not even the most anxious penitent could act. Everyone here must have winced when the click comes soon after the ringing tone, and our hoped-for interlocutor's voice pronounces 'I am not in at the moment, but if you would leave your name and your message, I'll get back to you as soon as I can. Please speak after the pips.' Such friendly monstrances underlie much poetry as well. From the Bible on to modern American Language Poetry we are frequently in receipt of highly sophisticated signals stored in answering machines. It is one of the responsibilities of poetry to discourage certainty, to act against the generic conveniences of philosophy. How much more attractive than

snatches of The British Grenadiers or achoic arpeggiated chimes are the
beautiful evasions of poetry.

I said before that we go to poetry to be told what we know already, but
if the vaunted phrase 'Make it New' has any meaning beyond a polemical
call-sign, it indicates that the familiar has another dimension, like the far
side of the moon. Take, for instance, mankind's oldest habit—that of
likening things, the method of metaphor. 'Odd that a thing is most itself
when likened', as Richard Wilbur put it. What happens when the search
for assurance is answered in poetry? I could give a thousand answers in as
many poems, but Wallace Stevens's 'The Motive for Metaphor' is as good
as any. The poem goes like this:

> You like it under the trees in Autumn,
> Because everything is half dead.
> The wind moves like a cripple among the leaves
> And repeats words without meaning.
>
> In the same way you were happy in Spring,
> With the half-colours of quarter-things,
> The slightly brighter sky, the melting clouds,
> The single bird, the obscure moon —
> The obscure moon lighting an obscure world
> Of things that would never be quite expressed,
> Where you yourself were never quite yourself
> And did not want nor have to be,
>
> Desiring the exhilaration of changes:
> The motive for metaphor, shrinking from
> The weight of primary noon,
> The A B C of being,
>
> The ruddy temper, the hammer
> Of red and blue, the hard sound —
> Steel against intimation—the sharp flash,
> The vital, arrogant, fatal dominant X.

The things we shrink from are the things we make poetry out of. In another
poem, Stevens asks 'How is it that / The rivers shine and hold their mirrors
up, / Like excellence collecting excellence'. This collecting of excellence is
the Recording Angel's work; it is going on everywhere in nature and occurs
in special ways in poetry. The millions of poems the world has so far given
rise to are all intimations which the steel of reality is set against. Intimations
are made in many different voices, and I shall devote most of my time this
afternoon to checking on them, trying to find the locus from which various
sorts of being may speak. If we would listen carefully we should be able,
as Caliban was, to hear all the island's frequencies, not just the official
announcements, the public concerts and the beguiling confessions.

In the play which contains to my mind Shakespeare's most orthodox achievenment in blank verse—the epitome of iambic pentameter—*King Henry the Fifth*, some of the finest poetry is found in the speeches of the Chorus. A Chorus is an old and easily understood device. It is the equivalent of the editorializing voice of the author in a novel or set of essays. Shakespeare used the Chorus to enrich the paucity of his stage scenery, and to cover shifts in time and place. 'Think when we talk of horses that you see them/ Printing their proud hoofs i' the receiving earth' . . . etc. . . . 'Turning the accomplishment of many years into an hourglass' . . . and so on. But is it just that the Chorus insists that ''tis your thoughts that now must deck our kings', or is this out-in-the-open mouthpiece up to something else? Isn't he really giving us a glimpse of what happens all the time in poetry (and in much prose as well)—namely, language pretending that its choice among the available epithets of reality is reality itself, free of the bias of the observer and compiler? I don't want to rush this into absurdity: in practice we experience little difficulty in responding to the Chorus's evocation of the eve of the Battle of Agincourt. Yet we might ask ourselves, 'What is the point of view of the speaker?' I'll quote a part of the opening of Act Four, since I think that lectures usually include all too little poetry and because I relish this richest of blank verse, even if it has to be in my own voice.

> Now entertain conjecture of a time
> When creeping murmur and the poring dark
> Fills the wide vessel of the universe.
> From camp to camp, through the foul womb of night,
> The hum of either army stilly sounds,
> That the fix'd sentinels almost receive
> The secret whispers of each other's watch:
> Fire answers fire, and through their paly flames
> Each battle sees the other's umber'd face:
> Steed answers steed, in high and boastful neighs
> Piercing the night's dull ear; and from the tents
> The armourers, accomplishing the knights,
> With busy hammers closing rivets up,
> Give dreadful note of preparation.
> The country cocks do crow, the clocks do toll,
> And the third hour of drowsy morning name.
> Proud of their numbers, and secure in soul,
> The confident and over-lusty French
> Do the low-rated English play at dice;
> And chide the cripple tardy-gaited night
> Who, like a foul and ugly witch, doth limp
> So tediously away. The poor condemned English,

Like sacrifices, by their watchful fires
Sit patiently, and inly ruminate
The morning's danger, and their gestures sad
Investing lank-lean cheeks and war-worn coats
Presenteth them unto the gazing moon
So many horrid ghosts.

That is half the Chorus's speech. He goes on to praise the king, telling of
how cheering the English soldiers find a visit from this paladin, with his
liberal eye, universal like the sun, giving them their 'little touch of Harry
in the night.' This last almost Monty Python phrase crowns the partisan
tone of the second part of the speech, but it's worth wondering what the
first section does to our sense of expectation. The partisanship here is not
predominently that of English versus French, but of a Cecil B. deMille-type
producer expending a lavish poetical budget on a nightpiece whose reality
might well put the theatre patrons off. Shakespeare's command of realism
misleads us beautifully: in telling the truth to our senses, he lies to our
understanding. I wouldn't have it any other way—if you want the truth
about war, you must fight in it and discover that any words further than
the blankest and most communiqué -like will misrepresent it. Whatever
one thinks of Yeats's attack on Wilfrid Owen's war poetry—'all blood,
dirt and sucked sugar-stick'—there is no good reason to believe Owen's
own assertion that the poetry is in the pity. He would have written very
differently had that been the case. The poetry is in the language. And
we are seeing at this moment, sadly, that the language of poetry cannot
match computerized technology. High Tech wars drain all poetry from
the world; they become video games leaving only charred bodies behind.
Even Shakespeare could do nothing with Baghdad and smart bombs.
The hard rule is that poetry has to be loyal to language, to Stevens's
'essential gaudiness.' Poetry was one of the consolations offered Adam
and his partner after their expulsion from the garden. It was the rainbow
of lies over Eden when the natural vision faded. Laertes, looking at mad
Ophelia, noted that 'Thought and afflictions, passion, hell itself/ She turns
to favour and to prettiness'. At this point I can hear the voice of George
Herbert, a poet whose genius might be said to derive from his passion
for truth—and then also of Samuel Beckett whose progress was from an
almost Yeatsian extravagance (I think Joyce is not to the point here) to
the nothingness of his last-breath last works. Yet what all these have in
common is a falsification which is built into language, and each knows
that beauty alone will justify their efforts—or, if not beauty, at least some
sort of pleasure in the shaping of truth beyond its commitment to right
behaviour. It is exactly if not precisely the voice inside the words which we
believe in, and which gives us the satisfaction we call art. A poem quite as

much as a painting, a piece of sculpture or a musical composition is a made object—its difference from these other artworks lies in the raw material it is made from—language, words and their couplings, mere symbols, not their own creatures. Right from the start poetry has had to put up a fight against meaning which painting and music have hardly been bothered by. In our century we have made this battle the very subject of poetry. It isn't easy to take sides honestly: just as you are about to rejoice in a juicy collection of non sequiturs in one of John Ashbery's poems, the voice of conscience calls you back to the obligations not just of meaning but of emotional congruity. The long poetic career of W. H. Auden reveals a steady tug of conscience away from Edenic arbitrariness to a dour reticence made up of short views and trust in God. But the Old Adam isn't suppressed so easily—witness Auden's habit of fitting up his later verses with a special camp or nonce vocabulary. His lexical sweet tooth remains in danger of becoming carious, to borrow a phrase of Stravinsky's. But he loves to warn us of the dangers of poetical independence which can so readily lead to showing-off and smugness. His poem 'September 1st., 1939' quickly became one of his most popular. Almost equally quickly it earned its author's distrust, especially the stanza which everyone loved to quote, and which Auden excised from the poem as soon as he could.

> All I have is a voice
> To undo the folded lie,
> The romantic lie in the brain
> Of the sensual man-in-the-street
> And the lie of Authority
> Whose buildings grope the sky:
> There is no such thing as the State
> And no one exists alone;
> Hunger allows no choice
> To the citizen or the police;
> We must love one another or die.

Ostensibly it was the last line which so offended the poet. That 'or die' should have been 'and die', he stated. I wonder though whether it wasn't the admission that all he had was a voice which stuck in Auden's throat. It is one of those boastful confessions poets love to make: we want to be contradicted or to be allowed to assert shyly that our voices are more important than Authority's buildings or the duties of citizens and policemen. The suppressor of this stanza is the Auden who found Pacifism dishonest and insisted on taking seriously his democratic duties of voting and doing jury service. But a poet can't turn his voice into that of a divine or a philosopher without surrendering his older oracular powers. The young Auden was certainly oracular—who is this new guy who's got into the landscape? Wyndham Lewis asked. The older Auden too reverted from time to time to warnings of a more paradoxical sort, as in the coda to his poem 'The Truest Poetry is the Most Feigning.'

> For given Man, by birth, by education,
> Imago Dei who forgot his station,
> The self-made creature who himself unmakes,
> The only creature ever made who fakes,
> With no more nature in his loving smile
> Than in his theories of a natural style,
> What but tall tales, the luck of verbal playing,
> Can trick his lying nature into saying
> That love, or truth in any serious sense,
> Like orthodoxy, is a reticence.

So, we are to attain Christian reserve by being playful—perhaps the only time Auden and Wallace Stevens might be thought to be speaking to the same text. I said earlier that the battle between poetry's atavism and literature's responsibility has hotted up this century. Both Modernism (a fairly unclear concept) and Post Modernism (a desperately unclear one) seem to me centred on the problem of meaning—*Voice versus Meaning* is an aesthetic current running through poetry since Robert Browning. It may even be glimpsed in Pope's medium-length essay-poems: compare the prose advertisements which Pope sometimes appends to them. The poetry flows with the brilliance of a sonata-form exposition: it feels utterly convincing, the sound leading the sense by the hand. It is, however, as the advertisement makes plain, a daisy-chain of argument put forward with little logic beyond its rhetoric. I find this the case with the *Moral Essays* and The *Essay on Man*, though not with the very early, perfectly crafted *Essay on Criticism*. In Pope's mature poems it is the Voice of The Master which the dog is devoted to, rather than the Master's message. Such anxiety can produce a kind of poetic paralysis. Perhaps I may justify my quoting two lines of my own poetry, by pleading my envious bafflement when reading modern virtuosi of the opulently oblique.

> Wonderful for those who keep away
> from meaning, living somewhere better –

That 'somewhere better' has always been with us, but only since Robert Browning has it appeared in its secular self-sufficency, not serving a larger cause. So many elaborate contrivances, often wreathed in tendrils of erudition, have been handed down to us by poets whose concern was to promote a theology, a world view or a commanding orthodoxy. I admit the case could be put the other way round: *Sir Gawain and the Green Knight* and *Orlando Furioso* might appear to serve Christianity in order that they can indulge in poetry. We have been warned very severely about this—'don't read the Bible for its prose', we're admonished. Attitudes like Neville Cardus's, who said that if he knew that his Redeemer liveth it was because Handel had asserted the fact, seem very outdated and Manchester Liberal. Yet I'm sure many of us wonder when we look at Pontormo's Deposition in Santa Felicità, Florence, or listen to Josquin's setting of Psalm 51 whether their depth of feeling must of necessity spring from dogmatic conviction. It is the service which counts: the reward for that service is a whole society, vocabulary and range of reference from which artistic constructions can be properly made.

The voice of poetry up until the nineteenth century was a Christian voice. It didn't matter too much how seriously the artist believed in his theology; he had no alternative but to employ Christian language and symbols. I don't think we should be nostalgic about this—I mean about some of us having lost such certainty. I deplore the sort of seriousness T. S. Eliot uses to reprimand Shakespeare's lines in *King Lear* 'As flies to wanton boys, are we to the gods;/ They kill us for their sport.' when set beside Dante's 'la sua voluntade è nostra pace'. To be fair, Eliot does not make his comparison on poetic grounds but on philosophical ones. Even so, I smell a sort of snobbery in his and Pound's elevation of Dante's alliegance to an organic Christendom over Shakespeare's local and proverbial loyalties. In practice, Shakespeare's plays rely on Europe's classical inheritance and on the Bible as much as *The Divine Comedy* does: think of the passage in *The Merchant of Venice* beginning 'When Jacob grazed his uncle Laban's sheep.' One could go on and cite Dante's Florentine spite as being more parochial than anything in Shakespeare. Shakespeare's fault for Eliot is his unwillingness to be prescriptive: he hears too many voices and speaks in too many accents to be trusted.

From the beginning of our verse, English poets have couched their poems in other men's and women's voices, but it is with Robert Browning that the monologue became dramatic and assumed the centre of the poetic arena. His practice tried not only to pack a whole play's dramatis personae into one usurping voice but also to allow that singleton to editorialize as it saw fit. This is to put a gloss on the view of the Browningesque monologue (and since Browning these have sprouted up everywhere) that it should be thought of as a key speech in a play which doesn't exist but which it creates around itself as ectoplasm. In his cruder moments we can see Browning lifting the stage directions up into the text—'put up your torches . . . No more wine, then we'll push back our chairs and talk' . . . and so on. But usually his technique is much subtler: he has led whole generations of poets to experiment by fitting analysis and criticism marsupially in their poems; Byron's 'Every poet his own Aristotle' almost achieved.

Browning's separation of the key speech from its context implied or immersed is, I believe, the basic technique which many contemporary poets employ. There is fairly general critical agreement that, despite his fondness for archaic diction and 'poetical' word-order, Browning is the father of Anglo-American Modernism. Pound thought so: Eliot kept off the subject, but relied heavily on Browning in poems such as *Prufrock* and *Gerontion*. However, the real revolution wrought by Browning was quieter than the noisy manoeuvrings of Pound. It wrested scope and seriousness from novel, play and biography—even from natural history—and gave it back to poetry. There was something to be done in poetry beyond satisfying the lyrical impulse, the sub-division of a whole landscape into its song lines, a task entrusted to *The Golden Treasury*. When the modern poet sits down to write he has Browning to thank for several circumstances which he probably takes for granted. Firstly, he can use any voice he pleases, and not necessarily have to identify it. Secondly, he can assume that the reader does not think that the world he evokes will be taken for objective reality. Thirdly, he can find his material anywhere, and weave it into his poem and so make it his own. The voice in modern poetry is tantamount to instant baptism: it makes poetical whatever it incorporates. It has no attitude to poetic stock; no preferred diction; and no prescribed ethical or aesthetic duty. Browning changed the coordinates by which poetry is recognized. Out went recitative and aria; in came the style the Germans call 'durchkomponiert', through composed, continuous melody. The chief gain was poetry's escape from a ghetto of appropriateness. The poet ate further down the table from the salt, but he ate more voraciously.

The least cluttered of Browning's monologues are soliloquies on which the reader is a simple eavesdropper. In 'Up at a Villa, down in the City' subtitled 'As distinguished by an Italian Person of Quality', you hear about Italian life but it doesn't matter who you are. 'Soliloquy in a Spanish Cloister', on the other hand, seems to be addressed to another and sympathetic colleague, one expected to share the speaker's distaste for Brother Laurence. The reader then becomes the second listener. 'Up at a Villa' is the better poem, but 'Soliloquy' is a more sophisticated structure. Sometimes in a Browning monologue the interlocutor is part of the *mise-en-scène*. Talking to one's own sort, 'One of Us' as you might say, a voice will more readily reveal its nastiness—a method beautifully illustrated in 'My Last Duchess'. The ideal listener might be God, on the other side of his universal confessional—or God being invented as the poem progresses. In 'Caliban Upon Setebos', Caliban wants God to congratulate him on some pretty good detective work. There is another sub-title, 'Natural Theology on the Island', and Caliban is trapped by the island's lush-growing hypotheses.

In Browning's hands the monologue becomes a Protean device, a path poetry may adopt to open the whole world to its investigations. There is no subject for which the poet cannot establish a relevant voice. From the one voice in charge of revelation come many voices, as Browning diversifies into highly complicated shapes. With his Tarnhelm on, Browning slithers into the various genres: 'Andrea del Sarto' (Vasari versified); 'Childe Roland to the Dark Tower Came' (bonsai ballad-opera); 'How It Strikes a Contemporary' (literary criticism); 'A Grammarian's Funeral' (literary theory); and the later 'Parleyings' (self-education as autobiography). One thing which strikes the reader of Browning each time he goes back to the poems is their bookishness. This is another reason for considering him the Father of Us All. Browning's English and Italian characters alike exhibit a convincing small-town worldliness, a conspiratorial scribblers' ambience, a freshly-coined opinionatedness. The world has been metamorphosed into talkative figures obliged to get everything down, and from all points of view. Apotheosis arrives with *The Ring and the Book*, that twelve-part *Rashomon*, suggesting that truth belongs to the garrulous. Browning satisfies the haranguer who is in each of us. We are born, we talk and we die. Chiefly we talk, and when we meet a good talker we listen. The world turns into words. The Recording Angel becomes our Chief Solliloquizer, and the message on the Answering Machine is 'Keep Talking.'

Fashion has changed since Browning's day. So when we look for his influence in poetry written this century we might miss it, thwarted by his Victorian love of inclusiveness, of preferring connections to cryptic omissions. Even here we should note that a poet may be mysterious to the point of eschewing Victorian accountability and yet preserve a Victorian opulence—I am thinking of John Ashbery's extended poem 'Self Portrait in a Convex Mirror'. This is the very model of the modern monologue, though its talking heads are hydra-like. They all sprout from one art-historical, philosophical neck. For all his shining New York stylishness, Ashbery might be called 'Le Browning de nos Jours'. He is as fond of writing about artists as Browning was. In 'Self Portrait', Parmigianino, for me and I guess for Ashbery as well, the most technically accomplished painter who ever lived, is in and out of Ashbery's own distorting mirror. The I of the poem is that modern I (not spelled eye) which we are certainly not to conclude is the poet, but which must include him. The other pronouns are likely to fail an identity parade as well. As the self breaks up in dreams, so in Ashbery's poem the true voice of feeling becomes a feast of ventriloquism. Everything is explained, but then we add another word—*away*. One American critic

has referred to the 'Self Portrait' as a mysterious and beautiful response
to Whitman's invitation to American poets to loaf and invite their souls.
But Parmigianino is more intellectual and more European than that and
Ashbery's poem is too dandified to be Whitmanesque. What the mirror
is to Parmigianino, the oil slick of associations is to Ashbery. You cannot
get any deeper, you can only go wider. The soul can't accept all its
invitations.

> The soul has to stay where it is,
> Even though restless, hearing raindrops at the pane,
> The sighing of autumn leaves thrashed by the wind,
> Longing to be free, outside, but it must stay
> Posing in this place. It must move
> As little as possible. This is what the portrait says.
> But there is in that gaze a combination
> Of tenderness, amusement and regret, so powerful
> In its restraint that one cannot look for long.
> The secret is too plain. The pity of it smarts,
> Makes hot tears spurt: that the soul is not a soul,
> Has no secret, is small, and it fits
> The hollow perfectly: its room, our moments of attention.
> That is the tune but there are no words.
> The words are only speculation
> (From the Latin *speculum*, mirror):
> They seek but cannot find the meaning of the music.
> We see only postures of the dream,
> Riders of the motion that swings the face
> Into view under evening skies, with no
> False disarray as proof of authenticity.
> But it is life englobed.
> One would like to stick one's hand
> Out of the globe, but its dimension,
> What carries it, will not allow it.

What I called the fight between Voice and Meaning is neatly placed in
this passage (one characteristic of Ashbery in seeming self-sufficient but
in fact a small part of a long poem). In imagination and in inspiration—in
the head or in the dream—you will find what Ashbery calls the tune.
But on the page there are only the words. The meaning of the music
will never, in any easy sense, be the meaning of the words. Which is
why poets go on writing. They are musicians by other means. I have
always been suspicious of analogies in the arts—poet as sculptor, frozen
music, unacknowledged legislator etc.—but I do find a useful parallel in
poetry's and music's use of thematic development. Also, I feel in my
bones that music is the 'Ur-Kunst', the one from which all the others
spring, despite its apparent late development as Europe's premier art.

The bias in any sort of scale, even in a twelve-note row, is a musical strait-jacket equivalent to the poet's, who has to use symbols (words) invented for purposes more utilitarian than his. Both poet and musician have to put up with the paradox that their opportunities for extravagance are less good in these free-thinking times than they were when every artist had to appear to serve a cause beyond himself. But as Ashbery, Stevens, and a whole range of modern poets show, the need for disguises is as great as ever. Today's inquisitors, however, are the aestheticians and theorists.

It may seem to many who have followed me so far that I have been playing about irresponsibly with serious matters—nothing less than poetry's power to move its readers and listeners, and its duty to promote good and demote evil. Anybody on his feet on an occasion like this should try to imagine what Milton would think of the course of his argument. But that would be Milton the law-giver, moral revolutionary and republican polemicist. Milton the poet is another matter. Though they hold strong views, like any other member of the public, poets do not necessarily keep those views in sight when they sit down to write. They look to criticism to help them follow their own track, to trace the voices in their words. Critics, of course, would rather grade them like eggs. There is no help for this. Another poem of Ashbery's makes it clear that a poet may be aware that his performance sets up difficulties of tone and language. It's titled *Paradoxes and Oxymorons*.

> This poem is concerned with language on a very plain level.
> Look at it talking to you. You look out a window
> Or pretend to fidget. You have it but you don't have it.
> You miss it, it misses you. You miss each other.
>
> The poem is sad because it wants to be yours, and cannot.
> What's a plain level? It is that and other things,
> Bringing a system of them into play. Play?
> Well, actually, yes, but I consider play to be
> A deeper outside thing, a dreamed role-pattern,
> As in the division of grace these long August days
> Without proof. Open-ended. And before you know
> It gets lost in the steam and chatter of typewriters.
>
> It has been played once more. I think you exist only
> To ease me into doing it, on your level, and then you aren't there
> Or have adopted a different attitude. And the poem
> Has set me softly down beside you. The poem is you.

Many people, myself included, find it tiresome that modern poets make 'the poem' the hero of their productions. But then we find ourselves doing it. The reason is that we have so many voices in our heads and levels of responsibility in our understanding, that we cannot be innocent listeners. The very art we practise has taken over the role of nascent reality. It would be good to see and hear things freshly, and perhaps we can only do that if we recognize all the programmes we've been listening to, whether we wish to recall them or not. As Stevens wrote, 'Tell X that speech is not dirty silence/ Clarified. It is silence made still dirtier.' In Ashbery's quatrains the poem which sits down next to his up-to-date Miss Muffet will certainly frighten her away. To learn about the self is usually frightening. It is hard to imagine any authorial disdain friendlier than Ashbery's. What distinguishes him from many fellow domesticated Surrealists is the authenticity of the material he makes his poems from. They are never the sayings of a man in an isolation ward, though they do insist on being heard in their own voice—that is, as interim statements, messages perhaps intended for bottles. Behind his highly aesthetic surface, the real muddled world of America lurks. But reality is judged as no more real than any other verbal manifestation. If imagination, rather than reality is to be celebrated, then the number of possibilities is limitless, and Ashbery is deliberately inclusive, though not in the Victorina mode. He is unworried by the most hair-raising of non sequiturs. In another poem he reminds us that the artist 'often . . . finds/ He has omitted the thing he started out to say/ In the first place . . .' To the eager anticipator of truth and beauty the answer on the machine is likely to be something completely different. The only thing a poem shouldn't be is less generous than its questioner.

One of the difficulties in talking about contemporary poetry seldom gets aired in serious quarters. It is too close to the bone. Namely, that we are too many, as Yeats observed in *The Cheshire Cheese*. Reference books exist which list more than 2,000 poets living and working in the English-speaking world alone. The usual, perhaps the humane, if not the generous, reaction to this is to narrow the field to a workable canon, and to neglect everything else. After all, Jonathan Swift observed long ago, 'Say, Britain, could you ever boast/Three poets in an age at most'. The combination of intense competition among poets and an absence of any universally agreed style greatly emphasizes the individual voice. Again—and this will be the last time – I'd like to quote from one of my own poems —

> the trouble is the shock,
> too much talent in the world, it can't absorb
> its own creation; there are queues in Heaven
> as the million dreams fight to be born
> and troop before the face of vindication —

It was all very well for Auden to say that originality was the last thing he looked for in poetry—in practice he was not so reactionary. It might even be worth asking whether the craftsmen who carved the face of Chartres Cathedral were as anonymous in their own time as historians sometimes say they were. A lingua franca may help a great artist find his individual voice, not bury him beneath its uniform outlines. The point remains, though, that as the next millenium approaches, we have no way of authenticating new verse beyond the resonance set up in us by its personal accents. Discussion of technique, of historical necessity and of prevailing theory will continue, but the critic will have to be more of a talent-spotter than a quality control inspector.

In attempting to delineate the way voice underlies and subverts meaning in poetry I have found it easier to traverse what one might call the flats and maynes of the twentieth century than to dwell on the larger achievements of the past—other than one foray into Shakspeare and a dip into Browning. (As a momentary aside, it is worth stressing that Shakespeare has the most compellingly individual voice of all, despite his shadowy biography and his indifference to publication. The more cryptic his utterance the more personal his sound. Compare his sonnets with Sidney's *Astrophel and Stella*. The difference is between the gamiest Freudian case-history and Amateur Night in the Petrarchan Academy. Shakespeare's poet-hero is the Rat-Man of the High Renaissance.)

I want to end by examining two well-known poems from the past where I believe some enlightenment may come from considering the voice or voices which inhabit them. First, one of Wordsworth's lyrics, 'A Complaint.'

> There is a change and I am poor;
> Your love hath been, nor long ago,
> A Fountain at my fond Heart's door,
> Whose only business was to flow;
> And flow it did; not taking heed
> Of its own bounty, or my need.
> What happy moments did I count!
> Blessed was I then all bliss above!
> Now, for this consecrated Fount
> Of murmuring, sparkling, living love,
> What have I? Shall I dare to tell?
> A comfortless and hidden WELL.
>
> A Well of love—it may be deep —
> I trust it is, and never dry:
> What matter? if the Waters sleep
> In silence and obscurity.

Such change, and at the very door
Of my fond Heart, hath made me poor.

Not being a Wordsworth man, I first encountered this poem when a student
in Perth Western Australia brought it to me and asked me what it meant.
At first, it didn't seem difficult. I was sure that it was not a love poem in
the usual sense. Nevertheless, it borrowed from that well-tried convention.
I decided it was an affecting example of the love poem directed to a side of
life all too little explored in poetry—collegiate loyalty, masculine sodality.
Which gave it a pleasant irony if you considered that Browning was to set
Wordsworth up as 'The Lost Leader' some years after this was written.
But I was too lazy to discover who Wordsworth had in mind. The tone and
some of the locutions interested me, however. A sort of selfish grievance
pervades the poem. There is no examination of why the fountain played
for him in the first place. In this the similarity to an erotic love poem is
strong—how dare you take away the bounty I've grown accustomed to.
'Whose only business was to flow' is a bit of cheek, though not taking
heed of its own bounty or his need does seem more generous. The final
couplet is hard to take if one wants to go on admiring Wordsworth. At
no time does he take his mind off his own need. Such a fond heart as his
might seem to others a rather greedy one. Lazy as I was, I suppose I knew
he was writing about Coleridge. My question now is whether identifying
Coleridge as the turned-off fountain makes any significant difference to
one's reception of the poem. Beyond this, there is the whole question
of the Theophrastian voice in poetry, and how far it underwrites any
particular set of circumstances. Thus, if I sit down to compose a poem
ostensibly descriptive of someone's inadequacy or felony, will I cunningly
put myself in the right by adopting well-tried modes of accusation? Further
off lurks the worry about all those pronouns poetry bristles with. The
second person pronoun has a long history of evasivensss in the accusatory
mouth of the first person pronoun, well before today's slippery lyrics. Yet
my initial reaction to Wordsworth's poem was not significantly different
from my more measured assessment once I'd read it up. Suspicion was
there from the start. Like Nipper with his head in the trumpet, I could
recognize something in this voice. Let me call it egotism, and perhaps
pompous outrage.

My second poem is by a man who has one of the most distinctive
voices in English verse—in fact, I think only Emily Dickinson's among
non-dramatic poets is as singular and powerful—that is John Donne.
Reading a Donne poem is an immediate test of what we mean by
sincerity. Stravinsky's aphorism helps as a start—Sincerity, he wrote, is
the *sine qua non* which proves nothing. All artists are sincere and bad

artists are sincerely bad. Therefore plain speaking and baroque elaboration are two kinds of sincerity. Donne's *Holy Sonnets* are especially alarming in that their strident arguing is conducted within the poet's own mind: it is not yet ready to appear dressed up as public rhetoric. The polemicist who was eager to be a bought pen for King James in his battles with the Continental Counter Reformation here turns on himself intemperately. The voice is hysterical, as is the sense of guilt. I find Donne's *idée fixe* of sin a baroque narcotic which limits my taste for these poems. I was able to understand them better once I appreciated that they are not spiritual exercises after ordination but come from the restless period of his life when he was still hoping for court preferment and was fighting a losing battle against the drift, king-propelled, directing him towards a career in the clergy. But, internal as the accusation is, we know it is tooling-up for the senate of world opinion. Those overbearing sermons are just over the horizon. You feel that in a secular age Donne would have been just as tortured—his way to God is through extremity, indeed flamboyance. He has no straight way as Herbert has. Though I don't trust this poetic voice, I can luxuriate in it. Here is No. 13 of Donne's *Holy Sonnets*.

> What if this present were the world's last night?
> Mark in my heart, O Soul, where thou dost dwell,
> The picture of Christ crucified, and tell
> Whether that countenance can thee afright,
> Tears in his eyes quench the amazing light,
> Blood fills his frowns, which from his pierced head fell.
> And can that tongue adjudge thee unto hell,
> Which prayed forgiveness of his foes' fierce spite?
> No, no; but as in my idolatry
> I said to all my profane mistresses,
> Beauty, of pity, foulness only is
> A sign of rigour: so I say to thee,
> To wicked spirits are horrid shapes assigned,
> This beauteous form assures a piteous mind.

Is this what Empson called 'argufying' or is it a piece of holy writhing? I am as uncomfortable with Donne's tone as I am when in the presence of Bernini's Saint Teresa. It's funny how the baroque fits music more happily than it does poetry or the architectural arts. The final couplet is a candidate for Auden's excising pencil—surely it is a sort of lie. Would you buy a map of penitence from this man? Yet could anyone with the temerity to imitate Christ so fulsomely adopt a more effective manner of doing it? It was while reading Donne that I first appreciated that meaning is the method and voice is the message. Such an insight may be poor criticism, but it is a useful nudge to composition.

There is, as I have acknowledged all thorugh this lecture, a world of seriousness which poets must serve which is not responsive to stylistic analysis. This is the harmonious world, the mathematical universe. It is largely deaf to poets' games and contrivances. You get a chilling glimpse of it in Rochester's brief translation of some lines from Lucretius.

> The gods, by right of nature, must possess
> An everlasting age of perfect peace;
> Far off removed from us and our affairs;
> Neither approached by dangers, or by cares;
> Rich in themselves, to whom we cannot add;
> Not pleased by good deeds, nor provoked by bad.

In the meantime, we serve an interventionist world, raising our voices and leaving messages for anyone who'll listen to them. I think again of Auden, parting from Stravinsky one night after much talk and drink; no doubt well past his usual bedtime. 'After all,' he remarked, 'we were put on this earth to make things'; His was the voice of poetry encouraging the voice of music.

*Proceedings of the British Academy*, **80**, 19–48

SIR JOHN RHŶS MEMORIAL LECTURE

# The Folk and the *Gwerin*:
# The Myth and the Reality of
# Popular Culture in
# 19th-Century Scotland and Wales

## CHRISTOPHER HARVIE
*University of Tübingen*

# I

IT MAY SEEM FLIPPANT to start with a 'Spot the *Gwerin*' contest, but it's useful as a means of providing a definition. Here are two candidates, separated by a century:

> A country where the entire people is, or even once has been, laid hold of, filled to the heart with an infinite religious idea, has 'made a step from which it cannot retrograde.' Thought, conscience, the sense that man is denizen of a Universe, creature of an Eternity, has penetrated to the remotest cottage, to the simplest heart. Beautiful and awful, the feeling of a Heavenly Behest, of Duty God-commanded, over-canopies all life.[1]

> We were a tribe, a family, a people.
> Wallace and Bruce guard now a painted field,
> And all may read the folio of our fable,
> Peruse the sword, the sceptre and the shield.

Read 7 March 1991. © The British Academy 1993.

[1] 'Sir Walter Scott' in the *London and Westminster Review*, Vols i-iv, 1837, reprinted in *Scottish and other Miscellanies* (London: Dent, n.d.), p. 71. I would like to express my thanks to Principal Kenneth O. Morgan FBA for the invitation to deliver this paper. As a non-Welsh speaker I have been greatly aided in preparing and revising it for publication by my friend Professor Ieuan Gwynedd Jones, Aberystwyth, whom I would particularly like to thank for his patience in translating Welsh terms and summarizing the arguments of Welsh writers. The mistakes which remain are my own.

A simple sky roofed in that rustic day,
The busy corn-fields and the haunted holms,
The green road winding up the ferny brae.
But Knox and Melville clapped their breaching palms
And bundled all the harvesters away,
Hoodicrow Peden in the blighted corn
Hacked with his rusty beak the starving haulms.
Out of that desolation we were born.

Courage beyond the point and obdurate pride
Made us a nation, robbed us of a nation.
Defiance absolute and myriad-eyed
That could not pluck the palm plucked our damnation.
We with such courage and the bitter wit
To fell the ancient oak of loyalty,
And strip the peopled hill and the altar bare,
And crush the poet with an iron text,
How could we read our souls and learn to be?[2]

Plainly the *Gwerin* – the Welsh image of popular democracy – in Prys
Morgan's definition,

> a classless society, progressing rapidly yet retaining a closeness to the soil,
> educated, religious, cultured, keen to own its own land and property,
> hard-working and methodical, law-abiding, temperate in drink, respecting
> the sabbath, and an example to the world . . .[3]

is present in the first, which is an extract from Thomas Carlyle's review
of Lockhart's *Life of Sir Walter Scott* (1838) – in the ideal of a religion-
penetrated people. In the second, Edwin Muir's 'Scotland 1941', the
poet indicts Calvinism with the destruction of the Scottish sense of
community, and locates it on an uncomfortable ground: it 'made us a
nation, robbed us of a nation'. That my task isn't an easy one, even these
citations show. Religious enthusiasts found Carlyle a disturbing, infidel
presence; Muir the Orcadian, as apprehensive in dealing with 'Scotland'
as any *Gwerinwr* confronted by 'cosmopolitan South Wales', regarded the
great industrial city, like Calvinism, as an alien intrusion on his ideal of
nationality.[4]

---

[2] Edwin Muir, 'Scotland 1941' in *Collected Poems* (London: Faber, 1960).

[3] Prys Morgan, 'The *Gwerin* of Wales – Myth and Reality' (1967), revised, translated and
rpt. in I. Hume and W. T. R. Pryce, *The Welsh and their Country* (Llandysul: Gomer
Press, 1986), p. 139.

[4] Edwin Muir, *Scottish Journey* (London: Heinemann, 1935), pp. 102-3, quoted in G. F. A.
Best, 'The Scottish Victorian City' in *Victorian Studies*, Vol XI (1967-8), p.330. Muir in 1948
became the first Principal of Newbattle Abbey College, which was consciously modelled on
Coleg Harlech.

In this exercise I hope I've shown that, in Scotland, something close to the Welsh myth of the *Gwerin* not only existed but both preceded and followed the flowering of the ideal in Wales, which Prys Morgan locates between the years 1880 and 1914. When David Jenkins translates the term as 'a man of the commonalty' the parallelism increases, both through the use of the figure 'John the Commonweal' by Sir David Lyndesay in his morality *The Thrie Estaitis* (1540) to embody the popular impulse which led to the Scots reformation, and through the use of the word 'commonwealth' by the Scots political scientist James Bryce to describe his democratic ideal in the later 19th century.[5]

This adds to the resonance of various 'is that a fact?' connections between the two countries at this time: the influence of Thomas Chalmers on Calvinist Methodist doctrine and culture; the sixth Marquess of Bute bankrolling various Scottish nationalist publications and groups out of his Cardiff income; Keir Hardie in Merthyr; the young Tom Jones in the Glasgow of Edward Caird and Sir Henry Jones; the young Christopher Murray Grieve imbibing the class struggle while a cub reporter on the *Monmouthshire Labour News*.[6]

'Is that a fact?' of course invites the response 'So what?' Is it worthwhile pinning down a myth? I think so. Myth can be used to 'order' reality. A Welsh historian writing about Scotland, Robert Anderson, takes the 'myth' of Scottish education seriously:

> The belief that Scottish education was peculiarly 'democratic', and that it helped to sustain certain correspondingly democratic features of Scottish life, formed a powerful historical myth, using that word to indicate not something false, but an idealization and distillation of a complex reality, a belief which influences history by interacting with other forces and pressures, ruling out some developments as inconsistent with the national tradition, and shaping the form in which the institutions inherited from the past are allowed to change.[7]

Myth, properly contextualized, is more than an ideological projection, it contributes not just to belief systems but to policy.

---

[5] David Jenkins, *The Agricultural Community in South-West Wales at the Turn of the Twentieth Century* (Cardiff: University of Wales Press, 1971), p. 35; and see Thomas Kleinknecht, *Imperiale und internationale Ordnung: eine Untersuchung zum Gelehrtenliberalismus am Beispiel von James Bryce, 1838-1922* (Gottingen: Vandenhoeck und Ruprecht, 1985), particularly pp. 59ff.

[6] H. J. Hanham, *Scottish Nationalism* (London: Faber, 1969), pp. 83-5; Thomas Jones, *Welsh Broth* (London: W Griffiths, 1951), pp. 1-80; Kenneth O. Morgan, *James Keir Hardie* (London: Weidenfeld and Nicolson, 1976), pp. 112ff.; Alan Bold, *Hugh MacDiarmid* (London: John Murray, 1988), pp. 63-7.

[7] R. D. Anderson, *Education and Opportunity in Victorian Scotland: Schools and Universities* (Oxford: Clarendon Press, 1983) p. 1.

The democratic 'myth' was always in the past placed in the dock by the 'economic interpretation of history': as one of the dodgier of the *faux frais* of production. For Gwyn A. Williams, writing in the 1970s, the *gwerin* was the 'pseudo-nation of Welsh dissent', an elitist means of disremembering both the sweeping population movements of the period and the industrial proletariat who were the true bearers of historical change. Matthew Price's academic task in Raymond Williams's *Border Country* (1961) is to 'measure the distance': to assess the social consequences of these population movements which, in Williams' implied judgement, the 'Welsh' tradition had ignored.[8]

By the 1960s this dismissal itself was under challenge, politically with the Liberal and nationalist intervention into two-party class-based politics, and academically through John Vincent's discovery of Ralf Dahrendorf and Peter Clarke's reanimation of the 'new Liberalism'. Economic class-consciousness was thereafter regarded as neither inevitable not actual; in Clarke's phrase: 'classes are essentially groups in conflict about power'.[9] In this context, Labour's rise at the beginning of the twentieth century had more to do with the malfunctions of ideology and 'organized', if not 'high', politics than with any dramatic change of allegiance at the grass roots. The *gwerin* were not dead but merely slumbering, like – who else? – Arthur and his knights under some interesting hill.

In the late 1980s this line received a boost from two apparently contradictory phenomena: the collapse of a self-proclaimed Marxian political order in East Europe, with the reinstatement of 'civil society' and the role within it of ethical judgement and 'public doctrine'; and the survival of patterns of political behaviour in Scotland and Wales which in the 1980s seemed simultaneously to transcend the decline of the economic structure of class politics and the acquisitive individualism of Thatcherite England. The miners marching back to Mardy Colliery in 1985 with their banners flying were the losers in an industrial conflict who seemed at the same time to breathe new (or old?) communitarian loyalties into life. Scots miners, with other Scots radicals in Holyrood Park in June 1987, cast a cool eye on Neil Kinnock while applauding the veteran Communist Mick McGahey as a symbol of the qualities which had just decimated the Scottish Conservatives. Both events seemed to echo not just the symbolism of 1926 – as potent in Scots as in Welsh culture – but the impact of the Penrhyn

---

[8] In Prys Morgan, art.cit., p. 146; Raymond Williams, *Border Country* (1961, Harmondsworth: Penguin, 1964), p. 333.

[9] See John Vincent, 'The Political Feelings of the People' in *Poll-Books: How Victorians Voted* (Cambridge Cambridge University Press, 1967), pp. 43-50; and P. F. Clarke, 'The Electoral Sociology of Modern Britain' in *History*, Vol.57 No. 189, (February 1972), pp. 32-55, esp. p.43.

quarrymen's strike of 1900-3, which became the rallying-point for a wider radicalism.[10]

Behind the activists, and the odd similarity of 'anti-Thatcher Britain' to Gladstonian Britain, stood more complex social reasoning. When David Marquand attempted to define the 'principled society', he cited the Scots theologian and philosopher Alasdair McIntyre's revival of Aristotelian politics against dogmatic individualism:

> On the traditional Aristotelian view such problems do not arise . . . There is no way of my pursuing my good which is necessarily antagonistic to you pursuing yours because *the* good is neither mine peculiarly nor yours peculiarly – goods are not private property[11]

If the Mardy and Edinburgh rallies seemed uncannily *gwerinol* in spirit, they also conjured up the young Ramsay MacDonald, whose biographer Marquand was, and that great Aristoteleian W. E. Gladstone himself.

The open society needs its myths every bit as much as the revolution, and a concept rather like that of the *gwerin* performed a function in late 19th-century Scotland similar to its role in Wales. Which should be a warning to us about the pitfalls of demotic pluralism. I have called the Scottish end of my subject 'the folk', but the Tory democrat John Buchan, in a *pasquinade* against a 1900s Liberal, formulated things rather differently:

> I have never listened to any orator at once so offensive and so horribly effective. There was no appeal too base for him, and none too august: by some subtle alchemy he blended the arts of the prophet and the fishwife. He had discovered a new kind of language. Instead of 'the hungry millions', or 'the toilers', or any of the numerous synonyms for our masters, he invented the phrase, 'Goad's people'. 'I shall never rest,' so ran his great declaration, 'till Goad's green fields and Goad's clear waters are free to Goad's people.'[12]

Along this road can lie the sentimentality and exploitation of the Kailyard – Tom Nairn's 'great tartan monster' – or Keynes' famous line on Lloyd George, as 'rooted in nothing', not to speak of Myles na cGopaleen's 'Plain People of Ireland'. If a rhetoric lacks any lodging in

---

[10] See R. Merfyn Jones, *The North Wales Quarrymen* (Cardiff: University of Wales Press, 1981) pp. 267-84; a fascinating light is shed on the differences in national *mentalités* from an English Conservative standpoint by Maurice Cowling in his two volumes of *Religion and Public Doctrine in England* (Cambridge: Cambridge University Press, 1981, 1986).

[11] Marquand, *The Unprincipled Society* (London: Fontana, 1988), p. 215; and see also Craig Beveridge and Ronald Turnbull, *The Eclipse of Scottish Culture* (Edinburgh: Polygon, 1989), pp. 99ff.

[12] John Buchan, 'A Lucid Interval' in *The Moon Endureth* (1912), rpt. in David Daniell, ed., *The Best Short Stories of John Buchan* (London: Michael Joseph, 1982) p. 30.

the process of production, it can degenerate into the vacuity typified by the politics of post-independence Ireland. (*Fianna Fail*, when you think about it, could be rendered as 'the *gwerin* of destiny'). What we are dealing with – *pace* those authorities on things Celtic Kingsley Amis, Bernard Levin and Lord Dacre – *could* be an alliance of cultural con-men, religious bigots and would-be local elitists. So we have to interrogate the tradition both through comparison and by assessing mutual contributions: in particular the influence of the Scots on the Welsh, through the vehicle of the religious and print-capitalist politics that they were the first to capture.

If we return to Prys Morgan's definition, we could examine the *gwerin* under the following main aspects: the *gwerin* is (1) progressive (2) educated (3) religious (4) cultivated (5) classless (6) law-abiding (7) linked to the soil, and (8) temperate. These dispute the gradations of English society – Dahrendorf's 'layer-cake of fine class distinctions' – but they also interdict the notion of a proletariat, whose self-definition situates itself on the line of economic division.[13]

We would also be here all night, so I plan to concentrate my analysis round what the *gwerin* generation themselves saw as the key activities of religion and education, and from these expand into considering the way in which the economic and social evolution of the two societies was affected by institutions of civil society, and by the state.

## II

> 'Tis true that her *gwerin*
> Own not an inch of her land,
> The Welsh are only pilgrims
> Upon the earth of beloved Wales,
> The arrogant conquered her,
> How often has she groaned! –
> The people which dwelled in her
> Live in dark deep captivity.[14]

The language of John Morris-Jones' *Cymru Rydd* ('Free Wales') is interesting, in that it's both powerful in its imagery, consonant with Welsh tradition, and deeply and ambiguously affected by an English religious/political discourse. The image of the landless pilgrim (later to be used so effectively by David Lloyd George) relates to Williams Pantycelyn – 'Guide me, o thou great Jehovah, Pilgrim through this barren land' – and

---

[13] See Ralf Dahrendorf, *On Britain* (London: BBC Publications, 1983), pp. 51-79.
[14] Cited in Prys Morgan, art.cit., p. 137.

of course to John Bunyan (first translated into Welsh in 1699). But the 'dark deep captivity' also suggests the passage in Ralph Lingen's education report of 1847, of their language trapping the Welsh:

> Equally in his new as in his old home his language keeps him under the hatches . . . his superiors are content simply to ignore his existence. He is left to live in an underworld of his own, and the march of society goes completely over his head.[15]

The Welsh nonconformist elite, as Ieuan Gwynedd Jones has written, accepted that while 'Welsh was the language of religion,' 'English was the language of science, business and commerce, philosophy and the arts.' Scottish presbyterians in the 1700s similarly accepted that the survival of their church required the Treaty of Union with England.[16] The pilgrim's politics, in other words, are of circumspect and measured assimilation, coupled with the retention of the 'marrow' of national identity (something which was never so strictly defined as to eliminate the prospect of getting on well elsewhere): the sort of thing which Nicholas Phillipson has described in 18th and early-19th century Scotland.[17] One is forcibly reminded that at Oxford Morris-Jones' (and Sir John Rhŷs') Jesus College is not a stone's throw from Lingen's – and Edward Caird's and A. D. Lindsay's – Balliol.

The pilgrim is central to the protestant culture of civil war England. The Irish had a quite different memory. But whatever a pilgrim was, he was unlikely to be found in his parish pew, touching his hat to a squire with a pass degree. Hugh Miller – surely the role-model as a religious journalist for Thomas Gee – wrote in his *First Impressions of England* (1847):

> The merry unthinking serfs, who, early in the reign of Charles the First, danced on Sabbaths round the maypole, were afterwards the ready tools of despotism. The Ironsides, who in the cause of civil and religious freedom bore them down, were staunch Sabbatarians.[18]

In case we get the wrong idea, the message is rubbed home:

> . . . the preponderance of enjoyment lies on the more credulous side. I

---

[15] Quoted by Saunders Lewis in 'The Fate of the Language' (1962), translated and published in *Planet* No. 4 (1971), p. 19.

[16] Ieuan Gwynedd Jones, 'Language and Community in Nineteenth century Wales' in David Smith, ed., *A People and a Proletariat* (London: Pluto Press, 1980), p. 61.

[17] Nicholas Phillipson, 'Nationalism and Ideology' in. J. N. Wolfe, ed., *Government and Nationalism in Scotland* (Edinburgh: Edinburgh University Press, 1969), pp. 167-88.

[18] Hugh Miller, *First Impressions of England* (London: John Johnstone, 1847), pp. 45-6.

> never yet encountered a better-pleased people . . . unthinking, unsuspicious, blue-eyed, fair-complexioned, honest Saxons.[19]

The English may have originated Puritanism, but the Scots, and later the Welsh, were better at it, being wired directly into the society of the Old Testament Israel, as in the great song of Scots radicalism, from the Covenanters to the Red Clydesiders, Psalm 124:

> Now Israel
>     May say, and that truly,
> If that the Lord
>     Had not our cause maintain'd;
> If that the Lord
>     Had not our right sustain'd,
> When cruel men
>     Against us furiously
> Rose up in wrath
>     To make of us their prey,
> Then certainly
>     They had devour'd us all . . .

This was sung on the moors, but also at St Enoch's Station – by the Glasgow Orpheus Choir – as Maxton, Wheatley and company went south in 1922.[20] Escape from the elite of the periphery – Jacobite, gentry, or Sir William Weir – came, not wholly owing to national efforts, but through a complex cultural diplomacy with the predominant partner.

The culture of religious dissent was on the face of it a factor common to Scotland and Wales. But the connections, while important, are complex. 'The chapels spoke as one', Kenneth Morgan writes, the nonconformity of Wales, which underpinned the notion of the *Gwerin* was 'a kind of unofficial established religion'.[21] Although Calvinistic Methodism resembles Scottish presbyterianism, the notion of any 'unofficial' establishment – a religion stemming directly out of the voluntary collaborations of civil society – was totally foreign to the Scots. In Scotland church-state relations were central, and in the mid-Victorian epoch, as before, *divided* presbyterianism in three ways.

First there was the Established Church. In Wales the overwhelming of episcopalianism by nonconformity was deemed 'progressive'; in Scotland the struggle over a formally presbyterian body was a different matter: about controlling it according to the letter of the Act of Union of 1707,

[19] Ibid., p.369.
[20] Iain MacLean, *The Legend of Red Clydeside* (Edinburgh: John Donald, 1983), pp. 98-9.
[21] Kenneth O. Morgan, *Rebirth of a Nation* (Oxford: Oxford University Press, 1981), p. 17.

through congregations and not landlords. This struggle was lost in 1843, although the creative treatment of the 'Disruption' by those whose defeat made them into Free Churchmen presented this as a victory for the Scots religious impulse. In reality it meant the end of a distinctive devolution of education and social welfare to the assemblies of the Church – and the transfer of this power to an English-style bureaucracy.

The 'Disruption' was also seen as a radical, anti-landlord act, although the conflict between the 'landlords' men' and the 'Godly Commonwealth' was not an overall phenomenon. William Alexander (1826–94) is a Scots novelist almost exactly co-aeval with Daniel Owen (1836–95); his *Johnnie Gibb of Gushetneuk* (1871) (subtitled 'a study of parish politics') rapidly became a Scottish classic, running into several editions by 1900. The eponymous crofter hero, fighting the 'muckle fermers' in the 1840s for his own livelihood and religious freedom, shows many *gwerin*-like characteristics, yet in the Aberdeenshire in which the novel is set, the 'Auld Kirk' continued to command general allegiance (70+% of the population) in an area where Liberals and radicals were politically supreme.[22]

For much of the 19th century, moreover, both the 'Auld Kirk' and the Free Church were 'united' in favouring the *principle* of establishment – something quite foreign to the Welsh tradition. They were strongly opposed by 'the Voluntaries', who attacked the state connection, yet even they stemmed from legalistic disputes about religious control. The Auld Licht Anti-Burghers, whom J. M. Barrie featured in his *Auld Licht Idylls* (1886), a strong influence on Caradoc Evans's *My People* (1915), were such a 'secession'. But where Evans's Methodists represented a nonconformist oligarchy, Barrie's Auld Lichts could be safely dismissed as an absurd remnant of 18th-century Calvinist extremism.[23]

'Dissent' could unite the non-Anglican *gwerin*; in Scotland for much of the century it divided the presbyterians, creating the bitter, nit-picking politics that the secularist and Liberal politician J. M. Robertson despised – 'the inherent reactionary bias of the ecclesiastical system had turned back the hands of the social clock'.[24] Yet this highly 'political' agenda linked religion closely to law and to some extent with statecraft, creating the possibility of a more intellectual, less disputative theology which could

---

[22] For a masterly study of Alexander in his literary-political context see William Donaldson, *Popular Literature in Victorian Scotland* (Aberdeen: Aberdeen University Press, 1986), pp.101-34.

[23] See Regina Weingartner, 'The Fight against Sentimentalism: Caradoc Evans and George Douglas Brown' in *Planet*, No. 75 (June–July, 1989), pp. 86-92.

[24] J. M. Robertson, *The Perversion of Scotland* (London: Freethought Publishing Company, 1886), p. 215.

venture out from Calvinism and create a discourse broad enough to
bridge the church-government divide – something evident in the theology
of Thomas Erskine of Linlathen, the friend of F. D. Maurice, Carlyle and
Guizot, and figures like John MacMurray and John Baillie in the 20th
century.[25]

In this context, it is interesting to look at Chalmers' influence on
the *gwerin*. Lewis Edwards (1809–87) studied under him at Edinburgh
and went on to found Bala College and, in 1846, *Y Traethodydd*,
which, consciously modelled on the *Edinburgh Review* and *Blackwood's
Magazine*, devoted much attention to Chalmers' theology and social
projects. One of its leading contributors, Owen Thomas (1812-91), whose
*cofiant* of Chalmers' contemporary and equivalent, John Jones Talysarn is
reckoned by some the best biography in Welsh, was also an Edinburgh
graduate. Their contribution reflects the power and contradictions of
Chalmers's approach: the commitment to economic individualism *and*
to the idea of community; to scriptural inspiration, but also to scientific
sophistication; to the 'select' nature of their own nationality, and to a
cosmopolitan world-view. Chalmers has been dismissed by historians of
a Fabian turn as a Tory arch-individualist (with saving graces in the social
casework line); the most recent biography, by Stewart J. Brown, rightly
sees his project of a Godly Commonwealth achieved through parochial
revival as something peculiarly Scottish.[26]

The concentration of the nonconformist intelligentsia – Lewis Edwards,
Michael D. Jones, later O. M. Edwards and Tom Ellis – around Bala,
its nonconformist colleges and linking position between rural mid-Wales
and the rapidly-developing slate-quarrying north, seems to have led to
un-Chalmersian modulation of the parochial ideal. Farmer- and minister-
dominated Welsh Unions, though stingy with their poor rates, but were also
notorious for rarely applying the workhouse test.[27] Communitarianism won
out over classical economics, providing a basis for *gwerinol* 'classlessness'.
But the Free Church also provided precedent for the Welsh confrontations
of the 1850s and 1860s: in its defiance of the landlords, its closeness to
Gaelic Scotland (over 20% of its clergy were Gaelic speakers), and the
democracy of the kirk session, the Scottish equivalent of the Welsh *seiet*.[28]

[25] See William Hanna, ed., *The Letters of Thomas Erskine of Linlathen*, 2 vols, (London:
David Douglas, 1877); and see Beveridge and Turnbull, op.cit., pp. 91-111.

[26] Stewart J. Brown, *Thomas Chalmers and the Godly Commonwealth in Scotland* (Oxford:
Oxford University Press, 1982), especially pp. 118ff.

[27] Anne Digby, 'The Rural Poor Law' in Derek Fraser, ed., *The New Poor Law in the
Nineteenth Century* (London: Macmillan, 1976), pp. 158ff.

[28] See Derick Thomson, ed., *The Companion to Gaelic Scotland* (Oxford: Blackwell, 1983),
p. 87; Sir John Rhŷs and David Brynmor-Jones, *The Welsh People* (London: T. Fisher
Unwin, 1900), p.589.

Coming after Rebecca, and after the depredations of the 'Scotch Cattle' (did this mysterious movement echo Scottish secret societies like the 'Horseman's Word?), both movements presented a reassuring legalism.

In Scotland the evangelical revival was not, as H. T. Buckle stigmatized it, a reaction against enlightenment, although it unquestionably mobilized some notable throwbacks to 17th-century bigotry, such as the social reformer, nationalist and ultra-protestant, the Rev. James Begg.[29] It was more of a continuation of the theistic, socially conservationist element in the enlightenment represented by the 'common sense' philosophers Thomas Reid and Adam Ferguson, whose position George Davie has described:

> . . . it is inherent in the nature of the belief in an external world or in the mathematical ideals to envisage facts not contained in the sum of the various elementary experiences involved in the genesis of these items of the common sense, and this peculiar and fundamental fact of self-transcendence is held . . . to be an ultimate irrational mystery.[30]

Yet the *étatisme* of Scots religion emphasized a further, social-psychological, difference. In Scots Calvinism conflicts between the churches, and between 'members' and 'adherents', detracted from that intense sociocultural hegemony exercised by religious bodies in rural and small-town Wales. The Scots equivalent of the *llythyr canmoliaeth* and sanctions against adulterers or loose women, for example, seems to have waned long before the kirk sessions lost power over parish relief after the passage of the Poor Law (Scotland) Act in 1845. With such a broad pallet of religious options on offer, the Scottish religious consumer was sovereign.

In part this can be put down to earlier industrialization and population change; in part to the fact that the kirk was part of a pluralistic political system. Thus in Scotland a pagan, hedonistic culture of dancing, storytelling, singing, drinking and bawdry coexisted with the Calvinist 'unco guid' – even in those areas dominated by the Free Church at its most fundamentalist, such as the Western Isles (still, notoriously, an area famed for record–breaking commitments to pietism and alcohol). The national consumption of 2.55 gallons *of spirits* per head per annum in the 1830s, was evidenced in terrifying detail in Dean Ramsay's best-selling *Reminiscences of Scottish Life and Character* (1857). The Kirk was not spared, with tales

---

[29] H. T. Buckle, *The History of Civilisation in England*, Vol.III (1861, London: Longmans Green, 1872); I deal with Begg, *inter alia*, in an essay on 'The Covenanting Tradition' in Tom Gallagher and Graham Walker, eds, *Sermons and Battle Hymns: Protestantism in Scottish Culture* (Edinburgh: Polygon, 1991).

[30] See George Elder Davie, *The Democratic Intellect: Scotland and her Universities in the Nineteenth Century* (Edinburgh: Edinburgh University Press, 1961), p. 27

of Presbyteries knocking the bottoms off their glasses before starting on an evening of serious drinking.[31] Rural Wales had a limited spirituous culture – as demonstrated by the brief and inglorious career of the country's only distillery and generally low sales of high-alcohol drink, even before the passage of the Welsh Sunday Closing Act (1881).[32] Scotland preceded Wales both in a popular temperance movement (strongly connected with moral-force Chartism) and in the legal enforcement of temperance, with the Forbes-MacKenzie Act of 1857, but illegal distilling continued on a huge scale in the Highlands and Islands, part of the 'bad weather culture' of a North European people, and an involvement with fishing, inshore and deep-sea, which with its dangers and spasms of relaxation, was quite different to farmers and quarrymen with their relatively settled lives. J M Robertson wrote accusingly in 1886:

> Austerity and joyless gloom on the one hand produce their natural corrective in dissolute mirth and defiant licence on the other . . . A moral duality, so to speak, runs through past Scottish life in a way that seems at times perplexing.[33]

The same year saw this dualism unforgettably dramatised in *Dr Jekyll and Mr Hyde*. This unrespectable culture, which the church only fitfully reached, had dimensions which astonished those who penetrated through to it – like the schoolmaster Gavin Greig and the minister Robert Duncan whose Carnegie-funded folksong researches in the 1900s were virtually swamped by the material they provoked.[34]

## III

The *gwerin* was never as seriously troubled by psychological dualism, although it was unquestionably *there*, in the biographies of O. M. Edwards and of Lloyd George. Welsh nonconformity exercised this sort of comprehensive cultural hegemony because it implied a counter-culture to

---

[31] See also T. C. Smout, *A Century of the Scottish People* (Glasgow: Collins, 1986), p. 135.

[32] W. R. Lambert, *Drink and Sobriety in Victorian Wales*, c.1820–c.1895 (Cardiff: University of Wales Press, 1983), p. 7.

[33] J. M. Robertson, *Perversion of Scotland*, p. 211.

[34] Trefor M. Owen, 'Community Studies in Wales: an Overview' in Hume and Pryce, coll.cit., p. 110; see also Ian A. Olson, 'Scottish Traditional Song and the Greig-Duncan Collection: Last Leaves or Last Rites?' in Cairns Craig, ed., *The History of Scottish Literature*, Vol.4, *Twentieth Century* (Aberdeen: Aberdeen University Press, 1987), pp. 37-48; and Hamish Henderson, 'The Ballad, the Folk and the Oral Tradition' in Edward Cowan, ed., *The People's Past* (Edinburgh: Polygon, 1980).

the British state, whereas Scots Calvinism had been statutorily incorporated into it. This was recognized by Queen Victoria's worship in the Auld Kirk in Scotland (Crathie Church was specially built for Balmoral in 1896, but the royal family had patronized the local kirk since 1854) instead of the Episcopalian chapels of the nobility, while being generally regarded as hostile to the Welsh.[35] The Scots, moreover, differed from the Welsh in their attitude to the military role of the state. The *gwerin* ideology was fundamentally pacifist, an importation into Wales of the values of 'militant' Old Dissent, via the Liberation Society and Peace Society, triumphing in 1868 with the election as MP for Merthyr in 1868 of the Rev. Henry Richard, 'the Apostle of Peace'.[36]

In Scotland the reverse was the case. The Liberation Society had no influence on Scottish politics, and from the 1850s on the Volunteer Force gained remarkable support. Hugh Cunningham has calculated that it involved 5.5% of the adult male population in Scotland in 1881 (against 2.6% in Wales and 2.8% nationally).[37] This was not simply a reflex of the belligerency of the Crimean War, 'Thin Red Line' period. The issue of a 'militia', an embodiment in arms of the Scottish people, had been a fixture of Scots political argument since the days of the Covenanters and Andrew Fletcher of Saltoun.[38] This military ethos seems to have affected the Free and Voluntary Churches as much as the Church of Scotland; indeed its most enduring traces were in the Boys Brigade Movement, founded by a Free Church elder and Volunteer officer, William A. Smith, in 1883, with the assistance of the scientist, preacher and Liberal Professor Henry Drummond. It numbered 44 companies (25 in Glasgow, four in England, none in Wales) in 1886.[39]

Seventeenth-century Scottish Calvinism, as Arthur Williamson pointed out, concentrated more on its civic mission – 'the Godly Commonwealth' – than on the millenarian/imperial appeal of being a 'protestant nation' that fixated the contemporary English.[40] In the 19th century this modulated into a myth of settler democracy: a small-farmer, radical-democrat, religious-dissenting ethos of the F. J. Turner pattern, often strongly moulded by

---

[35] Victoria paid only one visit to Wales, four days in 1889. See Sir Sidney Lee, *Queen Victoria* (Londom: Smith Elder, 1904), pp. 516-17.

[36] Ieuan Gwynedd Jones, 'The Liberation Society and Welsh Politics' in *Explorations and Explanations* (Llandysul: Gomer Press, 1983), pp. 236-69.

[37] Hugh Cunningham, *The Volunteer Force* (London: Croom Helm, 1975), pp. 46-7.

[38] See John Robertson, *The Scottish Enlightenment and the Militia Issue* (Edinburgh: John Donald, 1983).

[39] Olive Checkland, *Philanthropy in Victorian Scotland* (Edinburgh: John Donald, 1980), pp. 56-7.

[40] Arthur Williamson, *Scottish National Consciousness in the Age of James VI* (Edinburgh: John Donald, 1983), p. 35.

the 'gloomy memories' of persecution in and eviction from their native
land, and given a powerful thrust in Thomas Carlyle's *Chartism* of 1839.[41]
Scotland's was more of an emigrant than an immigrant culture, and
although they lacked a Madoc myth, Scots settlements were fairly thick
on the ground, particularly the Gaelic-speaking colonies in Cape Breton
Island, the Free Church's settlement in Otago after 1848, centred on
Dunedin and Port Chalmers, and the mission settlements on Lake Nyasa.[42]
The 1850s seem to have been something of a turning point, when after a
brief upsurge of romantic Scottish nationalism and associated Scots-English
sparring in the newspapers, the Crimea (the Thin Red Line), the Indian
Mutiny, the enormous success of David Livingstone as missionary hero,
and the raising of the volunteer regiments contrived to implant an imperial
enthusiasm which remained at least until the Boer War.[43]

Wales, as a royalist enclave, had not been subject to the 17th-century
debate on protestant destiny, and although a form of Welsh imperialism
certainly developed in the 19th century, it was overshadowed by the
successful and radical Welsh emigration to America.[44] Imperial enthusiasm
existed, in the Methodist community and in the effusions of mid-century
'bards' like 'Ceiriog'; there was no political unity in Wales over responses
to the Boer War, despite Lloyd George's position.[45] But a wholehearted
commitment was lacking, perhaps because too close a linkage with English
expansion was seen as inimical to the language. The 'Welsh colony' in
Patagonia had an ideological presence out of all relation to its size, while
Ulster – 'the most successful Scots colony of all time' – was something Scots
radicals wanted (and still want) to forget about.[46] Imperialism's role was to
determine Scottish identity at the margin, and in fact to produce a diffusion
of loyalties. This impressed the Free Churchman Buchan when he became
Governor-General of Canada in the 1930s; it may figure to some extent
in the current enthusiasm for the notion of an independent Scotland in a
united Europe.[47]

[41] Thomas Carlyle, *Chartism* (London: Chapman and Hall, 1839), particularly Ch. 10.

[42] Thomson, *Companion*, p. 215. There were 34,000 Gaelic speakers on Cape Breton in
1900, and of their 35 ministers, 29 preached in Gaelic; Keith Sinclair, *A History of New
Zealand* (Harmondsworth: Penguin, 1959), pp. 90ff.

[43] H. J. Hanham, 'Mid-Century Scottish Nationalism: Romantic and Radical' in R. Robson,
ed., *Ideas and Institutions of Victorian Britain* (London: Bell, 1967), pp. 143-79; and see H.
C. G. Matthew, *The Liberal Imperialists* (Oxford: Oxford University Press, 1973), p. 289.

[44] See Gwyn A. Williams, *The Search for Beaulah Land: the Welsh and the Atlantic Revolution*
(London: Croom Helm, 1980); compare with Gordon Donaldson, *The Scots Overseas*
(London: Robert Hale, 1966), pp. 34-44.

[45] For Ceiriog see Tony Bianchi, 'An Englishman and Something More' in *Planet*, No.69
(June-July 1988): Kenneth O. Morgan, *Rebirth of a Nation*, p. 45.

[46] Donaldson, op.cit., p. 29.

[47] Janet Adam Smith, *John Buchan* (London: Rupert Hart-Davis, 1965), pp. 422ff.

# IV

The path of the pilgrim had some unusual – but not impossible – termini. No less ambiguous, and longer lasting, was the educational impulse, something which was central – effectively a religion-surrogate – not only to the John Rhŷs, O. M. Edwards, Tom Ellis generation in Wales, but to Scottish cultural politics. In some ways the present nationalist revival stemmed intellectually from the publication of George Davie's *The Democratic Intellect* in 1961. Even in the 1980s the educational sociologist Andrew MacPherson could write that the essential module of Scots education in the *20th* century was the rural, all-ability secondary school, and something similar still appertains in contemporary Wales.[48] The rural bias of the *gwerin* was perhaps understandable, given that in 1880 the great urbanization of Welsh society had still to occur. But Scotland had had the most rapid urbanization rate in 18th and early 19th century Europe, so an ideal of progress based on a rural or small-town community seems paradoxical.[49]

Yet both tally with the ideals of 'improvement' which marked the Scottish enlightenment. Francis Hutcheson, in his *Address to the Gentlemen of Scotland* (1735) had seen the defence of Scottish identity as resting in its educational system, and charged the gentry of the country with its development.[50] Adam Ferguson (a Gaelic-speaker) and Adam Smith both stressed the essentially agrarian basis of society, and warned against the large-scale urban and industrial unit as something which could destroy the ideal of community, or Smith's vaguer 'social sympathy'. To both Ferguson and Smith, social progress came about by a dialogue between the market and the community, in which the excesses of the former – the automatism of the division of labour or of an individualistic arrogance – was compensated for by an ideal of the collective, by martial valour (hence the importance of the militia issue) and by access to public education.[51]

John Mullen has, for instance, attempted to explain the success of the bland and tautologous but enormously influential *Man of Feeling* (1771) by Henry Mackenzie:

[48] Andrew MacPherson, 'An Angle on the *Geist*' in Walter Humes and Hamish Paterson, eds, *Education and Scottish Culture, 1780-1980* (Edinburgh: John Donald, 1983): and see Tony Bianchi, 'R. S. Thomas and his Readers' in Tony Curtis, ed., *Wales: the Imagined Nation* (Bridgend: Poetry Wales Press, 1987).

[49] T. M. Devine, 'Urbanisation' in T. M. Devine and Rosalind Mitchison, eds, *People and Society in Scotland, Vol. 1, 1760-1830* (Edinburgh: John Donald, 1988), pp. 27-52.

[50] George Elder Davie, 'Hume, Reid and the Passion for Ideas' in Douglas Young, ed., *Edinburgh in the Age of Reason* (Edinburgh: Edinburgh University Press, 1967), pp. 25ff.

[51] Quoted in Duncan Forbes, 'Adam Ferguson and the Idea of Community' in ibid, p. 46.

the compensatory assurance of a potential for social solidarity was required by a culture which was learning to describe the effects of competition and self-interest. In Scotland, a nation whose propertied class had to find a substitute in politeness and intellectual cohesiveness for the political identity it had lost with the Act of Union, the ideal of sociability was particularly alluring and difficult.[52]

In Scotland education was more than an instrument of socialisation or an expression of nationality; it was something central to the institutions of the country's polity. As such it had its parties, its patronage, its own politics. Robert Anderson regards Davie's distinction between 'Scots' and 'Anglicisers' as something which oversimplifies all the various intersecting interests – bureaucracy, teachers, curriculum, class interests, politicians – which went into educational legislation and its enforcement.[53] With the Welsh, creating a system more or less from scratch made for a more homogenous approach. It would have been inconceivable for a Tory to have provided it with a central rationalization, as was the case in Scotland, where 'democratic intellectualism' was the coinage of Walter Elliot, Secretary of State, 1935–8, and in some ways the Scots' answer to Tom Jones.[54]

In both countries education presented continuing political challenges during the 19th century: 'Anglicising' assaults – in Scotland in the 1820s, in Wales in the 1840s – stimulated a 'national' agitation (but with an eye on the greater partner), then the 'acceptable' – but still mortal – compromise.[55] Did the Welsh take over the myth – already alluded to – of the indispensable links between Scottish education and the democratic nature of Scottish society? The Scots certainly insisted strongly enough that their successful industrialization stemmed from the 'improving' strengths of Scottish civil society – trained manpower, Calvinist work ethics and social control, a well–developed banking system – rather than from (as seems more likely) mineral wealth and low wages.[56] The Welsh national movement devoted itself with great energy – there is no-one in Scotland comparable to Sir Hugh Owen (1804-81) – to acquiring an educational system cognate with the Scots', and achieved success in 1889 with the Intermediate Education Act. It could even be argued that this put Wales ahead, as the new Welsh

---

[52] John Mullen, 'The Language of Sentiment' in Andrew Hook, ed., *History of Scottish Literature*, Vol.2, *1680-1830* (Aberdeen: Aberdeen University Press, 1988), p. 275; and see Ian Campbell, *Kailyard* (Edinburgh: Ramsay Head, 1981), pp. 18ff.

[53] R. D. Anderson, *Education in Victorian Scotland*, Appendix 1.

[54] Davie, *Democratic Intellect*, Preface; and see Colin Coote, *A Companion of Honour: The Story of Walter Elliot* (Glasgow: Collins, 1965), p. 16.

[55] See Anderson, op. cit., Ch. 2; and Donald Witherington, 'Scotland a Half Educated Nation' in Humes and Paterson, *Scottish Culture*, pp. 55-74.

[56] See T. C. Smout, *A Century of the Scottish People*, pp. 109ff.

educational establishment was more progressive than its Scots equivalent: the radicalism of O. M. Edwards (1858-1920) rather than the high Toryism of Sir Henry Craik (1846-1931), something reflected in the history books that both wrote.

More generally, we can use education as a paradigm of Ieuan Gwynedd Jones' useful approach – who was providing social overhead capital, and under what terms was it applied? In rural Wales this was crystallized in chapels, schools, halls, *eisteddfodau* and the 'People's University', a 'from the ground-up' business, with the occasional lucky break from a businessman of the David Davies sort.[57] In Scotland much of this capital was already in place: donated by an 'improving' aristocracy which, on account of this, survived as a factor in Scottish politics, educational and cultural life. R. B. Haldane, of a gentry-lawyer family which had been leaders of dissent in the 18th century, patronized the Fabians, promoted higher education, and chaired the Welsh University Commission, 1916-18.[58] John Sinclair, Lord Pentland (1860-1925) of the family which had earlier organized the massive *Statistical Accounts*, became both a popular Scottish Secretary, 1906-12, and – along with the Earl of Aberdeen – the patron of the polymath sociologist, regional planner and Celtic nationalist Patrick Geddes.[59]

Both countries were subject to increased social tensions as new urban areas expanded at the end at the end of the 19th century – particularly with the growth of port and commercial communities with their more cosmopolitan workforce. In Scotland this expansion was 'poured' into a long-lived and sophisticated urban tradition – the Convention of Royal Burghs had its origins in the 13th century, but in South Wales there was only a vestigial town tradition and the 'urban' – or employer/paternalist type of town – predominated over the 'civic' – or political/corporate type – until quite late in the century. The commercial provision of social utilities arrived with state action, in the shape of the Cathays Park complex, hard on its heels.[60] In this sense Wales seems to have followed Scotland, which had generated a civic movement comparable with that of America by the

[57] Ieuan Gwynedd Jones, 'Language and Community', pp.50-1.

[58] Eric Ashby and Mary Anderson, *Portrait of Haldane at Work on Education* (London: Macmillan, 1974) pp. 123-32.

[59] See Lady Pentland, *Lord Pentland: a Memoir* (London: Methuen, 1928); Lord and Lady Aberdeen, *"We Twa"* (London: Collins, 1925), pp. 188-90; for Geddes' influence on social studies in Wales see David Michael, 'Before Alwyn: the Origins of Sociology in Wales' in Glyn Williams, ed., *Crisis of Economy and Ideology: Essays on Welsh Society, 1840-1880* (Cardiff: Social Science Research Council and British Sociological Association, 1983), p. 24.

[60] Neil Evans, 'The Welsh Victorian City: the Middle Class and Civic and National Consciousness in Cardiff, 1850-1914' in *The Welsh History Review*, Vol. 12, No. 3 (June 1985), pp. 351-2.

1890s, but the ruralism and puritanism of the *gwerinwr* spoke against developments such as the 'establishment'–backed revival both of local ceremonies (Up Helly Aa! in the Shetlands and the Border Common Ridings in the 1870s), and the enormous expansion in Burns Clubs from the 1880s on.[61]

In Scotland the 'civic' was patent in the ambitious town planning schemes of the enlightenment period, replicated on a smaller scale in country burghs and landlords' model villages. The continuation of this tradition may owe something to the relatively greater fortunes made in Scotland in property, trade, brewing and banking. Major museum, art gallery and technical education projects were under way from the 1830s – financed in part by the Board of Manufactures created in 1727 as a consequence of the 1707 Act of Union. The universities expanded after 1861 – student numbers doubling to 6,798 in 1890, in a combination of state action with private philanthropy. The same factors supplemented the benevolence of Andrew Carnegie (who made his millions at a safe distance from Scotland) in providing opulent public libraries in 77 Scottish towns by the 1900s, and extensive grants to students in higher education.[62] Was this populist or elitist – or a contradictory combination of both?

Two major critiques have been made of such educational movements: one, that they elevated religion and culture above technical innovation; two, that they promoted ambitions which could not be bound by the national unit.[63] The former charge cannot fairly be laid at the door of the bureaucracy: both the Scottish Education Department and its Welsh equivalent tried to promote 'modern' studies and technical education, only to run into opposition from working-class bodies which suspected that they were being sold a lower-grade form of education.[64] The latter charge was guiltily evident in hackneyed Scottish jokes about all London Scots being inaccessible since they were all 'heids o' depairtments'. Both Scots and Welsh ran into 'unfriendly fire' from the pen of T. W. H. Crosland at about the time of Lloyd George (the tradition of English aggression towards the

---

[61] See Christopher Harvie and Graham Walker, 'Community and Culture' in Hamish Fraser, ed., *People and Society in Scotland, 1830-1914* (Edinburgh: John Donald, 1990).

[62] See Olive Checkland, op.cit, pp. 142-3; R. D. Anderson, op.cit., pp. 350-1 for statistics; pp. 287ff. for Carnegie.

[63] In 1900 the University of Wales conferred 60 degrees in Arts, only 10 in Science; in 1913 the figures were 114 and 27. See G. W. Roderick, 'Education, Culture and Industry in Wales in the 19th Century' in *The Welsh History Review*, Vol.13 (December 1987), No. 4., p. 443.

[64] R. D. Anderson, op.cit., p. 191; and see the opposition to O. M. Edward's plans for technical education in the South Wales valleys, in K. S. Hopkins, ed., *The Rhondda: Past and Future* (Cardiff, 1976).

non-Irish Celts deserves rather more attention than it's been given).[65] But this notion of the university as 'graduate factory' also damaged the fabric of working-class communities, as another Scoto-Welsh witness, Jennie Lee, wrote.[66] The 'positional goods' nature of Scottish education was to come under fierce attack – 'a land of second-hand thoughts and second-rate minds' – from G M Thomson and A S Neill, as well as many others, in the 1920s.[67]

# V

Their relationship to the Enlightenment caused major problems for the *gwerin* and the Godly Commonwealth. Both were ethics of conviction, social solidarity and an educational idealism which sought to embrace scientific progress, and the extension of higher education. At the same time their leaders feared the break-up that would be caused by the impact of the division of labour, scientism and mass-literacy. Thomas Chalmers was emblematic of this quandary. He had been reared in the rationalism of Edinburgh, which had stimulated his interest in science and economics; his later career attempted to equate this with evangelical Christianity.[68] Perhaps significantly, Chalmers on *Christian Revelation and Astronomy* (1846) was translated into Welsh in 1846, really the last of Welsh-language borrowings from Scots Calvinist theology. Few Scottish secular writers made the transition, although their works were summarised in Welsh periodicals like Lewis Edwards' *Y Traethodydd* (1846).[69]

The language issue is, of course, the major divergence. In both societies the 18th century saw a revival in native poetry and the native language, though for different reasons: Duncan Ban MacIntyre, William Ross and Alexander MacDonald in Scotland were shocked into lyrics of outstanding quality by the collapse of the clan society which had housed

[65] See T. W. H. Crosland, *The Unspeakable Scot, Taffy* ·(London: Grant Richards, 1900 and 1910).

[66] Jennie Lee, *This Great Journey* (London: Macgibbon and Kee, 1963), p. 89.

[67] G. M. Thomson, *Caledonia or the Future of the Scots* (London: Kegan Paul, 1926), p. 47; Trefor M. Owen, art. cit., p. 113.

[68] See S. J. Brown, *Thomas Chalmers*, Ch. 5.

[69] The popular devotional works of Thomas Boston – *The Fourfold State of Man*, *The Crook in the Lot*, and *The Covenant of Grace*, were translated between 1769 and 1824. *Y Traethodydd*'s index shows rather more substantial entries on Carlyle, Chalmers, Sir William Hamilton and David Hume than on 'Iesu Grist'.

them. Goronwy Owen and Williams Pantycelyn in Wa'es reflected a language which had ridden out attempts at acculturation and made peace on its own terms with 'vital religion', Atlantic identity, and print capitalism. The daring achievements in cultural construction of James 'Ossian' MacPherson (1736-96) in Scotland, and Iolo Morganwyg (1747-1826) in Wales reflected this divergence. MacPherson's exploitation of the juxtaposition of Gaelic and Lowland society – the 'militant' and the 'industrial' – helped 'sell' the enlightenment in continental Europe, *in English*.[70] Iolo, obviously deeply influenced by MacPherson's success, and by the patronage of English romantics like Southey whom 'Ossian' enthused, achieved his 'enlightened' ends in Welsh.[71] Politically, MacPherson wrote a threnody for a Scots Gaelic battered by political collapse, eviction and dispersal, whose literary witness would ultimately decline to the inconsistent genres of martial poetry, pietism and social protest.[72]

These proved only too easy to adapt to a sporting-and-tourism based culture of tartanry, sedulously fostered by the monarchy and the surviving, and surprisingly resilient, Scottish Tories.[73] Only in 1892 was a body similar to the National Eisteddfod Committee, An Comunn Gaedhealach, set up. Despite the fact that this followed the 'Crofters' revolt', which surely contributed precedents to the Welsh tithe war of 1887-8, its role was purely literary and aesthetic. Being largely under the control of the Conservative, 'Anglo-Gaelic' gentry of the Highlands, it could even be seen as an attempt to check the radicalism which had followed the third Reform Act. Lowland prejudice against the Highlanders, which had been almost as widespread earlier in the century as prejudice against the Irish, was diminished by migration into the cities and sympathy with the victims of landlordism, but by that time Gaelic had suffered the fate that, according to Brinley Thomas, Welsh would

---

[70] Murray H. Pittock, *The Invention of Scotland: the Stuart Myth and the Scottish Identity, 1638 to the Present* (London: Routledge, 1991), pp. 73-84.

[71] See Gwyn A. Williams, *When was Wales?* (Harmondsworth: Penguin, 1985), pp. 164ff. None of the standard works on Southey refer to Iolo, and only Jean Raimond, *Robert Southey: L'Homme et son Temps, L'oeuvre, Le Role* (Paris: Didier, 1966) draws attention to his interest in Ossian.

[72] Derick Thomson, 'Gaelic Poetry in the Eighteenth Century: the Breaking of the Mould' in Andrew Hook, ed., coll. cit., pp. 175-89; John MacInnes, 'Gaelic Poetry in the Nineteenth Century' in Douglas Gifford, ed., *The History of Scottish Literature*, Vol.3, *The Nineteenth Century* (Aberdeen: Aberdeen University Press, 1988) pp. 377-96; 67 books in Gaelic were published between 1750 and 1800, compared with over 1000 in Welsh. (Thomson, *Companion*, p. 245; Rhys and Brynmor-Jones, p. 533.)

[73] Andrew Noble, 'John Wilson (Christopher North) and the Tory Hegemony'in Douglas Gifford, ed., *The History of Scottish Literature*, Vol.3, *The Nineteenth Century* (Aberdeen: Aberdeen University Press, 1988), pp. 125-52.

have suffered in an non-industrial Wales. The numbers of Gaelic speakers slumped from about 20% of the Scots population in 1800 to about 5% in 1900.[74]

William Donaldson has argued for the continuing validity of lowland Scots as a vehicle of intellectual discourse – in local discussion circles, the local press, and in the realist novels of such as William Alexander. But even he sees this tradition in eclipse by the end of the century, overshadowed by the commercialism of the Kailyard, which transmitted a sanitized and sentimentalised Scotland to London and (particularly significant) to the USA after the copyright agreement of 1891.[75] 'Ian MacLaren's' *Beside the Bonnie Brier Bush*, the quintessential Kailyard product, was the first book to lead the American best–seller list, established in 1895. 'MacLaren' hid the identity of the Rev. John Watson, presbyterian minister in Liverpool (surely a strategic Scoto-Welsh junction) and President of the Free Church Federal Council, who was promoted by that other luminary of the nonconformist general staff, the Rev William Robertson Nicoll, Lloyd George's hot-line to the free churches he had long since left in spirit.[76]

The Kailyard had plenty of Welsh imitators among the authors of chapel prize-books. But one Scottish voice, however, remained significant and disturbing in the areas of religion and education for most of the second half of the 19th century: Thomas Carlyle. His impact on the generation of Disraeli and Dickens was vast, but by the time the Welsh national movement got going in the late 1860s his anti-democratic sourness had become rather embarrassing to the metropolitan *literati*.[77] Not so in Scotland and Wales, whose younger generation accepted Walt Whitman's more generous estimate of Carlyle's epic qualities.[78] In Geraint Goodwin's *The Heyday in the Blood*, his young writer rediscovers the books of his father

> . . . one of the Young Men of Wales. In his dark, bitter, fuming, eyes, his long narrow face, his lean spindle body, one glimpsed the passion that was to devour him. He came at a time when the country was turning anxiously, as though in sleep . . .

[74] Brinley Thomas, 'A Cauldron of Rebirth: Population and the Welsh Language in the Nineteenth Century', in *Welsh History Review*, Vol.13 (December 1987) No.4, pp. 418-37; and see James Hunter, 'The Politics of Highland Land Reform' in *The Scottish History Review*, Vol. 53 (1974), pp. 45-68.

[75] Donaldson, *Popular Literature*, pp. 146-9.

[76] See Christopher Harvie, 'Behind the Bonnie Briar Bush: the Kailyard Revisited' in *Proteus*, No.3 (1978).

[77] See Christopher Harvie, *The Centre of Things: Political Fiction in Britain from Disraeli to the Present* (London: Unwin Hyman 1991), especially Ch.2.

[78] Walt Whitman, *Democratic Vistas* (1871, London: Nonesuch, 1938), pp. 708-9.

The father had been a Methodist minister whose faith migrated from church to nation, something reflected in his library:

> Theological commentaries jostled one another along the shelves, political tracts, modern-day heresies. There was Locke and Spinoza, Hazlitt and William James, Cromwell's letters and speeches, a whole shelf of Carlyle . . .[79]

Advancing out of his books, the dead father plucks young Llew from fags and football and sets him down on his writing-desk. Something very similar happened to the young Henry Jones at Bangor and to David Lloyd George. As Frank Owen wrote, conflating Carlyle and Bunyan:

> It was Carlyle's *Sartor Resartus* which began to lead him back by a broad track from Doubting Castle to his own rather highly personal view of of the Delectable Mountains (for it describes a man who made a similar journey).[80]

Carlyle doesn't seem to have been much translated into Welsh (it was difficult enough to understand him in English!) but despite any expectation that religious unorthodoxy would heep him well out of the Calvinist-Methodist main line, he features prominently among the contents of *Y Traethodydd*. The 'devouring passion', the radical and anti-aristocratic spirit of his most popular writings must have made an impact:

> Did a God make this land of Britain, and give it to us all, that we might live there by honest labour; or did the Squires make it, and – shut to the voice of God, open only to a Devil's voice in this matter – decide on giving it to themselves alone? This is now the sad question and 'divine right' that we, in this unfortunate century, have got to settle![81]

This resounded along the debateable lands of the Anglophone border – and in Keir Hardie's Merthyr – with an impact similar to that which Carlyle had on Young Ireland or Giuseppi Mazzini, who in turn would exercise their influence on Tom Ellis's generation.[82]

---

[79] Geraint Goodwin, *The Heyday in the Blood* (London: Cape, 1936), pp.134-42.

[80] Sir Henry Jones, *Old Memories* (London: Hodder and Stoughton 1924), p. 94; Frank Owen, *Tempestuous Journey: The Life of David Lloyd George* (London: Hutchinson, 1954), p. 32.

[81] Thomas Carlyle, 'Baillie the Covenanter' (1841) in *Scottish and other Miscellanies* (London: Dent n.d.), p. 141.

[82] For Carlyle and 'Young Ireland' see Owen Dudley Edwards, 'Ireland' in *Celtic Nationalism* (London: Routledge, 1968), pp. 123-4; Nevil Masterman, *The Forerunner: the Dilemmas of Tom Ellis* (Llandybie: Christopher Davies, 1971), pp. 16-19; K. O. Morgan, *Keir Hardie*, p. 22.

## VI

The 'message' of Carlyle was essentially that of Adam Ferguson – the necessity of society:

> It is in Society that man first feels what he is; first becomes what he can be. In Society an altogether new set of spiritual activities are evolved in him, and the old immeasurably quickened and strengthened.[83]

A comparison of religion and education suggests the centrality in both countries of social *structure*: the mould into which politics has to be poured. The Scottish religious settlement partook more of the state, and this gave it a flexibility which could ride out the inconsistencies of 'vital religion', and resist the blandishments of the English *élite*, that beguiling mixture of goodwill, condescension, vague ethnic generalization masking tough metropolitan *realpolitik*, that is Matthew Arnold on *Celtic Literature*.[84] Preoccupation with a strategy which accepted Arnold's *étatism*, but tried to adapt it to the sort of compromise visible in Scotland, informed the Oxford-centred Cymdeithas Dafydd ap Gwilym generation, whose national and intellectual programme seems a Welsh version of the democratic nationalism of the *Essays on Reform* project twenty years earlier (which was actually edited by Albert Rutson, H. A. Bruce's private secretary.[85] Like them it was rooted in academic struggle – against the autocratic and anti–Welsh Principal Hugo Harper of Jesus College – and in an immediate political crisis, Gladstone's declaration for Irish Home Rule, which was overwhelmingly rejected by the Oxbridge and metropolitan Liberal intelligentsia.[86]

Indeed, if the *gwerin* and the folk have a comon political begetter, his name must be W. E. Gladstone. To Gladstone, the Scots Episcopalian, the Free Church 'Godly Commonwealth' of Thomas Chalmers was a reality, no matter how difficult it might be to square evangelical (or for that matter patristic) theology with scientific progress.[87] It showed the possibility of involving the laity in church government and, by analogy, in constitutional politics. This laity was the 'men' of the Scottish highlands; it could also be the 'fianna' of Celtic antiquity – masses, but also *convinced, empowered*

---

[83] Thomas Carlyle, 'Characteristics' (1831) in *Scottish and Other Miscellanies*, p. 194.

[84] Matthew Arnold, *The Study of Celtic Literature* (1867, London: John Murray, 1912), especially p. 13.

[85] See Christopher Harvie, *The Lights of Liberalism* (London: Allen Lane 1976), especially Ch. 6.

[86] Ibid, Ch.8; and see G. Hartwell Jones, *A Celt Looks at the World* (Cardiff: William Lewis, 1946), pp. 34ff.

[87] W. E. Gladstone, 'The Theses of Erastus and the Scottish Church Establishment' in *The Foreign and Colonial Quarterly Review* (1844), rpt. in *Gleanings of Past Years*, Vol.III (London: Murray, 1879), p. 38.

masses.[88] The 1860s were not a good decade, in terms of calculable support, for Gladstone; high-church Oxford rejected him in 1865; his backsliding on the American Civil War and reluctance over reform stigmatized him in the eyes of metropolitan radicals; English urban constituencies were insecure. One senses therefore that the popular mobilization in 1868 of Liberalism in Wales came to him as, literally, a godsend. A constituency existed which could be relied upon to back him, and for some time he paid it careful court.

Ieuan Gwynedd Jones has written eloquently of the groups mobilized at this time, about their cultural ambiguities and their political resolution. Such 'executive committees' of the *gwerin* could – like Gladstone himself – dissolve potential (and indeed actual) intellectual contradictions in political activism and in the common experience of struggle against landlords, Tories and clergy.[89] They were a major input into that dramatic initiative on the Eastern Question, which saw Gladstone first articulate his 'classes versus masses' theme. Thereafter, however, Gladstone, though geographically resident in Wales at Hawarden, realized that Scotland provided greater crowds, an English language press, greater malleability in terms of issues, and in Lord Rosebery a wealthy and hard-working patron.[90]

Cruder statistics of political calculation were – with Gladstone increasingly centralized party over which he presided – apt to take over, and thereafter did. *Gwerinol* ideology, after the 1884 Reform act and the brief efflorescence of *Cymru Fydd*, was in the cultural and 'social overhead capital' sphere successful, but politically – as the famous Newport confrontation of 1896 made brutally clear – it was upheld by an archaic political structure which might be tolerable to the Liberal Party but failed completely to cope with demographic change in Wales.[91]

In Scotland the population of the three industrial western counties – Lanarkshire, Renfrewshire and Ayrshire – was 21% of the Scots total in 1801, 27% in 1831, and 46% in 1911. These counties then returned 22 of the 70 territorial MPs. Between 1881 and 1911 the population of the two South Wales counties of Glamorgan and Monmouth doubled, while that of the rest of Wales rose only by 7%. Although Wales's electorate had been before 1832 more representative than that of Scotland – where scarcely 5,000 could vote – the proportion of electors to population in the

---

[88] See Christopher Harvie, 'Gladstonianism, the Provinces, and Popular Political Culture' in Richard Bellamy, ed., *Victorian Liberalism* (Oxford: Blackwell, 1989).

[89] Ieuan Gwynedd Jones, 'Merioneth Politics in the Mid Nineteenth Century' in *Explorations and Explanations*, p. 159.

[90] See Michael Fry, *Patronage and Principle: A Political History of Modern Scotland* (Aberdeen: Aberdeen University Press, 1986) pp. 92-3.

[91] Morgan, *Rebirth of a Nation*, p. 118.

new industrial areas lapsed badly by 1867 (from 8% to 4% in Cardiff, for example).[92] Later demographic change worsened matters, since it occurred *after* the last major redistribution of seats, in 1884. By 1910 the political map was grotesque. The single MP for Cardiff represented 186,000 people; the MP for Merioneth scarcely 20,000. Glamorgan and Monmouth, with 63% of the population, had only eleven (or one third) of the Welsh seats (five of which were Labour).[93] This might have been a fair reflection of real divisions in Welsh politics, marked by growing confrontation in the mines and on the railways. In fact, the country (apart from the above seats and two small collections of towns) belonged to the Liberals, like a huge pocket borough.

In Scotland the sequence of population growth was more consistent, because the various phases of industrial development – linen-cotton-iron-engineering – dovetailed fairly neatly into one another, and the major industrial area remained in the West of the Central belt. An earlier demographic shift meant that the electorate was a fairer reflection of the society. Although fewer working people were enfranchised than in England, Scottish politics were more sensitive to industrial and political change, to imperialism and tariff reform. But if an earlier urbanization produced relatively stable politics by the 1880s, it also bequeathed the appalling social problem of cramped and insanitary housing: patrolled and kept from crisis by the 'municipal socialism' of the towns, but never overcome. In the 1900s Labour's major issue in south Wales was the issue of control of the work–process, as in *The Miner's Next Step* (1910); in Scotland it was housing, whether handled by John Wheatley's schemes on Glasgow City Council or by the Royal Commission that the Scottish Secretary, MacKinnon Wood, granted in 1913 as the result of pressure from the miners in particular.[94]

How much was the raw, confrontational quality of labour relations in the South Wales coalfield the result of the inequities of the degree of parliamentary representation then available? How much was it the result of memories of struggles with landlords or quarrymasters being imported from rural Wales?[95] At any rate, in South Wales housing was not the powder-keg

[92] Ieuan Gwynedd Jones, 'Franchise Reform and Glamorgan Politics in the Mid-Nineteenth Century' in *Morgannwg*, Vol.II (1958), pp.47-64.

[93] Ieuan Gwynedd Jones, 'Franchise Reform and Glamorgan Politics, 1869-1921' in *Glamorgan County History*, Vol.IV (1988), pp. 43-69.

[94] See Maclean, *Red Clydeside*, pp. 165ff.; Ian S. Wood, *John Wheatley* (Manchester: Manchester University Press, 1990), pp. 36ff; Joseph Melling, *Rent Strikes: People's Struggle for Housing In West Scotland, 1890-1916* (Edinburgh: Polygon, 1983), especially Ch. 1.

[95] Hywel Francis and David Smith, *The Fed* (London: Lawrence and Wishart, 1980) see the Welsh-speaking element among the miners as conservative (p. 19) but also report some chapels as radical nurseries (p. 10).

it was in Scotland. Welsh 'by-law' housing was unimaginative but on the whole adequate. In Scotland the Commission found difficulty in 1917 in describing the awfulness of conditions which were, for a start, five times more overcrowded than in England and Wales:

> unspeakably filthy privy-middens in many of the mining areas, badly-constructed, incurably damp labourers' cottages on farms, whole townships unfit for human occupation in the crofting counties and islands . . . gross overcrowding and huddling of the sexes together in the congested industrial villages and towns, occupation of one-room houses by large families, groups of lightless and unventilated houses in the older burghs, clotted masses of slums in the great cities.[96]

The housing issue introduced a class note in Scottish politics, which the Wheatley act of 1924 made into a class interest. Public control of housing and subsidized rents were to remain pillars of a deeply functional and resolutely unimaginative Scottish politics until the 1960s.[97]

## VII

The mid-Victorian Scottish Liberal consensus was dissolving as the *gwerinwr* were getting into their stride. The split over home rule in 1886 went deeper than expected, revived the Unionist right, and drove Liberals to favour well-heeled southerners as candidates. A secular trading in votes by Scottish interest groups began in which the Unionists gave as good as they got and in 1900 even won a majority of Scottish seats.[98] This central fracture between an 'empowered people' and the structure of politics was reflected in both countries in ineffectual Liberal organization around the turn of the century, but by then the distinctive 'home rule' element in the Welsh revival had shot its bolt.

Scots home rule radicals could now leap-frog ahead, headed by the Young Scots, a body organized explicitly on the lines of Cymru Fydd.[99] But not for long. The war saw one *gwerin* leader boosted to world leadership, and the mobilization of the Welsh and Scottish industrial elites. It also propelled both economies into an enduring depression, knocking over the ideological, as well as social, supports of Liberalism. As the whole industrial project faltered, Calvinism itself was cast into question – an

---

[96] Report of the Royal Commission on the Housing of the Industrial Population of Scotland (London: HMSO, 1917), Cmnd. 8731, p. 102.

[97] T. C. Smout, *A Century of the Scottish People*, pp. 52ff.

[98] See I. G. C. Hutchison, *A Political History of Scotland, 1832–1922* (Edinburgh: John Donald, 1985), pp. 209-12.

[99] Ibid, pp. 232ff.

essentially corrosive ideology which had destroyed an earlier community of 'sympathy'. In Wales the redistribution of 1918, granting Glamorgan and Monmouth 24 seats, would have finished the old Liberal order, even without the havoc wrought by Lloyd George. The war took a further, savage toll in the rural areas of both countries, further wounding a Welsh pacifist element, already compromised by its acceptance of 'Lloyd George's Welsh Army'.

Oddly but in some ways appropriately, both Lloyd George and D. A. Thomas were taken over by the English imaginative tradition: Joyce Cary transposed Lloyd George to Devon in his 'Chester Nimmo' trilogy (1953-5); Arnold Bennett made Thomas into *Lord Raingo* (1926). John Buchan among others converted the Red Clydesiders into lovable House of Commons characters. Completing this process in the 1930s and 1940s, Aneurin Bevan became perhaps the one Labour politician who seemed to embody the triumph of class-consciousness over regional loyalties. But did this denationalizing process not reflect the fact that 'proletarian Scotland', and to a much greater extent 'proletarian Wales', had only eclipsed the *gwerin* – or 'Goad's people' – to be eclipsed themselves?[100]

This may explain why the nature of the post-war political–intellectual response was broadly similar in both countries. A Liberal continuum led into autonomous (but weak) home-rule movements, but younger intellectual activists rejected Mazzinian nationalism for a combination of Spengler and politicized French Catholicism, in the case of Saunders Lewis, or for Communist internationalism, as with Lewis Grassic Gibbon – or, as in the case of Hugh MacDiarmid, for *both*![101] Edwin Muir's juxtaposition of medieval (and thus Catholic) fruitfulness and Calvinist barrenness, in *Scottish Journey* (1935) and 'Scotland 1941' was something he had in common with Saunders Lewis, as had Compton Mackenzie and Fionn MacColla, who were also more involved in Gaelic, Catholicism and a conservative corporatism.[102] Yet, as much as Muir and MacColla, MacDiarmid himself stemmed from, and celebrated, a rural Scotland whose experience was a reality to less than a quarter of the population.[103]

The new nationalists were unsparing about the *gwerin*'s political inadequacies, limited though their own achievements were. On the other hand,

---

[100] See Harvie, *Centre of Things*, pp. 156-9.

[101] Hugh MacDiarmid, *Albyn, or Scotland and the Future* (London: Kegan Paul, 1927), p. 11.

[102] Mackenzie's 'Jacobite' political credo is given at great length in the first chapter of *The North Wind of Love* (London: Rich and Cowan, 1945).

[103] Emlyn Sherrington, 'Welsh Nationalism, the French Revolution, and the Influence of the French Right, 1880-1930' in David Smith, ed., *A People and a Proletariat*, pp. 127-47: and see MacDiarmid, *Albyn*, p. i.

the politics of post-1945 Scotland and Wales were essentially the creation of nationally-inclined 'progressives', who had matured in the *gwerin* period: Tom Johnston (one of Sir Henry Jones' pupils at Glasgow University) in 1940s Scotland; James Griffiths in 1960s Wales.[104] 'It is a heritage', wrote Walter Elliot in 1932,

> wherein discipline is rigidly and ruthlessly enforced, but where criticism and attack are unflinching, continuous, and salt with a bitter and jealous humour. It is a heritage wherein intellect, speech and, above all, argument are the passports to the highest eminence in the land. These traditions we should study, and their histories are the annals of the parishes, their ministers, and their elders.[105]

This is the *gwerin* ideology, but the fact that it was being articulated by a Tory, and referred to a religious tradition which was still a power in the land, suggests some reasons why it remained livelier in Scotland after 1918. The *gwerin* hegemony in Wales had ultimately been too dependent on political good fortune and the health of nonconformity. Indeed, the irony is that both traditions continued to be hypnotically effective, in a Kailyard, conservative-populist, modulation. The *Sunday Post* was founded in 1931, and remains rooted in a small-town Scotland: its famous comic strip 'The Broons' preserves an extended family of a type practically extinct sixty years ago. Richard Llewellyn's *How Green Was My Valley* became iconic after its first publication in 1939, despite the fact that it simplified and sentimentalized the *gwerin* past the limits of caricature. Yet in its almost wholly mythical re-creation of a civil society seemingly divorced from state action, Llewellyn's novel has proved as hard a nut to crack as the Dundee Press.[106]

## VIII

> *That* is The Land out there, under the sleet, churned and pelted there in the dark, the long rigs upturning their clayey faces to the spear-onset of the sleet. That is The Land, a dim vision this night of laggard fences and long–stretching rigs. And the voice of it – the true and unforgettable voice – you can hear on such a night as this as the dark comes down, the immemorial plaint of the peewit, flying lost. *That* is The Land – though not quite all.

---

[104] For Johnston see Graham Walker, *Thomas Johnston* (Manchester: Manchester University Press, 1988), Ch. 1; for Griffiths see Prys Morgan 'The *Gwerin* of Wales', p. 150.

[105] 'Scotland's Political Heritage' in *A Scotsman's Heritage* (1932), quoted in Coote, op.cit., p. 16.

[106] For the Dundee Press, tartanry, etc., see Tom Nairn, 'Old and New Scottish Nationalism' in *The Break-Up of Britain* (London: New Left Books, 1977), especially pp. 160ff.; for Llewellyn see *Planet* No. 76 (August, 1989).

> Those folk in the byre whose lantern light is a glimmer through the sleet
> as they muck and bed and tend the kye, and milk the milk into tin pails
> – they are The Land in as great a measure.[107]

'They' are the 'green international' that feeds the world. The power of
Lewis Grassic Gibbon's prose evocation of the thrawn, demotic radicalism
of the Scots crofter – something that far outpaces his ostensible, and
somewhat authoritarian, Marxism – is proof that, even in its *political*
decline, the notion of the 'empowered people' and the Carlyleian use
of language and drama to propel a social critique still had enormous
compulsion. The importance of schoolmaster-figures in the biography of
so many of the 'renaissance men' is a testament to the influence of *gwerin*
ideals; while even their ruralism and archaism helpfully coincided with the
reinstatement of anthropological and environmental concerns: making it
easier for them to latch on to Frazer, Freud, Jung and for that matter R.
D. Laing.[108]

In part the adaptation of the tradition was actually stimulated by the
War itself. In Scotland, for instance, the Scottish Women's Rural Institute
movement was set up under the *aegis* of the newly–created Board of
Agriculture for Scotland as part of its programme of agricultural planning.
Its aims were the creation of a rural 'community' which would bridge the
wives of 'muckle farmers' and farm labourers. In the following decade it
was to play the leading role in the significantly-titled Community Drama
movement. A leading writer of the 'kitchen comedies' which were its
stock-in–trade was the Fife miner, socialist and pacifist Joe Corrie, whose
play *In Time o' Strife* (1926) and poems like 'The Image o' God' predate
the Anglo-Welsh novels of the mining valleys in the 1930s.[109] In one sense
a loss, perhaps: in another the entry into a recognized social and political
role of half the population which the *gwerin* ideology had ignored. The real
'new departure' that the Scottish and Welsh 'renaissances' of the inter-war
years gave was a credible role for women: from popular writers like Annie
S. Swan – the first woman candidate in a Scots election – to Kate Roberts
and Naomi Mitchison.

Something of the paradox and peril of the whole mind-set is evident
in the testimony of a writer frequently featured in *Y Traethodydd*: Hugh
Miller, whose autobiography *My Schools and Schoolmasters* was published
in 1854. Miller was born in 1802 in Cromarty in Easter Ross, a seaport

---

[107] Lewis Grassic Gibbon, 'The Land' in *The Scottish Scene* (1934), rpt. in Ian S. Munro,
ed., *A Scots Hairst* (London: Hutchinson, 1967), p. 67.

[108] See Douglas Gifford, *Gibbon and Gunn* (Edinburgh: Oliver and Boyd, 1983), pp. 1-5;
and Beveridge and Turnbull, *Eclipse of Scottish Culture*, pp. 91ff.

[109] See Linda Mackenney, ed., *Joe Corrie: Plays, Poems and Theatre Writings* (Edinburgh:
7:84 Publications, 1985), pp. 75.

close to the great divide between Lowland and Highland. His father, a small ship-owner, was drowned and Hugh had to 'de-class' himself and be apprenticed as a stonemason, later working himself up to a bank official and journalist. He was psychologically torn and ultimately destroyed by cultural tensions. As editor of the Free Church's *Witness* after 1839 he had to be a moderate Liberal; as a gifted geologist he was hamstrung by his religious fundamentalism. Yet this greyness is banished by the vitality of his autobiography. The pressure-points of a changing Scotland are viewed by a man vertiginously on the edge of so many divides: on the edge of the highland line, the sea, the oral tradition, the working class, of sanity itself.[110]

We could compare it with Matthew Arnold on *Celtic Literature*, well-meaning, anxious about the philistinism of his own countrymen, but devoid of any notion about how societies actually work, continually lapsing into ethnic stereotype. Tom Hughes, 'the Doctor's' disciple, can be acquitted of this, but in *Tom Brown's Schooldays* (1857), we see the ascriptive ethos of English class society made plain, while Miller's 'open' commitment to experience and change conveys the sensuality of knowledge, the excitement of acquiring it, the near-inebriated condition of the adept. Both books value childhood, but where Hughes foresees a life governed by the rules of team games (parliament itself being an obvious example) Miller's voyage is towards an unknown region, possibly exciting, possibly (as in his own case) disastrous. Conscious that many Welshmen must have written like this, in their own language, and excusing my own limitations in this field, I leave the last word with him:

> 'You Scotch are a strange people,' said one of the commercial gentlemen.
> 'When I was in Scotland two years ago, I could hear of scarce anything
> among you but your church question. What good does all your theology do
> for you?' 'Independently altogether of religious considerations,' I replied, 'It
> has done for our people what all your Societies for the Diffusion of Useful
> Knowledge, and all your penny and Saturday magazines, will never do for
> yours: it has awakened their intellects and taught them how to think.'[111]

---

[110] For an introduction to Miller see George Rosie, *Hugh Miller: Outrage and Order*, (Edinburgh: Mainstream, 1980); and see Miller, *First Impressions of England*, pp. 16, 46.
[111] Ibid, p.11.

*Proceedings of the British Academy*, **80**, 49–71

SHAKESPEARE LECTURE

# Parks and Ardens

### ANNE BARTON
*University of Cambridge*
*Fellow of the Academy*

IN 1702, a play called *The Comical Gallant: Or, The Amours of Sir John Falstaffe* was performed at the Theatre Royal, Drury Lane. Its author, John Dennis, later claimed that because the actor entrusted with Falstaff failed to please, the audience 'fell from disliking the Action to disapproving the Play'.[1] Certainly, *The Comical Gallant* did not dislodge *The Merry Wives of Windsor* from the repertory. Shakespeare's comedy, un-adapted, had been one of the first plays performed after the Restoration. Revivals were frequent, and in 1704 Dennis had the humiliating experience of seeing Shakespeare's original, rather than his own 'improved' version, presented at court with a glittering cast that included Betterton, Mrs Bracegirdle and Mrs Barry. Yet he had worked hard to accommodate *The Merry Wives* to contemporary taste. Jeremy Collier's strictures in *A Short View* of 1698 clearly lie behind this Fenton's revelation to Master Page that he and Ann have not availed themselves (as they do in Shakespeare) of the confusion at Herne's oak to steal a marriage: having 'truly considered of the terrible consequences which attend the just displeasure of a Parent'.[2] Shakespeare

---

Read 23 April 1991. © The British Academy 1993.

Dates given for plays before 1700 are those suggested in *Annals of English Drama 975–1700*, by Alfred Harbage, rev. Samuel Schoenbaum (London, 1964). For the eighteenth century, I have relied upon the hand-list of plays supplied in Vol. 2 of Allardyce Nicoll's *A History of English Drama 1660–1900* (Cambridge, 1961).

In quotations from old-spelling texts, i/j and u/v have been regularized to accord with modern practice.

[1] John Dennis, 'The Epistle Dedicatory' to *The Comical Gallant: Or, The Amours of Sir John Falstaffe* [Cornmarket Shakespeare Series, vol. 42] (London, 1969).

[2] Ibid., p. 48.

had reserved Windsor Park as a setting until this final, nocturnal scene. Dennis insists that his play should not only end but begin in the park. Moreover, as the assembled characters cross and re-cross the stage in Act I, greeting one another, scheming, exchanging confidences and billets-doux or, in the case of Ann Page, slipping away from her mother to snatch a meeting with Fenton, it becomes apparent that what Dennis really has in mind is not Windsor but London's St. James's Park: the Mall, to be precise, shortly before mid-day, the time of the pre-dinner promenade.

In his softened and more cautious way, Dennis was following the example of a great many late seventeenth-century dramatists in gravitating to the Mall. By 1702, park scenes had for decades been a staple of comedies set in contemporary London. Several of them, indeed, had contrasted St. James in its fashionable daylight hours with the same place seen at night: *The Mall: Or, The Modish Lovers*, for instance, of 1674, probably the work of John Dover, or Southerne's *The Wives' Excuse* (1691) and *The Maid's Last Prayer* (1693). If Wycherley's character Ranger, in *Love in a Wood: Or, St. James's Park* (1672), can be trusted, 'the new-fashioned caterwauling', 'this midnight coursing in the Park' as he calls it, was à la mode by the early 1670s.[3] A risky activity, associated with the illegal pleasures (and dangers) of actual deer coursing after dark, it had been anticipated in the nocturnal park of *The Merry Wives of Windsor*—the first such scene, so far as I can tell, in English drama.[4] For Shakespeare's Windsor Park, where the younger generation deceives the old, and the heiress elopes with a libertine of 'riots past' and 'wild societies', is an oddly Restoration place.[5] Hence the anxiety it caused Dennis in 1702. Struggling to distance himself from the venery associated with parks, he omitted not only the clandestine marriage and all reference to Fenton's rakish reputation, but those shaggy-thighed satyrs originally involved in the hunting of Falstaff. Dennis's night park is more decorous than Shakespeare's. Partly for this reason, it brings into focus a real affinity between *The Merry Wives* and the urbane, tough-minded comedy of dramatists like Wycherley and Southerne—an affinity all the more surprising because of the rustic,

---

[3] Sir William Wycherley, *Love in a Wood: Or, St. James's Park,* in *The Plays of William Wycherley,* ed. Peter Holland (Cambridge, 1981), II.1.2–3.

[4] Hunting game (except for hares) at night had been illegal since the late sixteenth century. See P.B. Munsche, *Gentlemen and Poachers: The English Game Laws 1671–1831* (Cambridge, 1981), pp. 175–6. The Game Act of 1671 excluded deer—now regarded as a gentleman's private property and so covered by Common Law—from its protection, while effectively restricting the right to hunt game to the landed gentry.

[5] III.4.8. Subsequent references to works by Shakespeare have been incorporated in the text. All are keyed to *The Riverside Shakespeare,* ed. G. Blakemore Evans *et. al.* (Boston, 1974).

Warwickshire roots of this, as of Shakespeare's three other parkland plays.

What was the landscape of Shakespeare's boyhood? One haunted, I want to suggest, by the ghost of the Forest of Arden. In the thirteenth song of *Poly-Olbion*, published in 1612, Michael Drayton—himself a Warwickshire man—gave that ghost a voice: a lament for its destruction at the hands of those 'gripple wretch[es]' who spoiled 'my tall and goodly woods, and did my grounds inclose'.[6] Drayton's claim that Arden was once the greatest forest in Britain is often dismissed as antiquarian fantasy, sparked off by Camden's revelation that '*Arden* among the ancient Britans and Gaules signified a *wood*'.[7] A twelfth-century document, however, decisively supports Drayton. Colossal, on the scale of the greater French forests, Arden once covered Warwickshire and spilled over into Worcestershire and Staffordshire. It seems never to have been Crown property—protected by royal Forest as opposed to Common Law—and that, of course, was its undoing. Patchily but steadily, it was felled, cleared and cultivated, especially to the south of the Avon where the soil was more fertile.[8] Leland, writing in the reign of Henry VIII, observed that only the wooded country north of the river was still known as 'Arden'. It comprised the larger part of the shire, but by 1586 Camden, while recording the same division between felden (or fields) and wooded country, found that 'Arden', as a territorial name, had fallen into disuse. The part north of the Avon, 'much larger in compasse than the *Feldon*, . . . is for the most part thicke set with woods, and yet not without pastures, corn-fields, and sundry mines of Iron: This part, as it is at this day called *Woodland*, so also was in old time knowen by a more ancient name *Arden* . . .'[9]

Like Drayton's, Shakespeare's Forest of Arden in *As You Like It* has often been described as imaginary: a purely 'mythic and hypothetical' setting, as one critic puts it.[10] It is true that palm trees and olives, not to mention lionesses, are scarcely Warwickshire products. On the other

[6] Michael Drayton, *Poly-Olbion*, in *The Works of Michael Drayton*, vol. 4, ed. J. William Hebel (Oxford, 1933), p. 276.

[7] William Camden, *Britain, or a Chorographicall Description of the Most Flourishing Kingdomes England, Scotland, and Ireland, and the Ilands Adjoyning* . . . (English trans. of the 1586 edn, London, 1610), p. 565. See also the Warwickshire volume of *The Victoria County History* (London, 1908), vol. 2, 228.

[8] Oliver Rackham, *Ancient Woodland: Its History, Vegetation and Uses in England* (London, 1980), pp. 127, 175–82. See also Leonard Cantor, 'Forest, Chases, Parks and Warrens', in *The English Mediaeval Landscape*, ed. L. Cantor (London, 1982), pp. 80–1.

[9] Camden, op. cit., p. 565.

[10] David Young, *The Heart's Forest: A Study of Shakespeare's Pastoral Plays* (New Haven, 1972), p. 42. For an attempt to redress this view, see H. Stuart Daly, 'Where are the Woods in *As You Like It*?' (*Shakespeare Quarterly*, 34 (1983) 172–80).

hand, when Shakespeare, a man born and bred on the north side of the Avon, confronted the forest of Arden in his source, Lodge's *Rosalynde*, considerably more than just his mother's surname, or the French Ardennes intended by Lodge, must have sprung to mind. Shakespeare's Forest of Arden is the shifting and contradictory place it is because, unlike Lodge's, it compounds the fantastic with something native, real and intimately known. An 'uncouth forest' (II.6.6), a 'desert inaccessible, / Under the shade of melancholy boughs' (II.7.110–11), Arden presents itself initally to Orlando and Adam as untouched woodland. Wandering about helplessly, both nearly starve to death in a place apparently devoid of any settled human habitation. When Orlando fortunately stumbles upon Duke Senior and his fellow outlaws, he is anxious to know if they have ever been 'where bells have knoll'd to church' (II.7.114). And yet Arden is not only where William says he was born, the place he, Audrey, Corin, Silvius and Phebe call home, Touchstone has no difficulty in rustling up Sir Oliver Martext, 'the vicar of the next village' (III.43–4), and a chapel, when 'wedlock would be nibbling' (III.3.80–1).

Shakespeare's Arden, unlike that of Lodge, has experienced enclosure. In the source, Rosalynde and Aliena first encounter Coridon and Montanus sitting side by side 'in a faire valley', their two flocks of sheep feeding around them on common pasture.[11] As they talk, it becomes clear that Coridon is a tenant farmer who, as well as tending his 'landlord's' sheep on the common, supports himself by tilling arable land belonging to the cottage he rents. The landlord has now decided to sell, terminating the lease-hold. When Rosalynde and Aliena offer to buy both sheep and farm, Coridon gladly agrees to share the cottage he previously enjoyed alone, and relinquish to them the task of escorting sheep to the common. The position of Shakespeare's Corin is very different. A wage-earner, not a tenant, he is not only unable to 'shear the fleeces that I graze' (II.4.79)—the grazing itself—or 'bounds of feed' (II.4.83)—is up for sale too, along with the flock and the cottage. There is no 'landlord' in the case, only a churlish 'master' in whose cottage Corin, the labourer, is allowed a bed. Because this master is currently away, as Corin explains to Rosalind and Celia, there is almost nothing in this house on the 'skirts' (III.2.336) or 'purlieus' (IV.3.77)—Shakespeare uses the technical word for a cleared space on the edge of a forest—of Arden 'that you will feed on' (II.4.86), although he proposes to make them as welcome as he can.

Enclosure in Arden, unprotected as it was by Forest law, had begun early. Coridon's slide from tenant to hired man was a more recent phenomenon. In his study of 'Economic and Social Change in the Forest of

---

[11] Thomas Lodge, 'Rosalynde', in *Narrative and Dramatic Sources of Shakespeare's Plays*, vol. 2, ed. Geoffrey Bullough, (London, 1958), p. 182.

Arden: 1530–1649', the agrarian historian V.H.T. Skipp identifies a steady rise there towards the end of the sixteenth century in the number of landless labourers, proportions of about twenty per cent already registering in one parish by 1605.[12] It would be more than forty per cent by the middle of the century. The change seems to have been linked to Arden's gradual abandonment of its traditional pastoral economy, based on sheep and cattle, in favour of those 'green corn-field[s]' and 'acres of the rye' (V.3.18.22) characteristic of the other side of the river. And Shakespeare's play faithfully reflects it.

In their sylvan exile, Duke Senior and his court subsist on fallow deer—'poor *dappled* fools' (II.1.22)—an imported species, associated primarily with parks, where they tended to be kept at least as much to supply venison for the table as for sport. The wild red deer, the hart, from time immemorial the noblest of quarries, which Drayton depicts being hunted 'at force'[13] (that is, with hounds) through the spacious tracts of an older Arden, makes only a distant appearance in *As You Like It*, by way of Touchstone's parodic verses: 'If a hart do lack a hind, / Let him seek out Rosalind' (III.2.101–2). Warwickshire from medieval times had been particularly rich in parks and, of those established before the sixteenth century, fifty out of fifty-two were located north of the river.[14] Charlecote Park, bifurcated by the Avon, may not have been enclosed and stocked with deer in time for the young Shakespeare, 'much given to all unluckinesse in stealing venison', according to Richard Davies in 1695, to have chosen it as the scene of his depredations.[15] There were plenty of others in the vicinity, including (of course) Kenilworth, greatly enlarged by the Earl of Leicester, where Queen Elizabeth in 1575 had spent more time slaughtering deer than attending to the ingenious shows and entertainments with which these ceremonial hunts were entwined. Shakespeare may or may not, like his own Falstaff in *The Merry Wives*, actually have beaten keepers, killed deer, broken open a lodge, and then (as the legend has it) been obliged to flee Warwickshire and become England's greatest dramatist. But parks, during the 1590s, when he was still close to his Warwickshire youth, do seem to have been much on his mind.

---

[12] V.H.T. Skipp, 'Economic and Social Change in the Forest of Arden', in *Agricultural History Review*, 18 (suppl.) (1970), 84–111.

[13] Drayton, op. cit., p. 278.

[14] Cantor, op. cit., p. 80.

[15] Sir Edmund Chambers, *William Shakespeare: A Study of Facts and Problems*, 2 vols (Oxford, 1930), vol. 1, pp. 18–21, vol. 2, pp. 255–7.

I can find only one allusion to a park in Shakespeare's Jacobean work. The Queen, in *Cymbeline*, imagines all Britain as 'Neptune's park, ribb'd and pal'd in / With oaks unscalable and roaring waters' (III.1.19–20). The image is accurate, and ought never (though it often is) to be emended. In 1611, Arthur Standish, in *The Commons Complaint*, the first recorded book on English forestry, three slightly different versions of which, all dedicated to King James, appeared in 1611, 1613 and 1615, extended particular approval to park owners who reinforced their enclosures, whether hedge or the more usual cleft stakes, with living timber trees, a barrier of ash or oak, allowed to grow to full maturity, and 'once made, never to be made againe'.[16] The *Cymbeline* passage set aside, all Shakespeare's other park references or settings are Elizabethan: Talbot's dismayed exclamation in *1 Henry VI*, 'How are we park'd and bounded in a pale, / A little herd of England's timorous deer, / Maz'd with a yelping kennel of French curs!' (IV.2.45–7), Venus's unsuccessful attempt, in *Venus and Adonis*, to transform her body into a park, encircled by an 'ivory pale' (230), where Adonis might erotically and safely browse, or the complaint of Adriana in *The Comedy of Errors* about her husband's infidelities—'too unruly deer, he breaks the pale, / And feeds from home' (II.1.100–1). Other instances, literal rather than metaphoric, conjure up a shadowy park setting, just out of sight: Hotspur's park in *1 Henry IV* in which the crop-eared roan awaits his master, or Petruchio's in *The Taming of the Shrew*, where the servants ought to be lined up to welcome Kate. Editors of *The Merchant of Venice* usually indicate that Lorenzo and Jessica listen to music, just before Portia's return, in the open air of a garden or 'avenue before the house'. Judging from the fact that she and Nerissa left for Venice by coach from 'the park-gate' (III.4.83), Shakespeare may well, in an interesting anticipation of *The Merry Wives*, have imagined, without specifying, a night park.

Far more concretely realized are the paired park scenes of *3 Henry VI*. At the beginning of Act three, King Henry, fleeing from the battle of Towton, is taken prisoner by 'keepers' concealed in a thicket beside the 'laund' (or open space) of what editors usually designate as a 'forest', but which must, given the vocabulary used, be a park. Armed with crossbows, they are out 'culling the principal of all the deer' (III.1.4), but succeed in bringing down a different kind of royal stag. The scene has a carefully constructed obverse in Act IV, when the imprisoned Edward IV manages to escape from the Bishop of York's custody while walking in his park, despite the efforts of the 'huntsman' accompanying him. There is no indication in Shakespeare's sources that Henry was taken prisoner in either a forest or

---

[16] Arthur Standish, *The Commons Complaint* (London, 1615), D3.

a park. For his rival's evasion of captivity, there is only Halle's testimony that because Edward 'spake ever fayre to the Archebishop and the other kepers', he had liberty to go hunting, and one day met 'on a playne' with such a large body of his friends that 'neither his kepers would, nor once durst, move him to retorne to prison agayn'.[17] Shakespeare has availed himself of the suggestive word 'keper' to turn Halle's aristocratic gaolers into the single 'huntsman' responsible for showing Edward 'where lies the game' (IV.5.14). He also turns Halle's 'playne' into an enclosed park, at the 'corner' (IV.5.19) of which Edward's horse stands ready. Across the space of nearly two acts, Lancaster's capture and York's escape are counter-balanced structurally by way of their shared parkland setting.

The park in *Titus Andronicus* seems also to have been Shakespeare's invention. The hunt, with 'horn and hound', of 'the panther and the hart' (I.1.494, 493) in Act II is usually said to take place, quite simply, in a forest. Richard Marienstras, in his 1981 essay, 'The Forest, Hunting and Sacrifice in *Titus Andronicus*', makes much of it as 'a place predestined by nature to the release of savagery'.[18] That is partly true. But it is also true that, like Arden later, this forest keeps shifting its character and identity. 'The woods are ruthless, dreadful, deaf, and dull' (II.1.128), as Aaron says, but they are also—and not just in Tamora's imagination—'green' (II.2.2), a 'pleasant chase' (II.3.255), full of bird-song, 'cheerful sun' (II.3.13), and of wide and spacious 'walks' where 'the lovely Roman ladies' (II.1.113–14) can saunter at their ease, like those fifteenth-century Flemish beauties in the Victoria and Albert Museum's Chatsworth tapestries, while the hunt goes on around them. Tamora's two contrasting vignettes of the particular spot that is at one moment a *locus amoenus* and, in the next, a 'barren, detested vale' (II.3.93), merely polarize a general ambiguity, one reflected in the different terms used to describe the scene of the hunt: 'woods' and 'forest', but also (on two occasions) 'chase'—a small, managed forest in private hands—equipped, in this instance, on 'the north side' with a keeper's lodge (II.3.254–5). Finally, Marcus tells his brother Titus that he found the raped and mutilated Lavinia, straying, 'as doth the deer / That hath receiv'd some unrecuring wound', 'in the park' (III.1.88–90).

T.J.B. Spencer once remarked of *Titus* that Shakespeare seemed determined to include in it all the political institutions Rome ever had, not so much to get Roman history right, as to get it all in.[19] That impulse

---

[17] Edward Halle, *The Union of the Two Noble and Illustre Famelies of Lancaster and York* (London, 1550), 'The viii yere of Kyng Edward the iiii', fol. xiiij[r].

[18] Richard Marienstras, *New Perspectives on the Shakespearean World*, trans. Janet Lloyd (Cambridge, 1981), p. 44.

[19] T.J.B. Spencer, 'Shakespeare and the Elizabethan Romans', in *Shakespeare Survey*, 10 (1957), p. 32.

also seems to lie behind the hunt in this play and its setting. Titus's proposal to the emperor and his bride, 'Tomorrow . . . / To hunt the panther and the hart with me' (I.1.492–3), is startling, especially when surrounded, as it almost immediately is, with ceremonial detail—the horn call when hounds were uncoupled, the baying of what the stage directions suggest must have been real dogs, the different 'horns in a peal' described in Turbervile's *Noble Arte of Venerie* of 1575 as appropriate to call 'a companie in the morning'—all things associated specifically with the singling out and hunting, *par force des chiens*, of the red deer stag.[20] Shakespeare must have been aware that panthers are as impossible in Italy as lions in Arden, unless (of course) someone imports them, like those Elizabethan lions languishing in the Tower of London, for a purpose. Certainly a 'solemn hunting' (II.1.112), as this one is said to be, is implausible with both the panther and the hart as intended and simultaneous quarry. Or at least it is in a forest or chase. The enclosed park is a different matter.

At this point, the vexed issue of Shakespeare's 'small *Latine*, and lesse *Greeke*' becomes more than usually troublesome. Like the fallow deer with which they became so closely associated, parks were of eastern origin. Persia in particular was renowned for them. *Pairidaeza*, the Old Persian word for park—it means to 'shape' or 'mould around'—was first Hellenized by Xenophon, in the *Anabasis*, when he wrote about the great royal *paradeisos* of Cyrus, full of wild animals.[21] This Greek word was destined to become complexly entwined with the ancient Hebrew *pardes* and end up signifying both heaven and the garden of Eden. Meanwhile, according to Quintus Curtius, Alexander the Great, entering a great walled park in the heart of Asia which had not been touched for four generations, ordered all the beasts to be driven from their cover, and despatched single-handed the huge lion that attacked him. It was largely as a result of Alexander's progress through Persia that parks, enclosing beasts of various kinds, soon began to appear all over the Mediterranean.[22] Some were really menageries. Varro writes admiringly of the park belonging to the Roman orator Hortensius, where guests banqueting on an artfully raised triclinium watched a slave, dressed up as Orpheus, with a long floating robe, gather stags, wild boar, and a multitude of other quadrupeds around him with the music of his lyre.[23] This wonderful spectacle, Varro claimed, could be

---

[20] Hereward T. Price discusses the hunting music, and its precision, in 'The Authorship of *Titus Andronicus*,' in *The Journal of English and Germanic Philology*, 42 (1943), p. 61.

[21] A. Bartlett Giametti, *The Earthly Paradise and the Renaissance Epic* (Princeton, 1966), pp. 11–15.

[22] Russell Meiggs, *Trees and Timber in the Ancient Mediterranean* (Oxford, 1982), p. 272.

[23] Jacques Aymard, *Essai sur les Chasses Romaines, des origines à la fin du siècle des Antonins* (Paris, 1951), [Bibliotheque des Ecoles Francaises d'Athènes et de Rome], p. 71.

compared only to the great *venationes*, the hunts and other displays of the Roman circus, or at least to those which did not include African animals. They, according to Livy, had first appeared in the year 186 BC, in the form of a combat of lions and panthers.

In his *Historie of the Foure-Footed Beastes* (1607), Edward Topsell, assembling information from a wide range of classical and other sources, asserts that although the senators of Rome 'in auncient time' wisely forbade anyone to import panthers, the needs of the circus soon prevailed: Pompey the Great, we are told, brought in four hundred and ten of them, and Augustus four hundred and twenty.[24] These figures sound exaggerated, but there can be no doubt that panthers did feature prominently in the gory spectacles of the Roman circus, especially under the empire, and that a variety of other victims—including stags —were often hunted in the arena with them at the same time. In the most elaborate, moreover, of these *venationes*—they were known as *silvae*—the amphitheatre, at enormous expense, was landscaped: provided with trees and rocks, thickets, running streams, and artificial hills, so that the Roman crowd seemed to be looking down at a real forest or, given its protective barriers and circular shape, upon an enclosed park.[25] Some emperors—Nero, Caracalla—actually entered it themselves to display their prowess. I don't know whether Shakespeare had read or heard about the Roman *silvae* in Calpurnius and later Roman authors, but the mixed nature of the hunt, including the slaughter of human participants, in *Titus* eerily resembles them.

Tamora's son Demetrius assumes a shared experience of ordinary deer-stealing among Chiron, Aaron and himself: 'What, hast not thou full often strook a doe, / And borne her cleanly by the keeper's nose?' (II.1.93–4). But when he reminds Chiron that 'we hunt not, we, with horse nor hound, / But hope to pluck a dainty doe to ground' (II.2.25–6), he has ceased to be the human hunter and become the hound, one of those masterless 'whelps, fell curs of bloody kind' (II.3.281) that Saturninus, speaking more truly than he knows, later accuses of having murdered Bassianus. Lavinia, in Act II, describes Tamora as a tiger, but the honey-tongued and treacherous conciliatress of the play's first scene is more concretely emblematized by that panther Aaron persuades Titus's sons they can surprise fast asleep in the bottom of a pit. 'As a Lyon doeth in most thinges imitate and resemble the very nature of man', Topsell misogynistically recorded, 'so after the very selfe-same manner doth the panther of a Woman, for it is a fraudulent though a beautiful beast'.[26] Panthers in the wild, as Topsell

[24] Edward Topsell, *The Historie of the Foure-Footed Beastes* (London, 1607), p. 583.

[25] Aymard, op. cit., pp. 189–96, 354.

[26] Topsell, op. cit., pp. 581–2.

also records (following Oppian) were taken in pit-fall traps, baited with carrion; this 'subtile hole' (II.3.198), its mouth 'covered with rude-growing briers' (II.3.199), is the place to which two young men, lured by the panther, come unsuspectingly and, when they have fallen helplessly into its depths, discover human carrion.

The 'loathsome pit' (II.3.176) in *Titus*, a 'fell devouring receptacle, / As hateful as [Cocytus'] misty mouth' (II.3.235–6), was already complicated enough before the Freudians got hold of it. A natural cavity, a trap, a grave, hell-mouth, the entrance to the underworld, it also provokes thoughts of a Warwickshire saltory, or deer-leap: an excavation, usually combined with a steep bank, which allowed wild deer to enter a park through a gap in its palings, but not to get out again. Edward Ravenscroft, adapting Shakespeare's tragedy in 1686, rejected all these associations. He turned it into an ice-house. Unlike Dennis's *Comical Gallant*, Ravenscroft's *Titus* was a theatrical success. Establishing itself in the repertory as 'a Stock-Play', it not only replaced the original, but continued to be performed well into the eighteenth century.[27] One reason for its acceptability may have been the drastic—and revealing—measures Ravenscroft had taken when confronted with the peculiarities of Shakespeare's hunt and its locale. The hunt he abolished entirely; the ambiguous forest he transformed unequivocally into a park, or pleasure garden.

'Come *Tamora*', Ravenscroft's Saturninus says near the end of Act I,

> this is a day of Triumph,
> All Pleasures of the *Banii* shall delight thee,
> Where every Sense is exquisitely touch'd,
> Pleasures that not the World affords,
> And yet is only known to Roman Lords.[28]

I owe to Jeremy Maule the suggestion that 'Banii' represents Ravenscroft's attempt to Latinize the famous sixteenth century Bagnaia Gardens attached to the Villa Lante, outside Rome near Viterbo. He may have visited them himself, as John Evelyn did. But although the same dreadful things happen in Ravenscroft's Banii Gardens as had in Shakespeare's ruthless woods, they are everywhere coloured by suggestions of a place closer to home. Whatever may have been painted on the stage shutters, this scene of public promenade, but also of 'close walks' and 'private Groves', 'Grottoes', and retreats for lovers, where 'none may hear / Their Amorous talk', is again (like Dennis's Windsor Park) really London's St. James's.[29]

---

[27] Edward Ravenscroft, 'To the Reader', *Titus Andronicus: Or The Rape of Lavinia* (London, 1969), [Cornmarket Shakespeare Series; vol. 71].

[28] Ibid., p. 15.

[29] Ibid., pp. 17–18.

In his poem, 'On St. James's Park, As Lately Improved By His Majesty', published in 1661, Edmund Waller had paid particular attention to the marvel of the royal ice-houses: those 'deep caves', 'Winter's dark prison', whose 'harvest of cold months laid up, / Gives a fresh coolness to the royal cup'.[30] There was, as it happens, an ice-house in the Bagnaia Gardens. Its presence is clearly visible in an engraving of 1612–14, from the *Antiquae urbis splendor Roma*.[31] One needs, however, to remember that although common in Italy, and beginning to appear in France, ice-houses (as opposed to rudimentary snow conserves of the kind King James had at Greenwich Park and Hampton Court) were unknown in Britain until John Rose in October 1660 constructed the ones in St. James' Park on the model of those recently introduced at Versailles.[32] Ice-houses were sufficiently novel and also rare for the Royal Society to hold a special meeting on the subject in 1662, at which Robert Boyle gave a paper incorporating some of the observations made by Evelyn during his travels in Italy, and for Charles II in February 1664 to swear in one Simon Menselli (significantly, an Italian) in a newly-created post as 'Yeoman of O[u]r Snowe and Ice'. For London audiences, it would have been these celebrated ice-houses in St. James's Park, presided over by Menselli and his successors, with which Ravenscroft endowed Saturninus:

> on the more Remoter parts
> Dark Caves and Vaults, where water crusted Lyes
> In ice, all the hot season of the year.
> As Chrystillin, and firm as when
> 'Twas taken from the Winter's frost.[33]

It is to the deepest and most gloomy of these vaults, now containing the body of Bassianus, that the sons of Titus are decoyed. The attraction is not a panther, but what Quintus calls the 'pleasant Secret' of an anonymous letter:

> Quintus, as soon as this comes to your hands, find out your Brother Martius, Bring him with you into the Banii Gardens, and attend a while at the Mouth of the Vault which is called the Serpents-Den, where once the mighty Snake was found: Your Expectations shall be rewarded with the company of two

---

[30] Edmund Waller, 'On St. James's Park as Lately Improved By His Majesty', in *The Works of Edward Waller Esq. in Verse and Prose* (London, 1729), p. 208.

[31] The engraving by G.Lauro, showing the ice-house, is reproduced by Bruno Adorni in his essay, 'The Villa Lante at Bagnaia', in *The History of Garden Design: The Western Tradition from the Renaissance to the Present Day*, ed. Monique Mosser and Georges Tessot (London, 1991), p. 92.

[32] Sylvia Beamon and Susan Roaf, *The Ice-Houses of Britain* (New York, 1991), pp. 12–19, 34.

[33] Ravenscroft, op. cit., pp. 17–18.

> Ladies, Young, and in our own opinions not unhandsome, whose sight shall
> not displease you; Love gives the Invitation, and we believe you both Gallant
> Enough to know how to use it, and to conceal our favours.[34]

Here, and for several ensuing lines of dialogue, as the deluded brothers
await 'these kind and Loving ones', Ravenscroft begins to write Restoration
comedy: the kind of play—*The Mall*, or Southerne's *The Maid's Last Prayer*
are examples—in which one or two men are lured into St. James's Park by
a note (usually deceptive) of assignation.

Waller's encomium on St. James's Park, a 'Paradise', as he calls it,
another Eden, presided over by a benevolent shepherd king, had dealt
entirely with its daylight hours and cheerful, public pursuits: 'the lovers
walking in that amorous shade; / The Gallants dancing by the river's
side; / They bathe in summer, and in winter slide'.[35] A decade later,
in 1672, Rochester revisited the place, in his nocturnal 'A Ramble in
St. James's Park', and saw something very different: an 'all-sin-sheltring
Grove', where every 'imitative branch does twine / In some lov'd fold
of Aretine / And nightly now beneath their shade / Are Buggeries,
Rapes and Incests made'.[36] Ravenscroft has managed to invoke both
Waller's *paradeisos* and Rochester's surreal landscape of violence and lust,
translating Shakespeare's ambivalent forest into an equally ambiguous but
recognizable contemporary place.

*Titus*, *The Merry Wives*, and *3 Henry VI* were all adapted in the later
seventeenth century or early in the eighteenth. (Crowne's version of the
last, *The Misery of Civil War*, of 1680, omitted the scenes of Henry's
capture and Edward's escape.) *Love's Labour's Lost*—the fourth and
last of Shakespeare's parkland plays that I want to discuss—remained
untouched until 1762. Nor, although it appears (together with *As You
Like It*) in the long list of works, formerly the property of Shakespeare's
company at Blackfriars, that were 'allowed' to the King's Company at
Drury Lane in January 1669, does it seem to have been performed after
the Restoration. That, given its intransigently Elizabethan wit, combined
with a plotlessness exceeding even that of *As You Like It*, is understandable.
More surprising is the fact that this play, available only as a text for reading,
should have exercised such an influence on the best comedies of the period:

[34] Ibid., p. 23.
[35] Waller, op. cit., p. 207.
[36] John Wilmot, Earl of Rochester, 'A Ramble in St. James's Park', in *The Poems of John Wilmot, Earl of Rochester*, ed. Keith Walker (London, 1984), p. 64.

an influence, as I believe, far more profound than that of Fletcher or Shirley, whose comedies were frequently revived, and rivalled only by that of Jonson.

*Love's Labour's Lost* is usually said by its editors to be set entirely in the royal park of Navarre. That is not strictly true, although the unlocalized staging of Shakespeare's theatre must have blurred this fact. The anonymous author of *The Students* in 1762, however, who had experienced the comedy only on the printed page, displayed a rare flash of intelligence when he discriminated, in the scene headings of his version, between 'the fields' and 'the park'. The tents in which Shakespeare's Navarre lodges the Princess and her ladies stand in 'the wide fields' (I.1.93), somewhere close to that manor-house, the King's silent and 'un-peopled' court, whose gates they cannot enter. The park, abutting, as Armado tells us, on the manor's 'curious-knotted' garden (I.1.245–6), is a place slightly but significantly different. The women enter it for the hunt and then, at the end of Act IV, are escorted back to their tents ('from the park let us conduct them thither', IV.3.371) by men whose vows of asceticism and study have crumbled ignominiously in the parkland setting. It is a populous place, not only in terms of the deer, and the foresters in the 'lodge' who look after them, but because a variety of people like to walk there—the King and his three 'book-mates', Armado giving his melancholy some fresh air, Costard in amorous pursuit of Jaquenetta, or local villagers, the schoolmaster Holofernes and Nathaniel the curate, lost in erudite discourse.

The hunt arranged to divert a somewhat reluctant Princess is of the 'bow and stable', as opposed to *par force*, variety most often associated in the Tudor period with parks. As Queen Elizabeth did so often, she stands in an appointed place, armed with a cross-bow, while the deer are driven past, and her success is greeted by the shouts of assembled spectators. Meanwhile, Berowne is observing gloomily that while the King hunts deer, 'I am coursing myself', caught in a 'toil' of love he likens to the one set up in the park, the deer-haye forcing the animals towards the waiting archers (IV.3.1–3). This particular version of the Actaeon image (later elaborated by Orsino in *Twelfth Night*, in the context of a *par force* chase), in which the lover is both quarry and hound, is altogether more complicated than the brutally simple intention of Chiron and Demetrius in *Titus* to 'pluck down a dainty doe'. It links back, indeed, to the courtly love poetry of the fourteenth century, to Hesdin and the great *Jagd* of Hadamar—in which named hounds, sometimes in fell pursuit of the lover to whom they belong, are aspects of his self, or of his relationship with the lady. But it also looks forward to the Restoration.

It was once a critical fashion to assail even the best Restoration comedy for its supposed dullness and triviality, and to instance its repetitive imagery of the sexual hunt. This imagery is not, in fact, either as monotonous or as fatuous as was claimed—although it could be used to signal either the inappropriateness of the love chase to the old (Sir Oliver Cockwood and Sir Joslin Jolly in Etherege's *She Wou'd If She Cou'd* (1668), for instance) or the habituated response of fashionable young philanderers before they fall under the spell of a genuinely witty and interesting woman. Although usually, it is by no means invariably the language of men. Crowne's heroine Christina in *The Country Wit* (1675) intends to pursue the outrageous Ramble to his lodging 'And hunt him dry-foot thence:—would odds were laid me, / I did not rouse my wild, outlying buck / This hour, and catch him brousing on some common . . .',[37] and Farquhar's Lucinda in *Love and a Bottle* (1698), catching sight of the aptly named Roebuck, in one of the walks of Lincoln's-Inn Fields, goes in pursuit, thinking 'He may afford us some sport'.[38] A great many of these hunting images appear in scenes set in London's St. James's Park, which did as it happens still contain deer. Even when they do not, the presence of that park still tends to be felt behind them, as a focus of daily life in town.

Although Shirley's *Hyde Park* of 1632 was revived after the Restoration—Pepys saw it in 1668, apparently with live horses—and although a scattering of comedies visit the New Spring Gardens in Lambeth, Lincoln's-Inn Fields, or Greenwich Park, St. James's was overwhelmingly the preferred park setting. (The Mulberry Gardens, used by Newcastle, Sedley and Etherege, on the site of what is now Buckingham Palace, were merely an extension of it.) St. James's was not, in fact, any more fashionable or more frequented than Hyde Park in the period. The latter, however, although much mentioned in comedy, had become useless as a dramatic setting, for the simple reason that the 'done' thing there after 1660 was for people to sit in a coach, equipped with footmen and six Flanders mares, and ride round and round in up to twelve concentric and very dusty circles, each revolving in the opposite direction to the one flanking it. This was called 'The Ring' or 'Tour', and apart from being unstageable, it reduced conversation outside the cramped confines of each coach to what Etherege's Harriet in *The Man of Mode* (1676) dismisses contemptuously as 'the formal bows, the affected smiles, the silly by-words, and amorous tweers, in passing'.[39] Some signals could be given in the Ring: Charles II and the Duchess of Castlemaine formally greeting one another, as Pepys noted,

---

[37] John Crowne, *The Country Wit*, in *The Comedies of John Crowne*, ed. B.J. McMullin (New York, 1984), [*The Renaissance Imagination*, gen. ed. Stephen Orgel], I. 1.317–19.

[38] George Farquhar, *Love and a Bottle*, in *The Works of George Farquhar*, ed. Shirley Strum Kenny, vol. I (Oxford, 1988), I.1.130.

[39] Sir George Etherege, *The Man of Mode*, in *The Plays of Sir George Etherege*, ed. Michael Cordner (Cambridge, 1982), III.3.49–51.

at each revolution, or (on a different occasion) the Duchess expressing her superiority to the whole gilded and competitive show by allowing herself to be carried round fast asleep, with her mouth open. According to Stanmore in Shadwell's *A True Widow* (1678), Restoration Hyde Park had even invented a 'new method' of making love 'without speaking': 'your side glass let down hastily, when the party goes by, is very passionate. If she side *glass* you again, for that's the new word, ply her next day with a *billet doux* and you have her sure'.[40] It all depended, as Stanmore's interlocutor points out, on the two coaches *not* circulating in the same direction.

Etherege's Harriet, however, walking—as was the custom—in St. James's Park at 'high Mall', the second of the two fashionable times to be seen there, after the play and the Ring, observes that 'here one meets with a little conversation now and then'.[41] 'These conversations', her escort replies, 'have been fatal to some of your sex'. But Harriet likes to live dangerously. A moment later the park brings her face to face with Dorimant, the charismatic libertine of whom her mother is so terrified. Harriet has already seen and been fascinated by him at a distance. The Mall allows not only an introduction, but a tensely consequential crossing of verbal swords that she could have engineered nowhere else. It is also the arena Dorimant finds essential when he wants to quarrel with his mistress Mrs. Loveit, later in the same scene, severing their relations before the eyes of the whole town, and where she, at least briefly, is able to humiliate him.

'The hours of *Park-walking* are times of perfect *Carnival* to the Women', Sir Harry Peerabout later observed in an anonymous play of 1733 called *St. James's Park* and actually performed there 'Every Fine Day Between the Hours of Twelve and Two, During this Season':

> She that wou'd not admit the Visits of a Man without his being introduced by some Relation or intimate Friend, makes no scruple here to commence acquaintance at first sight; readily answers to any question shall be asked of her; values herself on being brisk at Repartee; and to have put him to it (as they call it) leaves a pleasure upon her Face for the whole day. In short, no Freedoms that can be taken here, are reckon'd indecent: All passes for Rallery, and harmless Gallantry.[42]

Almost half a century separates this passage from *The Man of Mode*, reflected not only in the later dinner hour and consequent advancement in the time of the morning promenade, but in the stiff response Peerabout's report of these manners elicits from Truelove: 'I should be sorry my Wife

---

[40] Thomas Shadwell, *A True Widow*, in *The Complete Works of Thomas Shadwell*, ed. Montague Summers, vol. 3 (London, 1927), p. 290.

[41] Etherege, op. cit., III.3. 49–51.

[42] *St. James's Park* (London, 1733), p. 3.

or Daughter were practis'd in them. But do any Women of real Honour take these Liberties?' The answer now, even from a Peerabout, is 'No'. It would have been 'Yes' before 1700, and not only in London's St. James's. Peerabout's account of raillery and repartee on slight acquaintance, bold skirmishes of wit in which women amuse themselves by putting down their male opponents, could also be a description of the Princess of France and her ladies, their mocking merriment at masculine expense, in that other royal park of Navarre.

Like Hyde Park, St. James's had been acquired and paled in by Henry VIII. He used it for hunting, as did Elizabeth.[43] Originally restricted to the royal family—St. James's Palace was incorporated in the grounds—it came under James I to be a place where other people, initially those attached to the court, came to stroll in the fresh air and admire not only the deer but the king's growing and expensive menagerie of wild animals. (The board of the elephant alone cost £273 a year, and that was exclusive of the gallon of wine a day his keepers said he required from September to April.)[44] Already fashionable under Charles I, St. James's continued to be frequented by Cromwell and his courtiers during the Commonwealth, and so escaped being sold off with the other royal parks. But it was only after the Restoration that it came into its own. Extensively re-designed and planted by Andre Mollet, 'Master of His Majesty of England's Gardens in His Park of St. James'—two copies of his book, *The Garden of Pleasure*, one with diagrams of the park, survive —this was the place where Charles II liked to exercise (and tended to lose) his spaniels, where he fed the ducks and played pall-mall, a form of croquet, on an avenue covered with powdered cockle-shells. Around him, Londoners with any social pretensions thronged to bask in the presence of this strikingly informal king and, even when he

---

[43] For Henry VIII's 'mania' for hunting in parks, see Oliver Rackham *Trees and Woodland in the British Landscape* (rev. edn, London, 1990), p. 158 and 'The King's Deer' [Nonsuch Palace Centenary Celebrations], which the author has kindly allowed me to read in typescript. See also E.P. Shirley, *Some Account of English Deer Parks* (London, 1867), A.S. Barrow ('Sabretache'), *Monarchy and the Chase* (London, 1948), and Susan Lasdun *The English Park: Royal, Private and Public* (London, 1991).
Edward Halle's account (op. cit. fol. iiii) of the festivities following Henry VIII's coronation ('The first yere of Kyng Henry the viii') includes a description of the 'faire house' erected in the Palace of Westminster, into which was brought a pageant in the form of a deer-park, 'paled with pales of White and Grene, wherein wer certain Fallowe Dere'. When its doors were opened, the deer 'ranne out therof into the Palaice, the greye houndes were lette slippe and killed the Dere: the whiche Dere so killed, were presented to the Quene and the Ladies' by Diana's knights.
[44] Jacob Larwood, *The Story of the London Parks*, Vol. 2 (London, 1881), p. 72.

was only symbolically there, to see and be seen, to observe the follies of others and commit their own.

Thanks to the efforts of Mollet, the park was wonderfully diverse.[45] Dominating it were the new canal, nearly half a mile long and one hundred feet wide, that extended down the middle, with an avenue of trees on each side, and the upper and lower Mall, the place of public promenade. But there was also a multitude of lesser walks, some of them named—the Green Walk, or Birdcage Walk, featuring some of the inmates of the royal zoo—others anonymous alleys or cross-walks lined with dwarf fruit-trees and leading to arbours or, in some cases, into what Mollet calls the 'wild Wood' at one end of the park and the artificial wilderness he had created at the other. Couples with something other than the promenade on their minds tended to arrange assignations in remote and specific areas: on the Duck-pond side, or at the mysteriously named Rosamond's Pond. The latter, at the west end of the park, had existed for centuries, but it was Mollet who surrounded it with trees and also constructed an artificial mount in the vicinity. An evening rendezvous at Rosamond's Pond, whether proposed or merely accepted by a woman, was usually regarded as tantamount to sexual surrender, something which might take place there and then. Not that Rosamond's Pond had a monopoly on such scenes. Courtall and Mrs. Wouldbee, in Dover's *The Mall*, are on 'the Duck-pond side' when she tells him, 'Sir, you have prevail'd, and overcome, but methinks this Bench is a very undecent place'. 'Oh Madam!', Courtall replies, 'There has been many a worse shift made'.[46] *Exeunt*, hand in hand.

It was, however, as a setting for the chase, rather than for consummation, that St. James's usually figured in comedy of the period. Women sometimes go there to spy upon and pursue erring lovers or husbands, as Lydia and Amanda do in Cibber's *Love's Last Shift* (1696) and Wycherley's *Love in A Wood*. Witty young heroines, cooped up at home by watchful parents or guardians, escape and range freely over the park in order to flush out and attract a young man to their taste. The young men themselves are the most habitual hunters. 'Yes faith, we have had many a fair course in this paddock', Freeman tells Ariana and Gatty in *She Wou'd If She Cou'd*, 'have been very well fleshed, and dare boldly fasten'.[47] Such predators often refer to their quarry as though they were female deer: 'does', a word that could mean 'prostitutes', but was also used of young women presumed to

---

[45] Andrew Mollet, *The Garden of Pleasure* (London, 1670), pp. 11–12. For the complicated history of this rare, posthumously published volume, see Blanche Henrey, *British Botanical and Horticultural History Before 1800* (London, 1975), pp. 198–203, 259.

[46] John Dover, *The Mall: Or, The Modish Lovers*, in *The Dramatic Works of John Dryden*, Vol. 8, ed. George Saintsbury (London, 1882), p. 537.

[47] Etherege, *She Would If She Could*, II.1.105–7.

be respectable.[48] Because upper class women, as well as whores, tended to wear vizard masks in the park, unless they were displaying themselves in the Mall, or were properly escorted, the chase often began with considerable uncertainty on the man's part as to the social standing, as well as identity, of the moving target. It was even possible to make the catastrophic mistake of pursuing one's own wife. The kind of embarrassment suffered by Navarre and his friends in *Love's Labour's Lost*, when the women mask and exchange love-tokens, and each man pays court to the wrong girl, is endemic in the park scenes of Restoration comedy.

But it is not only the masking and hunting in *Love's Labour's Lost*, its park setting and wittily realistic women, that make Shakespeare's play seem so uncannily to foreshadow those of a later period. As its title indicates, this is a work which concludes with the separation of people in love, with partings rather than marriage, and the reason is not to be found on the level of plot. The initial impediment—that league of study binding Navarre and his friends to shun female company for three years—crumbles midway through the comedy. What still holds Navarre and the Princess of France, Berowne, Rosaline, and the other two couples apart in Act V is not so much broken vows as attitudes of mind: chief among them, on the women's part, a deep distrust of the men's ability to sustain their love within marriage. That is why, in the final moments, they impose on their suitors penances designed to test the strength of their commitment and, in the case of Berowne, sent to jest a twelvemonth in a hospital, the validity of an accustomed social manner. Whether the men will return to claim their ladies at the end of the stipulated year of trial and waiting is unknown: something as much outside the limits of the play as the question of whether Etherege's Dorimant will survive his month of exile among the bucolic horrors of Hampshire and marry Harriet, or will flee after a fortnight, back to London and his bachelor life.

The ending of *Love's Labour's Lost* is unique in its period and, so far as I know, in English comedy generally before the Restoration. But between 1667 and 1700 versions of it turn up over and over again in plays by very different authors. In some comedies, the test is contained within the action. The man either passes it, or he fails. In the latter eventuality, if the woman accepts him, she does so with a measure of cynicism. In a number of plays, however, the ending is left open, as it is in *Love's Labour's Lost*. The woman turns aside the proposal of marriage finally elicited from the

---

48 Sir Mannerly Shallow, the rustic fool in Crowne's *The Country Wit* (1676), finds London's Whetstone Park, now built over, and notorious for its brothels, puzzling because devoid of grass and deer. 'I . . . spoke for a pasty; and they told me the strangest thing, they said their rooms were full of cold pasties, so big two people might sleep in one, and that if I had a mind to a doe, they would put me in a pasty, and put a doe to me' (III.4.107–10).

man she loves, for a definite or indefinite period. This is what not only Etherege's Harriet, but his Ariana and Gatty, for instance, do in *She Wou'd If She Cou'd*, Miranda and Clarinda in Shadwell's *The Virtuoso* (1676), Mrs. Sightly in Southerne's *The Wives' Excuse*, and Araminta in Congreve's *The Old Batchelour* (1693). A test, as the Princess of France puts it in *Love's Labour's Lost*, of whether an 'offer made in heat of blood' will 'bear this trial, and last love' (V.2.803), it can even (as in the Congreve and Southerne) suggest an impasse never to be broken.

Wellvile, in *The Wives' Excuse*, has been Mrs. Sightly's passionate, jealous but 'Platonick lover' for seven years. At the end, he offers to give up what he values most, 'my liberty'. Sightly, however, although she loves him, turns aside his proposal: 'This is too sudden to be serious'.[49] In the concluding moments of *The Old Batchelour*, when Bellmour and Belinda have agreed to marry, Araminta evades Vainlove's 'May I presume to hope so great a Blessing?' 'We had better', she tells him, 'take the Advantage of a little of our Friends Experience first'.[50] Bellmour's response to this—'O my Conscience, she dares not consent, for fear he shou'd recant'—is shrewd. Throughout the comedy, Vainlove has suffered agonies of desire for Araminta, but retreated in disgust as soon as he thought she might allow herself to be captured: 'I stumble ore the Game I would pursue.—'Tis dull and unnatural to have a Hare run full in the Hounds Mouth; and would distaste the keenest Hunter'.[51] Like Laelaps, the miraculous hound given by Minos to Procris, which never failed to pull down its prey—until it had the misfortune to meet up with an equally miraculous hare, which could never be caught—Wellvile and Vainlove seem forever frozen in pursuit, the distance between them and Sightly and Araminta impossible for either side to diminish. A situation frequently debated in those Restoration love poems which argue for and against 'fruition', it also reaches back to Hadamar's medieval *Jagd*, in which the lover, hunting in a park with fifty allegorical hounds, finds himself quite unable, when he has the deer at bay, to unleash the one called 'Consummation', but lets his quarry escape, to be once more and endlessly pursued.[52]

---

[49] Thomas Southerne, *The Wives' Excuse*, in *The Works of Thomas Southerne*, ed. Robert Jordan and Harold Love, vol. 1 (Oxford, 1988), V.3.294.

[50] William Congreve, *The Old Batchelour*, in *The Plays of William Congreve*, ed. Herbert Davis (Chicago, 1967), V.2. 172–6.

[51] Ibid. IV.1.175–80.

[52] For an account of this and related poems, see *The Stag of Love: The Chase in Mediaeval Literature*, by Marcelle Thiebaux (Ithaca, 1974). Also, for the symbolism of the hunt, see John Cummins, *The Hound and the Hawk: The Art of Medieval Hunting*, (London, 1988), esp. pp. 68–83.

In 1762, the anonymous adaptor of *Love's Labour's Lost* permitted the Princess to enter Navarre's park accompanied by a forester, but not to be so unlady-like as to shoot anything. He also closed Shakespeare's ending. Although the women try in the final moments to exact the year of trial and penance, Biron needs only to break into the 'Have at you then, affections men at arms' speech, from Act IV of Shakespeare's play, for them to abandon the whole idea. 'My liege', Biron complacently points out, 'you see how / Woman yields, when woo'd in proper terms'.[53] And as they all leave for France to get married, Biron neatly inverts the words of his Shakespearean original: 'Our wooing now doth end like an old play; / Jack hath his Jill; these ladies courtesie / Hath nobly made our sport a Comedy'. Imbecile though it is, *The Students* is nonetheless indicative of its period in its nervousness about truly independent and witty women, its rejection not only of the love chase, but of any suggestion that comedy need not end in marriage, and on male terms. I have been arguing not only for Shakespeare's special Elizabethan interest in parks, but for suggestive links between the ones in *The Merry Wives*, *Titus Andronicus* and *Love's Labour's Lost*, and those in some of the best comedies of the later seventeenth century: links which the three adaptations, by Dennis, Ravenscroft and the author of *The Students*, help (in their several ways) to define. In the course of the eighteenth century, that association was eroded, and so was a whole rigorous and sexually candid tradition of English comedy which had managed, in certain fundamental respects, to overleap the eighteen years of the theatre's interregnum.

Although St. James's (like Hyde Park) remained for some time fashionable, its appeal was gradually superseded by that of Vauxhall Gardens and the more various but theatrically not very assimilable entertainments in which it specialized. Fielding's Amelia, in 1751, takes the air in St. James's, but sees in Vauxhall the true *paradeisos*: fancying herself, on her first visit, 'in those blissful Mansions which we hope to enjoy hereafter'.[54] The transfer, under William and Mary, of the royal residence to Kensington (at least one park play, Leigh's *Kensington Gardens* of 1719 attempted to follow them) also diminished the centrality of St. James's. Most important of all, however, was what registers increasingly in eighteenth-century comedy as a real change and diminution in the comedic value of the park: one in which the imagery of the hunt was eventually to become obsolete. Already, in Steele's *The Lying Lover*

---

[53] *The Students: A Comedy altered from Shakespeare's Love's Labour's Lost and Adapted to the Stage* (London, 1969) [Cornmarket Shakespeare Series, vol. 33], pp. 74, 78.

[54] Henry Fielding, *Amelia*, ed. Martin C. Battestin [Wesleyan edition of the Works of Henry Fielding] (Oxford, 1983), p. 395.

of 1704, an assignation at Rosamond's Pond has entirely lost its sexual implications. The anonymous author of *St. James's Park*, in 1733, does almost nothing with an enormous cast of characters clearly intended to mirror his actual outdoor audience but have them walk up and down the Mall slandering each other. Some of the dialogue, genuinely funny, looks forward to Sheridan's *The School For Scandal* (1777). Nonetheless, when five of them decide to march abreast down the Mall and 'as Congreve says, *Laugh at the great Vulgar and the Small . . .* Sneer all the Men we meet that are Strangers to us, out of Countenance. And jostle all the Women', it is impossible not to remember that in *The Way of the World* (1700) these were the very minor voices of Petulant and Witwoud, whose proposal to do just this Mirabell treated with contempt.[55] Certainly St. James's Park in Congreve's play, that miniature forest of the passions, of dangerous *éclaircissements* between the sexes, and snatched private meetings, had been, as it was in so many late seventeenth-century comedies, the scene of something far more consequential than mere backbiting.

To talk about the declining fortunes of London's parks in eighteenth-century literature would require another lecture. I want only to remind you that the risk and potential anarchy of parks becomes increasingly prominent in novels of the period, and is associated there with a more timorous kind of heroine. Amelia's Vauxhall paradise rapidly turns nasty, even though she has two male friends with her, as a young rake forces his way into a place opposite her at table and gazes 'in a Manner with which Modesty can neither look, nor bear to be looked at'.[56] Fanny Burney's Evelina and her two companions have to be rescued, again at Vauxhall, from an insolent ring of bullies, 'laughing immoderately'.[57] Earlier comedy heroines had, on occasion, positively invited this kind of situation. Fiorella and Violante, for instance, in Mountfort's *Greenwich Park*, coolly approach and 'rally' with a group of blustering strangers, summoning assistance only when the men, no match for them verbally, resort to violence.[58] The later women, far from relishing such encounters, are terrified even by pale equivalents, and tremulously grateful to the noble gentlemen who spring to their aid.

No longer fashionable, London's parks, like those of almost all great cities, are now dangerous by day and can be deadly at night. Individuals, outside the special fraternity of dog-walkers and pram-pushers, tend to think twice about striking up an acquaintance with strangers. Sociologists

---

[55] *St. James's Park*, p. 17.

[56] *Amelia*, p. 396.

[57] Fanny Burney, *Evelina: Or, The History of a Young Lady's Entrance into the World*, ed. Edward A. Bloom (London, 1986), p. 195.

[58] William Mountford, *Greenwich Park*, ed. Paul W. Miller [Scholars' Facsimiles and Reprints] (New York, 1977), p. 4.

and psychiatrists produce complicated studies of why normal behaviour patterns should alter so radically within the gates of these public places. And parks have taken on a new and sinister lease of life as the setting for plays. Not even Rochester thought to list infanticide among the nocturnal crimes of St. James's, but in Edward Bond's *Saved* youths stone a baby to death in its pram, in a park 'at closing time'.[59] The London taxi-driver in Pinter's *Victoria Station*, whose cab has gravitated to the side of an unidentified 'dark park', is possibly mad; his woman passenger, silent and invisible on the back seat, seems to be dead.[60] When, in Pinter's *Old Times* (1971), Kate imagines a 'walk across the park', Anna shudders away from the memory: 'The park is dirty at night, all sorts of horrible people, men hiding behind trees and women with terrible voices, they scream at you as you go past, and people come out suddenly from behind trees and bushes and there are shadows everywhere . . .'[61] I want to end, however, with a different contemporary play: *Der Park* by Botho Strauss, an adaptation of Shakespeare's *A Midsummer Night's Dream*, first published in Germany in 1983, and recently performed at the Crucible Theatre, Sheffield.

Although Puck's wanderings, in Shakespeare, had taken him 'over park, over pale' (II.1.4) in Titania's service, the 'palace wood, a mile without the town' (I.2.101–2) appeared to be the equivalent of a royal forest. There is a forester in charge (IV.1.103), but no hint of any other human habitation, let alone of the sheep and goats pastured in Arden. Duke Theseus hunts there. Other people enter the wood on May Morning, or for special reasons such as an elopement, or the need to rehearse a play. Even the fairies are transients. When, in 1692, someone—possibly Betterton—turned Shakespeare's comedy into *The Fairy Queen*, a spectacular opera with music by Purcell, this forest setting survived for only one act. Titania then commands that everything should be transformed into Fairy-land: something which turns out to mean an enormous paradisal park, with grottoes, arbours, tree-lined avenues and delightful walks, a lake, a pretend forest, and a river with swans.

The park of *The Fairy Queen*, its different aspects revealed and changed through the use of movable scenes, stands in a fluid but organic relationship to the palace of Duke Theseus, where the opera ends. In the Strauss play, it has become a municipal green space paled in by an un-named city. Here, the stage is dominated by a large elder bush, its leafless twigs festooned with 'bits of paper, beer cans, tights, a shoe, a broken cassette-recorder with its tape flapping about, etc.'.[62] Animal noises emanate from the cages

---

[59] Edward Bond, *Saved* (London, 1965), scene 6.

[60] Harold Pinter, *Victoria Station*, in *Other Places: Three Plays* (London, 1982), p. 51.

[61] Pinter, *Old Times* (London, 1971), pp. 43–4.

[62] Botho Strauss, *The Park*, trans. Tinch Minter and Anthony Vives (Sheffield, 1988), p. 7.

of a sleazy circus. In the foreground: a shallow pit filled with dirty sand. Into this dispiriting setting, from some beautiful other planet 'where the wild thyme blows', comes Oberon, hunting Titania, his 'usual quarry', but also benevolently intent on teaching human beings how to make the most of the divine gift of sexuality. His project fails. The play's version of love in idleness only makes its quartet of young lovers more faithless and petty, while turning Titania into a bestial Pasiphae. The changeling boy, now a black park attendant, for whose sexual favours a gay sculptor called Cyprian (alias Puck) once competed with Titania, brutally murders Cyprian. Victimized and be-fouled by packs of young people who rove aimlessly through the park, the immortals gradually forget those talismanic Shakespearean lines about the 'bank where the wild thyme blows': the memory of which might enable them to return to their extraterrestrial paradise. They too are trapped, at the end, in a world epitomized by the litter-strewn city park and its elder bush, 'so dirty, sick and bare': a place from which wit and elegance have vanished as completely as the deer.

*Note.* I am grateful to Martin Biddle, Eric Griffiths, Eric Handley, Peter Holland, John Kerrigan, Jeremy Maule, Valerie Pearl, Oliver Rackham and Twigs Way for suggestions and help from which I have benefitted during my research for this lecture.

*Proceedings of the British Academy*, **80**, 73–103

CHATTERTON LECTURE ON POETRY

# Edmund Spenser, Poet of Exile

## RICHARD A. McCABE
*Trinity College, Dublin*

W.B. YEATS accounted Spenser 'the first poet who gave his heart to the State', the first, that is, to make the poetic service greater than the political god.[1] Or goddess, rather. In so far as she attempted to personify the state, 'fayre Elisa, Queene of shepheardes all' appropriated public service to personal cult, patriotism to private devotion.[2] To serve the country was to serve its Queen. As a result, expressions of frustrated political ambition frequently take the form of amorous pastoral complaint, *The Ocean's Love to Cynthia* being, perhaps, the most striking example.[3] Given his attachment to Raleigh and his exile from the lady they both hoped to serve, albeit in different ways, it is hardly surprising that Spenser's fictional *alter ego*, Colin Clout, should forever retain the *persona* of unrequited pastoral lover, humbly attributing his persistent failure to the social disparity between himself and his object: 'Not then to her that scorned thing so base,/ But to my selfe the blame that lookt so hie' (935–6). In fact, Spenser's position was a good deal more complex

Read 13 November 1991. © The British Academy 1993.

[1] W.B. Yeats, ed., *Poems of Spenser* (Edinburgh, 1906), p. xxxiv. All quotations of Spenser's poetry are from *The Works of Edmund Spenser*, edited by Edwin Greenlaw *et al.*, Variorum Edition, 11 vols (Baltimore, 1932–58), I–VIII. Prose quotations are from *Spenser's Prose Works*, edited by Rudolf Gottfried, Variorum Edition, IX (1949). Hereafter *Prose*.

[2] See E.C. Wilson, *England's Eliza* (Cambridge, Mass., 1939); Roy C. Strong, 'The Popular Celebration of the Accession Day of Queen Elizabeth I', *JWCI*, 21 (1958), 86–103; *The Cult of Elizabeth: Elizabethan Portraiture and Pageantry* (London, 1977).

[3] Donald Davie, 'A Reading of *The Ocean's Love to Cynthia*', in John Russell Brown and Bernard Harris, ed., *Elizabethan Poetry*, Stratford-Upon-Avon Studies, 2 (London, 1960), 71–90 (p. 73).

than Yeats allowed. Although commonly remembered as *the* Elizabethan
court poet *par excellence*, he spent remarkably little time at the court of
'Gloriana'. All genteel pretensions to the contrary, he was not a courtier
but a colonist. The years of his poetic and political maturity were passed not
at the centre but on the periphery of the Elizabethan state, not in the city
but in the wilderness.[4] Exile and the conditions of exile preoccupy much
of his canon. Paradoxically, one might say that the ardour of Spenser's
devotion to the state was born of exclusion from it. That being the case,
the subject of the present paper is the effect of Spenser's Irish experience
upon the form and content of his poetic work, the degree to which our
traditional 'English' Spenser is the product of an Irish environment, the
product of mortal conflict between two irreconcilable cultures.

For Spenser, the enterprise of Ireland was as much personal as political.
Ireland's 'savagery' was the planter's opportunity. As in the case of the New
World, to dismiss the indigenous population as 'savages' was *ipso facto* to
legitimize their conquest while at the same time insulating the conqueror
from the more disturbing implications of perceived cultural difference.[5] For
second sons, impoverished soldiers and indigent poets, Ireland afforded
the otherwise impossible prospect of ascent to the ranks of the landed
gentry. While the heroes of *The Faerie Queene* are careful to disclaim
all desire for 'meed', the persistent reference to land as 'commodity' in
*A Vewe of the Present State of Irelande* puts a somewhat unromantic gloss
upon the operations of Gloriana's knights.[6] 'The drifte of my purpose',
remarks Irenius, is 'to settle an eternall peace in that Countrie and allsoe
to make it verie *profitable* to her maiestie' (p. 197). The values of the
poetry are hereby costed in the prose, sometimes to the last pound. To
the more cynical Elizabethan observer, Spenser was one of those pitiable
have-nots who 'shifted' to 'the wolvish westerne isle' choosing to live, in
desperate pursuit of fame and fortune, 'among the savage Kernes in sad
exile'.[7] His condemnation of the Celtic clans for their failure to observe
the English code of primogeniture is thus richly ironic since many of his

---

[4] Pauline Henley, *Spenser in Ireland* (Cork, 1928), pp. 45–70, 168–91.

[5] David Beers Quinn, *The Elizabethans and the Irish* (Ithaca, N.Y., 1966), pp. 106–22; A. Bartlett Giamatti, 'Primitivism and the Process of Civility in Spenser's *Faerie Queene*', in Fredi Chiapelli, ed., *First Images of America*, 2 vols (Berkeley, 1976), I, 71–82; Nicholas Canny, *Kingdom and Colony: Ireland in the Atlantic World 1560–1800* (Baltimore, 1988), pp. 2, 33, 35.

[6] *Prose*, pp. 62, 115, 149, 181–3, 185–6; Edwin Greenlaw, 'Spenser and British Imperialism', *MP*, 9 (1911–12), 347–70 (p. 366); Raymond Jenkins, 'Spenser and the Clerkship in Munster', *PMLA*, 47 (1932), 109–21 (pp. 116–17); Alexander Judson, 'Spenser and the Munster Officials', *SP*, 44 (1947), 157–73 (p. 172). Simon Shepherd, *Spenser* (Atlantic Heights, N.J., 1989), pp. 9, 51–5.

[7] Joseph Hall, *Collected Poems*, edited by Arnold Davenport (Liverpool, 1949), p. 66.

comrades were its refugees, a point not lost upon contemporary Celtic commentators who frequently allude to the low social status of the so-called 'New English'.[8] In them, Spenser acquired a readership quite distinct from that of the home market, a readership for whom the imperial allegory of *The Faerie Queene* translated all too readily into oppressive colonial policy. By counterpointing their views against those of Spenser—for they were neither 'wild' nor inarticulate—one arrives at a clearer understanding of the complementary relationship between his poetic and political agendas.

The problem was that exile begat exile. The settlement of Elizabethan planters necessitated the dispossession from ancestral lands of people who could by no legitimate standards be described as savage, if only by virtue of the ancient Christianity which sufficiently distinguished them from the denizens of the New World. But popular reformation polemic allowed the appropriation of the term 'Christian' to the Protestant cause while relegating the hosts of Antichrist to that of pagan or 'paynim'. Thus *The Faerie Queene* envisages a world divided between civil Christians and barbarous Infidels, a pattern established in Ariosto and Tasso but ingeniously adapted to a new crusade far closer to home. As both poet and politician, Spenser needed a 'salvage' island—such as might be 'salvaged' by reformers like himself—and duly created one in the strident State Letters written on behalf of Lord Grey, in the harsh political injunctions of *A Vewe of the Present State of Irelande*, and the haunting, hostile landscape of *The Faerie Queene* whose beauty invariably proves inextricable from its peril.[9] By personifying the land while dehumanising its inhabitants, Spenser transformed poetic allegory into a powerful tool of colonial polemic, facilitating the presentation of violent conquest as civil reclamation.

Through the carefully deployed imagery of pruning and physic the destructive energies of violence are sublimated into charitable duties. We are given to understand that the *Vewe* undertakes no more than the cultivation of an estate gone to seed, the 'cure' of a sick body politic (p. 146), and 'wheare no other remedye maie be devized nor no hope of recoverie had', violent means 'muste neds . . . be used' (p. 148).[10] The very term 'plantation' suggests the cultivation of previously barren

---

[8] *Prose*, pp. 203, 210; Quinn, *Elizabethans and the Irish*, p. 39.

[9] For the State Letters see Raymond Jenkins, '*Newes out of Munster*, a Document in Spenser's Hand', *SP*, 32 (1935), 125–30; Raymond Jenkins, 'Spenser with Lord Grey in Ireland', *PMLA*, 52 (1937), 338–53; Raymond Jenkins, 'Spenser: The Uncertain Years 1584–89', *PMLA*, 53 (1938), 350–62.

[10] For a fuller account of these rhetorical strategies see Richard A. McCabe, 'The Fate of Irena: Spenser and Political Violence', in Patricia Coughlan, ed., *Spenser and Ireland: An Interdisciplinary Perspective* (Cork, 1989), pp. 109–25 (p. 114).

soil. Repeatedly in Spenser's usage, the figurative meaning draws moral support from the literal. Husbandry he deemed the 'moste naturall' (p. 216) of all human occupations, but in order to husband the soil one must 'plant' colonies of cultivators, and in order to 'plant' colonists one must 'plant' garrisons to protect them. Thus an agricultural image gradually develops military connotations with the result that dubious policies appear to acquire the validity of natural law: the iron man Talus who represents the force of Elizabethan military might 'scatters' the Irish landscape with the corpses of recalcitrant rebels, 'as thicke as . . . seede after the sowers hand' (V.12.7). By contrast, in one of the most celebrated of all Gaelic exile poems, 'Óm Sceol ar Ardmhagh Fáil' ('At the News from Fál's High Plain'), the Celtic poet and historian Geoffrey Keating inverts Spenser's imagery by comparing the proliferation of colonists to that of cockle in a wheatfield. The sole remaining hope is that a carefully winnowed Celtic harvest may be shipped overseas.[11]

Spenser ignored such consequences, presenting military conflict as a moral duty and colonisation as its inevitable consequence (p. 85). Thus he claims Ireland by right of ancient conquest—an achievement disclaimed even in Holinshed—while at the same time urging that it be conquered anew by his own contemporaries (pp. 55–6).[12] Despite its illogicality, however, the concept of conquest proved too potent to resist, associated as it was with the martial heroism central to national epic. By representing the possession of his own remote Irish estate as an act of conquest, Spenser afforded himself the somewhat illusory satisfaction of extending his English homeland rather than living in exile from it. Once the great work of 'reformation' was complete, Kilcolman would become an English estate and Edmund Spenser would indeed be 'home againe'. As matters stood, however, Spenser could neither regard Munster as home nor resign it to the 'meare' Irish whose gradual repossession of ancestral territories 'aliened' them from the English crown (p. 118).[13] His

---

[11] Religion too must be 'planted' in the wake of conquest, *Prose*, p. 221. For similar uses of this imagery see Nicholas Canny, 'Edmund Spenser and the Development of an Anglo-Irish Identity', *YES*, 13(1983), 1–19 (p. 15). For Keating see Seán Ó'Tuama, ed., *An Duanaire 1600–1900: Poems of the Dispossessed*, translated by Thomas Kinsella (Portlaoise, 1981), pp. 84–7.

[12] 'A conquest draweth . . . to it three things, to wit, law, apparell, and language. For where the countrie is subdued, there the inhabitants ought to be ruled by the same law that the conqueror is governed, to weare the same fashion of attire wherwith the victor is vested, and speake the same language that the vanquisher parleth.' *Chronicles of England, Scotland and Ireland*, 6 vols (London, 1808), VI, 5.

[13] 'Meare' in this context signifies 'pure' or racially unmixed but its pejorative meaning may also operate. 'The Irish generally', remarks Sir John Davies, 'were held and reputed *Aliens*, or rather enemies to the Crowne of *England*; insomuch, as they were not only disabled to bring anie actions, but they were so farre out of the protection of the Lawe, as it was often adiudged no fellony to kill a meere Irish-man in the time of peace'. *A Discoverie of the True Causes why Ireland was never Entirely Subdued* (London, 1612), p. 102.

proposal to transplant the Ulster clans to Leinster and their counterparts to Ulster—much as Prince Arthur lifts the emaciated Maleger from the native soil which 'as his life decayd,/ Did life with usury to him restore' (II.11.45)—manifests a determination to eradicate the very essence of Gaelic culture of which he ranks as possibly the most acute but certainly the least sympathetic of observers, displaying what one colonial historian has well termed 'the paradox of the understanding-that-kills' (pp. 178–9).[14] Since dispersal and dispossession were prime colonial aims, denigration of the Celtic bards, particularly skilled at relating genealogy to place, became a political necessity. Poet was set implacably against poet.

Amongst the most distinguished of Spenser's Gaelic contemporaries was Tadhg Dall Ó'Huiginn (1550–91) whose eulogy of the Maguire stronghold of Enniskillen, a 'fairy castle of surpassing treasure . . . full of poets and minstrels, from one bright, shining wall to the other . . . a mighty band of elfin youth . . . such that eye dared not regard them', paints a splendid portrait of Gaelic culture as remote from Spenser's 'salvage nacion' as well could be. Indeed, the bard's employment of a fairy mythology strikingly reminiscent of Spenser's own suggests an underlying similarity his English antagonist would certainly have been loath to admit. A distinguishing factor, however, is the grim premonition that the bard may outlive the culture which alone makes such poetry possible: 'would I had consumed the end of my days, lest I be longlived when all the rest have gone, it is perilous to survive one's world'.[15] Weighed against such humane sensitivity, the crude rhetoric of cultural inferiority may be seen to supply even more vital succour to the unconscious psychology of colonialism—to its desperate need for self-justification—than to its conscious politics. Ironically, however, the official prestige enjoyed by the Gaelic bards—to which Spenser attests with obvious discomfort (p. 124)—far exceeded that of their English counterparts as (apparently) did their public influence. The 'Enniskillen' poem celebrates a fully integrated society of chieftain, warrior, priest and poet of the sort to which Spenser himself vainly aspired; it was the presumed political efficacy of the Gaelic poets that rendered them so menacing. Thus, Celtic society confronted Spenser with the enticing

---

[14] Tzvetan Todorov, *The Conquest of America: The Question of the Other*, translated by Richard Howard (New York, 1982), p. 127. For the influence of the Munster Famine upon emaciated personifications such as Maleger see M.M. Gray, 'The Influence of Spenser's Irish Experiences on *The Faerie Queene*', *RES*, 6 (1930), 413–28 (pp. 423–8).

[15] *The Bardic Poems of Tadgh Dall Ó'Huiginn* edited and translated by Eleanor Knott, Irish Texts Society, 2 vols (London, 1984—first pub. 1922–6), I, 73–6, 79; II, 49–50, 52. Hereafter *Bardic Poems*. Occasionally it has proved necessary to revise Knott's very literal translations in order to capture something of the bard's poetic quality.

image of his own dearest ambitions and an element of peculiarly demonic
wish-fulfilment may have led him to attribute to his Celtic rivals far greater
influence than they actually possessed. Apparently it was comforting to
believe that somewhere in the world, if only in the wilderness, some poets
exercised power, albeit the wrong poets.

Literary historians disagree as to whether the Irish poets of Spenser's
day articulated a truly nationalist stance transcending the petty dynastic
factionalism of previous centuries. Bardic poetry, it has been argued, is
rigidly 'conventional' and conflicting claims of political primacy are made
on behalf of numerous chieftains in accordance with the varying demands
of individual patronage.[16] Yet context remains the best interpreter of
'convention', as Spenser was quick to recognise. Whatever the intention
of the bards, the reception of their work amongst the colonists is a separate
issue. Since *The Faerie Queene* itself employs a wide range of stock poetic
conventions to promote an urgent political agenda, there was no reason
to suppose otherwise of the bards whose work, Spenser concluded, tended
'for the moste parte to the hurte of the Englishe or mayntenaunce of theire
owne lewd libertie' (p. 125). His own insistence upon English nationalism
led him to dichotomise the Irish situation in such a way as to ensure a
nationalist reading of the Gaelic poets. Tadhg Dall's accomplished eclogue
casting Brian Maguire as a pastoral magus encircling Fermanagh with a
fiery wall would have the same topicality for Spenser's contemporaries as
the heavily 'conventionalized' eulogy of 'fayre Elisa' in *The Shepheardes
Calender*. The poem inciting Brian na Murrtha to unite Gaelic chieftains in
a march on Dublin until the Pale ran red with blood would merely confirm
such readings.[17]

Feagh MacHugh O'Byrne's father was credited by Tadhg Dall with
an invincible fairy lance—much like that wielded by Britomart—and
magic armour impervious to enemy blades—much like that worn by
Arthur and George.[18] Locked in the fastnesses of Glenmalure on the
very borders of the Pale, Feagh himself constituted an imminent threat
to its continued existence. Yet in a remarkable passage of the *Vewe*,

---

[16] Brendan Bradshaw, 'Native Reaction to the Westward Enterprise: a Case-Study in Gaelic
Ideology', in K. R. Andrews, N.P. Canny and P.E. Hair, *The Westward Enterprise: English
Activities in Ireland, the Atlantic, and America 1480–1650* (Liverpool, 1978), pp. 65–80.
T.J. Dunne, 'The Gaelic Response to Conquest and Colonisation: The Evidence of the
Poetry', in *Studia Hibernica*, 20 (1980) 7–30; Nicholas Canny, 'The Formation of the
Irish Mind: Religion, Politics and Gaelic Irish Literature 1580–1750', *Past and Present*,
95 (1982), 91–116.

[17] *Bardic Poems*, I, 86, 118–19; II, 57, 78–9.

[18] *Bardic Poems*, I, 254–5; II, 168. Richard Stanyhurst had compared Irish horsemen to
knights of the Round Table and Spenser himself endorses their prowess: Holinshed, VI,
68; *Prose*, p. 122.

indicative of a radical ambivalence underlying Spenser's attitudes, he is grudgingly praised for raising himself, 'to that heighte that he nowe dare front Princes And make termes with greate Potentates, the which as it is to him honorable so is to them moste disgracefull to be bearded of suche a base varlet' (p. 172). In this passage, Spenser's instinctive respect for heroic self-fashioning, the very stuff of his own fairy mythology, appears to have extorted a complimentary aside before the mentality of the public official reasserted itself in orthodox condemnation of a 'varlet'. The poets patronised by O'Byrne urged him to abandon factionalism and unite all local clans against the common enemy.[19] The call is doubtless time-honoured and 'conventional' but such was Spenser's regard for the effect of 'sweete invencions' upon 'braue yonge mindes' (pp. 125–6), for what Sir Philip Sidney terms the moral *praxis* of poetic convention, that he discovered in the bards a vitality and relevance frequently missed by modern commentators.[20] The very call for their suppression was a bizarre form of aesthetic appreciation.[21]

The Irish context of *The Faerie Queene* is established at the outset by dedicatory sonnets to Lord Arthur Grey, former Lord Deputy, Sir John Norris, Lord President of Munster, the Earl of Ormond, foremost of the Anglo-Norman peers, and Sir Walter Raleigh, Spenser's fellow planter. These attest to a desperate sense of artistic isolation in a 'savadge soyle, far from Parnasso mount' (Grey).[22] Despite similarities between his own literary career and that of Virgil in their common movement from eclogue to epic, it soon becomes clear that Spenser enjoys the patronage of no Augustus, that his position is, in fact, closer to that of the exiled Ovid. Nor is it merely a question of geographical distance but rather of the

---

[19] Bradshaw, 'Native Reaction', pp. 75–8. Tadhg Dall Ó'Huiginn remarks on the duty of the poets to give such advice: 'great unfriendliness were it did none of the poets . . . say to the men of *Fódla* that they should declare war upon the foreigner' (*Bardic Poems*, II, 73).

[20] G. Gregory Smith, ed., *Elizabethan Critical Essays*, 2 vols (Oxford, 1904), I, 171.

[21] For the ordinance of 1579 against 'rhymers, bards, harpers or such idle persons' see Henley, p. 106. For Spenser's endorsement of it see *Prose*, p. 219. In *The Faerie Queene* Malfont 'the bold title of a poet bad . . . on himselfe had ta'en, and rayling rhymes had sprad' (V.9.25–6). An Irish association is likely. In *The Romaunt of the Rose* Wikkid-Tunge's predilection for slander 'sat hym well of his lynage,/ For hym an Irish womman bar' (3807–11).

[22] His choice of names for his two sons, Sylvanus and Peregrine, points in the same direction. William Camden explains Peregrine as 'Strange, or outlandish' and Sylvanus as 'Woodman, or rather Wood-god', *Remaines Concerning Britaine* (London, 1605), pp. 67, 70. Peregrine and Sylvane figure as speakers in *A Book of the State of Ireland* (1599) apparently written by Spenser's neighbour Hugh Cuffe in imitation of the *Vewe*. See Rudolf B. Gottfried, 'Spenser's *View* and Essex', *PMLA*, 52 (1937), 645–51 (pp. 647–8).

cultural implications for *The Faerie Queene*'s avowed purpose to 'fashion
a gentleman or noble person in vertuous and gentle discipline'. Courtly
'fashions' rapidly transmute into colonial 'disciplines' when transplanted
to an environment 'through long wars left almost waste,/ With brutish
barbarisme . . . overspredd' (Ormond). Now it is the Celts who must
be 'framed and fashoned' (p. 240) to bring them 'from theire delighte of
licentious barbarisme unto the love of goodnes and Civilitye' (p. 54), and
the quality of the required 'discipline' alters considerably. Spenser has
made his own the Roman ideal of cultivating 'savage' peoples, formerly
espoused in Ireland by Sir Thomas Smith.[23] Had not Camden lamented
the Romans' failure to reach Ireland thereby rendering England's burden
all the heavier?[24]

Spenser's attitude to the cultural duties of conquest is largely responsible for transforming a national epic into a colonial romance.
Because of its engagement with current affairs, *The Faerie Queene*
functions not merely as a passive reflection of political events but as
an active expression of history in the making, an essential document
of the imperial ideal fashioned by one of its most articulate exponents.
Yet the practice of defining civil ideals by their 'savage' antitheses
is hazardous, particularly in the context of military conflict. In such
circumstances intended contrasts collapse all too easily into unintentional
comparisons, betraying the common heritage of 'civil' and 'savage', the
embarrassing kinship of self and other. It may then prove, 'that what
were conceived as distinguishing characteristics of the marginal are in
fact the defining qualities of the central object of consideration'.[25]
Throughout *The Faerie Queene* Spenser presents virtue militant rather
than achieved, embattled rather than secure, with the result that negative,
repressive energies frequently usurp their positive counterparts. In fact,
achievement invariably entails suppression. In the poem, cultivation of
civil selves necessitates suppression of savage others. In Ireland, the other
is identified with the Irish and the quest for civility with a struggle for
conquest ironically entailing the employment of 'savage' methods. Ireland
resembles the fairy realm in that the further inland one proceeds the

---

[23] Nicholas Canny, 'The Permissive Frontier: the Problem of Social Control in English
Settlements in Ireland and Virginia 1550–1650', in K.R. Andrews, ed., *Westward Enterprise*,
pp. 17–44 (pp. 18–19); Walter J. Ong, 'Spenser's *View* and the Tradition of the 'Wild' Irish',
*MLQ*, 3 (1942), 561–71 (pp. 564–5, 568).

[24] *Britain, or a Chorographicall Description of the Most Flourishing Kingdomes, England,
Scotland, and Ireland*, translated by Philemon Holland (London, 1610), p. 66. The Irish
section is separately paginated.

[25] John Sturrock, ed., *Structuralism and Since* (Oxford, 1979), p. 168.

greater, certainly, the possibility of self-discovery, but greater still the risk of self-disclosure.[26]

Within the poem celebration of national achievement is severely qualified by awareness of inter-racial failure: what might have remained culturally monolithic, if written from the perspective of the court, is fissured with the anxieties of cultural difference. As the poem stands, the wilderness is fully realised while the court remains abstract and remote. Hence one detects a constant sense of disorder and dislocation perceptible from the outset in the divergence between the plan set out in the prefatory 'Letter to Raleigh', centring upon Gloriana's court, and the text which proceeds to defy it. Of particular interest is the Fairy Queen's failure to make a single appearance in the poem that bears her name. She is discussed, desired, idealized, envisioned, fleetingly apprehended in a myriad of male and female surrogates, but never present. She is to the world of the poem what Elizabeth was to Ireland, a remote authority figure acting through deputies and substitutes. In England the 'cult' of Elizabeth was sustained by personal visibility, by progresses, processions, visitations and public speeches, none of which were accessible to her Irish subjects.[27] Not surprisingly, Spenser identifies the absence of the monarch (or an 'absolute' Vice Regent) as the single factor most detrimental to the struggle for 'civility' in Ireland (p. 55).[28]

During the 1580s, owing to the continued popularity of *The Shepheardes Calender*, Spenser was primarily acclaimed as a pastoral poet, yet the topography of *The Faerie Queene* marks a significant divergence from that tradition. The contrast illustrates the degree to which the earlier pastoral, despite its gestures towards rural almanacs, was primarily conceived as an exercise in courtly taste.[29] As employed in the 'July' eclogue, for example, the word 'kerne' possesses none of the savage connotations attributed to

[26] Ireland was one of the few places where trial by combat, of the sort common in *The Faerie Queene*, was still allowed and where knighthoods were conferred on active service. See Holinshed, VI, 455; Raymond Jenkins, 'Spenser and Ireland', *ELH*, 19 (1952), 131–42 (p. 133).

[27] Richard Helgerson, 'The Land Speaks: Cartography, Chorography, and Subversion in Renaissance England', in Stephen Grenblatt, ed., *Representing the English Renaissance* (Berkeley, 1988), pp. 327–61 (p. 356).

[28] Spenser calls for a supreme 'Lorde Liuetennante' (presumably Essex) with 'absolute' powers, *Prose*, pp. 188, 228–9, 428–9. For the absence of the monarch and the limitations of the office of Lord Deputy see Ciaran Brady, 'Court, Castle, and Country: The Framework of Government in Tudor Ireland', in Ciaran Brady and Raymond Gillespie, ed., *Natives and Newcomers: Essay on the Making of Irish Colonial Society 1534–1641* (Dublin, 1986), pp. 22–49 (pp. 30–4, 38).

[29] William Empson, *Some Versions of Pastoral: A Study of the Pastoral Form in Literature* (Harmondsworth, 1966—first pub. 1935), pp. 17–18, 22–3, 63; Louis Adrian Montrose, '"Eliza, Queene of Shepheardes", and the Pastoral of Power', *ELR*, 10 (1980), 153–82; Louis Adrian Montrose, 'Of Gentlemen and Shepherds: The Politics of Elizabethan Pastoral Form', *ELH*, 50 (1983), 415–59.

it in the *Vewe*: 'cruell and bloddye, full of revenge . . . Comon ravishers of weomen and murderers of Children' (p. 123).[30] In moving to Ireland Spenser transferred from pastoral as literary genre to pastoral as way of life—and despised it. Yeats captured the paradox brilliantly when he observed that, 'though he dreamed of Virgil's shepherds he wrote a book to advise . . . the harrying of all that followed flocks upon the hills, and of all the "wandering companies that keep the woods"'.[31] The quotation from the *Vewe* is particularly apt since its poetic cadence resists its polemic intent. Acting as colonial politician, Spenser determined to destroy what he had previously celebrated: the essential liberty of the pastoral life-style. Since he now contends that husbandry and urban settlement are the essence of 'civility', he persistently attacks as vagabonds, in the diction of the Elizabethan Statute Book, figures who might previously have inspired him to idyllic reverie.[32]

Not the 'enamell'd fields' of Renaissance pastoral but Ireland's 'wastfull *wildernesse*' informs the landscape of *The Faerie Queene* (I.8.50).[33] The hostile topography of Book One, for example, is everywhere redolent of the 'salvage' ethos beyond the the Pale with its treacherous forests, isolated cabins, and 'woodborne' 'salvage nation', 'a rude, misshapen, monstrous rablement', remarkably reminiscent of John Derricke's Irish 'woodkerne', who distort religious truth into superstitious idolatry (I.6.8–19).[34] 'Salvage nacion' is the phrase used of the Irish in the very first sentence of the *Vewe* thereby defining the work's cultural outlook. Little wonder, then, that Despair exploits a questing knight's desire to 'come unto his wished home in haste' (I.9.39). Religion lies at the heart of the issue since the supreme shepherd of this fallen Arcadia is 'the greate Pastor Peters successour' (p. 138). Living 'downe in a dale, hard by a forests side', Archimago is the typical caricature of an Irish seminary priest—'He told of Saintes and Popes, and evermore/ He strowd an *Ave-Mary* after and before' (I.1.35)—who would have St George 'drinke of that Cupp of fornicacion with which the Purple Harlot had then made all nacions drunken' (p. 137).[35] Even Spenser's most daringly Apocalyptic imagery bears specific relation to the one 'popish' country he actually knew, the one whose religious reformation was desired for primarily political reasons: fear of imperial

---

[30] E.K. defines 'kerne' simply as 'Churle or Farmer'.

[31] *Poems*, ed., Yeats, p. xxxiv; See *Prose*, p. 149.

[32] *Prose*, pp. 97–8, 128. See Quinn, *Elizabethans and the Irish*, pp. 55, 77, 123, 149.

[33] See Raymond Williams, *The Country and the City* (St Albans, 1975—first pub. 1973), p. 36.

[34] *The Image of Irelande with a Discoverie of Woodkarne*, edited in facsimile by John Small (Edinburgh, 1883—first pub. 1581), pp. 31–8, 51–5.

[35] 'They say alwaies both before and after their charmes, a *Pater Noster*, and an *Ave Maria*'. Camden, *Britain*, p. 146.

Spain and promotion of land-hungry planters—twin facets, perhaps, of the same acquisitive mentality (I.8.13–14).

Potentially Ireland was another Eden, 'a moste bewtifull and swete Countrie as/ anye is under heaven, seamed thoroughe out with manye goodlye rivers . . . sprinckled with manye swete Ilandes and goodlye lakes like little Inlande seas, that will carye even shipps uppon theire waters, adorned with goodly woodes fitt for buildinge of howsses and shipps so comodiously as that if some princes in the worlde had them they woulde soone hope to be Lordes of all the seas and ere long of all the worlde' (p. 62).[36] This is an extraordinary passage. Aesthetic appreciation of natural beauty gradually modulates, through plans for its commercial exploitation, into fantasies of world empire as beauty, money and power coalesce. Ideally the countryside should serve the court. As matters stand, however, Ireland's 'commodious' landscape is wasted upon 'idle' pastoral inhabitants who choose to leave it, contrary to the English practice, unenclosed and therefore 'wyld' and 'desart'. 'This Chieflye redoundethe to the good of the whole Comon wealthe', Spenser remarks, oblivious to the irony implicit in 'comon', 'to have the lande . . . enclosed and well fenced' (p. 135). Private property inspires his civil aesthetic, well-tilled fields rather than common pasture.[37]

Uncultivated landscape was all the more perilous because of its seductive beauty: the fascinating forests that dominate so much of the Irish countryside, as also that of *The Faerie Queene*, are places of mortal danger (p. 151).[38] The first episode of the poem sees St George plunging unwisely into the 'Wood of Error' to shelter from a storm: Spenser's first experience of the Irish campaign was Lord Grey's disastrous defeat in the woods of Glenmalure at the hands of the O'Byrnes and O'Tooles whose names, he believed, signified 'woddye' and 'hillye' (pp. 170–1).[39] Thus, through the semantics of cultural imperialism operative alike in poem and policy, etymology 'reveals' moral nature and scenic topography shades insensibly into moral topography. The indigenous population partakes of,

---

[36] Apropos 'little Inlande seas' and the Irish failure to exploit them, one notes that Phaedria operates in a 'wide Inland sea, that hight by name/ The *Idle lake*' (II.6.10).

[37] For husbandry, urban development and civility see *Prose*, pp. 216–18. The alternative lifestyle of 'wilfull want' in 'a little cottage, built of stickes and reedes/ In homely wize, and wald with sods around' represents a caricature of Irish practices (III.7.6).

[38] Spenser calls for 'the Cuttinge downe and openinge of all places thoroughe the wodes so that a wide waye of the space of C. yardes mighte be laide open . . . for the safetie of travellers'. *Prose*, p. 224. See Eileen McCracken, *The Irish Woods since Tudor Times: Distribution and Exploitation* (Newtown Abbot, 1971), pp. 26–9, 45. Gaelic poetry of the latter half of the seventeenth century laments the destruction of the woods.

[39] Holinshed, VI, 435–6; McCracken, p. 29; for references to Glenmalure see *Prose*, pp. 57, 171–2, 191.

and contributes to, the wildness of the place and epithets are commonly
transferred from one to the other denoting a symbiotic relationship of
outlaws and outlands. From the satyrs of Book One to the savages of Book
Six, the landscape of *The Faerie Queene* is populated by wild, ill-natured
subraces generally impervious to nurture: 'lawlesse people . . . That never
used to live by plough nor spade,/ But fed on spoile and booty' (VI.10.39).
Outposts of civility, such as the Castle of Alma, are besieged by marauding
hoards apparently spawned by the landscape itself, 'as when a swarme of
Gnats at eventide/ Out of the fennes of Allan do arise' (II.9.16). The very
precision of such detail attests to the pervasive power of the influence
behind it.[40]

The result is a poetry of intense suspicion in which every act and
thought requires unremitting vigilance. As in Ireland itself, the latent
violence of the landscape commonly erupts into savage confrontation:
'the danger hid, the place unknowne and wilde,/ Breedes dreadfull doubts'
(I.1.12). The landscape of *The Faerie Queene* is not just a backdrop but a
component of theme, a party to any incident occurring within it which may
at any time annihilate the distinction between person and place through
some bizarre stroke of Ovidian metamorphosis. Yet here, at what seems
the furthest remove of fantasy, the Irish influence is strongest since the
colonists' deepest fear was that of cultural assimilation, a fate that
had already befallen many of the Old Norman families according to
Irenius's account of the matter in the *Vewe*: 'for the moste parte of
them are degenerated and growen allmoste meare Irishe yea and are
more malitious to the Englishe then the verye Irishe themselves' (p. 96).[41]
The formidable Sir Satyrane, of both 'gentle' and 'brutish' antecedents,
'noursled up in life and manners wilde', 'exilde' from civil justice and
subjecting his savage environment to 'a tyrans law' (the charge most
often levelled against the Old Normans), well represents their ambivalent
cultural status (I.6.21–6). Were the Tudor settlers to suffer an equivalent

---

[40] Spenser had a house for several years at New Abbey in Kildare on the borders of the Pale
close to the Bog of Allen. The *Vewe* attests to the land's gradual repossession by the native
Irish (p. 57). See Jenkins, 'Spenser and the Clerkship in Munster', p. 117. For the nature of
Celtic warfare compare *Prose*, pp. 106–7; Gray, 'Influence of Spenser's Irish Experiences',
pp. 415–16.

[41] For cultural assimilation see Holinshed, VI, 4; Giamatti, 'Primitivism and the Process
of Civility', in Chiapelli, ed., *First Images of America*, I, 74–5. Just as the Old English
exploited the myth of the 'wild' Irish to good political effect, their New English rivals
found it increasingly expedient to employ the same weapon against themselves, hence the
many charges of 'tyranny'. See Nicholas Canny, *The Formation of the Old English Elite in
Ireland* (Dublin, 1975), pp. 18–29; Ciaran Brady, 'The Road to the *View*: On the Decline
of Reform Thought in Tudor Ireland', in Coughlan, ed., *Spenser and Ireland*, pp. 25–45
(pp. 32–6).

subversion, the programme of 'reform' would not merely be impeded but reversed.

Confronted by such a daunting prospect, Eudoxus asks in horror, 'is it possible that an Englisheman broughte up naturallye in such swete Civilytie as Englande affordes . . . shoulde forgett his owne nature and forgoe his owne nacion? howe maie this be?' (p. 96). A powerful poetic explanation of such 'daungerous *Lethargie*' is endeavoured at the conclusion of Book Two, where young Verdant, his courtly armour cast aside, reclines in the arms of the Circe-like Acrasia (Intemperance) who undoes the 'fashioning' of noble gentlemen by transformation into beasts (p. 115). Intemperance was part of the stock racial profile of the 'meare' Irish (p. 105) whose association with Acrasia may be inferred from Ruddymane's indelibly blood-stained hand, an oblique allusion to the Gaelic war cry, noted in the *Vewe*, 'the Red Hand Forever, that is the bloddie hande which is Oneles badge' (p. 103).[42] Guyon's failure to clense the child's hand with running water recalls Edmund Campion's allegation that the Irish left 'the right armes of their infants unchristened . . . to the intent it might give a more ungratious and deadlie blow'.[43] '*Mantled* with greene' (II.12.50), the landscape of Acrasia's bower suggests its subversive nature since the Irish mantle was 'a fitt howsse for an outlawe, a mete bedd for a Rebell and an Apte cloake for a thefe' while also serving as 'a coverlett' for the 'lewed exercises' of Irish prostitutes (pp. 100–1). According to Camden, defence of the 'Romish religion' was the 'mantle for all rebellion' in Ireland.[44]

Modern commentators have related the poetics of metamorphosis to the sociology of cultural assimilation, particularly in regard to the New World, but Spenser's contemporaries anticipated this development in drawing the same analogy with express reference to Ireland.[45] In this respect the best gloss upon the political implications of the Acrasia fable is supplied by Sir John Davies, equally concerned with the problem of cultural degeneration in his role of Irish Attorney-General. By adopting

---

[42] According to the account of Fr. Good, reproduced in Camden, the Irish were 'most intemperate, by reason of the distemperature of the aire, and the moisture both of the ground, and of their meats; in regard also that all law is exiled'. *Britain*, p. 143. Ruddymane's significance was first noted by John Upton who concluded that 'the rebellion of the Oneals is imaged in this Episode, who drank so deep of the charm and venom of Acrasia.' *Spenser's Faerie Queene*, edited by John Upton, 2 vols (London, 1758), II, 438. See Roland Smith, 'The Irish Background of Spenser's *View*', *JEGP*, 42 (1943), 499–515 (p. 504). A poem entitled 'The Red Hand of Ireland' current in Spenser's time was often attributed to Tadhg Dall. *Bardic Poems*, I, xvii–xviii.

[43] Holinshed, VI, 69.

[44] *Britain*, p. 123 (mispag. p. 111).

[45] See the valuable discussion in Stephen Greenblatt, *Renaissance Self-Fashioning from More to Shakespeare* (Chicago, 1980), pp. 180–8.

Irish customs, he complains, former English colonists, 'became degenerate and metamorphosed . . . like those who had drunke of *Circes* Cuppe, and were turned into very Beasts, and yet tooke such pleasure in their beastly manner of life, as they would not returne to their shape of men againe'.[46] Spenser's fable concludes with the swinish Gryll who resolutely refuses to abandon his new way of life, as did so many of the families castigated for having 'degenerated from theire firste natures' (p. 114). Prominent amongst them were the MacSweeneys whose name Spenser deliberately degrades into Mac*swines* thereby contriving an astonishingly apt accommodation of classical myth to contemporary circumstance (pp. 115–16).[47] The New World was commonly envisioned as 'virgin' territory ripe for the possession of European knights but in the Bowre of Blisse the opposite has occurred, the female has taken possession of the male and all hopes of conquest (symbolised by the rusting armour) perish. The effect is one of cultural 'depasturing' (II.12.73).[48]

In the case of Acrasia, as so often in Spenser, sexual seduction implies its political equivalent. Lord Grey had complained that the native Irish preferred to 'wallow in their own sensual government' rather than live by the moral code of English law and Spenser commonly employs the terms 'licentious' and 'libertie' in such a manner as to imply that Irish customs merely ratify personal licence.[49] In point of fact, the majority of the New English planters were hardly the cream of civil English society but single men of low social status whose likely intermarriage with Gaelic families posed the most serious threat of cultural assimilation.[50] In a very real sense, therefore, sex and politics were intimately related. John Derricke warned colonists to shun bewitchment by Celtic women,

> For why should men of Th'englishe pale,
>   In suche a Crewe delight
> Or eke repose suche confidence,
>   In that unhappie race:
> Since mischeef lurketh oftentimes
>   even in the smothest face?'[51]

[46] Sir John Davies, *Discoverie of the True Causes*, p. 182.

[47] See also Derricke, *Image of Irelande*, p. 11. Comparisons of the native Irish to swine are common (pp. 42, 54).

[48] See Louis A. Montrose, '*A Midsummer Night's Dream* and the Shaping Fantasies of Elizabethan Culture: Gender, Power, Form', in Margaret W. Ferguson, Maureen Quilligan, and Nancy J. Vickers, ed., *Rewriting the Renaissance: The Discourses of Sexual Difference in Early Modern Europe* (Chicago, 1986), pp. 79, 86.

[49] Jenkins, 'Spenser with Lord Grey in Ireland', p. 345.

[50] Nicholas Canny, 'Permissive Frontier', pp. 19–24.

[51] Derricke, *Image of Ireland*, p. 31. The vision of Irish maidens 'bathyng in their sweete delightes,/ so long thei doe remaine./ Till Cupid toul'th his sacryng bell,/ to enter other Rites' (p. 28) may well have suggested Guyon's encounter with bathing ladies (II.12.63–9).

Similarly, Spenser warns against 'licentious conversinge with the Irishe or marryinge and fosteringe with them' (p. 117). 'How cane suche matchinge but bringe forthe an evill race', he asks, 'seinge that Comonlye the Childe takethe moste of his nature of the mother besides speache, manners, inclynacion . . . for by them they are firste *framed and fashioned* soe as what they receave once from them they will hardelye ever after forgoe' (p. 120).[52] Thus, by usurping the very task Spenser had set himself, Irish Acrasias defeat English Guyons. The coincidence of phrasing reminds us, however, that cultural assimilation was adjudged 'contagion' only when it favoured the Celts (p. 117). What is lamented in the Old Normans is recommended for the 'meare' Irish. It was Spenser's hope that through a rigorous programme of suppression intended to obliterate Irish dress, language, customs, law and life-style, the native population would 'in shorte time learne quite to forgett his Irishe nacion' (p. 215). The Gaelic poets reversed the perspective, praising the Old Normans for their successful integration into Celtic society while sharply criticising their lowly born successors. 'I conceive not whence it is', remarked Geoffrey Keating, himself the scion of an Old Norman family berated by Spenser, 'that they do not contract alliance with the nobles of Ireland, unless it be from disesteem for their own obscurity, so that they do not deem themselves worthy to have such noble Gaels in their kinship'.[53] There is nothing 'savage' here except the satire.

But more important than the fact of assimilation were its implications for the fundamental distinction between the 'civil' and the 'savage' by which colonial theorists set such store. Ireland 'bred dreadfull doubts' of a more basic nature than the mere threat of violence since the phenomenon of assimilation betrayed the insecurity of English culture.[54] Matters were all the worse in that the decline of the Normans mirrored that of the Irish themselves who, in bygone times, had brought literacy to the Saxons. The island merely acts as a catalyst for a degenerative process endemic in the human condition and therefore common to 'self' and 'other'. 'One would not beleeve', remarks Camden, 'in how short a time some English . . . degenerate and grow out of kinde'.[55] The vision of the courtly Timias (alias Raleigh) deformed by an Irish 'glib', unable to utter his own name

[52] Derricke regarded the offspring of such marriages as beasts in human guise: 'Transformed now and then:/ From Bores to Beares, and yet sometyme,/ resemblyng honest men.' *Image of Irelande*, p. 29.

[53] Keating, *The History of Ireland*, edited and translated by David Comyn, Irish Texts Society, 4 vols (London, 1902–14), I (1902), 35.

[54] See Hayden White, 'The Forms of Wildness: Archaeology of an Idea', in Edward Dudley and Maximillian E. Novak, ed., *The Wild Man Within: An Image in Western Thought from the Renaissance to Romanticism* (Pittsburg, 1972), pp. 3–38.

[55] *Britain*, p. 148.

and unrecognisable to his former companions, represents the ultimate cultural horror, the inevitable effect of alienation from court (IV.8.12).[56] In attempting to grapple with the problem of how such things 'maye be', Spenser was forced to recognise that not the country but the colonists themselves were at fault: 'as it is the *nature of all men* to love libertye So they become Libertines and fall to all Licentiousnes of the Irishe' (p. 211). Since civility is not innate but imposed the last three words are redundant, there being no necessary association between 'nature' and 'nacion' such as Eudoxus imagines (p. 96). 'It is but even the other daye', Spenser concedes, 'since Englande grewe Civill' (p. 118).

This being so, the great anxiety is that of cultural regression.[57] In *The Faerie Queene* England first manifests a separate identity when it pulls free of the '*Celticke* mayn-land' (II.10.5)—the sole use of the word Celtic in Spenser's verse. Involvement in the enterprise of Ireland reverses that primal segregation, exposing fragile English 'civility' to a vibrant cultural alternative closely akin to its own 'barbarous' origins. The notorious Feagh MacHugh O'Byrne, Spenser notes *en passant*, is of ancient Briton stock—the same, that is, as his own King Arthur (p. 170).[58] To this extent the battle is internal and the Irish less savage in themselves than scapegoats for a savagery latent in all: the patron of Justice is a 'salvage' knight and Sir Calepine's place is supplied by a 'salvage' man in courtly armour who later proves indispensable to Prince Arthur, the very embodiment of English martial chivalry. Again and again, Spenserian poetry makes coalesce what Spenserian prose struggles to keep separate. The radical insecurity of both is apparent in the manner whereby persistent, intrusive digressions subvert main lines of argument and obsessive repetition of familiar *topoi* produces increasing indeterminacy rather than consolidation. In the first book of *The Faerie Queene*, for example, a fallen Eden is heroically saved by St George of Merry England—apparently the very paradigm of beneficent colonialism; in the second, however, a false Eden must be savagely destroyed in the interests of civil temperance—a disturbing reflection of actual colonial policy in Ireland and elsewhere; in the third book, the resulting struggle between creativity and destruction, metamorphosis and identity, continues interminably in the Gardens of Adonis where, in a reprise of the Bowre of Blisse, another Venereal figure 'possesseth' a young man 'transformed

---

[56] H.M. English, 'Spenser's Accommodation of Allegory to History in the Story of Timias and Belphoebe', *JEGP*, 59 (1960), pp. 417–29.

[57] *Prose*, pp. 56, 60, 117.

[58] The Trojan myth of origin served to obscure the common Celtic heritage of the two islands. See Hugh A. MacDougall, *Racial Myth in English History: Trojans, Teutons, and Anglo-Saxons* (Montreal, 1982), pp. 7–27.

oft, and chaunged diverslie' while the 'wilde Bore' ruts savagely beyond the Pale.[59]

Set in this context *Colin Clouts Come Home Againe* (1595) may be seen to occupy a pivotal position in Spenser's poetry of exile, indicative of changed moods and shifting attitudes, surveying familiar pastoral landscapes from an entirely unfamiliar perspective.[60] Symptomatic of this is the reappearance of the solitary, disconsolate Colin Clout, so 'alienate and with drawen' from pastoral contentment even in *The Shepheardes Calender* that he could not perform the eulogy of 'fayre *Elisa*' composed after the Virgilian model in premature expectation of a new Golden Age.[61] Reread in the light of Spenser's later career, such early work seems rich in proleptic irony. Though native to Arcadia, Colin endures a sort of internal exile in a pastoral setting that might have been the scene of wish-fulfilment but becomes instead an ironic backdrop to wish-frustration.[62] As month follows month his sense of unrequited love comes to symbolise nothing short of the vanity of human wishes, the inevitable disappointment of all idealistic aspirations whether personal or political.[63] By skilfully blending Skelton's satiric *persona* of Colin Clout with that of Clément Marot's elegiac Colin, Spenser 'shadowed' an highly discontented 'selfe'.[64] As 'October' makes clear, poetry enjoys no official status in Elisa's England nor may patronage

[59] Despite St George's victory, Spenser recognised that it was the very 'Englishness' of the Protestant cause that rendered it ineffective in Ireland, *Prose*, p. 221. See Alan Ford, 'The Protestant Reformation in Ireland', in Brady and Gillespie, ed., *Natives and Newcomers*, pp. 50–74. The hazardous sea voyage to the morally and culturally ennervating Bowre of Blisse (suggestive of the passage from Ireland to England in *Colin Clouts Come Home Againe*) reminds us that Grey is a 'wise Pilot' in the *Vewe*, *Prose*, p. 63.

[60] The dedicatory letter is dated 27 December 1591 but internal evidence suggests revisions possibly as late as 1594. See Sam Meyer, *An Interpretation of Edmund Spenser's 'Colin Clout'* (Cork, 1969), p. 150.

[61] For the political implications of Virgil's fourth eclogue see Laurence Lerner, *The Uses of Nostalgia: Studies in Pastoral Poetry* (London, 1972), pp. 68–70.

[62] For pastoral as the poetry of wish-fulfilment see Renato Poggioli, *The Oaten Flute* (Cambridge, Mass., 1975), pp. 1–41. For pastoral as the poetry of experience see Paul Alpers, 'The Eclogue Tradition and the Nature of Pastoral', *College English*, 34 (1972), 352–71; S.K. Heninger, 'The Renaissance Perversion of Pastoral', *JHI*, 22 (1961), 254–61. See also Harry Berger, *Revisionary Play: Studies in the Spenserian Dynamics* (Berkeley, 1988), pp. 277–89.

[63] For the immediate political context see Paul E. McLane, *Spenser's 'Shepheardes Calender': A Study in Elizabethan Allegory* (Notre Dame, 1961), pp. 13–26, 140–57. See also Helen Cooper, *Pastoral: Mediaeval into Renaissance* (Ipswich, 1977), pp. 157–61.

[64] See Annabel Patterson, 'Re-opening the Green Cabinet: Clément Marot and Edmund Spenser', *ELR*, 16 (1986), 44–70.

be relied on to supply the deficiency. In eclogue after eclogue shepherds travel 'homeward' but few, if any, seem to arrive, and Colin Clout is not of their number.

The title of *Colin Clouts Come Home Againe* is all the more arresting, therefore, in its apparent assertion of achieved security, in the implication that not merely epic heroes but epic poets are made in exile. But the *persona* of Colin Clout was far more complex now than in 1579, and the decision to revive it signals Spenser's willingness to explore increasingly problematic aspects of the relationship between fiction and reality, aesthetic ideals and practical necessities. For a start, all elements of anonymity had vanished. *The Shepheardes Calender* had run through four editions and the question, 'who knows not Colin Clout?', had on one level become entirely rhetorical. To a degree hitherto unique in English literature a fictional *persona* had been carefully cultivated into a personal trade-mark. But knowing that Spenser in some sense 'was' Colin Clout implied knowledge of the opposite, and Spenser deftly exploits this dual outlook in order to develop the *persona* both as a medium of self-expression and as a mechanism of self-transcendence. Now native to Ireland, not Arcadia, Colin Clout views Elisa's kingdom through the penetrating eyes of a stranger and returns 'home againe' in disgust. To him, England is 'another world of land . . . floting amid the sea in ieopardie' (272–3), the distant goal of a rough and hazardous sea voyage. But Colin's voyage out is Spenser's voyage home and subtle reminiscences of Ovid's *Tristia* evoke something of the ambivalent emotion the act of composition must inevitably have aroused.[65] The returning exile adopts the *persona* of an alien to gain clarity of vision. The suspicion that he may actually have become something of an alien in the process is neither endorsed nor refuted.

When first we encounter him, Colin Clout seems relatively contented where he is, 'desart' though the place be and unrequited though his love remains (91). The situation is completely altered, however, by the intrusion of 'the shepheard of the Ocean'—alias his fellow Munster planter, Sir Walter Raleigh—exiled from the court through unrequited love of Cynthia.[66] The obvious coincidence of circumstances qualifies Spenser's pastoral *persona* since the stranger is allowed to articulate 'Colin's' suppressed anxieties:

> He gan to cast great lyking to my lore,
> And great dislyking to my lucklesse lot:
> That banisht had my selfe, like wight forlore,

[65] Meyer, pp. 65–6.
[66] Stephen Greenblatt, *Sir Walter Raleigh: The Renaissance Man and His Roles* (New Haven, 1973), pp. 60–3.

Into that waste, where I was quite forgot.
The which to leave, thenceforth he counseld mee. (180–4)

The political connotations of 'banisht' slyly fuse the fates of these two ambitious expatriates, raising a spectre of public oblivion equally anathema to both. The passage is all the more potent in relation to Spenser's fear of cultural assimilation to the 'waste' world where even noble families lose their names and confound their genealogies, a fear apparent in Colin's fable of the river Bregog who 'did lose his name' through sexual assimilation into the waters of the river Mulla (155).[67] Spenser was particularly proud of the national heritage encoded in his surname—so much so that, once Colin arrives in England, he violates generic convention to remind us of the 'noble familie' of the Spensers of Althorp, 'of which I meanest boast my selfe to be' (538).[68] In this manner the personal pronoun 'I' is rendered intriguingly unstable, sometimes signifying Colin, sometimes Spenser, sometimes both, but never the supposed narrator since a pretence of detachment must always be maintained even though the whole exercise centres upon elaborately reflexive strategies of 'selfe-regard' (682).[69] In the present instance the jarring connotations of 'boast' and 'meanest'—almost oxymoronic in their context—bespeak the intensely personal dilemma at the heart of the issue. The 'Shepheard of the Ocean' ['he'] chooses his ground very well in urging 'Colin' ['I'] to accompany him to England and place his 'oaten quill' at the service of Cynthia. Raleigh had doubtless lent similar encouragement, but far more important than such factual correspondence is the tangled web of complex, conflicting emotions teased out through the apparently impersonal conventions of pastoral. The poem, I would suggest, is more powerfully autobiographical in its 'fiction' than its 'fact'.

Colin's first impression of England prompts bitter reassessment of the 'pastoral' landscape he has left behind: in England he discovers,

all happie peace and plenteous store
Conspire in one to make contented blisse:
No wayling there nor wretchednesse is heard . . .

---

[67] On the importance of names in the poem see Thomas R. Edwards, *Imagination and Power: A Study of Poetry on Public Themes* (London, 1971), pp. 56–7. For the fable of Bregog see John D. Bernard, *Ceremonies of Innocence: Pastoralism in the Poetry of Edmund Spenser* (Cambridge, 1989), pp. 128–9.

[68] Spenser particularly praises the three sisters of this family (536–71) to whom he had previously dedicated three poems from *Complaints*: *Mother Hubberds Tale* to Anne, Lady Compton and Monteagle; *Muiopotmos* to Elizabeth, Lady Carey; *Teares of the Muses* to Alice, Lady Strange. See also *Prothalamion* 130–1; Muriel Bradbrook, 'No Room at the Top', in Brown and Harris, ed., *Elizabethan Poetry*, pp. 91–110 (p. 108).

[69] Nancy Jo Hoffman, *Spenser's Pastorals: 'The Shepheardes Calender' and 'Colin Clout'* (Baltimore, 1977), 120–42; Terry Comito, 'The Lady in a Landscape and the Poetics of Elizabethan Pastoral', *UTQ*, 41 (1972), 200–18 (p. 204).

> No griesly famine, nor no raging sweard,
> No nightly bodrags, nor no hue and cries;
> The shepheards there abroad may safely lie,
> On hills and downes, withouten dread or daunger. (310–17)

As the prolonged technique of negative appraisal indicates, a remarkable transformation has overtaken the customary pastoral outlook. The mere act of comparison degrades Ireland completely and the tone of the speaker alters accordingly. The use of the word 'bodrags' (raids), unusual except in the Irish State Papers, is a case in point.[70] The traditional pastoral register gives way to that of the political tract, reminding us that *Colin Clouts Come Home Againe* is written, like *A Vewe of the Present State of Irelande*, 'by waye of a diologue', being no less engaged in the continuing dialectic of contemporary politics (p. 43). At this point the poem seems poised to defy one of the oldest conventions of pastoral—a perfect example of which is the 'September' eclogue—whereby shepherds journey abroad only to discover that true contentment resides at home. Arriving at the court of Cynthia, by contrast, Colin and the Shepherd of the Ocean appear to achieve the sublime goal of *The Faerie Queene*, the elusive nature of which Spenser attempts to capture through the use of increasingly abstract vocabulary and rarified, metaphysical symbolism difficult to relate to any political reality (605–8).[71] The closer one examines Colin's eulogy of the court, the more remarkable becomes its lack of specificity. Indeed it is precisely at the point of furthest abstraction that Spenser exploits the rhetorical mechanisms of the dialogue form to break the aristocratic spell and return us to mundane issues of salary and survival. Thestylis (alias Lodowick Bryskett, Spenser's fellow civil servant) abruptly enquires:

> Why *Colin*, since thou foundst such grace
> With *Cynthia* and all her noble crew:
> Why didst thou ever leave that happie place,
> In which such wealth might unto thee accrew? (652–5)[72]

The deliciously ironic possibilities of '*Cynthia* and all her noble *crew*' are admirably glossed in the appropriately mercenary, flat rhyme on 'accrew'—easily, and I suspect deliberately, one of the worst in the poem. Described as breaking the prolonged silence arising from the mystical description of Cynthia, this forthright query derives additional

---

[70] Also in a Celtic context see, 'The sundry bordragings/ Of neighbour Scots' at *Faerie Queene*, II.10.63. The relationship between the Scots and the Irish is discussed in *Prose*, pp. 82–4.

[71] On the quality of the language see Meyer, pp. 103–7.

[72] Bryskett had himself harboured dreams of pastoral retreat in Ireland. See Jenkins, 'Spenser and the Clerkship in Munster', p. 113.

force from its equal application to Colin and his creator.[73] It is the inevitable question suggested both by Spenser's career and the fictional manner in which he chose to represent it. Like throwing a stone through a stained-glass window, it shatters the fragile tracery of courtly fable, exposing majestic icons as mere ornament. As the perspective alters, all the apparently trivial qualifications covertly insinuated into Colin's expressions of wonder emerge into sudden prominence. It now appears that the reality betrays the ideal and Colin is forced from stylised panegyric to colloquial retraction: 'for sooth to say' (as though he had not said 'sooth' till now),

> it is no sort of life,
> For shepheard fit to lead in that same place,
> Where each one seeks with malice and with strife,
> To thrust downe other into foule disgrace. (688–91)

What is particularly remarkable is that many of the adjectives applied to the courtiers are identical to those applied to the 'wild' Irish: 'foule' (691), 'guilefull' (699), 'ydle' (704), 'wastefull' (762), 'laesie' (766), and even 'lewd and licentious' (787). There exists, it would appear, a sophisticated form of barbarity all the worse for its pretence to the sublime. The best that may be hoped for is the dissociation of Cynthia from her court, but that is like dissociating the spider from its web.[74] When the praise and the blame of the same institution are both absolute, the impression created is one of wilful dichotomy. Up to this point Spenser seemed personally engaged in the creation of the very myth that entices lowly 'shepheards' to seek out Cynthia's court where, in theory, 'learned arts do florish in great honor,/ And Poets wits are had in peerlesse price' (320–1). Since such poets 'do their *Cynthia* immortall make', they may now be regarded as victims of their own propaganda (453).[75] The condition of many is far from reassuring: Harpalus, 'woxen aged/ In faithfull service' (380–1); Corydon, 'meanly waged' though 'ablest' of all (382–3); Alycon, 'bent to mourne' (384); Palemon, 'that sung so long until quite hoarse he grew' (399); Alabaster, 'knowne yet to few' despite epic praise of Cynthia (401), and the Shepherd of the Ocean himself, 'that spends his wit in loves consuming smart' (429). Ominously the catalogue concludes with Sir Philip Sidney now 'dead and

[73] For an equivalent effect see, 'with that *Alexis* broke his tale asunder' (352). Alexis links praise of the Queen to the poet's elevation of his personal status, asking 'what grace' Cynthia afforded Colin—the central crux of the poem's autobiographical concern.

[74] For the court as a spider's web see Robert A. Brinkley, 'Spenser's *Muiopotmos* and the Poetics of Metamorphosis', *ELH*, 48 (1981), 668–76. Belphoebe is, however, conspicuously dissociated from the idleness of 'courtly blis' at *Faerie Queene*, II.3.40.

[75] The poem seems intentionally ambivalent as to whether greatness is innate (333–5) or ascribed, whether monarchs elevate poets or *vice versa*.

gone' (449). *Colin Clouts* was published with *Astrophel*, a pastoral elegy for Sidney with contributions from a variety of poets including Lodowick Bryskett, Spenser's 'Thestylis'. An essential unity may be seen to underlie the collection thus comprised through common concentration upon themes of lost potential and wasted opportunity. The lament for Sidney is really a lament for the England of courtly patronage he had come to symbolise, for his own inimitable version of pastoral. His cultural significance lends public resonance to the private grief of his early death. And Sidney, too, had sought to defend draconian but unsuccessful attempts to 'fashion' a civil Ireland.[76] Elegy, Spenser notes, invariably finds us 'mourning in others, our owne miseries'.[77]

At the conclusion to his catalogue of poets, Colin admits that Cynthia received him not for his 'skill' but for his patron's sake, thereby revealing the little esteem afforded 'oaten quills' however worthy. It is not in the least surprising, therefore, that Colin Clout 'chooses' to come home again since what Spenser actually 'shadows' under this *persona* is not himself but his poetic ambitions (672). The principal reason Colin comes home is that his creator cannot. Spenser signs the poem's dedication not from his 'home' (as its title seems to demand) but from his 'house' at Kilcolman. Colin is 'home' in Ireland, Spenser merely 'housed' there. Despite the poem's ostensible celebration of 'homecoming', little contentment is evident at the sombre Virgilian close when the company disperses under 'glooming skies'.[78] This is as it should be since we have heard far too much of Ireland's 'barren soyle' with its 'nightly bodrags' and 'ravenous wolves' to allow of any happier outcome. Colin's 'love' remains as unrequited as ever, much resembling his creator's relationship with his queen: 'So hie her thoughts as she her selfe have place,/ And loath each lowly thing with loftie eie' (937–8).[79] It would seem that Colin's heart-felt appeal for William Alabaster owes much of its intensity to a deep empathy in disappointment:

> O dreaded Dread, do not thy selfe that wrong,
> To let thy fame lie so in hidden shade:
> But call it forth, *O call him forth to thee*,
> To end thy glorie which he had begun. (406–9).

In the *Amoretti* published that same year, Spenser voices the fear that *The Faerie Queene* may never see completion, nor Gloriana ever enjoy poetic apotheosis (XXXIII).

---

[76] See the fragmentary *Discourse on Irish Affairs* in *Complete Works*, edited by A. Feuillerat, 4 vols (Cambridge, 1912–26), III, 46–50.

[77] *Dolefull Lay of Clorinda*, 96.

[78] The conclusion echoes that of Virgil's tenth eclogue ('gravis cantantibus umbra') but significantly omits the phrase 'ite domum'.

[79] David R. Shore, *Spenser and the Poetics of Pastoral: A Study of the World of Colin Clout* (Kingston, 1985), p. 129.

In view of England's presentation in *Colin Clouts Come Home Againe*, Ireland's prominence in the second instalment of *The Faerie Queene* (IV–VI), published the following year, was only to be expected. Indeed Spenser seems determined to make an issue of it; his engagement with historical detail grows increasingly explicit and the allegory correspondingly transparent. His sense of alienation was doubtless exacerbated by the poor reception accorded the poem amongst certain sections of the aristocracy, tantamount, in his eyes, to rejection by the very culture he had sought to celebrate.[80] It therefore becomes equally important to justify the poetry through the politics as the politics through the poetry; *The Faerie Queene* must be seen to be of national consequence. The effect upon the landscape is dramatic: the very terrain seems locked in ceaseless conflict as the vocabularies of polity and topography fuse:

> Like as the tide that comes fro th'Ocean mayne,
> Flowes up the Shenan with contrarie forse,
> And overruling him in his owne rayne,
> Drives backe the current of his kindly course,
> And makes it seeme to have some other sourse:
> But when the floud is spent, then backe againe
> His borrowed waters forst to redisbourse,
> He sends the sea his owne with double gaine,
> And tribute eke withall, as to his Soveraine. (IV.3.27)

Of particular note is the ambiguity as to the river's true 'source', an effect mirrored in the correspondent political analogies. Thus the ocean tide appears to usurp the Shannon in its 'owne rayne' although the Ocean is actually its true 'Soveraine' and the violent influx of foreign waters—'borrowed' by the river they seemed to oppress—eventually occasions the payment of double tribute, amply rewarding the expenditure of the invading 'floud'. The apparently unnatural effort to 'drive backe the current' of the river's 'kindly course' effects a paradoxical restoration of natural order analogous to the imposition of 'civility' through violence. A very comforting image, this, of the colonial enterprise. Yet latent within the imagery is the nightmare of perpetual recurrence. Several cantos later, inviting the Irish rivers to partake in Marinell's wedding masque, Spenser asks 'why should they not likewise in love agree?',

---

[80] Richard Helgerson, 'The New Poet Presents Himself: Spenser and the Idea of a Literary Career', *PMLA*, 93 (1978), 893–911 (pp. 896–7, 902–4).

only to answer his own question by summoning the 'balefull Oure, late staind with English blood' (IV.11.40–4).[81] As he describes them, Irish rivers invariably divide, submerge, overflow or run blood red: 'his corps was carried downe along the Lee,/ Whose waters with his filthy bloud it stayned' (V.2.19), the same Lee that 'encloseth Corke with his *devided* flood' (IV.11.44).[82] During Lord Grey's campaign in 1581 Sir John of Desmond's decapitated corpse was hung 'over the River Lee on the North Gate of Cork' while his 'blasphemous head' was impaled on a spike in Dublin. Pathetic fallacy struggles to accommodate political fact.[83]

Spenser's dilemma in these books is that he both promotes and deplores violence simultaneously thereby rendering further suspect the prime distinction between 'wild' Irish and 'civil' English—the 'sinister suggestions of Crueltye' attaching to Lord Grey's reputation being merely one case in point (p. 162). Many of the administrators he most admired acted beyond the bounds of English civil law, and his own appeal for the restraint of compassion, commonly regarded as an index of civility, erodes the moral basis of his argument still further (p. 163).[84] Mercilla enters his poem only to refuse the virtue she personifies, and the fearful paradox of savage knighthood implies submission to the very force it was designed to destroy: the Irish campaign forced Grey to such 'violence' that it 'allmoste Changed his verye naturall disposicion', almost made of him a wild creature of the borderland, a natural exile from court (p. 160).[85] Though more consistently allegorical than any of his predecessors, Spenser writes with a greater sense of immediacy, having personally experienced the events he records. His authorial voice is not that of Aristotle's detached narrator but

---

[81] See Jenkins, 'Spenser with Lord Grey in Ireland', pp. 341–2.

[82] Similar imagery is employed in the *Vewe*: the 'base' Irish have no wish to rebel but are 'carried awaie by the violence of the streame'; Elizabeth's 'compassion' impedes reform by stopping 'the streame of suche violence' as her Lord Deputy deems necessary. *Prose*, pp. 156, 159. See Roland Smith, 'Spenser's Irish River Stories', *PMLA*, 50 (1935), 1047–56.

[83] Henley, pp. 139–41.

[84] Canny, 'Spenser and the Development of an Anglo-Irish Identity', pp. 8–9. See also David J. Baker, '"Some Quirk, Some Subtle Evasion": Legal Subversion in Spenser's *A View of the Present State of Ireland*', in Patrick Cullen and Thomas P. Roche Jr., ed., *Spenser Studies*, VI (New York, 1986), pp. 147–63. According to Camden the mercenaries massacred at Smerwick cried out 'Misericordia, Misericordia' and Grey 'shed Tears' for the necessity of their slaughter but ordered it to continue nonetheless, *The History of the Most Renowned and Victorious Princess Elizabeth* (London, 1675), p. 243. Throughout the *Vewe* inconsistencies in Elizabeth's Irish policy are tactfully ascribed to excessive 'compassion' although 'greate faintenes in her maiesties withstandinge' the Earl of Tyrone is also recorded. In the *Brief Note*, however, 'compassion' is increasingly linked to political ineptitude. *Prose*, pp. 159, 166–7, 239, 242.

[85] For the notorious massacre at Smerwick see *Prose*, pp. 524–30. The Munster famine horrified many English observers, *Prose*, pp. 381–2, 396.

of an interested party; poet and planter coalesce.[86] The quality of violence in Book Five, remarkable even for the epic tradition, attests to the measure of Spenser's personal assimilation into the Irish problem—as though the verse were exploring the poetic implications of alienation from its own 'civil' values. The result is political poetry in the fullest sense; the poetry of man as political animal negotiating expedient strategies of *realpolitik* while at the same time seeking a moral basis for moral compromise.

If the 'Legend of Justice' represents an aberration in the poem's moral temper, it is largely because it also represents a perfect articulation of its historical vision.[87] In dealing with this problem, Spenser's principal recourse is to prefer motives to methods, to dissociate blood-shed from blood-thirst, but this is to justify means by ends and it soon becomes apparent that he is quite literally attempting to make a virtue of 'necessitye'.[88] The *Ius Politicum*, he informs us, sounding somewhat Machiavellian, 'thoughe it be not of it selfe iuste yeat by applicacion or rather necessitye is made iuste'. In public affairs, 'better is a mischief then an inconvenience' (p. 66).[89] All too often when 'necessity' dictates a choice between evils, the lesser (as Spenser conceives it) is presented as an absolute good, a process which subjects the poem's moral logic to severe strain. As a result, the 'Legend of Justice' becomes instead an enabling exercise in justification, in appropriating general ideals to particular policies, a procedural flaw latent in the grand distinction between the poem's 'general' and 'particular' intentions. Only through the careful interaction of politicized image and poeticized policy may the blood-soaked landscape of Book Five be presented as a serious instance of moral achievement.[90] Geoffrey Keating caustically remarks that 'being a poet' Spenser allowed himself, 'a poet's licence . . . framing and fashioning numerous poetic romances sweetly articulated to deceive'. In the original Celtic the phrase both imitates and parodies the rhythmic melody of Spenserian diction: 'do

---

[86] Spenser's views broadly correspond to those of his fellow Munster planter Richard Beacon, author of *Solon his Follie*, who presents a defence of Sir Richard Bingham comparable to Spenser's defence of Grey. See Brady, 'The Road to the *View*' in Coughlan, ed., *Spenser and Ireland*, pp. 37–9; Alexander Judson, 'Spenser and the Munster Officials', *SP*, 44 (1947), 157–73 (pp. 165–8).

[87] Richard A. McCabe, *The Pillars of Eternity: Time and Providence in 'The Faerie Queene'* (Dublin, 1989), pp. 39–47.

[88] For the principle of moral necessity see *Faerie Queene*, I.12.18–19.

[89] See Edwin Greenlaw, 'The Influence of Machiavelli on Spenser', *MP*, 7 (1909–10), 187–202; H.S.V. Jones, 'Spenser's Defence of Lord Grey', *University of Illinois Studies in Language and Literature*, 5 (1919), 151–219 (pp. 208–18); Felix Raab, *The English Face of Machiavelli: A Changing Interpretation 1500–1700*, (London, 1964), pp. 61–2.

[90] Michael O'Connell, *Mirror and Veil: The Historical Dimension of Spenser's 'Faerie Queene'* (Chapel Hill, 1977), pp. 156–60.

chumadh agus do chórughadh le briathraibh blasda, do bhreugadh an léaghthóra'.[91]

At times one detects in Spenserian allegory a deliberate confusion of tenor and vehicle calculated to obscure as much as it reveals.[92] Transposed to fairyland the colonial enterprise becomes a fairytale, a struggle between knights and monsters conventionally incapable of resolution except 'by the sworde' (p. 148). The unwary reader is led to forget that, translated back into real terms, such conflicts involve massive human casualties: 'for by the sworde which I named I doe not meane/ The Cuttinge of all that nacion with the sworde, which farr be it from me that ever I shoulde thinke soe desperatlye or wishe so uncharitablie . . . for evill people by good ordinaunces and government maye be made good/ but *the evill that is of it selfe evill will never become good*' (p. 148).[93] 'O, that we then could come by Caesar's spirit', remarks Brutus, 'and not dismember Caesar' (II.1.169–70). Allegory gratifies such impossible aspirations. Abstracted from the daily carnage, actual violence becomes conceptual 'powre' (or 'might'), an integral component of justice (V.4.1) and the concept which most often attracts the epithet 'imperial' in Spenserian poetry—closely followed by that of 'state'. Judging from the effect upon his writing, there can be little doubt that Spenser found violence aesthetically stimulating, evincing considerable imaginative sympathy with what, he knew, should properly be deplored, 'for bloud can nought but sin, and wars but sorrowes yield' (I.10.60). Nevertheless, 'fierce warres' must somehow 'moralize' his song; the solution must be found in the problem (I Proem 1). Artegall's enchanted 'sword' allegorises Lord Grey's 'thorough' policy, and month by month, from 1580 to 1582, his private secretary took toll of the casualties, fully aware of the compromise with 'civility' therein entailed: 'seinge that by no other meanes it is possible to recure them, and that these are not of will but of verye urgente *necessitye*' (p. 163). Moral necessity would thus appear to dispense with humanity and moral allegory to rationalise the dispensation.

Officially, of course, Spenser's policy was not repression but 'reform'. 'Irena', as its name implies, was intended as the Land of Peace (the eirenic land) as well as the Land of Ire, and Spenser's allegory of retributive justice duly gives way to that of civil courtesy, a virtue no less political proceeding from and returning to the court: 'so from the

[91] Keating, *History of Ireland*, I, 30.
[92] Donald Cheney, *Spenser's Image of Nature: Wild Man and Shepherd in 'The Faerie Queene'* (New Haven, 1966), p. 149.
[93] At one stage Spenser complains that Ireland is so 'full of her owne nacion that maye not be roted out' (*Prose*, p. 211). Whether 'maye' indicates moral prohibition or military impracticality remains problematic.

Ocean all rivers spring/ And *tribute* backe repay as to their *King*'—a superb gloss upon the heroic simile of the Shannon (VI Proem, 7).[94] The Patron of Courtesy is an armed knight inspired by the poetry of Colin Clout whose unexpected reappearance again signals his creator's personal involvement in the quest to restore 'Pastorella' to the gentle class to whom she rightfully belongs. As Calidore dons shepherd's clothing over his armour, romantic pastoralism reveals its imperial nature in the very act of disguise. Hugh O'Donnell complained that soldiers were being sent into his territory, 'under a colour of teaching his people civility', while Tadhg Dall Ó'Huiginn wryly observed that 'warlike men are left in peace but . . . Gaels of civil behaviour can expect no peace from the foreigners'.[95] The words 'wild' and 'salvage' occur more often in the sixth book of *The Faerie Queene* than any other, and its visions of pastoral tranquillity invariably degenerate into scenes of carnage. So potent is the influence of the Irish landscape that even the sudden emergence of Calidore 'out of the wood' is sufficient to dispel Colin's vision of gracious 'Civility' (VI.10.17). The book's most representative figure is the murdered Meliboeus who takes his name from the dispossessed, patronless exile of the Virgilian eclogue which, more than any other, haunted Spenser's imagination. Precisely because the 'seat' of courtesy is 'deepe within the mynd', the sense of alienation in Book Six is most acutely intimate.

Because of the perceived relationship of rebel and bard Spenser was particularly exercised by the power of the Celtic language, agreeing with Holinshed's *Chronicles* in recognising the indissoluble association of language and manners: 'the speache beinge Irishe the harte muste nedes be Irishe for out of the abundance of the harte the tongue speakethe' (p. 119).[96] Hence the objection to customs *never harde of* amongst the English (p. 50), cultural difference being precisely what gets lost in translation. The poet who had bardic verses 'translated'

---

[94] For the etymology of Eire see *Prose*, p. 417; Camden, *Britain*, p. 61; Roland Smith, 'More Irish Words in Spenser', *MLN*, 59 (1944), 472–7 (pp. 475–6). In Ireland reciprocal courtesy was displaced by reciprocal violence: 'The Irish after blood and murder is drawn and done upon them will never be reconciled, and will revenge with blood if they may'. *Calendar of State Papers Irish* (1588–92), p. 225. Spenser agreed, 'for it is not easie to thinke that they whoe have imbrewed them selves so deeplie in our bloud and inriched them selves with our goods should ever trust us to dwell againe amongste them: or that wee should endure to live amongst those peacablie without taking *iuste* revenge of them for all our evils'. *Prose*, p. 242. The concept of justice merely perpetuates the cycle.

[95] Camden, *Britain*, p. 125 (mispag. 113); *Bardic Poems*, II, 72.

[96] See Holinshed, VI, 5–6. See Stephen Greenblatt, 'Learning to Curse: Aspects of Linguistic Colonialism in the Sixteenth Century', in Chiapelli, ed., *First Images of America*, II, 561–80 (p. 562); Anne Fogerty, 'The Colonization of Language: Narrative Strategy in *A View of the Present State of Ireland* and *The Faerie Queene*, Book VI', in Coughlan, ed., *Spenser and Ireland*, pp. 75–108.

into English 'that I might understande them' subjected all other aspects
of Irish culture to similar 'translation' thereby precluding all chance of
genuine insight.[97] The adoption of the Irish language, and even Irish
surnames, by old Norman families disturbed him perhaps more deeply
than anything else: 'it hathe bene ever the use of the Conquerour',
he complains, 'to despise the Language of the Conquered and to force
him by all meanes to learne his' (pp. 118–19). Keating replied, 'he
who makes a Christian conquest extinguishes not the language which
was before him . . . and it was thus William the Conqueror did as
regards the Saxons'.[98] By establishing English as the language of civil
Christianity, however, Spenser represents the extinction of its rival as
a Christian duty even though, 'it is unnaturall that *anye people* shoulde
love anothers language more then theire owne' (p. 118). In so far as
the 'unnatural' becomes the ideal, the resulting paradox undermines the
whole colonial enterprise since it now appears that not the savagery but
the culture of the Irish resists it. The process would be simpler were they
savages indeed. The only alternative was to stigmatise the culture itself as
savage through a pseudo-anthropological investigation into its barbarous
'Scythian' origins, a far more comforting study for Spenser than that of
mutual Briton antecedents.[99] In the 'wylde desarts' of Book Six there
dwells 'a salvage nation . . . usde . . . to eate the flesh of men . . . and
straungers to devoure' (VI.8.35–6)—not realistic description, of course,
but a murderous metaphor for the residual savagery allegedly inherent in
Celtic society, and allegedly justifying its suppression.[100] The only instances
of actual cannibalism Spenser records in Ireland were occasioned by his
own policy of famine, 'in so much as the verye carkasses they spared not
to scrape out of theire graves' (p. 158).

The only savage capable of nurture in Book Six 'cannot expresse his
simple minde' (VI.5.30), just as the Celtic voice is rendered dumb or

---

[97] For Spenser's possible knowledge of Gaelic Chronicles see Roland M. Smith, 'Spenser,
Holinshed, and the *Leabhar Gabhála*', *JEGP*, 43 (1944), 390–401; Roland M. Smith,
'Spenser's Tale of the Two Sons of Milesio', *MLQ*, 3 (1942), 547–57.

[98] Keating, *History of Ireland*, I, 37.

[99] Thus Spenser supplies a perfectly cogent explanation of 'tanistrye', involving the avoidance
of primogeniture in Celtic society, but then discredits it through spurious association with
'those Barbarous nacions that overranne the worlde' in ancient times. *Prose*, pp. 49–51.
See Edward D. Snyder, 'The Wild Irish: A Study of Some English Satires against the
Irish, Scots, and Welsh', *MP*, 17 (1919–20), 687–725. For similar Spanish attitudes to the
American Indians see Todorov, *Conquest of America*, pp. 127–45.

[100] Sir Henry Sidney described the O'Byrnes as 'cannibals'. See *A Commentary of the Services
and Charges of William Lord Grey of Wilton . . . by Arthur Lord Grey of Wilton*, edited
by Sir Philip de Malpas Grey Egerton, Camden Society (London, 1847), p. 70. For similar
instances see Nicholas Canny, *The Elizabethan Conquest of Ireland: A Pattern Established
1565–76* (Hassocks, Sussex, 1976), p. 126.

inarticulate throughout the *Vewe* despite its pretence of open dialogue. Only by assimilating the Celts to the image of feral man can Spenser transform them into fit objects of the beneficent, Christian imperialism associated with the various foundlings of Book Six, infants recovered from the wilderness and fostered in civility. These constitute some of the poem's most compelling images of civil reclamation, yet behind them lies a prosaic determination to have the Irish 'compelled to sende theire youthe to be dissiplined' in English-speaking schools, 'whearby they will in shorte space growe up to that Civill Conversacion that . . . the Children will loathe the former rudenes in which they weare bredd and . . . theire parentes . . . perceave the fowlenes of theire owne brutishe behaviour' (p. 218).[101] Ultimately there would be no 'wicked' Celtic poetry because no Celtic language and the heart would perforce be English. It was even hoped that the imposition of English place-names upon newly created counties and shires would be complemented by the enforced abandonment of Irish surnames (p. 215). By such means the moral topography of self-cultivation, charted by the colonial allegorist, is made to legitimise the imperial cartography of conquest.

Within Spenser's lifetime, however, fortune favoured the 'savage'. The Blatant Beast proved indigenous to the pastoral landscape and like the Irish might not 'be roted out' (p. 211). Instead of celebrating Calidore's achievement, the conclusion to book six rehearses the damage done to its own 'gentle poet' by the malice of fellow countrymen, barbarians of another hue (VI.12.40–1).[102] Describing his situation in the *Prothalamion*, published in 1596, Spenser pens a powerful portrait in dejection, all the more effective for its setting upon the banks of his native Thames. Had he anticipated a better reception for the second instalment of *The Faerie Queene*, he was again to be disappointed since his presentation of Mary Queen of Scots infuriated James I, embarrassed Elizabeth, and caused the banning of the poem in Scotland. The latter mattered little in itself except for the prospect of a Stuart succession, the prospect that Gloriana's successor might regard *The Faerie Queene* as an anti-court poem, the antithesis of everything Spenser intended.[103] Worse still, many Irish Catholics eagerly anticipated the Stuart accession in the hope of negotiating some measure of religious toleration from the son of the

[101] Sir John Davies believed that by forcing Irish children 'to learne the English language' the next generation would 'in tongue and heart, and every way else, becom *English*'. *Discovery*, p. 272.

[102] For the definition of gentility see Montrose, 'Gentlemen and Shepherds', p. 428.

[103] Richard A. McCabe, 'The Masks of Duessa: Spenser, Mary Queen of Scots, and James VI', *ELR*, 17 (1987), 224–42.

'martyred' Queen Mary.[104] Little wonder, then, that Arlo Hill, located just twenty miles north-east of Kilcolman amidst some of the most treacherous woods in the province, provides the perfect venue for Mutability's challenge to Natural Law.[105]

Here, perhaps for the first time, the general and particular intentions of Spenser's allegory perfectly cohere. In so far as the ideal condition of Gloriana's court had always been presented as the earthly equivalent of the New Jerusalem, and she herself as the earthly equivalent of God, estrangement from court is equivalent to estrangement from heaven, and the Neo-Platonic doctrine of souls exiled in a world of matter corresponds to that of courtiers exiled in Ireland's 'salvage' wilderness.[106] The sometime 'holy-Island', now a fallen Eden haunted by the image of its lost potential, has finally come to symbolise the manifold disappointments of national and personal history. Replete with echoes of Spenser's previous works, the cantos expressly recall *Colin Clouts Come Home Againe* to introduce what was to prove his final Irish river fable, that of Arlo's daughter, Molanna, whose corruption by the wild god Faunus, patriarch of the woodland breed, led the goddess Diana ('soveraine Queene profest/ Of woods and forrests' though she be) to curse Ireland and abandon it to wolves and thieves, 'which too-too true that lands in-dwellers since have found' (55).[107] The choice of 'in-dwellers' is a masterstroke. In the Coverdale Bible Abraham tells the Canaanites, 'I am a straunger and an indweller amonge you' (Genesis 23:4). The King James version substitutes 'sojourner'.[108] Colin Clout is by no means home and the distance between shepherd and queen is at its greatest: in his final political writings Spenser implores her directly, 'to call us your poore subiectes alltogether away from hence that at least we may die in *our* Countrie' (p. 242). That Elizabeth had effectively abandoned Ireland, despite her 'professions' of sovereignty, by failing to champion her colonists' cause is clearly implied by accusations of 'temporizing' with

[104] Colm Lennon, 'The Counter Reformation in Ireland, 1542–1641', in Brady and Gillespie, ed., *Natives and Newcomers*, pp. 75–92 (p. 87).

[105] Holinshed, VI, 451–2; It is 'fowle Arlo' in *Astrophel* (96). The *Vewe* speaks of the repossession of Arlo [the Glen of Aherlow] by Irish 'outlaws' and calls for the stationing of a garrison close by. *Prose*, pp. 57, 194. See Smith, 'Irish Background of Spenser's View', p. 508.

[106] Gloriana's elusiveness has been related to the transcendence of the Christian god. See Jeffrey P. Fruen, '"True Glorious Type": The Place of Gloriana in *The Faerie Queene*', in Patrick Cullen and Thomas P. Roche Jr., ed., *Spenser Studies*, VII (New York, 1987), pp. 147–73.

[107] Early in the *Vewe* Eudoxus refutes the suggestion that Ireland labours under a divine curse, but the more experienced Irenius concludes that it was 'in olde time not Called amisse *Banno* or *sacra Insula* takinge *sacra* for accursed'. *Prose*, pp. 44, 145.

[108] Spenser was, however, still buying property in Munster as late as 1597. Judson, *Life of Spenser* (Baltimore, 1945), pp. 174–5.

the country's problems (p. 242).[109] She is at best a Lucretian goddess—if goddess at all in view of Mutability's effect on 'Cynthia'—shedding 'no one little beame' of her 'large mercie' upon her Irish planters, 'either for unworthinesse of us wreches which no way deserve so great grace, or for that the miserie of our estate is not made knowne unto you' (p. 236). The sour candour of the complaint is new but the sentiment merely confirms the sense of alienation and estrangement evident in *The Shepheardes Calender*, the *Amoretti*, *Colin Clouts Come Home Againe*, and throughout *The Faerie Queene*. The final stanzas of the *Mutabilitie Cantos* repose no trust in earthly goddesses but seek instead an escape from history itself into the 'stedfast rest' of eternity, an end to the underlying spiritual exile of which all others are merely reflections. It is, perhaps, indicative of Spenser's final state of mind that, of the many forms of address available, he invokes the deity as Lord of Hosts (Sabbaoth God) as though heaven itself were a well-garrisoned civil plantation in an otherwise 'salvage' universe.

[109] For the sinister connotations of 'temporize' see *Faerie Queene*, V.11.56.

*Proceedings of the British Academy*, **80**, 105–132

# Hattusha, City of the Gods and Temples: Results of the Excavations in the Upper City

PETER J. NEVE
*German Archaeological Institute*

In 1907, the German Archaeological Institute started its first excavation in the Hittite capital of Hattusha. The site, some 150 km east of Ankara near the Turkish village Bogazkale, is situated on a mountain slope rising more than 900 ft from a fertile plain in the north up to its highest point in the south. Deep gorges bordering the site to the east as well as to the west provide natural protection, which evidently was one of the main reasons why people preferred to settle here despite the less suitable rocky ground.

The earliest settlement of Hattusha, representing only a small residence of a landlord, dates back into the last decade of the 3rd millenium B.C. During the following years the place gradually grew up to be a rather prosporous landtown, which, within the 19th and 18th centuries B.C., became an important Assyrian trade centre like other places in Anatolia. About 1700 B.C. the town was destroyed by King Anitta of Kussara who, moreover, cursed the site in order that nobody should dare to settle there once more.

But, as proved by excavations, the town continued to exist. One hundred years later Greatking Hattushili I made Hattusha the capital of the Hittite Empire. During the following four centuries the site developed into large metropolis of more than 2 km² which finally, under the rule of Greatking Tuthaliya IV and his son, Suppiluliuma II, represented a mere official residence, consisting of the royal place and, in addition, of

Read 1 May 1991. © The British Academy 1993.

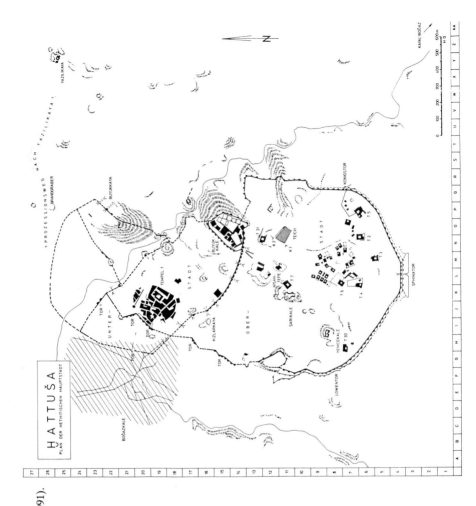

**Fig. 1.** Plan of the Hittite capital Hattusha (1991).

extensive temple quarters, while the normal population apparently settled in the surroundings of the town (Fig. 1).

Just at the summit of its development, about 1200 B.C., the capital collapsed in a tremendous conflagration, which also indicates the end of the Hittite Empire.

Then, the place seems to have been abandoned for centuries until the 8th century B.C., when it was settled by the Phrygians—but only with the size and function of a small landtown, as in Pre-Hittite times. In this state the site continued to exist during the following Hellenistic and Roman periods, at last being reduced to the size of its earliest stage of settlement.

Later, in Byzantine times, the area was occupied by single farmhouses and village-like units, indicating that the city of the periods before now was replaced by rather scattered rural settlements. After the fall of the Byzantine Empire in Anatolia the site of ancient Hattusha was left crude and empty.

Today it has been partly reoccupied by the Turkish villagers. But many efforts are made by the German Archaeoligical Institute to rescue and restore the ancient ruins as far as possible. Since 1987 Hattusha has been registered in the UNESCO World's Heritage List, and in 1989 was declared a National Monument by announcement of the Turkish Government.

The site was discovered in 1834 by the French archaeologist Charles Texier. In 1906, the German Hugo Winckler and his Turkish colleague Theodor Makridi succeeded in unearthing the first cuneiform archive in the royal citadel on Büyükkale, by which it became evident that the site must be the ancient Hittite capital Hattusha. In 1907, a joint expedition of the German Oriental Society and the German Archaeological Institute started the first excavations, which were continued in 1911/12 and, since 1931, work has been systematical.

## Hattusha, City of Gods and Temples

Following the excavations of large sections of the old city of Hattusha, including the royal palace on Büyükkale as well as the Great Temple and the surrounding residential areas in the so-called Lower City, the Bogazköy-Expedition has now focused its attention on the exploration of the Upper City.

Situated on a rising slope south of the old city and enclosing an area of over 1 $km^2$, from this section only the city walls and the few more or less visible buildings had been studied. This has now been rectified by the excavation of large areas of the site. The information gathered has contributed extensively to our knowledge of the construction and function of this part of the capital.

While the Lower City expanded naturally, the Upper City was from the onset a carefully planned area containing mostly temples and related buildings—in other words, we are dealing with a temple city. It was built during the last decades of the Hittite empire, that is during the reign of Greatking Tuthaliya IV (c. 1235–1216 B.C.) and his son Suppiluliuma II (c.1210–1190 B.C.).

The Upper City was enclosed by an extensive city wall, which, following an almost complete destruction, was rebuilt and reinforced by a second outer wall. It was pierced by five gates: the Sphinx Gate at the southernmost and highest point, the King's Gate at the eastern end and the Lions' Gate at the western end of the southern curve of the wall; two further gates, the so-called Upper and Lower Westgates, are situated in its northwestern part.

Of these gates the King's Gate and the Lions' Gate are symmetrically arranged to the east and west of the Sphinx Gate. Furthermore, all three are decorated with reliefs. Both these factors indicate without doubt, that these gates were allocated a special role, most probably as processional gates of a sacred route around the temple city.

The route left the city through the King's Gate and wound its way along the foot of the city wall's rampart towards the bastion of the Sphinx Gate, following a steep staircase at its eastern slope to the gateway on the top and then descended on the western side, continuing along the rampart until it reached the Lions' Gate, where it re-entered the city.

The very destination of the sacred route was quite obviously the Sphinx Gate. This can be deduced from its central location and the monumental structure of the pyramid-like bastion as well as from the existence of reliefs both on the inner and outer face of the gate, and, not least, by a long tunnel running underneath.

Turning to the settlement within the Upper City, the first aspect which must be noted is that its distribution takes into consideration both the symmetrical arrangement of these gates and the lie of the land.

Accordingly, the southern part of the city is divided into three sections corresponding to the three gates: in a central section at the foot of the Sphinx Gate's bastion, an eastern section beside the King's Gate and a western one associated with the Lions' Gate.

The northern part of the city was also integrated into this system. This is well established by the rock of Nisantepe, situated on the route from the King's palace on Büyükkale to the temple city; for this great mass of rock, which bears a hieroglyphic inscription by the Greatking Suppiluliuma II, is directly in line with the Sphinx Gate and its tunnel. Furthermore, it lies on the crosspoint of its axis with that which runs from the Lions' Gate, and there is no doubt that a similar axis was intended to run from the King's gate, despite the fact that it is somewhat out of line.

The Upper City was built in three phases (periods Upper City = O.St.4–2). It was during the earliest (O.St.4) that the first city wall was erected, and its destruction also marks the end of the first buildings phase. This catastrophic devastation may have been caused by internal dynastic struggles which led, probably during the reign of Tuthaliya IV, to a short interim period of rule by his opponent and cousin, King Kurunta of Tarhuntassa. The second phase (O.St.3) documents the rebuilding and extension of the temple city. The third and final phase (O.St.2) is represented by restoring activities and new, mostly secular, buildings, which partly destroyed the existing edifices.

Let us now turn to the individual sections and constructions in detail: The *central temple quarter* lies in an isolated wide depression, which extends from the Sphinx Gate north to Nisantepe. At the time of the first building phase this area contained only a single sanctuary, Temple 4. In the second phase further temples were erected, of which 24 (Temples 6–29) have been identified in lesser or better states of preservation. Looking at the gaps between the buildings and the still unexplored areas we can assume that the total number of temples was considerably higher (Fig. 2).

Despite their different sizes, all temples were designed and built according to an almost uniform plan. A characteristic feature of the layout is the inner courtyard from which one enters the cult rooms comprising of a small vestibule and a long main room. They did not face any particular direction, but were generally located so that they overlooked the valley. In all of the younger temples, this part was based on a cellar. A notable aspect of the temples is that they contain quite a large number of rooms, a fact which points to additional functions besides the actual cult (Fig. 3).

The construction of the temples is as follows: the foundations were made of rubble, the socles of dressed blocks. Horizontal and vertical spaces in the remaining walls show that they were constructed using a wooden framework with fillings of rubbles or mud-bricks, assembled all together according to a uniform measurement system. Fragments of painted plaster indicate that the temples were decorated with wall paintings.

The similarity in the design and construction of the temples is matched by the uniformity of their inventory. For the most the objects found fall into three groups: objects for daily use, objects for the cult and documentary inscriptions.

The objects of daily use are mostly represented by coarse kitchen pottery and tools of different sorts. During the last phase both were produced in the temple quarter.

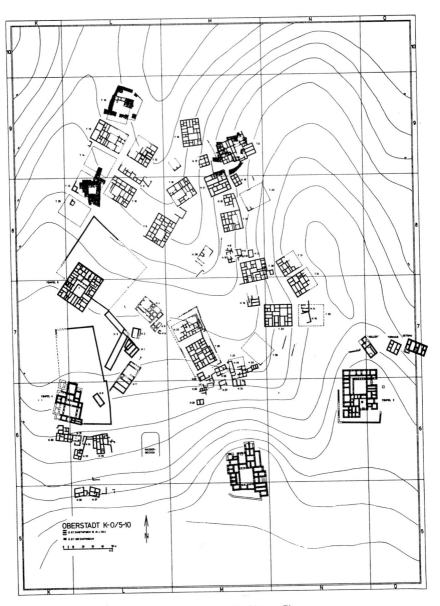

**Fig. 2.** Plan of the central temple quarter in the Upper City.

**Fig. 3.** View of the site with the remains of the temples.

Objects connected with the cult are principally votive vessels, the majority of which are miniature bowls and jugs, but also include arm-shaped libation vessels and so-called Spindle Bottles. All these vessels indicate connections with northern Syria which at that time was under Hittite rule. North Syrian influence is also attested by the fragments of terracottas, probably belonging to house altars, and by bronze and ivory figurines, which were used as votive gifts and amulets.

The documents comprise seals, sealed bullae and cuneiform tablets. The majority of the seals and bullae date from the younger Empire Period and come from people who apparently were employed as administrators or held other posts in the temples. The cuneiforms, on the other hand, are mostly older. They represent land donations and religious texts. Among the latter are Hurrian/Hittite bilinguas, which again point to connections with northern Syria.

According to the architecture and the inventory the temples cannot be considered as mere cult places. They, moreover, seem to represent divine residences, which, in some way like monasteries, had their own workshops, lands and archives, thus forming independent economic and administrative units.

Cuneiform inscriptions bear witness that the Hittite Kings took special care for transferring gods—including foreign deities—from abroad into the capital. It was mainly Tuthaliya IV, who did a lot of work in reorganizing and reforming religious life in the Hittite Empire, who was highly engaged with this matter, apparently motivated by the keen idea to settle all gods and cults of the country in the capital, which in view of the internal struggles mentioned before would, of course, contribute to strengthen his position as well as Hattusha's state as capital of the empire.

The most outstanding testimony of these activities is without doubt the rock sanctuary of Yazilikaya, where according to a cuneiform text the gods of the Hurrian pantheon assembled once a year to celebrate the ANTASUM feast. Looking at their number and the numerous temples in the central quarter of the Upper City one may assume that this was the place where Tuthaliya built their divine residences.

We have as yet no concrete evidence to support this assumption, but there is at least evidence that the quarter was built during Tuthaliya's reign. This is indicated by a stela which was found rebuilt in the wall of a Byzantine chapel erected on one of the temple ruins. The stela bears in genealogical order the hieroglyphic written names of Tuthaliya and three ancestors: of his father Hattusili (III), his grandfather Mursili (II) and of another Tuthaliya, probably Tuthaliya I, as eponym and founder of the dynasty (Fig. 4).

During the last phase (O.St,2) the central quarter suffered fundamental changes. The majority of temples were now abandoned and replaced by a less organized settlement comprising secular residences and workshops which served the needs of the people as well as of the few still existing temples. The reason for this change is probably to be found in the continuing decline of the political and economic situation in the capital and in the country brought about by the dynastic disputes among the members of the royal family. This in turn may have generated such a feeling of insecurity that the population who once lived and worked outside the city were now moved inside so that on the one hand they could be afforded protection and on the other guarantee for the maintenance of the rest of the temple city.

Further testimony of Tuthaliya IV's building activities in the Upper City is the *King's Gate precinct*. It comprises a temple, Temple 5, bordered on the east by a walled *temenos* which contains a number of other buildings and extends to the city wall.

Covering an area of almost 3000 m$^2$ this temple is without doubt the largest in the Upper City. Moreover, it contained two cult-rooms. An additional wing with numerous rooms in the north-west, which is similar in layout to the residential palace on Büyükkale, could indicate that the temple was in fact a combined temple-palace (Fig. 5).

**Fig. 4.**   Stela of Greatking Tuthaliya IV.

The *temenos* contained four separate structures: a group of three smaller buildings (houses A–C) in the northern edge, as well as a larger single platform (D) situated halfway between the three houses and the temple.

The houses A–C are all of the same type. They are identical in size and consist of only one room equipped with four pillars. On the basis of two objects discovered in house A and representing an altar and an image of a deified Tuthaliya, it seems possible that the buildings served as small chapel-like sanctuaries (Fig. 6). It is, in addition, certain that House A served a cult of a Greatking Tuthaliya in his role as a deity, which means, according to Hittite belief, a dead Tuthaliya.

Given that there are three chapels, it does not seem too far-fetched to connect the name of Tuthaliya with Tuthaliya I who is listed on the stela of the central temple quarter as the third ancestor in Tuthaliya IV's genealogical table. One therefore may assume that the chapels B and C

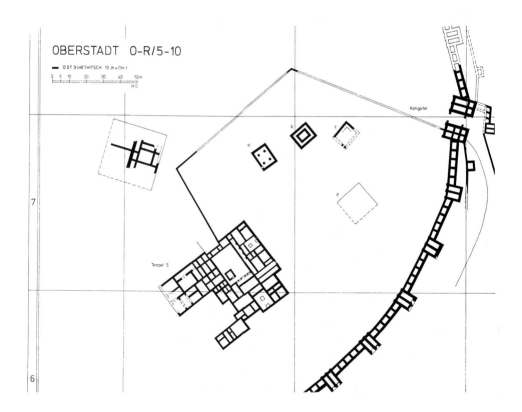

**Fig. 5.** Plan of Temple 5.

were dedicated to the other two ancestors mentioned on the stela. In chronological order this would mean we should associate House B with Tuthaliya's grand-father Mursili II and House C with his father Hattusili III. In connection with the chapels, Platform D could have been used to perform special cult services in the open air.

All in all, the total arrangement shows that the individual buildings of the temple precinct, i.e. the temple itself, the palace-like annex and the chapels, were all part of one extensive concept which could be interpreted as follows: in close proximity to the King's Gate with its relief of Sarumma, his protective god, Tuthaliya IV created a sacred district containing a temple, his personal residence and the shrines of his ancestors as the starting point for the procession route around the Upper City.

Also attached to this route were Temples 2 and 3 which lay southwest from Temple 5 and high above the central quarter. As both are identical in their layout and architecture they must be from the same period, and probably also from the same school. Both belong to the oldest building phase of the city.

Together with the first city wall, the two temples were destroyed, but

**Fig. 6.**   Relief of Greatking Tuthaliya.

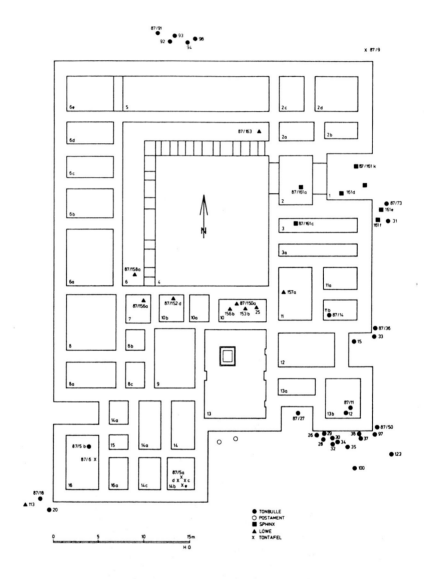

**Fig. 7a.** Plan of Temple 2 with distribution of finds.

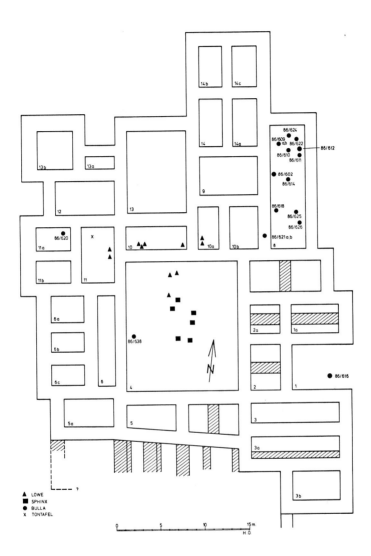

**Fig. 7b.** Plan of Temple 3 with distribution of finds.

they were immediately rebuilt—on the old foundations, but with new stone socles of the highest quality. An exceptional aspect of their architecture is that both temples, in contrast to all the other known temples in Hattusha, were decorated with sculptures. Numerous fragments were found on both sites and, judging from their find spots, it would appear that the sculptures once decorated the courtyard, the *porticus* of the cult room and the main entrance of the buildings (Fig. 7).

The majority of the fragments are from life-size lions. In addition, parts of two human heads, each wearing a horned helmet, were found in Temple 3. They apparently belong to sphinxes.

An orthostate with an unfinished relief of a lion shows that the fragments belong to door jambs and the socles of pillars. They are, therefore, similar to the architectural sculptures and reliefs as found in Hattusha on the gates of the Upper City, on Büyükkale as well as on Nisantepe and in Yazilikaya. All these works date without doubt to the period of the Late Empire; according to the archeological context in the case of Büyükkale and Yazilikaya most probably in the time of Tuthaliya IV, while those of Nisantepe are more likely to have been made during the reign of Suppiluliuma II. Furthermore, bullas found in Temple 2 and bearing his seal could indicate that both this temple as well as the neighbouring Temple 3 and their sculptures derive from the time of Suppiluliuma II, and are thus testimony to the building activities of this last Hittite Greatking in the Upper City.

The *Lion Gate temple-precinct* is similar to that of the King's gate in that it contained only a single sanctuary—Temple 30. Equally, the distance between it and the gate is the same, and it also had its own residence, which here was constructed as a separate building. A further complex comparable with that of the Temples 2 and 3 was planned but, apparently, remained unfinished.

Whereas these two temples were rebuilt following the first destruction, Temple 30 was completely abandoned. As in the central temple-quarter it was replaced by new buildings comprising simple residential houses and workshops. All that remains from the temple are the foundations and a few fragments of the socles (Fig. 8). Nevertheless, these are sufficient to give evidence that Temple 30 was similar in design to Temple 4 in the central quarter. Accordingly, a date from the first building phase of the Upper City seems plausible.

Further evidence to support the identification of the building as a temple is provided by votive vessels in the shape of the well-known miniature bowls and jugs, found in its debris, as well as some tiny cuneiforms bearing oracles. Unfortunately, the latter give no indication to whom the temple was dedicated. We are therefore left with the same situation as in all the other temples in the Upper City, since it has not been possible to connect a single temple with a particular god. The only exception is House A in the precinct of Temple 5, which was, as pointed out before, dedicated to the cult of the deified Greatking Tuthaliya.

Indications of a royal cult can also be found in the *precinct of Nisantepe* in the north of the Upper City. Evidence for this use is provided by the rock inscription by Suppiluliuma II as well as by the new dicoveries in the opposite area of the so-called South Castle.

Both places revealed remains of a Phrygian settlement of the 7th and 6th centuries B.C.; the South Castle represents a well fortified, akropolis-like stronghold with large official buildings, Nisantepe, on the other hand, the domestic equivalent with densely crowded small houses.

In addition to the inscription on Nisantepe, the rock beds and partly visible remains of walls, especially the presence of reused blocks, indicate that there also must have been an extensive Hittite settlement. This had always been assumed. Now, the excavations have proved it to be true (Fig. 9).

Two monumental viaducts—the oldest known examples of this type in the Ancient Orient—connected this area with the palace on Büyükkale. Built at different times, both were 85 m long and constructed as wide double walls which once rose up to a height of max. 10 m. Both spanned—in slightly different directions—the deep valley between the

**Fig. 8.**   View of Temple 30.

main gate of Büyükkale and the plateau in front of Nisantepe. That this gate is the starting point for the viaducts gives evidence that they were constructed together with the youngest palace, i.e. in the time of Tuthaliya IV or later.

Three buildings were situated on the plateau in front of Nisantepe which, as the remains of a surrounding wall would seem to indicate, belonged to a separated precinct. They are the so-called North and West Buildings, standing, as one can guess from their name, on the northern and western edges of the plateau, while the third one is on the rock of Nisantepe which closes off the southern end.

The North Building is 34 m long and 24 m wide and built on a

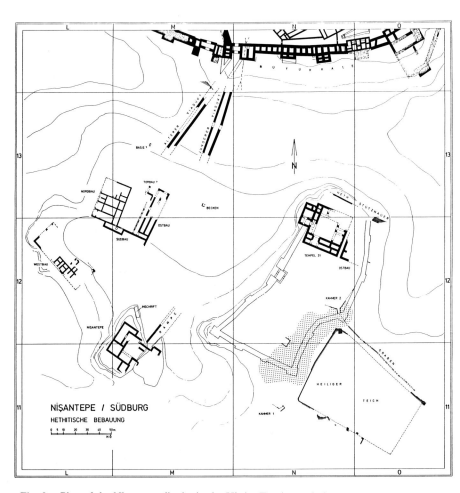

**Fig. 9.**   Plan of the Nisantepe district in the Hittite Empire period.

north-south axis. It is situated on the route which led from the older viaduct to Nisantepe. Remains of the route's pavement and a wide gateway where it passed into the precinct are still in existence. The plan of the house shows a narrower central part between two wider wings, of which the central part comprises the the main entrance, divided into a vestibule and a large corridor-like hall. According to this arrangement the building is a typical example of the Hittite 'Hallenhaus', which in this case, as is indicated by its location and the use of relatively expensive building materials, such as monolith door sills and stone blocks for the socles, was probably used for representative purposes. Because of the total lack of inventory a more precise identification cannot be made.

As a consolation for the fact that even less architecture has survived from the West Building, numerous objects were uncovered which provide valuable information on the use of this edifice. Situated on a long westerly stretch of rock with a steep slope to the south, it lies some 30 m away from the North Building. Apart from a few pieces of walls on the rock, all that remains are the burnt masonry stumps of the cellar embedded into the slope. But this is sufficient to allow us to estimate that the building was c. 45 m long and 25 m wide and had one, if not two, lower floors.

In three rooms (1–3) of the southern part of the basement more than 1000 bullae with seal imperessions and 11 cuneiform tablets, also sealed, were found (Fig. 10). Because of the fire which raged the building all were more or less burnt.

The majority of the bullae is stamped with the seals of Greatkings (Fig. 11). All rulers of the Hittite Empire are represented, beginning with the Greatking Suppiluliuma I, and followed by Mursili II, Muwatalli II, Urhitesup/Mursili III, Hattusili III, Tuthaliya IV, Arnuwanda III and Suppiluliuma II. Of these, more than half the bullae bear seals from Suppiluliuma I, Urhitesup/Mursili III and Tuthaliya IV. Suppiluliuma II is represented by only a single example, which moreover cites him only with the title king. Of special interest are two bullae showing seal impressions of the Greatking Kurunta. Their presence now definitely proves that he resided in Hattusha and can, accordingly, be included in the list of the Hittite Greatkings. Besides the bullae of Greatkings there are others bearing both the name of the Greatking and that of the Great Queen. In the case of Puduhepa, the wife of Hattusili III, one group of bullae just has her seal alone.

In addition to the Greatkings' bullae, a few hundred were also found with the seal impressions of court administrators, especially palace scribes. Interestingly, some of these officials bear the additional title of prince, showing them to be of royal lineage.

The cuneiform documents represent land donations sealed by Old Hittite

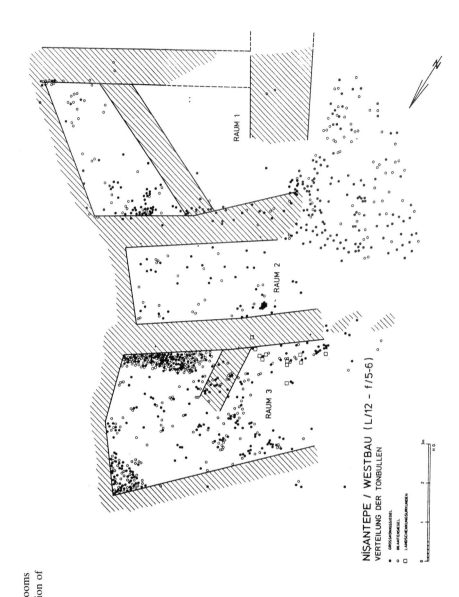

**Fig. 10.** Plan of the archive rooms in the 'Westbau' with distribution of finds.

NIŞANTEPE / WESTBAU (L/12 – f/5-6)
VERTEILUNG DER TONBULLEN

- GROSSKÖNIGSSIEGEL
- BEAMTENSIEGEL
- LANDSCHENKUNGSURKUNDEN

RAUM 1

RAUM 2

RAUM 3

**Fig. 11.** Bulla bearing seal impression of Greatking Kurunta.

**Fig. 12.** Cuneiform tablet with a land donation sealed by Greatking Muwatalli I.

Greatkings. The rulers named are the Greatkings Hantili, Huzziya and
Muwatalli I, who all reigned around the 15th century B.C. (Fig. 12). Holes for
strips in their edges indicate that the tablets were also attached to bullae.

The distribution of the bullae and the land donations show that they
were originally stored in different rooms of the cellar according to their
individual seals. As string holes indicate, and in a manner comparable with
the land donations, the bullae also may have been attached to tablets, but
wooden ones which burnt when the fire ravaged the building.

Contextually, this find is very similar to a deposit of seals found during
the first excavations in the palace on Büyükkale. From this we may
conclude that a further royal archive was housed in the West Building. If
so, perhaps the entire complex at Nisantepe served as an external precinct
of Büyükkale, which, as the inscription of Nisantepe and the absence of his
individual seals from the bullae collection show, only achieved its definite
form under the last Hittite Greatking, Suppiluliuma II.

Of the edifice on Nisantepe, which formed the third and most southern
part of the building-complex, only the rock beds and some architectural
remains at the base of the rock beside the inscription have survived. It
would seem that the latter belong to the socle of a monumentally designed
ascent to the building on the rock. Judging from extant fragments of an
unfinished lion and another still unidentified piece of sculpture the way
was decorated with reliefs. All these factors leave little doubt that the
Nisantepe with its building formed the actual centre of the entire complex,
be it as a palace or a separate sanctuary, or both.

Certainly a sanctuary which without doubt was built by Suppiluliuma
II proved to be the complex in the opposite area of the so-called South
Castle. It comprises an artificial lake with relating buildings in the castle's
eastern section, which even extend beyond its boundary, and two buildings
in the northern part.

From the lake only the western edge has been excavated, the rest
subjected to local sondages. Showing an oblong, slightly trapezoid from the
lake covers an area of over 5600 m². It was surrounded by a gently-sloping
paved embankment, which on the south side remains at its original height
of 2.1 m. Judging by a few stone blocks found *in situ* on top of it, the bank
was probably topped by a stone parapet.

The bottom of the lake was formed by the levelled natural bedrock
consisting of soft but non-porous serpentine. It was covered by a thick
layer of a grey clay sediment which evidently derives from the time when
the lake was in use. The water probably came from a still existing spring
located some 50 m away on the route to the King's Gate. Numerous
miniature vessels were found in the sediment. They are comparable not
only with those from the temples in the Upper City, but also with ones

found in similar circumstances in sacred basins on Büyükkale, which were most likely used in connection with the rain cult.

At the western end of the lake and extending beyond it to the north and the south a wide dam was constructed from the material which once covered the area of the lake. Four hundred years later, the Phrygians used the remains of this dam as the base for the east wall of the South Castle. Hundreds of Hittite paving stones found reused in this wall indicate that the outer bank of the dam was paved in the same manner as the bastion at the Sphinx Gate.

Three buildings were incorporated in the dam. One was located in the centre of its west side by following the longitudinal axis of the lake. The excavation brought to light a single room about 5 m wide and 4 m deep embedded in the filling of the dam. All that remains is the lower layer of the stone socle of the backwall and the two side walls, but it appears that some means of closing it off from outside existed. Because of its poor state of preservation nothing can be said about its function.

Fortunately, the two other structures provide more information on this. Both buildings contain a single vaulted chamber and are identical in size and layout. Located on the southern and northern end of the dam respectively, each chamber is equidistant from the middle building and so arranged that its longitudinal axis is in line with the relating corner of the lake.

Only tiny sections of the southern chamber (1) are *left in situ*, one part however, has survived as debris. The greater part of the building has fallen victim together with the dam to natural erosion or to farming activities. But despite its poor preservation, enough remains to prove that the chamber is identical with its pendant.

The northern chamber (2) was spared from drastic destruction, not least because of the fact that the wall of the Phrygian fortress was built on top of it (Fig. 13). As a result, a great deal of the structure is either *in situ* or remained where it fell into the chamber, while the rest is to be found in the immediate surroundings reused in the Phrygian wall.

The northward facing chamber measures 4 m in length, 2 m wide in the front narrowing to 1.6 m at the back. Its height is 3.3 m at the front, 3.1 m at the back. From the side walls three layers of stone blocks at most are still in place. They originally comprised four, at the entrance five, layers, of which the lowest is the vertical socle, while the remainder forms the shell of a steep parabolic vault. This was once covered by four keystones (Fig. 14).

From the originally vertical back wall, which now leans slightly inwards, the socle and a huge stone slab of over 1.5 m height are *in situ*. The top is missing. Just in front of the wall and cut into the floor which lies at least 1 m below the bottom of the lake, is a narrow pit once apparently covered by a lid. It is connected to a trench which runs eastwards parallel to the northern side of the lake. The trench is almost completely horizontal and lies about 2 m below the bottom of the lake. It is is filled with a reddish-brown clay.

The dam which once covered the chamber and the trench was supported by two retaining walls left and right from the chamber's entrance. Both additionally formed the side borders of a large square facing the two buildings in the northern part of the South Castle.

All three surviving walls of the chamber are decorated with reliefs. Immediately upon entering one was confronted with a figure on the back wall wearing a long robe, its head covered by the winged sun-disc (Fig. 15). Its right hand holds the 'ankh' sign, i.e. the symbol of life which the Hittites requisitioned from the Egyptian hieroglyphs. According to a comparable relief in Yazilikaya it is possible that this figure represents the sun-god of the sky.

A six-line hieroglyphic inscription covers the two lower stone layers of the west wall. Two blocks of it were found reused in the Phrygian citadel wall (Fig. 16). They originally come from the upper layer at the entrance. The inscription begins there with the upper first line from right to left, then continues bustrophedon down to the lower sixth line, which finishes half a length of the chamber.

According to D. Hawkins's analysis of the text, the inscription dealing with a 'divine stone/earth path into the underground' may relate to the

**Fig. 13.** View of Chamber 2 and its surroundings.

**Fig. 14.** Plan of Chamber 2.

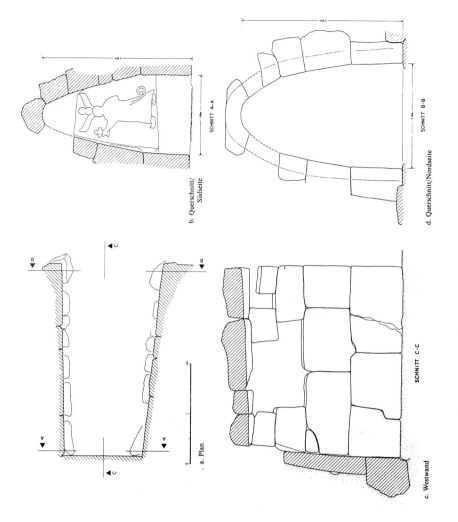

b. Querschnitt/
Südseite

SCHNITT A-A

d. Querschnitt/Nordseite

SCHNITT B-B

a. Plan

SCHNITT C-C

c. Westwand

building of the chamber and, moreover, to the trench as an entrance to the underground world. The frequent mentioning of Greatking Suppiluliuma in the inscription point to him being both the author of the text and the man responsible for the construction of the chamber as well as of the entire complex. Judging from the sherds found in the fillings of the dam and the debris of the chamber, which without exception are from the period of the Late Empire, the king has to be identified as Suppiluliuma II.

Incorporated in the Phrygian wall is a further relief which originally stood opposite the inscription on the east side of the chamber (Fig. 17). It shows the deified Greatking Suppiluliuma in a pose comparable with that of the Tuthaliya relief from Chapel A.

A remarkable feature of the two figurative reliefs of the chamber, especially when compared with the relief of Yazilikaya and that of Tuthaliya, is that they are worked in a very low relief showing almost

**Fig. 15.**   Chamber 2, relief of a sun-god.

only their outlines. Perhaps they were originally painted, but this cannot be proved as there are no paint traces left. Looking at chamber 1 which has no reliefs, and to judge from its rough wall surfaces were probably never completed, one may assume that the reliefs in chamber 2 also remained unfinished.

Somewhat apart from the lake, but in direct relationship to the dam and chamber 2 are the two buildings which occupy the northern part of the South Castle. They were built close together, almost 40 m from the entrance of chamber 2, and aligned in such a manner that they lie diagonal to the axis of the chamber but in a right angle to the dam.

Of these two buildings, the one lying to the west on a rock, with a steep drop on its north and west side, is relatively well preserved so that the most important features of its layout could be established. Its large interior courtyard and the adjacent west wing containing the mainroom with a vestibule show clear parallels to the layout of the temples, which indicate that this edifice most probably was also a temple, according to the number of known temples in Hattusha, i.e. Temple 31.

Its pendant was erected on an artificial terrace which joins the rock to the east and was supported by a high retaining wall. Except for the

**Fig. 16.**  Chamber 2, hieroglyphic inscription.

southwest corner none of the building has survived. Nevertheless, it does not seem to have been inferior in size to Temple 31 and, in regard to its close proximity, must have been functionally related to it.

Taking into consideration both their location and their obvious relationship to one another, there can be no doubt that all the buildings of the South Castle area formed a separate precinct which, in a manner similar to those of the central temple district and of temple 5, was developed in accordance with an overall concept (Fig. 18). The complex opened onto a large empty space to the west facing the dam and its buildings, Temple 31 and its pendant. Nothing is known about the entrance. Most probably it lay in the place where the Phrygians later erected their castle gate. In this case, it was not only located across from Nicantepe and its inscription but also points perhaps to a functional relationship between the South Castle and the Nisantepe precincts.

That the South Castle precinct was designed for religious purposes is evident from the presence of Temple 31, chamber 2 with its reliefs and the votive vessels found in the lake. Thinking of Egyptian examples, the lake itself may have represented a sacred lake. In which case it is by no means unique as a number of similar cult installations are known from the Hittite period. In Hattusha alone, nine, including the already mentioned

**Fig. 17.** Chamber 2, relief of Greatking Suppiluliuma.

basins from Büyükkale, have been found. They all vary in size, ranging from small ponds to rather large lakes.

Although there are a number of such installations outside Hattusha, only the large Karakuyu lake east of Kayseri shall be dealt with here. For this is the nearest parallel to our lake both in size and design as well as in the fact that it too had a plastered dam. While it was previously considered to be simply a water basin used for irrigation, it now has been connected with the cult of springs, not least because of a dedicatory inscription by Tuthaliya IV found there *in situ*.

The cult of springs probably also played a role in our cult precinct, looking at the inscription in chamber 2 perhaps in connection with the

**Fig. 18.** Isometric reconstruction of the sacred lake and its surroundings.

cult of the Underground World or, moreover, with the cult of the dead, as such an interpretation can be read from the reliefs showing the deified Suppiluliuma and the Sun God of Heaven, who according to Hittite belief rules over the eternal life. If the king shown on the relief and the author of the inscription are identical—an association which one would like to assume—then it is possible that the cult relates to Suppiluliuma II as the builder of the complex.

But a definite answer to this cannot yet be given. Nevertheless, the indications are such that the enormous building activity initiated by this ruler in the immediate vicinity of the palace as well as in other parts of the city—including the last additions to Yazilikaya—was not only a continuation of his father's work but also represented independent projects intended to demonstrate the power and importance of himself—projects which met with an abrupt end through the sudden destruction of the capital and the fall of the empire.

*Proceedings of the British Academy*, **80**, 133–148

ITALIAN LECTURE

# The Napoleonic Era in Southern Italy: An Ambiguous Legacy?

J. A. DAVIS

*University of Warwick*

WHAT ITALIAN HISTORIANS refer to as the *decennio* of French administration in the Mezzogiorno lasted slightly less than ten years (1806–15) and began when Napoleon declared from the Schonbrunn Palace in December 1805 that the Bourbon dynasty of Naples had ceased to rule. In January 1806 the Neapolitan rulers. Ferdinand IV and Maria Carolina, took refuge on British warships and fled to Sicily, where they were to remain under British protection until the collapse of the Empire. In February a French army led by Maréchal Massena entered Naples and installed Napoleon's brother Joseph as king. Joseph had accepted the Neapolitan throne with reluctance, and was to rule in Naples for barely two years before being translated—with equal lack of enthusiasm—to the throne of Spain. In March 1808 he was succeeded in Naples by his brother-in-law. Joachim Murat, the husband of Caroline Bonaparte, commander of the Imperial cavalry, Grand Constable of France, and for a brief season ruler of the Napoleonic Grand Duchy of Berg. Despite growing tensions with Napoleon, Murat ruled Naples until he became entangled in the dramatic events surrounding the collapse of the Empire—first defecting to the Allies in 1814, then rallying belatedly to Napoleon, and finally meeting his death before a firing squad in the Calabrian village of Pizzo in 1815 after a desperate last attempt to regain his Kingdom.[1]

The short but intense experience of French rule in the Mezzogiorno

Read 2 May 1991. © The British Academy 1993.
[1] See S.J.Woolf *The Napoleonic Integration of Europe* (London 1991), and J.Tulard *Le Grand Empire* (Paris 1983).

(but not Sicily)[2] was to prove a fascinating episode in the development of the Empire, and the tensions that developed between the Emperor and the rulers of Naples—in particular. Murat—revealed in often dramatic microcosm the deeper personal and structural contradictions embedded in the imperial system. But while the political and diplomatic relations between Paris and Naples and the role of the Neapolitan satellite Kingdom in the French imperial system have been closely studied by historians of the Empire, the impact of French rule on the longer-run development of the Italian Mezzogiorno has until recently received less attention. This paper will attempt to outline an assessment of the Napoleonic legacy in southern Italy.[3]

Writing shortly after the collapse of the Empire, the Neapolitan soldier and historian. Pietro Colletta, wrote simply:

> Never has a society been subject to greater convulsions that of Naples in the first years of the 19th century[4]

The most recent historian of the Napoleonic Kingdom of Naples. Pasquale Villani, reaches very similar conclusions:

> . . . the years between 1806 and 1815, the so-called 'French decade', were amongst the most dramatic and revolutionary in the entire history of the Kingdom of Naples.[5]

For all its brevity, the decade of French rule was one of intensive administrative and juridical reforms and the speed with which the French administrators set about dismantling the *Ancien Régime* state was remarkable. Within a short space of time they laid the foundations of a centralized, bureaucratic and autocratic monarchy, fashioned on the model that had finally emerged under Napoleon from the long experience of the revolution in France. The central clutch of reforms—the abolition of feudalism, the reorganization of the central and peripheral administrative institutions of the state, the restructuring of financial administration and of taxation—was pushed through in the first months of the occupation. During the summer and autumn of 1806 the massive task of redeeming and converting the

---

[2] For Sicily in this period see J. Rosselli *Lord William Bentinck and the British Occupation of Sicily* (Cambridge 1956), and R.M.Johnston *The Napoleonic Empire in southern Italy and the rise of the Secret Societes* (London 1904), 2 Vols.

[3] For the most complete recent appraisal see P.Villani 'Il *decennio* francese' in *Storia del Mezzogiorno* (Roma 1986), Vol.4. The older account by J.Rambaud *Naples Sous Joseph Bonaparte* (Paris 1911) is still the most detailed account of Joseph's administration and less dated in many respects than A.Valente *Gioacchino Murat e l'Italia Meridionale* (Turin 1941).

[4] P.Colletta *Storia del Reame di Napoli* ed. G.Capponi (Firenze 1848), Vol. 2, p.11

[5] Villani (1986), p.577

huge debt inherited from the former Bourbon rulers was begun, and preparations were made for the sale of former crown and church lands to fund the new debt. At the same time, French officials were also busy collecting data on every aspect of the southern economy, on the state of agriculture, on the potential for commercial development and on the types of industry established in the Kingdom.[6]

The legislative framework and much of the preparatory groundwork for the reform programme was laid by Joseph, while the more difficult task of implementing the reforms fell mainly to Murat. But the formulation and implementation of the reform programme has to be set against two different contexts. The first was that of the administrative and political models that had emerged from the Revolution. The second, and in many respect the more immediate, was determined by the situation which the French administrators inherited from their Bourbon predecessors. Leaving aside the problems posed by relations with France—which were laid down first by the terms on which Napoleon conceded the throne of Naples to Joseph, and then more stringently by the Treaty of Bayonne which governed the transfer of the crown to Murat in 1808—the most pressing problems facing the new rulers were those that had brought the Bourbon monarchy into crisis in the closing decades of the 18th century.

One clear indication of the extent of the crisis of the *Ancien Régime* monarchy was the vast debt of over 100 million Ducats inherited by the French rulers, against annual revenues of about 12 million Ducats.[7] But this was no more than a symptom of a deeper crisis that was facing many other European *Ancien Régime* monarchies in the second half of the 18th century.

At one level the crisis was essentially political. The Kingdom of Naples had become an independent dynastic state in 1734, and in attempting to transform the limited powers of their feudal monarchy the Spanish Bourbon rulers of Naples soon came into conflict with the most powerful forces in southern society—the feudal nobility and the Church. Similar struggles were being played out elsewhere in Europe, but nowhere else in western Europe were feudal jurisdictions as extensive. The struggles between the monarchy and the privileged orders were a consequence of the attempts to reorganize the administrative institutions of the Kingdom and above all to achieve adequate sources of revenues for the monarchy.

---

[6] See Rambaud (1911) pp.309–412, and A.De Martino *La Nascita delle Intendenze: Problemi dell'amministrazione periferica nel Regno di Napoli (1806–1815)* (Napoli 1984), pp. 7–111.

[7] The figures are based on the data collected by Roederer. See *Archives Nationales*, Paris (*ANP*), 29 *AP* 25, 31–2, and Rambaud (1911), pp. 309–42. The correspondence on the reorganization of the debt is in *Archivio di Stato*, Napoli (*ASN*), Min. Finanze f 2711, 2717, 2735 5581–95.

The bankruptcy of the Bourbon state was indicative of the failure of those efforts.

To make matters worse, the institutional and financial crisis of the *Ancien Régime* monarchy was paralleled by other changes that were beginning to erode the economic and social fabric of the *Ancien Régime* in ways that engendered fierce social conflicts throughout the Mezzogiorno. Growing demand for the staple products of southern agriculture—especially grain, olive oil, citrus fruits and spices—was one element of change, and in response to commercial demand, incentives to enclose land increased.[8] The expansion of private properties inevitably came into collision with two fundamental institutions of the agrarian economy: the feudal regime and the collective forms of land usage that focused around the common lands of the rural communities.

The critical juridical feature of land held in feudal tenure in the 18th-century Mezzogiorno was that it was subject to multiple use-rights. Since the largest properties were held mainly under feudal title in the 18th century (although feudal tenures were interspersed with allodial lands, known as *burgensatici*), it is not surprising that feudal landowners were often amongst the most enthusiastic enclosers. A second and often softer target was the common lands of the rural communities. In the 18th century feudal and non-feudal landowners joined in the onslaught on the village commons, and as these were enclosed the subsistence economies of many rural communities became endangered. Expansion of enclosed properties caused other conflicts too, especially where settled farming threatened the seasonal migrations on which transhumant sheep grazing depended.[9]

The agrarian tensions caused by these changes were exacerbated by unprecedented demographic expansion and also by the economic subordination of the rural areas to the towns and cities—and especially to the capital, Naples. Combined with the political struggles that had set the monarchy at odds with the most powerful social forces in the Mezzogiorno, these conflicts made for an explosive mix which found expression in the violent struggles that engulfed much of the Kingdom following the establishment of a Jacobin Republic in Naples 1799.[10]

---

[8] See P.Villani *Mezzogiorno tra Riforme e Rivoluzione* (Bari 1962), and P.Chorley *Oil, Silk and Enlightenment; Economic Problems in 18th-Century Naples* (Naples 1965).

[9] G.Tocci *Terra e Riforma nel Mezzogiono Moderno* (Bologna 1971); R.Trifone *Feudi e Demani: Eversione della Feodalita nelle Provincie Napoletane* (Milano 1909); D.Winspeare *Storia degli Abusi Feudali* (Napoli 1811).

[10] J.A.Davis '1799: The Crisis of the Ancien Regime in southern Italy' in J.A.Davis & P.Ginsborg (eds) *Society and Politics in the Age of the Risorgimento* (Cambridge 1991).

To what extent did the reforms and innovations introduced by the French rulers remedy the structural crisis of the Bourbon monarchy or alleviate the tensions had brought increasing levels of social conflict and instability to the Mezzogiorno in the closing years of the *Ancien Régime*? Fortunately the strategies adopted by the French administrators were nothing if not explicit. The principal advisers and administrators who accompanied Joseph Bonaparte to Naples—Miot de Melito, Cristoforo Saliceti and above all Pierre-Louis Roederer—were men of immense political and administrative experience who had survived the different phases of the Revolution in France to become well-seasoned imperial administrators. The administrative models on which they relied had been honed through the experience of the Revolution, and these were applied to the newly-won territories of the Empire with a missionary zeal that brooked no questioning of the validity or the appropriateness of the panaceas proposed.

The French reform programme was premised on the fundamental redefinition of the juridical character of the state itself which was achieved through the law of 2nd August 1806 that declared 'feudalism and all its appurtenances henceforth abolished'. The starting point for the broader operation of institutional and administrative reform was the abolition of the private jurisdictions and devolutions of power that typified the *Ancien Régime* state, combined with the assertion of the absolute authority of the state. This then opened the way for the reorganization of public administration in line with the French model of centralized and hierarchical bureaucracies. By abolishing feudal tenures, the law also asserted the exclusively private and absolute nature of property rights and the juridical premise for the introduction of a universal land tax (the *fondiaria*).[11]

These juridical and administrative changes were seen to be the essential prerequisites for any broader process of economic and social progress. By abolishing the unnatural and irrational restrictions and constraints imposed by feudalism, private enterprise would be able to flourish and what were believed to be the immense natural resources of the Mezzogiorno would be emancipated. Rational administration was a pre-condition for free enterprise and would establish a partnership that would unlock the path towards economic and social progress. This in turn could be expected to bring about significant changes in the relationship between state and society, and once public administration

---

[11] R.De Lorenzo *Proprietà fondiaria e fisco nel Mezzogiorno; La riforma della tassazione nel decennio francese (1806–15)* (Salerno 1984); Winspeare (1811), pp.86–95; L.Bianchini *Storia delle Finanze del Regno di Napoli* (Napoli 1859), Vol.7, pp.399–405; Trifone (1909), pp.181–203; Rambaud (1911), pp.402–12.

had been established on sound and rational principles, private and public interests would increasingly converge. This idea of a new partnership of public and private interests was a key *leitmotif* of French administrative and political strategy, and was readily endorsed by Neapolitan sympathizers like Vincenzo Cuoco—a former member of the Jacobin government of 1799 and later an ardent supporter of the Bonpartist regime:

> Facciamo che l'interesse privato cospirí col pubblico – Let us endeavour to ensure that public and private interests come into ever closer unison.[12]

To what extent were these expectations realized in the Mezzogiorno? In the short as well as in the longer term, the institutional and administrative reforms on which they were predicated proved far from easy to implement. By 1814 the administrative reorganization of the state was far from complete, while the social and economic consequences of the reforms that were implemented were often quite different to what had been intended.

Taking the issue of landownership first, the principal purpose of the law of 2nd August 1806 had been to establish the juridical premise for an autocratic and bureaucratic state. As a result it was concerned exclusively with the juridical aspects of feudalism, and so had little direct influence on the ownership of land. Those lands formerly held under feudal title were at a stroke transformed into private property, as were most feudal and seigneurial taxes. Although the law aroused great expectations, once it became clear that it had nothing to say on these complex and delicate issues, it soon gave rise to new tensions and disorder in the countryside.[13]

It was not the abolition of feudalism but the operations connected with the conversion of the Public Debt that had the most immediate implications for the distribution of landownership in the Mezzogiorno. The redemption of the huge debt inherited from the Bourbon monarchy was effected through a massive but well-tried and relatively simple operation. Credits against the old monarchy were transferred to new Debt, on which the government continued to pay interest at 5%. The operation was financed and consolidated through the sale of vast quantities of land belonging either to the Crown or to religious houses. Between 1806 and 1814 over 1,300 monasteries, convents and religious houses were suppressed, and

---

[12] Cf. P. Bevilacqua 'Acque e bonifiche nel Mezzogiorno nella prima metà dell'Ottocento' in A.Massafra (ed.) *Il Mezzogiorno Pre-Unitario: Economia, Società e Istituzioni* (Bari 1988), p.351: but the theme is omnipresent in the correspondence of the French administrators.

[13] Bianchini (1859), Vol.7, pp.400–1.

the land sales amortized about half of the original debt of 100,000,000 Ducats.[14]

Despite the scale of these sales, Pasquale Villani's research shows that they did not bring about a significant redistribution of land-ownership. Of the lands auctioned before 1808, some 66% of the total purchases were accounted for by only 7% of the total number of purchasers: mainly people with close contacts with the French administration in Naples. In this first phase, the beneficiaries were amongst the wealthiest groups in the Kingdom. After 1808 the sales were extended to the provinces and the profiles of the purchasers began to open out, especially in regions like Apulia where there was some relatively higher degree of prosperity. In these cases the sales of *beni nazionali* did strengthen the development of middling and smaller properties: yet there is no indication that small purchasers were anywhere able to acquire land.[15]

What about the creditors of the *Ancien Régime*? As yet there is insufficient evidence to reach firm conclusions, but it seems that while they certainly suffered losses, the French administrators did their best to protect their interests and with success. The worst damage occurred before the French arrived as a result of the collapse in value of the *arrendimenti* in the 1790s and the inflationary pressures at work in the second half of the 18th century. Considerable losses were sustained during the crisis of the *Ancien Régime*, but credits which were worthless at the time of the French occupation quickly recovered in value thereafter. These were transferred to the new Debt and although the titles initially circulated at 20% of face value or less, they did carry interest at 5% of nominal value. But providing that holders of titles on the new Debt were not obliged to realize their capital, they could then watch their market value rise steadily. There was no repetition in Naples of the disastrous inflation that had followed the issue of the *assignats* in France—thanks in part to the lessons which that experience had taught—and by 1808 the market value of the certificates had risen to 60%.[16] The difficulty of finding purchasers for the *beni nazionali* also caused the government to accept certificates in the Public Debt at nominal value in part-payment for purchases. In this way a substantial tranche of the old debt was liquidated and annuities were transferred into land, and since this was in any case being sold at extremely low prices

---

[14] Villani (1986), 614–16; L.deRosa 'Property rights, institutional change and economic growth in southern Italy in the 18th and 19th centuries', *Journal of European Economic History* Vol. 8, Pt.3 (1979).

[15] Villani (1986), 614–15; P.Villani *La Vendita dei Beni dello Stato* (Milano 1964), p.156; Rambaud (1911) pp. 357–60.

[16] O. Connelly *Napoleon's Satellite Kingdoms* (New York 1965), p82; on the arrendamanti see L.de Rosa *Studi sugli Arrendamenti del Regno di Napoli* (Napoli 1958).

the operation worked very much to the advantage of the creditors of the Ancien Regime.[17]

It would be wrong, therefore, simply to assume that the crisis of the *Ancien Régime* monarchy and the economic reforms introduced in the early stages of the French administration favoured the emergence of new social forces in the Mezzogiorno. If some new opportunities did emerge, the principal beneficiaries of the French reforms—in economic terms—were those who were already wealthy.

In terms of the wider economic impact of the new legislation, it has also to be remembered that the land sales in this period absorbed great quantities of capital in ways that made productive investment in agriculture more rather than less difficult. While the number of properties in the Mezzogiorno grew, so too did levels of mortgage debt.[18] One consequence was the formation in this period of the vast new *latifundia* in Calabria which would become one of the characteristic features of the southern agrarian economy in the 19th century. By no means a survival from the feudal past, the southern *latifondo* was a product of the land sales of the French period, and functioned on an economic logic which looked to extensive production and the exploitation of natural factors of production, including cheap and subordinate labour, to avoid the increased capital investment in production which more intensive methods of farming would have required.[19] The high mortgage debts incurred by middling and smaller purchasers also served to inhibit investment on the smaller properties that were formed in this period, so that in both cases the land sales probably perpetuated the low levels of agricultural productivity that had attracted the attention of the writers of the Neapolitan Enlightenment.

The sales of the *beni nazionali* did not bring about a significant redistribution of landownership, nor did they encourage changes in methods of farming. But the sales did substantially extend and consolidate the private ownership of land. In that sense, the French reforms gave juridical recognition to the dominant trends of the previous century and increased the precariousness of substantial sections of the rural population. Although there are no precise figures, there can be no doubt that sales of church

---

[17] Although the value of the Debt certificates was initially threatened by the impossibility of settling former credits in land; see *ANP* Fonds Joseph Bonaparte (FJB) 381 *AP* 3, Memo 15.3.1807, Roederer to Joseph

[18] See G.Della Valle *Della Miseria Pubblica. Sue Cause ed Indizi* (Naples 1833), p.35, and De Rosa, (1979) p.549; see also *ASN*, Min. Interni (1), f 183—Consigli Generali delle Provincie 1807–8.

[19] On the 19th-century origins of the latifondo see esp. P.Bevilacqua 'Uomini, Terra. Economie' in P.Bevilacqua & A.Placanica *La Calabria* (Turin 1985), pp. 205–17; M.Petrusewicz *Il Latifondo: economia morale e cita materiale in una periferia dell'Ottocento* (Venezia 1989), pp.34–57.

lands threatened the tenancies of thousands of peasant families, while the privatization of former feudal estates jeopardized the livelihood of many rural communities. One clear symptom was an increase in measures to combat vagrancy.[20]

Fear of serious rural disorder was one motive for the creation of the *Feudal Commission*, by Joseph shortly before his departure for Spain. Its task was to investigate the rival claims arising from use-rights exercised on former feudal estates. The *Commission* was empowered to adjudicate on all claims and to divide the estates proportionally amongst the previous users on the principle that the former feudatory would retain two-thirds of the land. The *Commission*—whose work was to be completed within two years—was charged with a further task: the recovery of the common lands belonging to village communities and their subsequent division amongst the inhabitants of the relevant villages and communities in the form of quit-rent (emphyteut) tenancies.

This was an immense task, but it was not until after the arrival of Murat that the *Commission* set to work. The first part of its brief proved to be more complex than expected and although judgements had been delivered on every single case relating to claims on former-feudal estates by 1811, the implementation of those judgements was to take very much longer. Appeals and litigation dragged on through the 19th century, and many were still outstanding in the 1920s when they were finally wound up by Mussolini's government.[21]

The reasons were partly technical, but they stemmed above all from the concerted opposition of the former feudal landowners. Whereas the ex-feudatories had warmly welcomed the abolition of feudalism in 1806 which deprived them of nothing and converted their limited titles into full property rights, they were much less enthusiastic about the partial dismemberment of their estates. Faced with that opposition, Murat's government—which by 1811 was increasingly at odds with the Emperor and therefore reliant on domestic support—backed off.

The second task, the planned division of the common lands, had hardly begun when the *Commission* was discharged in 1811. The project to reintegrate and divide the common lands was a massive undertaking, and one that was without precedent in the administrative experience of the Napoleonic Empire. For that reason even though it is generally recognized that its objectives were rarely achieved, it has often been seen as evidence of a radical reforming intent on the part of Murat's government—and above

[20] *ASN*, Archivio Tommasi, B.IV.
[21] Trifone (1909), pp.486–90; Tocci (1971), pp.146–57.

all as a fruit of the agrarian reform programme that had its roots in the Neapolitan Enlightenment.[22]

Such a view is strengthened by the presence on the *Commission* of Giuseppe Zurlo and other representative of the late-Enlightenment reform movement in Naples. There can be no doubt that Zurlo saw the *Commission* as a vital corollary to the abolition of feudalism and the attack on ecclesiastical mortmain. Through the re-integration of the village commons and their subsequent division into small farms Zurlo believed that a stratum on new small properties could be created which would complement the larger properties arising from the sale of the *beni nazionali*, bring elements of prosperity to the rural poor and so help stabilise the dangerous conflicts present in rural society.[23]

It is important to ask why Murat's government decided to support this ambitious and long-term project at a time when it was beset with pressing financial and diplomatic problems. The answer is that whatever the longer-term expectations of Zurlo and his Neapolitan colleagues, the government's expectations were more short-term and more explicitly fiscal. In fact, the projected restoration of the village commons cannot be separated from the problems posed by the reorganization of local administration, and the chronic indebtedness the local communities. The restoration of the common lands which historically were the principal source of local revenues was therefore an essential prerequisite for the reorganization of local administration. The creation of peasant emphyteut tenancies also offered the means to monetarize local revenues, while offering the Treasury an additional gain, since the tenant farmers would also become liable to pay the *fondiaria*.[24]

The scheme had a neat fiscal logic, but one that almost certainly undermined its practical success. In those cases where the divisions were actually carried out, the peasant farmers quickly fell victim to the combined weight of mortgage debts, payments of leases and the *fondiara*. At that point the land was bought up by wealthier landowners, so that a measure intended to widen access to the land in fact had quite the opposite effect. In this case too, the French reforms gave new force to processes already under way and by increasing the precariousness of the rural population undoubtedly exacerbated tensions and conflicts in rural society in the decades that followed.

---

[22] See Bianchini (1859), pp.401–5; Trifone (1909), pp.319–73; Villani (1986), pp.608–10. On Zurlo, see P.Villani 'G.Zurlo e la crisi dell'antico regime nel Regno di Napoli' in P.Villani *Mezzogiorno tra Riforme e Rivoluzione* (Bari 1962).

[23] See especially Zurlo's correspondence with the commissioners in *ASN*, Affari Demaniali, Carte Winspeare, f 81 & 89.

[24] *ASN*, Affari Demaniali, Carte Winspeare, f.89.

A balance sheet of the economic and social consequences of the liquidation of the feudal regime in the Mezzogiorno still contains many uncertainties. But it is not difficult to identify the losers—the greater part of the rural population, whose hopes of attaining some secure access to land were reduced. On the other hand, the principal beneficiaries of the removal of feudal constraints were the largest and wealthiest of the former feudal landowners, although those heavily encumbered with debts went to the wall. There was also some space for the formation of new properties, although these probably came into existence at the expense of the common lands rather than feudal properties and it was here that the southern gentry—the *galantuomini*—found their corner.

To what extent, therefore, did the French reforms mark a change in the outlook of the southern propertied classes? Despite the introduction of new administrative and juridical institutions, there is much evidence of continuity. For example, former feudal and seigneurial monopolies—over mills, baking ovens, rights to hunting, fishing or wood gathering—were in most cases simply carried forward as rents or private property. So too indeed was the vocabulary of feudalism, and throughout much of the Mezzogiorno large estates continued to be referred to as *'feudi'* down to the 20th century—including many that were formed during the French period.

This did not mean that the propertied classes of the Mezzogiorno remained unaffected by the new juridical order introduced by the French. It was generally agreed that the abolition of feudal entails (*maggioraschi*) seriously threatened the principles on which the marriage strategies and inheritance systems of the nobility operated. This had clearly been the Emperor's intention when he pressed on Joseph the need to abolish *maggioraschi*

> . . . bring the *Code Civil* into force: it will consolidate your power, and once in force all wealth dependent on entails will vanish, with the result that there will be no powerful families except those whom you chose to create as your vassals. That is why I have myself always argued the need for the *Code Civil* and why I have gone to such lengths to carry it through[25]

Whether the aim of abolishing entails was political rather than economic, the prohibition was widely circumvented. The practice quickly developed by which cadet sons voluntarily gave up their right to an equal share in the inheritance 'in the interest of the family', and received in turn an informal guarantee of a life interest.[26] The recourse to practices which effectively

[25] P. Umgari *Storia del Diritto della Famiglia* (Bologna 1974), p.103.
[26] See esp. P.Macry Ottocento *Famiglia, elites e patrimoni a Napoli* (Turin 1988), pp.29–35.

reinstated the mechanism of the entail in the interest of preserving the
integrity of family partimonies is especially significant since entails had been
one of the principal targets of the Neapolitan anti-feudal reform movement,
in which were represented—not surprisingly—a disproportionate number
of cadet noblemen. But not all families succeeded in finding voluntary
solutions, and in the Restoration period contemporary observers agreed
that the abolition of entails had dealt a fatal blow to the great aristocratic
*casate* of the previous century.[27]

Similar resistance to social engineering by legislative fiat was evident in
the powerful opposition to divorce. Indeed, so sensitive was the issue that
both Joseph and Joachim Murat succeeded for this reason in deferring the
introduction of the *Code Civil* until 1810, despite the Emperor's constant
insistence on its immediate introduction.[28]

Neapolitan hostility to divorce has generally been put down to the
clergy and the religious sensibilities of the propertied classes. The French
rulers in Naples had certainly no wish to give gratuitous offence to the
clergy, and in general the relations between the new regime and the
secular clergy (at least until the kidnapping of Pius VII in 1808) were
excellent. But the opposition came also from the landed classes since
divorce would have added a further and deeply unwelcome element of
uncertainty to the complex mechanisms that regulated the reciprocation of
dowries and marriage portions between propertied families over successive
generations

As Croce noted, even when divorce became available there was only
one application before 1814, and at the Restoration the legislation was
immediately abrogated. A similar fate befell another key stipulation of the
*Code Civil*: the obligation of partible inheritance, which was universally
ignored both by wealthy propertied families and by the poor.[29]

Such elements of continuity in the behaviour and practices of the
Neapolitan propertied classes should not be taken as evidence of the
absence of change in southern society, but as indications of the ways
in which southern agrarian capitalism developed from within the *Ancien
Régime*, rather than from its ashes. They do indicate, however, the limits

---

[27] M.Barbagli *Sotto lo stesso tetto: Mutamenti della famiglia in Italia dedal XV al XX secolo*
(Bologna 1984) p.514.

[28] eg. Napoleon to Murat 27.12.1808 in P.Le Brethon *Lettres et documents pour servir à
l'histoire de Joachim Murat* (Paris 1911–14), Vol. 6, p.470; on divorce see B.Croce 'Il
divorzio nelle provincie napoletane' in id. *Anedotti di varia letteratura* (Napoli 1942), Vol.3,
pp.67–85, and L.Parente 'Dibattito sul divorzio; Una battaglia politica nel Mezzogiorno
napoleonico' *Studi Beneventani* (Bevenento 1990).

[29] This is evident from recent studies on marriage strategies and inheritance customs in the
19th-century Mezzogiorno—but the reorganization of civil law remains one of the least
studied aspects of the *decennio*.

to the capacity or the will of the French rulers in Naples to put into effect the more radical aspects of imperial civil law. This might seem to contrast with a more radical stance on agrarian reform, but, as we have seen, the motives for the more radical measures of agrarian reform—the division of the common lands—were largely fiscal. When faced with sustained resistance from the landed classes, it is also clear that the French rulers were quick to abandon their projected reforms—to the anger of their Neapolitan administrators.

The reasons were quite simple. Although their political fate was always and directly dependent on the Emperor, both Joseph and Murat understood that the support of the Neapolitan propertied classes was critical if they were to achieve a degree of autonomy from Paris, and if they were to have any dynastic expectations for themselves and their families. From the moment that Joseph arrived in Naples there had been a clearly defined policy of *ralliement* with the propertied classes and with the great landowners. Joseph had hardly entered Naples in February 1806 when he wrote to the Emperor that 'all the great landowners have rallied to us'.[30]

Did the French rulers succeed in overcoming the rift between the monarchy and the most powerful forces in southern society which had brought chaos to the *Ancien Régime*? In looking to ally themselves with the Neapolitan propertied classes and to find a solution to the political crisis of the *Ancien Régime* monarchy, the French rulers in Naples sought to adopt and adapt the political formula of the Napoleonic regime in France—the 'regime of notables', in which autocratic government looked to involve the propertied classes in the business of government (through provincial assemblies and parliaments, through service in the state bureaucracy) without, however, conceding any real elements of power sharing.

Even in France this formula was pregnant with dangerous ambiguities, but in an occupied country like the Kingdom of Naples the prospects were even more difficult. Both Joseph and Murat did bring Neapolitans into the highest spheres of administration, and replicated the provincial assemblies of Napoleonic France. But such measures did more to reveal than conceal the absence of any real participation in government, and whetted rather than dampened expectations. The propertied classes resented the burdens imposed by administrative duties and obligations, which in general they avoided—thereby making it more difficult to implement the reorganization of local government.[31] At the same time, demands for some form of

---

[30] eg. Joseph to Napoleon, 22.2.1806, *ANP* AF IV 1714ᶜ.
[31] See esp. De Martino (1984); A.Spagnoletti 'Il controllo degli Intendenti sulle amministrazioni locali nel Regno di Napoli' in *L'Amministrazione nella Storia d'Italia* (Milan 1985), Vol.1; A.Scirocco 'I corpi rappresenttativi nel Mezzogiorno dal *decennio* alla Restaurazione: il personale dei consigli provinciali', *Ouaderni Storici* 37 (1978).

constitutional solution began to grow. These were strengthened first by the commitment to the creation of a national parliament made in the Treaty of Bayonne, and then by Bentinck's granting of a constitution in Sicily.[32]

Despite the serious deterioration of relations with the Emperor, Murat refused to concede constitutional government despite his growing political dependence on the Neapolitan propertied classes. His position was precarious, the more so because the new monarchy had failed to establish alternative political bases in either public administration or the army.

Both Joseph and Murat had received the enthusiastic support of the Neapolitan intellectual and professional classes, but the formation of an effective and cohesive new bureaucratic class proved extremely difficult. Many of the most outstanding figures in Neapolitan administration in the first half of the 19th century received their training in these years, but the development of a substantial class of public servants that might act as a *trait d'union* between the regime and the professional classes as a whole was limited. There were any number of constraints, not the least being Napoleon's insistence that the satellite bureaucracies existed primarily to provide work for French citizens. It was also, in practical terms and for political reasons, very difficult to carry out systematic purges of the *Ancien Régime* administrations without creating widespread professional unemployment. As a result, their employees moved to new branches of administration, without necessarily adopting new practices or mentalities. This meant that key sections of public administration, such as the magistracy, whose support would be critical for the success of an administrative revolution, were in practice more likely to blunt than sharpen its impact.[33]

The most serious obstacles to the formation of new bureaucratic cadres ideologically and materially committed to the new regime were financial and fiscal, however. The whole programme of administrative reform, indeed the whole concept of an 'administrative state', depended on the formation of a large, professional and technically proficient state bureaucracy. But this could only be achieved by increasing taxation, and in a relatively poor society this imposed severe constraints. The French innovations in this area proved extremely dangerous; taxation was increased, in many cases quite dramatically and in ways that provoked

---

[32] These developments are discussed in J.A.Davis 'La fin du royaume de Murat à Naples' in Y-M Bercé (ed.) *La Fin de l'Europe Napoléonienne; 1814, La Vacance de Pouvoir* (Paris 1990), pp. 219–34; on the Sicilian constitution see Rosselli (1956) and R.Romeo *Il Risorgimento in Sicilia* (1950).

[33] See A.Valente *Gioacchino Murat e l'Italia Meridionale* (Turin 1941), pp. 231–312, and the more recent appraisal in De Martino (1984).

growing popular protest and unrest, yet without yielding sufficient funds to enable new bureaucratic institutions to function.[34]

An alternative political base might have been created in the army, and this was something that Murat in particular had tried to achieve. But it was a policy fraught with ambiguities and above all dangers. First, because it attracted the suspicions of the Emperor and secondly because in so far as it succeeded it risked making Murat a prisoner of his own officers. Indeed, this was what happened in the closing days of the Kingdom when in the aftermath of the defeat at Tolentino in 1814 it was Murat's generals—Filangieri, Carrascosa, Colletta and Florestano Pepe—who demanded the immediate concession of a constitution as the condition for their continuing support. It was also in the army that the demand for constitutional government gave rise to the formation of the first Carbonarist cells.[35] The army proved to be, therefore, an extremely dangerous instrument by which to achieve the political and dynastic autonomy to which Murat undoubtedly aspired. Nothing revealed more clearly the persistence of those tensions between the propertied classes and the monarchy which pre-dated the arrival of the French rulers and would also be carried forward into the era of the Restoration.

If the administrative and juridical reforms introduced by the French rulers in southern Italy in this period consolidated and accelerated processes of economic and social change that had been evident for some time, the political reorganization of the state was to be the most ambiguous legacy of French rule in the Mezzogiorno. The terms of the political tensions that had brought the interests of the propertied classes and the monarchy into conflict in the last years of the *Ancien Régime* had changed, but their interests had not come into closer harmony during the period of French rule and reform.

The failure to find a political solution that would heal the conflict was to have important political repercussions which would be played out after the Restoration, when the demands for constitutional representation for the propertied classes quickly came to the fore. The failure of the Napoleonic *ralliement* between the monarchy and the propertied classes in the Mezzogiorno inhibited the development of a new 'administrative state'. Since the monarchy failed to win effective support from the propertied classes, especially at the periphery, the new administrative institutions remained weak and ineffective. Although the power of the state had in theory been immeasurably enhanced by the juridical and administrative

---

[34] See De Martino (1984), and A.Spagnoletti (1985), Vol.1; for complaints about taxation, see *ASN*, Min. Int. (1), f 183.

[35] J.A.Davis 'The political role of the Neapolitan army during the *decennio francese*' in A-M Rao (ed.) *Esercito e società nell'età rivoluzionaria* (Napoli 1990).

reforms of the French period (which was why none of the legitimist dynasties in Italy after 1814 sought to reverse those changes), in practice it remained weak in the Mezzorgiorno. Lacking the means to coerce, the powers of the state easily passed back into private hands. This of course was quite the opposite of what the French administrators had intended: indeed the central thrust of their reforms had been to bring to an end the devolutions of power that had been characteristic of the *Ancien Régime*. It was also the reverse of that new partnership between public and private interests which the French administrators had hoped to encourage. Where public and private interests did converge, it was too frequently on terms that were weighted heavily towards those who appropriated public institution for private ends. These were tendencies that pre-dated the experience of the French *decennio* but they were not resolved by the French reforms and thereafter the private exercise of public power was to remain one of the most distinctive features of political and social development in the Mezzogiorno.

*Proceedings of the British Academy*, **80**, 149–170

# The Codification of Commercial Law in Victorian Britain

ALAN RODGER
*Lord Advocate*
*Fellow of the British Academy*

IN 1904 Sir Courtenay Ilbert, one of the first Fellows, was asked to give a lecture to the Academy to mark the centenary of the Code Napoleon.[1] He tells us that he hesitated to comply since 'The subject of codification is vast; it does not much interest the present generation of Englishmen: one is tempted to think that all that is worth saying about it has been said already.' In the event Sir Courtenay was not deterred by his own warning. So, even though his words remain true today, I can at least claim to be following his example when I propose to examine one particular aspect of this dread topic.

The history of attempts at codification in nineteenth-century Britain is the history of a movement which largely failed. Perhaps for this reason it has been somewhat neglected by modern writers, though there are signs that this is changing, and a discussion of the period down to 1850 has recently appeared.[2] In that period, and indeed later, much effort was expended on the criminal law. So scholars have tended to concentrate on the draft criminal codes and on the codes prepared for use in India.[3] Nor is this surprising since the story is attractive and has a cast of well-known characters. It is set against a backdrop of the Indian Mutiny and other

---

Read 28 November 1991. © The British Academy 1993.

[1] Sir Courtenay Ilbert, 'The Centenary of the French Civil Code', (1903–1904) 1 *Proceedings of the British Academy* 253.

[2] M. Lobban, *The Common Law and English Jurisprudence* (Oxford, 1991), especially Chapters 5–7.

[3] For the criminal and Indian codes see, for instance, W.R. Cornish and G. de N. Clark, *Law and Society in England 1750–1950* (London, 1989), 598 *et seq.* with references.

troubles in India. There are clashes between strong-minded officials in London and others equally determined in Calcutta. Lord Macaulay, Sir Henry Maine, Sir James Fitzjames Stephen and Sir Courtenay Ilbert, all known from other exploits, succeed one another on the stage. Towards the end the scene switches back to London and we see the ubiquitous Frederick Pollock and Mackenzie Chalmers waiting to come on, clutching their digests on partnership and bills of exchange. Maitland, Sir Leslie Stephen and the Sidgwicks hover just off stage with Virginia Woolf and the Bloomsbury Group not far behind. Truly this is not mere legal history, but political, intellectual and cultural history in the grand manner.

It is also, if I may say so, extremely English. The various participants were at home in Oxford and London. They were involved in the affairs of the Empire. But there is little sign that they had any particular interest in Scotland or the law which applied there. Yet when Sir Mackenzie Chalmers' Acts on bills of exchange, sale of goods and marine insurance reached the statute book along with Sir Frederick Pollock's Partnership Act, they all applied to Scotland. In more recent years legal nationalists in Scotland have viewed these developments with less than complete enthusiasm and in particular the application of the Sale of Goods Act 1893 to Scotland has been portrayed as resulting from the 'imposition of foreign law' on the national legal system of Scotland.[4] As in all the best tales of national betrayal a native Scotsman—surprisingly enough Lord Watson—is portrayed as one of the blackest villains.[5] My aim this evening is to sketch a little more of the Scottish dimension and to suggest that in commercial matters at least we can better understand what happened if we look at the position in Britain as a whole.

To anyone with even a passing knowledge of British history the idea that businessmen in Victorian Scotland allowed English law to be imposed upon them may seem surprising. When we think of Scotland in that period, we think of Glasgow, the Second City of the Empire, and of the shipyards of the Clyde. We think of mighty shipping lines and of Sir William Burrell, so wealthy that he could devote himself to assembling the great Collection which bears his name. We think of Dundee magnates importing jute from India and amassing fortunes to build gracious mansions along the banks

---

[4] Sir Thomas Smith, 'Pretensions of English Law as "Imperial Law"' in the article on Constitutional Law, *The Laws of Scotland Stair Memorial Encyclopaedia* Vol. 5 (Edinburgh, 1987), para. 717. The complaint runs as a *leitmotif* through Sir Thomas Smith's work. Smith invokes some remarks of Koschaker, but he had been careful to confine them to the reception of a foreign legal system as a whole: P. Koschaker, *Europa und das Römische Recht* (Munich and Berlin, 1947), 138 n. 1. Whatever else may have happened, there has been no wholesale reception of English law in Scotland.

[5] See, e.g., T.B. Smith, *Property Problems in Sale* (London and Calcutta, 1978), 14.

of the Tay. In other words our impression is of booming commercial cities and of confident businessmen recognizing no superiors and few equals. If they were even remotely like that, then it would be surprising if this formidable mercantile community allowed English law to encroach against their will.

The picture has been obscured by a reluctance among some Scots lawyers to recognize that Scots law changed in character in the nineteenth century precisely because of the changes in Scottish society. Scottish businessmen were British businessmen who happened to work in Scotland; indeed in many spheres they were *the* British businessmen.[6] It was these Scottish businessmen, and not their English cousins, who were most insistent that the law which governed their transactions should be modern[7] and should help them trade in the larger English and Empire markets. They were practical men rather than romantic supporters of a native legal system of whose doctrines they would usually be entirely ignorant. So if any necessary change meant adopting a rule from English law, they saw this, not as some kind of defeat for Scotland and for Scots law, but as a step in the creation of that British commercial law which would help them sell their goods, to be carried by British railway companies or on British ships to British markets at home and overseas. In this way Scottish businessmen became enthusiastic supporters of a growing movement to assimilate the laws, and in particular the commercial laws, of England, Scotland and Ireland by embodying them in some kind of code. Although no such comprehensive code was ever produced, it is the existence of this current of opinion over many decades which explains why the four principal commercial law bills were all passed in a form which applied to Scotland. So far from there being any plot by English lawyers to impose their law on Scots Law, if it had been left to the English lawyers, this commercial legislation would almost certainly have applied to England and Wales only.

With pinpoint precision the Scottish institutional writer George Joseph Bell dated the rise of mercantile law in Scotland to 9 June 1772, when the first Scottish bankruptcy statute became law.[8] To that date also perhaps one could trace the start of the movement to assimilate the commercial

---

[6] On the development of Scottish industry see O. and S. Checkland, *Industry and Ethos Scotland 1832–1914* (second edition, Edinburgh, 1989), Chapter 1.

[7] For the mid-nineteenth century see the important passage in I.G.C. Hutchison, *A Political History of Scotland 1832–1924: Parties, Elections and Issues* (Edinburgh, 1986), 93–5. It is by no means insignificant that it was written by a historian rather than a lawyer.

[8] G.J. Bell, *Commentaries on the Law of Scotland and the Principles of Mercantile Jurisprudence* (seventh edition by J.A. M'Laren, Edinburgh, 1870) Vol. 1, ix–x, Preface to Author's Editions.

laws of Scotland and England. The differences between the bankruptcy régimes in the two kingdoms were keenly felt by businessmen. As early as 1814 a committee of London merchants reported on a bill for reforming the Scottish legislation[9] and, with neither system working well, for many years there were various proposals to develop a uniform scheme for both countries. Problems with bankruptcy were very much in the air in the middle of the nineteenth century, but by that time some people at least were beginning to think that other areas of commercial law should be assimilated.

If we imagine ourselves in the Advocates Library in Edinburgh in 1849, we shall see surrounded by books a gentleman who is not an advocate and not even Scottish. He is Mr. Leone Levi, a naturalized British subject settled in Liverpool, but by birth an Italian from Ancona.[10] As yet he is not a lawyer, though in due course he will become a member of Lincoln's Inn and a Professor at King's College, London. Despite his lack of formal legal qualifications, Levi is writing or compiling a huge work on Commercial Law in which he compares the mercantile law of Great Britain with the codes and laws of commerce of sixty other states and, he adds, the Institutes of Justinian.[11] When the work began to appear towards the end of 1850, at the front of the first volume he placed an address to Prince Albert in which he suggested that on the occasion of the Great Exhibition deputations from all over the world should be invited to London to discuss the feasibility of preparing an international code of commercial law for the whole world. The project would take about three years to complete. In replying[12] the Prince Consort invoked good constitutional principle to avoid commenting directly on the somewhat Utopian scheme, but despite this rebuff the publication of his giant compendium brought Levi some renown abroad and in certain circles in this country.[13] Buoyed up by this apparent success Levi pressed ahead with a scheme to assimilate the commercial laws of the

---

[9] *Report of the London Committee on the Scotch Bankrupt Bill, 1814.*

[10] Article on Leone Levi, *Dictionary of National Biography* Vol. 11, 1035 (J.M. Rigg). See also L. Levi, *The Story of my Life* (privately printed, London, 1888), 40. Cf. Note 103 below.

[11] L. Levi, *Commercial Law, Its Principles and Administration; or, The Mercantile Law of Great Britain Compared with the Codes and Laws of Commerce of the Following Mercantile Countries: Anhalt . . . Würtemburg, and the Institutes of Justinian* Vol. 1 (London, 1850), Vol. 2 (London, 1851).

[12] Vol. 2, xi–xii.

[13] *Dictionary of National Biography loc. cit.*; G. Cohn, 'The Beginnings of the International Assimilation of Commercial Law', *The Progress of Continental Law in the Nineteenth Century* (edited by J. Wigmore, London, 1918), 351 *et seq.* But in this country at least Levi was obviously regarded by some as a somewhat bizarre and comic figure. See, for instance, 'Scoto-English Law Commissions and Law Assimilations—Mercantile Law Reform', (1853) 49 *The Law Magazine* 318.

United Kingdom, and on this topic he lectured to public meetings up and down the country.[14]

At about this period the active political life of Lord Brougham was coming to an end and he was seeking other outlets for his boundless energy. Throughout his career he had been a tireless worker for reform, and at no time had he excluded his native Scottish legal system from his attentions. In pursuit of his aims he had been a prime mover in setting up the Law Amendment Society which, as its name suggests, was dedicated to law reform.[15]

In 1852 spurred on by Levi's efforts the grandly named Edinburgh Committee for the Amendment and Consolidation of Commercial Law called on the Law Amendment Society to arrange a meeting of representatives of Chambers of Commerce and others from the three kingdoms of England, Scotland and Ireland to discuss the assimilation of their commercial laws.[16] This suggestion was adopted and in November of that year a great conference was held in London with representatives from Edinburgh, Glasgow, Dublin, Liverpool, Birmingham, Manchester and many other manufacturing centres, though strangely enough commercial circles in London were not represented.[17] The week before, a meeting in the Glasgow Chamber of Commerce had given only a cautious welcome to an emissary of the London Committee for the assimilation of the commercial and bankruptcy laws of England and Scotland, who had used the occasion for the most part to promote a pet scheme of Lord Brougham to reform the Scottish law of bankruptcy.[18] But at the London conference, with Lord Brougham presiding, enthusiasm reigned and a series of motions was passed endorsing the need to assimilate the three systems of commercial law. Mr. Alexander Hastie, M.P., one of the Glasgow representatives, swept aside worries that England would swallow up Scotland in this matter since he was sure that the Law Amendment Society would wish 'to adopt that which was best in the laws of both countries.'[19] The meeting agreed to set up a committee to carry the views of the conference to the Government and the following afternoon Lord Harrowby led a deputation to Downing Street to meet Lord Derby. The Prime Minister appeared to be sympathetic to

---

[14] *Report of the Proceedings of the Conference on the Assimilation of the Commercial Laws* . . . (The Law Amendment Society, London, 1852), 22 (hereinafter '*Conference Report*'). For a text of his lecture to chambers of commerce in Leeds, Bradford and Hull, see L. Levi, *A Lecture on the Proposed National Code of Commerce* (Leeds, 1852).

[15] Cf. R. Stewart, *Henry Brougham His Public Career 1778–1868* (London, 1985), 348–9.

[16] *Conference Report*, 1. The Committee had been set up following a lecture to the Edinburgh Merchant Company on 24 March 1851. Cf. Levi, *The Story of my Life*, 44 *et seq.* and 66.

[17] *Conference Report*, 3–5.

[18] *Glasgow Herald*, 15 November 1852, 5.

[19] *Conference Report*, 10.

the idea of a commission.[20] Before anything could be done, however, the ministry fell and it was not till the following Spring that the matter could be taken forward with the new government under Lord Aberdeen.

The upshot was that in June 1853 the government set up a Royal Commission to 'inquire and ascertain how far the Mercantile Laws of the different Parts of the United Kingdom of Great Britain and Ireland may be advantageously assimilated'.[21] The Lord Advocate, James Moncreiff, who favoured the kind of assimilation which involved taking the best bits from each system, envisaged that the results of the Commission's work would probably be to 'lay the foundation of a general system of jurisprudence which, in the course of time, will be worked out to a consummation.'[22]

In the event the results were somewhat less dramatic. The Commission quickly produced two reports[23] which were only partly implemented.[24] Indeed it has been said that the legislation which followed in 1856 changed the laws of England and Scotland without in fact making them the same.[25] What is interesting to notice is that, when the Commission asked about the practical difficulties encountered by businessmen as a result of the differences among the various legal systems, the witnesses could give them few actual examples.[26]

For a time after 1856 attention turned away from the particular matter of commercial law. In England it was rightly seen that the statute book needed to be purged of out-of-date material and, though Lord Cranworth's scheme[27] for a Code Victoria came to nothing, at the beginning of the 1860s Lord Westbury's Statute Law Revision Acts made considerable progress in consolidating English statute law.[28] In a speech made at the time,[29] Lord

---

[20] *Conference Report*, 21–2.

[21] *First Report of the Royal Commission 1854* (P.P. 445), 3.

[22] Speech at Leith on 1 September 1853, *The Scotsman*, 3 September 1853, 3 (pages not numbered).

[23] *First Report 1854* (P.P. 445); *Second Report 1854–1855* (P.P. 1977).

[24] Cf. J. K (irkpatrick), 'On the Codification of Mercantile Law', (1880) 24 *Journal of Jurisprudence* 638, 640.

[25] His Honour Judge Chalmers, *The Sale of Goods* (London, 1890), viii. Much the same point was made, for example, in 'English Amendments of Scotch Law', (1858) 1 *Scottish Law Journal* 1, a generally hostile commentary on the 1856 Act. Levi felt extremely let down by what he saw as the meagre and unsatisfactory outcome of his efforts: Levi, *The Story of my Life*, 81–2.

[26] Introduction to the *Second Report*.

[27] House of Lords, 14 February 1853, Hansard Third Series Vol. 124, coll. 41 *et seq.*, especially at 58–66.

[28] For nineteenth-century developments see, for example, Sir Courtenay Ilbert, *Legislative Methods and Forms* (Oxford, 1901), 51–76.

[29] House of Lords, 12 June 1863, Hansard Third Series Vol. 171, col. 775; J.F. Macqueen, *Speech of the Lord Chancellor on the Revision of the Law* (London, 1863).

Westbury foreshadowed a more ambitious plan for an official digest of the statute and case law of England—no mention was made of Scotland—and in 1866 a Royal Commission was set up to see whether such a thing could be compiled. The importance of this scheme for present purposes is that it was seen as a possible way of securing the advantages of codification (for instance, a clear statement of the law within a manageable compass) without the disadvantages of a statutory code which might prove difficult to adapt to changing circumstances. Though the Commissioners reported in favour of the proposal and work was set on foot to draft specimen sections, the whole project eventually broke down.[30]

But while it was still active, it came to the notice of Mr. John Dove Wilson, a young Scotsman of ample means and Liberal opinions.[31] Since he features prominently in the story, it may be in order to introduce him slightly more fully. Having practised as an advocate for four years, in 1861 at the age of twenty-eight he was appointed sheriff-substitute (rather like a county court judge) in the small town of Stonehaven near Aberdeen. Being of an academic frame of mind, he soon began to devote his considerable leisure to the writing of legal textbooks. A new edition of a book on bills of exchange appeared in 1865[32] and a brand-new work on Sheriff Court Practice followed four years later.[33] With these substantial achievements behind him, in 1870 Dove Wilson was transferred to Aberdeen and seems quickly to have immersed himself in the life of that city where he was to spend the rest of his life. In 1890 he resigned as a sheriff to become Professor of Scots and Roman Law in the University of Aberdeen in 1891.

In 1870 shortly after moving to Aberdeen Dove Wilson published a paper under the auspices of the Scottish Law Amendment Society.[34] In it he argued that the proposed scheme for a digest of English case law, while admirable in itself, did not go far enough. What was required was to institute a similar scheme for Scotland and to compile a digest of Scots law on parallel lines. He drew attention to the 'intimate relations which bind Scotland and England' and to the 'great desirableness of assimilating the law of the United Kingdom'. He thought that, in particular for mercantile law, 'the parallel arrangement could be carried out almost to the minutest details', but that in any event the parallel digests would eventually allow

---

[30] Ilbert, *Legislative Methods*, 61 n. 1.

[31] S.D. Girvin, 'Professor John Dove Wilson of Aberdeen', 1992 *Juridical Review* 60; article on John Dove Wilson, Dictionary of National Biography (1901–1911) (A.H. Millar). I am grateful to Dr. Girvin for sending me a copy of his article before publication.

[32] R. Thomson, *Bills of Exchange* (second edition by J. Dove Wilson, Edinburgh, 1865).

[33] J. Dove Wilson, *The Practice of the Sheriff Courts of Scotland* (Edinburgh, 1869). In the Preface he suggests that the law of procedure is suitable for codification.

[34] 'On the Expediency of Forming a Digest of the Law of Scotland', (1870) 14 *Journal of Jurisprudence* 195.

codes to be developed which 'could be made to embrace the law of the United Kingdom on all matters on which it was really desirable that the law should be the same.'[35]

In arguing along these lines Dove Wilson was by no means an isolated figure on the Scottish legal scene. We have already come across Lord Advocate Moncreiff in 1853 favouring assimilation and he had spoken to the same effect at a meeting of the Association for the Promotion of Social Science, another vehicle for Lord Brougham's ideas, at Glasgow in 1860.[36] Dove Wilson's patron, the Solicitor General George Young, supported a large degree of assimilation in a speech in 1869.[37] Indeed he was widely suspected of favouring the total abolition of Scots law as a separate system.[38] At this period assimilation and codification were very much in the air and the legal press of Scotland recorded the discussions among Scottish lawyers and businessmen.[39] For instance in 1864 James Muirhead, the new Professor of Civil Law at Edinburgh, addressed the Chamber of Commerce there on the subject of 'Codification of the Mercantile Law',[40] pointing out that, even if codification of the whole legal system could not be contemplated, commercial law was an excellent place to begin. 'The mercantile laws of England and Scotland are both of comparatively modern growth;' he said 'neither contains anything that it would shock the affections of the people to see amended; the differences between them are insignificant, and with the assistance and under the guidance of calm, unprejudiced, rationally-minded merchants and jurists, might without much difficulty be reconciled and adjusted.'[41] We are told that his remarks were well received. Even Lord Deas, usually thought of as an archetypal old Scottish judge, said that 'he did not think that anybody could doubt the expediency of' assimilating

[35] Ibid., 200.

[36] J. Moncreiff, *Introductory Address on Jurisprudence and the Amendment of the Law* (Edinburgh, 1860), 18–23.

[37] 'Inaugural Address to the Scottish Law Amendment Society', (1869) 13 *Journal of Jurisprudence* 113, 122.

[38] G.W.T. Omond, *The Lord Advocates of Scotland Second Series 1834–1880* (London, 1914), 269–70.

[39] See, for example, 'Curiosities of the Statute Book. Codification', (1857) 1 *Journal of Jurisprudence* 404; A. Burrell, 'The Assimilation of the Mercantile Laws of England and Scotland—its Progress and Prospects' as summarized in (1861) 3 *Scottish Law Journal* 38; R.V. C(ampbell), 'A British Code', (1867) 11 *Journal of Jurisprudence* 400; 'On Codification', (1873) 17 *Journal of Jurisprudence* 188; H. G(oudy), 'Codification in Germany', (1873) 17 *Journal of Jurisprudence* 227; J.A. Dixon, 'The Codification of the Law', (1874) 18 *Journal of Jurisprudence* 305. There is, of course, a vast parallel literature in England on codification, but Scottish discussions generally have the added dimension of assimilation.

[40] J. Muirhead, *Codification of the Mercantile Law* (Edinburgh, 1864).

[41] Ibid., 17.

the mercantile laws of the United Kingdom 'in so far as it had been urged that night.'[42]

Muirhead's talk is perhaps particularly worth noting for the comparisons which he made with developments in Germany.[43] Speeches on codification all tend—even today—to contain historical and comparative sections which may for instance begin with Hammurabi and pay short uninteresting visits to Justinian, Francis Bacon, the Code Napoleon and many more besides. But by the 1860s events were stirring in Germany and these were particularly instructive.[44] The German Confederation was, after all, made up of many states, each with its own legal system and rules. But in spite of this, and particularly in the realm of commercial law, much had already been done to assimilate the laws of the different states and to embody them in a single code. Beginning with the law of bills of exchange, German jurists had managed by 1862 to produce a Common Commercial Code which was brought into force throughout the Confederation. This example was particularly compelling to advocates of codification in this country since the German problem had been so much more complex than the British. If a single code could be developed for Germany, it was hard to see how it could be impossible here.[45] Argument from the German experience recurs in many of the talks and, as the years go by and nothing is done, speakers contrast the lack of progress in this country with the great strides being made by the German Empire.[46]

But the simple fact was that, however many speeches were made or resolutions passed, it was a long time before any practical steps were taken to advance the cause of codification of commercial law. The subject first came to life again towards the end of the 1870s. Following the publication of his digest of the law of partnership, the young Mr. Frederick Pollock was paid £100 to draft a Partnership Bill for the Associated Chambers of Commerce.[47]

---

[42] Ibid., 19.

[43] Ibid., 15 *et seq.*

[44] See e.g. M. John, *Politics and the Law in Late Nineteenth-Century Germany* (Oxford, 1989), Chapter 2; F. Wieacker, *Privatrechtsgeschichte der Neuzeit* (second edition, Heidelberg, 1967), 458 *et seq.*; H. Coing, *Europäisches Privatrecht* Vol. 2 (Munich, 1989), 20, and 570–2. On mercantile codes generally see Coing, Chapter 26.

[45] See e.g. J. Dove Wilson, 'Concerning a Code of Commercial Law', (1884) 28 *Journal of Jurisprudence* 337, 343–4.

[46] See e.g. the article cited in the previous note and the paper of Mr. (later Sir) John Macdonnell cited in note 90 below.

[47] Executive Council, 13 December 1878; Law Committee, 25 January 1879; Executive Council, 14 February 1879, *Associated Chambers of Commerce of the United Kingdom (hereinafter 'A.C.C.') Minute Book (4 August 1876–3 October 1883)*. Manuscript 14,476.3, Guildhall Library. There is a not entirely accurate account of the involvement of the A.C.C. in commercial law reform in A.R. Ilersic, P.F.B. Liddle, *Parliament of Commerce* (London, 1960), Chapters 7 and 8. On codification see especially 86–7.

By June 1879 the bill was ready[48] and it was introduced later that session. Since it tried to do more than merely to restate the existing law, it ran into considerable difficulties and its progress was blocked for many years so that it did not reach the statute book until 1890.[49] In its original form it did not apply to Scotland but in the final stages of its passage through Parliament this was changed. The change was supported by the Faculty of Advocates who thought that the addition of a few words would be enough 'so to frame the Bill as to make it the means of effecting a complete assimilation of the laws of the two kingdoms on partnership.'[50]

No sooner had they launched their Partnership Bill on its troubled voyage than the Associated Chambers of Commerce turned their attention to codifying the law on bills of exchange.[51] Early in 1880 Mackenzie Chalmers was consulted[52] but the Associated Chambers soon became rather bogged down in trying to ascertain the French and German law on the topic.[53] They appear to have been rescued from this diversion in March 1881 when a letter arrived from Sir John Lubbock, the President of the Institute of Bankers, offering to share with the Associated Chambers the cost of drafting a bill to consolidate the existing law on bills of exchange.[54] The Institute had become interested a short time before as a result of a lecture by Mackenzie Chalmers.[55] The offer was accepted and by June a bill,

[48] Executive Council, 13 June 1879, A.C.C.; Resolution adopted by Special Meeting of the A.C.C., 24 August 1880: *Resolutions adopted at the Special Meeting of the Association of Chambers of Commerce of the United Kingdom . . . August 24th and 25th, 1880*, 8; Report of the Executive Council to the Annual Meeting February 1st, 1881 with Appendix adopted by the Annual Meeting, 1 February 1881: *Reports and Resolutions adopted at the Twenty-First Annual Meeting of the Chambers of Commerce of the United Kingdom . . . on February 1st, 2nd and 3rd 1881*, 12 and 19. Cf. also 31.

[49] Cf. F. Pollock, *The Law of Partnership* (fifteenth edition by L.C.B. Gower, London, 1952), Preface to the Twelfth Edition, xiv–xv. The A.C.C. was determined that the Bill should become law. For instance, the President, Colonel E.S. Hill, M.P., made a special effort to obtain a second reading for it in 1889: Executive Committee, 21 June 1889, *A.C.C. Minute Book (2 October 1883–14 June 1895)*. Manuscript 14,476.4, Guildhall Library.

[50] *Report of the Committee of the Faculty of Advocates on the Partnership Bill and other Bills relating to Companies*, 19 March 1890.

[51] Annual General Meeting, 17 February 1880, A.C.C.

[52] Executive Council, 12 March 1880, A.C.C. He was the author of *A Digest of the law of Bills of Exchange, Promissory Notes and Cheques* (London, 1878) which had been modelled on the work of Sir James Stephen and Frederick Pollock: Introduction iii.

[53] Executive Council, 21 May 1880, A.C.C. *Reports and Resolutions adopted at the Twenty-First Annual Meeting 1881*, 6, 19 *et seq.* and 33.

[54] Executive Council, 11 March 1881, A.C.C.

[55] Report of the Council to the Third Annual General Meeting of the Institute of Bankers on 18 May 1881, (1880–1) 2 *Journal of the Institute of Bankers* 422, 425. For the text of the lecture and discussion on 26 January 1881, see M.D. Chalmers, 'On the Codification of Mercantile Law, with Especial Reference to the Law of Negotiable Instruments', (1880–1) 2 *Journal of the Institute of Bankers* 113.

applying to England and Ireland only, was ready for Sir John to introduce in the Commons.[56] The bill made no progress until the following year. At that point up in Aberdeen Dove Wilson sprang into action and wrote to Sir John Lubbock. Calling upon his experience as the editor of a textbook on bills of exchange, Dove Wilson suggested that the bill both could and should be made to apply to the whole United Kingdom.[57] The Commons Select Committee were given power to extend the Bill to Scotland and at their invitation Dove Wilson first wrote an elaborate report and then, in June, travelled to London to give evidence to them. Having heard his evidence, the Select Committee immediately decided that the bill should indeed apply to Scotland.[58] The necessary amendments were made[59] and two months later it had received the Royal Assent. The Act proved an immediate success both in England and in Scotland and quite soon it was adopted in many parts of the Empire.

Dove Wilson's adventure with the bills of exchange bill brought him some immediate benefits. For one thing he had made contacts and come to know some of the leading commercial and legal figures of the time. Not surprisingly Dove Wilson was also able, if not to dine out, at least to lecture out on the basis of his exhilarating experience—an experience, moreover, which seemed to show what could be done if only matters were tackled with some vigour.

So in April 1884 we find him talking to the Aberdeen Chamber of Commerce 'Concerning a Code of Commercial Law' and calling for businessmen to demand a code of commercial law for the whole United Kingdom which, he reckoned, could be prepared within about five years.[60] The directors of the Chamber were so impressed by what

---

[56] Executive Council, 17 June 1881, A.C.C.

[57] Dove Wilson, 28 *Journal of Jurisprudence* 345–6. For the legislative history see also M.D. Chalmers, 'An Experiment in Codification', (1886) 2 *L.Q.R.* 125. It is proper to see the developments in Britain as part of a wider movement. Cf. J. Dove Wilson, 'Unification of the Law of Bills of Exchange' (1886) 2 *L.Q.R.* 297 and G. Cohn, in *The Progress of Continental Law in the Nineteenth Century* (Note 13), 362 *et seq.*

[58] *Report from the Select Committee on the Bills of Exchange Bill, with the Proceedings of the Committee 1882* (P.P.244).

[59] On the process of assimilation see the speech of Lord Avebury (Sir John Lubbock), 27 June 1900, *Official Report of the Fourth Congress of Chambers of Commerce of the Empire held in London on 26th, 27th, 28th, and 29th June, 1900* (London Chamber of Commerce [Incorporated], London, 1900), 39; cf. *Report by the Committee of the Faculty of Advocates on the Bills of Exchange Bill 1882*, 9 June 1882 and the *Report of the Committee of the Faculty of Advocates on the Sale of Goods Bill*, 20 March 1891, 1. See also the speech of R.V. Campbell cited in Note 83 below.

[60] 28 *Journal of Jurisprudence* 337, especially at 348–51.

he said that they immediately decided to petition the Prime Minister, Mr. Gladstone, and to circulate copies of Dove Wilson's speech to other Chambers of Commerce and to Members of Parliament.[61] Even more importantly they decided to submit a resolution on the topic to a meeting of the Associated Chambers of Commerce later that year.[62] This took place in Wolverhampton at the end of September and Dove Wilson was there to move the Aberdeen resolution calling for a Royal Commission to be set up to start the process of assimilating the commercial laws of the three kingdoms. The resolution was adopted and Dove Wilson was then deputed to prepare a memorial on the topic which was submitted to the Government in the name of the Associated Chambers of Commerce.[63]

In due course, but only with great difficulty,[64] arrangements were made for a deputation to see Lord Chancellor Selborne about the matter when the Associated Chambers met in London the following February. Naturally Dove Wilson was included in the delegation. Lord Selborne had a considerable record in law reform, not least for his Judicature Act 1873. So much may have been expected of him. As it happened, however, the timing of the meeting could hardly have been more unfortunate for General Gordon's death at Khartoum had been announced a few weeks before and the meeting took place on the eve of a censure debate on the Government's handling of the affair. In addition the failure of the proposed criminal law code to make progress in 1879 had highlighted the problems which any large-scale scheme of codification was likely to meet in Parliament.[65] Whatever the reasons, when he met the delegation the Lord Chancellor was completely unreceptive, dashing all hope of any grand scheme for codification.[66] Even if a code were drafted, he said, it would never get through Parliament which would wish to scrutinize every provision. The wiser course was to concentrate on codifying suitable branches of commercial law and, if private members came forward with suitable bills for that purpose, facilities would be afforded for

---

[61] Council of Aberdeen Chamber of Commerce, 29 April and 27 May 1884, *Minute Book of Aberdeen Chamber of Commerce* Vol. 3, 156–7, 164–5 and 166–7. Aberdeen District Council Archives.

[62] Council Meeting, 16 July 1884, *Minute Book* Vol. 3, 174–5.

[63] Special Meeting of A.C.C., 30 September 1884, *Supplement to the Chamber of Commerce Journal* 10 October 1884, 3–5.

[64] See the remark of C.M. Norwood, M.P., the President of the A.C.C. to the Annual Meeting, 24 February 1885, *Supplement to the Chamber of Commerce Journal* 10 March 1885, 2.

[65] Cf. Ilbert, *Legislative Methods*, 128.

[66] 'Codification of Commercial Law', (1885) 78 *Law Times* 321. See also E.S., 'The Proposed Mercantile Code', (1885) 29 *Journal of Jurisprudence* 186.

their passing. Addressing those whom he called 'the gentlemen from Scotland', he said that if they could suggest any difficulties which had not been removed by the reforming legislation of 1856, 'then he should be extremely happy to consider any suggestions on that subject, but he did not think a Royal Commission would be necessary for that purpose.'[67] Although the Lord Chancellor's attitude was heavily criticized in the press, there was nothing which could be done. Looking back on the débâcle, the Aberdeen Chamber concluded: 'it need not be disguised that it involves a loss of valuable time, in a question in which time is of the utmost importance, as it cannot be supposed that the condition in which the laws of the United Kingdom at present exist can long be tolerated.'[68]

Although Lord Selborne went out of office a few months later, no one seems to have thought it worthwhile resuscitating the grand scheme. Doubtless Lord Halsbury was not thought likely to be an obvious supporter. Rather, those who were interested in reform followed Lord Selborne's advice and brought forward piecemeal codifying measures usually under the tutelage of Lord Herschell.

So, as we have seen already, the Associated Chambers continued to press their Partnership Bill. They also initiated a bill to codify the law of arbitration but, despite Lord Bramwell's efforts, this ultimately came to nothing. More successful was the Factors Act 1889 which derived from a bill promoted by the London Chamber and the Institute of Bankers and which was applied to Scotland in 1890. Above all, the matter of sale was at last receiving attention. In 1888 Mackenzie Chalmers drafted a Sale of Goods Bill setting out the existing law for England and Wales[69] and it was introduced by Lord Herschell at the end of the session.[70] Modified and reintroduced in the Spring of 1889, this was the bill which eventually became the Sale of Goods Act 1893 and assimilated the laws of England and Scotland.

The idea that the bill was imposed on Scotland by English interests could hardly be less true. In fact the Scottish interests saw the risk that they would be left out and fought to make sure that the Bill was adapted to apply

---

[67] 78 *Law Times* 322.

[68] Report by Council to the Annual General Meeting of the Aberdeen Chamber of Commerce, 9 April 1885. *Minute Book* Vol. 3, 206–7. It says much for the determination of the Aberdeen Chamber that five years later they took the matter up again and submitted a motion on assimilation of commercial law for consideration by the A.C.C.: Council Meeting, Aberdeen Chamber of Commerce, 30 December 1890. *Minute Book* Vol. 3, 188 with 186. See further Note 75 below.

[69] Article on Sir Mackenzie Dalzell Chalmers, *Dictionary of National Biography (1922–1930)*, (F.D. Mackinnon).

[70] 9 August 1888, Hansard Third Series Vol. 330, cols. 70–71.

throughout the United Kingdom.[71] The first off the mark seem to have been the Faculty of Advocates. As early as June 1889 a Faculty Committee observed that a codifying bill which did not apply to Scotland would lose much of its value and they were reappointed to set about revising the Bill to make it applicable there.[72] Nothing much seems to have happened until the spring of 1891 when there was a flurry of activity in Scotland. The Faculty of Advocates again decided that 'with some verbal amendments' the Bill could easily be adapted to Scotland.[73] The Aberdeen Chamber of Commerce wrote round to other Chambers in Scotland urging them to join in petitioning in favour of the Bill[74] and a representative from Aberdeen spoke in favour of extending the Bill to Scotland at the Annual Meeting of the Associated Chambers of Commerce.[75] The Glasgow Chamber prepared a petition which referred to the 'great and general advantage' of assimilating the laws on sale of goods and sent it to Lord Watson for presentation in the House of Lords. Lord Watson presented the petition and in due course told the Glasgow Chamber that he would put down amendments to make the Bill apply to Scotland.[76] He duly did so at the end of July and they were contained in the Bill when it passed the House of Lords.[77]

The Bill made no further progress that session, but in May 1892 the Bill incorporating the Scottish amendments was reintroduced. The

---

[71] For instance Professor Richard Brown urged 'upon the legal profession in Scotland that they take up arms in the same way as they did in regard to the Bills of Exchange Act and insist that Scotland be included': *Is it Expedient to Codify by Statute the Leading Branches of Commercial Law? Report of Proceedings before a Commission of the Glasgow Juridical Society, On Wednesday, 17th December 1890* (Glasgow Juridical Society, Glasgow, 1891), 14. The 'Commission' answered the question in the negative. Much useful secondary material on the Sale of Goods Bill is gathered in the references to H. Macdonald and others, 'Law Reform' in the article on Sources of Law (General and Historical), *Laws of Scotland Stair Memorial Encyclopaedia* Vol. 22 (Edinburgh, 1987), para. 643.

[72] *Interim Report of the Faculty of Advocates Committee on the Sale of Goods Bill* adopted at a Faculty meeting on 1 June 1889. *Minute Book of Faculty of Advocates*, 593–4. National Library of Scotland. In the *Encyclopaedia* article cited in the previous note, the authors give the misleading impression, based on a secondary source, that the Faculty saw the application to Scotland as something which was likely to be imposed rather than something for which they were to aim.

[73] *Report of the Committee of the Faculty of Advocates on the Sale of Goods Bill*, 20 March 1891, 1.

[74] *Report of the Council to the Annual General Meeting of the Aberdeen Chamber of Commerce on 5 April 1892*, 9. The Aberdeen Chamber itself petitioned in favour of the Bill being applied to Scotland. For the text of the petition dated 14 April 1891, see *Minute Book* Vol. 3, 238–9.

[75] Speech of A.J. Brander, 5 March 1891, *Supplement to the Chamber of Commerce Journal* 10 March 1891, 23. See Note 67 above.

[76] *Report by Directors of Glasgow Chamber of Commerce to Annual General Meeting on 18 January 1892*, 12–13. Glasgow Chamber of Commerce.

[77] House of Lords, 30 July 1891, Hansard Third Series Vol. 356, col. 741.

amendments were not, however, satisfactory and the Glasgow Faculty of Procurators, who were in favour of the principle of the Bill, were very active in securing the introduction of many necessary changes during the course of the session.[78] The Bill fell again. It was introduced once more in 1893, but this time without the Scottish amendments. The Lord Chancellor, Lord Herschell, explained that the Bill could not possibly become law unless it were 'absolutely non-contentious'. He referred to the misgivings which had been expressed about some of the Scottish clauses the year before and indicated that he could re-introduce the Scottish amendments only if the position could be agreed.[79] Lord Watson replied saying that the differences of opinion were on 'comparatively trivial' points and he thought that agreement could be reached so that the Bill would not be put in danger.[80] About a fortnight later the Scottish amendments were back in the Bill[81] and there they remained until it reached the statute book in the following January.

Two comments seem in order. First, so far from wanting to impose the Bill on an unwilling Scotland, Lord Herschell actually preferred to confine it to England if there was any risk that difficulties with the law of Scotland would endanger its passage through Parliament. Secondly, the Bill enjoyed a wide measure of Scottish support from businessmen in their chambers of commerce and lawyers in their professional societies. Interestingly the Faculty of Advocates who had been the first to support the measure and who had maintained that support for four years suddenly withdrew it at the last moment when a Faculty meeting came down against the Bill. They apparently decided that the form of codification was unsatisfactory and that the English rule on the passing of property should not be adopted.[82] Not for the first time, nor indeed for the last time, the Faculty made its move too late to have any chance of affecting the outcome.

In truth the spirit of the age was against them. Codification of

---

[78] *Annual Report by the Committee on Bills of the Royal Faculty of Procurators in Glasgow to the General Meeting, 4 November 1892*, 4–12. Library of the Royal Faculty of Procurators, Glasgow.

[79] Speech of Lord Herschell, L.C., 21 February 1893, Hansard Fourth Series Vol. 9, col. 4.

[80] Speech of Lord Watson, Hansard Fourth Series Vol. 9, cols. 4–5.

[81] 6 March 1893, Hansard Fourth Series Vol. 9, col. 1069.

[82] Faculty Meeting, 10 March 1893 adopting the dissent in the *Report by the Committee of the Faculty of Advocates on the Sale of Goods Bill, 1893,* 10 March 1893. Among those who dissented was Professor Goudy. It would be difficult to detect this from his remarks a quarter of a century later: H. Goudy, *Address on Law Reform 3 July 1919 Society of Public Teachers of Law* (Oxford, 1919), 22–23.

commercial law was being promoted on all sides[83] and the rise of the New Imperialism encouraged an Empire-wide view of problems. So supporters of the codification of commercial law came to present it as a matter affecting the commercial health not just of the countries of the United Kingdom but of the Empire as a whole, an Empire which was having increasingly to compete with the growing commercial and industrial strength of Germany. Who better to tell forth this splendid theme than Professor Dove Wilson from Aberdeen? At least that appears to have been the view in London, for the Chamber of Commerce there specially asked the Aberdeen Chamber if Dove Wilson would move a motion on the codification of commercial law at the Second Congress of Chambers of Commerce of the Empire in 1892.[84] The Professor obliged and the resolution was safely carried.[85]

In Scotland the momentum in favour of codification was maintained the following year when the Edinburgh Merchant Company arranged a series of three lectures on the topic, each by an advocate and each in favour of codification. To a sceptical observer they may appear rather uninspiring, but the Merchant Company apparently thought otherwise since they had the lectures printed and copies circulated widely to Members of Parliament and others.[86] In 1895 the Merchant Company took up the matter again[87] and early in 1896 a circular letter was sent to mercantile and legal bodies in

---

[83] Indeed the Faculty itself had supported such a code of commercial law for the United Kingdom as recently as 1891: Faculty meeting on 20 March 1891 approving the *Report by the Faculty Committee on the Sale of Goods Bill*, 20 March 1891, 2. Minute Book of the Faculty of Advocates, 632. It would appear that the official attitude of the Faculty was in fact generally in favour of codification. See for instance the speeches of Aeneas Mackay and Richard Vary Campbell representing the Faculty, *Report of Conference of Delegates from Legal and Mercantile Bodies in Scotland 13th July 1896* (The Merchants' Hall, Edinburgh, 1896), 31–7 and 41–5 respectively. Sheriff Campbell in particular was anxious to dispel any impression of a lack of enthusiasm on the part of the Faculty. None the less it is interesting to note that on 21 November 1894 the Faculty set up a Committee 'to watch over any proposals that might be made for alterations in Mercantile Law . . .' The Committee was able to send delegates to meetings of legal bodies on the subject.

[84] Aberdeen Chamber of Commerce Committee, 9 June 1892, *Minute Book* Vol. 3, 367 referring to a letter of 31 May 1892 from the Secretary of the London Chamber.

[85] *Report of the Proceedings of the Second Congress of Chambers of Commerce of the Empire June 28th, 29th, 30th and July 1st 1892, Supplement to the Chamber of Commerce Journal* 14 July 1892, 47–9, reporting proceedings on 30 June 1892.

[86] H. Goudy, Ae. J.G. Mackay and R.V. Campbell, *Addresses on Codification of Law* (Edinburgh, 1893). For a contemporary comment on the lectures stressing the need to mobilize Parliamentary as opposed to mercantile opinion see 'A Word for Codification' (1893) 9 *Scottish Law Rev.* 203.

[87] Merchant Company, 15 October 1895, *Minute Book of the Merchant Company of Edinburgh* Vol. 19, 517. The Merchant Company, Edinburgh.

Scotland.[88] It is not perhaps surprising then that when the Third Congress of Chambers of Commerce of the Empire took place in June of that year Professor Dove Wilson was back in his place moving yet another motion on the need to codify the commercial law of the Empire.[89] The choice of Dove Wilson can be regarded as shrewd. He was recognized as something of an authority on the matter. More importantly, however, he could speak as someone coming from a country where English law did not prevail. For this reason he was well placed to argue that, if a code could be devised which could bridge the differences between English and Scots law, then surely it would easily bridge those gaps with other non-English systems in South Africa and Quebec, for instance. A code which could work in the United Kingdom could work throughout the Empire. So if only people would get on with codifying United Kingdom law, they would virtually simultaneously achieve the far wider goal of drafting a code for the Empire.[90] The main thing was to set to work quickly before the various countries of the Empire felt obliged to embark on their own codification schemes.[91]

Not surprisingly on this occasion Dove Wilson's motion was passed with acclamation, for the theme was seductive and fitted well with other resolutions calling for closer co-operation within the Empire. The tone of the congress had been set by a rousing opening address from Joseph Chamberlain in his role of Colonial Secretary.[92] It must have seemed to the supporters of codification that if only they could hitch their wagon to the popular theme of imperialism and enlist Chamberlain's support,[93] then they would at last overcome their major difficulty of arousing the interest of politicians in their proposals. As we have seen, it was precisely this

[88] Circular letter dated 25 February 1896. Cf. Copy Statement for the Master etc. dated 16 December 1895 appended to the minute of their meeting, 16 January 1896, *Minute Book* Vol. 19, 543 and 545 *et seq.* and the Copy Report appended to the minute of the meeting of the Master and others, 11 June 1896.

[89] *Official Report of the Third Congress of Chambers of Commerce of the Empire June 9th–12th 1896* (London Chamber of Commerce [Incorporated], London, 1896), 48–56. See also the remarks of Lord Herschell on the occasion of the Second Reading of the Sale of Goods Bill, House of Lords, 17 March 1891, Hansard Third Series, Vol. 351, coll. 1181 *et seq.*, where he plays down the practical advantages at home and stresses the advantages of uniform provisions for the Empire.

[90] *Official Report*, 49. Cf. paper by Sir John Macdonnell, 52 (first column).

[91] J. Dove Wilson, 'The Proposed Imperial Code of Commercial Law–A Plea for Progress', (1896) 8 *Juridical Review* 329, 344 and the speech of Sir John Macdonnell, *Official Report*, 55.

[92] 'Commercial Union of the Empire', *Mr. Chamberlain's Speeches* (edited by C.W. Boyd, London, 1914) Vol. 1, 365; *Official Report*, 4 *et seq.*

[93] Ibid., 367; Official Report, 4 (second column). By this time Dove Wilson was an active Liberal Unionist. Cf. *Glasgow Herald* 25 January 1908, 7 and *The Scotsman* 25 January 1908, 8. His confidence in Chamberlain shines through: *Official Report*, 49 (second column).

lack of political appeal which had caused all the previous schemes to fail since no-one was prepared to force the necessary legislation through Parliament.

After the Congress was over Dove Wilson stayed on in London to try to arrange meetings to give effect to the Congress resolution, but he found that the Agents-General for the colonies had gone off to a conference in Budapest and were not available.[94] So he returned to Scotland. But he was back in London on 6 August as part of a delegation which met Joseph Chamberlain and presented him with the Congress resolution. The meeting does not appear to have been a success since Chamberlain went no further than to suggest that, if they could tell him of any codifying measures already enacted in the United Kingdom which had not 'been adopted by the Colonies, he might possibly see the means of advancing the views of the deputation'.[95] This was a very far cry from support for a grand scheme of imperial codification.

Worse was to follow. In July, just after the Empire Congress, a meeting of Scottish businessmen and lawyers had assembled under the aegis of the Edinburgh Merchant Company and had enthusiastically endorsed the cause of codification of commercial law.[96] A committee was set up to raise the matter with the Government and they duly did so, forwarding a memorial to the Scottish Secretary and asking for a meeting. A curt letter was sent in return and the committee had to write again asking if he would meet them. In December the Scottish Secretary wrote declining to meet them and indicating that the Government had no plans to take up the matter of codification in its legislation for the next session.[97]

So far as one can see, this rebuff really marked the end of active campaigning for codification of commercial law. By now it must have been plain even to the greatest enthusiast that there was no prospect of a British commercial code in the foreseeable future. So it was back to the small things. The Marine Insurance Bill[98] staggered uncertainly towards the statute book and company legislation was consolidated. But the great vision had gone. When the motion on commercial codification came up yet again at the next Empire Congress in 1900, Dove Wilson was not even there and the matter was treated almost perfunctorily.[99] By that time the

---

[94] See the remarks of C. M'Combie, representing the Aberdeen Chamber of Commerce, *Report of Conference* (Note 83 above), 18.

[95] *The Times*, 7 August 1896, 6.

[96] *Report of Conference* (Note 83 above). For a useful summary see 'Codification of Commercial Law', (1896) 4 *S.L.T.* (News) 66.

[97] 'The Proposed Codification of the Mercantile Law', (1897) 4 *S.L.T.* (News) 176 *et seq*.

[98] For the history of the bill from its introduction by Lord Herschell in 1894, see for instance M.D. Chalmers, *Marine Insurance Act 1906* (first edition, London, 1907), Introduction.

[99] *Official Report of the Fourth Congress of Chambers of Commerce of the Empire* (Note 59 above), 39–40. The resolution was moved by Lord Avebury.

South African War meant that rather graver issues dominated the imperial agenda. A little later the radical programme of Mr. Asquith did not leave businessmen or parliamentarians much time to bother about the somewhat intangible benefits of a commercial code. The moment had passed.

In looking back at the story a number of observations occur.

First, it was businessmen who were most prominent in advocating a commercial code. But in the discussions Scottish businessmen and lawyers appear to have taken a very active role. The explanation of this phenomenon is, I believe, to be found in the relative indifference of English lawyers in particular. English lawyers work within a large system and have often been scarcely aware of the existence of any other. They will therefore not even perceive that differences exist between the Scots law and the English law on a particular topic. By contrast Scottish lawyers can never ignore English law and so they tend to see the differences. At some periods these differences may be cherished, but in the nineteenth century there was certainly a large body of opinion which thought of them as simply inconvenient. It would therefore be natural if Scottish businessmen and lawyers were particularly interested in any moves to eliminate them. The interest in assimilation in turn led to an interest in codification as a means of bringing it about. Scottish lawyers and businessmen therefore had this additional and arguably more practical reason for supporting codification of commercial law.[100]

It is indeed worth asking whether the campaign for assimilation and codification was designed to tackle a real problem which confronted businessmen of the time. It will be recalled that the Royal Commission on Mercantile Law could find few examples of actual problems. None the less the sustained active campaigning by chambers of commerce and others suggests that businessmen thought at least that the differences in the laws of England and Scotland caused actual difficulties. My impression is that with bills of exchange there may well have been actual problems. Partnership disputes on the other hand would not tend to cross the border, and so difficulties would be less likely to arise under that heading. So the incidence of real problems would vary from topic to topic.

Overall I incline to the view that proponents of codification probably exaggerated the difficulties which were experienced. After all, one of their own main arguments in favour of assimilation was exactly that, because commercial law was based on the practice of merchants, it really varied little between England and Scotland and so complete assimilation was

---

[100] As has often been observed, the desire to assimilate is a common driving force for codification. Cf. e.g. H. Coing, *Europäisches Privatrecht* Vol. 2, 19 *et seq.* and Ilbert, *Legislative Methods*, 160–2.

a relatively small step to take. In the end, as Maitland noticed, the differences between England and Scotland were not great enough 'to bring home to us in an acute form those evils which have plagued our neighbours.'[101] Because the evils were not acute, politicians did not give a high priority to formal assimilation in a common code and so it did not come to pass.

Secondly, I believe that events on the Continent played a very important role in shaping the views of the Scottish lawyers who were active supporters of codification. Much ink has been spilled in describing how in the eighteenth-century young men who wished to become Scottish advocates would go to the Netherlands to study and how, with the Napoleonic Wars, this came to an end, leaving Scots law cut off and ripe for domination by English influences.[102] Such a picture is rather over-simplified. What it overlooks is that, when Europe emerged from the Napoleonic Wars, young Scotsmen wishing to study law soon saw that German universities were in the forefront of legal scholarship.[103] So they wisely set off to learn their Roman law in places like Göttingen and Heidelberg.

The story is too long to tell here, but it is enough to say that during the nineteenth century we find a flow of intrants to the Faculty of Advocates who have had some of their education, usually probably just a semester, at a German university. This is conspicuously the case with many of those who supported codification. For instance, Professor Muirhead, who addressed the Edinburgh Merchant Company in 1864, had been to Heidelberg.[104] Similarly all three of the advocates who gave lectures to the same body in 1893 had studied in Germany: Aeneas Mackay and Richard Vary Campbell

---

[101] F.W. Maitland, 'The Making of the German Civil Code', The *Collected Papers of Frederic William Maitland* Volume 3 (edited by H.A.L. Fisher, Cambridge, 1911), 474, 477.

[102] E.g. T.B. Smith, 'Scots Law and Roman-Dutch Law: A Shared Tradition', *Studies Critical and Comparative* (Edinburgh and New York, 1962), 51–6.

[103] Cf. e.g. James Reddie, *Inquiries in the Science of Law* (second edition, London, 1847), vi. Incidentally, it was through his good offices that Leone Levi was introduced to Professor John More who took a leading role in advocating codification and who gained access for Levi to the Advocates Library. Cf. Levi, *The Story of my Life*, 39. His son John Reddie obtained the degree of doctor of laws at Göttingen where he matriculated on 1 October 1823: G. von Selle, *Die Matrikel der Georg-August-Universität zu Göttingen 1734–1837* (Hildesheim and Leipzig, 1937), 701 No. 30401.

[104] James Muirhead matriculated on 13 May 1854 and studied in the Faculty of Law. See G. Toepke, P. Hintzelmann, *Die Matrikel der Universität Heidelberg* Vol. 6 1846–1870 (Heidelberg, 1907), 225 No. 199. At this period Heidelberg under von Vangerow was particularly popular for the study of Roman Law. Cf. P. Classen, E. Wolgast, *Kleine Geschichte der Universität Heidelberg* (Berlin, Heidelberg and New York, 1983), 49 and the article on K.A. von Vangerow, *Allgemeine Deutsche Biographie* Vol. 39 (Leipzig, 1895), 479 especially at 481 (E. Landsberg).

at Heidelberg,[105] Goudy at Königsberg.[106] Dove Wilson was at Berlin in his youth and, when he was about to become a professor at Aberdeen in 1891, he prepared by going off to Leipzig.[107] This meant that these men were familiar with developments in Germany and indeed had sometimes been there when the German codes were under discussion. It is not surprising therefore that when they looked to the Continent they drew the lesson that there was a strong tide running in favour of assimilating what had formerly been divergent systems of law. After unification in 1871 Germany provided the best example, culminating in the Civil Code which was enacted just a fortnight after Dove Wilson spoke to the Empire Congress in 1896.[108] The lesson for Britain must have seemed clear: we too should move towards assimilating our systems and to do that we needed to have a code. The Germans had started with commercial law and we should do so too. So, paradoxically perhaps, those Scots lawyers who had studied abroad and been exposed to Civil Law influences became the most convinced of the need for English and Scots law to be united in a code based on the Common Law.

Finally it is legitimate to wonder just how popular codification really was among Scottish lawyers. Some of the main supporters seem to have been advocates who were not really in active practice: Dove Wilson was a judge, Goudy a professor. But others are not so easily dismissed: Aeneas Mackay combined literature with actual practice, while Richard Vary Campbell was very definitely among the leading practitioners at the Scottish bar at the time of his sudden death. So it would perhaps be too simple to classify the supporters of codification as practitioners in name only.

Yet one cannot avoid the suspicion that, when the Faculty of Advocates meeting came out against the Sale of Goods Bill in 1893, this was the voice of the ordinary members of Faculty that had never spoken yet.[109] Certainly

---

[105] Aeneas Mackay matriculated on 28 September 1862 and Richard Vary Campbell on 25 April 1863. Both studied in the Faculty of Law. See Toepke, Hintzelmann, *Die Matrikel der Universität Heidelberg* Vol. 6, 453 No. 251 and 465, No. 171 respectively.

[106] Cf. 'Professor Henry Goudy', (1893) 1 *S.L.T.* 113. The author remarks that Goudy 'has never lost the affection for the Fatherland, cherished by most of those who have known the romance of its student-life, spite of all the beer and tobacco.' The article referred to in Note 39 above is plainly the first fruit of Goudy's stay in Germany.

[107] Windscheid and Sohm attracted him to Leipzig: (1908) 15 *S.L.T.* 150, 151 (J.M. Irvine).

[108] John, *Politics and the Law in Late Nineteenth-Century Germany*, Chapter 7. In his *Rektoratsrede* delivered in the same year Lenel sounded a timely warning against exaggerated expectations of a flowering of German legal science and practice as a result of the new code: O. Lenel, *Das Bürgerliche Gesetzbuch und das Studium des Römischen Rechts Rektoratsrede*. Das Stiftungsfest der Kaiser Wilhelms-Universität Strassburg (Strasbourg, 1896), 15, 35–6; reprinted in O. Lenel, *Gesammelte Schriften* (edited by O. Behrends and F. D'Ipolito) Vol. 2 (Naples, 1990), 351, 371–2.

[109] Yet some at least, like Goudy and R.V. Campbell, were opposed to the particular Sale of Goods Bill rather than to the principle of codification.

Dove Wilson thought that, at best, proponents of codification could count on the acquiescence, rather than the active support, of practising lawyers. He always claimed that businessmen rather than lawyers had most to gain from codification and so they should do the most to promote it.[110] His lack of faith in the majority of legal practitioners was probably well founded.

However that may be, the efforts to introduce a commercial code failed. I cannot say that I am sorry, for I have never been convinced of the advantages of codification—least of all perhaps now when we have so many excellent textbooks and when Community Law is creeping into every nook and cranny even of our statute law. But though the idea of codification has been rather out of fashion for the past decade or so, it is once more stirring. Two years ago the Law Commission produced a large Criminal Code for England and Wales.[111] Having looked back at the events of last century, I shall watch with interest, when this new code eventually embarks on its voyage towards the statute book, to see how it fares in negotiating[112] those parliamentary rocks on which all the great vessels of codification have foundered in the past.

*Note.* I am grateful to the following bodies for permission to consult and use their records and for assistance in doing so: the Faculty of Advocates, the Society of Solicitors in the Supreme Courts, the Royal Faculty of Procurators, Glasgow, the Edinburgh Merchant Company, the Aberdeen Chamber of Commerce and the Aberdeen District Council Archives, and the Glasgow Chamber of Commerce. I am also grateful to the Hon. Lord Davidson for reading and commenting on an earlier draft of the lecture.

[110] (1884) 28 *Journal of Jurisprudence* 337, 348; (1896) 8 *Juridical Review* 329, 344–5.
[111] The Law Commission, *A Criminal Code for England and Wales* (Law Com. No. 177, 1989).
[112] Cf. *op. cit.*, Vol. 1, paras. 2.26 and 3.45–3.48. See the remarks of Lord Wilberforce seeking a new channel for such legislation: House of Lords, 6 November 1991, Hansard Vol. 532, coll. 274–5.

*Proceedings of the British Academy*, **80**, 171–199

PHILOSOPHICAL LECTURE

# Two Types of Naturalism

T. R. BALDWIN
*University of Cambridge*

A PROMINENT THEME of current philosophy is that of the 'naturalisation' of philosophy. Daniel Dennett has written that 'One of the happiest trends in philosophy in the last twenty years has been its Naturalisation'.[1] But anyone with even a slight acquaintance with the history of philosophy will know that, by itself, the invocation of 'Nature' is highly indeterminate. The situation is similar to that which is all too familiar from disputes about 'realism', and we may well be inclined to apply to the term 'natural' Austin's thesis concerning the term 'real', namely that 'it is the *negative* use that wears the trousers'.[2] Admittedly, it is equally indeterminate what is to count as 'unnatural' if we consider the matter just by itself; but the content of claims about what is 'natural' or not is given through a specification of the natural/unnatural distinction, and this is in fact often achieved by a specification of the negative term as, say, the *conventional,* the *social,* or even the *perverted*. Hume saw this clearly when, in his *Treatise of Human Nature* he wrote that 'when I deny justice to be a natural virtue, I make use of the word *natural*, only as oppos'd to *artificial*. In another sense of the word; as no principle of the human mind is more natural than a sense of virtue; so no virtue is more natural than justice . . . Tho' the rules of justice be *artificial*, they are not *arbitrary*.'[3]

---

Read 29 November 1991. © The British Academy 1993.

[1] Foreword to R. Millikan *Language, Thought, and Other Biological Categories* (MIT Press, London: 1984) p.ix. Other manifestations of the same trend include Sir. P. F. Strawson *Skepticism and Naturalism: Some Varieties* (Methuen, London: 1985), and S. Hurley *Natural Reasons* (Oxford University Press, Oxford: 1989).

[2] J.L. Austin *Sense and Sensibilia* (Clarendon, Oxford: 1962) p. 70.

[3] D. Hume *Treatise of Human Nature* ed. Selby-Bigge (Clarendon, Oxford: 1888) p. 484.

I shall propose that there are two different types of naturalism at work in current philosophy—what I shall call *metaphysical* and *epistemic* naturalism; they are not, I think, in conflict, and my chief aim is to discuss how they fit together. There may well be further interesting types of naturalism in philosophy—for example, in ethics (as in Hume's thesis that justice is not a natural virtue); but I shall not pursue such questions here. Central to the type of naturalism Dennett has in mind when he celebrates the 'naturalisation' of philosophy is the thought that 'since we human beings are a part of nature—supremely complicated but unpriveleged portions of the biosphere—philosophical accounts of our minds, our knowledge, our language must in the end be continuous with, and harmonious with, the natural sciences'.[4] Thus understood, naturalistic explanations contrast not only with 'supernatural' ones, such as those provided by traditional theology, but also with some 'Platonist' explanations, such as Frege's thesis that at a fundamental level we have cognitive access to abstract senses. For, at least as presented by Frege, such this hypothesis is not 'continuous with' those advanced by the natural sciences.[5] But it remains to be clarified just what this amounts to, and indeed, what the 'natural' sciences are.

Dennett's reference to philosophy's continuity with the natural sciences suggests a family tree of explanations: physics occupies the fundamental level because it deals with the most general properties of things; then other sciences offer higher level explanations which, because they invoke properties, such as environmental and historical properties, that do not occur at lower levels of explanation, are not necessarily reducible to them (and thus to physics), but which are nonetheless such that the processes involved are 'harmonious with' those described by lower level sciences. What, though, is this harmony? One interpretation will be just consistency. This may seem too weak—Cartesian psychology was supposed to be consistent with Cartesian physics. But the consistency requirement becomes more demanding if it is also assumed that processes explained by higher level sciences always involve changes to parts which can be described in terms appropriate to lower level sciences, and that under these latter descriptions, the changes must be explicable in terms of the lower level

---

[4] Dennett (1984) op. cit. p. ix

[5] Frege writes in his Logic manuscript of 1897 that grasping a thought such as Newton's law of gravitation 'is a process which takes place on the very confines of the mental and which for that reason cannot be completely understood from a purely psychological standpoint. For in grasping the law something comes into view whose nature is no longer mental in the proper sense, namely the thought; and this process is perhaps the most mysterious of all'—*Posthumous Writings* (Oxford, Blackwell 1979) ed. H. Hermes et al., translated by P. Long & R. White, p. 145.

sciences alone. Descartes' pineal gland would not satisfy this requirement. Yet this assumption is itself plausibly justified by the hypothesis that lower level processes should provide a 'mechanism' whereby higher level changes are accomplished in a given context, and this hypothesis is itself a better interpretation of the 'harmony' requirement. Although this hypothesis implies that all fundamental forces are physical, it is not a reductive position, since there can be an indefinite variety of mechanisms, not accommodated under a single bridge law, for accomplishing a single type of higher level change; furthermore higher order properties retain an autonomous causal role in setting up the contexts for changes which are accomplished by lower order mechanisms. I shall therefore adopt this account of the harmony requirement as a specification of 'naturalisation' in the sense suggested by Dennett. Since the underlying hypothesis here is metaphysical—it postulates a hierarchy of causal processes—I regard this position as a form of *metaphysical naturalism*.

On this account a naturalised philosophy of mind should abjure explanations of our abilities that are detached from the great chain of physical being; to be thus detached is to be, in this sense, unnatural. So a philosophy of language which postulates that we have the capacity to grasp abstract Fregean senses is suspect since such a capacity seems detached from any psychology that is harmonious with the other natural sciences. This case indicates the prime reason for accepting this kind of naturalisation—namely that the postulation of detached abilities threatens the unity of the self. Such a postulate seems bound to point in a dualist direction, whereby those abilities that are detached from our natural embodiment are held to be exercised by a non-physical subject—reason, perhaps, or a radically free will; and the *aporiai* of such dualist positions are too well known to need elaboration here. So it is not a crass 'scientistic' prejudice that motivates this kind of naturalisation of philosophy; it is instead the worthy motive of attaining a unified self-understanding that respects the fact of our existence as animals.

# I

Quine made the idea of a naturalisation of philosophy famous with his paper 'Epistemology Naturalised'.[6] But where Quine's hostility to the reality of mental content led him to maintain that naturalised epistemology can only be a branch of behaviourist psychology, other philosophers have sought

---

[6] W.V. Quine 'Epistemology Naturalized' in *Ontological Relativity and Other Essays* (Columbia University Press, London: 1969).

to provide an understanding of knowledge within a naturalistic context which is more receptive to mental states with content. Such an approach leads readily to the adoption of an *externalist* conception of knowledge, according to which what makes a true belief a case of knowledge is (to quote Armstrong) 'some natural relation which holds between the belief-state . . . and the situation which makes the belief true'.[7] This is rather vague, but Armstrong remarks that reliabilist theories are externalist in his sense, and that is enough to go on in the present context: for in their explanations of knowledge these theories rely on the existence of underlying causal processes of perception and inference to expedite the acquisition of beliefs.[8] By contrast, on the alternative *internalist* conception, according to which true beliefs are only knowledge where the subject recognises that she has evidence which justifies them, the notion of justification is not integrated into a broader understanding of the subject's psychology; so the resulting conception of knowledge is of a state whose explanation is detached from naturalistic explanations. As a result this conception is liable to give rise to accounts of knowledge which are either dogmatic, where some fundamental propositions are held to be inherently self-evident, or sceptical, if the claims to self-evidence are weakened.

Externalist accounts avoid this dilemma by permitting causal considerations to enter into the justification of claims to knowledge. Yet it remains unclear just what the implications of the adoption of an externalist conception are for traditional sceptical arguments. Where knowledge is regarded as (in Armstrong's phrase) 'a certain natural relation holding between the believer and the world', it looks as though sceptical arguments must be directed to raising doubts whether this relation really obtains. For example, perhaps the subject is hallucinating and her perceptual beliefs (even if correct) do not stand in the appropriate causal relation to the world. Yet it is not at first clear in what context a doubt of this kind is supposed to be being raised. Concerning any, or almost any, judgments a doubt can be raised: one *can* doubt whether snow is really white—but unless one has in mind a thesis about secondary qualities a doubt of this kind seems perverse, or neurotic, in the face

---

[7] D.M. Armstrong *Belief, Truth, and Knowledge* (Cambridge University Press, Cambridge: 1973) p. 157.

[8] As Edward Craig has recently shown, the notorious Gettier problem continues to plague many proposals of this kind—cf. *Knowledge and the State of Nature* (Clarendon, Oxford: 1990) section IX. But I remain hopeful that something can still be salvaged here—cf. the position developed by C. Peacocke in *Thoughts* (Blackwell, Oxford: 1986) ch. 9. The 'Gettier problem' comes from E. Gettier 'Is Justified True Belief Knowledge?' *Analysis* 23 (1963) pp. 121–3.

of massive evidence to the contrary. Similarly, one can doubt whether a subject stands in the appropriate relation to the world, e.g. whether her beliefs have been caused in the right way, or whether they have been acquired by reliable methods, with no false lemmas etc.; but in the face of evidence that she does stand in the right relation, doubt seems no more in place in this context than any other. If, as the externalist maintains, knowledge is just a natural relationship between between subject and world, then doubts concerning it would seem to have just as much, or as little, contextual propriety as doubts concerning any other natural state of affairs.

Thus at first sight it appears that an externalist conception provides little space for traditional sceptical arguments. This is not, I think, an altogether welcome result. For although we do not want to end up committed to a scepticism we cannot live, a satisfactory account of knowledge should not imply that sceptical doubts are just perverse or neurotic. However, there is a response available to the externalist at this point. He may observe that although any particular case of knowledge is just constituted by a natural relation between believer and world, the significance of describing that relation as a case of *knowledge* is that those who recognise it as such treat the subject as an *authority* on the matter; they regard themselves as *entitled* to act as if her opinions are true.[9] This normative aspect of the concept of knowledge is of course enshrined in the traditional account of it as true *justified* belief, and this normativity is quite compatible with naturalism. The externalist just takes the justification, where it exists, to be grounded in the reliability of the processes by which the relevant beliefs are formed.

The normativity of the concept of knowledge implies that there is a contextual element to the application of the concept: the standard of reliability we employ in one set of circumstances may not be acceptable in another: the standards appropriate to the public bar are not those appropriate to the court of law. As a result one can legitimately call into question a claim to knowledge on the grounds that the wrong standards are being applied, and this provides a way in which the externalist can seek to accommodate sceptical arguments. Hence even for the externalist there will be a difference between doubts about ordinary natural states of affairs and doubts about claims to knowledge; it is because knowledge is a normative concept that one can sensibly press doubts about knowledge in the face of evidence to the contrary in a way in which similar doubts about whether snow is white seem just just perverse.

---

[9] This aspect of the concept of knowledge is central to Craig's recent 'practical explication' of the concept (op. cit.).

This conclusion represents the philosophical sceptic as someone who, having raised the standards for knowledge to that ideal level which excludes the possibility of error, concludes that human beings have little, if any, knowledge at all. But it remains unclear what purpose is served by raising the standards for knowledge in this way, what context is being assumed which renders legitimate this kind of move. There are, certainly, contexts within which we rightly demand high standards for knowledge—criminal trials, for example. But the standards in these cases are high because we recognise that much depends on judgments reached in the light of the evidence presented. The attempt to represent philosophical scepticism as the result of pressing the standards for knowledge still higher, to the limit, would, therefore, seem to require that yet more serious implications should be attached to the results of philosophical deliberations concerning the limits of human knowledge. Yet, as we all know, the future of the human race, or the universe, does not hinge on the outcome of such deliberations. Hence, from this perspective, although philosophical scepticism is intelligible, it appears eccentric; it employs an absolute context for raising questions about human knowledge which has no place within the concerns of human life.

At this point externalists may be losing patience: if the external-ist conception does not provide a context within which philosophical scepticism touches on serious concerns, then, it will be said,[10] so much the worse for the traditional philosophical sceptic. He can still have the role of pointing out the snares inherent in internalist approaches to knowledge; but once externalism itself has been embraced, he can be dismissed from the company of serious philosophers. Yet this is, I think, too quick. A distinctive feature of traditional philosophical scepticism is that, in the first instance, it concerns itself with doubts concerning first-person claims to knowledge. The significance of this is that where a doubt is raised concerning a third-person claim to knowledge, e.g. whether Moore knows that there is a hand before him, and we apply to this claim an externalist account of knowledge, the doubt is typically focused on the issue as to whether Moore's belief stands in the appropriate causal relation to the situation in question—the presence of his hand before him. There is no need here to doubt that things are as Moore thinks them to be, that there is a hand in front of him. But if I doubt whether I know that there is a hand before me, my doubt concerns not only whether I am appropriately related to the presence of a hand before me; it brings with it a doubt

---

[10] cf. G. Stine 'Skepticism and Relevant Alternatives' *Philosophical Studies* 29 (1976) p.254; A. Goldman *Epistemology and Cognition* (Harvard University Press, Cambridge Mass.; 1986) ch.2.

about the presence of a hand before me. If I have reason to doubt the reliability of my belief, then I have reason to doubt its truth. Thus if I have reason to doubt whether I know that there is an external world, I have reason to doubt that there is an external world, and I cannot appeal to my convictions about the external world and my place within it in order to set aside my initial doubt without apparently begging the question. For my doubt concerns these beliefs as well as my belief that I have knowledge of the external world. So once a first-person perspective is adopted, it seems that the adoption of an externalist conception of knowledge does not by itself provide an immediate response to sceptical doubts. Furthermore, although the proponents of sceptical arguments press the implications of their arguments with greater rigour than we employ in ordinary life, once they adopt the first-person strategy they need not invoke any specially demanding standards concerning the vindication of claims to knowledge; their arguments do not presuppose the demand for absolute certainty which, I suggested, renders scepticism intelligible, but without providing any apparent motivation for it.

But why should one doubt whether one knows in the first place? Our own experience of our own fallibility certainly raises some such doubts in ordinary life. We typically banish them by considerations of coherence—by introducing other beliefs, beliefs both about the world and about our place within it, by reference to which we are able to exhibit the doubt as unreasonable. As I have indicated, if a doubt is sufficiently general, this procedure becomes questionable; for the beliefs by reference to which we may seek to banish it may themselves be called into question by the doubt. But what if I do not, in fact, have any such general doubts? Does the applicability of sceptical arguments depend upon a contingent proneness to such doubts? In order to provide us with reasons for general doubts the proponents of sceptical arguments typically describe possibilities which imply that our beliefs of some general kind, e.g. perceptual beliefs, do not stand in the right relationship to the world. But even as we recognise that it is not easy to find reasons for dismissing these possibilities, we also feel that they are themselves incredible (e.g. that our consciousness is just that of a brain in a vat). So it still needs to be explained why we should take these possibilities seriously, why they do not just give rise to intriguing puzzles with which we can amuse ourselves when we have nothing more serious to attend to.

I think the answer to this comes from the broader philosophical enterprise of attaining a reflective understanding of our place within the world (to which a commitment to the naturalisation of philosophy itself belongs). Once the normativity of the concept of knowledge is recognised, this enterprise will be seen to include the task of legitimating to oneself the possession of the kinds of knowledge one takes ourselves to possess; and once embarked upon this task the epistemologist can no more dismiss reasons for doubt fuelled by sceptical possibilities than can a political philosopher dismiss anarchist hypotheses without argument. In both cases the intellectual project requires one to extend serious consideration to relevant hypotheses whatever one's antecedent sympathies. An externalist who refuses to take sceptical arguments seriously because he finds sceptical possibilities incredible is a dogmatist who has turned his back on reason in order to protect his common sense faith.

Thus although the externalist is quite right to insist that his conception of knowledge implies that claims to knowledge need not run the gauntlet of sceptical argument, the broader context of reflective epistemological inquiry necessitates attention to these arguments even when it is conducted with an externalist conception of knowledge.[11] So there remains here a residue of Descartes' insistence upon the distinctively *theoretical* nature of philosophical scepticism even after one has abandoned his goal of finding absolutely certain foundations for knowledge.[12] The externalist might respond that this just confirms his suspicion that there is a lingering 'internalist' element within the philosophical project of attaining a reflective and critically coherent self-understanding that needs to be extirpated. But I think we can, and should, resist the demand that this reflective dimension in philosophical understanding should be abandoned. Such a demand is not implied by Dennett's naturalisation of philosophy; on the contrary, that is precisely the attempt to gain a reflective understanding of the way in which we ourselves, including our own thoughts and language, fit into the rest of nature.

It may seem that this adoption of a first-person epistemological perspective has produced a situation which is equivalent to the adoption of an internalist conception of knowledge. This is, however, not the case: since the internalist makes it a condition for the truth of a claim to knowledge that one should be able to justify to oneself what one claims to know, unless he can eliminate the sceptical possibilities which undermine such a claim, reflecting on his situation, he should judge that he does not know. The externalist, by contrast, does not make it a condition of the truth of claims to knowledge that sceptical doubts be silenced; for him, the truth of such a claim depends only on whether one's belief has been

[11] Here, therefore, I disagree with Marie McGinn who argues in chapter one of *Sense and Scepticism* (Blackwell, Oxford: 1989) that the significance of sceptical arguments requires nothing more than assumptions inherent in our ordinary conception of knowledge. McGinn's argument incorporates an internalist conception of knowledge.

[12] cf. *The Philosophical Writings of Descartes* vol.II transl. J. Cottingham, R. Stoothof, & D. Murdoch (Cambridge University Press, Cambridge: 1984) p.243.

formed by an appropriately reliable method. Sceptical argument gets its purchase here only by suggesting reasons for believing that one's belief might after all not have been been formed by such a method. In this context it will suffice if one can demonstrate that these doubts are, in fact, unreasonable.

This shows that, in vindicating claims to knowledge, the externalist has an easier task than the internalist, and thus that the adoption of an externalist conception of knowledge is an essential element in an anti-sceptical strategy. But given the scope of sceptical hypotheses, establishing that sceptical doubts are unreasonable is not a straightforward matter. Because these hypotheses call into question all the obvious counter-evidence, it is not easy to understand what one can appeal to without joining the ranks of those who have begged the question against the sceptic. Let me illustrate this point by considering a currently popular approach to the problem of induction, well exemplified by Hugh Mellor's recent discussion of 'The Warrant of Induction'.[13] Mellor takes knowledge to be true belief that is warranted by the believer's situation and evidence; but he insists that the facts which thus warrant belief do not have to be known by the believer in order to function as such. Thus, in the case of inductive beliefs, such a belief is warranted where it is prompted by an inferential habit that is, in fact, reliable—i.e. such that the believer's evidence does in fact give a high chance of truth to the belief to which it gives rise. This is an externalist account of inductive knowledge, and I have no quarrel with it. My disagreement with Mellor concerns his treatment of inductive scepticism.

The inductive sceptic introduces the possibility that the future will be entirely unlike the past; this hypothesis implies that our present inferential habits are unreliable, and thus, on Mellor's account of inductive knowledge, that we have no such knowledge. As I have argued, even if we find it difficult to take this hypothesis seriously, when we reflect critically on our epistemological situation we cannot dismiss it out of hand; and yet, as Hume observed, it is not easy to find any reason for rejecting it which does not assume its falsehood. It is clearly useless in this context to rely on the fact (supposing it to be such) that the future will resemble the past and thus that my evidence does in fact give a high chance of truth to my beliefs about the future. What I require is a non-question-begging reason to believe this. A better strategy is to appeal to the memory that up to now past futures have resembled past pasts; but, unless one wants to hold out for the *a priori* reasonableness of inductive inferences, the merit of any

---

[13] cf. D.H. Mellor *Matters of Metaphysics* (Cambridge University Press, Cambridge: 1991) pp. 254–68.

inductive inference from this to the nature of future futures is called into doubt by the sceptical possibility itself.[14]

Mellor, of course, recognises these familiar dialectical twists. But he takes it that he can avoid the need to grapple with them by his externalist treatment of knowledge; for he implies that it is only those who think that, if we know something, we know that we know it, who are caught within these snares.[15] If the argument of the earlier part of this lecture is correct, this is a mistake. As I reflect on my current situation, the thought that I might after all have knowledge of the future is no comfort to me if I can find no way to set aside my current reasons for doubt whether I have it. So although we may allow that Mellor's external warrants suffice for inductive knowledge, his appeal to them is either question-begging or fails to take account of the context within which the sceptic's argument is advanced.

## II

How, then, should one respond to sceptical arguments? I favour the Humean response, that 'Nature, by an absolute and uncontroulable necessity has determin'd us to judge as well as to breathe and feel'.[16] Hume's thesis that many of our beliefs are, in the first instance, spontaneous provides, I suggest, the first step in a response to the kind of scepticism I have been considering. The continuous, involuntary, gushing up within us of beliefs concerning the external world, the future, and so on, provides us with a way of breaking into the circle of argument which seemed to be closed off once the sceptical possibility was entertained. I can entertain the hypothesis that I might now be dreaming, and I can acknowledge that there is no way in which my experience alone enables me to eliminate this hypothesis; but the fact that I find myself, willy-nilly, believing that I am standing up and talking makes it impossible for me to sustain the sceptical hypothesis. My current perceptual beliefs provide me with ever new reasons for rejecting it, and although the sceptic within, my cognitive super-ego, may seek to dismiss these new beliefs as question-begging, the fact that they are spontaneous implies that, initially, I do not have the opportunity to do so. The initial spontaneity of belief, therefore, challenges sceptical doubt, by furnishing us with beliefs which give us reason to reject sceptical hypotheses without our acquisition of these beliefs being grounded in lines

---

[14] cf.C.Wright 'Facts and Certainty' *Proceedings of the British Academy* 71 (1985) p.447.

[15] Mellor op. cit. p. 266.

[16] Hume op. cit. p. 183

of argument that it has called into doubt.

We can, of course, modify our beliefs through reflection, and the initial spontaneity of a belief does not by itself establish the unreasonableness of sceptical doubt. Someone with paranoid beliefs about others will, it is to be hoped, find good reasons for rejecting them. It is at this point that considerations of coherence come into play, and the rejection of the conclusions of sceptical arguments requires a good degree of coherence. We need to be able to incorporate our spontaneous beliefs into a reflectively coherent conception of the world and of our cognitive relationship to it, albeit an inevitably incomplete and, in some degree, fragmented conception. In particular we need to be able to frame an understanding of the ways in which our own beliefs arise within the world, so that we can appreciate the causes of error on our own part and thus allow for our own fallibility instead of simply rejecting beliefs which do not cohere in a question-begging way. Nonetheless considerations of critical coherence are not by themselves sufficient to refute scepticism: if, in the light of a sceptical hypothesis, one were able to suspend judgment on all the matters concerning which the sceptical hypothesis gives one reasons for doubt, there need be no incoherence in one's resulting cognitive situation. Incoherence only enters when one finds that, however much one attempts to suspend judgment, one cannot prevent the arrival upon one's cognitive scene of fresh beliefs which conflict with the sceptical hypothesis.

This Humean strategy for responding to sceptical argument is by now familiar. In fact because of his commitment to the theory of ideas Hume remained a sceptic of sorts: 'if we are philosophers', he writes, 'it ought only to be upon sceptical principles'.[17] Thus the position I am proposing is closer to that of Hume's great critic Thomas Reid, who grasped the implications of Hume's position and presented a naturalised epistemology freed from Hume's commitment to the theory of ideas. Our natural *common sense* is, for Reid, the core of such a naturalised epistemology; he expressed its role in the following terms:

> Such original and natural judgments are therefore a part of that furniture which nature hath given to the human understanding . . . They serve to direct us in the common affairs of life, where our reasoning faculty would leave us in the dark. They are a part of our constitution, and all the discoveries of our reason are grounded upon them. They make up what is called *the common sense of mankind;*[18]

---

[17] Hume op. cit. p. 270

[18] *An Inquiry into the Human Mind* ed. T. Duggan (Chicago University Press, Chicago: 1970) p.268. It is arguable that Reid modifies his conception of common sense in his later *Essays on the Intellectual Powers*.

The concept of nature is explicit in both Hume's and Reid's formulation of this position, and it is common to describe it as a form of 'naturalism'. But is it just a further instance of the naturalisation of philosophy from which I started? Certainly, I think, it can be fitted in alongside the thesis of metaphysical naturalism. For it is important to the Humean position that it should include an account of beliefs and their content which is continuous with its account of the rest of the world. Were one to take the view that belief is a phenomenon quite detached from the rest of our animal nature it would no longer be clear how to fit the appraisal of one's own beliefs into the broader understanding of the natural world with which our beliefs furnish us. Thus the coherence condition of the Humean position suggests a commitment to a naturalised epistemology and, more generally, the theme of metaphysical naturalism; and I shall say more about this commitment below. Nonetheless the position is not just an instance of this theme. Instead it manifests a different type of naturalism, whose focus is not metaphysical, but epistemological: its primary concern is not with our continuity with the great chain of physical being but with the spontaneous availability to us of common sense beliefs which conflict with sceptical possibilities. Thus the sense of 'natural' in the description of the Humean position as a form of naturalism has the connotation of unreflective spontaneity; in this sense beliefs are unnatural where they are the outcome of reflective reasoning.

I shall mark this distinction by describing this second type of naturalism as *epistemic naturalism*. The existence of two such types, or varieties, of naturalism was proposed some years ago by Strawson.[19] Strawson, however, presented the situation as one in which, as theorists, we face a choice between a liberal accommodating naturalism whose perspective is essentially epistemological and a hard reductive naturalism whose perspective is essentially scientific and metaphysical. When the matter is put that way we are bound to favour the first alternative; but the protagonist of metaphysical naturalism will, I think, rightly protest that his position is not necessarily reductive, and thus that his variety of naturalism has not been accommodated within Strawson's categories. And the important point here is that there need be, and should be, no conflict between metaphysical and epistemic naturalism. I have been arguing, in effect, that the metaphysical naturalist needs epistemic naturalism in order to handle sceptical arguments;[20] and metaphysical naturalism equally

[19] Strawson op.cit. pp.1–2, 38–41.
[20] Perhaps this puts the point too strongly. I have only argued that metaphysical naturalism needs some further resource to handle sceptical arguments, and that epistemic naturalism suffices to meet this need. But there are other familiar strategies for handling sceptical arguments, e.g. transcendental arguments. Yet it may be doubted whether these are available to a metaphysical naturalist.

provides a way in which the epistemic naturalist can achieve a reflectively coherent understanding of his own epistemological situation.[21]

This latter thesis needs further development, and I should like to do this by looking briefly at the position Wittgenstein advances in *On Certainty*.[22] The broad similarities between some features of Wittgenstein's position and the Humean position I have called epistemic naturalism will be familiar.[23]But before myself discussing these I want to bring out a further feature of the epistemic naturalist's response to sceptical arguments. His reliance on spontaneous common sense beliefs concerning particular matters of fact implies that he offers no reasons independent of common sense belief for belief in the general conditions (concerning the reliability of the senses, the uniformity of nature and so on) whose obtaining would be required by his method of acquiring common sense beliefs were he to attempt to justify these beliefs by a process of non-circular reasoning from independent evidence. Thus there is a sense in which, according to the epistemic naturalist, these general convictions should strike us, when we reflect on ourselves, as ungrounded. For the only reasons we can offer for them are particular beliefs our acceptance of which would depend upon them were we to acquire these particular beliefs by a process of reasoning from evidence that does not include beliefs of the same type. So the best we can do is to say that the truth of these general convictions, which are not spontaneous, is implicated in the truth of particular beliefs which, in the first instance, we accept for no reason.

It is easy to see the similarity between this account and that which Wittgenstein offers of the status of 'Moorean propositions':[24]

> 136. When Moore says he *knows* such and such, he is really enumerating a lot of empirical propositions which we affirm without special testing; propositions, that is, which have a peculiar logical role in the system of our empirical propositions.

According to Wittgenstein these propositions are not a priori principles from which we reason. Instead they are implicit in our ways of forming particular beliefs, and our commitment to them derives from our attachment to the general picture of the world that we thereby form, an attachment

---

[21] Although Quine has, I think, much too restricted a conception of the naturalisation of epistemology, he gets this point right: 'There is thus reciprocal containment, though containment in different senses: epistemology in natural science and natural science in epistemology' op.cit. p.83.

[22] L.Wittgenstein *On Certainty* transl. G.E.M. Anscombe & G.H. von Wright (Blackwell, Oxford: 1969).

[23] Strawson op.cit. pp.14–20

[24] These correspond roughly to the truisms Moore set out in his 'Defence of Common Sense', which is reprinted in his *Philosophical Papers* (Allen & Unwin, London: 1959). Moore himself remarked on the 'strange' epistemological status of these truisms (p.44).

grounded in the way in which we lead our lives, in what we do (cf. section 204). One only needs to introduce Wittgenstein's own pragmatist account of belief (cf. sections 422,427) to connect his stress on the role of action to the epistemic naturalist's focus on that of our natural common sense beliefs.

The issue I want now to focus upon is that of the metaphysical status of these Moorean propositions, whose peculiar epistemological status has already been agreed. If the epistemic naturalist adopts the perspective of metaphysical naturalism he can accommodate this latter status by treating their truth as intrinsic to our methods of inquiry, so that there is no substantive question of our 'tracking the truth' with regard to them by means of these methods of inquiry. There is, however, nothing here to imply that these general propositions do not just state contingent general matters of fact of the same kind as other general empirical propositions. This result conflicts with the tenor of some of Wittgenstein's remarks about them. For he sometimes describes them as 'rules' (e.g. section 319), and raises doubts about the propriety of speaking of their 'agreement with reality' (e.g. section 199, 215). These remarks can be construed simply as expressions of the epistemological status of these propositions; but I do not want to argue the interpretation of the text. For Crispin Wright has unequivocally advanced the position Wittgenstein's remarks sometimes suggest—that once these propositions are accorded a special epistemological status, then they must also be denied the status of stating facts.[25]

Before discussing Wright's argument for this thesis, it is worth observing how problematic it is. How can the existence of the past (another Moorean proposition) not be a general fact? Surely such a fact is implied by lots of particular facts about the past—e.g. that the Battle of Hastings was fought in 1066—so can we not just run a simple Moore-type 'proof' of the existence of the past? Why, then, does Wright introduce his non-factualist thesis? He gives several reasons, but, in the present context, the crucial one is that he thinks that a plausible test for the factuality of a class of statements is whether 'appraisals of their acceptability can be legitimated within a satisfactory naturalistic epistemology'.[26] Wright argues that Moorean propositions fail this requirement because no naturalistic epistemology which legitimates our appraisals of them will be satisfactory to sceptics; by challenging our entitlement to confidence concerning the Moorean propositions, according to Wright, the sceptic undermines our entitlement to a naturalistic epistemology which represents us as having knowledge of the truth of these propositions. This does not seem to me persuasive. Certainly, in advance of the rejection of sceptical arguments by

[25] Wright (1985) op.cit. pp.455ff.
[26] Wright (1985) op.cit. p.455

reference to the epistemic naturalist position, there can be no satisfactory epistemology.[27] That was indeed my argument in the previous section. But once epistemic naturalism has been adopted, there is no reason why it should not enable a theorist, not only to repudiate sceptical arguments, but also to construct a naturalistic epistemology which shows why the epistemic naturalist position produces correct appraisals. Of course, acceptance of such a construction ultimately depends on the spontaneous common sense beliefs which the epistemic naturalist invokes; but the circle involved in legitimating the naturalist's favourable appraisal of such spontaneous beliefs is virtuous and not vicious. I conclude, therefore, that Wright does not give a good reason for supposing that Moorean propositions fail his test for factuality. Epistemic naturalism can be combined with metaphysical naturalism to defend the factuality of the Moorean propositions.

A different strand in Wittgenstein's remarks concerns the possibility of other forms of life, expressed by spontaneous beliefs which give rise to different Moorean propositions. A case which much concerns him is that of religious belief (e.g. sections 239, 336), and (whether or not this was Wittgenstein's own point of view) this can be considered from the point of view of an epistemic naturalist who is also an atheist. Such a person cannot deny that there are people with apparently spontaneous religious convictions, which give rise to Moorean propositions concerning the existence and attributes of a god. The atheist does not share these convictions, and therefore does not find himself committed to the same Moorean propositions. But the issue for him *qua* epistemic naturalist is whether the existence of these divergent natural cognitive dispositions puts pressure on the objectivity of the conception of knowledge that he is able to offer.

The epistemic naturalist's first line of defence must be to insist that his response to scepticism did not rely only upon the existence of natural cognitive dispositions; it also involved the possibility of attaining, with their help, a reflectively coherent understanding of their place within the world. Hence it is open to the atheist to maintain that the theist's cognitive dispositions, though genuine enough, cannot be accommodated into a coherent scheme, and for this reason do not pose a threat to the objectivity which he claims for his own, atheist, system. A theist will, of course, dispute this thesis; but what matters here is not who is right, but whether both sides should at least agree that they deny the other's claim. For the epistemic naturalist faces here an analogue of the traditional

---

[27] The terminology here is potentially confusing. Wright's 'naturalistic epistemology' is an epistemology viewed from the perspective of metaphysical naturalism. It is not the Humean epistemic naturalism.

objection to the coherence theory of truth,—the apparent possibility of incompatible systems of belief each of which is by itself coherent. If the epistemic naturalist really permits this, then it seems that he only picks us out of the sceptical frying-pan in order to cast us onto the relativist fire.

To deal with this objection I think the epistemic naturalist should reaffirm that the reflective coherence which he holds to be essential to the validation of natural cognitive dispositions includes a commitment to metaphysical naturalism.[28] For that commitment internalises the constraint that coherence cannot be attained in incompatible ways. One cannot hold both that one's own cognitive dispositions furnish one with a naturalistic understanding of oneself and the world which explains which dispositions are reliable methods for attaining beliefs about the world and, also, that other, conflicting, cognitive dispositions yield equally satisfactory, but conflicting, explanations of the reliability of human cognitive dispositions. For if there is a single phenomenon to be explained, in this case human cognitive powers, then, although there can be levels of explanation, the explanations must cohere as different descriptions of the same phenomenon. Thus, even though there is here no method for resolving all deep disagreements, a commitment to metaphysical naturalism brings with it an agreement that these are genuine disagreements.

This conclusion complements that which I made when discussing philosophical scepticism. In that context I argued that metaphysical naturalism by itself is inadequate to refute sceptical arguments, but that when supplemented by epistemic naturalism these arguments can be set aside. I have now argued that the relativist threat to epistemic naturalism should be answered by incorporating a commitment to metaphysical naturalism within cognitive naturalism. Thus although I insisted before on the distinction between these two types of naturalism, it turns out that they need each other.[29]

## III

I want now to apply this combination to a central issue of current philosophy of language and mind—the tension between, on the one hand, certain

---

[28] It may be felt that a commitment to metaphysical naturalism rules out the theist position. But as long as the metaphysical naturalist position is not assumed to be reductive I do not see why there cannot be a naturalised theology—along the lines of traditional conceptions of the 'immanence' of God.

[29] I should, however, acknowledge that I have not established here that each is both necessary and sufficient to solve the other's characteristic problem; in each case I have only argued for a sufficiency thesis. More work would be needed to establish the corresponding necessity thesis—cf. note 20.

supposed implications of Wittgenstein's rule-following arguments, and, on the other hand, the aspirations of those who wish to construct a naturalised philosophy of meaning. The tension will be familiar: the rule-following arguments have been taken, especially by Kripke, to show that there is no fact of the matter concerning what anyone means;[30] but a naturalised philosophy of meaning usually aims to identify the facts which constitute meaning. Reactions to this tension are varied: most naturalisers pass over Kripke's arguments in silence, though Dennett represents Kripke as an adherent of his own instrumentalist faith when he remarks that 'Kripke's ruminations on rule-following, which strike some philosophers as deep and disturbing challenges to their complacency, have always struck me as great labors wasted in trying to break down an unlocked door'.[31] On the other side, rule-followers have concluded that the approach to the understanding of language characteristic of traditional linguistic theory is seriously defective. Kripke, for example, maintained that Wittgenstein's argument implies that 'the *use* of the ideas of rules and of competence in linguistics needs serious reconsideration, even if these notions are not rendered "meaningless"'.[32]

This debate does not just concern the philosophy of language. Linguistic meaning is often taken to be internally linked to the contents of thought, especially beliefs and intentions. So if a naturalised philosophy of mind specifies natural facts which constitute the contents of beliefs and intentions, then there would seem to be material for an account of the fact of the matter as to what speakers mean.[33] The connection assumed here between linguistic meaning and mental content can be disputed. Philip Pettit, for example, has sought to insulate linguistic meaning from this kind of determination by proposing that although there are natural facts which constitute the possession of content by 'sub-personal' intentional states, including beliefs and desires, the fact that linguistic meaning involves deliberate rule-following ensures that it cannot be constituted by such sub-personal states.[34] Others, however, have argued in the opposite direction that the rule-following considerations can be applied directly to states such as belief to threaten naturalistic accounts of their content.[35]

---

[30] cf. S.Kripke *Wittgenstein on Rules and Private Language* (Blackwell, Oxford: 1982) ch.2.
[31] D.Dennett 'Evolution, Error, and Intentionality' in *The Intentional Stance* (MIT, London: 1987) p.294.
[32] Kripke op.cit. p.31. cf. C.Wright 'Wittgenstein's Rule-Following Considerations and the Central Project of Theoretical Linguistics' in *Reflections on Chomsky* ed.A. George (Blackwell, Oxford: 1989).
[33] cf. C.McGinn *Wittgenstein on Meaning* (Blackwell, Oxford: 1984) pp.144ff.
[34] P.Pettit 'The Reality of Rule-Following' *Mind* 99 (1990) pp.1–2.
[35] cf. P.Boghossian 'The Rule-Following Considerations' *Mind* 98 (1989) p.514. J.Sartorelli 'McGinn on concept scepticism and Kripke's sceptical argument' *Analysis* 51 (1991) pp.79–84.

Clearly, if this were right the rule-following argument would pose a serious threat to any naturalised philosophy of mind, and thus to metaphysical naturalism in the sense I have been considering.

What is the essential feature of the concept of meaning which is supposed to imply that it transcends any possible naturalistic theory? The answer, of course, is its supposed *normativity*.[36] It seems then that we have here a Humean 'is/ought' thesis—to the effect that naturalisers are guilty of another instance of the 'naturalistic fallacy' of thinking that one can derive a normative conclusion, in this case concerning meaning, from natural facts. But we should be wary of hasty judgments here; as we have already seen there is no incompatibility between a naturalised epistemology and the normativity of knowledge. To take matters further we need to understand better in what the normativity of meaning is supposed to consist. John McDowell has expressed this thesis in the following terms:

> We find it natural to think of meaning and understanding in, as it were, contractual terms. Our idea is that to learn the meaning of a word is to acquire an understanding that obliges us subsequently—if we have occasion to deploy the concept in question—to judge and speak in certain determinate ways, on pain of failure to obey the dictates of the meaning we have grasped;[37]

The idea here seems to be that in learning the meaning of a word we learn how we ought to speak; we learn under what conditions we ought, subsequently, to assent to, or dissent from, sentences containing the word and even assert such sentences ourselves. Clearly there are 'ought''s here; but are they, as Kant would put it, categorical or hypothetical? Surely they are only the latter. Learning the meaning of a word brings with it no categorical obligation to say anything at all; rather what we learn is what we ought to say if we want to express our desires, contribute to a conversation, impress the neighbours, and so on. Perhaps we can simplify here by saying that we learn what we ought to say if we want to speak the truth; but the imperative is still only hypothetical. The reason this matters is that hypothetical imperatives typically arise from the combination of a desire (broadly conceived) and some connection between the end desired and the current situation of the subject—e.g. if one wants to harvest one's broad beans in June, one ought to plant the seeds in March; and the fact that the conclusion is an imperative, an 'ought', does nothing to show that the connection is not a natural fact (though the connection can be conventional,

---

[36] cf. Kripke op. cit. p.37; Pettit op.cit. p.8.

[37] J.McDowell 'Wittgenstein on Following a Rule' *Synthese* 58 (1984) p.325. McDowell acknowledges that the 'contractual' simile comes from C.Wright *Wittgenstein on the Foundation of Mathematics* (Duckworth, London: 1980) p.19.

and in that sense not 'natural'). Hence, the fact that in learning the meaning of a word one becomes subject to a hypothetical imperative concerning how one should speak does not show that there is anything intrinsically normative, and thus not natural, about meanings. One can hold both that the concept of meaning characterises entirely natural (though perhaps also conventional) connections between language and the world, and that in learning the meaning of a word one learns how one ought to speak.

It seems, then, that the objection to a naturalised philosophy of language is not really an extension of the old 'is/ought' charge. Instead, if an objection is to be extracted from the discussion of normativity, it is that a naturalistic philosophy cannot accommodate the fact that in ascribing a meaning to a descriptive utterance we pick out certain conditions as truth-conditions for the utterance, whether or not these conditions actually obtain. For, certainly, if a naturalistic philosophy cannot accommodate this fact, then it cannot explain the conditional obligations to which a grasp of meaning gives rise. But the antecedent here remains to be established. The argument for it is that which Kripke employs when criticising the dispositional account of meaning—namely that naturalistic accounts cannot allow properly for the possibility of mistakes.[38] Kripke's challenge is certainly pertinent: for the possibility of mistakes is essential to many mental states—the very idea of a question would be incoherent if the content of a question were dependent upon its answer. In thinking about Kripke's challenge it is best to start from the issue of mental content, since *everyone* agrees that it is a conclusive objection to a simple causal theory of the content of beliefs that such a theory does not allow for mistaken beliefs.[39]

There is, however, no agreement on the way ahead. It would be silly for me to try to discuss fully here all the proposals that are currently on offer. But it is, I think, necessary to enter some way into this debate in order to exhibit the resources that are available to the naturalist programme and thereby undermine confidence in the anti-naturalist thesis that no such proposal can work. There are three general strategies for dealing with this matter: one can identify a belief's truth-conditions

**1** as those circumstances which produce tokens of the belief under ideal, or normal, conditions, or

[38] Kripke op.cit. pp.22ff.

[39] cf. D.Stampe 'Towards a Causal Theory of Linguistic Representation' in P.French, T. Uehling & H. Wettstein (eds.) *Midwest Studies in Philosophy* vol.2 (Univ. of Minnesota Press, Minneapolis: 1977) esp.pp.88–9. F.Dretske 'Misrepresentation' in *Belief: Form, Content and Function* ed.R.Bogdan (Clarendon, Oxford: 1986). J.Fodor *Psychosemantics* (MIT, London: 1987) pp.101ff. D.Papineau *Reality and Representation* (Blackwell, Oxford: 1987) pp.61ff. P.Godfrey-Smith 'Misinformation' *Canadian Journal of Philosophy* 19 (1989) pp.533–550.

**2** as those whose obtaining it is the belief's proper function to indicate by the occurrence of tokens of the belief, or

**3** as those whose obtaining would guarantee the success of actions caused by the belief and other true beliefs.[40]

The first of these strategies looks implausible; it requires a non-circular specification of ideal (normal) conditions, and it cannot be directly applied to non-perceptual beliefs, such as beliefs about the future. The second strategy is similarly restricted in its application, and, if it is supposed that the function of belief derives from a reliable correlation in circumstances which are important for the evolutionary success of the organism, then it runs into difficulties with apparent beliefs about the presence of predators that have an evolutionary role even though they are not reliably correlated with the presence of predators.[41] The third strategy, which draws on the pragmatist conception of belief,[42] is not vulnerable to these objections, and seems an essential ingredient of any satisfactory account. But it faces several difficulties of its own: in particular, the account of belief-content it implies seems too extensional (any description of the success-conditions will be admissable), and it does not incorporate any causal constraints, reflecting the history and cognitive capacities of the subject, upon the conceptual structure of beliefs.

One strategy at this point is to incorporate the pragmatist approach within a teleological theory, as has been proposed by Millikan and Papineau.[43] The central idea here is that successful action is the effect of belief which it is belief's proper function to produce; so where an action caused by a belief will be successful iff p, the belief will perform its proper function iff it is produced iff p, and this condition (namely that under which a belief performs its proper function) is taken to identify its content. By itself, however, this reinterpretation of the pragmatist approach does not help with the difficulties identified above, which suggest, rather, that the pragmatist approach should be incorporated within a causal theory which makes it a condition on the content of a subject's belief that the subject's belief-forming mechanisms (perception, memory, inference)

[40] Kripke himself suggests (**1**) (op.cit. pp.27–8), though only in order to reject it; for (**2**) cf. F.Dretske *Explaining Behaviour* (MIT, London: 1988) ch.4; for (**3**) cf. J.Whyte 'Success Semantics' *Analysis* 50 (1990) pp.149–157.

[41] Godfrey-Smith op.cit. pp.546–8.

[42] cf. C.S.Peirce 'The essence of belief is the establishment of a habit, and different beliefs are distinguished by the different modes of action to which they give rise' from 'How to Make Our Ideas Clear' reprinted in *C.S.Peirce: Selected Writings* ed.P.P.Weiner (Dover, New York: 1966) p.121.

[43] R. Millikan 'Thoughts without laws; cognitive science with content' *Philosophical Review* 95 (1986) pp.47–79. 'Biosemantics' *Journal of Philosophy* 86 (1989) pp.281–97, D.Papineau *Reality and Representation* (Blackwell, Oxford: 1987) ch.4.

should account for the subject having a belief with that content. On this suggestion, then, the content of a belief is that account of the conditions for the success of actions caused by the belief which explains, in the light of the subject's belief-forming mechanisms, why the belief is produced when it is. Since not any account of these success-conditions will thus explain the formation of the belief, the intensionality of belief-content receives here a better treatment than in the simpler theory.

This modified pragmatist account can be incorporated into a teleological framework: it could be said that the content of a belief is that account of the conditions under which it performs its proper function which explains why it is produced when it is. But this adds nothing obvious to the causal-pragmatist account with which I shall stick. This latter account needs to be supplemented by an account of belief-forming mechanisms, which, without providing a simple causal theory of content, elucidates the connections between perceptible features of the world and the occurrence of beliefs. Such an account will surely require the adoption of a version of the 'language of thought' hypothesis in order to provide a causal basis for inferential processes and our capacity to recombine old concepts in new beliefs, but I shall not speculate further about details. What does still require some attention is the account to be given of the content of desires, which is essential for a specification of what counts as success in action and thus for any pragmatist account of the content of belief. Although it is obvious that behaviour caused by desires reflects their content, since this behaviour is bound to be a joint effect of the subject's beliefs and desires, it is not easy to extract from an account of it a specification of the content of the operative desire without presumptions about the content of operative beliefs,—which is what the pragmatist needs. But, as a first approximation, this can be provided by reference to that effect whose achievement by action caused by a desire causes the desire to cease; for this feature of an effect of a desire reflects only the content of the desire and not those of the beliefs which also helped to produce it. This account will not quite work, for it is not the actual achievement of such an effect which puts an end to a desire, but the subject's perception of this achievement; so an account of perceptual content, still independent of belief, must also be provided. For this, however, I think we can have recourse to a teleological version of indicator semantics: the content of a perception is that cause of the perception which it is the perception's proper function to indicate.[44]

---

[44] For an account of perceptual content of this kind, cf. K.Sterelny *The Representational Theory of Mind* (Blackwell, Oxford: 1990) pp.124–7. In my account of the content of desires I largely follow J. Whyte except concerning the role of perception: cf. 'The Normal Rewards of Success' *Analysis* 51 (1991) pp.65–73.

I am well aware that this is over-simple; but it has been my aim only to sketch out the resources available within a naturalistic perspective in order to demonstrate the implausibility of the strong anti-naturalist thesis. Let me put these resources to work in a response to two arguments for the anti-naturalist thesis advanced by Boghassian[45]. Boghassian's first argument is that the naturalist is committed to supposing that, for every concept, there are ideal conditions under which, if subjects judge that the concept is instantiated, they are right; and he objects that this looks like an unacceptable verificationist conclusion. It will be clear that the pragmatist approach employed here altogether avoids this commitment; for on this approach the content of a belief is defined by its potential contribution, if true, to the success of the behaviour it causes, so the only commitment is that the truth of belief should guarantee success.[46] Nor does the causal constraint on the content of belief introduce Boghassian's commitment; for this only requires that there be a causal explanation as to how a belief was acquired, and this does not imply that there are any special circumstances such that beliefs acquired under them are bound to be true.

Boghassian's second objection is that the holism of belief makes it impossible for the naturalist to identify the right conditions for the occurrence of one belief without reference to other beliefs, which contravenes the requirement that content be determined by purely naturalistic properties. The reply to this must be that there is no reason why the holism of belief should not be accounted for by a holism of causal roles. It is no objection to the assignment of functions to parts of the human anatomy that they only have their proper function within a human body in which most other parts have their proper function. Similarly, therefore, it is no objection to the assignment of content to a belief as a mark of its distinctive causal role that that state only has this causal role within a system of interconnections between such states in which other states have related roles.[47]

At this point we encounter Pettit's point that even if a naturalistic account of the content of beliefs and desires can be provided, it does not follow that the self-conscious intentionality of beings such as ourselves can be comprehended within such an account.[48] The great chain of physical being somehow snaps just before it encompasses our own self-conscious common sense psychology. From a Darwinian perspective this seems a strange position to take up, but one can suppose that the concept of

---

[45] P. Boghassian op. cit. pp.538–40.

[46] This commitment is not unproblematic, as where one attempts the impossible. But these cases can be excluded by restricting attention to cases in which subjects can succeed.

[47] cf. R. Van Gulick 'Functionalism, Information and Content' reprinted in *Mind and Cognition* ed. W.G. Lycan (Blackwell, Oxford: 1990) esp.pp.118ff.

[48] cf. Pettit op.cit. pp.1–2.

meaning, and others that we employ in describing our own intentionality, are not straightforward explanatory concepts at all. But what reasons are there, connected with the rule-following arguments, for supposing this to be true? As I have already argued, it is not sufficient just to invoke the alleged normativity of the concept of meaning; further argument is needed to show that one cannot provide naturalistic accounts of the semantic connections between language and the world presupposed by the hypothetical imperatives of linguistic understanding.

The reason directly associated with the rule-following discussion is that of the alleged indeterminacy of meaning. Kripke's famous arithmetical example is intended to show that because all the natural facts associated with the past use of a word do not uniquely determine the truth-conditions of its future use, these truth-conditions, and thus the meaning of the word, are left indeterminate by the natural facts.[49] But once we have admitted, in line with rejection of the strong anti-naturalist thesis, that there are natural facts concerning the content of someone's non-linguistic beliefs, desires, and intentions, it is not easy to see how radical indeterminacy enters in once linguistic intentions are introduced. For the obvious naturalistic response to Kripke's argument is to appeal to the beliefs and intentions of speakers in order to specify what they mean.

## IV

These are rather brief remarks, doubtless too brief to be persuasive. But rather than pursue that debate, I want now to confess that I too, under Kripke's influence, have had that 'eerie feeling' when contemplating the rule-following argument that 'the entire idea of meaning vanishes into thin air'.[50] Am I bound, as a robust defender of a naturalistic philosophy of language, to dismiss this feeling as a mere illusion? I think not. Kripke presents his arguments as *sceptical*. Now, as I am well aware, the sceptical style of argument is employed by Kripke only as an artifice of exposition; he writes that 'merely epistemological scepticism is *not* in question.'[51] But suppose one were to make this the question? That is, suppose we introduce a gruesome possibility—that the meaning of 'David Holdcroft' is such that in future the name refers to Margaret Thatcher—and now ask ourselves, how can we tell that this possibility is mistaken? Does a commitment to the kind of naturalistic philosophy of language I have been defending

---

[49] Kripke op.cit. pp.38–9.
[50] Kripke op. cit. pp.21–2.
[51] Kripke op. cit. p.39.

provide us with an answer to this sceptical challenge? If the first part of this lecture is correct, we should be prepared for a negative answer. For the naturalistic philosophy of language is an application of metaphysical naturalism, and I argued that metaphysical naturalism remains vulnerable to sceptical arguments. But the issue here needs to be examined on its own merits.

Once it is 'merely epistemological scepticism' that is at issue, the dialectical strategy will be somewhat different from that followed by Kripke's sceptic, who is permitted to occupy God's point of view. For the metaphysical naturalist does claim that there are facts, presumably accessible from that point of view, which render meaning determinate. Instead, the sceptical thought worms its way into the first-person point of view of each of us to destroy our confidence that we know what we mean. For, once gruesome possibilities are introduced, and recognised to be consistent with all our past practice, how are we to eliminate them? Did we intend to convey beliefs about the addition of two numbers when we employed the plus sign—or was it beliefs about their quaddition? Did we intend to convey the belief that the grass is green when we used the word 'green'—or the belief that it is grue? Once we entertain these sceptical possibilities we find that the semantic and intentional facts have been obscured behind a gruesome veil. The situation of the sceptical thought itself is then, admittedly, rather delicate: for it implies that it itself is located behind the veil. But I do not think that we should regard this as showing that the sceptical thought is self-defeating; as elsewhere, the sceptical strategy can be formulated as a reductio ad absurdum of our pre-sceptical self-confidence.

What resources are then available to the subject to enable her to exhibit the sceptical doubt as unreasonable? There is perhaps content-less introspective evidence—sensations, imagery, and unspoken words. But, for reasons which Wittgenstein stressed, none of this evidence has determinate implications for semantic hypotheses.[52] What, however, about the facts in terms of which the naturalistic account of intentional content was set out in the previous section? Entertaining gruesome possibilities does not seem to give us reason to doubt our ability to gain knowledge of these facts. Hence, it would seem, metaphysical naturalism does in this case provide the subject with resources to cope with a sceptical argument.

The trouble with this response is that without some antecedent understanding of our own beliefs and intentions, we lack the ability to conduct rational inquiries into, among other things, the content of our own thoughts. For rational inquiry involves the adoption of hypotheses

---

[52] cf. e.g. L. Wittgenstein *Philosophical Investigations* sections 141, 154.

and their scrutiny in the light of evidence. Yet how can I follow such a procedure without some presumptions concerning what hypothesis I do, in fact, entertain? If I cannot rule out gruesome interpretations of a hypothesis concerning my own thoughts, I cannot conduct any rational inquiries to determine what I am thinking. The third-person route to self-knowledge offered by the metaphysical naturalist's account of intentional content turns out to be illusory; for we cannot pursue such a route without an understanding of our thoughts as we attempt to direct our inquiries along it. Since, *ex hypothesi*, we start off with no such understanding, we can learn nothing about ourselves that way. Hence we need to have a way of acquiring this self-understanding without relying on the kinds of inquiry characteristic of the third-person route to knowledge of oneself. It is therefore a mistake for Dennett and Millikan to attack this claim, which they call 'meaning rationalism', as a misguided relic of Cartesianism, to be abandoned by all true naturalisers.[53] In the face of sceptical argument the 'meaning rationalist' claim is certainly problematic. But to abandon it is to abandon all hope of avoiding the sceptical conclusion that we have no knowledge of our own thoughts and meanings.

My previous discussion will indicate which type of response to this sceptical challenge I favour—the Humean epistemic naturalist's response of invoking our spontaneous beliefs about our thoughts and meanings. Although I am again not concerned to argue for an interpretative thesis, this is, I think, part of the response that Wittgenstein himself favoured. In a famous paragraph in his *Philosophical Investigations* he wrote

217 'How am I able to obey a rule?'—if this is not a question about causes, then it is about the justification for my following the rule in the way I do. If I have exhausted the justifications I have reached bedrock, and my spade is turned. Then I am inclined to say: 'This is simply what I do'.

It is worth noting that in this passage Wittgenstein allows that there can be a 'causal' question about rule-following distinct from the issue of justification. This distinction fits well with my view that the sceptical challenge in this area is epistemological, concerning questions of justification, and not metaphysical; Wittgenstein does not deny that there is a causal story about rule-following.

When discussing the epistemic naturalist strategy before. I emphasised that it was not enough just to invoke spontaneous cognitive dispositions; if a title to objective knowledge is to be made defensible, then the subject needs to be able to develop these dispositions into a reflectively coherent conception of the world and her place in it which incorporates

---

[53] Dennett (1987) op.cit. p.313; Millikan (1984) op.cit. pp.91–3.

something along the lines of the account of these dispositions offered by the metaphysical naturalist. So, where this strategy is applied to the case in hand, it implies that we can vindicate our attributions of non-inferential self-knowledge where we can combine our spontaneous self-ascriptions of thoughts and meanings with our understanding of the world and our situation to develop a psychology which shows how it is only to be expected that we should have this kind of self-knowledge. Such a theory seems bound to attribute to us an 'inner sense', whereby we can gain reliable, though not infallible, beliefs about our own mental states. This hypothesis is, however, liable to arouse considerable hostility from those who think that it is just a hangover from the Cartesian tradition; so it is worth looking briefly at two alternative accounts of self-knowledge. Once one appreciates how unsatisfactory they are, it is, I think, easier to become reconciled to the inner sense model.

Wright, who holds that the rule-following arguments undermine the naturalistic conception of meaning and content presupposed by the 'inner sense' model, has proposed an account of self-knowledge based upon an analogy with the familiar secondary-quality conception of colours.[54] He argues that, because, according to this conception, the fact of an object's being blue 'is constitutively' the fact that under cognitively ideal conditions we are disposed to judge it to be blue, our judgments of colour have a priveleged status in determining what colours things actually are. Similarly, therefore, according to Wright we should account for the authoritative status of our first-person attributions of thought by assigning to these judgments a similar 'extension-determining' role. We should not think of a subject's intentions as 'some *independently constituted* system which the subject's opinions at best reflect'; instead 'what determines the distribution of truth-values among ascriptions of intention to a subject who has the conceptual resources to understand these resources and is attentive to them are, in the first instance, nothing but the details of the subject's self-conception in relevant respects'.[55]

This account obviously challenges the account of mental content I have espoused, but if it were to provide a satisfactory account of self-knowledge that would be a reason for rethinking the matter. I do not think, however, that Wright's proposal will work. One difficulty concerns the attribution of beliefs and intentions to lower animals who lack the capacity to attribute them to themselves. On Wright's account it would seem that these attributions get their sense from counterfactuals concerning the content of the self-attributions that these animals would make had they

---

[54] Wright (1989) op.cit. pp.246ff.
[55] Wright (1989) op. cit. p.253.

the capacity to do so. This seems to tie the employment of these concepts to nursery tales; yet serious animal ethologists employ them to explain animal behaviour without any such fantasies. Another difficulty is that if the constitutive account is to work, the ideal conditions under which the subject's self-attributions have their constitutive role must themselves be independent of the subject's thoughts; but since (as Wright himself notes) one of the cognitively ideal conditions is the absence of self-deception, it is not clear how this requirement is to be met. But the fatal difficulty is that an infinite regress arises concerning the content of judgment, or belief. On Wright's account, the content of a belief is determined by the subject's judgment, under ideal conditions, as to what she believes. How then is the content of this judgment determined? On Wright's account, it can only be by a higher-order judgment concerning that judgment—and so on. This regress is vicious: at each level we find a judgment (actual or potential) whose content depends on the content of a higher-level judgment (actual or potential). Thus, in seeking to determine the content of a bottom-level belief, we are referred progressively up the hierarchy with no prospect of relief; we never, so to speak, find a firm hand-hold.[56]

A different approach is proposed by Davidson. He has argued that the process of radical interpretation, through which (according to him) meaning and intentional content are determined, presupposes that speakers normally know what they mean; and since we can also assume that speakers normally know which sentences they hold true, we can conclude that they normally know what they believe.[57] As with Wright's proposal, Davidson's position conflicts with the naturalistic philosophy of mind I have defended. But where Wright is neo-Lockean, Davidson is neo-Kantian; on his view the radical interpreter, like the Kantian understanding, brings her a priori principles to make sense of physical behaviour that is not meaningful simply in virtue of its physical properties, since, according to Davidson, there are no psychophysical laws. Attributions of meaning and intentional content have, therefore, always to be understood with reference to the perspective of a potential interpreter; and since, Davidson argues, such an interpreter must presume that her subjects, the native speakers, normally know what they mean, we arrive at an account of self-knowledge without relying on the inner sense model.

Davidson's approach appears vulnerable to the regress argument

---

[56] Suppose, somehow, that the account of colour was such that the colour of something depended upon the colour of a subject's judgment concerning the thing's colour: then a similar vicious regress would apply to the account of colour.

[57] D. Davidson 'First Person Authority' *Dialectica* 38 (1984) pp.101–11; 'Knowing One's Own Mind' *Proceedings and Addresses of the American Philosophical Association* 1987 pp.441–58.

that undermines Wright's account. For Davidson makes the content of native thoughts dependent upon those attributed to them by the radical interpreter. But how, then, is the content of the latter's interpretative attributions determined? Again, we seem to be pointed upwards to ever higher meta-interpretations with no prospect of relief. Furthermore Davidson's main argument for his position is, I think, unpersuasive. Davidson wants to establish, without relying on any antecedent presumption of self-knowledge, an asymmetry thesis—'a presumption that speakers, but not their interpreters, are not wrong about what their words mean'.[58] But this thesis fails to take account of the fact that most language is not simply expressive; instead speakers choose the words which they believe will enable their audience to grasp whatever they wish to communicate, and they can be mistaken about the meaning of the words they thus employ. A visitor to a foreign country who wants to order a cup of coffee is not well advised simply to make this request in his own tongue and hope that the natives catch on: he would do much better to listen to the natives and try to copy their words when, as he thinks, they are ordering a cup of coffee. Clearly, in this latter situation there is no presumption that the speaker knows what he means.

Perhaps Davidson's reliance upon knowledge of language, whose meaning is in some degree a social, and not merely individual, phenomenon, can be omitted; one might well argue that interpreters are bound to presume that those whom they can make sense of as rational agents possess considerable self-knowledge. Yet this now looks like an unhelpful conditional; if rationality implies self-knowledge then ascription of the former implies ascription of the latter. But this does nothing to show what makes it correct or not to make sense of a being as rational, or possessed of self-knowledge. It seems to me, therefore, that Davidson's account of self-knowledge is no more satisfactory than Wright's, and this failure lends support to the view that self-knowledge can only be adequately substantiated within the metaphysical naturalist's model of an inner sense.

The question that remains, therefore, is how this model should be developed. This is essentially a task for cognitive psychologists, and not philosophers, but a crucial move towards rendering this model acceptable was made by Armstrong, when he compared introspection to the 'silent' bodily senses, such as proprioception.[59] The traditional 'Cartesian' conception of introspection as an inner analogue of vision, the inner eye, is vulnerable to the objections that there is no organ of introspection, nor any

[58] Davidson (1984) op.cit. p.110.
[59] D.M. Armstrong *A Materialist Theory of Mind* (Routledge, London: 1968) ch.15.

characteristic introspective experience comparable to visual experience. But once the comparison is made with proprioception, which provides us with beliefs about our body without any organ that we can control or much in the way of sense-experience, the idea of introspection should be less troubling. It should be understood as a capacity we possess to acquire beliefs about our own mental states, and given the advantages to us of such a capacity, which is essential for rational reflection, it ought not to be mysterious from a naturalistic perspective that we have developed it, even if we remain largely ignorant how in fact it is accomplished. Thus although faith in such a capacity remains to a considerable extent a cheque drawn on the metaphysical naturalist's account that cannot yet be cashed, it is not unreasonable for the epistemic naturalist to write such a cheque in presenting his response to the argument of the Kripkean sceptic. My conclusion here, therefore, is that just as before my two types of naturalism need each other.

*Proceedings of the British Academy*, **80**, 201–219

KEYNES LECTURE IN ECONOMICS

# Incomplete Market Economies

### FRANK HAHN
*University of Cambridge*
*Fellow of the British Academy*

MARKET ECONOMIES are now widely praised, sometimes in quite unlikely quarters. There are of course important 'Hayekian' reasons which account for this as well as the lack of success of alternative economic arrangements. I shall not be concerned with these arguments. Indeed I have no intention of arriving at some final judgment of what may be the 'best' economic arrangement. My aim is much more modest: it is to re-examine the fundamental notion of 'market', to consider whether and in what sense there may be 'too few' of these and to study the modifications of economic analysis of market economies which such an examination suggests as needed.

It will probably be useful to begin with an outline of where I am going and why I consider the subject matter of this lecture to be important.

Adam Smith taught us to regard markets as the central device for co-ordinating the actions of a large number of self-interested agents. They provided the 'invisible hand'. Not only would markets prevent chaos, they would also be beneficial in other ways, for instance in permitting the division of labour. In late twentieth-century economics one of the beneficent consequences of a market economy is summed up by the first Welfare Theorem. It tells us that if every item which enters either into agents' preferences or into their production activities can be traded at a given price, then the resulting equilibrium is Pareto-efficient.

Pigou was one of the first to provide an analysis of cases where

Read 26 February 1992. © The British Academy 1993.

important items of preference or technology are not tradable. These are the items connected with external economies and diseconomies. Thus there is no market in pollination services of bees nor in nectar, nor are there markets for air. One can continue. Coase later taught us to regard the market insufficiency as due to deficiencies in property rights, but did not go on to ask why they might be deficient. For instance, it is not clear how property rights could be established for unborn generations which will suffer from our polluting propensities. But in any case 'the problem of externalities' is not only a problem of market economy inefficiency but also of incomplete markets. Economists have had no difficulty in proposing non-market intervention in those cases where I include taxes and subsidies and marketable licences under that category. The point is that all these instruments are employed by a collective and not by the self-seeking agent.

But externalities of the kind familiar from textbooks are only one example of incomplete markets. There are others. In particular there may not be a sufficiently rich array of intertemporal markets and of insurance markets. I shall later give some reasons why this may be so. It is with this kind of incompleteness that I shall be concerned this afternoon.

Take a familiar example. Keynes maintained that 'savings were not a demand for future goods'. But they are undertaken with a view of one's own or one's heirs' eventual consumption. If the saver at the time of saving could also signal his future demand at various dates which these savings represent, many central planks of Keynesian theory would be lost—and he knew it. This is even more true if we allow for uncertainty. Agents care about it and on completeness arguments should be able to trade in it—that is, there would have to be adequate insurance markets. Thus savings in a complete market economy would give rise to trade in goods for conditional forward delivery. For instance one would buy a water bottle or doctor's services with part of one's savings, to be delivered if one is sick next year while nothing is delivered if one is well. In such an economy savings would not be diverted to 'precautionary money balances' and once again little would remain true, or even relevant, of Keynesian theory.

The example suggests that the study of incomplete market economies and the recognition that they need studying may be important. I shall later remind you of an important further problem which incomplete markets present. Students are taught that firms maximise profit. Except for certain extreme cases, this cannot mean that firms are only interested in today's receipts and costs. So it is explained that it is the present value of profit that is maximised. But if goods cannot be traded forward today, then this maximand depends on price expectations. Those may be different for different shareholders. Once we are in the realm of expectations we must also consider risk aversion. But that may differ amongst shareholders. In short, we have no justification for what we tell students unless markets are complete. Should students not be told? Should advisors to Chancellors not be alerted?

But there is another important consequence of incompleteness on which I shall dwell more fully later. Incomplete inter-temporal markets give rise to an economy with trading at every date—a 'sequence economy'. The stage is set for monetary theory. It cannot be studied in a complete market economy. But even more significant is the impossibility for the economist of neglecting price expectations. Yet another stage is set on which Keynes can play a star role. For one must now consider equilibria as equilibria of beliefs and this, as we know from the 'sunspot literature', is a departure from orthodoxy for which equilibria are reflections of 'fundamentals'.

So there are a lot of rather important questions to be answered. But so far I have taken markets to mean what the textbooks call 'perfect markets'. Not only that, these markets are conjured up but not analysed. Most transactions are mediated transactions. For instance by shops and wholesalers. Of course one might think of a market for some good as just an opportunity to trade it. But that gives too little structure although no doubt there are goods which are traded directly. I think sufficient generality is ensured if we say that a good has a market when it is traded through mediators. The latter to some extent perform the role of the fictional auctioneers of theory, although they are 'real' auctioneers. But that analogy must not be taken too far and the mediator, just because he is not fictional, may well bargain with either his supplier or demander. All of these matters are taken up in the second part of this lecture, but you must be warned that I do not get as far in the analysis as one would like.

I shall now start off in the more traditional way which does not concern itself with the mechanism of exchange, but simply assumes what the textbook calls 'a perfect market'. I do so because I want to report on some of the new results in the analysis of such economies for which the market is incomplete. They certainly are of intellectual interest on their own account. But they also have what I consider at least two important messages. The first is that incomplete market equilibria are not only Pareto-inefficient, which is obvious, but *constrained* Pareto-inefficient. The second is that equilibrium analysis may not buy us much because it may be that there are not only many, but a continuum of equilibria. If these propositions are true for the idealised economy here studied, then one would be surprised to find that more realistically based models perform better. Of course they might. But that is not all. The idealised model has been much used by empirically minded economists—not least by 'classical macro-economists'. For them these new results should be of peculiar interest.

## I. The Tradition

It is useful to start with what we know. In received theory (as I have already noted), to assert that a good has a market is equivalent to the claim that agents can trade in that good to any extent at known and given terms. The market structure of an economy is then given by the array of prices that agents face. It does not seem that classical and neo-classical economists differ much here.

From my point of view the first important step is to consider the classification of goods. We want to distinguish one object from another if it is distinguished either in preferences or in technology. In general this means that goods need to be distinguished by location, date of delivery and state of nature as well as by physical characteristics. Perhaps to some the only unfamiliar item here is 'state of nature'. Savage thought of a state of nature as a particular history of the environment which is independent of the actions of agents. If this history brings rain today then an umbrella will be valued differently than it would have been had it been fine. In principle a good at any location and date must be distinguished by all states of nature between which agents can distinguish and for whom the distinction is economically relevant. It now follows that if all goods so distinguished have markets in the traditional sense it is equivalent to all goods having a price. If one picks a particular date, location and state, as the 'present' then all these goods must be priced in the present. In that case markets are said to be 'complete' although I shall argue shortly that this may be a misnomer.

Since this way of thinking of goods and markets may not be familiar to everyone, I give an implication of complete markets, by way of example. Consider a firm. We think of it now of making a contingent production plan. That is, it decides on its inputs and outputs for each date and state of nature. It buys and sells claims to these goods in the present. For instance it makes a contract in the present for labour to be delivered next year if it does not snow, and pays for it in the present. It also sells the output of this labour in the present, that is what that labour will produce next year if it does not snow. If it does snow no labour or output will be delivered. It is clear that the firm will be fully insured against unpredictable states of nature and that the future is collapsed into the present. If such a firm maximises profit, that is the revenue from all goods sold minus the revenue from all inputs bought, then it is easy to show that this is exactly what each shareholder of this firm regards to be in his or her best interest. In textbooks this rather weird scenario is rarely spelled out but it underlies the rationale of profit maximisation.

Now let us note that there is an obvious moral hazard problem with contingent forward contracts. The moral hazard problem and its consequences are perhaps less well known and certainly not yet fully understood. Strictly speaking, forward contracts are promises, and promises can be broken. They may be broken deliberately or because of mis-calculation. Until quite recently the matter has not received proper theoretical attention. As we shall see this difficulty may account for incompleteness of markets. But it also reminds us of the necessity of thinking of a market theory as firmly embedded in a legal system. For instance bankruptcy and default laws are clearly relevant. To give an example, privatisation of the Czechoslovak economy is at the moment retarded by a lack of adequate bankruptcy laws which, for instance, are required to attract foreign investors.

Suppose we now, as in the textbook, ignore all these caveats (including externalities), and return to what is misnamed a complete market economy. An equilibrium of such an economy is by its nature an equilibrium through time. Once transactions have been completed, the actual economy unfolds as time and states of nature unfold. Deliveries are made at each date and in each state as agreed beforehand. Of course this long run equilibrium is not necessarily a steady state, nor even a stochastic steady state. For instance it could manifest itself cyclically. But under suitable assumptions we know that such an equilibrium exists and what is more, that it is Pareto-efficient. To this last result, even in the purest cases, we need to add a caveat—we are speaking of finite economies, that is, economies over a finite future. If the indefinite future is included then some further conditions are needed to ensure Pareto-efficiency. We also, of course, have the subtler second Welfare Theorem which tells us that in suitable circumstances every Pareto-efficient allocation can be decentralised into a competitive equilibrium.

It is unlikely that many people will regard this abstract theory as yielding an adequate base from which to mount arguments in favour of market economies. As stated it is plainly false: for instance such an economy could have no use for money as a medium of exchange, because all transactions are carried out once and for all in the present. But there are other counter-factuals to which I return.

However it is possible to make the story somewhat less unrealistic, although, as I shall argue, not much less so. This modification is due to Arrow (1953). Suppose we consider a date t. Now if it rains at t we will call this an event: it is all the states of nature—histories of the environment—which have rain at t. We then call t and rain a 'date-event pair'. So far we have assumed that all goods, whatever their appropriate 'date-event' pair, have markets in the present. Arrow suggested that we can do with far fewer markets. In particular if we had in the present as many securities with independent payoffs in the date-event pairs, as there are date-event pairs, then that economy would have the same equilibria as the one with many more markets. Once certain assumptions are made the argument is straightforward.

Suppose there are only two dates, the present (when the state of nature is known) and tomorrow. Suppose it is not possible to have any conditional forward transactions in the present. Suppose further, and that is crucial, that everyone knows with certainty what prices tomorrow will clear all markets for every possible event. Note that there are now only spot prices for goods and that agents will no longer to able to complete all their transactions in the present. However, knowing tomorrow's market clearing prices, say if it rains, there is a certain amount agents would wish to have available. If there is a security which pays a certain amount of numeraire if it rains tomorrow they can make sure of their wealth for this date-event pair by buying an appropriate amount of it in the present. If it does not rain, perhaps that security pays nothing, but there is another which pays if it hails. In that way all the insurance open to agents in the complete markets is also open to them in the Arrow-security economy. Moreover there are no new opportunities and so the same choices will be made in both economies.

Arrow has thus shown us a way in which the economy with all transactions in the present can equally well be thought of as a sequence economy with transactions in every date-event pair. Completeness now means that the security pay-offs 'span' the set of all date-event pairs so that any combination of wealth across these can be attained by a suitable present portfolio. However this equivalence of the equilibria may, and indeed has, obscured certain important differences between the two economies.

In economies in which goods markets are complete any given economy is adequately describable by preferences, endowments and technology together with the commodity space and consumption sets. This is not a sufficient description of the Arrow-sequence economy. For the latter we have also to specify spot price expectations—that is the prices expected for any date-event pair other than the present pair. At this stage Arrow introduces an assumption which has since become very popular—he assumes that there is perfect foresight of market clearing prices for each date-event pair. This is not only a strong assumption and one which I shall argue is not unambiguous, but it is an assumption which is not needed in the complete goods market economy.

A second difference arises between these two types of economies if we take account of transaction costs. Since there are fewer markets in one than there are in the other, one would expect equilibrium transaction costs to differ between them. Taking account of such costs in both economies will generally yield different equilibria which one would expect to differ with respect to Pareto-efficiency.

The ambiguity in the expectation hypothesis arises from the likelihood of multiple equilibria. Consider a two-period economy. Second period spot prices which clear markets given an event will generally not be unique simply because the conditions necessary for uniqueness are pretty restrictive. If that is so, then in specifying price expectations held in the present we must arbitrarily pick one possible equilibrium from amongst what may be a large set of equilibria. There is thus an important *ad hoc* element. It should however be noted that a full Arrow-Debreu economy may have a unique equilibrium even when the associated sequence economy with complete securities has multiple second period equilibria.

Before I discuss this further I want to take a short detour to rational expectations models as used particularly by macro-economists. In that literature, expectations are said to be rational if the price (of the single 'representative good') is equal to the mathematical expectation of this price, conditioned on the agents' information plus an error term of zero mean and fixed variance. Note that all price differences over states of nature are captured by the error term. Note also that since these authors seem to postulate risk neutrality as a matter of course, there is no desire to trade across states of nature. Finally note that, like Arrow, agents are assumed to know which of a number of possible equilibria will occur. It is not easy to see why any of these assumptions are justified. Moreover there is the unfortunate fact that a theory designed to rescue us from the '*ad hockery*' of Keynesian practitioners is thoroughly *ad hoc* itself.

Returning to the main theme one notices that in the Arrow-sequence economy such spot price uncertainty as there is in the present is entirely based on state uncertainty. The state is a random variable but the spot prices are single-valued functions of the state. As I have said, this is a possible assumption but it is not descriptively persuasive. It is, for instance, not fanciful that in the present the agent is uncertain of the market clearing price of wheat next period, if it rains. This uncertainty may be based on the understanding the agent has that there are a number of market clearing prices of wheat if it rains and that the one which will prevail will depend on the beliefs of other agents which will determine the wealth which they transfer to the state 'rain' next period.

I have now come to a point in the argument where I pause to admire an important Keynesian insight. For neo-classical theory of the sort that I have been dealing with, the market economy is a non-distorting reflection of the reality encapsulated in preferences, endowments and technology. Accordingly, a market equilibrium reflects this reality faithfully if markets are complete. For Keynes a market equilibrium is an equilibrium of beliefs which may or may not reflect reality. This insight has only recently resurfaced in sunspot theory and in game theory. If my foregoing arguments are correct and the economy has multiple spot equilibria, then the Arrow security equilibrium is what it is because everyone believes that that is the equilibrium and not because the underlying reality demands it. It is somewhat surprising that many politicians seem to understand the basic idea here—think of the arguments for joining E.R.M.—while economic theory until recently has taken no notice of it.

But this line of argument leads to certain, not exclusively technical, difficulties with the notion of complete markets and indeed with that of equilibrium.

Suppose for the sake of simplicity that second period market clearing prices are formed by auctioneers of the usual tatonnement story. But each one of these auctioneers guides the economy to one of the possible second period equilibria. Then agents can be thought to have expectations of which auctioneer will be in charge. In the usual way let us think of these beliefs as probability distributions. There is now uncertainty concerning the state of nature and concerning the auctioneer in charge. One is now tempted to say that we shall need securities to span not just the states of nature but the joint 'state' of states of nature and auctioneer. One thus would need more securities. I shall now distinguish between 'Savage States of Nature' which are the states I have discussed so far and the 'Augmented States' which include the auctioneers.

However completion with respect to augmented states leads to a serious problem. It is easy to show as before that the completion of securities in this sense would once again lead to an equivalence between the complete goods market economy and the sequence economy. That is, there would be implicit prices such that it is possible to think of this economy as completing all of its transactions at a single date. But households' utilities depend on the amount of each good they have in each state of nature and not at all on which auctioneer performs in the second period. If these households are risk-averse expected utility maximisers, then their present choice of goods for any state of nature in the second period cannot be different when auctioneers are different. That is so because if it were so dependent the expected quantity of these goods over auctioneers would dominate the supposed choice.[1] This is a simple consequence of risk-aversion. Hence markets completed for price uncertainty leads to the conclusion that there can be no price uncertainty.

The arguments here are closely related to the sunspot literature.[2] The different auctioneers are like sunspots in the sense that agents' endowments and preferences do not depend on them. The uncertainty arising from multiple second period equilibria is extrinsic, i.e. not deriving from 'fundamentals'. We know that if we include extrinsic uncertainty with states of nature and have complete markets, then there cannot be an equilibrium with extrinsic uncertainty. Sunspot equilibria are not possible in an Arrow-Debreu economy which is derivable from a complete securities sequence economy.

We have come to an interesting conclusion. Assuming that second period spot equilibria are not unique, completing the security market rules out multiplicity. But then the extra securities which the spanning of the augmented state space seemed to require, will be redundant. From this I conclude that equilibrium with complete securities spanning the augmented state space implies that there is only one second period equilibrium for each Savage state. But that means that there cannot be multiple second period price equilibria, which is what I started with.

All of this sounds like airy-fairy theory topped with technical froth. But even though it sounds like that, it is of considerable practical relevance. Market economies may expose agents to uninsurable uncertainties which cannot be insured by creating insurance possibilities. Even quite casual acquaintance with the citizens of countries making the transition to market economies will convince one that they are vividly aware and sometimes resentful of the extra uncertainties they impose. My claim is that these may be intrinsic and not just traceable to Savage states of nature which of course also impinge on a command economy. If it is indeed true that typically people are risk-averse, then we know that they would be willing to trade mean income for a reduction in risk. It is thus an important policy question whether completely free market institutions are what one wants. To answer that one would have to undertake a careful analysis of possible uncertainty-reducing public policies which could be pursued in a basically market-oriented economy.

I now conclude this line of thought by reporting briefly on traditional incomplete market theories in which it is assumed that all agents know

---

[1] Utility depends on consumption c(s) in various states s = 1 . . . S. Risk aversion implies that if it is possible for the agent he will want to consume the same amount c(s) whatever the price vector p(s) which clears markets.

[2] I owe the direction of my thoughts here to a conversation with Andreu Mas-Collel.

with certainty what second period equilibrium is for each Savage-state of nature. The economists who have recently made most progress here are Radner (1972), Geanakoplos and Mas-Colell (1989), Geanakoplos and Polemarchakis (1986), but there are other contributors, in particular an early one, namely Cass (1984).

Radner was the first to provide an explanation for incomplete markets. This turned on asymmetric information. A contract where payment was conditional on a state which one party could verify while the other could not would be exposed to moral hazard and so, Radner argued, could not be made. Nowadays we would put this differently: asymmetric information requires contracts whose terms ensure incentive compatibility. That is, they make it in the interest of the better informed party to be truthful in the report of the realised state. If this is possible the contract will not be of the sort which we find in Arrow-Debreu theory. Radner thus was right in saying that Arrow-Debreu contracts may be impossible to make under asymmetric information, but he was not right in thinking that no contracts could be entered into by differentially informed parties.

A second reason for incomplete markets is the existence of transaction costs. Brokers and insurance companies do not come free. I argued this a good time ago (1965). But transaction costs pose problems for traditional theory, and it is best to postpone their discussion.

The line taken by research is to take the degree of incompleteness as exogenous. This is clearly unsatisfactory and the closing of this intellectual gap must be high on the agenda. So far it has not been possible to do so satisfactorily.

If we stick to a world where all insurance is by means of securities, we must distinguish between at least three pure kinds: securities whose pay-off is denominated in unit of account, those that are denominated in numeraire, and those that are denominated in goods. There are conclusions peculiar to each of these. If pay-off is in unit of account and securities are incomplete in S Savage states, then (generically) there is an (S–1) dimensional set of equilibria.[3] This is indeterminacy indeed and gives much scope to Keynesian bootstraps. For the numeraire case there is only the possibility of isolated equilibria. On the other hand all of these are generically constrained Pareto-inefficient. By that one means that they are inefficient even taking account of the constraints that all insurance must be by means of securities. The inefficiency is best understood by remembering that with incompleteness, the marginal rates of substitution of wealth over states will generally differ between agents. A small, initial

---

[3] I.E. The set of equilibrium allocations is generated by a differentiable function from (S-1) dimensional Euclidean space.

wealth preserving redistribution of securities between agents will then generally affect equilibrium prices. That is, a social planner would have to take this externality into account in allocating securities.

In the final kind of security there are difficulties with existence proofs first noted by Hart but since resolved in a surprisingly highbrow way.

It is seen that incompleteness is not just a theoretical toy. It has for instance important policy relevance. A good example is provided by Newbery and Stiglitz (1981) in their analysis of agricultural price stabilisation schemes and many more in a survey paper by Newbery (1989). The 'indeterminacy' results of course throw doubt on the usual rational expectations macro-models and so on forecasts and policies based on them. In particular the assumption that 'agents know the structure of the true model' even if accepted is now a quite inadequate foundation for these models. Indeed indeterminacy suggests that the formulation of learning hypotheses and adjustment processes may be essential to the usefulness of macro-economic models. But I leave this analysis carried out in the framework of traditional value theory in order to consider some more radical difficulties.

## II. Some Steps Towards Realism

The traditional, let me call it 'textbook' treatment of markets has the virtue of simplicity, but the drawback that it is incomplete and also in various ways unrealistic. To say that some good has a market is to claim no more than that it may in some circumstances be exchanged for something else. This is not very precise nor informative. For instance is there a cost involved in the exchange act? Is there only a limited number of goods against which it can be exchanged? Do agents know that an exchange is possible on certain terms or do they have beliefs on this? And so on. Evidence for the incompleteness of the textbook account is its inability to provide an exchange role for money and its neglect of a large and important group of agents which consists of middlemen.

One could attempt an abstract formulation of the market structure of an economy of which the textbook case would, I believe, be a very special instance. This way of proceeding accords best with my inclinations but, on reflection, seems inappropriate to this occasion. I shall accordingly concentrate on certain elements of a whole collection which may eventually add up to a satisfactory account. My particular aim is to give a more plausible and also perhaps more interesting account of incompleteness.

I shall concentrate on mediation. There have been a number of fine technical accounts of economies where agents are confined to bilateral exchange and where exchange partners' meetings are random. Particular notice here is owed to the very fine work of Douglas Gale (1986). But his intention was quite different from my present one. He was concerned to establish that in certain cases the stationary outcome of exchange encounters would be the textbook one. My concern at the moment is to make theory descriptively more adequate and bilateral exchange does not provide that. To this I am bound to add that Gale paid little attention in this work, although he had done so elsewhere (1982), to problems of trust which arise in inter-temporal exchange.

The reason why exchange à la Gale is comparatively rare is that it leaves open a profitable, but unfilled, niche. This is especially so for a monetary economy. The best and simplest example is an estate agent. He collects offers to sell or offers to sell conditionally on an agreed price. This is plainly to the advantage of buyers and sellers. Both would be willing to pay for the informational services provided. Notice further that the estate agent's existence does not exclude eventual bargaining between buyer and seller once they have found each other. In other words the institution of middlemen provides information for which other agents are willing to pay. There is naturally also a cost to mediation and whether particular exchanges are mediated by a middleman will then, of course, depend on an obvious cost and willingness to pay condition.

By increasing the chances that a willing buyer will meet a willing seller, middlemen of course reduce transaction uncertainty. In many cases middlemen can reduce the buyer's transaction uncertainty significantly by holding inventories and so becoming the proximate sellers. This is particularly true for standardised goods. They may also enable futures contracts to be entered into which would not be possible in bilateral exchange. The reason is that large numbers can make risks of default acceptable. All of these roles, to be fully understood, require formal modelling and here they should not be treated as more than suggestive.

But it may be helpful to show the possible importance of some of these suggestions in the context of familiar search theory. To fix ideas consider labour search. The worker knows the distribution of offers but not any particular one. He searches for an offer at a wage which is no less than a critical one. The latter depends on the distribution of offers and on search costs. Now imagine a mediator in the form of an employment exchange. Since these theories assume homogeneous labour it is pretty clear that the distribution would collapse. On the other hand, workers would save search costs. It is not difficult to see that the employment exchange may be able to charge workers as long as there is no private transmission of the information which it has. In fact the employment exchange would make this market very close to that described in the textbook.

Or consider Diamond's (1982) very interesting approach. It will be recalled that this is a model of search for bilateral exchange partners. He noted that increasing the number of searchers, by raising the probability of partners finding each other, would be Pareto-improving. He thus identified what appears as an important externality and a potential source of co-ordination failure. Yet here also there are unexploited profits to mediation. In his particular example all a middleman need do is to provide a list of all those willing to exchange, while crossing out names as exchange proceeds. This would involve some costs both for him and the agents who must give their names and tell him when to cross them off. But it would be surprising if not everyone involved were not better off than in the Diamond world. There is co-ordination failure because there is no co-ordinator even though a co-ordinator could cover his costs.

It is seen that allowing for mediators can affect the conclusions we reach. But while a glance at statistics will quickly convince one that mediation is a surprisingly large fraction of G.N.P., there are also obstacles to mediation.

An important obstacle is that it is almost surely subject to increasing returns. This fact alone would reinstate Diamond's externality although it would now be of slightly different origin. But significantly increasing returns may make mediation altogether unprofitable for specialised goods with few traders. This would seem to apply to goods conditional on idiosyncratic states of nature where 'idiosyncratic' here means that these states are pay-off relevant to only small groups of agents. Moreover, if asymmetric information requires that exchange be carried out by means of incentive compatible contracts, then mediation may be inhibited by the cost of devising such contracts for heterogeneous traders.

I should now like to propose that by incomplete markets we mean incomplete mediation. This proposal is motivated by the notion that by a market we really understand the possibility for exchanges. But it is not easy to think of goods for which exchange is strictly impossible, except where there are legal constraints. It may be costly in search time and thus finally not profitable, but that is something different. The advantage of my proposal is that it will in an obvious, but by no means simple, way make incompleteness endogenous. It will also bring it closer to what is ordinarily meant by the claim that such and such a good has no market. The reason why an exact implementation of the proposal will not be simple is this. One will need to decide whether the existence of what I have called a profitable niche is sufficient for it to be filled. But profitability itself will not be straightforward: one particular niche may only be profitable if some other niche has been filled. We are familiar with this kind of problem in attempts to make the variety of goods endogenous. In the present case increasing returns add further complications.

There is also the very difficult question of competition between mediators. Increasing returns alert us to well known problems here. There is the additional fact (recently emphasised by Stahle [1988] and Yanello [1989]) that mediators deal with both sides of the market and that there will thus be competition in both sides, and that competition will be by price-setting. Particular cases may yield to analysis relatively easily, but it will not be easy even to define, leave alone prove, the existence of an economy-wide equilibrium.

But there is a further caveat. The proposal, as indeed the whole story of mediation, only makes sense in a monetary economy. One can imagine mediation of barter, but it is likely to be very costly. We now have a very satisfactory literature which has made the very old arguments showing the efficiency gains of monetary exchange precise. (e.g. Ostroy and Starr, [1990], Darrell Duffie [1990]). But I believe that these efficiency gains are themselves closely related to mediation. This seems particularly clear in Duffie's contribution which, incidentally, also seems to identify 'market' with mediation.

Suppose now that mediation is complete. It will not ensure the Pareto-efficiency of an equilibrium. That is so for two reasons. Mediators make their return from a spread between selling and buying price. This spread will put a wedge between the marginal rates of substitution of buyers and sellers. The second reason arises from increasing returns to mediation. For instance there may be a Pareto-improvement possible from making a 'thin' market 'thick'. But as long as it is thin and costs are high, agents are deterred from using it and there is no obvious decentralised mechanism to remedy the situation. There is here an externality for which there does not appear to be a Coasian remedy by means of property rights.

Of course care must be taken with the appropriate notion of Pareto-efficiency. Reallocations themselves will incur mediation costs. Nonetheless, taking account of this, there are generally Pareto-improving reallocations from equilibrium. That would be true even without increasing returns to mediation. The reason is, just as in the incomplete securities case, that the social planner would need to include in any decentralisation rule, changes in relative equilibrium prices resulting from a reallocation; private agents do not take account of these.

I believe that we are now on the way to a richer analysis of incompleteness. When I gave an account of what I have called the 'textbook view' it was clear that it was taken for granted that spot markets were costlessly mediated or behaved as if that were so. But that assumption removes a number of problems of considerable economic importance. If goods are durable then generally their date of birth matters. If goods are purpose-specific, they may have a narrow market or no mediation at all. That means the purchasers of new durables or of specific goods run considerable transaction risks if there is no mediation for them in subsequent periods. Considerable costs may be required for their exchange. This is a familiar problem of illiquidity and inflexibility. The risk is two-fold: there being no mediation it is not plausible to suppose that there is a known price. But there is also the cost of finding an exchange partner at all. These risks of incomplete mediation have been ignored in the incomplete market literature. They may have serious consequences.

To sum up. I have argued that the textbook notion of 'market' is unsatisfactory, not only because of its lack of realism but also because it leaves an extremely important range of activities unexplained. I have proposed to distinguish between mediated and non-mediated exchange. Completeness now refers to mediated exchange. Because of increasing returns to most mediation, we would not expect a counterpart to the first Welfare Theorem to hold. One also expects that this is a further source of multiplicity. Lack of mediation exposes agents to uncertainty which is different from state of the world uncertainty, and which may be more important. A theory of the economy from the standpoint here taken concerns a monetary economy since one can take it that, because of the high cost of doing so, mediation in a barter economy would be much restricted.

## III Remarks on Production and Imperfect Competition

So far I have been largely concerned with pure exchange economies. Production raises new problems which I can touch on but not resolve.

I have already noted that when markets are incomplete we cannot rely on shareholders' unanimity to justify the assumption of profit maximisation. Except for some special cases (e.g. Dreze [1987], Grossman-Hart [1979]), the principal-agent problem becomes peculiarly opaque. Many of the difficulties point towards a managerial theory of the firm. That is to a theory in which the organisation and perhaps ethos of a firm, as well as its information flows, become central. There are such theories, but much remains to be done. One part of this will have to deal with the constraints in which managerial decisions operate. Here incompleteness will again be important. We believe that management must pay some attention to share prices (because of take-overs), but except for the case of risk-neutral investors, we cannot rely on the 'efficient market' hypothesis. Share prices will reflect not only estimates of profits but also attitudes to risk. It is for instance not at all clear how managers should evaluate the effect on the price of their shares of increased expenditure on R and D.

It may now be argued that while these observations are largely correct it is nonetheless unlikely that the hypothesis of profit maximisation will be seriously misleading when, for instance, used as a basis for comparative statics. Thus, it may be said, there is no reason to suppose that managers will not wish to produce efficiently, so that for instance well known substitution effects of changes in relative input prices will continue to be validly predictable. I have some sympathy for this view but there are reservations. These are that this kind of 'as if' methodology will leave many important phenomena unexplained and indeed unpredicted. For instance risk-aversion, together with incompleteness, seems important for an understanding of investment which is postponed until some uncertainty is resolved. Hence at the very least I would take 'as if' far enough to endow the firm with a utility function. This sloppy way out is perhaps the best we can do now—but it is very much a second best.

But in many ways a more serious problem is raised by the perfect competition postulate. There is a limit to 'as iffery', and here we have probably reached it. Certainly the assumption stops us asking important questions or explaining important phenomena. For instance it rules out any meaning to a claim that effective demand is too high or low and of course it makes a theory of price adjustment by economic agents impossible. At the very least it must be worthwhile attempting theories not so much at variance with the world. Of course I cannot do so here and I confine myself to only a few remarks on non-perfect competition and incomplete markets.

Once one takes the courageous step to do without the perfect competition assumption one also begins to feel that 'state of the world incompleteness' may not be the only, or even most important, form of incompleteness. That is because non-perfect competition thinking quickly leads one to recognise externalities which have nothing directly to do with property rights and do not seem to lend themselves to market-like cures. It is here simplest to think of game theory. There the externality—that is, the effect of the actions of other players on the pay-off of a given player—is of course of the essence. Not surprisingly it has been found that very often games have multiple Nash equilibria which can be Pareto-ranked. One may ask whether this could be avoided by redesigning the game without making it a co-operative one. The intrinsic externalities one here encounters and the 'co-ordination failures' which they lead to have been the subject of useful papers for example by Heller (1986).

As far as I know, no one has yet succeeded in formulating an economy-wide market game in which firms, workers and consumers are players. It certainly will be a formidable task. But one conclusion seems to me pretty certain to be reached. Arrow-securities, even if complete, will not yield the required co-ordination. That is so because firms need to know not only next period's price (for each state) but also next period's demand at that price and state. Not just that they need to know demand functions. The Arrow-securities markets will not convey that information. So if we were designing a market game for this world we would, I believe, need all the Arrow-Debreu goods markets plus something else. That something else would require knowledge of the consequences of deviating from the given price. Prices are not now 'called' but set. Negishi (1960) took the first step here and I followed him with the idea of a 'conjectural equilibrium' (1978).

But the difficulties with these notions are still very severe. For even if in some sense conjectures are 'correct', there seem to be very many equilibria with correct conjectures. Once again only more insistently, we need to think of an equilibrium of beliefs. The so-called 'fundamentals' of the economy will be seen only through a glass darkly.

But that markets do not provide a sufficiently rich language by which agents can communicate is a conclusion which I consider to be of some importance. To return to the Keynesian theme of my opening, not only is savings not a demand for future goods, neither is the supply of labour. That is, an individual firm hiring more labour will not know whether the extra output can be sold at the going price. Some forward markets for labour in the form of labour contracts exist, but these have only been studied under the perfect competition hypothesis. One should, it would seem, combine these with proper forward markets for goods. While these would still leave us exposed to the indeterminacy arising from beliefs, it may just be possible to show that, for instance, a central Keynesian problem could be avoided—at least if that is interpreted as the efficient use of labour.

This is as far as I can go. I hope I may have convinced you that the problems raised by incomplete markets are real and not just purely theoretical problems. I believe that many of these, perhaps not in the form which I have given them, exercised Keynes. He has been declared out of date and wrong by the very simple device of ignoring and assuming away all of the difficulties which he thought to be important. But they will not go away. When, as now appears to be the case, they are again recognised, economists will again become more circumspect in their judgment of market economies. It is unlikely that we shall find that *The General Theory* provides all that we need. But it will again be seen as pointing to the right questions.

It may well be that Keynes' insights, from liquidity preference to the role of effective demand, are now best understood as the 'economics of missing markets'.

*Note.* I am greatly indebted to Kenneth Arrow, Robert Evans and Robert Solow for comments on a first draft.

# References

Arrow, K. J. (1953): Le rôle des valeurs boursières pour la repartition la meilleure des risques', *Econométrie, Colloques Internationaux du Centre National de la Recherche Scientifique* 11, 41–7. English translation, *Review of Economic Studies* 31 (1964), 91–6.

Cass, D. (1984): 'Competitive Equilibrium with Incomplete Financial Markets', CARESS Working Paper 85–16, University of Pennsylvania.

Diamond, P. (1982): *A Search-Equilibrium Approach to the Micro-Foundations of Macroeconomics* (The Wicksell Lectures 1982), Massachusetts Institute of Technology.

Dreze, J. (1987): 'Pseudo Equilibria of the Firm' in Jacques Dreze; *Essays on Economic Decisions under Uncertainty*, pp. 271–3, Cambridge University Press.

Duffie, D. (1990): 'Money in General Equilibrium Theory' in B. Friedman and F. Hahn (eds.), *Handbook of Monetary Economics*, pp. 82–100.

Gale, D. (1982): *Money: In Equilibrium*, Cambridge Economic Handbook, Cambridge University Press.

Gale, D. (1986): 'Bargaining and Competition Part I: Characterisation', *Econometrica* 54, 785–806.

Gale, D. (1986): 'Bargaining and Competition Part II: Existence', *Econometrica* 54, pp. 807–18.

Geanakoplos, J. and Polemarchakis, H. (1986): 'Existence, Regularity and Constrained Suboptimality of Competitive Allocations when Markets are Incomplete', in Heller, Starr and Starrett (eds.), *Essays in Honor of Kenneth Arrow*, Vol. 3, Cambridge University Press.

Geanakoplos, J. and Mas-Colell, A. (1989): 'Real Indeterminacy with Financial Assets', *Journal of Economic Theory* 47 (1), 22–38

Grossman, S. and Hart, O. (1979): 'A Theory of Competitive Equilibrium in Stock Market Economies', *Econometrica* 47, 293–330

Hahn, F. H. (1965): 'Equilibrium with Transaction Costs', *Econometrica* 39, 417–39.

Hahn, F. (1978): 'On Non-Walrasian Equilibria', *Review of Economic Studies* 45, 1–17.

Heller, W. (1986): 'Co-ordination Failure under Complete Markets with Applications to Effective Demand', in Heller, Starr, Starrett (eds.), *Equilibrium Analysis*, Essays in Honor of K. J. Arrow, Vol. 2, pp. 155–76.

Negishi, T. (1960): 'Monopolistic Competition and General Equilibrium', *Review of Economic Studies* 28, 196–201.

Newbery, D. and Stiglitz, J. (1981): *The Theory of Commodity Price Stabilization (A Study in The Economics of Risk)*, Clarendon Press, Oxford.

Newbery, D. (1989): 'Missing Markets: Consequences and Remedies', in F. Hahn (ed.), *The Economics of Missing Markets, Information and Games*, Clarendon Press, Oxford.

Ostroy, J. and Starr, R. (1990): 'The Transaction Role of Money', in B. Friedman and F. Hahn (eds.), *Handbook of Monetary Economics*, pp. 3–62.

Radner, R. (1972): 'Existence of Equilibrium of Plans, Prices and Price Expectations in a Sequence of Markets', *Econometrica* 40, No. 2, 284–304.

Savage, L.J. (1954): *The Foundations of Statistics*, John Wiley, New York.

Stahle II, D. (1988): 'Bertrand Competition for Inputs and Walrasian Outcomes', *The American Economic Review* 78 (1), 189–201

Yanelle, M.O. (1989): 'The Strategic Analysis of Intermediation', *European Economic Review* 33, 294–301.

*Proceedings of the British Academy*, **80**, 221–231

# Antony Andrewes
# 1910–1990

ANTONY ANDREWES was the eldest son of Percy Lancelot Andrewes and Ursula Andrewes (*née* Freeman), and was born in Tavistock on 12 June 1910. His father was an art dealer who subsequently became a teacher of mathematics. Although they soon moved to Brighton, his affection for Dartmoor remained throughout his life. Much of his mother's family life was based on the area, and it was the centre to which they all returned for walking holidays even before his father took a post at Kelly College, Tavistock. It was a musical family, and he played duets, both on the cello and on the piano, with his father and brother; the range was wide, though Schumann was a particular favourite, and the piano at least remained important for him. It was in the home too that he laid the foundations of his wide reading in English and European literature. Later he regularly acquired more languages by starting from their major classics; Dante was particularly important.

He was educated first at Horris Hill, outside Newbury (where his younger brother Richard subsequently became a headmaster) and then at Winchester to which he won the top scholarship in 1923. At Winchester, he came under the influence of the 'eager, even uproarious,' teaching of Alan Blakeway, who, there and at Oxford, first fertilised traditional Oxford approaches to archaic Greek history with strong archaeological interests.

The tutors he found at New College could not live up to this standard, and he did not later talk much about them, even about Stanley Casson, the most obviously relevant; he made exceptions for Eric Yorke for Mods and Alick Smith for philosophy. He has given his own account of Greek History at Oxford in the 1930s in his memoir of Wade-Gery,[1] to whose iconoclasm and vivid historical imagination he owed as much as to Blakeway. This was

[1] *PBA* 59, 1973, 419–26.

A. ANDREWES

one field of Oxford classics which was already bubbling at the arrival of the German professionals who did so much to toughen them. What he does not recount there are the disasters, the deaths of Humfrey Payne in 1936, Alan Blakeway in 1937, the promising Robert Beaumont in 1938. The coda to these premature losses was the death of Tom Dunbabin, a professional in both history and archaeology, in 1955. Finding ways of keeping archaeology in Oxford Greek History alive, particularly at undergraduate level, is still a struggle.

Elected soon after Greats in 1933 to a Fellowship at Pembroke, he went off for a year in Athens. The year gave him the foundation for a wide knowledge of Greek topography, particularly of the Peloponnese, and to have lived through the procession of the seasons was a radical enlightenment about Greek life. He made many new friendships, most of which terminated prematurely, but Martin Robertson at least remained an important source of artistic and archaeological counsel throughout his life.

In 1934 he got into harness, and rapidly made his mark as a don who, despite doing serious work, had time to drink with and talk to undergraduates. Though his University Lecturership, then in short supply, did not come through until 1939, young tutors were expected to lecture. For his first two years, he could very much please himself and, both in 1935 and in 1936, he offered luxury courses on 'The Greeks in Egypt' and 'Argos', the first at least surprising in relation to his later interests. 1937 produced sterner stuff, two double courses on 'The Seventh Century B.C.' and 'Athenian Democracy'. He threw away all his pre-war lecture notes, and knowledge of his development can only be deduced from his articles.

Two papers present totally pre-war work. He could hardly have avoided an early interest in archaic Sparta, dominant in British minds since the *Artemis Orthia* publication in 1929 had revealed normality, even luxury, in seventh-century Sparta. Blakeway had taken a position in a review (*CR* 49, 1935, 184–5), which his own first paper (*CQ* 32, 1938, 89–102) developed more widely, reassessing the word *eunomia* and the accounts of archaic Sparta in Herodotus and Thucydides in the light of what now seemed the most likely sequence of events.[2] A similar operation on an apparently disjointed Herodotean narrative (*BSA* 37, 1936–7 [1940], 1–7) started well and ended fairly wildly.

Besides trying to see whether Herodotus and Thucydides were telling the truth about archaic history, his interest in Argos led him, not only to

---

[2] There are strong connexions with Wade-Gery's more developed position (*CQ* 37, 1943, 57–78; 38, 1944, 1–9, 115–26).

further exploration on the ground in 1937, but to the question of what could be said about later historical tradition on mainland Greece. The most profitable approach was to try to explore the work of the lost, but influential, Ephorus. Two papers related to Argos which did not appear until well after the war[3] represent this line of work.

The war gave him access to wider fields of human experience. Dropped into the north-west Peloponnese, he had ample opportunity to contemplate Greeks, Italians and Germans under pressure and the gap between ideas in Cairo offices and realities on the ground. 'He immediately made himself at home with people of all ranks and social levels, knew everybody's story and was immediately loved and revered by all who were capable of such feelings. To the Greeks he was simply Toni—a name very properly considered to be Greek from the start.'[4] 'Research has revealed glimpses of the recruit to the Special Operations Executive attending a demolitions course at Arisaig and practising the art of sticking limpet mines on ships in Mallaig harbour; of his acquiring the art of subversive living in the depths of the New Forest, riding a motor bicycle through the battered streets of Southampton and shadowing presumed secret agents in crowded saloon bars; of his travelling from Freetown to Lagos in a Norwegian merchant vessel manned by a Chinese crew and eating birdsnest soup with undiminished bonhomie; of his showing the skills of a contortionist while undergoing parachute training on the summit of Mount Carmel; of his arriving in the Peloponnese and gathering a band of "faithfuls" to act as his runners, guides and suppliers; of his accepting the surrender of two German battalions at Patras and passing on by jeep to liberate Monemvasia; and, last but not least, of his ability to relax *à la grecque* when the appropriate time came. "When God sent a cheerful hour", it is said, "he did not refrain".'[5] About all this he seldom spoke later, except on the odd occasion when a wartime thought was relevant to classical campaigning.

In 1946 he came back from the war with an M.B.E. to a Tutorial Fellowship of New College, with which, with a switch from tutorship to professorship, he stayed in a close bond of affection, tempered by amusement, till his death. He was not an ideal tutor, though he inspired great personal loyalty. If a pupil bored him, he had no hesitation in saying so, and this was not always an effective technique. But he responded to those who worked and, even after becoming professor, enjoyed small doses of tutorial work.

---

[3] 'The Corinthian Actaeon and Pheidon of Argos', *CQ* 43, 1949, 70–8; 'Ephorus Book I and the Kings of Argos', *CQ* N.S. 1, 1951, 39–45.

[4] *The Times*, 15 June 1990.

[5] *New College Record for 1976–77*, 1–2, but he himself attributed the Patras coup to Eric Gray.

The first large-scale task which he took on in 1946, together with Russell Meiggs, was a revision of G.F. Hill's *Sources for Greek History B.C. 478–431*, long out of print, somewhat wastefully organised, and totally out of date epigraphically. Progress was slow, and publication did not come until 1951. It is long out of print, but still useful, not so much for its collection of the texts as for the meticulous arrangement of the indices, which make it easy to establish rapidly the primary evidence for any particular topic. This was the great age of Attic fifth-century epigraphy, the years of the creation of *The Athenian Tribute Lists*. Andrewes was never as deeply involved as Wade-Gery or Meiggs in these matters and never worked on actual stones, but, with reinforcement from a stay with Meritt in Princeton in the winter of 1949–50, he could cope easily and constructively with epigraphic argument.

In 1953, he was elected Wykeham Professor of Ancient History in succession to Wade-Gery. Though Meiggs was the senior man, he had more devotion to college and tutorial life, and everyone was happy. Andrewes' lectures, ingeniously constructed, had probably always been more effective than his tutorial work, and he now gave more of them, rewriting them in full virtually every year and hardly ever refusing a request, though managing to avoid any course later than the battle of Leuctra. He took a great deal of trouble with his graduate students, with patchy results, chiefly because he had a tendency to pass on those who were both good and efficient and keep the problems; his best were particularly prone to prolixity and have still not established their full stature. The most memorable features of his tenure of the chair are various major seminars, in which careful planning broke open new fields, and in which he did most of the work himself or with a single colleague; the current fashion is rather different. Administration he faced without fuss, and could be relied upon to find a way out of trouble, by diplomacy or, on occasion, by decisive and unconstitutional action.[6]

A lecture-course on 'Aristocracy and Tyranny', which had been developing and changing at least since 1946, eventually resulted in *The Greek Tyrants* (1956).[7] This book will have been many people's first introduction to serious work on Greek History, and can still be read with profit at all levels. It was still very much in the tradition of Blakeway, tempering the scattered and unsatisfactory literary evidence with injections from the archaeological picture and a sense of realism. It was thus a substantial contrast to its predecessor, P. N. Ure's *The*

---

[6] In one *cause célèbre* the examiners had disagreed about a thesis. He short-circuited discussion and months of further red-tape by telling the Faculty Board that he had voluntarily worked through the thesis himself and that it would become a standard work; the prediction was amply justified.

[7] His election to a Fellowship of the Academy in 1957 followed on this.

*Origin of Tyranny* which had pressed (and sometimes tortured) every scrap of evidence into arguing for an origin of tyranny in capitalists who had profited from the expansion of trade in the early archaic period. There was no attempt to destroy this picture except by substituting another; it is even a shade surprising that there is no reference to Hasebroek's anti-modernist operations on archaic trade.[8] The problem of why Greek tyranny started in the north-east Peloponnese received a very different answer. Aristotle's information about Pheidon of Argos, the king who went beyond his inherited rights, was linked to recent work by Miss Lorimer (*BSA* 42, 1947, 76–138) on the origins of the hoplite phalanx. Tyranny and hoplites seemed very close in date, and, since Lorimer insisted that all elements of hoplite warfare must have come into use simultaneously, it was attractive to link its introduction with the powerful military figure of Pheidon[9] and its spread with the spread of tyrannies elsewhere, particularly at Corinth. Suggestive though the thesis was, it did not survive long in this form, except in examination scripts; there was too much evidence for the employment of individual items of the hoplite's repertoire before the introduction of the phalanx.[10] It remains possible, even likely, that a larger supply of metals brought by trade was broadening the social groups which had a part to play in war, but, as Andrewes admitted from the first, there was no necessary connection between that and tyranny; Sparta was a counter-example. Spartan avoidance of tyranny had been the theme of his mature and wide-ranging inaugural lecture of 1954, *Probouleusis: Sparta's Contribution to the Technique of Government*, arguing that it had been achieved by a controlled recognition of the rights of the popular assembly, from which other Greek states had eventually learned.

Discontent with working from literary and archaeological scraps in the archaic period had been setting in for some time. For choice, he ceased to lecture on the early period, except on Athens; further work on Sparta was purely classical. By the early 1950s the interest in Ephorus had turned to a later period, where there were at least coherent stretches of Diodorus to represent him; the appearance of a new papyrus of the *Hellenica Oxyrhynchia*, a work related to Ephorus and Diodorus, encouraged exploration and revaluation. Notes and repeated drafts started to accumulate on Diodorus and the historiography of the Peloponnesian

---

[8] Lecture-notes of 1946 and 1947 show that he then thought that Blakeway's refutations of Hasebroek's travelling potters constituted all that there was any need to say about Hasebroek.

[9] He had already tidied the various ancient datings of Pheidon in *CQ* 43, 1949, 70–8. Not everybody has been satisfied with his solution, and the questions remain open.

[10] *The Greeks* (1967), 149, 277 represents a fairly rapid capitulation in the face of Snodgrass, *JHS* 85, 1965, 110–22.

War after the end of Thucydides's narrative; real history of the period got into print in a paper of 1953, particularly satisfying, because a problem was actually solved and stayed solved.[11]

The American visit of 1949–50 had given him an affection for America, its institutions and individual Americans which never left him; he repeated it several times. In the early 1950s the affection could only be tempered by concern about political and intellectual developments there. One result of these was to bring to England in 1954 Moses Finley, then virtually unknown and out of a job; after a term in Oxford and one in Cambridge he had the choice of two. They struck up an immediate rapport, and correspondence and frequent meetings lasted until Finley's death. Finley was fascinated with the formidable technical equipment of British Greek historians, much though he disapproved of their total lack of theoretical baggage and their tendency to speculate on inadequate evidence. For Andrewes, the attraction of Finley was not so much his theoretical interests as the liveliness which he brought into all discussion and his determination to cut through the sources to reality. The author of *The World of Odysseus* had much to offer to someone who had been approaching the archaic period in rather different ways. His exposure to non-Oxford ways was enhanced by the arrival of Geoffrey de Ste Croix at New College to succeed him in his tutorship; there was fruitful interaction here too.

He had, we have already seen, become discontented with his way of doing early Greek history. He now moved into work on archaic social institutions based on survivals and anthropological consultation, and two key papers[12] cleared away much dead wood and pointed the way to much later work. His later work on archaic history was more or less confined to Athens, in two superb chapters of synthesis in the *Cambridge Ancient History*.

The work on social institutions formed one of the most substantial contributions in *The Greeks* (1967; *Greek Society* as a Penguin, 1971), perhaps the best general introduction to Greek society ever written, free of the idealisation of Greek life prevalent in such works up till then, and again widely read. He himself was liable to refer to it as 'the plumbing'. Good though it is, he hated the job; the prescription suggested by Finley, to write first and think afterwards, was not always helpful. He came near giving it up on grounds of conscience and was only kept going by 'a moral talk from Meiggs'; fortunately, by July 1966, 'Plumb's reply suggests that, if I can only keep Moses under

---

[11] 'The Generals in the Hellespont, 410–407 B.C.', *JHS* 73, 1953, 2–9.
[12] 'Phratries in Homer', *Hermes* 89, 1961, 129–40; 'Philochoros on Phratries', *JHS* 81, 1961, 1–15.

reasonable control, I may be almost at the end of that awful enterprise, to the relief of everyone except those unguarded enough to read the result'.

The sequence just described overlapped with one even more substantial. Between 1959 and 1962, he published four major papers[13] which reshaped the debate on the development of Thucydides' thinking. The first of these recast with great power the thesis of Eduard Schwartz that Thucydides had changed his mind about the causes of the Peloponnesian War and had modified the original structure of Book I. Jacqueline de Romilly had in 1951 made a very strong and enticing case for an unitary Book I and there are still few questions which divide Thucydidean scholars more. Even among analysts other approaches are possible, but Andrewes' case remains compulsory reading. The third paper took up the inequalities of Thucydides' treatment of Persia, and drew the inevitable but then unfashionable conclusion that Books VI and VII had reached virtual 'completeness' at a very early stage. The two others are more speculative in their attempts to fit major set-pieces in the History into relatively late stages of Thucydides' thought. The purpose of the Melian Dialogue is a problem for all except the most simple-minded, and continued wrestling with it led Andrewes in his latest work for the *Cambridge Ancient History* to even more unpalatable conclusions. That the Mytilene Debate is a late work has never been particularly easy to believe, but the article on it has become a classic, since it also contains particularly sensible doctrine on Thucydides' practice in speech-writing and substantive discussion on the Athenian demagogues (Finley simultaneously produced a complementary paper on this).

He was thus well prepared to join Kenneth Dover in the completion of Gomme's *Historical Commentary on Thucydides* when Gomme died in 1959. With subsidiary studies, this took fifteen years or so, and is his most substantial achievement. Dealing with Gomme's extensive but incomplete drafts on Book V was particularly arduous and raised worries about methods of presentation and the numerous places where 'the comment sometimes becomes a dialogue in which one party is unfairly prevented from answering back'; it was with relief that, at last 'dégommé', he could turn to Book VIII, for which Gomme had left no notes. Nothing normal to a commentary was shirked, and the minutiae sometimes took most time; worries about the topography and purpose of

---

[13] 'Thucydides on the Causes of the War', *CQ* N.S. 9, 1959, 223–39; 'The Melian Dialogue and Perikles' Last Speech', *Proc. Camb. Phil. Soc.* no. 186, 1960, 1–10; 'Thucydides and the Persians', *Historia* 10, 1961, 1–18; 'The Mytilene Debate: Thucydides 3.36–49', *Phoenix* 16, 1962, 64–85.

the fort on Eëtioneia persisted for several months. Good judges found his feeling for Greek and patience with the transmitted text superior to that of Gomme.

As he worked through the commentary, dissection was becoming increasingly unfashionable. There had always been those who had seen Thucydides as a flawless genius, and these were reinforced by a new generation of those who insisted on seeing the work as a completed literary whole to be read in order from beginning to end. He observed of one book on these lines, by someone he personally liked: 'This is not at all my world . . . sympathy with the notion that Thucydides's thoughts continually developed is seriously strained when the development has to be forwards from ii.65 to viii.97'. He could not accept what seemed to him to be flying in the face of observable fact. Enforced close attention to the particularly puzzling Books V and VIII could only strengthen his beliefs. The relationship of documents to text in Book V was a long-standing puzzle, and the old thesis that Book VIII contained parallel narratives which had not been pulled together looked more and more plausible the more he looked at it.[14] Giving far closer attention to the text than most, he never overlooked a problem or an incoherence in it. This did not result in a crude dissection into strata; it did pay close attention to what could be discerned about the processes of composition involved in writing a long work over a long period. In his hands and those of Dover, Thucydides has become a personality, not a monolithic authority.

As work on the commentary came to a close, he came under increasing pressure, particularly from Finley, to write a book on Thucydides, but resolutely refused on the grounds that other lower-level problems were more suitable to his age. This was regrettable, and surviving material is not sufficient to plug the gap, though there is a tempting batch of three or four lectures on the subject from 1963 or so ending 'He was certainly a great impressionist; whether he deserves the title of scientific historian is another matter.'

Apart from one or two small articles, his last completed work was for the *Cambridge Ancient History*, two chapters on the history of the Peloponnesian War from the Peace of Nikias to its end; they continue to show new thinking.

The project he selected for his final work almost brought him full circle. The work on Ephorus originally undertaken for the sake of Argos and the 'more extended survey of the sources for the period after 411, which in

---

[14] For an attempt at refutation see H. Erbse, *Thukydides-Interpretationen* (1989), which the state of his eyesight kept him from.

the event was postponed for the sake of the commentary on Thucydides'[15] would be subsumed in a book on Diodorus. He could not love him for his own sake, but found his use of his predecessors a satisfyingly tough subject. For the purpose, at 77, he applied himself to the problem that he always wrote everything at least twice,[16] and took to word-processing. He started with the topic which offered some hope of a solution, Diodorus' use of his chronographic source, and found Diodorus, though manifestly incompetent, at least more innovative than had been thought. He then moved on to characterise Ephorus in a substantial, though incomplete, piece. Though there is surely matter to salvage here, there is no real hope of getting a book out of what remains: chapter 1 consists of the first five lines (with two pages of notes), and he had embarked on an extensive course of reading on Diodorus' reputation across the centuries when his eyes began to give trouble and the first signs of his final illness appeared.

This renewed work followed a relatively fallow period caused by personal circumstances, and involved considerable will-power. He had always been particularly conscientious about personal obligations, and one could name many which he acknowledged and on which he spent time and energy. Above all, there had been the rising tide of concern for his wife Alison, the widow of Alan Blakeway, whom he had married in 1938. She had broadened him in ways which can now be only dimly discerned and brought a special flavour of fun and devilry to the household in Manor Place, but her last years took a great deal of energy, and he gave it unstintingly. After her death in 1983 there was a new start to be made, but he managed to fill his life effectively, and not only on Diodorus. Passionately interested in the pursuits and occupations of his two daughters and their husbands and children, he continued to contemplate the problems of his garden and look forward to the next opera. He took a variety of holidays, including a last one in America, offered counsel to friends in academic tangles, and did the rounds of Oxford's seminars.[17] These kept his critical faculties well up to scratch. Though he maintained his longstanding reluctance to conduct in public any argument which might take a personal tinge, he did not cease in private to express his extreme distaste for manifestations of pretence or pretentiousness. He set himself high intellectual standards and expected them of others.

---

[15] *JHS* 102, 1982, 15.

[16] The second draft was never all that similar to the first; it was not just a matter of removing adjectives, since he had never put many in in the first place.

[17] *The Greek City from Homer to Alexander* (1990), edited by Oswyn Murray and Simon Price, is dedicated to 'the most senior member of our seminar, who missed not a single meeting, and whose wise counsels have continued to guide each generation of Oxford graduates in Greek history for thirty years'.

This inner hard core was not visible in the courtesy and consideration which are the main memories of his more distant colleagues and the younger members of his Senior Common Room, which he frequented much more after Alison's death. These were confronted with what seemed an immensely tall figure, who turned out to be exceptionally mild of manner. They first had to learn how to 'interpret that distinctive Androvian style of utterance—a kind of vocal Linear B, allusive, elliptical and, above all, orotund. What the pebble was reputed to have been for Demosthenes a hot potato seemingly was for Tony—except that in his case so far from transforming his voice production it became an integral part of it'.[18] Once past that, they were entranced by the range of his conversation, based on wide and continually refreshed reading and listening. There were few things which did not interest him. One may single out music and opera, liable to produce a wide range of reminiscence extending back to Bayreuth in the 1930s, and the minutiae of politics. Essentially of the moderate left (never further, even in the 1930s), he had clear views about particular matters, but was seldom active.[19] Of North American politics he was simply a connoisseur, but a knowledgable one. The day before he died, on 13 June 1990, he was complaining of an imbalance of reporting which was denying him adequate understanding of the Canadian constitutional crisis.

It would be totally misleading to leave an impression of pure intellect. He had had more to absorb in the way of premature deaths and disasters of friends and contemporaries than most people, and they never left him unmoved. In the sunny periods, he maintained relations and affection, if only by a battery of unusual postcards, with a wide variety of people. They will remember not only his intelligence and his curiosity, but his humanity.

D. M. LEWIS
*Fellow of the British Academy*

*Note.* I have had particular help from Helen Forde, Judith Hunt, George Forrest and Herbert Nicholas, and have drawn on a file of correspondence covering over thirty years, some of it now too cryptic to interpret.

---

[18] H. G. Nicholas at Andrewes' funeral.

[19] His *Times* obituarist tells us that his Commandership of the Order of the Phoenix, conferred in 1978, showed appreciation of his less overt but no less effective support for a later Greek resistance movement.

*Proceedings of the British Academy*, **80**, 233–243

# John Gordon Beckwith
# 1918–1991

JOHN BECKWITH formed part of a group of scholar-curators who, after the Second World War, established the English National Museums as centres of academic excellence with a steady stream of erudite articles and more wide-ranging books aimed at the educated public.

He was born on 2 December 1918. Tragedy struck his family two years later, when his mother died giving birth to his brother Peter. His father, unable to cope with the burden of bringing up the two boys alone, deserted them and it was left to their paternal grandmother to raise the children. By all accounts she did this successfully: John sometimes recounted how his gift for languages was nurtured from an early age under the tutelage of a close friend of his grandmother's, Mimi Turnbull, and how French was often spoken at meal times in her house at Whitby. His affection for the town remained strong: I remember innocently asking him in 1980 whether he had visited the great Viking exhibition then being held at the British Museum and being taken aback by his typically robust and revealing riposte—'No, nor do I intend to. Those barbarians destroyed my beloved Whitby'. It was as if he had witnessed the destruction himself and the memory was still fresh.

He was sent to Ampleforth, and the education he received there was to shape his future. He was clearly extremely happy at the school and retained a fondness for it throughout his life which went far beyond most people's feelings for their old school; it served as a second home and no doubt provided him with a security which had been missing since the loss of his parents. He spoke often of his love for the place, and it was his hope that he might be offered a home in the grounds in later life. This never came to pass, but his special closeness to Ampleforth has now been marked permanently with the bequest of his library to the Abbey. In addition to his talent for

J. G. BECKWITH                    *Hon. Nicholas Sellicre*

French, at an early age he developed an interest in History and excelled at it, so that a place at Exeter College, Oxford, was duly offered.

He went up to Oxford in 1937 as a Loscombe Richards Exhibitioner, reading Modern History, but after two years as an undergraduate his studies were interrupted by the outbreak of the Second World War. He immediately joined up and remained in the Duke of Wellington's Regiment throughout the War. The War dealt two further serious blows to the young Beckwith: his brother was killed in 1941 and he himself was severely wounded after the D-Day landings in the battle for Le Parc de Boislande on 17 June 1944. His right hand was permanently injured and disfigured, forcing him to write with his left hand and to give up playing the piano, one of the great loves of his life. This must have been a heartbreaking turn of events. After a long period of convalescence, and now without any close family except for his cousins and aunt (his grandmother had died in 1938) he returned to Exeter College to continue his studies. At university he made a number of friends with whom he would remain on close terms for many years: foremost amongst these were Fr. Gervase Mathew, who encouraged in John an interest in things Byzantine, and who was to advise and help him over a long period; Denys Sutton, later to become the influential editor of *Apollo* magazine, for which Beckwith would write numerous short and pithy book reviews; and Ralph Pinder-Wilson, with whom he was to share a profound interest in Islamic art. He was also much influenced by the lectures of Otto Pächt, who was later to become a good friend. Graduating in 1947, he embarked on a D.Phil. on an aspect of medieval constitutional history, but this was abandoned when he applied for and was offered a job at the Victoria and Albert Museum the following year. By the time he came to make a career decision John was, by the standards of today, quite old (at 30) to be entering employment for the first time. He had already devoured a huge amount of both literature and historical material, but decided in the end that a university career was not the life for him. He briefly dabbled with the idea of diplomatic service, where he could have exercised his abilities for language, but instead was persuaded that a post in one of the national museums offered greater potential for his particular blend of talents. Consequently he went in 1948 for an unofficial talk with John Pope-Hennessy at the Victoria and Albert Museum, and shortly afterwards joined the Museum as one of the first batch of Assistant Keepers to be appointed after the War, together with John Hayward, Terence Hodgkinson, Jonathan Mayne and Peter Ward-Jackson. He was to remain at the Museum for his whole working life.

Posted initially in the Department of Textiles, under the Keepership of George Wingfield Digby, Beckwith took up responsibility for the Coptic, Byzantine and early medieval material. The study of these textiles had

moved on remarkably little since the endeavours of Thomas Kendrick
in the 1920s and he was able to build up a detailed knowledge of them
in a remarkably short period of time. He combined a sound historical
knowledge with a close inspection of the textiles themselves, in the
classic curatorial manner, and by the early 1950s he was recognised in the
international scholarly community as a force to be reckoned with, speaking
with authority at many conferences, taking up a Visiting Fellowship
at Harvard University's Centre for Byzantine Studies at Dumbarton
Oaks in Washington in 1950–1 and becoming a Member of the Centre
Internationale des Études des Textils Anciens at Lyon in 1953. He travelled
tirelessly on study trips, especially in the Middle East, becoming familiar
with the monuments of Istanbul and greater Turkey (he had an extended
stay at the British Institute of Archaeology in Ankara), and in the
Lebanon. By this time he was fluent in French, German and Italian
and had gained a good reading knowledge of Latin, Greek and some of
the Slav languages. He started work on a comprehensive catalogue of the
Byzantine silks in the Museum's collection but this, unfortunately, was to
remain uncompleted. Wingfield Digby, from an older school, was uneasy
with Beckwith's rigorous academic approach and was perhaps jealous of
his younger international network of colleagues; relations between the two
became strained, resulting in the latter's transfer, while on annual leave
and against his wishes, to the Department of Architecture and Sculpture
in 1955. Although his curatorial responsibilities now covered medieval
sculpture his expertise was not surprisingly still called on by students of
textiles and he continued to publish in that area.[1]

John now turned his energies overwhelmingly towards the study of
medieval ivory carvings, largely because the Victoria and Albert Museum
houses one of the most comprehensive collections in the world, but also
because there seemed much to do on the subject. Then, as now, all
scholars depended to a very great extent on the *corpora* of Adolph
Goldschmidt on early medieval ivories published between 1914 and 1926,
on the two volumes on Byzantine ivories published by the same author
in conjunction with the young Kurt Weitzmann in 1930–4, and on W.F.
Volbach's *Elfenbeinarbeiten der Spätantike und des frühen Mittelalters*
(then in its second edition of 1952). Although these catalogues provided
a solid foundation for study, Beckwith set out in his first ten years in the
Department to publish new discoveries, refine problems of dating and
localisation, and to make the early medieval and Byzantine collection of

---

[1] Most notably 'Coptic Textiles', *Ciba Review*, XII, no. 133, August 1959, pp.2–27, and
'Byzantine Tissues', *Actes du XIVe Congrès International des Études byzantines*, Bucharest,
1974, I, pp.33–44 (both reprinted in John Beckwith, *Studies in Byzantine and Medieval
Western Art*, London, 1989, pp.1–70).

ivories at the V&A known to a wider constituency through more popular publications. In the first two areas he wrote a large number of important articles, in some cases on ivories which he himself had acquired for the Museum;[2] in the latter category he published five titles in the attractive and useful V&A Museum Monograph series, concentrating on *The Andrews Diptych* (1958), *Caskets from Cordoba* (1960), *The Veroli Casket* (1962), *The Basilewsky Situla* (1963) and *The Adoration of the Magi in Whalebone* (1966).

Outside the Victoria and Albert Museum Beckwith was the co-author, with Professor David Talbot Rice, of the catalogue accompanying the highly important exhibition of Byzantine art, held in Edinburgh and London in 1958. His involvement with the exhibition, which included not only writing much of the catalogue but also selecting the objects and arranging the installation in London, was to be his first experience of this type of large exhibition; it gave him the opportunity to show a talent for display which he was to reveal on a number of later occasions in the permanent galleries of the Victoria and Albert. The selection of the objects and the opportunity to study them at close quarters also provided the basis for much of the material covered in his first book, *The Art of Constantinople*, published by the Phaidon Press in 1961. In this book he employed a formula which he would return to again: a selection of objects of the highest quality, usually in good condition and often commissioned by the imperial court, were illustrated and discussed in the context of their historical background, with special emphasis being placed on the more notable and important personalities. He was blessed with a lucid and flowing prose style, which always makes his books a pleasure to read. At least one of the reviewers missed the point of the book, which was to make the subject more accessible to the educated public, to interpret rather than to break new ground. Within these parameters it was manifestly successful, and it sold well.

His next book, on Coptic sculpture, was published by the firm of Alec Tiranti in 1963 as one of their pioneering 'Chapters in Art' series, which

---

[2] 'An Ivory Relief of the Ascension', *Burlington Magazine*, XCVIII, 1956, pp. 118–20; 'An Ivory Relief of the Deposition', *idem*, pp.228–35; 'The Werden Casket reconsidered', *Art Bulletin*, XL, 1958, pp. 1–11; 'Sculptures d'ivoire à Byzance', *L'Oeil*, 51, March, 1959, pp.19–25; 'Some Anglo-Saxon carvings in ivory', *Connoisseur*, CXLVI, 1960, pp. 241 ff.; 'An Ivory Relief of the Crucifixion', *Burlington Magazine*, CIII, 1961, pp. 434–7; 'Mother of God showing the Way: A Byzantine ivory statuette of the Theotokos Hodegetria', *Connoisseur*, CL, 1962, pp.2–7; 'A rediscovered Italo-Byzantine carving in Ivory', in *Miscellanea pro Arte. Festschrift für Hermann Schnitzler*, Dusseldorf, 1965, pp.168–70; 'A Game of Draughts', in *Studien zur Geschichte der europäischen Plastik: Festschrift Theodor Müller*, Munich, 1965, pp.31–36; 'Problèmes posées par certaines sculptures en ivoire du Haut Moyen Age', *Les Monuments Historiques de la France*, nos. 1–2, janvier-juin, 1966, pp.17 ff.; 'A rediscovered English reliquary cross', *Victoria and Albert Museum Bulletin*, II, 1966, pp.117–24.

also included George Zarnecki's three influential little books on English Romanesque sculpture. It was clearly a subject of specialist interest, but Beckwith presented the material clearly and cogently (with an excellent selection of about 150 good photographs) and avoided making it a dry discussion of concern only to a handful of scholars. Although unashamedly a history of style, it remains the only general survey of Coptic sculpture and the first point of reference for any student with an interest in the subject.

John was at the height of his powers in the 1960s, in demand as an exceedingly entertaining lecturer and as a Visiting Professor at Harvard (the Fogg Art Museum) in 1964 and at the University of Missouri at Columbia, Missouri, in 1968–9. His expert knowledge and good eye enabled him to make a number of fine acquisitions for the V&A (the most outstanding being the beautiful English eleventh-century walrus ivory pectoral cross, bought in 1966 and published by him in the same year), and his flair for display transformed many of the Museum's galleries. His favourite gallery at the Museum, and the one he himself considered to be his greatest success, was the Early Medieval Court near the main entrance, which he redisplayed in the mid 1960s and which became known in the Museum as 'Beckwith's basilica'. This remained a testament to his taste for twenty years, until it in turn was refurbished in 1986. He was to say later that the 1960s were his happiest days, working in a department with such internationally-recognised scholars as John Pope-Hennessy (Keeper of Architecture and Sculpture 1954–66, Director of the Museum 1967–74), Terence Hodgkinson (Keeper 1967–74) and the young Michael Baxandall. His standing in the academic community had been recognised within the Museum in 1958, when he had been promoted to Deputy Keeper, and in the 1960s, with a relatively light administrative workload, he was able to write an enormous amount and to lecture widely, both in this country and abroad. He was also involved in the organisation of a number of the great Council of Europe exhibitions of medieval art, most notably those on European Art around 1400 (Vienna, 1962) and on Charlemagne (Aachen, 1965), and he was on the European advisory committee for the planning of the important exhibition *The Year 1200*, held at the Metropolitan Museum in New York in 1970. He was made a Fellow of the Society of Antiquaries in 1968.

In 1964 Thames and Hudson published Beckwith's third book, *Early Medieval Art*, in their extremely popular 'World of Art' series. Covering the Carolingian to Romanesque period, this book has been on the reading lists of undergraduates since publication and has been reprinted many times. Its enduring popularity has to do with its sureness of touch, its clarity and easy-to-read authority; it is to my mind his best book and a model of how a short survey of a particular artistic period should be written. Its coverage is well-balanced, the buildings, paintings, manuscripts, sculptures and works of art are all placed in their historical context, the circumstances of their commissioning are lucidly explained, and the stylistic analyses are brilliantly succinct. Few museum curators of Beckwith's generation could have written such a wide-ranging volume on a potentially difficult subject which would appeal to such a large audience.

He was, then, by the mid sixties highly thought of and uncommonly productive. However, it seems that despite an outward appearance of great gregariousness in public he remained essentially a solitary person. He had a large number of acquaintances but few close friends. Sir Steven Runciman noted that 'he was immensely hospitable and took enormous trouble to entertain and look after scholars from abroad; and he delighted to see his old friends, who were often roped in to help him with some lady professor from Belgrade or some monk from Armenia'.[3] He is remembered by many as being wonderfully entertaining company, with a quick, witty and often wicked tongue, and a letter written to his Department from Harvard in 1964 bears this out:

> Last week I was asked to a medieval dinner by Radcliffe (the girls' college) which started with sickly sherry at 5.30 p.m., went on to grilled chicken wing (everybody had a wing, no legs to be seen) served by some of the students wearing the tall *hennin* decked out with scarves, with Renaissance music belting out from the stereo-hi-fi, and an old chasuble (Spanish, 17th century cut with 16th century embroideries) draped like a banner over the grand piano, and ended at 8.0 with coffee-bar coffee and that was that. I trudged along Garden Street, avoiding the piles of snow and the lakes of slush to get to my apartment at 8.30 ready for the party to begin. Yesterday evening I was invited to a sherry party at 5.0, which ended at 6.30, given by the President of Harvard to all new comers and their 'spouses' (as you know I don't have one) which entailed pinning a large label to oneself which gave one's name in red ink and one's profession (mine said 'F.A. Fogg' and I had to say to anyone interested that I liked it that way). Others had 'Govnt' and 'Ed' and there was a Jap with 'Psycho phys' which I found intriguing . . .

> Then there are the students: they audit this and they credit that, they major in science and audit in culture, or major in Cubism and credit in Rembrandt. And they are terribly nice. The girls are clever, attractive, and anxious to show that they care; the boys are bright, outrageously dressed (even at Harvard), and determined. The Byzantine world goes down well with them; it is so strange and remote and really beyond their comprehension. They like anything new, fresh, and lucid. And they write it all down. It comes back, as I expected, packaged, refrigerated, and slightly out of focus. But then how can you expect someone from Pensacola or Wisconsin or even Boston to tune in straightaway to the Emperor Constantine VII Porphyrogenitus?

[3] *Burlington Magazine*, CXXXIII, 1991, p.315.

> What is nice about them is that they realise it too and they are wonderfully
> receptive. They know that they are not getting it quite right and I find
> that refreshing. The visits away, New York, Cleveland, Toledo, are like
> royal progresses. These are the times when I find myself on a pedestal
> and I look down to find someone is there *polishing*. The adulation rises
> like incense.[4]

But beneath this sociable and confident *persona* there was a certain
loneliness and a need for reassurance. He was consequently susceptible
to flattery, gradually becoming less aware of current research and
resistant to new approaches. Perhaps a close companion—which John
never had—could have prevented the almost imperceptible slide, both
intellectual and physical, which started in the late 1960s. Always a heavy
smoker and fond of drink, he was the more vulnerable for living alone.

In recognition of his ability to construct elegant and erudite surveys
he was commissioned by Nikolaus Pevsner to write the *Early Christian
and Byzantine Art* volume in the prestigious Pelican History of Art series,
which duly appeared in 1970. It was written remarkably quickly and has
perhaps not stood the test of time as well as *Early Medieval Art*. It is one
of the shorter volumes in the Pelican History of Art series and although
Beckwith emphasised in the foreword to the book that it was 'neither
dictionary nor encyclopedia, neither catalogue nor hand-list', its modest
scale means that it inevitably suffers in comparison with other volumes
in the same series, most notably Richard Krautheimer's *Early Christian
and Byzantine Architecture*, which is now in its fourth, revised edition,
and which combines a magisterial treatment of the survey with numerous
new observations. Nevertheless, it too has entered the reading lists of all
those studying the art of the period and it continues to sell steadily, twenty
years on.

Beckwith's last book, *Ivory Carvings in Early Medieval England*
(published by Harvey Miller in 1972), was the result of twenty-five years'
study of Anglo-Saxon and English Romanesque ivories. It brought together
material he had published elsewhere in articles and in exhibition catalogues
and introduced a good number of little known pieces. Half introduction to
the subject, half catalogue, it at once aroused controversy because of the
large numbers of ivories included. Beckwith was aware that this might be
the case, and said as much in the preface. Now that a reasonable time
has passed since its publication, and with the benefit of the exhibitions of
Anglo-Saxon and English Romanesque Art held at the British Museum
and the Hayward Gallery in 1984, where many of the ivories discussed in
the book were exhibited, it has to be said that up to a third of the 166

---

[4] This letter was published in full in *The Art Newspaper*, April 1991.

catalogue entries in the book are not now regarded as English by those working in the field.[5] Be that as it may, it still remains an extremely useful reference book and its publication played a large part in stimulating interest in the subject. Lord Clark was so impressed by the book and the beauty of the objects illustrated that he immediately suggested that an exhibition should be organised to present them to the general public. Beckwith was charged with re-casting the book into three-dimensional form with the help of the Arts Council and the exhibition took place two years later in the Victoria and Albert Museum. It was widely acclaimed as a triumph of design, as the entrance hall of the Museum was transformed into an intimate space reminiscent of the Palace Chapel at Aachen; every object was beautifully displayed, and although it was a comparatively small exhibition—there were only about sixty pieces—it left not only scholars but also non-specialists enchanted.

In the same year (1974) Beckwith was promoted to Keeper of the Department of Architecture and Sculpture and elected a Fellow of the British Academy. Because of his pre-eminence in his chosen fields he had also become a member of the consultative committees of *The Burlington Magazine* and *Pantheon*, the German art-historical periodical. Perhaps by this time he felt that he had no more mountains to climb; the five years of his Keepership were not marked by any special distinction and in contrast to his earlier years he wrote very little. Unlike his colleagues John Pope-Hennessy, who went on to direct the V&A and the British Museum, and Terence Hodgkinson, who became Director of the Wallace Collection, he felt no desire to manage change in a large institution and he harboured an aversion to all forms of bureaucracy. However, when he was invited by his old university to become the Slade Professor of the Fine Arts for the academic year 1978–9 he was jolted out of his self-imposed inertia to write at length again. The title of his Slade Lectures—*Early Medieval Art and the Imperial Ideal*—encapsulated Beckwith's over-riding interests and his approach to works of art produced in the courtly *milieu*, while the subject of the art of the imperial court both in the West and the East was at the heart of his studies and interests throughout his working life. Always concerned with high quality, he cared less for humbler products and could be scornfully dismissive of what he considered to be second-rate works of art.

On retirement in 1979, at the age of 60, he was offered a Visiting Senior Fellowship at Dumbarton Oaks, but by this time he was not

---

[5] For a balanced review of the book by S. Heslop see *Burlington Magazine*, CXVI, 1974, p.413; see also Peter Lasko's review of the exhibition which came out of the book, raising many questions of dating and localisation (*idem*, pp.426–30).

prepared to live abroad for a year and did not, in any case, have a particular research project which sufficiently interested him. His Slade Lectures would have needed a considerable amount of work before they could be turned into a book and by this time Beckwith's appetite for such work had sadly diminished. Unlike others who retire only to join committees or to write the books they had never had time to complete while in full-time employment, he instead withdrew to his small flat in Ladbroke Grove, which he had been renting since taking it over from Otto Pächt shortly after moving to London and which he was now able to buy. He bought a television set (never having owned one) and read and re-read his favourite biographies and novels, especially Trollope. He was surprised at how much his circle of acquaintances had shrunk now that he no longer worked at the Museum, and although he wrote the occasional review and acted as guest lecturer on one or two tours abroad in the early 1980s he gradually lost touch with most of his old colleagues. He did, however, take a keen interest in events at the Museum and was always anxious to be kept informed of any changes. He retained his strong Catholic faith and served on the fabric committee of Westminster Cathedral for many years, which gave him great pleasure, and he kept in contact with his old school at Ampleforth. But the intellectual momentum built up in the 1960s had slowed and stopped, and various ailments plagued him. By the late 1980s he was a shadow of his former self, and when the Pindar Press decided to publish a selection of his articles under the title *Studies in Byzantine and Medieval Western Art* he was unable to write the preface and additional notes which are the norm for such publications. This task was taken out of his hands and he was delighted when the volume was eventually published in 1989.

Shortly afterwards he experienced difficulty in swallowing and it was discovered that he had contracted cancer of the throat. After chemotherapy in the Charing Cross Hospital he was looked after in two nursing homes in London but was allowed to return to his flat when it appeared that he had made a satisfactory recovery. This was a huge blessing to him, and he had cause to be even more thankful when he discovered that he could rely on the assistance of a kind neighbour who had moved into the next flat while he was away. Elizabeth Tarrant turned out by an extraordinary twist of fate to be the mother of a boy still at Ampleforth, and her attention to John in his last months was an example of selfless charity rarely seen today. He died peacefully in his flat, surrounded by his books and his small collection of ceramics and pictures (many of them by his friend Marian Wenzel) on 20 February 1991.

PAUL WILLIAMSON
*Victoria and Albert Museum*

*Note.* The author wishes to acknowledge with gratitude the assistance and information he has received from Mrs Angela Greatorex (John's cousin), Terence Hodgkinson, Ralph Pinder-Wilson and Dom Alberic Stacpoole OSB of Ampleforth. Mention should be made of obituaries in *The Guardian*, 25 February 1991 (Professor Michael Kauffmann), *The Independent*, 23 February 1991 (Diana Scarisbrick), *The Times*, 27 February 1991 (the present author), *The Burlington Magazine*, CXXXIII, 1991, pp.314–15 (Sir Steven Runciman), and *Exeter College Association Register*, 1991, pp.6–10 (Dom Alberic Stacpoole).

*Proceedings of the British Academy*, **80**, 245–260

# Frederick Fyvie Bruce
# 1910–1990

FREDERICK FYVIE BRUCE died on September 11, 1990, shortly before what would have been his eightieth birthday. He held a number of academic posts before coming to the Rylands Chair of Biblical Criticism and Exegesis in the University of Manchester which he occupied from 1959 to 1978. He was first and foremost a Pauline scholar, but his interests were widespread.

He was born on 12 October, 1910, the son of Peter Bruce, in Elgin, Morayshire, in the north-east of Scotland. From his earliest years he displayed outstanding intellectual gifts, and it was natural that as 'a lad o' pairts' he should proceed from Elgin Academy to the University of Aberdeen where he distinguished himself in the study of the Classics, taking a First-Class Honours degree and winning various awards including the Ferguson Scholarship and the Croom Robertson Fellowship. He then proceeded to the University of Cambridge where again he was the most distinguished graduate in Classics in his year; he was awarded the Sandys Studentship (1934). Among the teachers who most influenced him in these days he lists Alexander Souter—'I suppose that, among all my university teachers, he is the one to whom I owe most'[1]—in Aberdeen and Peter Giles in Cambridge.

At this stage in his career he appeared to be set to follow an academic career in Classics. He therefore spent a year (1934–5) in the University of Vienna and studied Indo-European philology; it was here that he picked up his knowledge of the Hittites. At this point he was contemplating a second year in Vienna and the possibility of a Ph.D, but there came the possibility of a teaching post in Edinburgh. The attractions of getting into teaching—and also of an earlier marriage than would otherwise have

---

© The British Academy 1993.

[1] F. F. Bruce, *In Retrospect. Remembrance of Things Past*, Glasgow: Pickering and Inglis, 1980, 48.

F. F. BRUCE                    *Desmond Groves*

been possible—sufficed to change Bruce's plans. He took up a terminable appointment as an assistant lecturer in Greek (1935–8), with Sir William Calder as his Head of Department. From there he moved to a permanent appointment as lecturer in Classics in the University of Leeds (1938–47).

Somewhat surprisingly he published scarcely anything in the area of Classical Studies. Although he wrote a dissertation for the Croom Robertson Scholarship on 'The Latinity of Gaius Marius Victorinus Afer', it was never published,[2] although Bruce retained an interest in him and wrote articles on his work.[3] His doctoral studies remained unfinished, although they did lead to a couple of articles on Roman slave-names.[4] At that time the attainment of a Ph.D was not regarded as the essential passport to an academic career which it has now – unfortunately in Bruce's eyes—become.

Already at this point his scholarly interests were shifting to biblical studies in general and New Testament studies in particular. He carried further his study of Hebrew and gained a Diploma in Hebrew (1943). (He had also won the Crombie Scholarship in Biblical Criticism awarded by the University of St Andrews in 1939.) At the same time, the opportunity came to give some teaching on the Greek New Testament and he began to produce scholarly work in the field of New Testament. In particular, he commenced his commentary on the Greek text of Acts.

Consequently, when the University of Sheffield opened a Department of Biblical History and Literature in 1947, he was well-equipped by self-education to apply for the Headship, and he was duly appointed. The fact that he was not a clergyman, but a layman, was apparently one of the points in his favour at a time when there was a suspicion of Christian theology in the University and a certain fear on the part of some that an ordained person might not be wholly objective in the study of the subject.

Over the next twelve years Bruce built up the work of the tiny Department which consisted of himself and one other colleague with

---

[2] There is a copy in the Manuscripts and Archives Section of Aberdeen University Library.

[3] 'Marius Victorinus and His Works: In Memory of Alexander Souter', *Evangelical Quarterly* 18, 1946, 132–53; republished in *A Mind for What Matters*, Grand Rapids: Eerdmans, 1990, 213–32; 'The Gospel Text of Marius Victorinus', in E. Best and R. M. Wilson (ed.), *Text and Interpretation. Studies in the New Testament Presented to Matthew Black*, Cambridge University Press, 1979, 69–78. Bruce also wrote on the works of another Victorinus (Victorinus of Pettau) in 'The Earliest Latin Commentary on the Apocalypse', *Evangelical Quarterly* 10, 1938, 352–66 (*A Mind for What Matters*, 198–212).

[4] 'Latin Participles as Slave Names', *Glotta* 25, 1936, 42–50; 'Some Roman Slave Names', *Proceedings of the Leeds Philosophical Society: Literary and Historical Section* 5, 1938, 44–60.

some part-time help. His own scholarly reputation was such that he was appointed to a Chair in Biblical History and Literature in 1955, and his own University awarded him a DD in 1957. To the best of my knowledge he was one of the youngest persons ever to be so honoured by Aberdeen in this century—and he a layman without a degree in theology! In 1959 he was invited to occupy the Rylands Chair in Manchester, where he remained until his retirement. He served as Dean of the Faculty of Theology in 1963–4.

Such is the outline of his scholarly career. it included the normal tasks of undergraduate teaching and administration, but it also involved the successful supervision of a remarkable number of postgraduate students, especially at Manchester, where, it is said, he had more than any other teacher of biblical studies at that time. The many published theses produced under his supervision testify both to the quality of the students whom came to work with him and to his own expertise in stimulating and developing their scholarship. He was also in great demand as a lecturer in other institutions in Britain and all round the world.

The appointment of a person to a university post is generally understood to be both to teach and to do research. If we interpret 'research' in a fairly broad sense to cover scholarly work and writing that is not necessarily original in character, Bruce's contribution was phenomenal by its sheer extent. His list of publications is quite prodigious. He produced a vast amount of scholarly material of all kinds, much of it more of a textbook character, and some of it at a popular level (but never lacking in scholarly quality). He also did a quite remarkable amount of the kind of work behind the scenes which wins few public plaudits but is essential nonetheless. Among the earliest references to such work is the brief comment in the second edition of the Oxford Classical Texts version of *Novum Testamentum Graece* (1944), where the editor, Bruce's former teacher Alexander Souter, expresses thanks to him for reading the proofs *qua est summa doctrina diligentiaque*—a phrase which well sums up the man. In this connection one remembers his immense task of proof-reading the whole of the English translation of G. Kittel and G. Friedrich's *Theologisches Wörterbuch zum Neuen Testament* (10 volumes), said to have been accomplished mostly while travelling daily in and out to Manchester from Buxton on the train. But this work represents only the tip of an iceberg. The number of other works, published and unpublished, that Bruce read or corrected, the number of scholarly queries that he dealt with in correspondence, and the promptness with which he answered correspondents generally in his own hand or on a portable typewriter—these are almost incredible.

A couple of formal features of his writings may be noted before we look at the contents. First, Bruce was one of the best contemporary popularisers of biblical scholarship, expressing himself in simple terms for the benefit of a wide public. There is sometimes a certain scholarly haughtiness towards so-called popularisers, and the impression is fomented that what they are doing is not real scholarship. One rather suspects that those who criticise in this fashion are like the fox in Aesop's fable; unable to write well at a popular level themselves, they pour scorn on those who can. But it must be forcefully urged that writing for a popular audience is an important aspect of scholarship. Far too often the accusation is heard that the pulpit is fifty years behind the teacher's rostrum, and the pew even further out-of-date. Some of the blame for this situation undoubtedly rests on a scholarship which does not trouble to communicate with both pulpit and pew in a way that both can understand. In any case, to write at a popular level is not inconsistent with a truly scholarly approach, and it may be argued that one test of a person's scholarship is the ability to express arguments and conclusions in a manner that is generally intelligible. That the more popular works of Bruce represent the fruit of worthy scholarly labours is proved beyond cavil by the fact that even the advanced scholar will find profitable material in them. Bruce's work is in no danger of being confused with that of the populariser whose work is second-hand and cheap. This is apparent, for example, in Bruce's contribution to more than one one-volume Bible commentary where his comments on the text proved that he knew what really needed explanation and provided it succinctly, and where the scholar will read with ease between the lines Bruce's mind on matters of controversy and debate.

Second, at whatever level he was writing, Bruce expressed himself with superb clarity and ease. His work is always a delight to read, so smoothly does it flow. He is never guilty of obscurity, and he is a master of the apt phrase. All this is the mark of a writer who has carefully thought out what he wants to say and is thus able to express it neatly and unequivocally. Here is something worthy of praise in an age when dullness, and even vagueness and obscurity, sometimes seem to be the hallmarks of scholarship. The clarity and utility of his writings is demonstrated by numerous translations into European and Asian languages.

Bruce belonged to what may be called the conservative wing of New Testament scholarship. This approach is characterised by its recognition of the generally reliable character of the New Testament from a historical point of view and by its understanding of its theological teaching as finding its appropriate systematic expression in the outlook of the Protestant Reformation. No doubt Bruce was influenced here by his upbringing in the Christian Brethren, who are among the more right-wing groups in

Protestant orthodoxy.[5] This fact will inevitably raise the question in some people's minds whether his conclusions in matters of biblical study and theology were not dictated by his presuppositions rather than being the result of objective study of the evidence. To this question various points may be made.

First, it is increasingly accepted that no scholar is entirely free from presuppositions which affect the way in which a text is read or a problem is solved, and that the right approach lies in recognising and allowing for one's presuppositions as much as possible and in entering into dialogue with scholars with different presuppositions.

Second, it follows from this that the legitimacy of different approaches must be recognised, and the decisive test of the validity of any conclusions is whether they rest on a fair reading of the evidence; in other words, a scholar's conclusions cannot be rejected simply because 'you would expect him to say that in view of his presuppositions', but they must be examined in the light of the evidence; when presuppositions replace evidence and cogent argument, then is the time to criticise.

Third, it is important to observe that Bruce was concerned not only to uphold his own interpretation of the New Testament over against a more 'liberal' approach but also to help people in his own tradition to move out of the kind of 'fundamentalism' which is antithetical to any kind of biblical criticism into the 'conservative evangelicalism' which recognises that the Bible is open to historical and literary study.

This last point deserves some development. Prior to Bruce's work there had been little in the way of first-class scholarship from this wing of the church since the turn of the century. The prevailing theological climate was that of a liberalism which looked at the Bible so much from a human point of view that it was in danger of depriving it of its character as a source of divine revelation.[6] Admittedly, the rise of the kind of theology associated with the name of Karl Barth did much to restore the balance between the character of the Bible as the words of man and the Word of God.

---

[5] It may be necessary to comment that the group to which Bruce belonged is to be sharply distinguished from the so-called Exclusive or Closed Brethren and similar sectarian groups. His own account of the 'Open' Brethren will be found in *In Retrospect*, 313–17. It must be admitted that at the time when it was originally published (1961) it represented an ideal of freedom and openness which was by no means universally maintained, and it is certain that the influence of Bruce himself has had a lot to do with the fact that the Brethren of today are much closer to it.

[6] This point has been increasingly recognised by later scholars standing closer to that tradition. See, for example, T. W. Manson, 'The Failure of Liberalism to interpret the Bible as the Word of God', in C. W. Dugmore (ed.), *The Interpretation of the Bible*, London: SPCK, 1944, 92–107; J. Smart, *The Strange Silence of the Bible in the Church*, London: SCM Press, 1970.

Nevertheless, the general effect of liberalism was that Christians of a more traditional outlook concluded that the results of criticism were entirely negative, and therefore that the method itself was fundamentally flawed. Biblical criticism and assaults on the faith appeared to be synonymous to them, and the result was a fairly complete withdrawal by traditionalists from the field of biblical study.

If the situation has now changed, it is in large measure due to the work of Bruce who has demonstrated to his fellow-evangelicals that biblical criticism can help them to understand the Bible better and can lead to positive conclusions as well as negative ones.

At the same time he has equally shown to students of a more liberal persuasion that there is an intellectually respectable case for a view of the human character of Scripture and its composition which is fully compatible with the claims made for it as divine revelation. More than anybody else Bruce has demonstrated that it is possible to approach the Bible in a spirit of critical study and to find that it stands up to critical scrutiny. This does not mean that Bruce's work always leads to an acceptance of traditional conservative conclusions. He shared, for example, critical doubts about the authorship of the Pastoral Epistles, and he adopted positions in Old Testament scholarship which were not always readily acceptable to many of his more conservative friends.

In all this Bruce was something of a bridge-builder between different schools of scholarship. Unlike many more traditional Christians who avoided all contact with those from whose views they dissented, Bruce was prepared to join in the common scholarly enterprise and was respected by those who might reject his conservatism but could not mistake his scholarly integrity and capability coupled with his eirenic spirit.

What, then, were the particular qualities and interests that character-ised Bruce's approach?

In the first place, he brought to his biblical studies the background of a sound training in the Latin and Greek Classics and several years of experience in research and teaching in a university setting. This meant that he was familiar with the principles and methods used in the study of ancient literature, in particular the literature of the Hellenistic world which formed the environment of the New Testament. He was able to approach the New Testament from the standpoint of one who knew how to evaluate Greek literature and what to expect from it. Consequently, he could study the New Testament 'like any other book' and was not hindered by theological prejudice (whether conservative or radical) from a dispassionate examination of its contents.

Bruce thus found himself in that group of Classicists who have directed their attention to the New Testament and reached a positive verdict on its historical worth. It is surely no coincidence that Bruce did his early classical training in the University where Sir William M. Ramsay had once taught Humanity. It is true, of course, that Bruce had no need to undergo a conversion like that of Ramsay from a negative estimate of the historicity of the New Testament to a positive one, but this is no reason to regard his position as any the less objective. The work of both scholars is to be judged by its quality and not by irrelevant psychological considerations. The significant fact is that classical scholars often do seem to have a higher estimate of the historical worth of the New Testament than do the professional theologians—and this is not because they are ignorant of the work of the latter. Bruce himself comments:

> The NT writings were not, of course, designed as historians' source material, and apart from Luke-Acts are not written in historiographical style; but historians will not be deterred on that account from using them as source-material; nor will they be intimidated by theologians who assure them that their task is impossible and illegitimate.[7]

Second, we may link with Bruce's classical outlook his stress on the importance of archaeology. Classical archaeology has an important contribution to make to the understanding of the New Testament, especially in Acts whose detailed background can be illustrated and substantiated to a remarkable extent from archaeological discoveries. Bruce's earliest book, *Are the New Testament Documents Reliable?*,[8] makes ample use of this method within the framework of a general treatment in which he takes full account of other types of critical study. In it he stated:

> I have written as a teacher of classics, with the purpose of showing that the grounds for accepting the New Testament as reliable compare very favourably with those on which the classical student accepts the authenticity and credibility of many ancient documents.[9]

To be sure, such an approach may lead to scepticism about the historical reliability of parts of the NT,[10] but it certainly indicates that in places where control is possible the historicity of many details in Acts in particular can be upheld.[11]

---

[7] F. F. Bruce, *New Testament History*, London: Nelson, 1969, 159 n. 1. See further his presidential address to Studiorum Novi Testamenti Societas, 'The New Testament and Classical Studies', *New Testament Studies* 22, 1975–76, 229–42.

[8] First published in 1943. Republished as *The New Testament Documents: Are they Reliable?* and frequently reprinted.

[9] Ibid. iii.

[10] As in the case of classical scholars who have compared Acts with ancient romances; R. I. Pervo, *Profit with Delight: The Literary Genre of the Acts of the Apostles*, Philadelphia: Fortress, 1987.

[11] See the work of Bruce's pupil C. J. Hemer, *The Book of Acts in the Setting of Hellenistic History* (edited by C. H. Gempf), Tübingen: Mohr, 1989.

Bruce's interest in archaeology was not confined to the Graeco-Roman world. He gave the Tyndale Old Testament Lecture in 1947 on *The Hittites and the Old Testament*,[12] and he wrote the chapter on 'Tell el 'Amarna' in a survey volume produced by the Society for Old Testament Study.[13] He succeeded S. H. Hooke as editor of the *Palestine Exploration Quarterly* (1957–71), where his regular 'Notes and News' added greatly to the value of the journal, and his interests even extended to editorship of *Yorkshire Celtic Studies* (1945–57).

But the area where he made his own chief contribution is in the assessment of the Dead Sea Scrolls. Bruce characteristically produced a 'popular' book on the discoveries—*Second Thoughts on the Dead Sea Scrolls* (Exeter: Paternoster Press, 1956)—which is second to none as a reliable and readable account of the matter. He also produced a brief and original study of *The Teacher of Righteousness in the Qumran Texts*[14] and, more importantly, a detailed and constructive monograph on *Biblical Exegesis in the Qumran Texts* (London: Tyndale Press, 1959) which greatly illuminated the sect's understanding of their Scriptures. He served as editor for the material on the Dead Sea Scrolls in the *Encyclopaedia Judaica*.

Third, Bruce has recognised that the New Testament must be understood in the light of the OT and of Judaism. In his earlier days as a teacher he was responsible for dealing with both Testaments—and he was one of the few contemporary scholars with the breadth of expertise to be able to do so. *Israel and the Nations* (Exeter: Paternoster Press, 1963) is a competent survey of the history of the period, now no doubt dated in comparison with more modern studies. Bruce's main interest, however, was in the interpretation of the Old Testament in the New, and several publications took up this theme, especially *This is That* (Exeter: Paternoster Press, 1968); *The Time is Fulfilled* (Exeter: Paternoster Press, 1978).

This combination of Classical, archaeological and Old Testament studies formed the background for Bruce's main work in the field of New Testament. His achievements in this area can be considered under four heads: the history of New Testament times; the Book of Acts; the career and letters of Paul; and the rest of the New Testament.

**1** Among Bruce's earliest works was a trilogy, based on extra-mural lectures, which brilliantly portrayed the early history of the church. The three books, *The Dawn of Christianity* (London: Paternoster Press, 1950),

---

[12] London: Tyndale Press, 1947.

[13] D. Winton Thomas (ed.), *Archaeology and Old Testament Study*, Oxford University Press, 1967, 3–20.

[14] London: Tyndale Press, 1957. It was originally presented as The Tyndale Lecture in Biblical Archaeology, 1956.

*The Growing Day* (1951), and *Light in the West* (1952) were combined into one volume as *The Spreading Flame* (1953). One of the original impetuses to this work was the aim of showing that the facts concerning *The Rise of Christianity* differed in very significant respects from the presentation of them in the book of that name by E. W. Barnes, the very liberal Bishop of Birmingham (London: Longmans, 1947).[15] The result was a brilliant, eminently readable survey of the New Testament period which Bruce was then persuaded to carry on into the sub-apostolic period and right through to the conversion of Britain.

At a later point he wrote an entirely fresh volume on *New Testament History* (London: Nelson, 1969) which deals with the NT period and its background in considerable detail; its strength indeed lies in the mass of detailed information, but it lacks discussion of controversial matters in the record of the actual events of Christian history. While Bruce was able to present a picture of Christian origins which many will find coherent and persuasive, and which is corroborated by a number of recent, similar investigations[16], it is to be regretted that he did not really enter into debate with advocates of an approach which finds the New Testament record much less straightforward.[17]

**2**   A study of *The Acts of the Apostles: The Greek Text with Introduction and Commentary* (London: Tyndale Press) naturally fits in with this historical interest. It was, as we have noted, the first major area to claim Bruce's attention. The commentary was published in 1951, and it is not too much to say that it marked the real beginning of conservative evangelical scholarship as well as setting a high standard for others to follow. Intended as a textbook for students, it was characterised by careful attention to detail in matters of textual criticism and Greek syntax. Its basic approach was historical; it gave a coherent interpretation of Acts as an authentic history of the early church written by Luke, the companion of Paul. Here certainly Bruce was fully aware of the historical problems, as they had been posed at that time and dealt faithfully with them. It is noteworthy that his preparations for the volume included a lecture on *The Speeches in the Acts of the Apostles* (London: Tyndale Press, 1943) in which he dealt with the objections to their historical basis not only from H. J.

---

[15] Bruce was not the only scholar to attempt a refutation of the bishop's views. On a much smaller scale, see F. G. Kenyon, *The Bible and Modern Scholarship*, London: Murray, 1948.

[16] E.g. F. V. Filson, *A New Testament History* (London: SCM Press, 1965); B. Reicke, *The New Testament Era* (London: Black, 1969); L. Goppelt, *Apostolic and Post-Apostolic Times* (London: Black, 1970).

[17] E.g. H. Conzelmann, *History of Primitive Christianity*, London: Darton, Longman and Todd, 1973.

Cadbury, whose work was well-known in the English-speaking world but also from M. Dibelius whose work was scarcely known outside Germany (as indeed it continued to be during the war years until it was translated in 1956).[18]

If from the perspective of today the commentary had a weakness, it was that it was too narrowly linguistic and historical and was lacking in theological content. True, it was written just before the point when the recognition began to prevail that a New Testament commentary must be primarily theological because the nature of the subject matter requires it to be so. Nevertheless, the real explanation of the omission lay in the fact that Bruce was simultaneously engaged on a commentary on Acts for what was known in the UK as the New London Commentary and elsewhere as the New International Commentary; this series was intended to present a running exposition of the text at a non-technical level with scholarly detail relegated to footnotes. The pattern was congenial to Bruce, and the commentary paid much more attention to theological matters than was the case with the earlier one *(The Book of the Acts* (London: Marshall, Morgan and Scott, 1953). If readers in the 1990s feel nevertheless that it does not deal sufficiently with the theology of Acts, and that, while theological points are discussed, the question of the relation between the theology of the author and that of the early church is not really raised, it can justly be urged that these questions reflect the concern of contemporary scholarship and that Bruce wrote before they had become as dominant as they now are.

What Bruce was doing is showing that a positively evangelical approach to the text of the NT makes sense of it. After all, the test of any kind of understanding of a text is whether it arises from the text and is demanded by the text or has been forced upon it at the expense of failure to do justice to the text. In Rudolf Bultmann's commentary on the Fourth Gospel, for example, the exegesis is conducted on the basis of the assumption that the Gospel is to be understood in terms of Existentialism; hence Bultmann continually expresses what he thinks John really means in Existentialist language. But this approach may not do justice to what John says; it may be plausible for some parts of the Gospel, but there are others which

[18] The Lecture was the first to be given under the auspices of the Biblical Research Committee of the Inter-Varsity Fellowship (which was the predecessor of the Tyndale Fellowship for Biblical and Theological Research established in 1945), of which Bruce was a founder member and Chairman from 1942 to 1951, and which has been mainly responsible for the revival of biblical scholarship among conservative evangelical Christians. It was to this group that Bruce volunteered to write his commentary on Acts as early as May, 1939. Throughout his life Bruce was a strong supporter of the Inter-Varsity Fellowship (now the Universities and Colleges Christian Fellowship), serving as its Honorary President in 1955.

will not yield to this treatment, and so the whole enterprise is rendered questionable.[19]

Now one can raise the criticism that evangelical Christians like Bruce may assume too easily that their understanding of the gospel flows directly from the text and that their language is the best for expressing its meaning. They may take it for granted that the thought-forms of the past will still be meaningful today, and that the essential message of the New Testament does not need any correction or reformulation in the light of succeeding centuries. So far as Bruce is concerned, however, he was clearly aware of these questions even if he did not bring them out into the open as much as he might have done. For example, in a discussion of the heavenly intercession of Christ, as it is presented in Hebrews, he wrote:

> If we translate this emphasis into terms less pictorial than those which the writer to the Hebrews uses, we may say that the death of Christ, and the spirit in which he accepted death, constitute an abiding force in the eternal order, powerfully acting in defense of mankind.[20]

Nevertheless, Bruce would equally firmly claim that for Christians the New Testament is part of the authoritative revelation of God, and there can be no question of evading its authority.

This same general approach can be found in his work as a whole.

**3**    From Acts we turn to Paul. Here is the area of the New Testament where Bruce found himself most at home. He wrote commentaries on varying scales on *Romans* (Tyndale NT Commentaries, 1963, [2]1985); *1 and 2 Corinthians* (New Century Bible, 1971), *Galatians* (New International Greek Testament Commentary, 1982), *Ephesians* (New International Commentary, 1984; he also wrote a shorter exposition published independently by Pickering and Inglis, 1961); *Philippians* (Good News Bible Commentary, 1983; republished in the New International Biblical Commentary, 1989); *Colossians* and *Philemon* (New International Commentary, 1957, [2]1984), *1 and 2 Thessalonians* (Word Biblical Commentary, 1982). Of these the major works are those on Galatians and 1 and 2 Thessalonians, both of them based on the Greek text and discussing it in considerable detail, and the commentary on Galatians is perhaps Bruce's best work. It combines acute linguistic discussion with profound discussion of theology, and the whole is suffused with the warmth that comes out of sympathetic understanding of the text. It is doubtless written on more conventional lines than the equally important work of H. D. Betz which appeared almost simultaneously, but its very freedom from conjecture may well make it more of an abiding contribution to the literature on the epistle.

---

[19] As is argued in the equally meticulous and scholarly commentary by R. Schnackenburg in Herders theologischer Kommentar zum NT.

[20] F. F. Bruce, 'The Interpretation of Hebrews', *Interpretation* 23, 1969, 3–19, cited from 9.

In addition Bruce wrote at length on the career and thought of Paul. Part of the impetus to this may well have lain in the obligation of the Rylands Professor to take his share in the public lectures of the Rylands Library. A regular stream of essays on different aspects of Paul's life and thought and on the Book of Acts were delivered in public and published in the Bulletin right up to 1986 when health problems restricted his public activities. These formed the basis for a major study of *Paul: Apostle of the Free Spirit* (Exeter: Paternoster Press, 1977) in which Bruce summed up his understanding of Paul. The work is not a 'theology of Paul', but it places his thought, as expressed in his letters, in the context of his career and the world in which he lived. The stress on freedom, reflected in the title, is something that was increasingly congenial to Bruce.

4   Fourthly, there is Bruce's contribution to the study of the rest of the New Testament. Here his commentary on *Hebrews* in the New International Commentary (1964, ²1990) must be reckoned a major achievement. He also wrote on *The Epistles of John* (Glasgow: Pickering and Inglis, 1970) and the *Gospel of John* (Glasgow: Pickering and Inglis, 1983), in both cases on the level of a more popular type of exposition which dealt admirably with the meaning of the text but which eschewed the technical problems which would have been foreign to the kind of audience which he was addressing. There is no denying that to a considerable extent the shape of Bruce's writing was determined by the character of the audience; he had to start from where they were, and the kind of people in his constituency would not have coped with the technicalities and critical problems which he dealt with in his more learned works. But even in the New International Commentary series Bruce was adept at keeping the text non-technical and providing the more scholarly material in footnotes.

Bruce was less at home in the Gospels, although he wrote at a more popular level on the life and work of Jesus, and never without illumining the subject. *Jesus and Christian Origins outside the New Testament* (London: Hodder and Stoughton, 1974), *The Real Jesus* (1985), and *The Hard Sayings of Jesus* are among his writings in this area. One of his earliest works was a series of essays on *The Books and the Parchments* (Glasgow: Pickering and Inglis, 1950, ⁴1984), in which he surveyed at a popular level the story of the various ancient versions of the Bible. More recently he produced the standard account of the history of *The English Bible* (London: Lutterworth, 1961; revised as *History of the Bible in English*, New York: OUP, ³1978/London: Lutterworth, 1979) tracing the story up to the publication of the New English Bible. Still more recently there is his work on *The Canon of Scripture* (Glasgow: Chapter House, 1988) which is noteworthy for discussing both Testaments together.

All these—and others not listed here—constitute a formidable enough list of publications—some fifty books in all. Add to that the fact that in his last years he carefully revised several of his earlier works to bring them up to date.[21] Besides all these, there was a wealth of contributions to collective volumes on all kinds of biblical subjects; they frequently offered a shrewd assessment of currently fashionable ideas and gave well-founded reasons why they should or should not be accepted. There was a regular stream of writings in more popular religious journals; for years he contributed a series of answers to questions by readers in the Brethren monthly magazine, *The Harvester*, and something like a thousand of these short pieces were gathered together in *Answers to Questions* (Exeter: Paternoster Press, 1972). The same journal saw his memoirs published month by month, eventually shaped into his book *In Retrospect: Remembrance of Things Past* (Glasgow: Pickering and Inglis, 1980), which is written with typical dry wit and offers a fascinating commentary on his early life in north-east Scotland as well as on his experiences south of the border. His last work, *A Mind for What Matters* (Grand Rapids: Eerdmans, 1990), originally intended to be published as a tribute on his eightieth birthday, is a collection of mainly previously published essays, including a couple on the history of Brethren thought which reveal his specialist knowledge in that area. He was associated with *The Evangelical Quarterly*, first as Associate Editor and then as Editor for thirty-eight years up to 1980. He also edited the *Journal of the Transactions of the Victoria Institute* (1949–57), a periodical devoted especially to questions on the interface between science and religion.

F. F. Bruce may not go down in history as a highly creative, original thinker. His name will not be associated with any brilliant new thesis in biblical scholarship, in the way in which, for example, his predecessors in Manchester, C. H. Dodd and T. W. Manson, have given their names to 'realised eschatology' and the corporate aspects of the Son of Man image respectively. His gifts were of a different order and perhaps more akin to those of the first holder of the Rylands Chair, A. S. Peake, who was also responsible for the high-level mediation of biblical scholarship to the Christian church. Bruce's contribution lies more in his encyclopaedic knowledge and interests, combined with a phenomenal memory and a brilliantly lucid and engaging written style (strangely different from his

---

21 Thus he revised his volume which included Colossians and Philemon in the New International Commentary fairly substantially (and contributed a fresh treatment of Ephesians in place of the previous one by his colleague, E. K. Simpson), as also the volumes on Acts and Hebrews (1984, 1988 and 1990 respectively). His last major work was a thorough revision of his first major publication, the commentary on the Greek text of *The Acts of the Apostles* (Grand Rapids: Eerdmans, 1990), where he was not afraid to alter his judgment on such an important matter as the dating of Acts.

rather dry delivery as a speaker), which enabled him to present fresh information at every point rather than to weave and conceive major new hypotheses. He was able to sift the work of others, to weed out what was doubtful or ephemeral, and to present in solid and convincing form a picture of the real state of affairs. New Testament history and thought alike are thus placed on a firm basis; the readers know that they will learn much from the presentation and not be exposed to daring and unlikely hypotheses. It should need no argument that this is among the proper tasks of a scholar, and that, while one is grateful for the stimulus of new hypotheses, it is of supreme value to be presented with sound learning and sober conclusions.

The high respect given to Bruce as a biblical scholar is evident from the honours which he received. In addition to the Aberdeen DD already mentioned he received an honorary doctorate (D Litt.) from Sheffield (1988). In 1973 he was elected a Fellow of the British Academy. He was particularly delighted to be awarded the Academy's Burkitt Medal; for Biblical Studies in 1979. He was president both of the Society for Old Testament Study (1965) and also of the Societas Novi Testamenti Studiorum (1975)—a rare double honour shared with Matthew Black. He received two Festschriften, one from colleagues and one from former students, and an issue of the *Journal of Semitic Studies* was dedicated to him.[22]

This tribute is not the place to comment on his life outside his scholarly career in any detail. He was married in 1935 to Betty Davidson, a fellow student in Aberdeen, and they had two children, Iain and Sheila. Throughout his life he enjoyed the happiest of home life with his wife and family. He enjoyed travel and listed it among his recreations. Some people found him difficult to get to know, for he was not a master of small talk, but colleagues and students alike have testified to his genuine friendship and care expressed in many ways; he demonstrated his interest in them and their families, and was as ready to play on the floor with their children as to talk with them on social occasions. He was completely lacking in pride and ready to learn from people of every shade of opinion. Only in his last three

---

[22] W. W. Gasque and R. P. martin, *Apostolic History and the Gospel* (Exeter: Paternoster Press, 1970); D. P. Hagner and M. J. Harris, *Pauline Studies* (Exeter: Paternoster Press, 1980); C. E. Bosworth and S. Strelcyn, *Studies in Honour of F. F. Bruce: Journal of Semitic Studies* 23/2, Autumn 1978. Some account of Bruce's life and influence can be found in *The Journal of the Christian Brethren Research Fellowship* 22, 1971, which was devoted to aspects of his work and Christian witness. The present obituary incorporates the substance of the author's contribution on 'F. F. Bruce as a Biblical Scholar', ibid., 5–12. See also Frederick Fyvie Bruce: An Appreciation', by Laurel and Ward Gasque, in *Aware*, November, 1990, 1–6, and the obituary in the *Journal of Semitic Studies* 36, 1991, 1–6, by A. R. Millard (to whom I am indebted for much valuable information). Lists of his major writings can be found in the two Festschriften and of his minor writings (to 1971) in the CBRF Journal.

or four years did he experience ill-health, but even then his capacity and zeal for scholarly work did not desert him; as late as the end of August 1990 he despatched a contribution to an as yet unpublished collection of *Documents from New Testament Times*, and he continued to work until a matter of days before his death. The University of Manchester held a memorial service on 13 March, 1991, at which his academic career and achievements were particularly remembered. Earlier, on 27 October, 1990, a memorial service of a more personal character was held in Brinnington Chapel, Stockport, where Bruce was an elder. Perhaps there is space even in a British Academy obituary for the story of the building site worker who joined Brinnington Chapel after becoming a Christian, and who was confronted by his work-mates with difficult questions about his new-found faith. He produced the most excellent and well-informed answers until at last his mates asked him where he got all his answers to their questions. 'O well,' he said, 'there's an old fellow in our church called Fred. He seems to know all about these things.'

I. HOWARD MARSHALL
*University of Aberdeen*

*Proceedings of the British Academy*, **80**, 261–273

# Norman Davis
# 1913–1989

THE DEATH ON DECEMBER 2, 1989, of Professor Norman Davis, MBE, FBA, D. Litt., deprived the Academy of one of its most distinguished members, the the world of medieval English scholarship of one of its most influential figures, and his friends of a witty and convivial companion.

Norman Davis was born in Dunedin, New Zealand, on May 16, 1913, the only child of James John and Jean Davis (née Black). The family, like many in this part of New Zealand, had deep Scottish roots. Three of the grandparents came from Scotland. James Davis's father (from a Gloucestershire family) had come to New Zealand from Tasmania at the age of seventeen; he worked on the big stations as a boundary rider, and was renowned for his stories of the 'early days'. Eventually he purchased a farm, 'Bellevue', in Central Otago (still owned, a hundred years later, by a Davis cousin). His wife was a Highlander, Margaret Cameron. Jean Black's parents were both Lowland Scots. Norman Davis's parents were both brought up in Central Otago, in the Maniatoto (a region now perhaps more widely known outside New Zealand because of the novelist Janet Frame). However, when he was aged about twenty, James Davis moved to Dunedin to work with Reddells Men's Tailoring, a business which he was later able to buy. Both parents are remembered as lively and witty people: it is likely that Norman Davis inherited some of his dry and quizzical sense of humour from them.

His childhood was a happy and secure one. The family was firmly Presbyterian—and also teetotal. Although in later life he became an agnostic, and was also prone to make jokes about 'wowsers' (an Australasian term for those fanatically opposed to strong drink), the family atmosphere seems to have been far from oppressive, and certainly did not make him into an early rebel. He was fond of both his parents, and was deeply influenced by them.

N. DAVIS

B. J. Harris (Oxford) Ltd

Holidays were often spent at a beach house in Karitane, north of Dunedin, and on the farm in Central Otago, where he helped with the mustering and the work in the wool shed, and enjoyed the company of his cousins. He once spent a period of three months on the farm when the Dunedin schools were closed because of the polio epidemic in the 1920s. His experience of New Zealand farming remained with him. Later in life he would occasionally give a graphic account of the shearing or slaughter of sheep; he was also fond of using the phrase 'I am only a simple farming lad, of course, but . . .' to introduce and emphasize a decidedly unsimple remark. His cousins recall these early days with affection—swimming, rowing on the Waikouaiti River, or playing tennis at the farm. Although his eyesight had been affected by a severe early attack of measles, he made up for this in games by his quick wittedness. He and his two cousins caught minnows from the creek in a tin bath, and set up their own business (for the production of mud pies, etc) called 'We, Us and Co.' (Norman Davis was We, his cousins Violet and Dorothy Us and Co.). Later, reading and 'tramping' were his preferred pastimes. He was a keen tramper, and spent much time walking in the mountainous region now called 'Fiordland'—in the Hollyford Valley and around Milford, capturing the spectacular scenery with his camera. This part of New Zealand, while it has been to a certain extent developed for tourism, still has some extremely remote and virtually inaccessible areas. In those days, when there were hardly any roads or tracks, there were even more: he used to recall the thrill of coming over a ridge and seeing a valley which he felt sure had never been seen by a human being before.

The resourcefulness and self-reliance developed in these early years were to prove of particular value to him in a later period of his life. His academic inclinations were also developing. Besides his love of reading, he gave early evidence of a penetrating mind, and an insatiable intellectual curiosity. He entered Otago Boys' High School, a school of high academic reputation, where he developed a taste for languages and for debating, and ended as dux and the winner of a university scholarship. In 1930 he went to Otago University, the oldest of the New Zealand universities, and one which was proud of its Scottish tradition of academic excellence. In those days the B.A., on which he first embarked, was a three-year unclassified degree, involving more than one subject; it was possible to follow it with a further one-year M.A. course, which was classified. He studied English Language under a remarkable duo—Professor Herbert Ramsay, originally a St Andrews classicist, a deeply committed scholar with a distrust of humbug, and, most remarkably for a university in a town of distinctly Presbyterian leanings, a deeply committed atheist; and MacGregor Cameron. The writer Dan Davin, a near-contemporary of Norman Davis at Otago, later to become Academic Publisher to the

Oxford Press, remembered him as a natural scholar, one who 'seemed secure in himself, strong in that natural good sense that . . . never left him'. He had, says Davin, 'a natural sense of what scholarship really is': 'the rest of us . . . looked at what we were doing as a means to an end and not as an end in itself . . . We had little notion of the passionate dedication to learning which burnt in Ramsay's mind like one of those peat fires that never go out, and recognized in Norman's mind at least a spark of that same fire.' He was a hard worker as well as a brilliant student, who found his relaxation in tramping and climbing rather than in more goliardic student activities. His career at Otago culminated in a First and the award of a Rhodes Scholarship (with characteristic modesty he had not contemplated applying for this until it was strongly suggested to him by Mrs Ramsay).

In 1934 he came to Oxford. This was a major turning point in his life. Oxford was to become his true intellectual and emotional centre, and his later visits to New Zealand were rare and relatively brief. However, New Zealand, and Dunedin and Central Otago in particular, were never forgotten, and he kept in close contact with his relatives and early friends. He was too sceptical and too level-headed a person to become a professional expatriate. Just as he enjoyed revisiting his native land, so he enjoyed expatiating on its characteristic defects and virtues—such as the anti-intellectualism he remembered vividly, or its development, in a later, more enlightened period, of excellent wine. After a whisky or two he might quote, with ringing voice and mischievous eye, the lines of the nineteenth-century Otago writer Thomas Bracken : 'Go trav'ler, unto others boast / Of Venice and of Rome, / Of Saintly Mark's majestic pile / And Peter's lofty dome, / Of Naples and her trellised bowers / Of Rhineland far away: / These may be grand, but give to me / Dunedin from the Bay.'

Oxford was an important centre for English philological studies. Among his teachers were H. C. Wyld, J. R. R. Tolkien, then Professor of Anglo-Saxon at Pembroke, C.T. Onions the lexicographer, and Kenneth Sisam (himself a New Zealand expatriate of an earlier vintage). Tolkien in particular proved to be a sympathetic and inspiring mentor, and later a lifelong friend. It was producing a series of talented philologists: its recent graduates in English Language included G.V. Smithers (1933) and Angus McIntosh (1934). Davis's own college, Merton, was in those days a nest of English philologists from the Antipodes—his stay overlapped with that of Jack Bennett from Auckland and Eric Dobson from Sydney. The three of them shared friendly academic rivalry and, later, fame (Bennett became a professor at Cambridge, Dobson at Oxford). Norman Davis took a First in English in 1936, and followed it with a Diploma in Comparative Philology.

He learnt much else at Oxford besides historical philology. When Dan
Davin met him again there in 1936, he found that 'he had become an
enthusiastic rowing man, he had an unexpected and unrivalled command
of the bawdy verses familiar to sporting and sparkish undergraduates, and
he had acquired an extensive and profound knowledge of the subtly varying
qualities of vintage clarets and burgundies.' He had been able to receive an
education in the finer points of wine while staying with his uncle (of the New
Zealand Dairy Board) and aunt who were then living near London. It was
during this period that he came to know and to appreciate good food. He
not only enjoyed a good dinner, he remembered it, and would recall it in
loving detail years later.

In 1937 he was appointed to a Lecturership in English at Augustaitis
University in Kaunas, Lithuania. He celebrated this by a European grand
tour in the Antipodean manner, visiting Germany, Italy, Switzerland and
France before taking up his post in September. Always an excellent linguist,
he added another language to his store. He shared the affection which all
Indo-European comparative philologists have for the Lithuanian language,
and was particularly delighted to find his surname being declined on the
pattern of the Lithuanian noun. He had to eke out his meagre salary
by giving private lessons in English. (One of his more interesting pupils
was the secretary general to the Foreign Ministry, Urbšis, who became
the last Lithuanian Foreign Minister before the Soviet annexation, and
survived fourteen years of Russian imprisonment, eleven of them spent
in solitary confinement.) The political situation in Lithuania was looking
increasingly uncertain, and Davis approached the British Council about a
job. In July 1938 he heard that he had been successful in gaining a British
Council Lecturership in the University of Sofia. Here, in typical manner,
he added good Bulgarian—and what he called a basic 'common Slavonic'
for use in other parts of the Balkans—to his skills.

The shadow of war was now very threatening. He marked the end of
peace with a memorable motoring tour of France with Eric Dobson and
two friends, in which cathedrals and restaurants ('we had some excellent
meals') were equally prominent. With the advent of war he resigned from
the British Council, taking the post of Assistant Press Attaché to the
British Legation in Sofia. He had in fact also by now been recruited by the
Department which later became the British Special Operations Executive
'for the conducting of clandestine warfare against the Axis powers'. Those
of us who knew him only in his later years find it extremely difficult to
imagine the Merton Professor of English Language and Literature involved
in the dark world of sabotage, but his resourcefulness, quick wittedness and
linguistic talent made him a very successful practitioner. When later, after
many years of discreet silence, he could be prevailed upon to talk about

this period, he would always stress his youth, the fact that there was 'a war on', and that 'it was a long time ago.'

Sofia made a suitably louche Balkan setting for the beginning of his adventures. In 1957 the memoirs of the British ambassador, Sir George Rendel, gave a brief and cautious account (with the participants cloaked, as was still necessary, under the pseudonyms Stevens and Ivanoff) of Norman Davis's most spectacular exploit. The background to this event, which took place in 1941, a year which was to prove a turning point in the war as well as an *annus mirabilis* for the young Norman Davis, went well beyond the diplomatic life of Sofia. With the fall of France, and the entry of Italy into the war the Allies were faced with the threat of a German move south through Bulgaria towards Greece. In Bulgaria German influence was growing, and pressure on King Boris increased. Eventually, German troops began to infiltrate disguised as 'tourists' or 'technicians'. Davis remembered calling on a surprised British ambassador with the news that reliable sources had reported German staff cars and transports inside the Bulgarian frontier: this was the first intimation Rendel had had of his Assistant Press Attaché's secret life. It was soon impossible to deny the increasing German presence. In February the *New York Times* reported German general staff officers wearing civilian clothes staying in a leading hotel in Sofia—and watching a student demonstration against the German occupation of Bulgaria.

The only consistently anti-German group in Bulgaria was the Agrarian Party led by Dr. G.M. Dimitrov (because of the German-Soviet pact the Bulgarian Communist Party was urging resistence by 'non-cooperation, but not by force'). Dimitrov fiercely opposed any pact with the Germans. Davis had made his acquaintance and kept in secret contact with him. When eventually the Bulgarian Government formally allowed the entry of German troops, Dimitrov's life was at risk. He was quickly arrested, but managed to escape, and turned to Norman Davis. They met on the evening of February 22nd, and agreed that Dimitrov had to leave the country. A plan was devised, to which Ambassador Rendel agreed, with the warning that he would have to disclaim all knowledge of it if it ever came to light. The British Legation was making preparations for leaving, and the files were to be taken out of the country by truck under diplomatic immunity. And so, in Norman Davis's own words:

> I got a large packing-case, a large peasant quilt, some oranges for Dimitrov to eat . . . We picked him up in the middle of the town in the middle of the night (25 Feb 1941), put him in the packing-case inside the truck, put the quilt round him, and round the packing-case we stacked the legation files. At the last moment Dimitrov said he wanted a gun. We gave him a gun. And off we went . . .

(though not without causing considerable anxiety to others, since the building was watched: 'if', said Rendel later, 'you wish to smuggle someone in a packing-case out of a country by night and there are police about, use screws and not nails.') It was an extremely dangerous and tense journey, since the notional 'immunity' would certainly not have stretched to the contents of the case. With some irony they were in fact occasionally escorted by motorized police. The truck's driver had been kept in total ignorance of the real purpose; remembering the journey, Dimitrov remarked 'I could overhear the conversation between the driver and the English professor, who was distracting his attention so that he would not notice if I should cough behind his back . . .' Then there was a hitch at the frontier crossing—Rendel's instructions for clearance without inspection had not been received by the frontier guards, and there a delay of several hours while permission was sought. During the long wait Norman Davis spoke loudly so that the secret passenger would know what was going on—but, he said, 'I have never been so anxious in all my life'. Permission eventually came, and after thirty hours Dimitrov was at last released in the British Legation in Istanbul. Both he and Norman Davis, disguised as King's Messengers, then went by rail through hostile territory to Belgrade, where he could establish contact with colleagues and allies.

Later that year Dimitrov was charged in absentia in Bulgaria with plotting to overthrow the government, and acts of sabotage involving English agents, including Davis. After a long and well-publicised trial, he was sentenced in absentia on December 25, 1941 to be hanged, along with ten others, one of whom was Norman Davis, described as 'that architect of British subversion'. When the news of this sentence eventually reached New Zealand, a friend of his father came to commiserate with him about the report that young Norman had been sentenced to death in absentia; 'by the way,' said the friend, 'where is absentia?' But before this much else was to happen.

Belgrade now became the setting for more stirring events. After the signing of the Three-Power Pact in Vienna on 25th March, there was an officers' coup which ousted Prince Paul (an Anglophile Quisling-malgré-lui) and installed the young King Peter in his place. This took place on the night of 26/7 March. 'I was duty officer in the SOE annexe to the legation that night,' Norman recalled, 'with a camp bed, and incendiary device with which I was meant to destroy secret files, some sandwiches and a bottle of beer. I heard a racket outside and looked out. I saw a tank and a whole lot of soldiers with rifles . . . so I prudently went back to bed. This was the coup d'état taking place in the city'. This made a German invasion inevitable, and ten days later the Luftwaffe attacked Belgrade.

The British Legation had been warned to prepare for a sudden evacuation. Davis had to collect petrol, a car, tinned food ('and this damned machine gun which we put in the back') in readiness. On the night of 5th April he, Hugh Seton-Watson (also working for SOE, and also later a Fellow of the Academy), and other friends had 'an extraordinarily good dinner'—'the main course was smoked Ochrid trout which was very beautiful'—and more to drink 'than we should have had if we had known what was going to happen.' He recalled driving back in the middle of the night in a state 'of which I would not now approve'. In the early hours of the morning of the 6th he was roused by a naval attaché with the news that German planes had crossed the frontier. He woke Hugh Seton-Watson with some difficulty ('I said, 'Get up, the war's on', and nothing but a grunt emerged'), and they and their colleagues set off ('Hugh went off to his rendez-vous and I said, "Well, heigh ho, see you later"'). The plan was that they should all meet at Avala, a few miles outside Belgrade, and sort themselves out into convoys. Davis's task was to drive Dimitrov and a lieutenant of his, Kostov, who 'had been given British passports and were supposed to be French Canadians'. After reaching Avala, he made further trips back into the bombed city to rescue men and equipment. They then set off in convoys for Kragujevac and Sarajevo, which they reached on the 10th after a difficult and dangerous drive. The roads were full of refugees and groups of soldiers, and at night they had to drive without lights on very rough roads ('I couldn't see where I was going and I owed a good deal to Basil Davidson for looking out and saying "If I were you I'd go a bit to the right, we're nearly going over the edge"'). At Mladenovac they were stopped and told to jettison all their belongings to take on more refugees. He recalled a particularly tricky situation at Višegrad :

> I had a couple of chaps in my car the Germans mustn't get hold of, and we slept in the local square because we couldn't find a room. The place was absolutely crowded and again, a very hair-raising event in my young life was that I was at the wheel, and the two Bulgarians were in the back, and . . . we were of course supposed to be British. In the middle of the night a policeman came round checking the cars . . . so I said, 'You know, this is a diplomatic car; we are British diplomats.'

But one of his passengers began to talk in Serbo-Croat —

> and the car was supposed to be full of British diplomats . . . and I had to cover. Well, the policeman was a simple-minded rustic and he didn't pick it up, but oh dear, oh dear. So there it was . . .

The situation in the country was now chaotic. Sarajevo was severely bombed, and on the 13th the party set off for the coast. Davis was told to drive directly to Kotor on the Adriatic coast with a colleague, Tim Watts (one of those who had enjoyed the smoked Ochrid trout back in Belgrade), who had been seriously wounded by a bomb splinter and was likely to need medical attention on the way (his permanent passenger Dr Dimitrov was a physician). He picked him up. 'I remember driving through the broken glass and wire and things in Sarajevo' he said modestly. A journalist who was there gave a more dramatic account of the event :

> though the bombardment was now heavy and continuous, Norman Davis calmly parked his car there and carried Watts out. Watts was not yet out of danger, and there was a chance of his losing his sight. Norman Davis therefore drove through the bombardment as slowly as a funeral, whistling rude airs to himself, while the rest of us scudded through the town at some speed.

On the 14th he reached Kotor, and rejoined the rest of the Legation party. There were other adventures :

> I was driving Hugh [Seton-Watson] . . . in the dark with no lights along the short distance from Kotor to where we were to be billeted. I hit a bridge in the dark and burst a tyre. Hugh and I sat on the rocks by the sea shore waiting to be picked up, and I said, 'It occurs to me that there's a bottle of White Horse in that bag and we'd better just bring it down with us'. So we did, and we sat there sipping whisky until we were duly picked up. I remember this little vignette, Hugh and I sitting there, sipping whisky on the rocks in the Boka Kotorska, a most improbable scene.

The party waited at Kotor for the flying-boats they had been told were coming from Athens to pick them up. It had by now grown considerably; it included 'consular people from Split and places up the coast, and odds and ends, mining engineers, British Council people', and two or three airmen who had been shot down. On the 16th one flying-boat turned up, and those who were thought to be in danger were loaded on to it : 'that included my two Bulgarians and Tim Watts, and people who were held to be compromised, very largely Yugoslavs'. The remaining eighty or so were left behind, hoping to be picked up by a destroyer or a submarine. However, on the 18th, they were captured by the invading Italians.

The diplomats were taken by bus and military trucks to Scutari, and eventually to Durazzo, where they were lodged in the Hotel Durres, 'quite a good hotel'. They were to be flown to Italy, and on April 30th the first group were taken to Tirana for a plane, but one was not available, and they had to go back to Durazzo and wait until the following day. On the evening of their return to Durazzo he experienced one of the worst moments in his wartime career. On April 30th the Albanian Italian language newspaper *Tomori* carried an item headed 'Intrighi Serbi scoperti a Sofia' which reported the opening of Dimitrov's trial in absentia, linked him with the former British Legation, and identified 'un certo Norman Davis' as the 'principale organizzatore del terrorismo' who had distributed explosives with his own hands. 'Apparently they didn't realize it was me', said the principal organizer of terrorism. Most alarmingly of all, it was brought to his attention in the vestibule of the hotel as they came in by one of the party who had remained there waving it and saying 'Oh what fun!' :

> The foyer was full of detectives. The Italians had my passport—it would have been quite easy for them to have taken me back to Sofia so I was a little nervous at this point. Nobody noticed the connection, and just to show how extraordinarily foolish and vain one is I had a copy of the newspaper and I brought it with me and have it to this day.

The following day the nineteen diplomats were flown across to Foggia in small Caproni bombers. Into the first were put those who were in any way compromised, including Hugh Seton-Watson and Norman Davis ('and I was considerably compromised by that time').

Some sighs of relief were heaved when they reached 'as it were . . . the mainland of Europe, the first time for a long time'. Foggia had a big Luftwaffe base, and they were not allowed out of their hotel, but they were given lunch in a private room :

> in order to get to this room we had to walk through the dining room which was entirely full of German Airforce officers, in uniform, and there were 19 of us, not in uniform, and we were led through the 100 or so German officers. In our private room we had an excellent lunch, just a good Italian midday meal. At intervals along the table were bottles of excellent Brolio, and beer . . .

And when they tried to pay, the proprietor said, 'Gentlemen, you are my guests. I will not take any payment'—'we thought that was very good.' They were taken by train to Chianciano, where they maintained this standard of good living (contriving to drink the hotel's cellar dry). Eventually they were taken by train through Vichy France to Spain, and then by a convoy from Gibraltar to the Clyde, arriving in London on 13th July 1941. After only twelve days' leave, Davis was flown out to Cairo, and went on to Istanbul, where he operated under a new identity—'James Cameron'—and with a new appearance. Photographs of him in disguise now have a faintly comical air, but since the disguise apparently deceived Ronald Syme, it must have been effective. He also served for some time in GHQ, Cairo. He ended the war with the rank of major, and was awarded an MBE (Military). In 1944, resuming his true identity, he married Magdalene (Lena) Jamieson Bone, whom he had known since his time in Sofia. The marriage was to prove a very long and happy one. Lena shared his shrewd and detached view of the world, as well as his interest in good food and drink. They were devoted and inseparable companions.

The extraordinary events of the war years inevitably demand a prominent place in any obituary of Norman Davis, and a biographer of Romantic inclinations might find his return to academic life something of a comedown. He, however, in his typically down to earth way, regarded his wartime SOE period as a necessary (and often entertaining) temporary interlude. He was glad to be able to return to what he had really wanted to do all along, and he was delighted that he could now do it in Britain. He taught in London for a short period as lecturer in medieval English at Queen Mary College (1946), and then back at Oxford, as a lecturer at Oriel and Brasenose Colleges (1947). In 1948 he became University Lecturer in Medieval English. Then, in 1949 a far-sighted and enlightened decision made him Professor of English Language in the University of Glasgow, a post which he held for ten years.

This was a very happy period. He enjoyed a warm and effective relationship with Peter Alexander, the Professor of English Literature, and he built up his own Language Department and reshaped the syllabus. He liked Glasgow, and, naturally, had no difficulty in adapting to the pattern of a Scottish university. He was a good lecturer, and a superb administrator. There was much time to make up, and evidence of his scholarly distinction now began to appear in published form. First came reviews—and these continued in a steady stream throughout the rest of his career. He was an excellent reviewer, judicious and authoritative, severe if he thought it necessary, but only then. Then came a series of articles and notes, beginning in 1949 with a piece on the text of Margaret Paston's letters, and continuing with offerings on topics as diverse as the Middle English Bestiary and 'Hippopotamus' in Old English. There were many on the Paston Letters, a subject he made increasingly his own : in particular, 1955 saw the publication of a major British Academy lecture (the Sir Israel Gollancz Memorial Lecture, 1954) on 'The Language of the Pastons'. Longer works also began to appear: in 1953 the revision of Sweet's *Anglo-Saxon Primer* (in fact a totally new work which proved a reliable and indispensable guide to generations of students) and in 1958 a Selection of the Paston Letters in the Clarendon Medieval and Tudor Series. He was by now a leading authority on the language and texts of the Middle English period, and especially of the fifteenth century. In 1959 he succeeded Tolkien as the Merton Professor of English Language and Literature at Oxford.

His return to Oxford began the happiest phase of his career. He was an Oxford man through and through, and as one of the most loyal of old Mertonians, he was delighted to be able to occupy a Professorial Fellowship at that college. The long tenure of the Merton chair (from which he retired in 1980) was an unqualified success. He was able to devote himself totally to his work for the Faculty and to an increasing number of devoted graduate students. In these years the skills he had developed in earlier years came to fruition. He became increasingly influential in medieval philological and textual studies. Already in his Glasgow days he had become joint editor (with Peter Alexander) of *The Review of English Studies* (a position he held from 1954 until 1963) and Honorary Director of the Early English Text Society (1957–1983). He later became a Delegate of the Oxford University Press and a general editor of the Oxford History of English Literature. To these enterprises he devoted his wide learning and considerable energy. He excelled in a kind of 'collaborative' scholarship, maintaining an unrelenting gentle moral pressure on his authors or collaborators, and painstakingly commenting on everything they produced. Selflessly, he would put much of himself into the work of others. The only tangible memorials to this remarkable achievement are to be found in the prefaces of many books (and, as he would jokingly point out, in the EETS and *RES* instructions to authors and contributors, where the date of his birth was enshrined as a model).

This period saw an impressive flow of scholarly work. Among many important articles may be mentioned 'Styles in English Prose of the Late Middle and early Modern Period' (1961), which raised grave doubts about R. W. Chambers's views on the 'continuity' of English prose, and 'The *Litera Troili* and English Letters', in which he used his knowledge of epistolary formulae to illuminate a passage in Chaucer. Others appeared on topics ranging from 'The Epistolary Uses of William Worcester' to 'Sheep-farming terms in Medieval Norfolk' or 'William Tyndale's English of Controversy'. The Glossary which he provided for *Early Middle English Verse and Prose* (ed. J. A. W. Bennett and G. V. Smithers, 1966) demonstrated another area in which he excelled. As a glossator, he had a remarkable sense of the precise contextual nuance of a word. This quality was seen again in the glossary of his revised edition of the Tolkien and Gordon edition of *Sir Gawain and the Green Knight* (1967)—again, what was modestly called a 'revision' was a completely new work. Another practical and useful project of this kind was brought to completion in 1979 in the collaborative *Chaucer Glossary*. The idea was entirely his; he organized and oversaw the work with his customary skill and meticulous accuracy. In 1970 there appeared his EETS edition of *Non-Cycle Plays and Fragments*, and in 1971 the first volume of his *magnum opus*, the edition of *Paston Letters and Papers of the Fifteenth Century*. Volume II of this was published in 1976. It was a great sadness to us all that Volume III, with further notes and the glossary, did not appear, but the two volumes that did represent a magisterial and definitive achievement. After his retirement he produced distinguished pieces on late medieval English, and on Chaucer's language (in the Riverside edition). He also took part in a number of recorded readings from Chaucer with Nevill Coghill, John Burrow and Lena. These arose from a highly successful series of readings for undergraduates in Oxford, in which John Burrow was a dashing Troilus, and Norman Davis read Pandarus with considerable zest.

Over the years honours of various kinds came to him. He was elected to the Academy in 1969. In 1977 he became a Corresponding Fellow of the Medieval Academy of America, and in 1984 he returned to Dunedin to receive an honorary D. Litt. from the University of Otago. He had apparently settled into a happy retirement in Oxford when he was plunged into deep sadness by the death of Lena in 1983. It took him a long time to recover from this, though he was helped by his visit to his New Zealand relatives. Eventually, his inner strength reasserted itself, and he regained much of his former cheerfulness, helped by the constant kindness of his college, Merton, the attentions of his group of friends in Oxford and elsewhere, and the renewal of his old friendship with Mary Seton-Watson, the widow of Hugh, his former SOE colleague.

His death following three months in hospital after what had been thought to be a simple hip replacement operation greatly saddened his friends. Always firm in the face of death, his steadfast refusal to have any memorial service would no doubt have pleased his old academic mentor, Professor Ramsay.

Norman Davis was a fine scholar, with a genuine modesty that is not always found in academics. His friends remember the quizzical look and the sceptical turn of phrase, and, above all the wit and geniality of his companionship. As a host he demonstrated the wide and humane range of his interests. There would be entertaining dinner-table disquisitions on etymologies, sometimes punctuated by visits to the *OED*, and superb imitations of the speech patterns of Glaswegians, New Zealanders, and others. For him life and scholarship were not separate compartments. His vitality and his imagination contributed in no small measure to that quality which was so characteristic of him: 'a natural sense of what scholarship is'.

DOUGLAS GRAY
*Fellow of the British Academy*

*Note.* I am indebted to Mrs V. Mathewson and Miss D. Davis, and to Mrs Mary Seton-Watson for extensive information about Norman Davis's earlier career, and to the following published sources: an interview with Norman Davis in *The NZ Listener* May 9 1981; Dan Davin, 'Norman Davis: the Growth of a Scholar' in *Middle English Studies presented to Norman Davis in Honour of his Seventieth Birthday* edd. Douglas Gray and E. G. Stanley, Oxford, 1983; Charles A. Moser *Dimitrov of Bulgaria* 1979; Sir George Rendel, *The Sword and the Olive* London, 1957; David Walker, *Death at My Heels*, London, 1942.

*Proceedings of the British Academy*, **80**, 275–287

# Meyer Fortes
# 1906–1983

MEYER FORTES was in the first rank of that distinguished group of scholars who virtually created the subject of social anthropology in Britain between the two wars. Created, that is, the subject as a form of comparative sociology based upon field observations, bringing their intensive research to bear upon problems, mainly of non-European societies, that related to cultural, psychological, historical, demographic, political and administrative matters, in all of which, with the exception of the historical, Fortes took part.

His father, Nathan, was born in Melitopol, Crimea, which he left at the age of 16 to escape being drafted into the army. He walked to Hamburg and took the boat to England where he stayed for a year to earn enough to pay for a passage to America. There he worked as a peddler before settling down in Memphis and marrying a young Jewish widow who owned a bar. A daughter was born, he prospered and was joined by two brothers. But his wife died and, after some trouble in the bar, he left for England where he worked in the clothing industry in Leeds. There he was joined by his parents and their other children. Nathan emigrated to South Africa where he married Bertha Kerbel from Lithuania and settled down as an innkeeper in the Afrikaans-speaking township of Britstown, some 500 miles inland from Cape Town. The couple had four sons and two daughters, of whom Meyer was the eldest, being born on April 25, 1906.

From 1918 to 1922 he attended the South African Collegiate High School, dominated by Scottish teachers to whom he was always grateful. With the aid of various scholarships he studied for a B.A. in English and Psychology at the University of Capetown and received the Noble scholarship as the best graduating student of the year 1925. He then took an M.A. with distinction in 1926 and received the highest postgraduate

M. FORTES

*Ramsey & Muspratt*

award which he used to go to London to register for a Ph.D. degree in Psychology. There, with the South African situation in mind (he had become interested in the education of Cape coloured adolescents), he worked first with the sociologist Morris Ginsberg but then decided to carry out research on non-verbal intelligence tests for inter-racial use under G.E. Spearman under whom he took his Ph.D in 1930 at University College.[1] At the same time he started working voluntarily under the psychiatrist Emmanuel Miller at the first child guidance clinic in the East End of London, funded by the Jewish Health Organisation, on the effects of sibling order on adolescent behaviour, research that led him increasingly to concentrate on the social dimensions of psychology.[2] His association with the clinic and his meeting with J.C. Flügel resulted in a permanent interest in psychiatric and psychoanalytic theory, especially as it affected interpersonal behaviour within the family.

It was through Flügel that Fortes met the man who was to have the greatest influence on his life, the anthropologist Bronislaw Malinowski. He describes his encounter as a chance meeting but chance had a directional quality about it.[3] In the first place he had a number of introductions from Cape Town, which he assiduously cultivated. Secondly, he lived in Bloomsbury at a time when even research students could afford rooms in Central London and when, in Raymond Firth's words, that area had some of the characteristics of the Quartier Latin, or anyhow the Left Bank, in Paris. As a bright young man with the right contacts he met many of the leading intellectuals of the day as well as the major figures in the social sciences. In Cape Town he had been given the names of Ginsberg and Miller. Miller, who founded the *British Journal of Delinquency*, had been taught at Cambridge by W.H.R. Rivers, a man who combined an interest in psychology, psychoanalysis and anthropology, as Fortes was later to do in a different way, and who trained the Cambridge psychologist Sir Frederic Bartlett, author of *Remembering*. It was Bartlett who acted, a little reluctantly, as a referee when Fortes later applied for a Rockefeller Fellowship in 1932.[4] Fortes also speaks of a chance meeting with C.K. Ogden which gave him the opportunity to translate a ponderous but authoritative work on the *Gestalt Theory* by B. Petermann for that remarkable series, *The International Library of Psychology, Philosophy*

---

[1] The tests Fortes devised at this time contributed to the Raven IQ tests.

[2] The work Fortes did at the Clinic was published in *Economica* (1933).

[3] He had in fact met Malinowski on a previous occasion but this is when he was invited to join his seminar. See the accounts given to John Barnes in S. Drucker-Brown, Notes towards a biography of Meyer Fortes, *American Ethnologist* 16 (1989): 375–85.

[4] Bartlett had been an examiner of Evans-Pritchard's doctoral thesis on Azande wichcraft, with the viva being conducted on the phone according to the candidate.

*and Scientific Method*, Ogden was the author, with I.A. Richards, of the *The Meaning of Meaning* which contained an important contribution by Malinowski on 'The problem of meaning in primitive languages' and called for 'a Science of Symbolism and Meaning'. Another figure who crops up as a referee, this time in Fortes' application to enter the Gold Coast to carry out field research, is that of Lancelot Hogben, whose works on social aspects of mathematics achieved great popularity. These intellectual contacts give some idea of the milieu in which he lived and worked when he started to study anthropology, a subject to which he was drawn by his liberal, Jewish background in South Africa and his increasing concern with the social aspects of psychological phenomena.

Malinowski's seminar in 1931 was clearly an intellectual and professional turning point for Fortes. His original intention was to carry out psychological research on the African family, but his plans were strongly modified under the influence of Malinowski's teaching, the friends he made and lastly the financial opportunities for research. It was through the seminar that he met E.E. Evans-Pritchard, and through him in August 1931 Radcliffe-Brown who was on his way to take up a Professorship in Chicago and had come to London to attend the centenary meeting of the British Association for the Advancement of Science as President of the Anthropology Section. His long-standing friendship with Evans-Pritchard was of the greatest importance. They met at the time when his interests in cross-cultural psychology led him in the direction of anthropology, just as his involvement with racial tests and juvenile delinquency pushed him in the direction of sociology and, in particular, of studies of family and kinship. At this time he was working in the clinic in East London and teaching for the London County Council Evening Institute which he had been doing since 1929. Evans-Pritchard at once began negotiating for his appointment as head of a new department of experimental psychology at the University of Cairo, where he himself was teaching at the time.[5] When he applied for a Fellowship at the International African Institute, it was Evans-Pritchard who sent a very strong letter in his support. When he eventually went to the field in West Africa, Evans-Pritchard wrote to him constantly, offering suggestions for topics to investigate, asking for information on matters that interested him, sending gifts of food and of reading matter. They sent each other draft papers to read and made severe comments on each other's work. In 1941 when Evans-Pritchard was trying to persuade Fortes to take up a post in South Africa, he commented 'I can't do without the inspiration of your mind.'[6] Despite a cooling of the friendship in the late

[5] Evans-Pritchard to Fortes, 29 August, 1932.
[6] Evans-Pritchard to Fortes, 18 February 1941, Malakal, Sudan.

1940's, partly as the result of a disagreement about Fortes' observations on the contemporary family published in a popular journal, they continued to correspond throughout their lives. The relationship went on being important to both of them, with Evans-Pritchard asking Fortes' advice on psychological matters and Fortes looking upon Evans-Pritchard as his 'elder brother' in anthropology.

The most significant factor in enabling Fortes, and many others, to carry out research in Africa was the sudden access of funds for anthropological research which came from the Rockefeller Foundation of New York. In 1926 the Foundation extended its fellowship scheme to anthropological fieldwork and operated in the Pacific through the Australian National Research Council and Radcliffe-Brown at Sydney. Some years later Malinowski approached the Foundation with a view to instituting a scheme for research in Africa centred on the International African Institute, which it was already supporting in other ways. His success enabled the Institute to offer a number of fellowships to established scholars for field research in Africa, in many cases on condition that they carried out a year's training with Malinowski in London beforehand. The year 1932–3 brought together Fortes, S.F. Nadel from Austria via Berlin and S. Hofstra from Holland, all of whom were preparing to carry out research in West Africa and who were required to work out a joint scheme for theoretical and empirical collaboration. In addition there was Lecoeur from France, killed in the Second World War, who carried out work in Tibesti. These were the active members, the 'mandarins', of Malinowski's famous seminar at the London School of Economics, attended not only by his advanced students such as Audrey Richards and Margerie Perham, but by scholars from abroad, such as Talcott Parsons and Alison Davis.

As a result of his apprenticeship, Fortes' project to study the African family from a comparative psychological point of view moved in a more sociological direction. Despite his difficulties with Malinowski, which were more than shared by Evans-Prichard, his research plans were greatly influenced by him in many ways. While Evans-Pritchard kept his distance, obtained his research funds from elsewhere and had an independent income, Fortes was more closely tied to his patron through the Institute which provided him with generous support over a period of five years.

That support enabled him to undertake research in the Gold Coast with his wife, Sonia Donen, a fellow student at Cape Town, whom he had married in 1928 and with whom he collaborated in writing about the domestic economy. The actual location for the work among the Tallensi of the Northern Territories was decided upon after discussion with R.S. Rattray, the well-known administrator-anthropologist who had already visited their ritual centre in the Tong Hills. Fortes had considerable difficulty in entering the colony, partly because Malinowski insisted on him doing longer preparation than he wanted, partly because the colonial authorities were suspicious of his radical and Jewish background which was not helped by the fact his wife had been born in the USSR and had been a Young Komsomol member.

They eventually set sail for Africa on the same boat as Nadel and his wife in December, 1933. The research he carried out no longer took the focussed form of his earlier proposals but extended widely across the whole spectrum of the social life of the people, although he did give special attention to some of his early interests. His initial papers covered a wide variety of themes. The first was on 'marriage laws' and was published by the Government Printing Office. He also wrote on 'incest', on 'communal fishing festivals' (in a Durkheimian manner), on demography, on the domestic economy (with Sonia Fortes), on culture change (the theme of the Rockefeller project) and especially on *Social and Psychological Aspects of Education among the Tallensi*, a valuable contribution whose approach to learning theory was praised by many, including the American psychologists, Dollard and Miller.

Fortes returned to London temporarily in 1935 and again attended Malinowski's seminars. Before he left he was invited by the new head of the colony's model secondary school at Achimota to join the staff in order to help prepare the way for coming social changes. The administration was not keen on the idea, although by now Fortes was viewed not so much as a radical, wanting to change the world, but as a conservative anthropologist, wanting to keep all as it is. In the event, Fortes preferred to continue his fieldwork which he did until 1937.

Fortes returned from the field in mid-August after spending some time in South Africa on the way. He then applied to the International African Institute for an extension to his Fellowship until August 1938 so that he could write his book on Tallensi 'social structure', which he now decided was his priority. 'My plan is to do a book dealing mainly with that segment of the culture of the Tallensi which is of most immediate concern to people working the area, officials and others. Its topic will be the social structure: Local and kinship grouping, political organization, the economic system, law and family government'. And he adds, 'Apart from utilitarian considerations there is sound theoretical justification for dealing first with the social structure'.[7] While it is true that Fortes was attracted by practical concerns, and while most anthropologists hope that their work

---

[7] Application of Dr Fortes, Document C for item 2 of the Agenda of the 16th meeting of the Executive Committee of the International African Institute, 12–13 October, 1937.

may be of some 'use' to the local population and its administrators, his main interest was undoubtedly 'theoretical', in a sociological sense. At this point he seemed to have set aside his earlier psychological and psychoanalytic interests under the influences of Durkheim, Radcliffe-Brown, Malinowski and his contemporaries. Fortes has himself suggested that the 'brilliant success of the sociologically oriented fieldwork of the 'functionalist' contingent (Firth, Evans-Pritchard, Richards, Schapera, Hogbin *et al.*)' led to 'a marked hostility to having dealings with psychoanalysis' (1978: 7–8). But there was also, under broader Durkheimian influences very apparent in Evans-Pritchard, resistance to the so-called confounding of sociological and psychological levels of explanation. So that although Fortes was initially encouraged to carry out psychological research, he decided that he had first to analyse the social structure along the lines of his colleagues.

At this point in his career it was understandably difficult to obtain yet further funds for research and, in the absence of available academic posts, Fortes had to look round for part-time teaching which he found at the London School of Economics. By this time Radcliffe-Brown had been appointed the first Professor of Social Anthropology at Oxford in 1937 while Evans-Pritchard had already been giving lectures there for three years. The latter persuaded Fortes to join them to write up his notes, envisaging his move as the beginning of the creation of 'a school' which would be more scholarly, more scientific, less applied, than that of Malinowski. Plans were made for their active collaboration, the first material evidence of which was *African Political Systems*, a series of studies published by the International African Institute in 1940, with a preface by Radcliffe-Brown and an introduction by Fortes (mainly) and Evans-Pritchard. Like the companion volume on *African Systems of Kinship and Marriage* (1950), which had a long theoretical introduction by Radcliffe-Brown, these works exerted an important influence on world anthropology, not simply of Africa, for years to come.

The introduction to the first volume attempted to lay out a broad framework for the analyses of political systems in the simpler societies by putting forward a tripartite distinction between states, segmentary or acephalous societies and 'primitive hordes'. The distinction between the first two owned much to Durkheim, who was concerned, as Spencer and many philosophers before him, with 'the problem of order', in particular how it was possible to maintain social control in the absence of legal institutions such as the courts of Europe. The problem went back to Locke, Hobbes and Rousseau, and it was one that gave rise to a useful discussion as well as further investigation in anthropology on the nature of 'law', on the role of the lineage and on alternative fields through which social

control might be maintained. For at this period in time it was still possible
to enquire into political systems that had not been overly transformed by
the advent of colonial rule and its successor, the nation state.

This early collaboration was soon interrupted by the outbreak of war.
The two men worked out a scheme, which they subsequently felt failed
to get Radcliffe-Brown's complete approval, whereby they would be sent
to the parts of Africa they knew, partly to carry out research, partly to
further the war effort.[8] The plan did not work out but Evans-Pritchard
took off on his own for the Sudan to engage in a minor guerilla war, while
Fortes stayed in Oxford, took over Evans-Pritchard's work and completed
his two-volume manuscripts on the Tallensi.[9] Eventually he went out to
Nigeria in connection with Lord Hailey's *African Survey* and was caught up
in intelligence activity in the Gold Coast. He also became heavily involved
in moves towards the development of higher education in that country,
looking in the utopian way characteristic of wartime Britain, towards the
future of Africa and the world.

At that time he was himself being considered for a post at Achimota.
He had earlier been asked by the Principal to help draw up 'a comprehensive scheme for the establishment of an Institute of West African Culture',
which would make provision for the teaching of 'West African sociology
and arts and crafts'. Fortes wrote a memorandum indicating how such
a programme might be linked to the proposed University level teaching
but the whole project was postponed until after the war. At that time
the situation was more favourable, with the allocation of considerable
funds for development. In 1943 Fortes wrote two other memoranda,
one for a West African Institute and another for a new University of
which the Institute would be a part. When the Institute (WAIASS) was
established Fortes became its first director and organised one of its first
and certainly its most important research project, namely the Ashanti
Social Survey of 1945–6, an interdisciplinary scheme directed by Fortes
himself, by Robert Steele, a geographer, and by Peter Ady, an economist,
as well as recruiting some 40 local field assistants. He had long wanted
to study the matrilineal Ashanti as a contrast to the patrilineal Tallensi,
especially as he had been interested in such forms of social organisation
through Malinowski. The survey enabled him to do this but it was also

---

[8] When their scheme for sociological research on modern political systems in Africa
(essentially following up *African Political Systems* which was about to appear) was put
before the Hebdomadal Council on 8 March 1940, Radcliffe-Brown expressed his 'very
strong support'. But Evans-Pritchard felt he had not done enough.

[9] Evans-Pritchard's account of this war is given in the *Army Quarterly* for 1973 (pp. 470–97).
The article has been discussed by Clifford Gertz in a chapter of his book, *Works and Lives;
the anthropologist as author*, Stanford, 1988.

one of the first major socio-economic enquiries in a non-literate culture, making use of the most modern techniques of data processing. Apart from the publications of Steele and Ady, the project led to two major articles by Fortes, one a general analysis of Ashanti kinship and marriage, the other a study of social change. More generally his work there served as a continuing source of interest and contributed a considerable part to the Morgan lectures, which he delivered at the University of Rochester.

The early war years had enabled him to complete his two major monographs on the Tallensi, *The Dynamics of Clanship among the Tallensi* (1945) and *The Web of Kinship among the Tallensi* (1949). The first had been largely written in 1938 and analysed the workings of this social system at the macro level, with the hugely complex intertwining of political, religious and kinship relations in which each boundary was contextually important but there were no clear-cut tribal groupings or levels of hierarchy. Much attention was paid to the minute analysis of descent groups, especially the patrilineal lineage; the result was a brilliant presentation of the overall structure of the workings of a political system in pre-colonial times, his research being carried out within some thirty years of the conquest.

But it was on the second volume on the family that Fortes was to bring his expertise most powerfully to bear. Influenced by the studies of Raymond Firth, the work achieves a subtle marriage of quantitative data on the composition and cyclical structure of domestic groups with an extremely perceptive analysis of the social and psychological relationships of its members. Having worked among a related group of people, I am well aware of the skill that has gone into its construction; indeed I doubt if we have any monograph about the family in any part of the world that can stand comparison.

It was on the promise of these two volumes that Fortes had been appointed to a Readership at Oxford in 1946. Together with Evans-Pritchard, Gluckman and Srinivas, they built up a powerful department which attracted students from all over the world at the moment when anthropology, and particularly African anthropology, was expanding rapidly. that period of intense co-operation was short. In 1949 Gluckman accepted a Readership in Social Anthropology at Manchester, with the prospect of a Chair, and in the following year Fortes was appointed to the William Wyse Professorship at Cambridge with Evans-Pritchard's strong support, and became a Fellow of King's College. This post he held until his retirement in 1973, during which time he built up the Department to become arguably the most prominent in the country, having made the imaginative appointment of E.R. Leach to a Lectureship as soon as a post became free.

At the beginning these were tough but exciting years for Fortes.

Competent social anthropologists at Cambridge were few and he did most of the teaching and training of graduate students himself. But he soon established field research as an important feature of the department, attracting lively speakers, organising a post-graduate seminar, stimulating the publication of the results in *Cambridge Papers in Social Anthropology* and in the monograph series, *Cambridge Studies in Social Anthropology*. He thoroughly reorganised undergraduate teaching, introducing a specialist degree in social anthropology as well as encouraging options in social psychology, statistics, linguistics and development economics. Administration was not much to his liking, but he played a notable part in bringing distinguished sociologists to Cambridge and indeed in extending the social sciences themselves.

In terms of his own research, one aim was to complete a volume on Tallensi religion and towards this end he gave a number of named lectures, which were later published. Outstanding among them was the Frazer Lecture for 1957, *Oedipus and Job in West Africa* (published 1959). In 1966 he gave a presidential address to the Royal Anthropological Institute on 'Totem and Taboo', in 1972 the Emmanuel Miller Lecture to the Association for Child Psychology and Psychiatry on the subject of 'The first born' (published 1974) and in 1973 a memorial lecture for Ernest Jones, the biographer of Freud, entitled 'Custom and conscience' to the British Psychoanalytic Society.

These titles already indicate the continuing role of psychological ideas which became most explicit in his later studies on religion. That was especially true of his work on ancestor worship, which had early on fascinated him as a link between the domains of kinship and religion, an acting out of familial conflicts on a supernatural plane. In this he was stimulated by his second wife, Doris Meyer, M.D., a psychiatrist whom he married in 1960, four years after the death of his first wife, and with whom he collaborated in writing on mental problems ('migrant madness') among the Tallensi. The broad outline of his approach had already been sketched out in his major monographs in which the political and jural role of the cult of the ancestors was fully analysed. In *Oedipus and Job* he pursued the theme in a more subtle manner, attempting to explicate what Horton has called the 'social psychology' of the Tallensi, including their conceptions of the spiritual and psychic make-up of human beings. Such an enquiry entailed a deep knowledge of the language and behaviour of the people themselves, a knowledge which few scholars of non-literate societies have possessed to the same degree. While this analysis, like much of Fortes' work, does not make for easy reading, it has had a pervading influence on the field. But he did not complete the book on Tallensi religion he had hoped and these essays were gathered together after his death under the title of *Religion, Morality and the Person* (1987), a phrase that gives a flavour of his major interests in the field, that is, in the moral consequences of religious practice and belief, and in the notion of a person, essentially a moral person for whom kinship and the family were of supreme importance.

It is for his studies in the field of kinship and the family that Fortes is best known. Following his monographs on the Tallensi, his major published work was an expansion of the lectures appropriately given at the University of Rochester in the name of Lewis Henry Morgan, entitled *Kinship and the Social Order* (1969). The empirical material on which the book is based derived from his research among the Ashanti of Ghana. But the lectures themselves were a wide-ranging investigation of the sphere of kinship studies, as he saw it, dwelling in particular on the role of the lineage (in this case, matrilineal) and on what he called 'the principle of amity', the cathectic aspect of kinship relations which had impressed him from his early studies and no doubt from his earlier background. Fortes' work on both the political-jural and domestic aspects of the lineage have been seminal for countless scholars, both those working on Africa, in New Guinea (where comments have been made on the introduction of 'African models') and on Chinese studies, initially through the research of Maurice Freedman. The influence came not only from his empirical and general work on the lineage contained in his monographs and in a much-quoted theoretical article on 'The structure of unilineal descent groups' (1953), but also from his studies on the associated aspect of ancestor worship, which is what drew him to Chinese and Japanese studies. Once again it was the complex contribution of the ancestral cult to the maintenance of moral behaviour on which he dwelt, the function of filial piety in social life.

In stressing the role of the lineage, some social anthropologists may have been led to underplay the role of domestic groups as such. Fortes worked in lineage societies and with Evans-Pritchard, so that he was inevitably impressed with the nature of their operation. But he was also deeply interested in the domestic domain, in the effects of demographic variables (as in his insightful contribution to Lorimer's *Culture and Human Fertility*, 1954) and to its psychological components. One of his most influential contributions was on cyclical change among domestic groups (1958), including the family, an interest that derived from developmental psychology but which was given an important sociological and demographic dimension. As with notions of morality, the ancestors and family life, his interest was embedded in his first research proposal to the International African Institute, well before he had undergone his anthropological apprenticeship. But it was the ability to combine the sociological and the psychological that enabled him to analyse interpersonal relations among the Tallensi and the Ashanti in such a profound manner.

Both at Oxford and at Cambridge, Fortes supervised the post-graduate work of an array of students, mostly Africanists, from a variety of countries. He was always glad to be able to contribute to the training of those from the Third World and was especially proud of having taught Kofi Busia, author of *The Position of the Chief in the Modern Political System of Ashanti* (1951), first Professor of Sociology at the University of the Gold Coast, and later Prime Minister of Ghana. His other Ghanaian student was Alex Kyeremateng who wrote on Ashanti law and rituals of royalty, but he also encouraged others outside social anthropology to pursue academic careers, always seeking to instill high academic standards. Although he was also interested in wider social problems, he became sceptical about developmental studies and, possibly with Malinowski in mind, did not greatly welcome anthropologists becoming engaged in work of this kind. Like many of his contemporaries he was also hesitant about admitting students who wanted to carry out research on modern or modernising societies, being worried in both cases of a descent into the higher journalism (the very charge levelled by Malinowski at his first research proposal and later on by Evans-Pritchard). He was equally wary of the belle-lettrism and of the intuitions of many 'cultural' approaches as well as of the scientism of 'billiard-ball' sociology. That did not prevent him using case-histories, psychological deductions, linguistic and statistical data. But there was nothing in his view that could match the understanding derived from linguistically competent, intensive fieldwork within a sociological framework, directed not so much to problem as to topic. He was above all committed to the interlinking of empirical observation and theoretical analysis; one without the other was of little interest to him.

Meyer Fortes died in Cambridge on 27 January 1983. He was the recipient of two festschriften, *The Character of Kinship* (1973) and *Changing Social Structure in Ghana* (1975). He was elected to the British Academy in 1967, became an Honorary Foreign Member of the American Academy of Arts and Sciences, received honorary degrees from Chicago and Belfast, and was especially proud of being an honorary fellow of the London School of Economics (1975) and of King's College, Cambridge.

Meyer Fortes played a prominent and responsible part in the running of anthropological affairs. He was President of the Royal Anthropological Institute, to which he was much attached, partly because of the efforts made by Charles and Brenda Seligman, his early allies in the struggle with Malinowski, for its support. He was equally devoted to the International African Institute, which had supported his fieldwork and published his major monographs, serving on its Council until he retired from the

William Wyse Chair in 1973. He played an important part in founding the Association of Social Anthropologists and later became its Chairman. He delivered most of the distinguished lectures in the field, the Frazer lectures, the Morgan lectures in the United States and was widely known, through his work and through visits, throughout the English-speaking world. As the result of his work and that of a handful of other scholars, mostly from overseas, social anthropology in Britain led the field for the three decades between 1930 and 1960.

JACK GOODY
*Fellow of the British Academy*

*Note.* I am grateful for the help of Doris Fortes, John Barnes, Raymond Firth and M.N. Srinivas.

*Proceedings of the British Academy*, **80**, 289–304

# Morris Ginsberg
# 1889–1970

MUCH OF MORRIS GINSBERG'S EARLY LIFE remains unknown, for he refused to record his memories and could be got to talk about his youth only in snatches. The following account is derived from personal knowledge as a former student and colleague at the London School of Economics, supplemented by information in the School's archives and by the published and unpublished recollections of other former students and colleagues.[1]

Morris Ginsberg was born on May 14 1889, the son (but not the only child—a sister is known to have survived him) of Meyer Ginsberg, tobacco manufacturer in one of the smaller Lithuanian Jewish communities of the Russian empire. His mother tongue was Yiddish and he was educated as a Talmudic scholar in classical Hebrew. He remained entirely Yiddish speaking until he came to this country at about the age of 17. He earned his living in the business of relatives in Manchester whilst preparing himself for entry to London University. He mastered English readily enough, but mathematics was another matter. The subject had no place at all in his early education and he later declared that had never in his life worked so hard as for the mathematics papers of the London University Matriculation examination. He entered University College London in 1910 to read for a degree in Philosophy, with a modest but indispensable scholarship for which he more than once in later years expressed his profound gratitude. His first acquaintance with English society had been, he recalled, through a Hebrew translation of George Eliot's *Daniel Deronda* (which, he insisted, read better in Hebrew). He

---

[1] Obituary notices by Professors T. H. Marshall and D. G. MacRae in the *British Journal of Sociology*, December 1970 and in *The Times* newspaper of 1 and 14 September 1970 (unsigned); entries in the *Dictionary of National Biography* (A. H. Halsey) and the *Encyclopaedia Judaica* (unsigned); also contributions to *A Memorial Volume for Morris Ginsberg*, ed. R. Fletcher (1974).

M. GINSBERG                                    *J. Russell & Sons*

now, in 1910 at the age of 21, embarked on a transforming life-long career in British academia.

His Jewish foundations were overlaid but never suppressed. He never lost his Yiddish or his classical Hebrew (which enabled him to cope with the modern Israeli version). His style of life ceased to reflect the ritualised Judaism in which he was reared, but he was never alienated from Judaism. All religion was to him a sociological mystery and he sought within it the rational and the ethical. He and his wife Ethel (née Street), whom he married in 1931, brought up their daughter by informal adoption in the Jewish faith as practised by the unorthodox. He was actively interested in Jewish problems and was associated with the World Jewish Congress. His substantial and learned essays on *Anti-Semitism* and *The Jewish Problem* were published by the World Jewish Congress in 1944; and in 1956 he delivered the Noah Barou Memorial Lecture for the Congress: *The Jewish People Today. A Survey*. He co-edited, with the anthropologist Maurice Freedman, the *Jewish Journal of Sociology* founded in 1959, and contributed articles and reviews including, in the first issue, an essay 'On Prejudice', which he had delivered as a lecture in a memorial series for Jacques Cohen, *Über Vorurteile*, organised by Max Horkheimer.

Ginsberg was driven intellectually and emotionally to a belief in conquering rationality and the unity of mankind grounded in interconnect- edness, interdependence and moral convergence. But he was acutely aware of anti-semitism, endemic even in liberal England. He once remarked that his seniors at University College had 'treated him very fairly'—with the implicit rider 'despite my being a Jew'. Faced with the horrors of the Holocaust he evinced a characteristically Jewish *Weltschmerz*: a quiet sadness and an instinct for the worst outcome of events. T. H. Marshall recalled: 'Anyone who heard him deliver his Hobhouse Memorial Lecture on "The Unity of Mankind" will remember what a moving experience it was to listen to those closing passages, even though the nearest he got to an explicit statement of faith and hope was in the sentence: "Great as are the obstacles to human unity and deep-seated as are the antagonisms between men, we can find no justification in sociology for an attitude of fatalistic pessimism."' This was in 1949. By 1956 he was writing: 'In reviewing the development of ethical theories we cannot help being overcome by a certain feeling of despondency. The advances seem so small when viewed in relation to the terrifying problems facing mankind.' He wondered: 'Has there been a failure of ethical insight? Or is it the lack of agreement about what I have called the middle principles of morals, combined with the growing scale and complexity of the problems and our ignorance of the forces at work, that is the source of our failure? Or is it that knowledge is not enough, that evil is not entirely due to ignorance?' Despondent he was, but not despairing. 'The grounds of hope remain. The problems facing humanity are of old standing. But they undergo continuous change, and in the character of the change there is evidence of real hope.'

Ginsberg graduated from University College London BA with first class honours in Philosophy and obtained his MA in 1915. He undertook his first teaching duties in 1914 as University Lecturer in the Department of Philosophy and made the philosophy of Malebranche his specialism. His first contribution to the Aristotelian Society (of which he became President in 1942–3) appeared in the *Proceedings* for 1916–17: 'The Nature of Knowledge as conceived by Malebranche'; and his translation of the *Entretiens* appeared in 1923: *Dialogues on Metaphysics and on Religion*, with an appreciative Preface by G. Dawes Hicks and a substantial Translator's Introduction analysing and discussing Malebranche's work, in particular, his account of causation.

G. Dawes Hicks was head of the Department of Philosophy at University College London in Ginsberg's time. He was well-known as a philosophical Realist in the '80s and '90s, when the philosophy of the British Idealists was dominant at Oxford and in the English and Scottish universities generally. Ginsberg came to intellectual maturity under his auspices and imbibed a philosophical outlook compatible with the natural, and by extension the social, sciences and prepared to give full weight to them.

He came under the powerful and enduring influence of L. T. Hobhouse, 25 years his senior, who had been appointed in 1907 to the Martin White chair of Sociology at the London School of Economics. Ginsberg attended his lectures and seminars as an undergraduate from University College in preparation for the sociological requirements of the philosophy syllabus. On graduating, as well as teaching in the Department of Philosophy at University College, he participated, as Martin White scholar and research student, in the major sociological investigation on which Hobhouse was at that time engaged. Hobhouse had come to regard the scientific side of sociology as especially concerned with the problem of correlating the various aspects of social life reflected in social institutions. For the 'simpler' societies he had elaborated a method for correlating the various forms of social institution with economic status as measured by the degree of control attained over natural forces; and this led to the extensive statistical investigation in which Ginsberg collaborated. The results appeared in 1915 in the monograph *The Material Culture and Social Institutions of the Simpler Peoples. An Essay in Correlation*, attributed jointly to L. T. Hobhouse, G. C. Wheeler and M. Ginsberg.

In 1916 Ginsberg enlisted under the Derby scheme and served in France from 1917–19. At one time he was a sergeant engaged in the dangerous business of bringing ammunition-laden mule teams up to the line on the Western Front. After demobilisation he returned to academic life in London, moving eventually from University College (of the Fellowship of which he was very proud) fully to LSE where, in due course, he became Martin White Professor of Sociology in succession to Hobhouse, who retired in 1929. He occupied the chair until 1954 and as Professor Emeritus taught actively at the School thereafter, until 1968. By his death in 1970 at the age of 81, British sociology lost one who for many years was its only professor, its master teacher and its acknowledged and widely respected spokesman.

Ginsberg wrote prolifically and authoritatively in his spare, clear style continuously throughout his career, to within two years of his death, on a range of topics all stemming from his central preoccupations: the diversity of morals; the theoretical and practical problems and prospects of a rational ethics; the philosophy, psychology and sociology of morals; the ethical aspects of social organisation; sociological theories and methods; and the processes inherent in the genesis and development of social structures. He wrote for colleagues in the professional journals read by philosophers, economists, sociologists, anthropologists, political theorists and psychologists. He wrote also for a wider, non-professional or non-specialist audience (in journals such as *Nature*, the *Rationalist Annual*, *Politics and Letters* and *Scrutiny*) on problems of interest to layman and student alike, in which questions of value and questions of fact are closely interwoven: the causes of war; national character; German views of German mentality; prejudice and anti-semitism. Whatever the occasion and whatever the audience his writing displayed those merits of scholarship, precision and attention to detail which were his hall-mark. Fifty or so papers were assembled in *Studies in Sociology* (1932), *Reason and Unreason in Society* (1947), *On the Diversity of Morals* (1956), and *Evolution and Progress* (1961).

Ginsberg wrote a small book *Psychology of Society* in 1921 which went into nine editions, the last of which (a revised edition) appeared in 1964. In 1932 his *Sociology* appeared in the Home University Library. By virtue of their brief compass, learning in the European tradition of the subjects and their succinct force, they remain classics—and implicitly reproachful reminders of the high standards of undergraduate university study once taken for granted. *On Justice in Society* appeared in 1965. Ginsberg applied himself at length and in detail to one specific problem: the relation between law and morals, illustrated with reference to the justice of educational systems, the ethics of sexual relations, types of marriage and so forth. T. H. Marshall, a sympathetic critic, remarked of this book that though in it Ginsberg 'is as wise and shrewd as ever in his comments and criticisms, it is doubtful whether it succeeds in lifting the subject to a new level.' This is as it may be; but Ginsberg's aim was probably more modest, namely, to demonstrate the synthesis—not the fusion, he would insist—of sociology and social philosophy for the effective handling of social problems. The influence of Sidgwick is very strong. The arguments against ethical relativism are set out and the view defended that ethical judgments are genuine propositions, susceptible to truth claims, and not not merely expletives, commands, commitments or expressions of subjective preferences; and there is a good statement of radical egalitarianism. The book is still read by undergraduates in the Faculty of Social Studies at Oxford.

As teacher, professor and head of the Department of Sociology at the School, Ginsberg established and fought to maintain a tradition in the subject well described by Donald MacRae as one of 'rigour, order, clarity, cosmopolitan scholarship, creative doubt and humane concern'. The going was hard: he faced not only the widely prevalent mistrust of reason, to which his students in general were not immune, but also the passion and impatience of the militantly anti-fascist and, especially, the Marxist students, among whom were many refugees from Nazism. They were out of sympathy with his scholarly preoccupations and found his lectures austere, uninspiring, overly critical and exegetical. He was not helped by the arrival at the School of Karl Mannheim, under the auspices of the Academic Assistance Council for colleagues driven out of Germany, for which he had worked untiringly. Unexpectedly (for Ginsberg knew and respected his work on *Wissenssoziologie*, had welcomed him and his wife and had put them up at home until they found somewhere to live) Mannheim came to personify for him the carelessness of the very professional standards and intellectual integrity he was dedicated to promoting among his students. He sought to limit the damage, as he saw it, by restricting Mannheim's teaching to postgraduate students and relations became very bad. He was greatly relieved when Mannheim left the School for a chair in the Sociology of Education at the London Institute of Education.

Ginsberg underrated his own influence as a teacher. It distressed him in his later years to feel that little remained to show for his efforts. He was far from regretting, still less resenting the fact that, inevitably, a great deal in British sociology came to lie outside the areas in which he worked. But he had no patience with research that seemed to him to be concerned with trivialities and to have no ulterior purpose; or with sociologists who brought psychological arguments into their explanations without having properly mastered the subject; or who undertook comparative studies without a well-grounded general knowledge of human societies, their institutions and their history.

It must be said that these criticisms were not directed at and most definitely did not apply either to his successor in the Martin White chair, Professor Donald MacRae, or to other members of the Sociology and related departments. Ginsberg foresaw and feared the threat to his conception of the subject posed by the great sociological explosion of the post-war era. His pessimism was not rooted in blind conservatism; he believed, with good reason, that without the fundamental values and virtues of the tradition that he defended, the subject would lack substance, purpose and some of the qualities essential to a science. The rapid development of the subject after 1945 and the shift of the centre of gravity from Europe to America did not, as has been suggested, pass him by. He kept himself informed; he knew what was taking place and he did not like it. He was firmly dismissive of much American sociology: ('There's nothing in it, you know!'). He regarded most of its leading exponents as verbose and pretentious and much of its empirical work as trivial. He conceded little or nothing in his teaching to the eagerness of post-war students to come to grips with American empiricism and American 'grand theory', so that his influence on those who were to help man the imminent expansion of the subject in British universities was conveyed through the style rather than the substance of his teaching. He was gentle but unassuming and intellectually assured rather than forceful in his dealings with students. At a departmental meeting not long after the end of the war the talk was of teaching methods. Some enthusiasm was expressed for the 'democratic' procedures adopted in the discussion groups for the Forces run by the Army Bureau of Current Affairs, aptly described by enthusiasts and cynics alike as 'no teaching, only learning'. Ginsberg said nothing and after a time was asked for his opinion. With a deprecating smile, 'I don't let them waste their time in talking—I tell them' he said.

Ginsberg professed a suspect subject but in his hands it could not attract the conventional slights and he himself was widely admired and much honoured. He held honorary degrees from the universities of London, Glasgow and Birmingham and was an honorary Fellow of University College London, and of the London School of Economics. He was Frazer lecturer in 1944, Conway Memorial lecuturer in 1952, Clarke Hall lecturer in 1953, in which year he was elected to the Fellowship of the British Academy, received the Huxley medal and gave the Huxley Memorial lecture. In 1956 he gave the Comte Memorial Lecture at the LSE and in 1958 the Herbert Spencer lecture at Oxford.

In his Introduction to the first of the three volumes of his collected essays, *On the Diversity of Morals*, published in 1956, Ginsberg explained that the main aims of his work on the side of philosophy were to explore the possibilities of a rational ethic and to bring out the importance of the distinction between facts and values. On the sociological side he aimed to maintain and exemplify the view of sociology as concerned with the structure of societies, their genesis and development.

In ethical matters he took a non-naturalist view of moral judgments. 'I do not believe that the moral can be elicited or constructed from the non-moral, or that psychology or sociology can ever take the place of ethics.' On the other hand, it is within the field of social and psychological facts that moral rules have their application and here he argued *naturwissenschaftlich* procedures were appropriate. Ginsberg therefore worked, so to say, on two fronts—as philosopher and as sociologist. He proceeded on the assumption that a rational ethic is possible, and in the belief that the building up of a rational ethics turns to a large extent on questions of psychological and sociological fact: 'on knowledge of human needs and potentialities and of the ways in which the means available for their fulfilment, including the mode of their distribution, are likely to affect the ends and ideals aimed at.'

As philosopher, he took for granted the unity of human reason and the possibility of a rational ethics. He therefore rejected any relativistic view of either knowledge or morals. He argued that there is no necessary connection between the diversity and the relativity of morals: the diversities are not arbitrary and lend no support to ethical relativism in any of its forms. The comparative study of moral codes reveals a fundamental similarity of content 'due to the circumstance that human needs and impulses are much the same everywhere'. 'At one point or another we must assume primary valuations which are not further reducible.' The concept of 'ideal' is essential to the understanding of moral development. Moral values take shape as ideals which transcend, though they arise from and are related to, fundamental human needs. The ideals differ because they are coloured by historical processes and contemporary situations and are marked by confused and irrational thoughts. The task of reason is to clear from them the accretions that have gathered round them. That the subjection of ethics to this kind of rational analysis would reduce the diversity in the unanalysed situation is certain. But 'whether any fundamental divergences in moral outlook will remain when the facts have been clarified and the ideals elucidated remains to be seen.'

Apart from differences in content and the possibility of residual differences in outlook, there are actual differences of structure: differences in the clarity with which principles of conduct are elicited and examined; in the ways in which they are balanced and contribute to the total order or way of life; and in the detail of their application. 'Looked at in this way, the diversities are far from arbitrary and they lend no support to subjectivist or emotionalist interpretations of morals.' They do, however, imply differences in the level of moral development. 'It seems to me that no-one seriously believes that all cultures are "equally valid", though what we mean by differences of level is a very difficult question.'

By a rational ethics, Ginsberg meant one that is based on a knowledge of human needs and potentialities and of the principles of justice: that is, principles designed to exclude arbitrary power and to secure an equitable distribution of the conditions of well-being. He argued that when we speak of a movement from lower to higher levels in moral development we have in mind such criteria as comprehensiveness, coherence and articulation of principles and assumptions; objectivity and disinterestedness; and the range of persons to whom moral rules are applied. It is true that in this we are influenced by the view of morals prevailing in the 'higher' societies and are allowing these societies to be judges in their own cause. It is they that decide that they are 'higher' and that moral development is synonymous with moral progress, or progress in morals: 'But I fear this cannot be helped'. Ginsberg dismissed what is today regarded as the deep and worrying interpretive problem of being inexorably caught up in a hermeneutic circle. He would have been unmoved by the criticism of, say, Max Gluckman's study of Barotse jurisprudence or Richard Brandt's study of Hopi ethics, that they consist in cross-cultural investigations of the extent to which the Barotse or the Hopi accept principles like our own.

The expanding role of rationality, Ginsberg argued, is the main operative factor in the development from a lower to a higher level in human affairs generally. This is obvious in the case of knowledge, science and technology and can be demonstrated as true also of morals. Insofar as it can be shown to be true of law, this is evidence for the reality—in a broad sense—of social progress. 'The movement from unreflective custom to the declaration, systematisation and codification of law, thence to deliberate legislation and the critical scrutiny of the ethical basis of the law, unquestionably constitutes growth in self-direction and the rational ordering of life.' The motives behind the drive to systematisation are not only technical and logical but also ethical: they comprise principles of high generality, such as the general principle which excludes arbitrariness and insists that like cases must be treated in like manner, but also, increasingly, the 'middle' principles which attempt to define what constitutes arbitrariness in a given context. 'It is in the field of the "middle" principles that knowledge of the ways in which institutions affect the individuals concerned, directly or indirectly, is of vital importance.' Such knowledge (in which ethics most needs the co-operation of the social sciences) does not alone suffice; it offers no apocalyptic visions—but 'it can do something to help man to make his own history before the end'.

T. H. Marshall recalled 'a lunch at UNESCO held to bring Ginsberg and Raymond Aron together and persuade them to collaborate in planning a symposium on development. Ginsberg wanted the role of rationality to be the guiding light in the proceedings. Aron objected on the grounds that the thesis underlying the idea was untenable. He brought all his big intellectual guns to bear, but in vain. In the end he was completely baffled by this stubborn champion of rationality who, as it appeared to him, was quite impervious to reason.'

Aron's arguments for the contention that the thesis underlying Ginsberg's idea (that the concept of development in human affairs must express the expanding role of rationality) are not recorded. It must be said, however, that there was nothing in Ginsberg's position to suggest that he was impervious to reason. He felt deeply the widely prevalent reaction against reason and the cult of the irrational, but this set-back was not in itself a reason for abandoning a theory of social development as progress in the building up of a rational ethics. There is an ineluctable ethical or normative component in any idea of human social development.

Ginsberg did not suppose that the concept of a rational ethics implies a fixed code or one uniform for all peoples. As our knowledge of and sensitiveness towards human needs grows and as greater control is achieved over the conditions of development, the system of rights and duties must undergo change. 'There will never, in all probability, be a universal code of morals, though the history of moral development supports the possibility of agreement on a minimum code of the kind now trying to find expression in a list of human rights.'

In the psychology of morals he wrote briefly but informatively and perceptively on the English moralists of the eighteenth century and on contemporary writers who stood nearest to them—in particular, Samuel Alexander and Edward Westermarck; and also on Bergson. He devoted more time and attention to Freud. He was persuaded, no doubt under the influence of his friends Dr Emanuel Miller and Professor Aubrey Lewis, that psycho-analysis had much to contribute to the study of morals—short, of course, of committing the naturalistic fallacy. He devoted his Conway Memorial Lecture in 1952 to 'Psycho-analysis and Ethics'. In an appreciative but not uncritical review of Freudian theory he suggested that it might be used to throw light on the natural history of morals; to provide the material for a comparative moral pathology, which would facilitate inquiry into the causes making for variation in moral codes and for social conformity and deviance on the part of individuals; to assist in the building up of a rational ethics, by disentangling the unconscious elements in moral experience, clarifying it by ridding it of the magical elements that have gathered round it in the course of its history and ridding it of fear, hate and anger.

In an essay on 'Psychoanalysis and Sociology', contributed to *Politics and Letters* in 1944, he was severely critical of Freud as social psychologist and social theorist. In the sociology of morals he gave close and critical attention, in particular, to Durkheim's theories of ethics and religion as illustrating the value and limitations of applying 'the method of positive sciences' to the study of morals; and to Pareto's denial of human progress, resting on his disbelief in any rational ethics and his view that history has disclosed no significant changes but only oscillations.

At the first Annual General Meeting of the British Sociological Association in 1952 Ginsberg devoted his Chairman's address to the idea of progress. This address, in the expanded form in which it was published in 1953 as *The Idea of Progress: An Evaluation*, appears in Volume III of his collected essays, *Evolution and Progress*. Ginsberg began by quoting the French historian A. Javary, writing in 1851, to the effect that the idea was so firmly established that no one any longer would contest it and all that remained to be examined was the conditions under which it was realised. A hundred years later he was obliged to report that the belief in progress was seriously weakened. Nevertheless, the idea persists and Ginsberg was able to show without much difficulty that its critics frequently lapse into inconsistency and do not, in fact, entirely reject it. The theories of its protagonists he sorted into three groups: Marxism, which he regarded as the only nineteenth-century philosophy to remain influential; the theory associated with L. T. Hobhouse and especially the views advanced in *Morals in Evolution*; and a more generalised theory of evolution which includes the field of human history and an emergent morality.

Ginsberg devoted a chapter of his study of progress to eighteenth-century theories of perfectibility, another to Comte, and still another to Hegel and Marx, both of whom he found unimpressive on the subject. He himself favoured the generalised evolutionary theory, though he was fully aware of the complexities involved (see his Introduction to the seventh edition of *Morals in Evolution* [1950]; two essays on the subject in *On the Diversity of Morals* [1956] and one in Michael Banton [ed] *Darwinism and the Study of Society* [1961]). He drew a distinction between evolution and development. Evolution is a term that is sometimes used to mean any orderly change and especially in biology, where new forms arise in a process of differentiation from the old. Development, an older term, is a process in which what is potential becomes actual. Neither one is progress but Ginsberg offered a definition in terms of both of them: 'progress is development or evolution in a direction which satisfies rational criteria of value'. Evolution itself cannot supply such standards. He agreed with T. H. Huxley that 'from the facts of evolution no ethics of evolution can be derived'.

No plausible general laws of social development or progress have as yet been formulated. Nevertheless, it is possible to enquire if there are particular trends in history or society which exhibit 'advance'. Ginsberg identified two significant trends: the emergence of law; and the unification of mankind, by which he meant interconnectedness and interdependence. In discussing the unification of mankind he arrived at a monistic interpretation of civilisation. As to whether it is approaching unity in the sense of unity of goal or purpose, Ginsberg disagreed with both Whitehead and Toynbee. He denied that religion in general or Christianity in particular has exhibited an 'upward trend'; but he found evidence for moral progress. 'The case for moral progress rests above all on the persistence of the quest for justice in the history of mankind, spurred on by the sense of injustice.' He agreed with the eighteenth-century philosophers who saw progress as a movement towards reason and justice, equality and freedom.

In addressing the British Sociological Association in 1952 on the subject of progress, Ginsberg had chosen the topic closest to his heart but least likely to inspire his audience. Legislation in the Welfare State was a powerful and articulate agent of social change; members of the Association, which included social workers, teachers, doctors, psychiatrists and psychologists as well as academics, were concerned to demonstrate the importance of social research for the effective handling of social problems and to bring its results to bear on social policy. Ginsberg had understandably strong and persuasive views on the adverse implications, for the theory and practice of social research, of the divorce in the universities of teaching in philosophy and teaching in the social sciences: on the one hand, lack of training in critical scrutiny of the nature and validity of the methods employed in social research; and on the other hand, the inculcation of a superficial, even misleading conception of the nature and requirements of ethical neutrality. 'There can be no doubt that much confusion has been caused by failure to observe the distinction between things as they are and things as they ought to be, and insofar as the present attitude of the social sciences is intended to guard against this confusion there is clearly much to be said for it. Yet I am not sure that the grounds of the distinction have been accurately stated or that ethical neutrality is observed in practice'. This had been the theme of an address to the British Association for the Advancement of Science in 1937 and he might well have reiterated it in 1952. *Naturwissenschaftlich* procedures in the social sciences are not plain sailing in theory or in practice.

As regards practice, the empirical work which flourished at the LSE, especially after 1945, was very much after Ginsberg's heart, concerned as it was, on the one hand, with the problems and prospects of radical egalitarianism in the context of modern social structures, viewed historically and comparatively (the changing occupational structure; the distribution of wealth and income; social class differences in fertility, morbidity and mortality, family size, measured intelligence, educational opportunity and achievement) and, on the other hand, with the psychology of class and status; the nature and distribution of attitudes and opinions; electoral behaviour and so forth. He took no part in this work. The survey methods and statistical techniques of analysis had become specialisms in their own right and were a far cry from the simple but immensely laborious procedures he had adopted in 1929, in his pioneering investigation into 'interchange between the social classes'. He could no longer participate but he was interested and appreciative of the departmental enterprise and ready to make use of the results in his lectures for the paper 'Ethical Aspects of Social Organisation' which, at his suggestion, was introduced into the revised syllabus for the B.Sc. (Econ) degree in 1962.

Volume III of his collected essays *Evolution and Progress* contains the Herbert Spencer lecture he delivered in Oxford in 1958 on the subject of Social Change, and the five lectures he delivered in Tokyo in 1955, the year after his retirement.

By social change he understood changes in social structure, such as in the size of a society, the composition or balance of its parts or the type of its organisation. And he concerned himself in this lecture with 'fundamental problems involved in all sociological and historical analysis but which require reformulation from time to time in the light of current thought'. In a learned, wide-ranging and effective discussion he considered problems of causality in the social sciences, such as the role of human purpose, the significance to be attached to the concept of 'social forces' and the problem of teleology arising from the occurrence of changes which look as if they were designed but in fact have not been designed or foreseen. He discussed the view around which the *Methodenstreit* had raged in Germany at the end of the nineteenth and the beginning of the twentieth century: that the natural and the cultural sciences differ radically in their aims and methods. This view had been fully discussed in England by Collingwood but was again being taken up vigorously by both philosophers and social scientists. He argued with the aid of examples closely analysed that the causal relationship has much the same significance in the social as in the natural sciences; but went on to show from consideration in detail of the various important differences between social and physical causation that the social sciences are inherently, not contingently incapable of achieving the universality, certainty and precision characteristic of causal propositions in the natural sciences.

Among the Tokyo lectures, those on the comparative method and social morphology are of interest as valuable discussions of the methodological problems of the synoptic study of society and social development favoured by Ginsberg. In a final lecture he reviewed the work of the 'formal' and 'interpretative' schools of sociology. The formalists, following Simmel, proposed to give sociology a distinctive role among the social sciences in confining it to the study of the forms of association and social relations in abstraction from their content. Ginsberg's accounts of the work of Vierkandt and von Wiese are brief but cogent. The same is true of his accounts of the interpretative approach of Tönnies and Max Weber: but whereas it would be fair to say that the work of the post-Simmel formalists does not suffer from a treatment purely from the point of view of method, the same cannot be said of Tönnies and Max Weber. Ginsberg's account of Weber's *verstehende Soziologie*, of his use of 'ideal type' heuristic constructions and his classification of types of social action is lucid, accurate and helpful; but it is subjected to a totally misleading critique, to the effect that though not itself psychological, the method implies a sharp separation of the social sciences from psychology and rests on a confusion of the familiar with the intelligible—on an assumption that 'what we know within our minds is somehow more intelligible than what is outwardly observed'. This is a surprising misunderstanding of Weber's concept of *verstehen*.

In seeking to evaluate Ginsberg's scholarly achievement the obvious comparison that comes to mind is with Edward Westermarck, his senior colleague at the School until 1930 when he retired from the personal chair in Sociology which he held simultaneously with the chair of Moral Philosophy at Helsingfors. The two men were well-matched intellectually, though very different in temperament. They held each other in high regard. Westermarck wrote enthusiastically and perceptively about Ginsberg's suitability as candidate for the Martin White chair of Sociology in succession to Hobhouse; and when Westermarck died in 1939, Ginsberg wrote an admirably full, intimately knowledgeable study of his life and work.

It might seem at first glance that the palm should go to Westermarck as practitioner of the comparative study of morals who put an ethical theory to work, in the grand manner never attempted by Ginsberg (or for that matter by Hobhouse), on the fruits of massive erudition and bold fieldwork. His influence on the relativist outlook of anthropologists between the wars was considerable; and he anticipated the relativist arguments developed by present-day writers such as J. L. Mackie, John Ladd and Kai Nielson. However, his reputation as a sociologist inevitably suffered a decline as the inherent difficulties of the comparative method, due to the need to detach and isolate cultural phenomena from their context, have come to be perceived as posing conceptual and practical problems far greater than those he acknowledged and supposed himself to have faced satisfactorily.

Ginsberg, on the other hand, was a cautious theorist and learned exponent rather than a systematic practitioner of the comparative method on a large scale. He admired and, in general, accepted Westermarck's use of the method, whilst recognising that some of his material was 'vague and ambiguous'; but he had shrewd and significant reservations about his contribution to ethical theory which, he saw, seriously weakened his interpretations of his comparative material. He successfully criticised Westermarck at his weakest, namely in his unsatisfactory account of the part played by 'reflection' or reason in morals. He set himself to analyse the nature of moral diversity and the sources of moral bewilderment and conflict, to raise the discussion of the part played by reason and experience in morals to a more satisfactory level and, building on Hobhouse, to formulate a theory of social development incorporating rational criteria of moral progress.

All this he succeeded in doing; and in the process he demonstrated the possibility and the requirements of a disciplined and creative comparative study of social institutions. It seems safe to say that his legacy might have proved more enduring but for the eclipse of the Enlightenment-inspired belief in the possibility of a rational ethics and the general acceptance of a view of moral diversity as contingent 'value-pluralism', as a plurality of conflicting and incommensurable conceptions of the good.

Ginsberg quietly resisted the sea-change of *Zeitgeist*. His sociology remained handmaiden to his unchanging philosophy. He read Marx as an unimpressive theorist of social development and Weber as an original but unsatisfactory methodologist who did not put the principles of his *verstehende Soziologie* into practice. At no point in his teaching or writing did he orient himself to their understanding of what they were about, or himself attempt to grasp the essence or distinctive character of modernity. He acknowledged the significance of Marxism, writing in 1932: 'Whatever estimate may be formed of the value of the Marxian theory of social development, its heuristic importance cannot be doubted and it has in fact affected recent workers in history and sociology profoundly.' But he never gave it sustained critical attention in any of its aspects, or sought to explain its heuristic importance. He confined himself to references in general terms, as was relevant in the context of his own immediate concerns. Nor did he ever address the social and moral implications of the spread of instrumental rationality which Weber identified as the hall-mark of modernity; and it seems in retrospect extraordinary that he paid no attention at all to the alleged 'negative dialectic of the Enlightenment' that so troubled the sociologists of the Frankfurt school between the wars. Several prominent members of this school sojourned briefly at the LSE in exile *en route* for the United States, generating unforgettable intellectual excitement and much confusion among the native young. Yet Ginsberg sat quietly by. Perhaps despondency and the effort to resist despair in face of the triumphs of vile irrationalism induced a kind of lassitude, a deep reluctance to do fresh battle on the new fronts which had opened up. This would account for the decision to lecture in Tokyo in 1955 on 'Aspects of European Sociology *in the Early Twentieth Century*'.

JEAN FLOUD

*Note.* The Academy is very grateful to Mrs Floud for taking over the task of writing this obituary in December 1990.

*Proceedings of the British Academy*, **80**, 305–317

# Eugénie Jane Andrina Henderson
# 1914–1989

EUGÉNIE HENDERSON was born on October 2nd 1914 at Newcastle, where she spent her early years. She took pride in being a 'Geordie', and she claimed some skill in the local dialect. Her father, William Henderson, was a civil engineer and, *inter alia*, made himself responsible for the construction of the Singapore docks between the two wars. He was also a respected amateur football player in his local team.

After school in London, Miss Henderson enrolled in the English course at University College, London, graduating with first class honours. During her studies in English she took advantage of the regulations then in force to take brief courses in a number of European languages and in general phonetics. In this she attracted the attention of Daniel Jones, Professor of Phonetics in the University of London, who encouraged her work in phonetics and persuaded her to take an interest, which proved lifelong, in the languages of Southeast Asia. In 1938 she was appointed to a junior post in Jones's Department of Phonetics.

At the outbreak of war in 1939 the Department moved out of London, and she took up a temporary post in the Ministry of Economic Warfare. But as soon as the Japanese entered the war at the end of 1941, she was recalled to the University to undertake teaching in different types of Japanese in Professor J.R. Firth's Department of Phonetics and Linguistics at the School of Oriental and African Studies. Not unexpectedly the Service Departments had assumed that, should Japan become involved against England, they would have enough language experts in that field for operational purposes. This was by no means the case, and for the whole of the rest of the war the School became virtually a language teaching unit for the three services, with Japanese the principal, but not the only, language taught. For some, no doubt good, reason the Far East Department dealt

E. J. A. HENDERSON

with Army personnel and the Department of Phonetics and Linguistics took charge of students from the Navy and the Royal Air Force.

These courses were at first concentrated on Japanese phonetics for R.A.F. people who would be engaged in intercepting and recording Japanese radiotelephone messages between aircraft and other aircraft or ground stations. Rightly or wrongly it was assumed that the Japanese, proud of the uniqueness of their language, would make far more use of messages *en clair* than the armed services of other belligerents would be expected to do. These courses were considered urgent and only lasted about eight weeks, enrolment for them going on throughout the year, without regard for academic terms and vacations. Later 'translators' courses', lasting six months, were introduced for those intended to deal with captured documents and the cryptographic tasks of the Government Communications Centre, then located in Bletchley. Much of this course teaching was targeted on a probable year and a half of continuing war in the Far East after the defeat of Germany. Much of this latter work proved operationally unnecessary, but some of the trainees were important components of the forces of occupation, and a number continued with Oriental studies in civil life.

During the three war years 1942–5 Miss Henderson was one of the most active members of the departmental staff, together with her colleagues and former teacher Eileen Evans (later Mrs. Eileen Whitley). All service students who passed through the Department of Phonetics and Linguistics took some of her Japanese phonetics courses, and many recall with pleasure the stimulation of her teaching.

She had been a Lecturer in Phonetics on a temporary basis in 1942 at the start of her wartime work, and this was made permanent until 1946, when she became a Senior Lecturer. In 1953 she was appointed Reader in Phonetics in the University of London, and she became Professor of Phonetics in 1964 until her retirement in 1982.

Eugénie's services to the School and to the University were and remain outstanding. Her research and publication extended over general phonetic and phonological theory and studies in more than one language family and area. In this Memoir this part of her work will be considered below in greater detail.

She served on several important committees of the School and the University; and the revival of the Department of Southeast Asia after the war was largely in her care as far as the languages of the region were concerned. Lecturers in specific Southeast Asian languages were appointed straight from those holding first degrees in other subjects; there was scarcely any other source of young people to fill such positions. The School was then expanding rapidly under the favouring wind of the report of the Scarbrough Commission, which had been set up just before the end of the war to review the provision of university teaching and research in the languages and cultures of the peoples of the Orient and of Africa (along with the languages of Eastern Europe). In one year four new Lecturer's posts in Southeast Asian languages were created and filled; and the expansion of universities in general and of the School in particular and the numbers of staff appointments made in the early postwar years seem almost incredible and unimaginable in today's stringent climate.

Newly appointed Lecturers in the Southeast Asia Department spent their first four years in the Department of Phonetics and Linguistics under the direct charge of Miss Henderson, with their own regular seminar over which she presided, before their first visit to their own language areas and subsequent membership of the Southeast Asian Department. From 1960 to 1966 she served as Acting Head of this latter department while retaining her senior position in her own. After the appointment of a separate Head of Southeast Asia she was Head of Phonetics and Linguistics until 1969, when she was succeeded by the present writer. During her years as Head of Southeast Asia a wider interest in the languages, cultures, and histories of the Southeast Asian area was promoted by the introduction of a first degree in Southeast Asian Studies, under her encouragement and guidance. She was made an Honorary Fellow of the School in 1985 and elected a Fellow of the British Academy in 1986. A member of the Philological Society from 1945, she served on its Council and was Treasurer from 1966 to 1974, holding office during a period of financial difficulty for the Society. From 1984 to 1988 she was the Society's President and a Vice-president thereafter. She was also elected to the Chair of the Linguistics Association of Great Britain from 1977 to 1980.

Within the Department of Phonetics and Linguistics she saw herself all the time as a phonetician and phonologist. *Phonetics* was the title of her University appointment, and *The domain of phonetics* was the title of her Inaugural Lecture in 1965. But she always involved herself with phonetics as a part of a much wider general linguistics. In her younger days, during the 1930s and 1940s some phoneticians quite legitimately concerned themselves with articulatory and acoustic phonetics, transcriptions, and the extreme accuracy of recording and classifying the pronunciation of the words and sentences of languages, leaving grammar and semantics to others. There is nothing wrong with this, and such phoneticians strengthened the reputation for accuracy of audition and pronunciation for which Daniel Jones's department in University College was rightly famous. But this, for all her phonetic abilities, was not for Eugénie Henderson; phonetics and phonology made up a part, and a vital part, of linguistics, whether in general theoretical terms or in the description of languages, and it was this understanding of her subject upon which she concentrated.

In this sense the highly situationally bound practical language teaching of the war years suited her own inclinations well, and she was entirely in sympathy with the linguistic philosophy of J. R. Firth, Head of the Department of Phonetics and Linguistics, expressed in such aphorisms as 'linguistics at all levels of analysis is concerned with meaningful human behaviour in society (Firth 1957:117). Henderson's Inaugural Lecture sets out clearly her own conception of her subject in her mid-career (1965a:4): 'Let me say at once that in my view there can be no question but that phonetics forms a part—an extremely important part—of the wider field of general linguistics'; (1965a:7): 'The phonetician cannot close his eyes to grammatical considerations if he wishes to give the most helpful account of the use made of phonic features in a given language'; and (1965a:9): 'the most useful work' in the field of acoustic phonetics) 'may be expected to result from teamwork between phoneticians and psychologists'. Later in the Lecture she set forth her interpretation of her subject as part of the teaching and research work of the School of Oriental and African Studies. This should embrace the languages of the Orient and Africa, though not exclusively. It should be complementary to the language teaching of other departments, not necessarily directed to the same aspects of the languages shared by the language departments. This, she said at the end of her Lecture (1965a:29): 'is worth the attempt, in order to maintain our somewhat perilous but exhilarating stance astride the two cultures' of the sciences and the humanities'.

In her research, seen in seminars and publications, her interests lay primarily, though not exclusively, in Southeast Asian languages and in general phonetics and phonology, at their peak of prominance in the years 1945–60. Though Japanese was the language of her war service, her interest in Thai and other Southeast Asian languages had begun under Daniel Jones's influence while she was still at University College.

In the School, during Firth's headship, of a young and expanding department phonetics and phonology were dominated by prosodic theory to an astonishing intensity. Firth expounded it, as he also expounded contextual semantics, with an almost religuous fevour, and this was followed with enthusiasm by his colleagues, several of whom cut their phonological eye-teeth on the development and application of its principles and methods. The vigorous and sometimes deliberately polemic support given to prosodic phonology in these years seems somewhat strange today, though it may be compared with the single-minded devotion bestowed on Chomsky and transformational grammar (as it then was) in the early 1960s. Prosodic theory continues to arouse interest at the present time, and linguists continue to publish prosodically orientated phonological analyses. It is, moreover, to be seen underlying, though often without acknowledgement, some current generative approaches to phonology, especially in such fields as autosegmental and metrical phonology.

At the time Firth's theoretical outlook was new and revolutionary, though he always claimed its kinship with the thinking of Henry Sweet, the nineteenth-century Anglist and pioneer phonetician. As Firth's phonology was the main impetus behind Henderson's phonological work, it will be relevant to state the main principles here (but for a fuller account see Palmer 1970:ix–xvi).

Firth's theory was one of the first reactions against the two dominant versions of phonology during the 1940s and early 1950s, the conservative phonology of Daniel Jones, whose interpretation of the phoneme as the basic unit of phonological structure was sometimes rudely referred to as the 'Joneme', and the 'structuralist' phonemics widely accepted in America and elsewhere at the time. Intended to be the application of Bloomfield's principles, it was embodied in a number of once standard textbooks. Basic to it was the demand for the absolute 'autonomy' of phonemic analysis, to be exhaustively completed before any statements were made about morphology, syntax, or the lexicon, and grounded on the working out of a phonemic transcription of the language, giving rise to the necessary 'biunique' relationship between phonemic analysis and narrow transcription, established independently from all other analyic considerations

Prosodic analysis ran directly against these prevailing views in two respects, which perhaps we see more clearly today than in Firth's own time. Firstly, he rejected the 'autonomous' status of phonology. He envisaged linguistic analysis as being set out at a number of levels, movement between which (the use of data from one level to justify analysis at another) was not only permissible, but desirable. But essentially phonology was the interlink between grammar and lexicon on the one side, and phonetics on the other, substantially the later outlook of the generative grammarians (and others).

Secondly Firth intended to decouple phonological analysis from broad transcription, which had always been the matrix and the guide for phonemic phonology. A broad, or phonemic, transcription was a graphic necessity, but for Firth it was not the most revealing analysis of the parts played by the various sound differences in the phonological system and structure involved in words and sentences.

Instead of one basic unit, the phoneme, Firth insisted on two, the purely segmental phonematic (*not* phonemic) units and prosodies at various levels related to structures, whether grammatical or phonological. So one could set up word or morpheme prosodies as well as syllable prosodies, phrase prosodies, and sentence prosodies; and in consonance with this approach to phonology there could be prosodies abstracted from separate word classes (e.g. verbs), separate types of morpheme (e.g. prefix, suffix), and lexically separate prosodies of loan words as against inherited and assimilated words where this would lead to a more revealing analysis. Prosodies could relate to their structures in two ways, by actual phonetic extension of a feature over more than one segment, as when a nasalized vowel always follows a preceding nasal consonant or when a syllable is marked by length, pitch (tone), or stress, and demarcatively when the occurrence of a sound feature, e.g. aspiration, though located at a certain place in a structure serves to delimit it by signalling initiality or finality.

This brief overview of Firth's prosodic phonology is relevant to this memoir because it was Henderson's phonology no less. Indeed, it has been maintained by teachers that as an introductory exemplification of prosodic theory Henderson's *Prosodies in Siamese* (1949) is one of the best texts available, far more explicit and accessible than the programmatic and obscure article by which Firth (1948) officially inaugurated his theory and its methodology (cp. Palmer 1970:xiii).

Palmer refers to Henderson's article as 'the neatest and, in some ways, the most convincing of all the articles' written in the framework of prosodic analysis. It will serve as an illustration of the theory and as an example of Henderson's phonological analysis; she saw it (Palmer 1970:27) as a working application of Firth's 'Sounds and prosodies' to a specific language.

She lists the sounds heard in the language in 'general phonetic terms' (Palmer 1970:28) as twenty-one consonants in syllable initial position, seven in final position, nine vowels, six of them with contrastive length, and sixteen diphthongs. In her analysis she sets up as phonematic units seven consonants and twelve vowels. To these belong only those features that are treated as strictly segmental in scope. The remaining features are assigned to prosodies of syllables and syllable parts, or to larger structures:

**1**   Prosodies of intonation (one of seven) superimposed on the lexical tones, and 'sentence prosodies' applicable to certain particles carrying general sentential functions.
**2**   Prosodies of phrases and polysyllabic words, such as loss of stress and tonal neutralization.
**3**   Prosodies of syllables as wholes: quantity, tone (one of five), stress, labiovelarization and yotization in diphthong formation.
**4**   Prosodies of syllable parts, marking initiality: plosion, affrication, friction, voicing, rhotacization, aspiration, lateralization, labialization; marking finality, unreleased closure.

As an example of this the syllable (and word) *khrai* with level tone, come, is analysed as:

**1** Syllable prosodies: shortness, tone 1, yotization
**2** Syllable part prosodies: plosion, aspiration, rhotacization (all prosodies of initiality
**3** Phonematic units *k a ʐ* (zero).

Table 1 (from Palmer 1970:51) provides further exemplification.

Though *Prosodies in Siamese* makes specific reference to Firth *Sounds and prosodies* (Firth 1948), her thoughts had already been turning in a prosodic direction in her research on the phonetics of Lushai (Henderson 1947–48), in which she identifies tone and length as syllable features and yotization and labiovelarization as features of syllable initiality and syllable finality.

Her attention was concentrated on phonetics and phonology, but she also produced a fuller linguistic analysis of a language of northwest Burma, Tiddim Chin (Henderson 1965b) as the product of a field visit among its speakers in 1954. Subtitled *A descriptive analysis of two texts*, it subjects its material to syntactic, morphological, and phonological description, the phonology in prosodic terms.

Tiddim Chin is not an isolating language like Vietnamese and Thai (Siamese), on which she spent so much time, but has a recognizable morphology of word structure. In her description she made the syllable the basic structure with 'placed' (phonematic) units characterizing or demarcating the whole structure (Henderson 1965b:19); tone, quantity, syllable initial features, and syllable final features. Intonation is superimposed on lexical

**Table 1.**   Prosodic analysis of a passage of Thai.

| Prosodies of Sentence | Sentence Tone C | | | | |
|---|---|---|---|---|---|
| Prosodies of Polysyllables and Sentence Pieces | | Contrast of 'neutral' tone and 5-tone system; Contrast of no-stress and stress | | Contrast of 'neutral' tone and 5-tone system Contrast of no-stress and stress | |
| Prosodies of Syllables | Length | Shortness | Shortness | Shortness | Length |
| | Tone 3 | 'neutral' tone | Tone 1 | 'neutral' tone | Tone 1 |
| | Labiovelarization | No-stress | Stress | No-stress | Stress |
| Prosodies of Syllable Parts | Plosion | Labialization | | | Plosion |
| Phonematic Units | *ʐaʐ* | *ʐiʐ* | *mon* | *naʐ* | *ʐeɳ* |
| Broad transcription | ʔa:u | wi·mon | | na·ʔe: ɳ | |
| Translation | 'Ah! There you are, Wimon' | | | | |

Adapted from Henderson 1949; Palmer 1970:51.

tone, as in Thai, and below sentence intonation she identified a specific intonation and other prosodic features relating to phrases and 'figures', sequences smaller than phrases but potentially larger than words (52). At the level of individual words certain distinctions, particularly of tone, separate verbs from nouns, and she treated these phonological distinctions under the grammatical headings of the word classes concerned. Likewise the syllable structures of prefixes are described under that grammatical heading (99).

Henderson was a phonetician and a phonologist, but her account of Tiddim Chin embraces all levels of description. After a brief chapter on spelling and pronunciation (9–14), the phonetic material is handled in two principal chapters, syllable structure (15–28) and the grammatical structure of the (unmarked) 'narrative' style (29–105), in which phonological categories are successively related to the syntactic and morphological analysis already made. A short chapter (106–17) points out some grammatical and phonological differences pertaining to the 'colloquial' style in parts of the texts. The book ends with a detailed word by word analysis of the texts themselves.

Henderson by no means confined herself to the typology of isolating languages nor to the area of Southeast Asia. In 1949 and 1970 she published two articles on the phonetics of Caucasian languages, whose structures, with their high morphological complexity, are about as far removed as possible from languages like Thai and Vietnamese. Her second article (1970) in this field is now one of the classic texts on the instrumental analysis of the phonetics of languages of this type.

Most of her work took the form of articles in a wide range of journals, but in addition to her *Tiddim Chin* she edited and introduced a selection of Sweet's many writings (Henderson 1971). Like Firth she saw in Sweet's work a significant anticipation of prosodic theory in his contrast between analysis and synthesis, the former foreseeing the later phonemes of Daniel Jones and others, and the latter taking in the sorts of features subsequently to be treated as prosodies (Sweet 1906:44). One may notice the use of Sweet's term *synthesis* in the subtitle of her article on Siamese (Henderson 1948). She entitled her selection of texts from Sweet *The essential foundation*, using Sweet's own words (Sweet 1871:v), and this book serves excellently as a presentation of his many works on phonetics and on other aspects of general linguistics within a moderate compass (329 pages). Later (1981) she edited jointly with R.E. Asher a festschrift for Professor D. Abercrombie, which took up his particular interest in the historical development of phonetics in its title *Towards a history of phonetics* a topic in which she also had an interest.

Eugénie Henderson travelled widely on the Continent of Europe, in in

America, the Far East, and in her own specialist area of Southeast Asia, and she achieved an international reputation in the quality and value of her published work. Towards the end of her professional life she was honoured with an invitation, gladly accepted and fulfilled, to address the Plenary Session on phonology at the Thirteenth International Congress of Linguists in Tokyo in 1982. Her paper was published in the *Proceedings* of the Congress in 1983.

Professor Henderson retired in 1989, but retirement for her did not mean a diminution of her research. One may take note of the continued work on her projected dictionary of Karen (another language of Burma). This was unfinished at her death, but it is hoped that colleagues in the School will be able to see it through to completion and publication.

She was an invigorating teacher. In the matter of holding the attention of a class and of maintaining her stance perhaps she gained something from her experiences in the last full year of the war, when, huddled in corridors to avoid injury from broken windows during flying bomb attacks, she had to shout down her colleagues holding their own classes at the same time. In her interpretation of her professorial duties she regularly gave an introductory course on phonetics and phonology for first-year students throughout the academic session, covering a wide survey of principles and methods. One recalls such vivid techniques as bringing into the classroom a three-dimensional model of a chemical compound to illustrate distinctive feature theory.

She had many students under her supervision during her years as a teacher, mostly Ph.D. candidates from Southeast Asia, working on one or other aspects of their own languages. They were successful, and they remembered her and the years spent under her care with affection, on several occasions making sure of seeing her again on a visit to their own countries. Hers was not just academic supervision, but personal help and friendship; her students visited her home in Hertfordshire with its extensive garden, and she recalled with amusement one Thai girl, brought up on English literature, including Wordsworth's *Daffodils*, who could scarcely contain her excitement on seeing masses of them in bloom in her lawn. While she lived in the country, as Head of Department she gave a garden party each summer to her departmental colleagues.

Her academic career was marked not only by her research and teaching, but by an abiding administrative efficiency on committees and as Treasurer of the Philological Society, displaying in all matters a consistent sense of values and general commonsense. Later in her life it is no secret that she was approached with the prospect of being head of an Oxford or Cambridge college, a post that she would have filled with acclaim but which at the time for personal reasons she felt she must decline.

In a Memoir such as this, one must concentrate on her public and academic life, but some account of her private and family life must be included if one is to give a proper perspective of her and of her personality. She was a member of the first generation of women scholars who sought to combine their profession with their duties of family care. The generation preceding hers had seen women into professions traditionally occupied by men, in universities, for example, as students and then as teachers. These had on the whole remained unmarried. Henderson faced the problem of the necessarily double life of the professional wife and mother. Her family was by modern standards a large one, four sons, and a daughter who tragically died while still a child. As a mother she was loving and well loved, managing to satisfy her obligations fully at home and at the University. It was noticeable that when she was a Head of Department women colleagues found it more embarrassing to plead 'benefit of clergy' to be excused academic engagements for family reasons with her than with male heads.

Though she insisted on the right of women scholars to make progress in the academic world on an equality with men, and her own success in her career makes this manifest, she was never a 'feminist' in the political or social sense, deliberately eschewing male pronouns and the like. Amusingly in the opening paragraph of her Inaugural Lecture, on the place and the duties of a professor of phonetics, the pronouns *he* and *his*, referring to her own position, occur no less than twelve times in all. She was rather surprised that this should be pointed out to her after the lecture was finished.

In fact she combined a number of roles, each of which might have satisfied one person. Apart from her academic and her family life she was an accomplished pianist continuing to practise and attain to higher grades throughout her life. She also regularly attended theatres and concerts, and she enjoyed, and produced, good cooking and good wine. For a time she ran a small home dairy farm, referring to herself in this role as a 'cow keeper'. While she invited students and colleagues to her home, in general she kept the two sides of her life apart, not normally discussing private and family matters among colleagues nor turning her house into just an extension of her room in the School. Perhaps typically, she had two names for herself among those with whom she was on first name terms; to us, her colleagues, she was 'Eugénie', at home and among friends she was 'Gene'.

As a scholar and as a supervisor of graduates she was meticulous and exacting, but in her general bearing she was delightfully free of self-importance and she could never be accused of 'pulling rank'. The photograph attached to this Memoir, taken while she was at the height of her university career, nicely portrays her levity and slight cynicism about herself. Some anecdotes in this connection are illustrative of this. When she had retired and was living in Hampstead, she had to shelve and classify her numerous academic books. These shelves were labelled by such headings as *syntax*, *phonology*, *historical linguistics*, and so on; a shelf of unclassified books bore the title *rhubarb*. On one occasion during a lunchtime conversation, when someone insisted on acting 'on principle', she interjected 'I do so distrust people who act on principle'. At another time she took part in a series of public lectures on linguistics, dealing herself with phonetics and phonology; each contributor was asked to supply brief personal details, including 'hobbies'. She wrote 'Bringing up a family of four sons'.

Her charm and her unceasing energy, undimmed by age and by certain health problems, made her sudden death a great shock to all who knew her and had worked with her. Such was her bearing right to the last that one thought (and perhaps she thought) that she could never die. I myself recall her company at the British Academy summer dinner, which she thoroughly enjoyed; the conversation turned to the venue for the 1992 International Congress of Linguists, with Canada and Australia as possible host countries (in the event Canada was chosen). Henderson at once put in: 'I do hope Australia is chosen; I have always wanted an excuse to go there'.

As a conversationalist she was unique. She could hardly open her mouth without saying something interesting, provocative, or stimulating. When we were having lunch together on the day of the Academy dinner, I happened to mention the (then) recent film of *Little Dorrit*. Immediately she said: 'I am sure the most intersting difference between the book and the film is the different lights in which Clennam is presented'; this was typical.

Her death on July 27th, 1989, was sudden and unexpected. It was a shock to her family and to all her colleagues and friends. But it was painless and therefore happy; prolonged invalidism was something she could not easily face. The funeral took place on July 31st in Hampstead, and a Memorial Service was held for her in the University Church of Christ the King on October 20th. A friend to all who knew her, she has left us with a sense of affection and admiration, and of great loss.

R. H. ROBINS
*Fellow of the British Academy*

# References

A complete bibliography of Professor Henderson's publications may be found in *Southeast Asian linguistics* (Davidson 1989:5–9).
Firth, J. R. (1948) Sounds and prosodies. *TPS*: 127–52.

—— (1957) Ethnographic analysis and language with reference to Malinowski's views. In R. W. Firth (ed.), *Man and culture*. London: 93–118.

Henderson, Eugenie J. A. (1948) Notes on the syllable structure of Lushai. *BSOAS* 12:36–79.

—— (1949) Prosodies in Siamese: a study in synthesis. *Asia Major* (n.s.) 1:189–215.

—— (1949) A phonetic study of Western Ossetic (Digoron). *BSOAS* 13:36–79.

—— (1965a) *The domain of phonetics*. London.

—— (1965b) *Tiddim Chin: a descriptive analysis of two texts*. London.

—— (1970) Acoustic features of certain consonants and consonant clusters in Kabardian. *BSOAS* 33:92–106.

—— ed. (1971) *The indispensable foundation: a selection from the writings of Henry Sweet*. London

—— ed. with R. E. Asher (1981) *Towards a history of phonetics*. Edinburgh.

Palmer, F. R. (ed.) (1970) *Prosodic analysis*. London.

Sweet, H. (1871) *A handbook of phonetics*. Oxford.

*Proceedings of the British Academy*, **80**, 319–332

# Kenneth Hurlstone Jackson
# 1909–1991

PROFESSOR KENNETH HURLSTONE JACKSON, Hon. Fellow of St John's College, Cambridge, died on 20 February 1991. He had held the Chair of Celtic Languages, Literatures, History and Antiquities at the University of Edinburgh from 1950 until his retirement in 1979, and could have claimed to be a world authority on most of the varied subjects that the Chair, the most ambitiously named in the British Isles, called upon him to profess. It is certain that no previous holder of the Chair, distinguished as several of them were, could have made such a claim, and it is doubtful whether any future holder will make any pretence to it. Indeed, with the increasing extension and proliferation of the branches subsumed under the name 'Celtic Studies', it may very well be impossible in the future for any one to claim distinction in as many branches as Professor Jackson could. His achievements inspired unqualified admiration among colleagues of his own age and reverential awe in those who aspire to succeed them.

He was born on 1 November 1909 at Melville, Lavender Vale, Beddington, Surrey, the son of Alan Stuart Jackson and Lucy Jane Hurlstone. Alan Stuart Jackson came from a south London family, many of whose members had been in the past clergymen and latterly civil servants: he himself had gone into 'the City' on leaving school and became the head of a very conservative stockbroking firm. The Hurlstones are represented in the DNB by two artists, Richard Hurlstone (*fl.* 1768–80) who was great uncle to the other, Frederick Yeates Hurlstone (1800–69). F.Y. Hurlstone was elected President of the Society of British Artists in 1835 and again in 1840, retaining the office until his death. He married a fellow artist, Miss Jane Coral, by whom he had two sons, one of whom was also an artist. Lucy Jane Hurlstone, Professor Jackson's mother, had a brother, William Yeates Hurlstone, a composer of promise who died aged 30 from the effects

K. H. JACKSON

*Walter Bird*

of bronchitic asthma just after being appointed Professor of Harmony and Counterpoint at the Royal College of Music in London.

Professor Jackson inherited an interest in art: his sister who was older, was trained at the London College of Art, but he did not develop that interest. He also inherited or developed during his childhood a propensity for asthma and this meant that he was unable to attend the local primary school (Hill Crest, Wallington)—the family had moved by that time to Trelawn, 1 Sandy Lane South, Wallington—regularly during the winter and had frequent spells in bed. This meant that he received much of his early education from his mother who passed on to him her family's interest in music, art and literature. Naturally he was encouraged to read and he read extensively. His reading prompted him to write and apparently he compiled an illustrated 'book' on heraldry. He was also urged to go out in fine weather and to explore on foot and by bicycle the surrounding countryside and this he did to good effect with a small Brownie camera—apparently some exercise books have survived in which snapshots of local landmarks have been pasted with careful annotations in fading ink. Exploring the surrounding country remained one of his interests throughout his later life. As his friends can testify, he explored the Cambridge, the Bangor and the Dublin countryside as he was later to explore the Harvard, the Bermuda and the Edinburgh countryside. In *Who's Who* he gives his recreation as 'walking'. He continued to cycle well into his Edinburgh years. It is on record that he 'coxed' for one of the rowing boats at Cambridge during Lent Term 1930. In his younger days he also played some tennis. But 'walking' was his passion and preferably walking, or if that was too much, travelling to an archaeological site. It is not surprising that his son Alastar is a historian.

Jackson attended, albeit irregularly, Hillcrest School, Wallington, from May 1916 to December 1919. He then attended the County School, Surrey, from January 1920 to July 1920. He does not seem to have been happy there and he was transferred in September to Whitgift Grammar School, Croydon, where he remained until July 1928. As the name implies, Whitgift Grammar School had been founded in 1596 by Archbishop Whitgift and true to the tradition of the best grammar schools it gave Jackson a thorough grounding in the Classics. He must have been an excellent pupil for in June 1928 he was elected a scholar of St John's College, Cambridge, where he had a most distinguished career. He was placed in the First Class not only in the Classical Tripos, Part 1 (1930), but also, and with special merit, in the Classical Tripos, Part II (1931) when he graduated BA and was named 'Senior Classic'. In the meantime he had won the Sir William Brown Medals for Greek Ode and Latin Epigram in 1930 and for the Greek Ode in 1931.

In view of his achievements in Greek and Latin verse we are not surprised to find him writing poetry in his native language. A few of his poems were published in *The Eagle*, but he probably wrote more. We venture to say this because the best, 'Two Partings', is a kind of love-poem addressed, we assume, to the young lady whom he had met through mutual friends in Cambridge and whom he was to marry in 1936, Janet Dall Galloway of Hillside, Kinross, Scotland. Another poem, 'Mount Caburn', reflects the author's interest in prehistory. Two prose articles are of special note. 'A Forgotten Painter' is on the Belgian artist, Antoine Joseph Wiertz, and is written with the authority of one who has studied painting and can compare the work of one artist with that of another. 'The Cambridge Cottage' which includes an illustration, testifies to the fact that its author, true to the habit formed in childhood, had explored Cambridgeshire. There are also translations which reflect the author's wide-range of interests, e.g., 'Coming Night. From the Rig-Veda'. Of particular interest to us are the 'Irish Translations', 'The Drowning of Coning Mac Aedan' (*c*.720 AD), and 'Autumn Song' (*c*.850 AD) in *The Eagle*, June, 1931.

In his Classical Tripos, Part II, Jackson specialized in Comparative Philology and we would have expected him to proceed with Classical Studies and Comparative Philology. Instead of that he switched over to Celtic Studies. When asked the reason he would answer that he thought at the time that the Classics were overworked: the implications of the discovery of Hittite, etc., had not been realized, although it is interesting to note that Pedersen turned his back on Celtic to devote attention to Hittite, Tocharian, etc. Jackson never attended the lectures of A.E. Housman. The textual work done by the latter, brilliant though it was, held no attractions for him. More congenial was the work done by his tutor M.P. Charlesworth, not so much on the history of the Roman Empire as on the history of Roman Britain. One can readily believe that he eagerly joined and enjoyed immensely the visits to Roman sites organised by Charlesworth.

There must have been other reasons for the switch to Celtic Studies. On one occasion he remarked on his discovery that Old Irish *sechitir* corresponded exactly to the Latin *sequuntur*, thereby illuminating for him at one stroke the Indo-European character of Old Irish. On the same occasion he said that he must have been about nine years old when he read Alfred Nutt's *Cuchullain. The Irish Achilles* (1900) and Eleanor Hull's two books, *The Cuchulinn Saga in Irish Literature* (1899) and *Cuchullain. The Hound of Ulster* (1909), to find them all enthralling, 'marvellous stuff'.

The importance and the influence of H.M. Chadwick at Cambridge during Jackson's years as a graduand no doubt had more than a little to do with the switch from Classical Studies to the Archaeological and Anthropological Tripos, Section B, to study Anglo-Saxon, Norse and Celtic. It will be recalled that Chadwick had succeeded W.W. Skeat in the Elrington and Bosworth Chair of Anglo-Saxon in 1912 and that he was fond of reminding his students of the founder's wish that the subject should not be Anglo-Saxon only but 'the languages cognate therewith together with the antiquities and history of the Anglo-Saxons'. In pursuit of this ideal, Chadwick had transferred English studies from the school of modern languages, and at the same time had reshaped the study of the origins and the background of English literature so as to make philological scholarship serve the knowledge of history and civilization. In 1927 he had transferred his department to the new Faculty of Archaeology and Anthropology where his group of studies, like the Classics, could constitute an independent discipline. Eventually it came, in Jackson's words, to be 'an investigation of the total range of history and literatures of the British Isles in the period between the Roman and Norman Conquests.'

All this was very much to Jackson's taste as a scholar. Naturally, he went for the languages, but one paper in Archaeology was compulsory, and he attended the lectures on anthropology as well. Some will recall that a few of Jackson's earliest papers were published in the anthropological journal *Man*.

Jackson has written of the course:

> the Chadwicks' pupils all testify to the intellectual excitement of this course. After the then comparatively narrow range of the Classical Tripos, in which, having specialized in comparative philology, not in 'Literature', I came away wholly ignorant of, for example, Classical manuscripts and palaeography, Section B was a most thrilling and liberating experience. Four new languages and literatures, together with the history and the archaeology of their speakers. As for the rest, the pre-Roman and Roman archaeology of Britain has remained, I am sure, with all 'Chadwickians' as an abiding life long interest.

He proceeds:

> I well remember, forty years since, the excitement of cycling the dark and windy miles down the Newmarket Road to the Paper Mills, penetrating the inner fortress, crossing the bridge, negotiating the 'savage' dogs and listening entranced for an hour while 'Chadders' gave his evening lectures on Early Britain and 'Mrs Chadders' sat at the epidiascope projecting pictures of Bronze Age leaf swords . . . The same excitement extended to the reading of works like the *Growth of Literature*, the excitement of finding likenesses and connections between subjects where none had been thought of before.

Needless to say, Jackson was placed in the First Class, with special distinction, in the Archaeological and Anthropological Tripos, Section B, and was awarded the Allen Research Student Scholarship for 1933 and 1934.

Notwithstanding his enthusiasm for the course Jackson must have been aware from the beginning of its weakness for he seems to have taken steps to compensate for it. The weakness was in the teaching of the languages involved. Chadwick had apparently taught himself German as a schoolboy on the eight mile journey to school at Wakefield and back every day and he expected his pupils to teach themselves the four languages required for the course. When Jackson went to him for a reading list he was told that he would probably find Welsh easier than Irish and he rather dumbfounded him when he returned to say that he found Irish easier than Welsh, not surprisingly, if the experience of others is taken into account. Apparently some help was given by the Department in Old Irish. Mrs Chadwick prepared *An Early Irish Reader* (C.U.P., 1927), an edition and translation, with introduction, notes and glossary, of the Old Irish 'Story of Mac Dathó's Pig'. It was savagely reviewed by Professor Osborn Bergin, but, as he himself informs us, Jackson 'must have been one of the earlier students in the famous Chadwickian "Section B" . . . who cut his first Celtic teeth on this edition.'

However, he was not to be handicapped by the deficiencies of the Department. He has described how he read Wade-Evans, *Welsh Medieval Law*, with the help of a Modern Welsh-English Dictionary (?Spurrells) where the obsolete words were marked with a dagger. If he had not been convinced before, the experience must have convinced him that he had to go to places where Welsh and Irish were spoken languages. He spent a month in Ireland and a month in Wales in the Summer of 1932. Pontargothi in the old Carmarthenshire was the place where he spent the month in Wales, and it was there that he collected the 'Coracle Fishing Terms' which he published in the *Bulletin of the Board of Celtic Studies*, vol. VI, part iv (May, 1933). He had spent the previous month in the Great Blasket. Although the first two stories he published ('*Dhá Scéal ón mBlascaod*') in *Béaloideas*, IV, iii (1933) were taken down from the lips of Peig Sayers in June 1933, he had started recording her tales the previous year, as his note appended to *Scéala on mBlascaod*, published in *Béaloideas*, VIII, explains:

> The foregoing stories and poems were collected between the years 1932 and 1937 on the Great Blasket Island, Kerry. With the exception of nos 18, 20, and 35, they are all from Peig Sayers, the Blasket *seanchaidhe* who has become famous recently through her autobiography *Peig* . . . It was originally planned by Dr. Flower and myself to publish the present material jointly with his own famous collection of her stories recorded on

the ediphone, as the complete *Tales of Peig Sayers*; but as pressure of other work is likely to prevent Dr Flower's part in this being ready for some time to come, it has been decided to bring out my stories separately.

Jackson acknowledged his debt to Robin Flower in the interview he gave to Patrick Sims-Williams and some of the latter's students: Flower, he said, had made it much easier for him to learn Irish. Flower lived at Croydon where Jackson was then living and they may have come to know each other as neighbours or through M. P. Charlesworth or through the British Museum where Flower was deputy keeper of MSS as well as being honorary Lecturer in Irish at the University College of London. Flower's connection with the Great Blasket is too well-known to be more than mentioned here and we can take it for granted that it was he who introduced Jackson to the Great Blasket Island and its people. In the interview already referred to, Jackson described how he and Flower went once to the island together but in separate coracles, dipping and rising with the strong Atlantic waves, Flower sitting up with the inevitable cigarette dangling from his mouth, himself crouching back and held tightly by the powerful arms of the island's schoolmistress, so tightly indeed that he woke up next morning with aching ribs. However, he seems to have coped well with the primitive conditions on the island and to have established excellent rapport with Peig Sayers, then quite old. There is a charming photograph of the old Gaeltacht lady and the young Cambridge graduate in Bo Almqvist, *Viking Ale* (1991).

Flower must have had a far greater command of the Irish language at that time than Jackson, but it is both significant and revealing that whereas the former recorded Peig's stories on an ediphone, the latter took them down orally in a modification of the International Phonetic Script, and indeed recommended the use of phonetic script not only as a means of recording tales but also as a means of learning the language. He used to take down the 'chatter' of the Blasket women whom he found much more talkative and articulate than the men, and then checked what he had written by reading it back to them. This must have been most effective, for, as he admits, it gave the impression that he knew more Irish than he did. The tales he took down from Peig he afterwards published in a simplified Irish orthography based on the traditional spelling but adapted to the dialect. He must have had complete confidence in this method for he took down and published in much the same way Gaelic stories later in Nova Scotia and later still in Harris, Scotland. The results justified the method, but Jackson must have had a very good ear and very good training if not an innate aptitude for this effective use of the International Phonetic Script.

The *Scéalta ón mBlascaod* included Romantic Tales and Adventures, Anecdotes, Moral Tales, Saints and Miracles, and tales of the Supernatural, and it is worth emphasizing that Jackson never lost interest in folktales and folklore. He lectured on them while he was at Harvard and also published on them, his most substantial contribution being perhaps *The International Popular Tale and Early Welsh Tradition* (1961).

To resume our account of Jackson's academic career. He spent his first year as Allen Research Student in Bangor at the University College of North Wales attending the lectures of Professor Ifor Williams on early Welsh poetry and those of his assistant Thomas Parry on the Mabinogion and Dafydd ap Gwilym. It was an exciting time to be at Bangor University College. Ifor Williams was preparing his edition of *Canu Llywarch Hen* (1935). Jackson was quick to see its importance and rendered English scholars a service by writing an article on it, 'The Poems of Llywarch the Aged', in *Antiquity* IX (1935). He was to render a similar service when he wrote on Ifor Williams' *Canu Aneirin* in 'The Gododdin of Aneirin' in *Antiquity* XIII (1939). But in addition to attending lectures Jackson was pursuing research with Ifor Williams' assistance on a subject suggested to him by H. M. and N. K. Chadwick, Celtic Nature Poetry, and succeeded in publishing the results of his research work at Bangor and Dublin in the two volumes which appeared in 1935, *Early Welsh Gnomic Poems* and *Studies in Early Celtic Nature Poetry*.

It was rumoured that Jackson went first to Bangor rather than to Dublin because of the savage review by Bergin on N. K. Chadwick's *An Early Irish Reader*. However, as a classics scholar, he must have been welcomed by Bergin with open arms, for, as I well remember, Bergin used to preface his course on Old Irish with the remark that to study the subject successfully one should have at least a sound knowledge of Greek and Latin and ideally some Sanskrit as well. And I should not be at all surprised that Jackson for this reason got from Bergin, if not more, at least as much as any of his other students, for in the introduction to his edition of *Cath Maige Léna*, he acknowledges his debt: 'I wish to record here my best thanks to Professor Osborn Bergin who read the whole book partly in MS and partly in proof, for his generosity in giving me the benefit of his great learning and for his invaluable help in correcting the many errors which were made'.

As one who, like Jackson, studied at the feet of Ifor Williams and Bergin, I should like to endorse Jackson's judgment that they were both great scholars and to add that had they lived to see Jackson's achievements they would have derived great satisfaction from them.

After the second year as Allen Research Student in Dublin Jackson returned to Cambridge where he was elected Fellow of St John's College and appointed first assistant, and then full Lecturer in Celtic in the Faculty of Archaeology and Anthropology.

In December 1938 he was appointed Lecturer in Celtic in the University of Glasgow but for some reason did not take up the appointment. The following year, however, he was made Lecturer in Celtic at Harvard where he was soon promoted to be Associate Professor 1940–8 and finally Professor (1949–50).

He seems to have been almost as much at home in Cambridge, Mass., as in Cambridge, England. He found the students there tremendously enthusiastic and intellectually curious although not very well prepared by their previous education. His best attended course was that on the International Folk Tale. In the more linguistic courses students found his demands rather exacting and the majority withdrew after the first few classes. Eric P. Hamp, perhaps his best known student, although not among the earliest, found it impossible to read all the texts prescribed by him, especially in conjunction with all those prescribed by Joshua Whatmough, and when he telephoned Jackson to say so, the only reply was a laconic 'Oh! that is very unfortunate!' On the other hand, the company of some of the staff was most congenial. F. N. Robinson, the well-known editor of Chaucer's work and the not less well-known author of 'Satirists and Enchanters in early Irish Literature', used to hold 'Celtic Conferences' regularly.

World War II supervened and Jackson was sent to do war service in the British Imperial Censorship, Bermuda, in the 'Uncommon Languages' section (1942–4) and in the U.S. Censorship (1944). His knowledge of the Celtic languages was not greatly exercised: only one letter in Welsh appeared, and that written by a Patagonian, but his knowledge of the Romance Languages was extended to include Rumanian, and he was asked to learn Yiddish, only to find that there were already four persons in the section who knew the language. (Oliver Padel has written that Jackson qualified as a censor in 23 languages, and once said that he had learnt Japanese in three weeks.) True to the habit formed in childhood, Jackson explored the countryside thoroughly, but he must have been glad to return fully to the academic work he had managed to continue in his spare time.

His appointment to a full professorship at Harvard in 1949 was soon (1950) followed by appointment to the Chair of Celtic in Edinburgh. In those days, as in these, it was unusual for a scholar to relinquish a Chair at Harvard for another, and Jackson's decision to leave excited some curiosity among the local journalists, but he guarded his privacy with his usual tenacity, as we can gather from the comment by one Frank Oliver, the *Daily Record* Correspondent in Washington: 'Since coming to America, [Professor Jackson] has wrapped himself completely in his work at Harvard and has consistently shunned all publicity.'

Jackson had taken an interest in Scottish Gaelic before his appointment to the Edinburgh Chair. He had published notes on the Gaelic of Port

Hood, Nova Scotia, and tales from Port Hood, in *Scottish Gaelic Studies*, but the appointment meant that he had to take a far deeper interest.

Naturally he introduced changes in the Department. His successor in the Chair, William Gillies tells us that in the early 1950s,

> There was little demand for the teaching of Gaelic to learners at University level. Gradually that pattern was to change, and from the late 1960's demand was such that Kenneth and Willie Matheson . . . took two steps which transformed the numbers and the consistency of the student body when they introduced 'Celtic, Type II', one of the first intensive beginners' courses in a modern language at Edinburgh; and, for postgraduates, the M.Litt. in Celtic Studies, which was shrewdly designed to give access to Celtic to the increasing numbers of home and overseas students who had solid grounding in some allied subject but had not been able to take Celtic as their primary degree. This transformation brought Kenneth great satisfaction, despite the greatly increased workload—a satisfaction, which he retained until his last days as he followed the successful careers of his ex-students, many of whom also became fast friends.

If as an outsider I may add a gloss on Professor Gillies' remarks, it was characteristic of Jackson that he shouldered the extra-workload for the most part himself. I cannot believe that there were many departments in the University of Edinburgh that, like the Celtic Department, did not take advantage of the extra money available during the 60s to increase the number of staff appreciably.

Naturally Jackson took part in the activities of those societies which dealt with the wider aspects of Celtic, e.g. the International Congress of Celtic Studies of which he was President from 1975 to 1984, the English Place-Name Society of which he was Vice-President from 1973 to 1979 and Honorary President from 1980 to 1985, and the Council for Name Studies in Great Britain and Ireland. His enthusiasm for the study of place-names was intense; until recently the volumes of the English Place-Name Society were offered to him for comment before publication and the Celtic material in such volumes as those on Cheshire place-names benefited greatly from his detailed criticism.

As a life-long student of Roman and Pre-Roman Britain Jackson was naturally appointed one of H. M. Commissioners for Ancient Monuments for Scotland and served from 1963 to 1985.

More immediately connected with his Chair was his work for the Linguistic Survey of Scotland. This was initiated under the late Professor Myles Dillon during the session 1949–50 when he was at the University of Edinburgh. Jackson took over in 1950 and began collecting material, with the help of a questionnaire to elicit phonological and morphological data. By 1959 all areas other than the Outer Hebrides had been covered and by 1963, 192 points had been researched. In 1960 Magne Oftedal (Oslo) was appointed co-editor of publications, and Jackson undertook to write a history of the dialects. Oftedal who resigned in 1969 was succeeded by Máirtín Ó Murchú who resigned in 1970 to be succeeded in turn by D. Clement. Jackson did not give up his work on the Survey until his retirement from the Edinburgh Chair, and, as was said at the time, after making a greater contribution than any one until then to the Survey. His Sir John Rhŷs Memorial Lecture, *Common Gaelic: the Evolution of the Gaelic Languages* (1951), may be said to have cleared the way for the Survey and his *Contributions to the Study of Manx Phonology* (1955), no.2 in the Monograph Series of the Linguistic Survey of Scotland, was an indirect contribution. His paper on 'The Pictish Language' in F. T. Wainwright, ed., *The Problem of the Picts*, can also be reckoned as a contribution to our knowledge of the linguistic history of Scotland.

But it is an indication of the extent of Jackson's contributions to scholarship that he, followed by us, regarded all these publications as *parerga*. His first *magnum opus*, *Language and History in Early Britain*, appeared in 1953. He had planned it as early as 1944 as a work which would describe the development of Brittonic Celtic into the later languages, Cumbrian, Welsh, Cornish and Breton, and would ascribe dates to the various stages in the development, and which would, by correlating these changes with the changes in Anglo-Saxon and Irish, give an overall picture of the language and history of early Britain. The linguistic changes in Brittonic Celtic which had produced Welsh, Cornish and Breton were broadly known thanks to Pedersen's monumental *Vergleichende Grammatik der keltischen Sprachen* but these changes had to be more minutely identified, analysed, and described in their various stages in the light of more recent knowledge, and, above all, they had to be dated with the help of facts which were not easily accessible even after the most thorough research. With characteristic perspicacity, Jackson had seen the relevance of Mac Neill's articles on the Latin loanwords in Irish and had become aware of the crucial importance of the evidence of place-names. It must have come as a considerable shock to him to find that another scholar had been working on that evidence and had already published an epoch-making volume. That scholar was Max Förster and his volume was *Die Flussname Themse und seine Sippe. Studien zur Anglisierung keltische-Eigennamen and zur Lautchronologie des Altbritischen*, 1942. Unfortunately, owing to wartime circumstances it was not until 1947 that Jackson was able to obtain a copy. By that time his own researches were far advanced and his preliminary conclusion already formulated. He realised that in some matters Förster had anticipated his own results, in others they differed fundamentally in their conclusions, while yet in others he had answered questions which Forster had ignored.

Jackson called Förster's work 'monumental' and it is a shame that it has not received the attention that it deserves, but on the other hand it must be said that Jackson took a wider field to research than Förster and carried his research much further. One has to agree with every word of D. A. Binchy's tribute to the volume:

> *Language and History in Early Britain* is one of the most important contributions to Celtic scholarship that have appeared in our time. Its main purpose is to trace the historical phonology of the British dialects of Celtic from Roman times down to the twelfth century. A formidable task, indeed, owing to the scanty and scattered nature of the evidence, but one to which Professor Jackson brings unique qualifications. Almost every page illustrates his wide and accurate knowledge not only of all the Celtic languages but of Vulgar Latin and Anglo-Sazon, a combination which no other scholar has hitherto possessed. When one finds allied to all this a profound historical sense and a highly developed critical faculty, it is safe to conclude that the book supersedes all previous contributions to the subject and will long remain the standard work of reference.

Although several *parerga* were to appear before Jackson's second *magnum opus*, *A Historical Phonology of Breton* (1967),—in addition to those already named one should mention *The Oldest Irish Tradition. A Window on the Iron Age* (1964)—it must have been started immediately after the first had been completed. In a way it was an offshoot of the first, the second volume, as it were, based on the foundations laid in the first, but the more one studies it, the more one realizes that it was much more difficult to write, and although the author does not make much of the difficulties, he touches upon them. Primitive Breton is virtually unrecorded. For the earlier period of Middle Breton, down to the middle of the 15th century, our information consists almost solely of names in cartularies and such documents. There is controversy as to when Middle Breton became Modern Breton. And the most important source for our knowledge of the Breton dialects, Le Roux's great *Atlas linguistique de la Basse Bretagne* in six parts, 1924, 1927, 1937, 1943, 1953, 1963, excellent though it is for the study of present day dialects, should be used sparingly and with the greatest caution as a basis for speculation about their history in the past. However, in spite of these and other difficulties, Jackson succeeded in achieving what he set out to do, in producing,

> a consistent and methodical framework in which all the chief historical problems are raised and discussed; and within the scope of which it may be possible for future research to lead to criticisms, additions, substractions, adaptations, removals of error, and other improvements in the course of time, until by the collaboration of many scholars a fairly definitive and generally agreed picture is finally agreed. Nothing like an overall treatment

of Breton phonology throughout its history has been tempted before, and it seems evident that such a work is needed and that the time is now ripe for a first essay in this direction.

Jackson had two other *magna opera* in mind, a 'Historical Grammar of Irish' and an edition of the 'Vision of Mac Conglinne', and when he retired from his Chair in 1979, having published in the meantime *The Gododdin* (1969) and *The Gaelic Notes in the Book of Deer*, it seemed that he could finish both works. Indeed, when he was presented with a second *Festschrift* in the form of volumes XIV/XV of *Studia Celtica* (1979/80)—the first was composed of articles written by former pupils and presented to him in a bound typescript volume to mark the completion of his 25 years' tenure of the Chair of Celtic at Edinburgh—both he and his friends were looking forward with confidence to their completion. Unfortunately ill-health supervened—he suffered a stroke in 1984—and in the event he was only able to publish *Aislinge Meic Conglinne* (1990) with the help of friends, in particular Professor Brian Ó Cuív, at the Dublin Institute for Advanced Studies. The Appendix on the language of the text is an excellent introduction to Middle Irish, and the Glossary, far from being a mere vocabulary, is a concordance of the language and the key to the whole. It fully deserves to be called Jackson's third *magnum opus*.

It goes without saying that Jackson's amazing achievements compelled international recognition. In addition to being a D.Litt. of the University of Cambridge he had honorary doctorates conferred upon him by the National University of Ireland, the University of Wales and the University of Haute Bretagne. He was made a Fellow of the British Academy in 1957, and Honorary Member of the Royal Irish Academy in 1965. He was appointed CBE in 1985.

Faced with such prodigious achievements in scholarship and publications, one would like to find an explanation in extraordinary energy, tremendous industry, exclusive application to work or such. No doubt Jackson had both energy and industry but his working life was very much like that of other scholars. He used to work on his research in the mornings; he lectured or went for walks in the afternoons and he spent the evenings in reading scholarly books and journals with an occasional dip into a detective story. He was always available to his two children, Alastar and Stephanie, and delighted not only in telling them stories from his vast knowledge of folklore but also in taking them with Janet his wife to visit places of historical interest. Janet and he loved to entertain friends and students and many recall with gratitude their generous hospitality. No; energy, industry, application to work do not provide a satisfactory explanation. Jackson must have had quite exceptional ability, a brain of unusual power and a strong character to make the best use of it.

He was never less than a demanding teacher. A perfectionist himself he could be harshly critical of incompetence while at the same time deeply appreciative of excellent work by a student or by a colleague.

There was an old-fashioned aspect to his character and behaviour. One student wishes me to stress that he treated his women students with the chivalry of a world long-dead.

In his memorable address at the funeral service, Gordon Donaldson, H. M. Historiographer in Scotland, said that he knew Jackson almost exclusively as a friend, that he had known little of his scholarly achievements until then, but that he had been always impressed by his modesty, his courtesy, his kindness and his generosity. He concluded his remarks: 'Kenneth Jackson of course leaves the work he has done. But, what is dearer to his friends, with the fever of life over and his work done, he goes, as Ecclesiasts has it, to his long home, but he leaves in his friends' minds memories that will endure.'

Great scholar as he was, one of the greatest ever among Celtic scholars, Professor Kenneth Jackson would have appreciated that tribute. *Suaimhneas síorai dá anam.*

J. E. CAERWYN WILLIAMS
*Fellow of the British Academy*

*Note.* I gratefully acknowledge the help given me in the preparation of this Memoir by Professor Jackson's widow, Mrs Janet Jackson, her son, Alastar, his former pupils, Miss Margaret Bird, Dr Kay Muhr, Dr A. T. E. Matonis, Professor William Gillies and Dr Oliver Padel. I am especially indebted to Dr Patrick Sims-Williams, Fellow of St John's College, Cambridge, who in recent years kept Professor Jackson in touch with his Alma Mater and enjoyed his friendship and respect. A list of Professor Jackson's published works will be found in *Studia Celtica, XIV/XV* (1979–80) with 'Addenda' in *Studia Celtica, XXVI–XXVII* (1991–92).

*Proceedings of the British Academy*, **80**, 333–348

# George Williams Keeton
# 1902–1989

PROFESSOR KEETON was an energetic man. A considerable proportion of anyone's effort must go into the ephemeral daily round, but the enduring evidence of Professor Keeton's achievements is of a quantity to excite an exclamation. How did he do it all in a mere eighty-seven years? (Or fifty if you lop off minority at the beginning and rest at the end, for he was neither Mozartian in precociousness nor Shavian in endurance.) He was not a mysterious person, but there is a mystery. How did Professor Keeton do his vast and varied work without ever appearing to be in a hurry? Lawyer and historian, textbook writer, biographer and novelist, teacher and administrator, sportsman and gardener, he was a relaxed, kindly, sociable man. He must have read, taken in, thought and written extraordinarily quickly, as he was forever enjoying himself with friends, colleagues, students and former students, discussing law, politics, current affairs or any topical subject; reading a newspaper or book; playing on the tennis court or at the bridge table; in front of the television set; and away on holiday. He enjoyed himself, as he did everything, with zest.

George Williams Keeton was born in Sheffield, United rather than Wednesday, in 1902, son of a silversmith, and died at home in Princes Risborough in 1989. He left behind a library of law reports, journals and other books on many subjects, most of which have been given by his widow to grace the court in Luton, a charming souvenir of his work and friendship with Judge Keith Devlin dating from their time together at Brunel University. He also left behind as one of the permanent reminders of his industry almost a library on its own of his authorship.

After coming down from Gonville and Caius College, in the year 1924 George Keeton acquired a readership at Hong Kong University and his first wife, Gladys, with whom he had been going out since schooldays in

G. W. KEETON

*Camera Press Ltd*

Sheffield. There was no Law Faculty in Hong Kong until much later. The young reader, though, edited and wrote on an extensive variety of subjects for the *Hongkong University Law Journal*. He also wrote for *The South China Times* and was a member of the North China Branch of the Royal Asiatic Society.

His teaching responsibility in Hong Kong was international law and relations. That interest and its location appear in an early book, *The Development of Extraterritoriality in China*, and in papers written in Hong Kong for English periodicals. It survived George Keeton's return to England in 1927 and his conversion into one of the country's leading academic exponents of the law of trusts and other aspects of equitable jurisdiction. During the thirties and forties he wrote many articles on international law and relations, book reviews galore and several more books, including *China, the Far East and the Future* and, with Georg Schwarzenberger, a friend, colleague and collaborator over a long period, *Making International Law Work*.

When at University College, London, Professor Keeton fostered the development of a thriving group of international lawyers powered by Professor Schwarzenberger. Keeton was Principal of the London Institute of World Affairs from 1938 to 1952 and President from 1952 onwards. The purpose of that Institute, as given in the preface to the first *Year Book* in 1947, is to provide an independent international forum for the critical and constructive discussion of, and research into, problems of world affairs. Schwarzenberger was his co-editor of the *Year Book*, an addition to the quarterly, *World Affairs*, and occasional books (the *Library of World Affairs*) already published by the Institute.

In 1927, George Keeton left Hong Kong University, which later conferred an honorary doctorate of laws on him, and in the following year was called to the bar by Gray's Inn. Unlike many academic lawyers, who attain a professional qualification and never use it, Keeton did practical legal work as well, but he was primarily a scholar. Assistant tutor to the Law Society and supervisor in law at Clare College, Cambridge in 1927, when he was awarded the degrees of Master of Arts and Master of Laws, after call to the bar he spent 1928–31 as a senior lecturer in law at Manchester University. During that early period Keeton's academic development owed much to the guidance and help of his former Cambridge tutor, (later Lord) McNair. From Manchester came the translation to London. Although that university was not his last, Keeton was at University College for the longest and most influential period of his career. It began in 1931 with a readership. In 1932, he was awarded his substantive doctorate of laws (to which Sheffield and Brunel Universities, as well as Hong Kong, added honorary ones). *The Development of Extraterritoriality in China*, published in two volumes in 1928, was the work which earned the doctorate, but another four years had to elapse after the candidate's graduation before Cambridge University was allowed by its own regulations to make the award. In 1937, Dr Keeton exchanged that title for professor, which is how practically everyone will remember him. He had charge of the fortunes of the University College Faculty of Laws in Gower Street, Aberystwyth, Cambridge, Foster Court and Endsleigh Gardens until reaching in 1969 the magical age of 67 at which UCL people turn into something else.

As a part-time practising barrister, attached to different chambers at different times, Professor Keeton did not appear in court as an advocate but wrote opinions and drafted documents. It is difficult, even in London, to combine court work with full-time law teaching and its appointed hours of lectures, tutorials and meetings. Over the years, he gave advice on many legal subjects, from overseas as well as originating in England.

His advice to association football authorities and clubs was but one component of his consultative work. It was a happy component because of his interest in the game itself. He reconstituted the rules of the Football Association, was adviser to the Football League and was co-founder of the Metropolitan and Hellenic Leagues. Although supporting Sheffield United in the various divisions to which it was allocated by fate, he was far from sharing the delusion that only professionals play. He was an organiser of clubs as well as leagues at the most local, amateur, level. In 1949, he drew up the memorandum and articles of association of Headington United Football Club Co. Ltd and was the first subscriber of the memorandum. The main team then played in the Spartan League, but he saw it through the Southern League and into the Football League as Oxford United. In 1951, his book *The Soccer Club Secretary*, a practical manual with a foreword by Sir Stanley Rous, was published. In 1972, came *The Football Revolution*.

Winter sports in England only last from mid-August to mid-May, and Professor Keeton's attention turned readily to cricket and tennis as the seasons dictated. The seasons of man also change, though they seldom recur, and require that watching shall supersede participation and that television shall supersede presence in the stand. Professor Keeton was interested in everything frivolous, diverting and amusing as well as in everything earnest. If there was something to do or watch, he did or watched it. When the war started in 1939, Professor Keeton was building his own boat. It was never finished, but he was Commodore of the Amateur Boat Builders Association and edited their journal. Before the war, he sailed a boat of someone else's construction, lost in the Dunkirk rescue. That was the novelist period. *The Speedy Return*, a version of a true story of piracy between Scotland and England in the reign of Queen Anne prior to the Union, appeared in 1938. In 1940 he published a book for boys, *Mutiny in the Caribbean*, also based on an actual incident.

The 1930s were scarcely a period of development in university law schools, but significant innovations in law publishing happened then. The *Modern Law Review,* now in its fifty-fifth year, was inaugurated by the enterprise and at the financial risk of a group of London law teachers (including Professor Keeton, who was co-editor from 1937 to 1939 and a member of the editorial committee thereafter until 1955). *The Solicitor,* deceased in 1965 shortly after a change of name and style, was founded under Professor Keeton's editorship. His own durable books, *The Law of Trusts*, now in its twelfth edition, and *An Introduction to Equity* (entitled *Equity* in editions published after the book was expanded twenty years ago) appeared in Pitman's *Equity Series*, of which Professor Keeton was the general editor.

Pitman's were Professor Keeton's main publishers for several decades, but they lost interest in law in the 1970s. Their activity in publishing law books has since revived, but new editions and new books meanwhile had to go elsewhere. In the event, they were spread. The upheavals and take-overs in law publishing of the last thirty years, which in the 1980s reached a frantic pitch resembling the later stages of a game of musical chairs, led to much novation. Professor Keeton did strike up a lasting relationship with Barry Rose, the Chichester publisher who maintains hallowed values and who is now the principal producer and distributor of the Keeton books still in print.

One of the consequences of Hitler's grotesque rule which had an impact on university law schools during the 1930s was the migration to England (and the United States of America) of lawyers retreating from Nazi Europe. The common law of England and the countries to which that law has been exported is, quite apart from language, distinct in technique from the legal systems of continental Europe and was even further away from their methods before the evolution of European Community law and consequent harmonisation. The immigrant lawyers had to learn or improve their command of English even if they were to confine their interests to universal subjects like international law and legal philosophy, but mostly they went the whole hog and became scholars of the common law. In addition to Georg Schwarzenberger, Professor Keeton brought Wolfgang Friedmann, who became a renowned exponent of legal philosophy, to University College, London. Friedmann later moved, via Melbourne, to the chair of jurisprudence at Columbia University and was murdered by muggers just outside the Faculty of Law there.

The second world war sent University College, London on its travels. The Law Department went to Aberystwyth for the phoney war and the armed struggles ending with Dunkirk, back to London for a brief encounter with the battle of Britain (during which the College was severely damaged) and then to Cambridge until the bombs, the V1s and the V2s were silenced by the demise of their progenitor. The return from Aberystwyth to London, which seems to have delighted West Walians and Londoners alike, took place during a period of jitters about spies and the fantasy of the imminent arrival of German paratroops disguised as nuns. Unknown to Professor Keeton at the time, the door of the vehicle in which he was travelling came ajar and papers and pamphlets on international law and relations escaped. What had happened came to the attention of Keeton only when he was stopped by police investigating reports of the distribution of enemy propaganda in the Welsh mountains.

Gladys went with their sons Peter and Michael to New Zealand for the war. That was the effective end of that marriage save for the post-war divorce proceedings. Meanwhile, George had met Marian and they were married towards the end of 1947. It is impossible to believe that there could be a couple better suited to each other. George's zest was well matched. His and Marian's interests were coincident. They did practically everything together. Even the publications were a co-operative effort for Marian, though not a lawyer, is a first class typist and proof reader. Many authors will appreciate how important it is to have copy read and reproduced by an intelligent, interested and critical person. Together, George and Marian set up the household in Princes Risborough and made their large garden beautiful and productive. Amongst George's other talents was the ability to make things grow; and he was something of an expert in grafting fruit trees. There is no modern twist to the story: the marriage remained a happy and loving mutual admiration society.

In October 1945, University College, like a great deal of London, was a shambles. To reopen the Law Faculty there, using makeshift accommodation, an unregenerated library and depleted academic staff, required a considerable feat of organisation. Much of that fell upon the shoulders of Professor Keeton as Dean of the Faculty and Head of the Department. The burden—or joy—was increased by the addition of ex-servicemen, many of whom had passed examinations for part of a law degree before or early in the war and now aimed to complete their studies as quickly as possible, to the population of students who left school to go up in that year or were already reading law. One by one the staff who had been in the forces or on other national service came back, their knowledge of the law often in the disrepair that results from lack of routine maintenance. There was much to keep up with as well as catch up with, for a Labour government was initiating a flood of legislation and Lord Denning was already on the bench. Through all the tasks of rebuilding and reshaping the Law Department, Professor Keeton took a full share of the teaching of undergraduate and postgraduate students.

Even in the midst of gathering together the pieces, invention was alive. In 1947, London University created the Institute of Advanced Legal Studies, the brain-child of Professor David Hughes Parry, then Vice-Chancellor of the university as well as a professor of law at the London School of Economics and Political Science. Professor Keeton, along with other London professors, was for many years a member of the management committee. Mainly a library and teaching premises for postgraduate students, the Institute is also a national and international meeting place. The enterprise began in old houses in Russell Square, easy to use but difficult to manage, and is now housed in spacious premises built for the purpose a few doors away.

Also in 1947, University College inaugurated the series of public lectures called *Current Legal Problems* which results in an annual published volume. The lectures, under Professor Keeton's chairmanship, were delivered in the Eugenics Lecture Theatre, perhaps because it was the warmest place in the College, central and intact. The lecture series is still going strong, and the annual publication nowadays includes articles specifically written for it without concomitant oral delivery. Although at a high level, suitable for lawyers and law students, those public lectures are related to Professor Keeton's general and abiding interest in adult education. He taught for the Workers' Educational Association and for Extra-mural Departments of universities one-year extension courses and three-year tutorial courses in international affairs and relations from Manchester days until shortly before retiring from University College. For many years he was chairman of the University of London Extra-mural Council.

One person who was often in the Eugenics Lecture Theatre during the public lunch-time series of lectures also inaugurated by Professor Keeton was a little old lady dressed in old-fashioned style. Many people wondered who she was. Professor Keeton took the trouble to find out and visited her in her bleak flat in Waterloo Road. She, it appeared, did indeed attend in order to come in from the cold. It is a commentary on the economics of little old ladies that when she died a considerable estate was revealed. It is an unusual reward for disinterested kindness that she left it to the Law Faculty at University College.

Professor Keeton's period of deanship of the Faculty of Laws at University College, London, 1939–54, was of a length which has become unusual but was quite normal then. In faculties of law with only one chair, the professor would habitually combine contractually permanent headship of the law department with continuous office or periodic re-election as dean of the faculty, but even the larger law schools generally had long-serving deans. For whatever reason that habit died, whether due to the embracing of notions of democracy or to the increasing size of academic staffs, the splitting of the duties of deanship of the faculty and those of the headship of the department proved a satisfactory response to the changing scope of organisational functions when the demand for university legal education burgeoned, even in universities where faculties of law were not divided into several departments. The deanship began to circulate around the professors at the University College, London Faculty of Laws, but Professor Keeton remained Head of the Law Department until he retired from the service of the college.

Professor Keeton's administration of legal education at University College, London measured up to the highest standard by which organisers can be tested: that students were unaware that it was going on. When administration becomes obstrusive, there must be inefficiency or squabbling or both. Essential disagreement, debate and innovation do not produce that effect. For some years after the second world war, law teaching at London University was intercollegiate. No doubt that required considerable intellectual endeavour by makers of timetables (who sometimes took an optimistic view of public transport or the middle-distance running of students). Despite a slight taint of disloyalty, those University College students who chose to read optional subjects taught at the London School of Economics and Political Science or King's College did not find their careers blighted. Intercollegiate teaching of undergraduates was abandoned long ago, and London University colleges with faculties of laws even have diverse syllabuses for their bachelors' degrees.

During the course of thirty-eight years as a law teacher at University College, London, Keeton tutored and noticed many students who followed his footsteps into an academic career, including quite a few who were taken on at his college or in other parts of London university. Some achieved the highest eminence; some were among his remote successors as dean. The fifties saw the beginning of the process of establishing new faculties of law in the Commonwealth, a process which gathered pace in the sixties—a decade when many new university and polytechnic law degree courses were also set up in the United Kingdom. There were numerous overseas students at London University long before they were courted by universities generally as a source of wealth. Both at home and abroad, Keeton's former students from home and abroad have been influential in the development of legal education. Sir Roy Marshall, for example, who was a candidate for the degree of Doctor of Philosophy under Professor Keeton's supervision after reading for his bachelor's degree at Cambridge University, and taught law at University College, London, was Vice-Chancellor of the University of the West Indies when the Caribbean law faculty was established (later Vice-Chancellor of Hull University, he is now Barbados High Commissioner in London and accredited as ambassador to several European countries). The maintenance of contacts all over the world kept Professor Keeton in touch with emerging and growing law faculties, brought him consultative legal work, generated invitations to lecture and inspired the book of large geographical scope, *The Comparative Law of Trusts in the Commonwealth and the Irish Republic*, published in 1976. Of course, many more law graduates who studied in Keeton's department pursued careers in practice as solicitors or at the bar and in diverse other walks of life than went into teaching and research; and eminence was achieved in many directions.

For his thirty years as Head of the Law Department at University College, London, Keeton was naturally the main participant in making, or declining to make, appointments to the academic staff. There were those who joined university College as young lecturers and stayed until retirement as professors. Others left for rapid advancement elsewhere in Britain or overseas. In international law and in the law of trusts particularly, teaching and developments in many countries can be related back to a base in Keeton's department. Several members of the academic staff of University College, London migrated directly or indirectly to Canada, including Professor Donovan Waters, whose big book on the *Law of Trusts in Canada* is cited judicially so often as to have become almost a work of binding authority throughout the Provinces. The preface to Keeton's *The Comparative Law of Trusts in the Commonwealth and the Republic of Ireland* records the personal contacts all over the Commonwealth from whom help was received in the research. The last name listed is from Cyprus, which not only provided Professor Keeton with consultative work on its law of trusts but also became, for a period, a favoured holiday destination for George and Marian and the provider of good wines for the dining table in Princes Risborough.

Professor Keeton, though a good judge of intellect and potential, was, like everybody else, fallible: not everyone he chose bore out his predictions or fulfilled the promise they had shown, while people he overlooked or decided against occasionally invalidated his judgment too. One of his weaknesses—or charms—was a tendency for his loyalty to protégés to outlast its justification. One of his strengths was that he was capable of adjusting his opinions in either direction when the evidence became strong.

At the outset of the decade of the sixties, Professor Keeton was President of the Society of Public Teachers of Law, the learned society founded in 1909 with a membership of persons teaching law at United Kingdom universities and at the professional law schools of the Inns of

Court and the Law Society. The presidency of the society is the highest honour that can be conferred on an academic lawyer solely by the volition of fellow workers. It is an office which makes continuing demands throughout its tenure and ends with the annual conference at which the presidential address is usually, but not necessarily, envisaged as an opportunity for the speaker to express views on legal education. On 20th September 1962, President Keeton delivered a presidential address, described immediately afterwards as 'topical' by Professor Hanbury, leading the discussion, on the behaviour of the judiciary in the quarter of a century before, during and just after the deposition of King James II. That was one of a number of works in which Professor Keeton sought to correct the previously received judicial history of the period and to provide an apologia for much of the career of Bloody Jeffreys. 'Judge Jeffreys as Chief Justice of Chester' had appeared in the *Law Quarterly Review* the previous year; 'Judge Jeffreys: Towards a Reappraisal' was published in the *Welsh History Review* in 1962; and in 1964 *Cheshire Life* carried 'Bloody Jeffreys.' That phase of Professor Keeton's work culminated in 1965 in the publication of a substantial book, *Lord Chancellor Jeffreys and the Stuart Cause.*

Professor Keeton's historical writings are sometimes biographical in form. The lives under review are set in the context of the state of the law and of the legal developments of the time in which they were lived. In that category come, in addition to the works on Jeffreys and the downfall of the Stuarts, a number of articles and these books: *A Liberal Attorney General: being the Life of Lord Robson of Jesmond 1852–1918* (1949) and *Harvey the Hasty—A Mediaeval Chief Justice* (1978). In two of his books the historical basis is literary. Professor Keeton analysed great dramatic legal conflicts in *Shakespeare and His Legal Problems* (1930) and *Shakespeare's Legal and Political Background* (1967). Their roots were in his schooldays. In 1918, adolescent Keeton was secretary of the Sheffield Central Secondary Boys' School Shakespeare Society, *The Merchant of Venice* being performed four times in December of that year. Secretaries had no time to act, but he trod the boards before and after. An account of the Society is given in *All Right on the Night* (1929), a book edited and partly written by Keeton. Facing page 140 is a photograph which includes the editor making his stage debut in 1917 as the first Sicilian lord in *The Winter's Tale.* (Turn on a couple of pages for a more mature representation in orthodox dress.)

In his various textbooks on equity and trusts there is a wealth of historical material illuminating the origins and development of doctrines operating today (as well as superseded doctrines without knowledge of which precedents still cited on other points often cannot be fully understood). *The Modern Law of Charities*, first published in 1962, was occasioned by the enactment of a wide-ranging Charities Act for England and Wales in 1960. The 'modern' law of charities means the law as it is, but that may be taken as having begun when the first major legislation was enacted, and the first charity commissioners were provided for, in the Statute of Charitable Uses, 1601. In his book, Professor Keeton does indeed treat 'modern' as 1601–1960, with the accent on 1960, but he also informs his readers of the Tudor precursors of the great statutory changes of 1601 and shows how charity in England evolved from mediaeval times to the state in which it was a constituent of the social problems facing the policy makers of Elizabeth I.

As both historians and lawyers should, Professor Keeton insisted on the best evidence in his research. In 1948, during a conversation about *Sambach v. Dalston*, a case decided in 1634 and correctly regarded generally as a keystone in the structure of the modern law of trusts but briefly and poorly treated by the law reporters, he initiated a visit to the Public Record Office to substitute, if possible, knowledge for speculation. The manuscript record of the proceedings in fact settled everything that had been under discussion, and that is a lesson which should be re-learned whenever overlooked. It is essential to use originals, in preference even to what purport to be reproductions of originals, for, unless reproduction is by a photographic process, reprints import misprints. Reform of the law of charities, not undertaken theretofore since 1601, was a recurring public issue during the first half of the nineteenth century (as it has been recently, despite the Act of 1960, and will be in the twenty-first century notwithstanding the enactment of the Charities Act 1992). In *The Modern Law of Charities*, Professor Keeton made extensive use of governmental and parliamentary papers and the reports of commissioners throughout the nineteenth century. Judging by how dirty the work was, not many people had been there before. His work was seldom lightened by research assistants: grants to support legal research, including research into legal history, were hard to come by. Amongst the exceptions was *The Comparative Law of Trusts in the Commonwealth and the Irish Republic*. A two-year fellowship awarded to Professor Keeton by the Leverhulme Trust enabled him to employ assistance in the research for that book. He did sometimes collaborate with co-authors or co-editors. In the case of several of his books on equity and trusts, he did all the work himself in the first place, a co-author being enlisted only for new editions. Legal history he wrote alone.

The British Academy elected Professor Keeton to fellowship in 1964, when the limit was two hundred fellows under the age of seventy-five. The opinion expressed in the citation was:

> Professor Keeton is now the senior member of the University of London Law Faculty. He has been Principal of the London Institute of World Affairs since 1938, a field in which he has an international reputation; and through the Institute he has stimulated much original work. His numerous books on

legal philosophy, equity, and the law relating to charities constitute important contributions to legal learning; his lucid analysis of difficult problems has also made them popular with law students. In addition to his books he has had many articles in the *Law Quarterly Review, Current Legal Problems, Transactions of the Grotius Society, British Year Book of International Law, and Year Book of World Affairs*.

There follows a list of his principal publications.

The allusion to the stimulation of much original work deserves to be picked up. Despite the massive quantity of research and writing he did himself, Professor Keeton had too many ideas for one person to bring to fruition on his own. They were liberally articulated. Consequently, as well as a prodigious author, Professor Keeton was a facilitator and stimulator. It was not only methods and standards that were derived from Professor Keeton by students and colleagues: expressly or by implication they learned of countless things that ought to be done and which they found they would like to do.

Around the time of Professor Keeton's sixty-fifth birthday, 'the worldwide circle of former students and other close friends' conceived a desire 'to express, however inadequately, their affection for him and their appreciation of his attainments as a scholar and academic teacher.' The product was a symposium of essays, *Law, Justice and Equity*, published in 1967 under the editorship of Messrs. Code Holland and Schwarzenberger (from whose preface the quotations are taken). The volume includes a selected bibliography of Professor Keeton's writings on law and international relations thus far, compiled by Sultana Saeed. The frontispiece is a reproduction of a portrait of Professor Keeton, an evocative likeness painted by Julia Heseltine, which had been presented to the Faculty of Laws of University College, London by Dr George Webber, formerly Reader in English Law there, and which now hangs in the Keeton Room of the faculty building.

The bibliography compiled by Sultana Saeed shows the range of Professor Keeton's authorship. The headings she used, under all of which there are entries for numerous articles, notes and reviews, are: *administrative law* (including one book, *Trial by Tribunal*, 1960); *charities* (including one book, *The Modern Law of Charities*, 1962 and subsequent editions from time to time); *company law; comparative law* (comprising Asian, European, American and South African topics); *conflict of laws; constitutional law* (including one book, *The Passing of Parliament*, first published in 1952 and meriting a second edition in 1954); *criminal law, courts and procedure; English law* (including one book, with other contributors, *The United Kingdom: The Development of its Laws and Constitution*, 1955); *equity* (including two books, *An Introduction to*

*Equity*, 1965, current as *Equity*, 1987 edition, and Cases on *Equity and Trusts*, 1959, with another edition in 1974); *industrial law; international law and relations* (including seven books written alone or with co-authors, *The Development of Extraterritoriality in China*, 1928, *The Problem of the Moscow Trial*, 1933, *National Sovereignty and International Order*, 1939, *Making International Law Work*, 1939, with a second edition in 1946, *The Case for an International University*, 1941, *Russia and her Western Neighbours*, 1942, and *China, the Far East and the Future*, 1949, with a second edition in 1953); *jurisprudence* (including two books, *The Elementary Principles of Jurisprudence*, 1930, with a second edition in 1949, and, with Professor R.A. Eastwood, Dean of the Faculty of Law at Manchester University, *The Austinian Theories of Law and Sovereignty*, 1929); *law of contract and tort; law of succession; law reform; legal education and profession; legal history* (including six books, being, in addition to the four already mentioned, *Trial for Treason*, 1959, and *The Norman Conquest and the Common Law*, 1966); *property law;* and, of course, *trusts*.

By the time of the occasions of honour by the British Academy and by the worldwide admirers, Professor Keeton's chair at London University had only a few more years to run. Early retirement and the fashion of parting company prematurely with their best scholars had not yet been embraced by United Kingdom universities. The operative scheme then was an arbitrary retiring age (sixty-seven at London University) designed to rid universities, without managerial embarrassment by judgment or argument, of employees whose powers were failing. So far from any of Professor Keeton's powers failing, they increased in those closing years. In 1966, he embarked upon a three-year term as Vice-Provost of University College, London, a post in which his experience, knowledge of the college and the university, invention, firmness, kindness and common sense were fully deployed. So it was that in 1969 Professor Keeton's retirement was from a dual role in the college.

That was the close of a long and illustrious chapter, not the end of a career. In the prime of life, commanding the energy many a younger academic would envy, the emeritus professor swapped one employer for two. From 1969 to 1977 he was responsible for the courses pursued in London by law students of Notre Dame University during their annual expatriation. From 1969 to 1977 he was involved in the development of legal education at Brunel University. The journey from Princes Risborough to Uxbridge is more convenient than commuting between Princes Risborough and Bloomsbury, but now Florida came into the regular itinerary too. Professor Keeton's zest for travel was unabated, as was his enthusiasm for lecturing. During the 1970s he accepted an invitation to deliver the most prestigious series English-speaking Asia has so far had, *The Tagore*

*Lectures*. He did prepare them, a considerable work; unfortunately, due entirely to difficulties in India, the lectures were never given.

Starting a new university teaching department is an exciting venture for everyone who participates in it. Planning syllabuses, acquiring a library, recruitment of the first staff and students, securing professional recognition for graduates and, perhaps above all, ensuring that the new block fits comfortably as well as usefully into the university structure, are all challenging tasks. If the project becomes manifestly successful, excitement may diminish but an equally pleasurable sensation replaces it.

As at Hong Kong University and University College, London, Professor Keeton participated at Brunel University in the founding of a periodical. The *Anglo-American Law Review*, published by Barry Rose and edited at first by Professor Keeton and Keith Devlin, first presented itself to the public in 1972 and is now in its twentieth volume.

Even misfortunes can have a sunny aspect. One sad episode threw up an unusual instance of judicial notice. A student of economics and law at Brunel University was denied progress towards his goal of becoming a lawyer because he repeatedly failed examinations in economics. Some of the academic lawyers at Brunel (not, as a matter of fact, including Professor Keeton, who knew nothing of the case) used their good offices to arrange the student's transfer to another university at which he could read for a degree in law alone. The candidate failed there as well and eventually sued the second university and the head of its law department for conspiracy. The fanciful case was, in effect, that the defendant professor had conspired with Professor Keeton to bring about the plaintiff's failure in economics and consequent transfer from Brunel to the other university in order to wreak undeserved disaster on the plaintiff at closer quarters. Appearing in person, the plaintiff asked the defendant in cross-examination whether he was intimately associated with Professor Keeton and wrote books with him. The judge did not catch the name at first and the witness re-enunciated it for him. 'Oh, Professor Keeton,' said the judge, 'he's very well known.'

In 1976, Professor Keeton and I planned the only book on which we worked together from scratch, as opposed to my joining him as co-author when the work was already under way or proceeding to a new edition. Dr W.G. Hart had much material on which the Trusts Bill, 1908, to codify the law of trusts was based. The Bill was not enacted, and in 1909 Dr Hart published the material as a book entitled *A Digest of the Law relating to Private Trusts and Trustees*. We decided to write a new book following Dr Hart's form of articles of a possible code, followed by commentary and illustrations drawn from decided cases. In addition to taking account of over half a century of new legislation and judicial precedent, we added sections on charitable trusts, custodian trustees and trust corporations, all outside Dr Hart's scope. In the academic year 1976–7, Professor Keeton was still at Brunel University and I was a Commonwealth Visiting Professor in Canada, based at the University of Manitoba. The scheme we adopted was for me to draft the articles of the code and the commentary and post the drafts to Professor Keeton, whereupon he would return them with criticism and drafts of the illustrations for my criticism. The work went well in that way and in the spring of 1976 I was able to deliver a first version of the book to our publisher when he visited Manitoba. His enthusiasm for the project seemed to cool when, on an outing, I drove our car along a track into some supernaturally adhesive mud, but his willingness to publish survived. I had found the work tough going to fit in with my responsibilities as a visiting professor and writing a couple of articles for Canadian legal periodicals and imagined that Professor Keeton, doing his share in his spare time, had found it demanding too. It should have come as no surprise to me that, when we had finished the *Digest of the English Law of Trusts*, Professor Keeton presented me with a copy of *Harvey the Hasty*, which he had written at the same time. Three years ago, a Japanese translation of the *Digest* appeared. It looks beautiful, but we had reluctantly to forgo the kind invitation of the translators to comment on their work.

That was the last book Professor Keeton wrote on the law of trusts. The first was a textbook, published in 1934 and entitled simply and informatively *The Law of Trusts*. The twelfth edition is about to be published, many of the earlier editions requiring reprinting and supplements. I had used *The Law of Trusts* as a student, and later as a teacher, but it was not until I joined in the preparation of the tenth edition twenty years ago that I appreciated fully the depth of insight commanded by the original author. There are a number of current works on trusts of high quality, but the contribution of Professor Keeton to contemporary knowledge of the subject would be difficult to overestimate.

Sometimes, as with that book, his careful treatment of history and development has misled observers into thinking that Professor Keeton was more concerned with the past than with the present state of the law. Nothing in his writings supports that superficial conclusion. In fact, news often stimulated him into an article, and some of his books on trusts are distinctly rooted in the time at which they were written: *Social Change in the Law of Trusts* (1958), *The Investment and Taxation of Trust Funds* (1964) and *Modern Developments in the Law of Trusts* (1971). With the assistance of Professor Ernest Scamell, he also edited the the 1960 edition of Williams on *Executors and Administrators*, the leading practitioners' reference work.

A sturdily built person, normally robust in health, Professor Keeton suffered a bout of influenza or some such illness during his seventy-eighth winter. For some undiagnosed reason, but most probably because of worry about his wife's prolonged and more serious illness, he was in a depressed state for some time afterwards. With the completion of *Harvey the Hasty*, he lost interest in writing. He did not participate in the production of the subsequent editions of his books or engage in any work from then on. He lost the taste for travel and for social intercourse with anyone but the few intimate friends whom, tiring quickly, he liked to see for short periods. At no stage did he falter in mental capacity, in keeping up with current affairs or in his sense of humour. His memory was unfailing and he remained an entertaining raconteur, but with a lack of gusto which was a curious sensation for those who had known him well before the illness. Happily the depression eventually lifted as the years went by and his interest in investment intensified. Although following a more constricted routine than before, the last part of his life, until the final, unpleasant but brief, struggle with cancer, was contented.

As a trusts lawyer should be, even if only on behalf of persons seeking advice or in the pursuit of scholarship, Professor Keeton was knowledgeable about investments. Despite living fully and in material comfort, never appearing to stint his family or himself, he generated spare resources upon which to bring his knowledge and flair to bear. George Keeton did not start with any wealth behind him, but he earned a great deal besides his academic salary. His investments, like his grafted fruit trees, prospered and also provided yet another occasion of intellectual engagement and diversion.

George Keeton was a radical. That is not to say he was a man of the left. Politically, he was probably best classified as an old fashioned liberal, leaning, if he leant, more to the conservative than to the socialist trend of opinion. He had a wide acquaintance among politicians. To his amazement, representatives of each of the three main political parties approached him to stand as a candidate for Parliament in the general election of 1945. That is evidence not of being all things to all men but of being nobody's conformist.

His thought was radical, and he was an innovator as well as a historian. It is scarcely to be expected that his books will remain for ever tools in daily use by those who work on law or history: hardly anybody's do. The journals, institutions and facilities of legal education which he established, joined in creating or inspired will have an enduring influence. What he accomplished was varied as well as large in quantity, and everything he did he did very well.

L. A. SHERIDAN

*Proceedings of the British Academy*, **80**, 349–359

# Neil Ripley Ker
# 1908–1982

NEIL RIPLEY KER was born in Brompton, London, on 28 May 1908, the only child of Robert Macneil Ker and Lucy Winifred Strickland-Constable. He was educated at home by his mother until he was ten, and then for two years at a preparatory school in Reigate before going to Eton. He was there at the same time as Francis Wormald and Roger Mynors, although each in a different house and year and so did not know them there. And only once, in his last year, was he entertained to dinner by the Provost, M. R. James, whom he greatly admired but whose work as a medievalist he was then unaware of. He went quite often to the College Library in the hour or two a week it was open to the boys and did not remember seeing any manuscript books on exhibition, only documents, but with the printed books 'we could just browse on the shelves, which was heaven'.[1]

In 1927 he entered Magdalen College, Oxford, to read Philosophy, Politics and Economics with the idea of a career in the Foreign Office, but, on the advice of C. S. Lewis, changed to English Language and Literature, in which he obtained a second-class degree in 1931. His interest in manuscripts had already begun as an undergraduate (when he is said to have chosen to read Old and Middle English texts in that form): 'The Laudian collection was my first love in Bodley. I can still remember browsing through the catalogue and the Summary Catalogue addenda about 1929–30 (?) and the sort of romantic aura there was about "Jesuits of Würzburg", that especially for some reason'.[2] And in 1929–30 he had attended the classes of E. A. Lowe

[1] Letter to T. J. Brown, 29 July 1972, from Professor Brown's papers in the Department of Palaeography, King's College, London, made available to me by Miss S. Dormer; quoted by kind permission of Mrs Jean Ker, like subsequent extracts from his correspondence.
[2] Letter to R. W. Hunt, 10 June 1974, from Hunt papers, Bodleian Library, Oxford, made available by Dr B. Barker-Benfield.

N. R. KER

*Professor K. D. Hartzell*

in palaeography.[3] His B. Litt., 1933, guided by Kenneth Sisam, and influenced by his belief that study of the manuscripts offered new prospects for Anglo-Saxon studies, was on the additions and alterations in Bodley MSS 340 and 342 of Aelfric's homilies. Having failed to get a Research Fellowship at Magdalen in 1934 and spent some time at the family home near Glasgow and looking at (and being allowed to foliate) manuscripts in the University Library there, he was asked in 1935 by the Oxford English Faculty to give regular lectures on Anglo-Saxon manuscripts.[4] By 1937 he had begun the comprehensive catalogue of ones containing Old English which was to be published eventually in 1957, dedicated to Sisam, whose long encouragement he specially acknowledged.[5] In 1938-9 he made three tours of continental libraries for the purpose (in the course of which he met Berhard Bischoff in Brussels) and had intended to go to the U.S.A. for the same purpose in September 1939, but was prevented by the war, not getting there till 1968-9.[6]

Meanwhile he had become involved, together with R. W. Hunt, J. R. Liddell and R. A. B. Mynors, in the scheme of publishing lists of all books known to survive from medieval British institutional libraries, and of their catalogues, got off the ground by C. R. Cheney in November 1937. Ker already had, like the others (whose relationships in this matter have been well described by Sir Richard Southern),[7] a collection of such identifications and had also 'been through a good many sale catalogues'. Initially it appears he provided somewhat fewer entries (3-400) than each of the other three (Cheney 6-700), Mynors most of all (1200), but when the latter declined the general editorship and he and Cheney were taken for war service in 1940, Ker rather reluctantly accepted the responsibility.[8] When however Cheney wrote to him in 1941 approving the draft preface and suggesting the title *Medieval Libraries of Great Britain* he said that it was the unanimous opinion of the collaborators that Ker's name alone, under which it has since been known, should stand on the title-page: 'you have done so much more actual research than any others of us and you have had most of the burden

---

[3] Record reported by Professor R. J. Dean via Dr M. B. Parkes, from Lowe papers, Pierpont Morgan Library, New York.

[4] Letters to R. W. Hunt, 28 October 1934, 5 November 1934, 5 June 1935, 29 October 1935.

[5] See also his memoir of Sisam, *P. B. A.* 58 (1972), 409-28, esp. 413-14, 420.

[6] Letters to R. W. Hunt, 1937-9.

[7] Memoir of R. W. Hunt, *P. B. A.* 67 (1981), 371-97.

[8] Letters from C. R. Cheney to R. W. Hunt, 12, 18 November 1937, Hunt papers; letters from Hunt to Cheney, 14, 30 November 1937, presumably passed by Cheney to Ker, in box on origins of *MLGB* assembled by the latter, Ker papers, Bodleian Library, made available by Professor A. G. Watson.

of the final editing'.[9] And although they and others went on to contribute corrigenda and addenda for the master file of cards, housed in the Bodleian Library, it was under Ker's prime care and it was by him that the second edition in 1964 was greatly enlarged, including now the extant holdings of cathedral and college libraries, and a digest and index of persons connected with the medieval acquisitions (as desired by Cheney in 1940); he also prepared most of the supplement, completed by Andrew Watson, which came out posthumously in 1987. Nevertheless he was unhappy as late as 1974 'about the card index . . . being called Mr Ker's', and particularly about Cheney's original share not having been made clear enough in the later edition.[10] It was this work of a very happy convergence of interests and talents in Oxford in the 1930s and a remarkably rapid compilation steered to press by Cheney (as Literary Director of the Royal Historical Society) that has not unjustly made Ker's name most widely known, long envied and more recently emulated in other parts of Europe.[11] With future supplements and no doubt eventual reissues, if the studies it condenses continue to flourish, it will always be an indispensable guide to the evidence for intellectual and artistic history, when used in the ways he indicated.

In 1941 he had been formally appointed Lecturer in Palaeography and although in 1942 he was registered as a conscientious objector and directed to full-time work as a porter at the Radcliffe Infirmary (which he enjoyed except for night duty), he was nevertheless able to get on with a few of his own studies, publishing a number of notes and articles on various subjects, and even hoped to do his lecturing 'if I have any pupils', though he also helped to prepare other pacifists for their tribunals.[12] During the war years he was also able to visit some provincial libraries, such as Worcester Cathedral,[13] Ushaw College and Downside Abbey, and to 'spend what spare time I have' on descriptions of the Magdalen medieval manuscripts, where he gradually developed his methods and criteria: 'I've learnt that all manuscripts need looking at in the way that Lowe has looked at the oldest manuscripts, with due attention to the pricking, ruling, etc., and that a small book needs to be written on the subject'.[14] Though he himself regrettably never carried out the last notion, apart from making an

[9] Cheney to Ker, 1 April 1941, Ker papers.

[10] Ker to Hunt, 14 April 1974, Hunt papers.

[11] E.g. E. Van Balberghe *et al.*, 'Medieval Libraries of Belgium', *Scriptorium* 26 (1972), 348–57; 27 (1973), 102–6; 28 (1974), 103–9; S. Krämer, *Handschriftenerbe des Deutschen Mittelalters*, Mittelalterliche Bibliothekskataloge Deutschlands und der Schweiz, Ergänzungsband I, 2 vols (Munich, 1989).

[12] Ker to Hunt, 4 October 1942, 2 July 1943, Hunt papers.

[13] Ker to Hunt, 15 February 1941: at Worcester 'I saw about 180 manuscripts in three days'.

[14] Ker to Hunt, 16 January 1944, and list July 1944.

unpublished list of periods of changing practices, from the beginning of the twelfth century to the fifteenth, which he must have used in his teaching, the introduction to his *Catalogue of Manuscripts containing Anglo-Saxon* (1957) has a masterly account for its centuries, many such observations occur in *English Manuscripts in the Century after the Norman Conquest* (1960), some are found in the introduction to *Medieval Manuscripts in British Libraries*, volume 1 (1969), and many are indicated in the facsimiles and editions to which he contributed palaeographical matter, as well as in individual articles, notably that on above and below top line (1960), the findings of which have recently been freshly and more extensively vindicated.[15]

It was also during the war that he followed up Mr James Fairhurst's discovery, amongst the remains of John Selden's and Sir Matthew Hales's collections, of Patrick Young's, James I's librarian's, catalogues of the manuscripts of five cathedral libraries, of which Ker edited three, enabling him to identify additional items from their medieval collections and to trace the occasions and agents of losses; and the whole area of early post-medieval ownership of manuscripts was one (led by M. R. James) which he developed in showing the value of, in specific cases, such as those now at Antwerp, Thomas Allen's, Sir John Prise's and others.

In 1945 he was elected a Fellow of Magdalen and in 1946 he succeeded Lowe and Denholm-Young as Reader in Palaeography. Besides manuscripts of the Anglo-Saxon period he normally gave classes on writing in England from 1100 to the sixteenth century and on the description of manuscript books, leaving other Latin topics to Richard Hunt as a part-time lecturer besides being Keeper of Western Manuscripts in the Bodleian Library. Ker's modesty of manner meant that as a teacher he was most effective by example, and as much through influence on people who had never sat in his classes but who asked him about particular manuscripts or read with attention what he wrote.[16] When questioned he was usually reluctant to risk generalisation, except by way of report on his own experience, but what emerged from his acute and systematic observations has frequently more than narrow applicability.

His interest and expertise were not primarily in script, despite his very sharp eye and memory for its details, but in the ensemble of evidence about the making and history of medieval manuscript books, effectually

---

[15] M. Palma, 'Modifiche di alcuni aspetti materiali della produzione libraria latina nei secoli XII e XIII', *Scrittura e Civiltà* 12 (1988), 119–33. The comments by Jacques Lemaire, *Introduction à la codicologie* (Louvain-la-Neuve, 1989), pp. 164–5, concerning earlier and later occurrences, miss the limits of Ker's observations.

[16] The present writer cannot speak at first hand of his official teaching, only of a single seminar and a lecture (that published on cathedral libraries), which was very well received.

codicology, before the word was invented or imported.[17] Nonetheless in the field of pure palaeography he made without fuss specific advances ranging from the late ninth to the fifteenth century, and was adept in demonstrating crucial scribal identities in diverse conditions (e.g. Aldred, 1943, and William of Malmesbury, 1944). His establishment of the term 'anglicana' (with medieval precedent) for the traditional English cursive script of the thirteenth to fifteenth centuries, after a period when he had used the ambiguous 'chancery' for it (in private notes), was affected by growing awareness of the continental discussions of nomenclature, through the Comité International de Paléographie, of which he became a member;[18] yet, like his complementary naming of the competing late fourteenth- and fifteenth-century 'secretary' script (from its Tudor descendant), it was chiefly from the wish to characterise more distinctly the types and mixtures of writing he found in the late medieval books he wanted to catalogue.[19] Similarly, he decided it was desirable, in order to avoid ambiguity, to refine his form of stating broadly mid-century dates from that (s. xiii) in the first edition (1941) to that (s. xiii med.) in the second (1964) of *Medieval Libraries*.[20]

During the war, as a result of his work for *Medieval Libraries*, he had got to know the book-collector J. P. R. Lyell, who at his death in 1949 left 100 of his medieval manuscripts to the Bodleian Library and an endowment for an annual Readership in Bibliography at Oxford, of which in 1952–3 Ker was the first holder. The first lecture, by the donor's wish, was on Lyell's collection (published in the introduction to the catalogue of the Lyell manuscripts by Albinia de la Mare in 1971), and the remainder appeared as *English Manuscripts in the Century after the Norman Conquest* (1960). This was perhaps his most discursive work; hearers and readers may, like the present writer, have wished that it had been longer, revealing even more of his perceptions and reflections about books produced in that era.

His intimate knowledge of Oxford libraries, and that not simply of material in Oxford, was shown in an innovatory work, *Pastedowns in Oxford Bindings* (1954), which both identifies over two thousand fragments of medieval manuscripts (some of copies recorded in early catalogues),

---

[17] The French term is said to have been introduced by A. Dain, *Les Manuscrits* (Paris, 1949), in a more restricted sense than its later usage; the first instance in English in the Supplement (1972) to the Oxford English Dictionary is of 1953.

[18] G. Battelli *et al.*, *Nomenclature des écritures livresques du 9e au 16e siècle* (Paris, 1954).

[19] *Medieval Manuscripts in British Libraries*, I (Oxford, 1969), xi–xii, II (1977), vi; elaborated by M. B. Parkes in an Oxford B. Litt. thesis and *English Cursive Book Hands* (Oxford, 1969), pp. xiv–xxiv.

[20] This of course could hardly apply to datings he had not reviewed in the interval and, out of step, the older form is used in *MMBL*, I (1969), vii, much of the work for which however had been done in the earlier 1960s; for the revised form see II (1977), vii, III (1983), vii.

utilised by Oxford binders in the sixteenth and early seventeenth centuries, and dates and groups the tools they used and the colleges they worked for, with ample indexes; it was soon followed by the Sandars Lectures at Cambridge in 1955 on 'Oxford College Libraries in the Sixteenth Century' (not published till 1959) and an exhibition with a catalogue, 1956, on Oxford College Libraries in 1556; later came *Records of All Souls College Library* (1971) and posthumously 'The Provision of Books' in the History of the University, volume III, on the sixteenth century (1986). He was intended to contribute the parallel chapter to volume II, on the middle ages, a task taken over by M. B. Parkes after his death, but he already had drawn up, as a piece of the ordered documentation on which all his work is based, a chronological list of cautions, notes of book pledges in loan chests, incorporating contributions from Graham Pollard (with whom over the years he exchanged much other information on the university book-trade), which should be published eventually.[21] He also left notes on early sixteenth-century Cambridge bindings which have manuscript pastedowns. The results of his regular rubbing of early English blind-stamped bindings wherever he came across them, and any evidence of their provenance, had long been communicated to J. B. Oldham, and names of graduate book-owners to A. B. Emden, to the benefit of their respective publications.[22] And the significance of other binding details (such as marks of chaining) in relation to provenance is just one of the aspects he drew attention to in a number of articles and catalogues.

The *Catalogue of Manuscripts containing Anglo-Saxon* (1957), and a *Supplement* (1976) reissued with it (1990), definitively replaced the corresponding portion of the survey by Humfrey Wanley in the *Catalogus Librorum Septentrionalium* (1705), for which Ker had great esteem, but added many more items, describing most of them minutely at first hand, with full notice of previous discussions and editions, and relating them to each other, contemporary charters (excluded from the catalogue) and wholly Latin codices. One may now overlook how greatly this stout volume, with its packed introduction and elaborate index, transformed the palaeography and codicology of the field and promoted further research.[23]

From a very early stage in his career Ker seems to have resolved to see all the medieval manuscript books in British repositories outside the major centres, and any printed books which could have evidence of

---

[21] Bodleian Library, Ker papers.

[22] J. B. Oldham, *English Blind-Stamped Bindings* (Cambridge, 1952); *Blind Panels of English Binders* (1958); A. B. Emden, *A Biographical Register of the University of Oxford to A. D. 1500*, 3 vols (Oxford, 1957); *1501–40* (1974); *Cambridge* (1963).

[23] Evidence may be seen in the Supplement (1976) and the annual bibliography of *Anglo-Saxon England*.

fifteenth- or sixteenth-century British ownership, including early bindings, which meant constant journeying throughout his life. From this as a by-product came much of the information in the influential report on *The Parochial Libraries of the Church of England* (1959). By 1960 he was already engaged on cataloguing in London libraries for his last and largest enterprise, *Medieval Manuscripts in British Libraries*, intended to deal with all institutional collections not yet adequately described in print, with the exception of the British Library, the Bodleian, Cambridge University Library and a few others for which separate catalogues were known to be in preparation. The first volume, for London, appeared in 1969, the year after he took early retirement from Oxford in order to concentrate on this work. The second volume, Abbotsford – Keele, came out in 1977; in 1982, when he had completed all but the introduction of the third, Lampeter – Oxford, he anticipated that the remainder might take a further five years. Volume 3, then in proof, finished by his literary executor Andrew Watson, appeared in 1983, and volume 4, Paisley – York, for which Ker's drafts were all checked with the manuscripts and augmented, and descriptions for Parkminster and some in other places done *ab initio*, by A. J. Piper, has been published in 1992. Although adopted by the Manuscripts Sub-Committee of the Standing Conference of National and University Libraries, it was done entirely at Ker's own initiative and largely at his expense, including heavy subsidies for the printing of the first two volumes, though the Committee obtained British Library and Academy grants towards the third and fourth. Indexing of this huge assemblage of information still remains to be done, an urgent need of users all over the world, for the contents are as much European in origin as British, and deserves to be done as well as the compiler himself would have done it or seen it done. As Julian Brown said in a moving memorial address, Ker's bent, from his first publications, as a schoolboy, of churchyard gravestones, was to catalogue, as faithfully as possible, what he saw, while he showed in it fresh patterns of significance. It would be more difficult to draw these out of the miscellaneous matter of his last great work than from the coherent categories of his other catalogues, but he certainly would have been able to point to instructive instances of contrasting practices in different places and centuries, and varieties of format in relation to custom and function, in his quiet way.

In a work of such a wide reach, carried out over twenty years and in diverse conditions, published in instalments, there will be inevitably some inconsistencies, unconscious and conscious, as he learned more and adapted his methods, and possibly some failures to cite relevant literature, although Ker went back everywhere to check and fill out his first descriptions, in the light of researches he had to pursue elsewhere:

'I am bad at getting to the point where I don't need to see a described manuscript again'.[24] Many of the manuscripts included were of foreign origin, some of types with which previously he had not many dealings, and with texts or annotations in difficult hands and spellings, but he usually knew when and where to get help with them. Despite his remarkable visual memory, and his meticulous description of the details of the hierarchy of decoration, he explicitly limited his listing of illustration,[25] and generally avoided giving stylistic judgements related to region and period of origin, unless cited from another authority. This was presumably deliberate in an area where, surprisingly, he did not feel confident of his own assessment or realise the sorts of help enquirers want. More understandably he eschewed venturing on watermark identification before the techniques had been more fully developed. And over his whole career he concentrated on manuscript books, not documents (significantly having declined F. M. Powicke's suggestion of succeeding Cheney as Reader in Diplomatic in 1945), though he did not hesitate to discuss their contents and forms if apposite, and to use telling evidence from the content of archives.

His correspondence grew as his publications and the range of his expertise became gradually known throughout the world, and his readiness to reply rapidly and helpfully. Indeed he frequently took the initiative: as Sir Richard Southern writes, 'he remembered what everyone was doing and sent abrupt little notes about any discoveries he had made that would help; I imagine he did this for scores of people'.[26] There was however nothing abrupt in the following-up and continuing relationships. One looked forward keenly to what one would learn from his letters and visits. Acknowledgments to him appear in innumerable prefaces, introductions and footnotes. More than one obituarist remembered his Sunday mornings devoted to letter-writing and remarked on his personal approachability by young students and foreign scholars. His usual informality of dress and manner went with the happy division of his time and attention between lecture room, libraries and study on the one hand, and family and outdoor activities on the other. On a visit of more than a night to a place with manuscripts he would try to fit in afternoon or evening walks as he did at home, and he travelled with very simple luggage, though often burdened with annotated copies of crucial books. As an undergraduate he had been President of the University Mountaineering Club and he continued to resort to Switzerland and Scotland (where there were family homes), eventually retiring to the latter, and by a sad aptness it was on a walk there with his

---

[24] Letter to T. J. Brown, 21 July 1973, Brown papers, Department of Palaeography, King's College, London.
[25] *MMBL*, I, xii–xiii; cf. M. R. James's lengthy lists.
[26] Letter to present writer, 8 January 1991.

wife, looking for bilberries, that he had his fatal fall, on 23 August 1982, in the midst of undiminished activity of mind and hand.

He had a remarkable capacity for switching from and back to unperturbed concentration on a task, to produce systematic and accurate, if at first sight untidy, notes, transcripts or typing. Although disinclined to some forms of sociability and academic life, he rarely betrayed it, was extremely unwilling to criticise other people, and took a due share of college responsibilities. He was Librarian of Magdalen, succeeding C. T. Onions, from 1956 to 1968, but already active in cataloguing its manuscripts and assisting enquirers, and he was Vice-President in 1962–3, playing his part in college business and entertaining guests at High Table then, as at other times, very conscientiously and kindlily. He was a Curator of the Bodleian Library from 1949, and a member of the Standing Committee from 1960 (meeting fortnightly), until 1968, a length of service reflecting the value of his interest and support, as a long and constant reader, college librarian and frequent benefactor. It was not only the Bodleian but also other libraries and archives outside Oxford to which he gave books and documents and offered timely sums towards purchases thought particularly suitable, and through Bodley he helped institutions lacking their own facilities to get manuscripts and bindings repaired. He also served in the 1960s and 1970s on the Sub-Committee on Manuscripts of SCONUL, which besides making representations on such questions as export controls and arranging training seminars and conferences, took on the sponsorship of *Medieval Manuscripts in British Libraries* and the catalogues of dated manuscripts in Britain for the Comité International de Paléographie, of which the other British members sat on the Sub-Committee, under the chairmanship of Richard Hunt. Ker himself became the first chairman of the British Academy's Corpus of British Medieval Library Catalogues when it was eventually established in 1979, forty-eight years after the first notion of it was voiced by Roger Mynors, though the first volume did not appear until after both their deaths, in 1990. He was a Vice-President of the Bibliographical Society from 1966 till his death but declined the Presidency when it was his turn because of his removal to Scotland and wish to concentrate on *MMBL*. It was a handsome gift of money from him in 1977 that helped to revive the union catalogue of printed books up to 1700 in the cathedral libraries of England and Wales begun by Miss M. S. G. Hands in 1944, of which the first volume was published in 1984 and the second may appear in 1993.

The distinction of his work was recognised by his election as Fellow of the British Academy, 1958, a Corresponding Fellow of the Mediaeval Academy of America, 1971, and of the Bavarian Academy in 1977, conferment of honorary doctorates at Reading, 1964, Leiden, 1972, and Cambridge, 1975, the Israel Gollancz Memorial Prize of the British Academy, 1959, the Gold Medal of the Bibliographical Society, 1975, and the C.B.E., 1979. Friends and pupils presented him with a Festschrift in 1978[27] and after his death an appeal (to which besides friends and pupils his family contributed generously) has provided a permanent endowment for a Memorial Fund administered by the British Academy giving grants annually to assist research, travel and publication concerning medieval manuscripts, especially ones connected with the British Isles.

In 1938 he married his second cousin, Jean Frances, daughter of Brigadier Charles Bannatyne Findlay; she survives him, with a son and three daughters. Many British and foreign scholars enjoyed their hospitality in Oxford, at Kirtlington, in Edinburgh and Perthshire, and other kindnesses.

It is not easy to write a wholly fresh memoir after a lapse of nine years, since a number of admirable obituaries appeared then which cannot now be bettered in expressing the professional and personal characteristics of the subject, one of which may most appropriately be quoted: 'It is no exaggeration to say that in the field of medieval manuscripts he was the greatest scholar that Britain has ever produced. His output matched that of M. R. James in volume and far surpassed it in authoritative precision'.[28]

There can be few scholars who have done more enduring work and merited more gratitude.

A. I. DOYLE
*Fellow of the British Academy*

---

[27] *Medieval Scribes, Manuscripts and Libraries*, ed. M. B. Parkes & A. G. Watson (London, 1978): includes a list of his publications pp. 371–9; supplement in the selection of his essays, *Books, Collectors and Libraries: Studies in the Medieval Heritage*, ed. A. G. Watson (London, 1985), pp. xiii–xiv.

[28] [B. Barker-Benfield] *Bodleian Library Record*, vol. 11, no. 2, May 1983, pp. 64–5; in fairness it may be noted that though the list of M. R. James's publications is shorter than Ker's, he must have catalogued at least twice as many books, and he published more than as much again on other subjects. The other obituaries I have seen are: [G. R. C. Davis] *The Times*, 25 August 1982; T. J. Brown, Address at memorial service, 13 November 1982, edition of 300 copies, Glendale (California), May 1983, also (with errors) in *Magdalen College Record*, 1983, pp. 35–40; P. Robinson, *Mediaeval English Studies Newsletter* (Tokyo), no. 7, December 1982, pp. 1–2; [A. I. Doyle] *The Library*, 6th series, vol. 5, no. 1, March 1983, pp. 171–3; C. R. Cheney, *Archives*, vol. 16, no. 9, April 1983, pp. 86–7; R. J. Dean, P. J. Meyvaert, J. C. Pope, R. H. Rouse, *Speculum*, vol. 58, no. 3, July 1983, pp. 870–2; H. Gneuss, *Jahrbuch der Bayerischen Akademie der Wissenschaften*, 1983; T. Webber, *Dictionary of National Biography 1981–85* (Oxford, 1990), pp. 221–2. Besides friends mentioned here and in notes above my thanks are also owing to Dr G. L. Harriss and several others I have consulted.

*Proceedings of the British Academy*, **80**, 361–370

# Russell Meiggs
# 1902–1989

RUSSELL MEIGGS' last book, *Trees and Timber in the Ancient Mediterranean World*, is dedicated to the memory of his grandfather John and his great-uncle Henry, 'timber merchants in New York State'. The family, originally from Dorset, had been established in America since the seventeenth century. Henry, born in 1811, joined the movement to California in 1849, but to establish sawmills, not to search for gold. Being skilful, vigorous, enterprising and persuasive, he rapidly achieved distinction in San Francisco and after a few years there ran for Mayor. Unfortunately, he overreached himself financially, and arrived in Chile in 1854 as a fugitive from Californian justice. He made a fresh fortune in Peru, displaying a genius for engineering management, notably in the Trans-Andean railway, the highest point of which runs under a mountain still called Mount Meiggs. His younger brother, to whom the *Dictionary of American Biography*, in two columns devoted to Henry, does not do justice, had joined his enterprise in San Francisco (but without falling foul of the law) and joined him later in Peru, where (as contemporary documents show) his exceptional managerial and financial talent was greatly respected. About the time of Henry's death John moved to London, where he enjoyed great wealth, was highly regarded in English society, and set up a company for railway-building in Argentina. Political events there wrecked this enterprise, and John died almost destitute, having sacrificed everything in the interests of his creditors.

His son William Meiggs, the fourth of his nine children, eloped in 1897 with Mary May to Argentina. Their first child, Helen, was born in Buenos Aires the following year, but they were in London by 1902, when Russell was born. There was no inheritance from John. If William had employment, it did not last long; nor did his association with his family, for he was back in

R. MEIGGS

Argentina by 1904. From there he sent postcards signed 'Uncle Willy'. It seems likely that Russell as a child was led to believe that his father was dead; William did not in fact die until 1939 (in England), but Russell felt no obligation towards him. Mary brought up her children in poverty, but William's elder sister secured a place for Russell at Christ's Hospital.

He said later in life that he 'owed everything' to Christ's Hospital. The headmaster from 1919 to 1930 was Sir William Hamilton Fyfe, who, like Meiggs, had been brought up in poverty by his mother. Fyfe was a committed Christian, all his life a giver and not a taker, a breaker of barriers between classes and ages, combining a strong sense of duty with a considerable sense of humour and an alarmingly sane disrespect for convention. His influence on Meiggs was profound; he was in fact a splendid substitute for an unsatisfactory father, and their friendship endured until Fyfe's death in 1965. Meiggs, an all-rounder, became Head Grecian and Head Boy, and won an exhibition to Keble. There followed the predictable Firsts in Mods and Greats, and in 1925 the Pelham Studentship at the British School in Rome. He remained an all-rounder, and displayed his talents as actor and producer in the Keble Players; and through the long friendship with Leslie Banks which was rooted in that activity he kept in touch for many years with the theatrical world.

After Rome he taught for two years at Christ's Hospital, but returned to Keble as a tutor in 1928. He was elected to a fellowship in 1930 and was Dean from 1935 to 1939. While he was at Keble he edited the *Oxford Magazine*, visited the Soviet Union, and went to the United States to raise support for the Keble appeal. His unique combination of candour, firmness and kindness, and the speed and penetration of his thinking, whether it was applied to historical problems, contemporary political situations or delinquent undergraduates, made a profound impression on senior and junior members of the college. He maintained that 'teaching is a branch of the acting profession'; and if more dons of the 1930s had taken the proposition seriously, their teaching would have been a good deal better than it was.

In 1938 he was invited by Balliol to take over from Duncan Macgregor (who as a tutor was fading out) some of their Ancient History teaching for Greats. Balliol thought so well of him that in the following year they offered him a tutorial fellowship, and he accepted it. Nowadays it would be unusual for a fellow to move from his own college to a position of the same category at another college, but at that time Keble was used to it; H. M. D. Parker, Meiggs' own tutor in Ancient History, had made a similar move to Magdalen in 1927. What chiefly determined Meiggs' move was that at Balliol he would no longer have any significant degree of responsibility for the Pass

School, which at Keble, he felt, had taken up an inordinate amount of his time.

Early in 1940 he was recruited by the Ministry of Supply and became Chief Labour Officer in the department concerned with the production of timber. One consequence of that period was a thorough knowledge of trees and the techniques of those who turn them into timber; a second was a book little known in the Classical world, *Home Timber Production* 1939–1945 (London 1949); the third, and most important, was his marriage in 1941 to the historian Pauline Gregg. They were both at Warwick in the Ministry of Supply, both devoted some of their spare time to amateur theatricals, and they first met when she was playing Elizabeth Barrett and he Robert Browning.

As Praefectus of Holywell Manor from 1945 until his retirement from his fellowship in 1969 he got to know generations of research students at Balliol, irrespective of subject. Wherever one goes in the world, one has a good chance of meeting people who remember the Meiggses with great affection. He lived up to the standards of the very best 'housemaster' dons of the previous generation, and in that respect he earned a reputation as an 'archetypal don'. Academically, though, he improved greatly on the archetype; neither his teaching nor his research was cast in the traditional mould, because his intellect was both restless and resolute.

New pupils found his appearance formidable on first acquaintance; a mane of long hair (many years before it became fashionable, and regarded with great disapproval by some of his more conventional colleagues at Balliol), a complexion which suggested many seasons of baking and desiccation under a desert sun, bushy eyebrows, craggy features and thin lips gave an impression which was reinforced by an incisive way of speaking, and the subtle inclination of the mouth which betrayed that he was smiling was not easily observed until one got to know him better. His criticisms of imperfect work were sharp, and could sometimes be wounding when they were meant to be cheerful and jocular. He pushed pupils to their limits, but he was a very good judge of what an individual's limit was, and he did not try to push past it. With those who had been away from academic work for four or five years he was merciless, and in that he was quite right; it would have been very bad for us if such excuses had been allowed, and we recognised, when we stopped to think, that in teaching one period of Greek history and two of Roman he had far more to catch up with than we had. Anyone in real trouble found him patient, sympathetic and generous with good, practical advice. It was characteristic of his tutorials that he compelled us to ask awkward questions to which neither the sources nor the secondary literature gave direct answers, and always to think of the Greeks and Romans—whether eminent politicians or anonymous stonecutters and sailors—not as chessmen to be moved around in an intellectual game but as real people dealing with real predicaments. His prodding was sometimes facetious ('How did they get enough ostraka for an ostracism? Did you break up the jerry before you went to the assembly, or what?'), sometimes more emotional, as when he expressed his admiration for the self-discipline which made transaction of business by a very large citizen-assembly possible.

The years immediately after the War were years of peculiar excitement in Greek history. The first volume of the *Athenian Tribute Lists* had been published in 1939 and the first volume of Gomme's *Historical Commentary in Thucydides* in 1945 (Gomme describes it in his preface as 'virtually a 1939 book', but he took full account of *Athenian Tribute Lists*). Meiggs' experience at Ostia strongly inclined him to put documentary inscriptions at the very heart of historical studies and then to see how far the literary 'authorities' could be reconciled with them—he was not among those who grumbled 'the tribute-lists haven't really told us anything we couldn't learn from Thucydides'—though the relative paucity of material makes that a harder approach for the Greek historian than for the Roman. He was University Lecturer in Greek Epigraphy from 1949, the year of Marcus Tod's retirement, to 1957, and his skill and judgment in the handling of inscriptions were strongly reflected in his teaching.

Three projects in which he took a large share were designed primarily with the needs of students in view. The first was the revision of J. B. Bury's *History of Greece*, the second edition of which dated to 1922 but was still the standard one-volume Greek history used by sixth-formers and students. For the new edition (1951) Meiggs had to work under the severe constraint of retaining the original pagination, but for the fourth edition, which appeared in 1975, the publishers agreed to a new format, and Meiggs was able to rewrite substantial portions, shifting emphases and inserting material which was not, and in some cases could not be, appreciated in Bury's time—for example, the tribute assessment of 425. Sir George Hill's *Sources for Greek History, B.C. 478–431* (Oxford 1897, 2nd ed. 1907), another standby of undergraduates reading Greats, needed not only substantial expansion on the documentary side but reconsideration of its selection of excerpts from literature. Meiggs produced a new *Sources* in collaboration with Anthony Andrewes. It still bore the name of Hill on its spine, but the literary sources were rearranged, the epigraphic portion was transformed, and five massive indexes divided into sections and subsections provided a panorama of the Pentekontaetia in which users can quickly spot the precise topics of their choice. The rate at which new inscriptions of importance were being discovered made a revision of Marcus Tod's *Selection of Greek Inscriptions to the End of the Fifth Century*

*B.C.* (Oxford 1933; reissued with an appendix, 1947) an urgent necessity, and Meiggs and David Lewis did this in collaboration. Their new *GHI*, published in 1969 (second edition, 1989), contained, out of a total of 95 documents, 22 which had not been in Tod, shedding in the process three long documents which are now available in *Athenian Tribute-Lists* and a few from which nothing could be learned except that some people well known from literature had really existed. No less than half the new items had been found since Tod's original publication.

One product of Meiggs' epigraphical interests was a magisterial article, 'The Dating of Fifth-Century Attic Inscriptions', (*Journal of Hellenic Studies* lxxxvi [1966]). It had been vigorously argued, particularly by Professor Mattingly, that the generally accepted dating of Attic documents had relied far too much on a dogma that the three-barred sigma gave way completely to the four-barred at a point in time in the mid-440s. In his article Meiggs catalogued the forms of β, ρ, σ and φ attested in inscriptions which are securely dated on other grounds, adding a list of those which are not so dated but contain letter-forms which are putatively early. He was in no way hastening to the defence of a dogma, because he recognised that where many stone-cutters are concerned we cannot expect letter-forms to change universally and irreversibly overnight, but presenting the evidence as a basis for the assessment of probabilities, and he showed how enthusiasm for the revision of accepted chronology could lead to the adoption of a later historical context for a document when an earlier context is at least equally plausible and in some cases demonstrably more so. In an appendix he points out the superficiality of Sir Moses Finley's criticism of historians for their preoccupation with 'the date when the Athenian stone-cutters began to carve the letter sigma with four bars instead of three'. The issue is in fact vital to the reconstruction of the history of Athenian imperialism, and 'Finley has made a molehill out of a mountain'. Meiggs would have understood, and possibly Finley would not, how and why laborious dissection of small fossils from the Burgess Shale matters to evolutionary biology.

During his year at Rome as Pelham Student his imagination was captured by Ostia. He made several further visits before the War, and by 1940 had prepared a short book about it; but he dropped this project during the busy years immediately after the War, resumed it in 1951, and paid many further visits to Ostia, where his talent, integrity and warmth of personality made friends of all those concerned with the site. By then he had a much more comprehensive book in mind. *Roman Ostia*, which was published by the Clarendon Press in 1960, is undoubtedly his greatest book. It was unanimously acclaimed in the reviews (except for one in *Classical Philology*, written from the standpoint of a social historian who deplored the 'lack of organization' in what Herbert Bloch, whose own experience of Ostia put him in a good position to judge, praised as 'excellent organization'), although Meiggs' decision not to include a folding map was no less universally regretted. Bloch thought the book a 'masterpiece', and Jocelyn Toynbee called it 'an object-lesson in ancient history'. Although there was plainly much more of Ostia to be excavated and much more to be found out about it (as proved to be the case at the end of the 1950s), the most systematic campaign of excavation had been completed in 1942, by which time two thirds of the town had been exposed and the interest of the Italian directors had rightly shifted to interpretation and conservation. *Roman Ostia* was the right book at the right time. A new edition appeared in 1972, in which many points in the original edition were amplified in the light of new data, particularly new inscriptions, and the most significant revision was owed to the accidental discovery, in the course of roadworks for the airport at Fiumicino, of a substantial synagogue, which overturned Meiggs' conclusion (justified on the evidence available in 1960) that there was no Jewish community at Ostia. His style was plain, muscular and vivid. His task demanded equal competence in the handling of many different types of evidence. What makes *Roman Ostia* 'an object-lesson in ancient history' is the clarity with which it describes historical change, the acumen displayed in the choice of relevant data, and conciseness in explaining their relevance. These qualities are especially notable in the chapters which deal with the archaeology of the Claudian and Trajanic harbours, the analysis of the governing class, the operation of the guilds (emphasising that they were combinations of employers and not analogous to trades unions), the process by which Christianity came to predominate in the course of the fourth century AD, changes in artistic taste, and the gradual shift of population and prosperity from Ostia itself to Portus.

A shorter book on Ostia, designed for a series entitled 'Ancient Sites', exists in typescript; the publisher abandoned the series, but Meiggs' book, with a certain amount of editing and up-dating, may yet appear.

He began work in 1961 on *The Athenian Empire*, which was published in 1972. It is hard for anyone whose enthusiasm for fifth-century Greek history was aroused by reading Greats in the Post-War years to open the book anywhere without a pang of nostalgia; but perhaps that is not entirely a good thing. It is an unhappy fact that neither *Journal of Hellenic Studies* nor *Classical Review* reviewed the book (though both acknowledged receipt of a copy). Conceivably potential reviewers felt that it was an old-fashioned book and would have found it embarrassing to say so. Certainly the reference on the first page to 'the unrivalled authority of Thucydides', and phrases such as 'the best tradition says . . .', 'our earliest authorities . . .' and '[had this occurred] he must have mentioned it' are out of keeping with attitudes to ancient historiography which were taking shape by then. Chapters 21 and 22, on how the empire was regarded in the fifth and fourth centuries, are sound enough on the issues which ancient sources themselves thrust under our noses, but miss (for example) the gruesome implications of Isocrates' dismissive reference (*Panathenaicus* 70) to 'insignificant islands' and fail to probe the Funeral Speech deeply enough to uncover its exultation in aggression. He was baffled by Herodotus' evasive allusion to Kallias' mission to Persia, for which Professor Badian (*Journal of Hellenic Studies* cvii [1987] 7f.) has now provided an explanation which has very far-reaching implications for fifth-century history and historiography. If we consider *The Athenian Empire* as a 'state of the art' book on a very large subject charged from beginning to end with controversy, we may well doubt whether anyone could have done the job better than Meiggs. It is, after all, a splendidly lucid and concise presentation, simultaneously candid and courteous, and always informed by sensible judgment, of the problems and arguments at the point they had reached by 1970. There is a characteristic touch of self-deprecating humour in one entry in the index: 'Probably, *passim*'.

After retirement in 1969 he turned to a subject which originated in his years in the Ministry of Supply: timber in the ancient world. From time to time he had mentioned to friends his ambition to write a book about it one day, and *Trees and Timber in the Ancient Mediterranean World* appeared from the Clarendon Press in 1982. Wood was of such fundamental importance to the ancient world that it may seem surprising that there was a gap to be filled; but, after all, there cannot ever have been many good Classicists who had Meiggs' intimate knowledge of the qualities of different woods and the practicalities of moving great timbers from source to destination. He comprehended under 'the ancient Mediterranean world' regions as far east as Assyria, but not those west of Italy. The surviving remnants of ancient wood (often carbonized) are enough to answer some questions and create some surprises, but any attempt to give a comprehensive account of the woods used by the ancients for this purpose or that is bedevilled by semantic uncertainties. There is no general agreement on what the Egyptians meant by *aš* and *meru*, inconsistencies and regional variations in the Greek words for different kinds of oak were observed by Theophrastus, and poets (to say nothing of prose authors on unfamiliar ground) are notoriously careless of distinctions which mattered less to their original audiences than they do now to historians. Ancient cities and rulers were alive to the perils of deforestation in the areas on which they were accustomed to draw for timber, and they knew that deforested mountain-slopes are subject to landslides which expose bare rock and leave the land useless, but population growth, the corresponding demand for ever more agricultural land, and the consumption of wood in fuel and building materials brought great changes before the end of antiquity to forests which were readily accessible from cities or situated near a sea-coast. In a masterly chapter on deforestation, using illuminating evidence from medieval and modern times, Meiggs shows that goats, whose consumption of new growth has made them the villains of the story in modern tradition, are comparatively innocent; it is simply growth of population and consumption in the last two centuries to which really serious and irreversible devastation must be debited.

For a substantial part of his career Meiggs had to combat a cyclic depression which first struck early in 1946. In the depressive phase he became lethargic and apathetic, unresponsive in tutorials and faltering in giving the lectures which when he was well had so powerfully impressed audiences by their vividness and spontaneity. He was treated several times by electro-convulsive therapy; a few days after each treatment, some hidden switch in his brain was turned and he became irrepressibly active, effervescing with new (mostly good, and never unrealistic) ideas and projects—until the next occasion on which the switch was turned, in a matter of minutes, the other way. In the mid 1960s a new medication (lithium carbonate), unknown at the start of his illness, smoothed out the ups and downs into a welcome stability. The symptoms of depression are in large measure the same, no matter whom it attacks, but the characters of those who suffer its invasion are not, and Meiggs' own extraordinary strength of character not only enabled him, during the years of recurrent illness, to serve on the Hebdomadal Council and pay enjoyable visits to the University of Ibadan and Marlborough College, Vermont, but also ensured that even when deeply depressed he did not become suspicious or hostile in his dealings with other people; nor was he ever inclined to self-pity.

He was a Christian, who read the Bible daily and prayed on his knees until he was too old to kneel. In college business he was always a peacemaker, immune to the temptations of intrigue, malice and slander. He forgave readily, and was prompt in giving helpful advice (which even Lord Balogh sought from him on occasion). Yet the religious faith which underlay his treatment of his fellow humans was never allowed to obtrude; no one could ever have been less sanctimonious, and no one less likely to imagine that charity required him to praise where praise was not due. He was in fact an extremely shrewd judge of personalities and motives, and in private conversation would commonly express himself in terms which sounded cynical but lacked the essential ingredient of cynicism in that they squared with the evidence. Candour was always to be expected of him. He once told a young research fellow, 'No, you shouldn't get that job. [X] is much better than you are'. Some years later, meeting the same person, he remembered and made amends: 'I was wrong about you'. Occasionally he lapsed into the donnish habit of summing up a person as 'beta minus', but that sounded out of character. In the late 1950s, lamenting a certain lack of enthusiasm for ancient history among undergraduates reading Greats, he exclaimed 'Martin Frederiksen is the only *real* historian I've taught since the War!' (Noticing that I must have heard him, he hastily qualified the statement, but he need not have done).

In 1960 he was invited to Swarthmore College, Pennsylvania, as a Visiting Professor. The College gave him an honorary doctorate in 1971 and invited him back, after his retirement, in 1974, 1976 and 1977. He endeared himself to faculty and students alike not only by the standard he set in teaching but by his readiness to talk to anyone about anything. His colleagues' children loved him, and he evoked astonishment and admiration by rolling in deep snow, wearing only bathing-shorts (physical hardiness was one of many attributes which he shared with Bernard Ashmole). A Cedar of Lebanon was planted on the Swarthmore campus in his honour.

He had a strong belief in the handwritten letter as a bond between people, and although his letters were not easy to decipher—his handwriting looked at first sight like hasty Egyptian Demotic—they were well worth the labour of decipherment. Margery Allingham, a friend of many years, declared, 'He taught me how to write letters'. Thanks to his enjoyment of the art, he was able to keep contact with his former pupils at Swarthmore as fully as he did with his Oxford pupils.

He lived at Garsington from 1969 onwards, where his ability to insert himself into a community was quickly manifested. He had an exceptional rapport with people of all ages, and the whole village was anguished by his death. His capacity for work had been progressively reduced by immobility (an operation on one hip was reasonably successful, but the operation on the other was not) and failing eyesight (he lost one eye in an accident) and memory (he suffered a series of strokes from 1982 onwards). Yet neither his humour nor his curiosity was extinguished, and he continued to reflect on intractable problems in Herodotus long after he knew that he would not be writing any more. There are few scholars of his generation to whom so many pupils, colleagues and friends owe so much.

KENNETH DOVER
*Fellow of the British Academy*

*Note.* I am indebted for much helpful information to Mrs Meiggs, Mr Barry Williamson, and Professors A. G. Dickens, D. M. Mackinnon, Helen North and Martin Ostwald.

*Proceedings of the British Academy*, **80**, 371–401

# Roger Aubrey Baskerville Mynors
# 1903–1989

ROGER AUBREY BASKERVILLE MYNORS was born on 28 July 1903, slightly ahead of his twin brother Humphrey. Their father, Aubrey Baskerville Mynors, then rector of Langley Burrell, Wiltshire, was later secretary to the Pan-Anglican Congress held in London in 1908. The Congress was years in the preparation, and it was not until 1920 that Aubrey produced the little book that described the spending of the money it raised. But he had by then long reverted to the tranquil life of a parish priest. He died in 1937 at the age of 71.

It is conjectured that the Mynors family took its name from Les Minières not far from Breteuil-sur-Iton, south-west of Évreux. In England they can be traced back to the twelfth century, when they are associated with land at Burghill, north-west of Hereford. The connection with Treago in the same county, which Roger was to inherit, goes back at least to the fifteenth century. Humphrey's book on the family suggests no particular intellectual strain before the twentieth century, though plenty of local honour and rural sports. The more interest, therefore, attaches to Aubrey's wife, a strong personality, who came of a family of squires from Kent. She was Margery Musgrave, born in 1878 daughter to the Rev. Charles Musgrave Harvey, Prebendary of St Paul's; among her surviving brothers, all of them successful, was Sir Ernest Musgrave Harvey, Bt, who held, as Humphrey later did, the post of Deputy Governor of the Bank of England.

Roger and Humphrey had an elder sister Winifred; two further brothers were born later, and all four boys were to win open classical awards at Oxford or Cambridge. The twins were much in the country even when their father held a living in Bristol, for they spent holidays at Llanwarne in Herefordshire, where Aubrey's brother was rector, as their father had been before him, and where Aubrey and his wife are buried. Aubrey, who

R. A. B. MYNORS

had a remarkable collection of eggs, instilled a knowledge of birds, as well as of ecclesiastical architecture; an influential governess, Miss Jose, taught a love of wild flowers. Roger remembered watching the work in the smithy: he was always, he said, 'fascinated by men doing things'. But the major influence came from the clerical background on both sides of the family, and from the serene frugal life of a country vicarage, where politics was never mentioned and responsibility to parishioners was a matter of course.

The twins were very close, and remained so all their lives. They were famously alike, at least till middle age; Humphrey is said to have remarked: 'Yes, we are still very much alike, I suppose because we have both lived sheltered lives.' When they were separated by education, it is well attested that Humphrey once attended chapel at Eton in Roger's place, only the Head Master noticing; but quite untrue that Roger rode a bicycle round the Court at Marlborough, explaining, when challenged, that he was not a member of the school.

Roger, who had earlier been at Summerfields in Oxford, went to Eton as a scholar in 1916. In the same selection were J. C. S. (now Sir Steven) Runciman and Denis Dannreuther, who went on to Balliol with Roger and became a barrister and Fellow of All Souls. Junior to them were, amongst others, Robert Longden, the ancient historian, and Eric Blair, better known as George Orwell. The Eton of this period is veiled in myth, much of it purveyed by Cyril Connolly's *Enemies of Promise*. Connolly's contemporaries viewed his account with scepticism, but there seems no doubt that Dannreuther, as captain of the school, together with Longden and Mynors, brought a civilising influence to a world of 'bullying, beating, fagging [and] . . . militarism', and Roger was apparently very happy. He was no sportsman. But he got into the Lower Boats on the Fourth of June, and was twelfth man in the St Andrew's Day Wall Game in 1921: 'Has had bad luck in staying out during the greater part of the Half. Knows what to do and how to do it, and has a long reach.' In 1922, at the Fourth of June Speeches, he read from the second *Georgic*, 'most kindly and wisely using the old pronunciation'. The future was coming into focus.

Homer and Virgil were at this time the pillars of an Eton education. English was not formally taught, though it was unofficially encouraged, and when Mynors went up to Balliol the college commented on his 'really astounding knowledge of English poetry'. He later spoke of 'what so many of us inarticulately feel, the gratitude to those who taught us when we were young', but it is difficult to be sure where he felt his chief obligations lay. It is probable that the Head Master, C. A. Alington, who taught Latin to the upper forms, communicated his unusual enthusiasm for Latin written after 200 A.D. Even more important was M. R. James, who became Provost of Eton in 1918. 'This genial and amusing super-uncle', as John Lehmann described him, was a lover of P. G. Wodehouse and 'laughed his teeth out' over him. He was also, Mynors felt, rather too keen on Gilbert and Sullivan. Yet he was a leading authority on Biblical studies and on medieval manuscripts, with, at his elbow, a wonderful college collection that he had himself had the run of as a boy. He became a family friend of the Mynors. Roger was to visit him at Eton for a week in 1935 to show him some of his work on the Balliol manuscripts: 'the great man was cheerful, affectionate and communicative. What a man!' (Hunt 5.4.35). It is to be presumed that Mynors, who followed so many of his paths and was to inherit some of his books, was well known to James at Eton, went to his breakfasts, and benefited from his learning and encouragement. Certainly he must have warmed to a man who could tell boys: 'But as to knowing, finding out about things, this is the time of life when you have most chance of beginning to do that . . . There are, providentially, so many things in the world to be observed and watched and noted and collected.'

Mynors won only an exhibition to Balliol. The College wrote to Eton that 'his work was full of cleverness all through . . . We did feel that there was a lot of verbiage about him and that he would want pruning in the end'. No one ever made that complaint again; and Eton wrote a surprised reply. Soon, however, he became the first holder of the closed Robin Holloway scholarship from Eton. It was Dannreuther who got the open scholarship, just as later he was preferred at All Souls. None of this soured Mynors's affection for Balliol: 'my heart,' he wrote on election to an honorary fellowship in 1963, 'has always been, and will be, in the College, to which I owe more than I can express' (Keir 4.6.63).

He found himself in distinguished company when he went up to Balliol in 1922. In his year were, besides Dannreuther and Cyril Connolly from Eton, Jack Westrup, Robert Birley, Walter Oakeshott and Graham Greene. Older, but still in residence, were W. F. R. Hardie, Richard Pares and C. J. Fordyce. Balliol was a stronghold of the classics. Seven other Balliol men joined Mynors in the first class in Honour Moderations, six in the first class in Greats. He was Hertford Scholar in 1924, and in the same year Craven Scholar when T. B. L. Webster won the Ireland. At Balliol, as at Eton, it is unclear which teachers, if any, captured his imagination. Cyril Bailey, who taught him and was later his colleague for many years, hardly mentions him in his unpublished autobiography. Much later Mynors wrote to C. M. Bowra: 'It is you who have taught me all I know about the classics.' As to social life, one of his contemporaries writes: 'My general impression is of a man whom nobody did know very closely. I think he was on the fringe of a number of groups of which he never became wholly a part. . . . One of the things well-known about him was his "archaic smile".' He could row; and a contemporary said tartly: 'I cannot understand why

Roger Mynors can like getting drunk with rowing men.' It is possible that he played the Almighty in a Nativity Play. He was also briefly connected with the Balliol Players, and on their tour of 1923 played Cassandra in the *Agamemnon* and Mistress Ford in *Merry Wives* (Humphrey understudying Falstaff). 'Roger's Homeric laughter and his Homeric striding about the buck-basket' are recalled in the official account of the Players published in 1933.

Mynors's academic successes led to his election as a Junior Research Fellow of Balliol in 1926 and then Tutor in Classics and a full fellow a year later. He did not become a University Lecturer until 1935, but he was already by Hilary Term 1928 lecturing three times a week on the *Eclogues* and *Georgics*. Virgil dominated his lectures for fifty years, though he also treated Cicero, Juvenal, Lucretius (at Harvard), Propertius ('beastly difficult poet'), Plautus, Horace and Catullus. In his memory the years at Balliol came to seem a golden age. In one of his more public expressions of regret at his move to Cambridge, he said: 'I accepted a chair at one of our ancient universities and gave up teaching, a decision made with reluctance which (as far as the teaching goes) I have never for one moment ceased to regret.' In a private letter he wrote: 'I am hopelessly imbued with the Balliol principle that it's the working College tutor in the Oxford sense who matters' (Watt 17.11.46). But in the same letter he expresses horror at the 22 pupils taught by a Balliol classics don in 1946: 'here [in Cambridge] you would be restricted to 12 which is badly overdoing it.' Exactly how much Mynors taught in the thirties at Balliol is uncertain; but he remarked in 1935 that he had fifteen pupils, even though it was Trinity Term (when the Mods don's life was easiest). The pabulum at least is known; as at other colleges at that time, it was an unvaried diet of proses and verses (hence his remark, in sending Richard Hunt [18.4.29] his marks in Mods: 'your standard in both proses is a bad advertisement for your tutor'). At least for the best pupils, the meat came after the composition had been returned: 'he just talked', and often about his own research. For the rest, he was clearly liked by his pupils. One tells of 'not infrequent walks . . . when he introduced me in the lightest possible way to whole fields of knowledge which were largely new to me'. Another recalls how he arrived in Balliol in July as a late candidate and was told Mr Mynors was expecting him: 'He showed me to my room in college, saying he would come and see me in the morning . . . Come he did—and *with a cup of tea* . . . and with directions to the bath-house.'

A notable part of Mynors's life up to the war, and an important link with the young, was F. E. ('Sligger') Urquhart's Chalet des Mélèzes (dubbed des Anglais) in the French Alps. Urquhart had taken reading parties there since 1891, and Mynors, who was clearly in the 'Sligger' circle and may have owed to him his interest in pictures, went regularly from 1924 on. He did a lot of reading there, but took much exercise also. Even to reach the chalet in those far-off days was a major effort, and once there very long walks (not to speak of extempore games) were customary; for example, an expedition with Richard Pares and C. G. Eastwood in 1924 that started at 5.15 a.m. and ended only at 9.50 p.m. Humphrey Mynors occasionally came too, and well-known names are sprinkled through the Chalet Book. On Urquhart's death in 1934, the chalet was left to Mynors. Though he did visit it once with his wife in 1950, he largely disassociated himself from it after his move from Balliol, and eventually the place was handed over to trustees, who still run it for undergraduate reading parties. As late as 1987 Mynors could write: 'How that place does get under one's skin! I think about it as little as I can, and cannot fail to think about it constantly. My so-called mind is like a house with several rooms that I cannot bear to go into. Like Queen Victoria, I make up the Prince Consort's bed every night' (Kenny 14.10.87).

Mynors lived in II.5, a room looking out, Janus-wise, on the front quadrangles of both Balliol and Trinity. Here he taught and entertained undergraduates: one of whom, Christopher Fremantle, took up a light suggestion of his to try his hand at murals there, with pre-Raphaelite results that are still to be seen. But 'Roger as a young don struck me as shy, always pleasant and polite but not obtruding himself into undergraduate society'. We glimpse him 'walking about the college with enormous enthusiasm', and, during a short period as Dean, dealing tactfully with an errant dining club. Meanwhile in the Senior Common Room he made enduring friendships, especially perhaps with Humphrey Sumner. A very junior colleague still recalls with gratitude the generosity of a timely cheque. Yet even here the note of separateness is struck. Sir Richard Southern has 'bright memories of small incidents. . . . But somehow our friendship never blossomed—it was like a string of bright beads all the same size'. Something of Mynors's ultimate inarticulacy at this period comes over in a recollection of an Australian research fellow of Balliol: 'We went up into Hall by a staircase from the Senior Common Room. At the foot of this staircase was a newel post. The top piece of this post was loose and the post itself was not as firm as it might be. Roger, before he climbed the staircase, was accustomed to give this post a good shake, producing from this action a rather loud clanking noise, which he would greet with his shy smile. It always seemed to me that this act of his was the playful gesture of a man of feeling, expressing in this small way something of his fondness for the place and all its associations.'

Mynors, however, most obviously went his own way in his research. He seems not to have known well the Oxford classicists of his day, with the exception of Bowra. It was not that men of distinction and learning were lacking in the twenties. But several restricted themselves to the art of composition (J. G. Barrington-Ward, A. N. Bryan-Brown, T. F. Higham). Others favoured the commentary, but had little time for manuscripts (Cyril Bailey, A. S. Owen, M. Platnauer). Others, again, wrote about literature, and with wide horizons (C. M. Bowra, Gilbert Murray). Many of these were in any case primarily Hellenists, and none served as a model. Indeed 'the University provided my tottering steps with no guidance or supervision of any kind whatsoever' (Hunt 4.12.45). Mynors acted on his own principle, as he enunciated it later, that 'it is good for the young to be working at a book, and much better practice as a rule to edit a text than to enstodge a treatise' (Hunt 7.2.47). It would seem that the text chosen from the start was Cassiodorus's *Institutiones*; the edition was certainly well under way in 1931. But we hear of a 'notebook I filled in Lyons in the summer of '27 and Paris in the spring of '28' on the ninth-century poet and theologian Florus of Lyons: 'I've always felt uneasily that I ought to go back and finish—the food in Lyons was capital, and I spent the Fête Nationale on an expedition to Paray le Moniel [*sic*] and Cluny—an appropriate day for the thoughtful inspection of monastic ruins' (Hunt 4.12.45). Such topics show Mynors from the start drawn powerfully away from the ordinary classical stamping grounds. He could easily have grafted a Jamesian enthusiasm for manuscripts on to classical studies, and in the fifties he did so. But the later period called insistently, again perhaps because of James. And, while James had concentrated on English manuscript collections, it was perhaps the travel requirements of the Derby scholarship, which Mynors won in 1926, that opened his eyes to continental manuscripts and to the ways of continental medievalists.

In the *Institutiones* 'Cassiodorus Senator, in the middle years of the VIth century, set himself to compile for the monks of his foundation at Vivarium an Introduction to their studies'. For one interested in manuscripts, a book that seemed to describe its author's own library and that certainly instructed scribes in their task of copying must have held a special fascination. The tradition was intriguing too. One notable manuscript is famously subscribed 'Codex archetypus ad cuius exemplaria sunt reliqui corrigendi'; and the several recensions, authorial and other, challenged the skills of an editor who was always interested in lay-out, typography and printing convention. Mynors's edition was the only one that had (or has) appeared since 1679. But the field was not unworked. Scholars on the continent, not least Paul Lehmann, had recently concerned themselves with the complex story, and its main outlines were already clear. Mynors's introduction, written in English though originally drafted in Latin, sheds new light mainly on the later manuscripts; it does not solve the most pressing problem, the disentangling of the exact process of the expansion of Cassiodorus's original text. That remains unsolved, perhaps insoluble. It was the manuscripts that held Mynors's attention most closely. He travelled widely to see them ('the Laurenziana and Ambrosiana came since I last wrote—I entered them in fear and trembling': Hunt 30.7.33), though he seems oddly not to have at this stage visited such great collections as those at the Vatican, Munich and Leiden. His sole aim, he wrote, was 'to establish the relationship of the manuscripts to one another, and to provide at last the materials for a text that can be trusted'. Much remained to be done from other angles, as a tart review in *Gnomon* pointed out. Mynors's disclaimer of the requisite knowledge for a commentary was not mere modesty. But an appended translation and notes on the difficulties of interpretation would have added to the utility of the volume immeasurably.

The book finally appeared in 1937, after characteristic delay in the final stages and proofs. It was always Mynors's custom to work with passion on what he was interested in at the moment, but then, its back broken, to turn to new projects. On this occasion the tempting Siren took the shape of English medieval library catalogues. Even before the departure of his pupil Richard Hunt to research under Lehmann at Munich he had discussed this matter with him. And on Hunt's return, first to Oxford and then to a job in Liverpool, the two became deeply involved in a scheme that ultimately arose from a study published by M. R. James in 1922 of a fifteenth-century bibliographer known to him as John Boston of Bury St Edmunds. The chequered history of this project has been authoritatively told by Sir Richard Southern in his memoir of Hunt (*P.B.A.* lxvii [1981], 378–89) and does not need to be repeated here. A vast amount of work was done, but its fruits were slow to appear. One was the first edition, in 1941, of *Medieval Libraries of Great Britain*, the work of Neil Ker, another Etonian palaeographer, whom Mynors first met in 1935, and who with Hunt and Mynors became pivotal in the reshaping of British medieval studies described in Southern's memoir. The original 'Boston' project lost impetus around 1937, when Mynors began to express despair at its endless ramifications. He occasionally harked back to it after the war, and he contributed a chapter on it to the Saxl Festschrift in 1957. But he and Hunt were glad, after they had both retired, to hand over their dossiers to Richard and Mary Rouse in 1974. In 1981 the Academy adopted the Corpus of British Medieval Library Catalogues, a series foreseen by Mynors in the early thirties, and he took a keen interest in the progress of the first volume, K. W. Humphreys's *The Friars' Libraries* (1990). The second is the Rouses' *Registrum Anglie de libris doctorum et auctorum veterum*, 'the text established by R. A. B. Mynors' (1991). Its first chapter tells the absorbing tale of the long battle with this recalcitrant material, and records the part played not only by Roger Mynors but also by his brother Humphrey, who, as we know from a letter to Hunt (17.5.37), had 'plotted the complete order of monasteries on an outline map stolen from the Bank of England', cracking the code of the library numbers.

Mynors took his first Balliol manuscript from its shelf in 1926. He became the college's Librarian in 1929, and was soon at work on the manuscripts. The bulk of the first draft of the Catalogue was done by 1940, but the usual delays, caused partly by the desire to amass comparative material from Oxford and Cambridge college libraries, postponed publication until 1963. It is deeply indebted, as Mynors frequently acknowledged, to Hunt and Ker. One qualified to judge it says that 'it represents a high-water mark of thoroughness and detail which will, largely for economic reasons, probably never be surpassed'. It is strong where James would have been weak, in the treatment of obscure scholastic texts; but it suffers from its minimal index (something that remained on Mynors's conscience). His ideal was 'a catalogue in three dimensions, not just the bibliographer's flatland' (Thomson 16.9.83), and the most striking feature of the extended introduction is a detailed treatment of the life and books of William Gray: 'the more I think of Wm. Gray,' he wrote to Hunt in 1935, 'the more interesting his collection gets for Kulturgeschichte, as a mixture' (5.4.35). Mynors's only published article fills in a detail of Gray's story, and incidentally provides another point of contact with the work of M. R. James. The Catalogue illuminates its author's dictum that 'more and more, I attach chiefest importance to *Form* in publication of this kind' (Hunt 2.12.37). And Eduard Fraenkel used to read it aloud to his wife.

The Durham Catalogue was conceived later than the Balliol, but published much earlier (in 1939). It took its rise from a letter from the Dean in 1935 'saying they can't yet afford a regular librarian, but could I be induced to go and work a few weeks in the Library this summer and report on it anything that occurs to me' (Hunt 30.4.35). The Dean was Mynors's old Head Master, C. A. Alington, who had moved from Eton, with seventeen furniture vans, in 1933; and M. R. James no doubt also had a hand in the arrangement. We soon hear of a 'preliminary memorandum on publication of Durham MSS . . . which has gone down all right so far and is to be discussed with MRJ' (Hunt 10.8.35). The project began as a series of reproductions of early Durham manuscripts, for which Mynors was to provide brief notes, but it expanded to include descriptions of all the older manuscripts at Durham or associated with it. The collection has its grandeurs ('now for Lindisfarne Gospels!—shall I have to wear morning-dress?': Hunt 18.1.38), and no fewer than eleven books still at Durham precede the ninth century. Hence the excitement with which Mynors greeted the appearance of *Codices Latini Antiquiores* II (Great

Britain and Ireland): 'I got my copy as they came to the Press depot at 5.30 p.m. on Dec. 31st, so they only just made 1935' (Hunt 3.1.36), and his copy bears his comment 'the first copy in circulation'. He had attended some of Lowe's seminars in Oxford (one term with Fraenkel and one other), and repaid his debt by compiling two of the indexes to the whole series that appear in the Supplement of 1971. The Durham Catalogue itself is produced more lavishly even than *C.L.A.*, and paints a uniquely vivid picture of a rich twelfth-century library. Later, in 1956, Mynors wrote about the Stonyhurst Gospel for a Durham publication, *The Relics of St Cuthbert*.

Two general comments may be made on this flood of work on late and medieval topics. One is to stress the unremitting industry it entailed. An editor today is bound to spend long hours of collation, but, thanks to comparatively cheap and easily available microfilms he can often do this in convenient instalments in the comfort of his study. Sixty years ago, it was possible to obtain 'rotographs' of manuscripts, but they were almost prohibitively expensive. The alternative was prolonged work in libraries. 'Last Thursday, I left here [Ross on Wye] before breakfast and drove over to Cambridge for one night. It took just 10/11 hours steady going to check Sister J.'s transcript of Peterhouse 169 . . .' (Hunt 7.10.35; it is true that even after the war Mynors preferred to see and collate his books *in situ*). Nor should the transformation wrought by the advent of the Xerox machine be forgotten. 'Many thanks for the de Ghellinck article,' Mynors wrote to Hunt in 1936. 'It must have been a bore copying it out' (25.10.36).

Second, the concentration on post-classical matters set up a tension that continued in one form or another until Mynors's retirement. It seemed less urgent in 1933: 'Meanwhile I've read nothing—certainly no Mods work;—but am in the middle of Raby . . . and Lehmann's "Johannes Sichardus" . . . And Cyprian's letters' (Hunt 30.7.33). By 1937 he is writing: 'I don't want to go on with Boston indefinitely; my University lectureship *in Classics* weighs on my conscience . . . I *must* read the classics and get down to those Georgics' (24.3.37). From Harvard in 1938 he wrote: 'Virgil worries me deeply . . . There is such a temptation to try a big edn. of Ecl. & Georgics, and I feel (rightly or wrongly) I could do one, up to the standard, say, of Butler and Barber's Propertius: but that's not really good enough for Virgil, and it would mean dropping for good all this messing about with MSS, which I'm very loth to do' (Hunt 24.10.38). Matters were made worse by his acceptance of the Jowett Lectureship at Balliol in 1940 'on condition of working at a specified *classical* subject with a view to publication': 'I have specified the Ecl. and Georgics, and am very excited about them' (Hunt 7.2.40). We shall see the theme developing.

Despite Mynors's evident bias towards medieval studies, he was considered for purely classical jobs in the thirties. He found it easy enough to refuse to think of the editorship of *Classical Review* in 1935 and the Latin chair at Manchester in 1936. But he was more torn in 1939 over the possibility of a Readership in Palaeography, a plan apparently originating in F. M. Powicke: 'A stormy scene with Fraenkel on Tuesday over the readership in palaeography, as I expected. I fear he is right, that it would mean giving up any hope of being good at Latin (uncle Ed. offered me the reversion of the chair at either Oxford or Cambridge, neither of which I want, needless to say), and that I must refuse; but I daren't face FMP' (Hunt 3.3.39). Such things are unsettling, and Mynors had been unsettled enough by a few months in Harvard (Sept. 1938 – Jan. 1939). He lectured there on Lucretius as well as Virgil, and seems to have done a good deal of purely classical reading. '. . . do not look forward to returning to the round of Greek and Latin proses again . . . how extraordinary it is to live in an atmosphere in which it's taken for granted that everyone is writing an article, if not a book' (Hunt 24.10.38). The stay at Harvard was a success in itself, and it was prefaced by an exciting hurricane in New England and followed by a trip across the States to California. But it eventually became clear that he had been invited as a trial run for the succession to E. K. Rand's chair: 'Roger felt embarrassed not to be able to accept; he thought that perhaps he was there under false pretenses.' On his return he found 'Oxford is awful hard to settle into after Harvard. Feeling much is expected of one makes one about twice as good at the job; return here, where you are a nobody, and you behave like a nobody. Nor can you even keep warm. . . . But I shall get into my stride again soon' (Hunt 22.2.39). So, it seems, he did, and he found his 1939 freshmen 'as intelligent and attractive a lot as I have ever had to teach, and gloriously determined to have a crack at the humanities while they can' (Hunt 22.10.39). They included A. E. Douglas, D. F. Pears and D. A. F. M. Russell. But Balliol was upside down, the Library 'piled in two sitting-rooms, to make way for the books and press-cutting files of Chatham House which has taken over most of the College' (Hunt 16.9.39). The world was upside down too. In June 1940 Mynors went to the Exchange Control Department of the Treasury as a temporary Principal.

His first lodgings were in Margaretta Terrace, Chelsea; but he soon moved to Chelsea Square, to live with his old Eton fag, Balliol pupil and friend Anthony Wagner (now Sir Anthony Wagner, Clarenceux King of Arms), two maids, billeted sailors, and a barrage balloon. The Treasury demanded long hours of hard work ('9.30 to 8 in a steam-heated room': Ker 9.2.41).

Mynors is said to have been concerned variously with the coining of Maria Theresa dollars to pay Ethiopians, the financing of the Vatican, and the establishment of the Deutschmark. He for some time belonged to the Home Guard. In the evenings he fought fires, and sang with Wagner songs from the Oxford Songbook. He characteristically became interested in heraldry, and during a precious week's leave in 1943 cycled round Herefordshire churches 'for Papworth'. There was little time for scholarship of other kinds. '. . . plan notes on the Eclogues in bed at night' (Hunt 18.5.42). But by 1944, no doubt stimulated by Galbraith's plans for Nelson Medieval Classics, he is reading for the first time Bede, Jocelin of Brakelond and Walter Map ('and was ravished by them all') and 'am now wallowing in Aldhelm' (Hunt 21.3.44). The tension between classics and medieval studies was eased by an ingenious argument: 'reading the Classics is a responsible affair, not to be undertaken by one half asleep after a day in the office which seems to get longer and longer' (ibid.). And, though Oxford started to re-assert itself (Mynors seems to have become a Curator of Bodley for a short time in 1944), that only added to the temptations: 'as long as there are College MSS uncatalogued, I shall be half torn from my Classics by the lust to go a whoring after them' (ibid.).

But Oxford had to wait; for in 1944 Mynors, on the persuasion of Eduard Fraenkel, accepted the offer of the Kennedy Chair of Latin at Cambridge. He left the Treasury in January 1945, and moved 'resentfully' to Cambridge almost at once. 'My mandate is to revive Latin studies.' But Galbraith provided the other side of the equation, adding a new twist: 'You go to Cambridge to do two things, publish the Balliol catalogue, and get married' (Hunt 26.11.44).

Marriage was the speedier matter. When C. A. Alington became Head Master of Eton in 1917, his daughter Lavinia was six. Her brother Giles was to become a Fellow of University College, Oxford, and a sister, Elizabeth, later married Alec Douglas-Home. Their mother, 'a truly remarkable person' (with whom Roger Mynors was later 'besotted'), was a daughter of the fourth Lord Lyttelton. 'Her way of expressing herself was unique' (to quote Lord Home again), and not only when she was employing the private language of the Glynnes, the Lytteltons and the Gladstones, 'Glynnese'. Lavinia was, and is, no less remarkable, and no less idiosyncratic in her expression. She had taken a first in Mods in 1931, and then changed to medicine. Roger was acquainted with her over a long period. By 1940 he was appealing to his family for advice: he wanted to marry Lavinia, but did not wish to upset her career. Late in the war, two trips by Lavinia to Cambridge sealed the friendship. They were married in Durham Cathedral on 12 December 1945. No one who saw them together later in life could doubt their entire happiness in each other's high qualities.

The couple soon moved into a 'half-house' (1A Belvoir Terrace, Trumpington Road): 'staining floors and screwing up coathooks does seem to take a lot of time' (Hunt 18.5.46). But Mynors had for some time been concerned with the practicalities of a far bigger property. 'In the same week of hearing I was to become a Civil Servant, I heard I was also become a squire, with a country house and some 1250 acres of farmland and woods, best part of a small village; the house built (by my father's family) not later than s.XV and with some charm' (Hunt 18.5.42). This was Treago, near St Weonards, south of Hereford, inherited from a cousin, a high-spirited and (in her youth) adventurous lady. The house at first continued to be let; it was occupied from 1950 to 1958 by Lavinia's parents, and from 1958 until 1969 by Roger's sister. At first it was the estate that engrossed: '. . . planning farm water supply and other improvements, in which my whole heart is, could one only raise the money and the labour' (Hunt 29.9.43). 'I have developed a perfectly hopeless passion for milking sheds' (Hunt 23.10.45). 'I am turning a derelict brewhouse into a milking-shed, sign of the times?' (Hunt 28.8.48). Later, the house itself claimed attention: 'we took over possession of my Country Seat on 1st Jan., which needs Any Amount doing to it and takes a bit of time' (Hunt 18.1.51). Throughout Mynors's professorships Treago took time, and gave deepening pleasure.

Mynors never hid the sense of loss he felt in going to Cambridge. It was, it seems, the teaching he missed, and the life of a tutorial fellow. In Cambridge 'I am expected to supervise two men researching in Propertius (heaven help them) and lecture on the textual criticism of the last five satires of Juvenal and examine every year unpaid in University Scholarships . . . and never see an ordinary pupil, nor what is worse have any contact with the ordinary life in College such as alone makes it possible to play any part in the Collegiate system' (Watt 17.11.46). Phrases such as 'a bad dream', 'rent from my beloved Balliol', 'fundamental error', 'idiot mistake' recur in his letters to the end of his life; and he even toyed with re-applying for his old job at Balliol should it fall vacant. He was made a fellow of Pembroke; a colleague was Sir Ellis Minns, his twin's father-in-law, himself a distinguished palaeographer. But 'one takes a little time to get used to a small college at Cambridge full of strangers however friendly in lieu of a large College in Oxford full of friends (however strange), with the added embarrassment of being professor in a subject with which I am but imperfectly acquainted' (Hunt 19.2.45). Against such a background, his failure in 1949 to become Master of Balliol in succession to A. D. Lindsay must have been a sore blow. In the final stage, 14 voted for D. L. Keir, 13 for Mynors. He seems later to have declined a Cambridge headship.

A further objection to Cambridge was, not that it was dominated by scientists, but that the arts dons were, in Mynors's view, so spiritless a minority. Spirit, too, he found lacking in the Library Syndicate, on which, as on the Fitzwilliam Museum Syndicate, he was active. Personally, however, Mynors found the University Library, and the college libraries that James had catalogued, a standing temptation. There was also talk of a 'composite catalogue' of manuscripts in Oxford college libraries. Pleading to himself that he was looking for comparative material for the Balliol catalogue, he was a familiar figure in Cambridge libraries ('my entertainment at the moment . . . is the MSS of Peterhouse . . . I check MRJ's descriptions with what care I can': Hunt 13.8.46). A fruit was his contribution on Peterhouse book-markers to the Powicke Festschrift. Later 'this summer I've put all I had into helping Pink with the Cat. of Add. MSS in ULC' (Hunt 8.9.48). Not surprisingly 'I am in considerable difficulty over the split between bibliography and classics; hope to keep both going by devoting the afternoons only to MSS' (Hunt 3.3.45, with an ambiguously placed 'only'). Or again: 'efforts to close down the medieval Department of RABM have recently received a series of rude knocks' (Hunt 8.10.46). Work on the Balliol catalogue, even so, remained fitful. Towards the end of his time, Mynors began to have the manuscripts removed to Cambridge in batches; but the catalogue appeared only in 1963. It seems only to have been in Oxford that Mynors seriously began to redress the balance with classics; and he produced almost nothing in either field over his own name while at Cambridge.

That does not mean that he was unproductive. A great part of his energies was devoted to Nelson's Medieval Classics (later Texts), from 1967 Oxford Medieval Texts. Though this association extended long after his return to Oxford, the story may conveniently be told as a whole here.

The series took its rise from a meeting in an Edinburgh club. V. H. Galbraith, Professor of History in Edinburgh from 1937 to 1944, was having a drink with H. P. Morrison, once a director of United Steel in Sheffield, now Managing Director of Nelson's. Galbraith turned down the idea of a history of England under his editorship, but suggested instead a series of medieval texts with facing translations. Morrison agreed, and Galbraith became General Editor on condition that Mynors joined to provide the Latin expertise. He agreed in 1946. The partnership, distinguished as it was, did not always flow easily. Galbraith was not convinced of the need for newly edited texts ('you can toss it off in the Long Vac.'); Mynors, aware of the shortcomings of some historians in Latin and in acquaintance with manuscripts, tended, at least where a book interested him, to take over the text for himself. But there was full agreement on the scope of the series. 'Vivian's most emphatic point in the beginning (and how right he was!) was that unless people have English to face their texts, they will give up reading their texts altogether, and his second point was that the texts must be complete. . . . At first nothing was said about *historical* texts but with Vivian's background it was inevitable that they should predominate' (Brooke 20.8.65). Mynors thought of it as 'a series of which I like my friends (some history dons and some classical schoolmasters) to ask me "What's your next one going to be?"' Standards were to be high, but 'we try never to become *inhumane*' (Brooke 31.12.65). Towards the end of the joint editorship, Mynors was complaining that he was more and more becoming the general administrator, particularly during 'that awful year when VHG went off to California leaving EIGHT volumes in various stages on my table' (Brooke 14.10.59): 'VHG, as you can imagine, doesn't give [the programming of the series] two minutes' thought' (Brooke 15.3.59). C. N. L. Brooke, joining the General Editors in 1959, did not have an easy ride. Mynors seemed happy neither to be consulted nor to be bypassed. In 1962 it was announced that Mynors would now be only an 'advisory editor'; yet four years later he was still complaining to Galbraith about the amount of work he was doing for the series: 'it's not the tedium of all this I mind, though sometimes excruciating; it's the way it interferes with the work I am really supposed, and am paid, to do, like editing Virgil. . . . I am really borne down by it all' (Galbraith 16.10.66). Previous resignations from the editorship had been smoothed over, partly because, though a new Latinist was clearly desirable, 'Galbraith won't have one'. As late as 1970, Mynors was writing: 'I propose to RESIGN AGAIN when I reach retirement age this Fall' (Brooke 2.2.70); and the replacement of both Galbraith and Mynors followed. But for all the later difficulties, which show how the balance of Mynors's interest was at last turning decisively to classics, the series was close to his heart: 'the fact that I was privileged to help [Morrison and Galbraith] on the Latin side meant a great deal to me' (Brooke 16.5.75).

Mynors's participation in the books published in the series varied greatly. His remark to the Classical Association that 'I have been privileged occasionally to help one or two medieval colleagues with the technical aspects of their texts' is a marked understatement. With some of the editions, like Charles Johnson's *Hugh the Chanter* (1961), he regrettably seems to have had nothing to do. But in several others he collated the manuscript or manuscripts involved, often establishing the text, constructing the apparatus, and writing an account of the tradition under his own name: so H. E. Butler's *Jocelin of Brakelond* (1949), F. M. Powicke's *Life of Ailred of Rievaulx* (1950), K. R. Potter's *Historia Novella* (1955), Charles Johnson's *De Moneta* (1956), and Rosalind Hill's *Gesta Francorum* (1962). Mynors played a crucial part in Potter's *Gesta Stephani* (1955). At an advanced stage of the edition, which was then based on an early printed text, Mynors found, in a Valenciennes MS he was consulting for the continental version of William of Malmesbury's *Gesta Regum*, a more complete text of the chronicle; this he collated, transcribing the new material. He gave 'many marvellous supervisions' to Christopher Brooke when he was at work, from 1952, on the first volume of the Letters of John of Salisbury: 'when he had worked out that the marginal numbers in Claudius B.ii related to another collection of John's letters he was so excited he had to leave the MS room and walk round the courtyard before he could resume work.' He gave important help to J. H. Harvey in his *Itineraries* of William Worcestre (1969). And he felt especially close to C. R. Dodwell's edition of Theophilus's *De Diversis Artibus* (1961): 'it is one of the few volumes that are all my own invention (including the editor)' (Brooke 28.3.60).

Two texts named Mynors on the title-page. The later, Map's *De Nugis*, had its roots far in the past. When retyping the Latin in 1965, Mynors remarked that he had been at work on it thirteen years before (Brooke 31.12.65), and long delays were still to ensue before it was finally published in 1983. The book was close to Mynors's heart, not merely because 'the patron of Map's living of Westbury-on-Severn was *Roger de Miners*—doubtless an old Herefordshire chum' (ibid.), but especially because it was a revision of M. R. James. Brooke's notes and introduction completely replaced James's. Mynors's text improves on James in exploiting the evidence of seven English manuscripts of the *Dissuasio Valerii*, which had been published separately by Map. And he contrived delicate pastiches of James's style for passages in the translation ('the best English trans. I know of any Latin text': Brooke 14.10.59) which had been left in the obscurity of the learned language.

More important was Bede's *Historia Ecclesiastica*. 'I have also been thinking about Bede's *History* for the Medieval classics, to be edited probably by B. Colgrave (with some help from me on the collations?)' (Hunt 23.7.52). In the event Colgrave did the translation, Mynors the text. This is no place to rehearse the unhappy story of their collaboration. Colgrave died before the volume appeared in 1969, and Mynors was left feeling he had been pressed into premature publication. 'I *loathe* my introduction, and already have a lot to add to it' (Galbraith 29.9.66). The project was perhaps misconceived from the start. The text, as Mynors readily admitted, hardly differs from Plummer's, and the apparatus is starved of material (Mynors was looking forward to spreading himself further in a volume of *Corpus Christianorum* that never materialised). We are left with a masterly survey of the tradition of the book from the eighth to the fifteenth century, the fruit not only of Mynors's own expertise but of his ripened association with the great Bernhard Bischoff, whom he had known at least as early as 1937.

Mynors also contributed to the Preface of the facsimile of the Moore Bede (Copenhagen, 1959).

Even this is not the end of Mynors's medieval work. A major effort went into the long and intriguing text of William of Malmesbury's *Gesta Regum*. Stubbs had long ago recognised the existence of three versions of this history, at least two of them authorial. Mynors found in a hitherto unexamined manuscript at Troyes what he saw to be a fourth: it is chronologically the first, and forms the basis on which the A-text was founded around 1125. The Troyes version is closely related to an abbreviated continental tradition of the *Gesta*, whose witnesses Mynors was investigating when he stumbled on the new *Gesta Stephani*. The history of the project is characteristic. 'We still hope to find someone ready to do *G.R.* for the "Medieval Classics"' (Hunt 14.9.52, written when he was just about to go to Troyes), followed by 'VHG is trying to bully me into translating the *Gesta Regum* for Nelson's, with notes by himself (!)' (Hunt 21.11.52). In the end Mynors both edited and translated the long book. The notes were to be by Sir Richard Southern; but the scheme had become becalmed as early as 1961. Mynors typed out the final pages of the translation in his last years, when he was handing over the whole to a new triumvirate. It is his first extended essay at an art that came more and more to absorb him. William he regarded very highly; and, as with Map, there was a family connection—one manuscript of the *G.R.* describes a suit in the King's court between the monks of Gloucester and Gilbert de Mineriis.

Mynors's letters occasionally refer to active if temporary interest in other medieval authors. 'Alistair Campbell tackled me the other day about Ethelwulf's poem on those Northumbrian abbots (of which I have actually made a new text myself, but have no wish to publish it)' (Brooke 5.5.64); Campbell's edition was judged unsuitable for N.M.T., and was diverted to the Oxford University Press. Or again: 'Collated half the CCCC transcript of Asser last week—we shall be able to improve Stevenson's text here and there' (Brooke 21.5.62: this refers to a proposed edition of Asser by Galbraith himself; but nothing came of the idea). Mynors also made some progress (especially in 1949) with the Latin version of the Shepherd of Hermas, and did some abortive work on the Latin Aristotle.

To complete the picture of Mynors's medieval work, something should be said about his association with the *Dictionary of Medieval Latin from British Sources*. The story of this project is told by H. C. Johnson in the Preface to the first fascicule (1975). Mynors had long been a member of the committee, and he was a prime mover in the adoption of the dictionary by the Academy in 1963 and in the setting up of a new committee to oversee its progress. For many years his correspondence with the Dictionary concerned slipping he was doing for it, very far from a mere mechanical labour, considering the nature of the texts in question, the *Hisperica Famina* and the Glossaries. Finally, in 1967, 'the Academy have told me to be Chairman of the Med.Lat.Dict.Ctee, and of course I have said yes, tho' I wish they had appointed someone more useful' (Johnson 9.3.67). He was an admirable chairman, tactful but expeditious; behind the scenes he was warmly supportive of R. E. Latham and his successor as Editor, D. R. Howlett: 'I think about you a good deal and wish you well with all my heart' (Howlett 22.9.73). He resigned as chairman in 1973, and left the committee in 1977. He also frequently attended the annual meetings of the Union Académique Internationale, which amongst other things coordinates European medieval Latin dictionaries, and was its president in 1955.

Mynors returned to Oxford as Corpus Professor of Latin in 1953. He and Lavinia lived at 14A Merton Street, where, after 8 a.m. service at the University Church, young relations (of whom he was passionately fond) would foregather for a morning's talk and Sunday lunch. Mynors rarely visited Balliol, and even during his work on the college glass for the Academy's Corpus Vitrearum Medii Aevi tended to slip in anonymously. At Corpus the Common Room was a markedly classical place. Mynors's predecessor, Eduard Fraenkel, of whom he always spoke with the deepest admiration, was constantly in the college till his death in 1970, and dinner was often dominated by him, the other resident classicists, the President W. F. R. Hardie, R. G. M. Nisbet and Hugh Lloyd-Jones, and their guests. Mynors did not continue the famous classes held by Fraenkel, who indeed did not stop them on his retirement. He was not an enthusiastic examiner. But he showed his customary speed and courtesy in chairing the Sub-faculty of Languages and Literature. He lectured still on the *Eclogues* and *Georgics*. It is difficult adequately to convey the fascination he commanded even for the less enthusiastic lecture-goer. He seemed to have no notes, and did not disdain a touch of the histrionic; his voice, with its attractive timbre, filled the vast School with no effort. Those who expected answers to the 'problems' that loomed so large in the then Virgil special subject were disappointed. Instead, and more importantly, they heard the mature reflections of one who loved his author and loved the countryside he described. One was advised to go to the Parks to look for specimens of a plant or tree. There were charactistic dicta, informative ('tom-cats with pink eyes are invariably deaf') or mildly polemical ('questions one is often asked by people who ought to know the answers by now'). It was all very unfamiliar. Mynors also had research students, though not very many. He was not interested in reading drafts or even completed theses. If one asked advice one was invited to dinner at Corpus, introduced to legendary figures, and taken back to Mynors's room for disquisition on his own researches. He taught—perhaps not even with any conscious intent—by being himself, lucid, wonderfully wide in learning, unaffected, enthusiastic, drawing the uninitiated into a conspiracy of scholarship. One went away without the answer to the question, but heartened to press on.

It was from Oxford that Mynors produced the distinguished succession of Oxford texts that were during his lifetime the sole fruit of his purely classical scholarship. The Virgil naturally posed special problems. But the others are marked by a determination to be personally familiar with as many manuscripts as possible, to give their evidence in brief and elegant form, and to print a text that is, within the conditions set by the different traditions, neither over-conservative nor startlingly innovative. Himself disinclined to emend, Mynors felt strongly that the conjectures of others, especially when enshrined in manuscripts, should be properly attributed. Where other editors might shelter behind the stigma, he cited a manuscript and if possible a name. Of one admirable corrector of the *Panegyrics* he says: 'cuius nomen pudet me nescire'.

The attribution of emendations, particularly those dating from the fifteenth century, is perhaps the most valuable feature of the first text, the Catullus (1958). Eight groups of emending manuscripts, ordered by date, are distinguished by Greek letters; a reviewer calculated that of 800 emendations admitted to the text, no less than 322 are thus attributed to Renaissance manuscripts. This part of Mynors's work has not been much improved. Higher up the stemma complaint was made at the time, and a good deal of work, not all trending in the same direction, has been done since. Mynors naturally relied on three manuscripts, all known to previous editors but never so well reported, the Oxoniensis, to the facsimile of which (Leiden, 1966) Mynors contributed a Latin preface, G and R. Philip Levine's review judged that Mynors 'errs gravely' in not distinguishing in R the hands of the 'variants and other additions by one or more hands different from that of the first scribe', especially as one of the correctors seems to be Coluccio Salutati, the known owner of the book. The offence is hardly heinous in an apparatus of such conscious brevity, whatever view is taken on the still disputed matter of the corrections in R; the technical considerations involved are largely, if not entirely, irrelevant to the establishment of the text. Descending the stemma again, Mynors had said that all the other manuscripts (of which he had handled more than eighty) 'a codicibus OGR originem aut duxerunt aut, quod nobis idem ualet, duxisse possunt'. That is mere assertion, and one feels here the need for a supporting monograph, that could also have given what Levine missed, discussion of the reasons for at least some of Mynors's textual choices.

That Mynors should depart in eight hundred places from the reading of the lost Veronensis does not, in so corrupt a tradition, make his text innovative. Even the edition later produced by G.P. Goold, though as a whole markedly unlike any text of Catullus ever published, does not print anything that had not been somewhere proposed before. It seems clear that Mynors could profitably have mentioned more rejected conjectures than he does. Several reviewers attributed the brevity of his apparatus, in this and other respects, to the strict conventions of the Oxford Classical Text series. In fact, the austerity would appear to have been self-imposed. Instructions were (and are) not issued to editors in this series, and the precedents could have led in another direction: Mynors's predecessor for Catullus, Robinson Ellis, had produced an apparatus of 'opulent confusion' (so D. F. S. Thomson; compare Mynors's own remark, in a letter to Hunt dated 3.3.45, on *Catalepton* 13.21: 'a very obscene passage, I fear, but not as revolting or as unnaturally vicious as Ellis's apparatus'). It is difficult to imagine that if Mynors had wished to provide a fuller apparatus he would have met with any obstacles from the Press.

Mynors prints no emendations of his own: 'mihi nec doctrinam neque ingenium ad [uersus deprauatos] tandem enucleandos suffecisse uix est cur moneam.' Reviewers found this excessively modest, but the words seem to conceal a life-long distaste for textual emendation. Even in the editing of medieval texts from unique manuscripts, Mynors was very slow to apply his own remedies, and the emendations printed in his *Panegyrics* come as something of a surprise (though even in 1948, re-reading his own Jocelin of Brakelond, he remarks: 'I think on looking thro' it again I was too conservative in the text' (Hunt 8.9.48). It was as though the meticulous establishment of the *lectio tradita* exhausted his curiosity as to what the author actually wrote. His judgement on the changes made by others was praised by as radical a critic as Goold, but he seems to have felt no impulse to continue along the path they had shown.

In 1963 came the Letters of the Younger Pliny. The tangled tale of how the scholars of the Renaissance built up their knowledge of this text from a nucleus of a hundred letters to a complete corpus is told in some detail in Mynors's preface. He begins and ends by acknowledging his debt to others: there was room only 'ut hic illic zizanium aliquod euellatur e segete'. That is not mere modesty. The outline of the story had been known to Keil already in 1870, and many details had been filled in by

Merrill and by Stout (Mynors's review of whose edition seems to be the only review he ever wrote). It was left to Mynors to assert firmly, but again without argument, that the old Paris manuscript lying behind the β family is partly available to us in the sixth-century fragment in the Morgan Library in New York; that this is so cannot, naturally, be seen from Mynors's apparatus, in which β is eliminated where Π is present, but comparison with Keil's makes the point clear. He was also able to find a superior witness to the elusive θ tradition, and to fit a number of subsidiary manuscripts into the general picture. Though Mynors 'shows his working' to an unusual extent in the Preface, a more extended treatment of certain aspects would still have been welcome. Reviewers commented justly on the way in which Mynors merely *tells* us what γ read (again Keil's apparatus helps to show what lies behind the scenes). As for the text, if Mynors was too mechanical in following the indications of his stemma in choosing between variants, it is only very rarely that this might seem to be leading him into serious error.

The labours involved in this edition must have been prodigious, given Mynors's determination to handle as many of the manuscripts as possible and considering the work implied by the simple word *contuli* for a text of such length. The fact that at the same time he was completing an edition of the *Panegyric* of Pliny, together with the eleven encomia associated with it in a tradition quite different from that of the letters, is little short of miraculous. This text appeared only a year after the other; Mynors had typed out every word on his ancient typewriter, as was sometimes his custom with medieval texts, to provide a clean copy for what he felt was a long-suffering Press. It is true that the tradition was a good deal less complex here, and that the main lines of it had again been laid down by predecessors, principally the Baehrens, father and son. Mynors, again concerned to inspect the books where at all possible, was able to fit further manuscripts into the picture, and he brings new order to one corner of the stemma by assuming (without any full statement of the evidence) the descent of the Cluj manuscript from Harley 2480 and of the Uppsala manuscript from the Cluj. A favourable review in *Gnomon* praised his re-collation of the sixth-century fragment in Milan, and his judgement of the worth of Cuspinianus's edition. The text, about which historians occasionally express reservations, is marked by an unusual efflorescence of the editor's own emendations, which are often, though by no means always, prompted or supported by rhythmical considerations. In all his work on Pliny, Mynors gave proper weight to clausulae, internal as well as final, and tried so far as possible to let the punctuation follow the rhythm.

The final fruit of these *anni mirabiles* was a new O.C.T. of Virgil, to replace Hirtzel's of 1900, whose judgements, as well as whose plates, had become worn with time. 'Restat fere integer poeta: *non illum nostri possunt mutare labores*', writes the editor in one of several felicitous quotations from his author. But the apparatus, discumbered of ancient junk, gives, besides succinct citation of secondary evidence and convenient indication of the witnesses available at each point, readings from a dozen ninth-century manuscripts. That these ω-texts occasionally anticipate later conjecture or agree with the indirect tradition against the capital books does not seem to give them an independent value that could stand opposed to the old witnesses; nor does Mynors's practice suggest that even he thought they did. It would seem that his investigation of the ninth-century tradition might more elegantly have been hived off into an article or monograph, clearing the apparatus of a good deal of unnecessary material. At the same time, Mynors did not look systematically at later manuscripts, and here alone he is content with the general 'recc.'. As to the text, the occasional acceptance of a modern conjecture is a proper reminder that there is nothing sacrosanct about the text of Virgil: although the fact that the *Aeneid* was left unfinished and unrevised makes that a special case.

It is perhaps not unfair to say that these four texts are only in minor ways improvements on their predecessors in their treatment of the manuscript tradition, and that their apparatuses, though technically superior, are hobbled by their brevity. It should be emphasised that the prime merit of all four lies in their unfailing application of mature *iudicium*. Only close working with the texts and their apparatuses, and careful comparison with rival editions, will show the care that Mynors took over every aspect of the editor's task.

Such were the fruits of the second period at Oxford. Mynors largely forewent the delights of bibliography, at least once the Balliol Catalogue was published, and his passion for manuscripts diverted itself into the laborious investigation of the tradition of classical authors. But quite apart from this, the round of professorial duty and the constant call of Treago, Mynors lived a busy life, one that does much to explain his well-known elusiveness. He was frequently abroad on the business of the Academy. He gave the Jackson lectures at Harvard in 1966 (and failed to make a book of them). He acted as Curator of the Bodleian Library from 1953 to at least 1971, and was chairman of the Standing Committee of the Curators for many years. His retirement from his chair was marked by an exhibition 'Duke Humfrey and English Humanism in the Fifteenth Century'. In the Foreword to the Catalogue Robert Shackleton wrote: 'His energy, enthusiasm and imagination have been applied to housekeeping details not less than to the occasional purchase of a splendid manuscript. He has placed many members of the Library staff in his debt, and none more so, or more lastingly, than the Librarian. His confidence in the future of the Library has matched his loyalty to its past.' Finally, he was on the literary panel of the New English Bible (first published as a whole in 1970). Some of the meetings were held in the Tower Room at Treago, where the translation of Job was completed. 'I had two solid days last week in the Chapter House of St Paul's, translating the Prophet Jeremiah—how's that for an alibi?' (Brooke 12.4.60).

Mynors wrote in 1963: '. . . until we retire and go and live in our country seat, as Lavinia always maintains we shall' (Brooke 24.7.63). Lavinia was right. Having for some years camped in the adjacent stables, they finally moved into the big house in 1970, together with Roger's mother, who lived on for another four years, Humphrey, and Humphrey's wife Marian. The house is big, but intimate. 'We live what they call simply. If such a thing is possible' (Winterbottom 30.4.87). Under a strict division of labour, Lavinia was cook. Roger was in his study by 7 every morning, and worked there till lunch (and often at night also). But the afternoons he always spent, whatever the weather, out of doors; often he was not home till dark, sometimes to the alarm of the others. The woods on the estate, their nurture, replacement and extension, form a constant background to his scholarship. '. . . young trees don't answer back or criticize—they just grow, and look like outliving one, and get no less beautiful with age—all the things one cannot do oneself' (Hill 25.1.76). It was hard labour: '. . . the unprecedented mildness of the winter which has made it possible, and therefore necessary, to work out of doors (23 acres of young trees to weed . . .)' (Latham 11.1.72); but that came naturally enough to someone who thought nothing of a twenty mile walk in his forties and was still striding up Garway Hill in his last decade. A special concern was the development of 'Roger's stamp-collection', a remarkable arboretum in the Wilderness, which covered old quarry workings above the house.

Apart from endlessly generous hospitality to house-guests, there was the round of local social life: 'a busy time for country-dwellers—nettle-cutting, punctuated by sherry with the high sheriff and the village fête' (Winterbottom 20.6.87), and, in particular, the church. The Mynors regularly attended St Weonards church, where Roger often read the lesson. On two Sundays a month they worshipped at Hereford Cathedral. For fifteen years from 1979, Roger was chairman of the Friends of the Cathedral. He served on the Advisory Committee for the library, and in 1988 a book fund was set up in his name, for the purpose of acquiring valuable or rare works of permanent interest. The controversy over the proposal to sell the Mappa Mundi darkened his last years. He endeared himself equally to the under-twelves who once listened spell-bound as he talked about a manuscript on which he was working in the chained library, and to a Friend to whom he gave a book ('I think you said this was a gap—may we have the pleasure of filling it?').

The Mynors continued to the end to pay regular visits to the Homes on the Tweed, and to travel abroad, especially in Italy and Spain, living frugally and using local transport. One of the many benefits of his marriage was that Roger was forced to take holidays (Brooke 28.4.71: 'my wife carries me off this week for a fortnight's holiday in Madrid and Toledo'). Before the war, apart from physically and mentally demanding stays at the Chalet, we hear only of a day or two in Langdale ('on high hills in thick cloud mostly and quite deep snow—ice-axes, and I am a new man': Hunt 3.1.36), the result apparently of doctor's orders following 'a very mild sort of brief collapse' in late 1935. Even after the war he was subject to 'a mysterious complaint that proves life-saving every eighteen months or so when I've been slightly overdoing it, in which my temperature goes up (sometimes to 103) and the doctor asks in vain whether I haven't had malaria' (Brooke 1.3.66): nature asserting itself in a very fit man always liable to overwork. 'I don't think I could possibly work harder—it might pay in the long run to take more holidays' (Brooke 5.5.64).

There were, in first retirement, a few remnants of university cares. Mynors continued to lecture at Oxford for some years, and he was also the first Longman Visiting Fellow at the University of Leeds in 1974–5. But after 1978 private research took over completely. Far the most important preoccupation was the Erasmus project. Mynors had, as we have seen, greatly admired M. R. James's translation of Walter Map; and he shows the same rather archaic felicity in the unpublished translation of the *Gesta Regum*. But it may have been his experiences with the New English Bible that particularly turned his thoughts towards the theory of translation, of which he would often speak in his later years. 'Translation as a most perilous and most enjoyable art takes so much of my thoughts these days' (Brooke 5.12.61). He grew more and more convinced that the translator should be flexible, unliteral, bold: 'humble people don't always realise that they *must* adopt a more domineering attitude towards the style or syntax of their author, and bully him into writing English' (Brooke 12.2.60). Translation was, in any case, important for him, as a means of passing on the classical and medieval torch to ages when Latin would be little studied.

Mynors came to Erasmus by way of a short-lived association with the

Amsterdam Erasmus series, for which he edited the *In nucem Ovidii* and the *Libanii declamatiunculae* (1969). But in the same year he took a step that influenced the whole of the rest of his life, by joining a committee whose mandate was to produce a translation of the principal works of Erasmus for the University of Toronto Press. Mynors went out to Toronto annually until 1982, going on to Harvard to stay with Wendell Clausen; he 'became invisible' in Hart House, his natural elusiveness increased by his habit of working by English time, five hours ahead of the local clock. He was responsible for the translation of a very large number of the Letters (some in collaboration with D. F. S. Thomson). But it was in the *Adages* that he found the greatest fulfilment, in facing the challenge of identifying the sources and sorting out from the various editions of Erasmus's work the way in which the collection evolved. The volume of Prolegomena, which would have told the complex story, was never written, but much work was done towards it. As to the translation, two of six volumes have already appeared (one with Mynors's annotations, the other translated and annotated by him): the third was found entire after Mynors's death, and the other three in various stages of completion. His association with the project was marked by an honorary LL.D. at Toronto in 1982.

But the passion for manuscripts was never stifled. When R. M. Thomson was working on the Lincoln catalogue, Mynors wrote to him: 'O how I wish I could help!—am much tempted to slip over to Nottingham for the day, just for the pleasure of having a few nice unknown MSS in my hands and of getting some inkling of what awaits you' (16.9.83). And it was appropriate that Mynors was working on the Hereford manuscripts on the last day of his life (17 October 1989). He had fitfully concerned himself with this local collection, again in the footsteps of M. R. James, who had written the introduction to Bannister's catalogue; and it was a solace in the sad last year. A successful cataract operation had relieved worries about his sight, but others supervened. His brother Humphrey died in the summer of 1989, a grievous blow. The Treago ménage was broken up, and Roger and Lavinia moved back to the newly converted stables. The remains of his last work at Hereford show a failing of powers, and he was distressed at the deterioration of his clear and characterful handwriting; but his joy in life and scholarship remained. Meryl Jancey, the Cathedral's Honorary Archivist, tells how 'on the last day of his life, he left the Library full of pleasure at the thought of the good day he had had, and with plans for what he would turn to next. . . . As he left, we spoke of Bede. He told me he was glad that he had translated for the Oxford Medieval Texts the account of Bede's death, and that Bede had not ceased in what he saw as his work for God until the very end.' Driving home the few miles to Treago that evening, he was killed instantaneously in a road accident.

The commentary on the *Georgics* was what the classical world had been waiting for from Mynors: and the wait had been a long one. We have already found him talking of the need to 'get down to those Georgics' in 1937, and in 1938 thinking at Harvard of a commentary that would cover the *Eclogues* also. Later, Wendell Clausen took over the *Eclogues*. It is not clear when the bulk of the work on the *Georgics* commentary was done. But it was sent to press in the early eighties, and set up in proof. The delay of several years was caused, it seems, by Mynors's inability to write an introduction; on his death only a few scraps remained. He apparently knew no way in which to express what he felt with an instinctive and deep emotion, the greatness of Virgil's poetry; he was not accustomed to making judgements of that kind, either verbally or on paper. But there was also a characteristic lack of faith in his own work. He repeatedly spoke of the commentary as beta plus, and once, even more dismissively, as 'my famous commentary on the *Georgics*, which was to have been a masterpiece and now looks like an extinct volcano in use as the town tip' (Howlett 9.1.87). There was perhaps also the thought, as the years passed and *Année Philologique* grew thicker with each volume, that his approach was becoming outmoded. When the book was published in 1990 with a brief introduction by his successor at Oxford, R. G. M. Nisbet, it was opened with intense curiosity.

In the event the commentary seems timeless. It eschews any parade of secondary literature (Mynors once wrote to Clausen that his ideal commentary 'would . . . never mention a modern author (other than Pauly Wissowa and *Thes.*) except where one has an obligation to acknowledge—grossly unprofessional conduct'). And it sidesteps the antithesis of pessimism and optimism that has dominated recent work on the poem by stressing the practical and technical side of the *Georgics* (he once told Nicolas Barker that 'he was the latest person to read Virgil for practical advice'): though, beyond that, he regarded 'the subject as Man and his place in Nature etc., with a less attractive (to me) foreground of ethics and politics, for all of which agriculture, weather etc. is the chosen vehicle' (quoted by Clausen). On every page there are signs of Mynors's knowledge of a peopled and cultivated countryside: 'you can still tell a good farmer by the shine on his tools' (on 1.45–6); 'had V. seen the wild-oat standing head-and-shoulders above the crop, as it still does?' (1.154); 'the farmer who sees animals in his grain "damage-feasant", as our lawyers used to say, will mend his fence in the face of the whole college of pontiffs' (1.270). Mynors might have added to his note on 2.189 the advice he once gave to the writer's wife, with supporting detail: 'Cull bracken on 3 June.' But it is more than the writer's knowledge that comes through. He shares Virgil's *energy*, or imparts his own: 'The effect is almost that of a visit to the fold-yard with our instructor: "You must learn to fumigate all this. Those mangers ought to be moved, or you'll get snakes in here—look, there's a *coluber*, what did I tell you? Down with it! There it goes!"' (3.414). The range of reading is everywhere apparent; and the man 'who could spend all day in front of a picture' brings Delacroix and Claude Lorraine to a discussion of 3.271–9. There is even a reminiscence of the youthful athlete (or oarsman?): 3.105–6 '*haurit*: of that familiar empty feeling before a race'—combined characteristically with a quotation from Tennyson.

The literary criticism is unstated and implicit, in Mynors's habitual manner. He adopts the persona of the moderate and not too adventurous critic: irony glances at the extravagances of 'some sensitive modern ears' (1.491, cf. 328–9). He remains, so far as he can, in the realms of what is there and can be shown; but the commentary places the poem unobtrusively within the cultural heritage of Western Europe. In his lectures, as a perceptive reviewer observed, Mynors 'flattered his hearers by speaking as an educated and passionate lover of poetry to an audience which must surely (he implied) be the same'. This flattery is at work in the commentary also, as it often was in Mynors's conversation. Indeed the book, more than most, talks to us.

Charm was Mynors's most obvious characteristic, and few who met him were untouched by it. His normal manner was mild, even bland. If one said something silly or trivial, he would often not reply, smiling, his head slightly on one side, masking his thoughts. At least till his last years, he was unwilling to speak of the bad or the sad, just as he avoided talk of religion or of the beauties of Virgil. He switched off in the face of stupidity, or from time to time lapsed into memorable anger. Some were frightened of him, some offended by his fitfulness as a correspondent (another Jamesian trait) or by what they saw as his remoteness and occasional insensitivity to their feelings. He had, a colleague wrote, a 'disconcerting way of letting you know that he knew more about you than you had supposed and than you might care to think'. But for many he had a 'gift for creating comfort' and 'extended an unswerving bond of trust'. To those of whom he approved, and especially to the young, often from overseas, with their way to make, he was unendingly encouraging: 'one was made to feel that one was significant, and that one had a great deal to do and should get on with it'. Criticism and compliment was, like so much else, implied rather than directly stated. But one always felt one was learning from him, not only on scholarly matters: 'he was constantly teaching ethics.' There were a few gods in his universe, people 'sent to us from another planet', Neil Ker, for instance. There were demons too, the ignorant and pretentious and those who would not take the trouble to get things right. For though he was oddly unsure of himself, and often spoke of his inadequacies as a scholar, he knew very well that usually he could do a thing better than another would.

Mynors once wrote to Ker: 'I fear I am *dotty* about pictures. Perhaps I should have been an art critic—certainly not a professor' (17.9.47). D. J. Allan, on the other hand, thought he should have been a scientist: certainly he had the instinct to collect and organise data. But, as has been seen, the division felt by Mynors within himself was between medieval and classical studies. The medieval side was complex. He was clear what he was not: 'God forbid I should try to become a palaeographer' (Hunt 24.10.35, when he was setting out on his Durham catalogue). He thought of himself rather as a bibliographer ('this hobby of medieval bibliography': Hunt 26.11.44). But though he could contrast bibliography and classics (Hunt 3.3.45), he also once significantly writes: 'no one in his senses would profess Latin . . . who can plant trees or try to learn some history from the original sources' (Ker 21.9.46). His interests went well beyond the page of the manuscript, to embrace the story it told, the people whose lives it illuminated. In a tribute to the codicologist Bob Delaissé he said: '. . . if it [scholarship] is . . . to throw light on the world we all of us have to live in, as it *can* and *ought to*, it does this by never forgetting that it is dealing in the last resort with men like ourselves.' That, of course, is a principle applicable, and by Mynors applied, to work on Virgil also. His division of interests was only harmful if, as he sometimes feared, it led to a failure to do justice to either side of his work. It would be foolish to attempt a judgement on a matter over which Mynors himself agonised throughout his life. But it is worth remarking that it was in medieval studies that he made his closest friends, and had his most important influence on the course of scholarship. And it was on a medieval topic that he wrote words that best exemplify his vigour of expression, his concrete imagination, his encouragement and his implied criticism, his good humour and his lack of affectation, his depth of knowledge and his wide horizons. He is sketching the sort of preface that Ker might have written, but did not write, for *Medieval Libraries of*

*Great Britain* (3.3.41, written with the correction of a single letter 'hard on midnight, and I didn't get to sleep till half past three this morning'):

It would be nice to start with a purple patch; to sketch the history of the British medieval library from Benedict Biscop returning laden from Rome with stained-glass windows and stately tomes in uncial, or Bede on his deathbed enriching Jarrow with St Mark in the vernacular, down to Leland (was it?) watching the loose leaves of the books of Malmesbury blowing across the churchyard, and being picked up by the fellow-citizens of William Stumpe—unworthy townsmen of Aldhelm—to patch their draughty windows and fire their bakers' ovens. To explain that this is not a Book but contains material for many books—a raw coral atoll fresh from the insect, on which others must make the palm-trees grow; give us our schools of writing and illumination; trace the waning of an interest in Old English, the arrival of texts from the new Universities of the Continent—ousting the Fathers who will have their turn again in the XIVth century,—the amount of attention given in monastic houses or by Tudor collectors to history or law or works of piety and romance in French and English; tell us why it is that monastic books are collected in the XVIIth century by the bourgeoisie, in the XVIIIth by peers, and in the XIXth by bankers. I should like to see you put on your dressing-gown and fill your pipe with shag, and tell us (I your Doctor Watson) how it is you perform these incredible feats of detection—for in your second article (for which I shall long remain in your debt) you have really surpassed yourself—and Dr Lowe. For that is the real justification for putting this highly specialist and unreadable book into the unwilling—let us hope acquiescent—hands of every pie-faced Fellow of the R.Hist.S.: that there are all these stories waiting to be told of the literature and art and economies of our forefathers . . . —and the spadework of this list is the essential preliminary to their telling. And published in the middle of a fearful war? Yes, because these survivor books are the best evidence we have of what happens in the change from one epoch to another, such as we live in today, and rightly interpreted can show us how men like ourselves in past time have built a new world many times over out of the ruins of the old.

As this letter is getting every moment more like the inaugural lecture of the Seeley W. Mudd Professor of Bibliography, and my Pegasus is in need of a second wind, I will dismount.

MICHAEL WINTERBOTTOM
*Fellow of the British Academy*

Roger Mynors was knighted in 1963. He was elected to the British Academy in 1944; he was its Vice-President in 1955–6 and its Foreign Secretary from 1958 to 1961. He was an Honorary Fellow of the Warburg Institute, of Balliol and Corpus Christi Colleges, Oxford, and of Pembroke College,

Cambridge. He was an Honorary Member of the American Academy of Arts and Sciences, the American Philosophical Society and the Istituto di Studi Romani. He was an Hon.D.Litt. of the Universities of Edinburgh and Durham, an Hon.Litt.D. of the Universities of Cambridge and Sheffield, and an Hon.LL.D. of the University of Toronto. He was President of the Classical Association in 1966.

*Note*: This memoir could not have been written without the encouragement, cooperation and manifold kindnesses of Roger Mynors's family, in particular his widow Lavinia, his twin's late widow Marian, Mr David Mynors, Mr Tom Mynors, Mrs Joanie Wilkes, Dr K. V. Wilkes, and Sir Richard and Lady Mynors. I am indebted to the family and to surviving recipients for permission to cite from Roger Mynors's letters (which I identify by recipient and date); those in the Balliol Archives are published with the permission of the Master and Fellows of the College, those in the Bodleian Library, Oxford with the permission of the Keeper of Western Manuscripts (R. W. Hunt and N. R. Ker papers) and, for the letters to Ker, Professor A. G. Watson, those in the archives of Oxford Medieval Texts with the permission of Professor C. N. L. Brooke and the present General Editors (I am especially grateful to Miss Barbara Harvey for her patient help), and those in the archives of the Dictionary of Medieval Latin from British Sources with the permission of the editor, Dr D. R. Howlett. Anne Borg took endless trouble with the typescript. I am also indebted to many others who helped me in various ways: the staff of Balliol College library, Mr Nicolas Barker, Dr B. C. Barker-Benfield, Professor J. Barnes, Mrs Georgina Battiscombe, Miss Joan Bookham, Professor C. O. Brink, Professor C. N. L. Brooke, Mr R. W. Burton, Mr Basil Butcher, Mr D. S. Colman, the Rev. R. E. Davies, Mr M. M. Davis, the late Professor Ralph Davis, Mr A. E. Firth, Mr J. H. Gleason, the late Mr J. G. Griffith, Mr C. G. Hardie, Mr A. S. Hoey, Mr M. Hutchinson, Mr M. W. Ingram, Miss Meryl Jancey, Dr J. H. Jones, Professor E. J. Kenney, Mr F. A. Lepper, Mr Philip Mason, Dr J. K. McConica (who gave invaluable assistance on the Erasmus project), the late Miss Penelope Morgan, Professor R. G. M. Nisbet, Professor R. W. Pfaff, Mr Paul Quarrie (who kindly sent me details from the archives of Eton College), Mr V. Quinn, Mr L. D. Reynolds, Professor M. D. Reeve, Dr Richard Sharpe, Professor Richard Rouse, Sir Richard Southern, Dr J. B. Sykes, Mr Arnold Taylor, Canon John Tiller, Dr R. M. Thomson, Sir Anthony and Lady Wagner, Professor W. S. Watt, Mr G. K. White and Mr G. Yeates.

## Published Writings of Roger Mynors

*Cassiodori Senatoris Institutiones* (Oxford, 1937)
*Durham Cathedral Manuscripts to the end of the twelfth century* (Durham Cathdral, 1939)
'Some book-markers at Peterhouse,' in *Studies in Mediaeval History presented to*

*Frederick Maurice Powicke*, ed. R. W. Hunt, W. A. Pantin, R. W. Southern (Oxford, 1948), 465–8

'A fifteenth-century scribe: T. Werken,' *Transactions of the Cambridge Bibliographical Society* 2 (1950), 97–104

'The Stonyhurst Gospel (a) Textual description and history of the manuscript,' in *The Relics of Saint Cuthbert*, ed. C. F. Battiscombe (Durham Cathedral, 1956), 356–62

'The Latin Classics known to Boston of Bury,' in *Fritz Saxl 1890–1948*, ed. D. J. Gordon (London, 1957), 199–217

*C. Valerii Catulli Carmina* (Oxford, 1958)

*The Moore Bede*, preface by Peter Hunter Blair with a contribution by R. A. B. M. [pp. 33–7] (Copenhagen, 1959)

*Catalogue of the Manuscripts of Balliol College Oxford* (Oxford, 1963)

Review of S. E. Stout's edition of the letters of the younger Pliny, *Classical Review* 13 (1963), 304–5

*C. Plini Caecili Secundi Epistularum Libri Decem* (Oxford, 1963)

*XII Panegyrici Latini* (Oxford, 1964)

*Classics, pure and applied*, Presidential Address to the Classical Association (London, 1966)

*Catullus Carmina Codex Oxoniensis*, praefatus est R.A.B.M. (Leiden, 1966)

*Bede's Ecclesiastical History of the English People*, edited by Bertram Colgrave and R. A. B. M. (Oxford, 1969)

P. Vergili Maronis Opera (Oxford, 1969)

*Opera omnia Desiderii Erasmi Roterodami* I.1 (Amsterdam, 1969), 139–74 (Commentarius Erasmi in Nucem Ovidii) and 175–92 (Libanii aliquot declamatiunculae Latinae per Erasmum)

*Collected Works of Erasmus* vols 1–9: *The Correspondence of Erasmus* in 9 vols (Toronto, Buffalo [London], 1974–89), the first six vols with D. F. S. Thomson

—— vol. 32: *Adages* [Vol. 2] (Toronto, Buffalo [London], 1989), translated and annotated by R. A. B. M.; the first vol. (1982) was annotated by R. A. B. M.

*Walter Map De Nugis Curialium* edited and translated by M. R. James, revised by C. N. L. Brooke and R. A. B. Mynors (Oxford, 1983)

*Virgil Georgics* (Oxford, 1990)

*Proceedings of the British Academy*, **80**, 403–423

# Michael Joseph Oakeshott
# 1901–1990

MICHAEL JOSEPH OAKESHOTT was born in Chelsfield, Kent, on 11 December 1901. His parents belonged to the educated middle class and enjoyed a modest financial independence. His father, who was a civil servant in the Inland Revenue, had an interest in Fabian socialism and was a man of studious tastes; his mother engaged at various times in charitable social work and seems to have had a more active temperament than her husband. There were two other sons, both of whom lived into old age. By all accounts the household in which Oakeshott grew up was cultivated and serious in outlook, though not in any way an intellectual hothouse. The family moved house several times in order to be near to suitable schools. At the age of eleven Oakeshott was sent to St George's School, Harpenden, a somewhat unusual coeducational school, founded by its headmaster, the Revd Cecil Grant. It provided an environment favourable to the growth of intellectual curiosity and the stimulation of aesthetic sensitivity, whilst at the same time sustaining a respect for the individual's moral obligations in society and for the conduct of his or her own life. To judge from Oakeshott's friendship with Mr Grant (lasting until the latter's death in the 1960s), the school made a lasting contribution to the shaping of Oakeshott's moral perceptions and to his conception of education.

At school Oakeshott received a fairly conventional academic education. This included classics, and for the rest of his life he was to reveal the abiding influence of classical thought, especially as expressed in the Latin language. He went to Gonville and Caius College, Cambridge, in 1920 as an Entrance Scholar in History, and gained distinguished results in 1922 and 1923 in Parts I and II respectively of the History Tripos. In the liberal atmosphere of those times gifted students were not expected to throw themselves into some specialised groove. From the beginning Oakeshott displayed

M. J. OAKESHOTT

*Angus McBean*

an interest in philosophy and attended J. M. E. McTaggart's lectures in that subject. No doubt this served to nourish his growing interest in philosophical Idealism. But alongside this developing concern with philosophy there were other intellectual preoccupations—with theology, with literature and, increasingly, with the history of political thought. After completing the Tripos he gained the Christopher James studentship at Caius and was then able to spend some time in Germany during 1923–4, and probably again in 1925. He was also for a short time a schoolmaster teaching English at Lytham St Anne's Grammar School. Meanwhile he prepared a dissertation which gained him a Fellowship at Caius in 1925. He was to retain this status, one which he probably prized more than any other, until his death sixty-five years later.

Oakeshott undoubtedly absorbed quite a lot of German philosophy and literature on his early visits to Marburg and Tübingen, but it is doubtful whether this owed much to any systematic course of study. Some have asserted that he heard lectures by Heidegger who was then engaged in the preparation of *Sein und Zeit* (1927), but to others Oakeshott denied this. Whilst his thinking undoubtedly reveals debts to the world of German thought and sensibility, apart from his acknowledgement of Hegel Oakeshott was never very explicit about what he owed to that source. Indeed, after his early visits he rarely went back to Germany and in later years preferred to take his holidays in Italy and above all France. There is even a passage in which he mocks the Germans for their propensity to fall for a *Weltanschauung*. In his feelings towards Europe Oakeshott was essentially an eclectic and tolerant Englishman. He owed most to the cultural heritage of his own country and was proud of it. But he also saw England within a wider European tradition and was always ready to draw on whatever elements in that tradition caught his imagination and excited his interest.

By the end of 1925 Oakeshott had embarked on the life of a Cambridge don. Initially he had only research duties, but he soon began to teach history to undergraduates. In 1931 be became a College lecturer, and then in 1933 University Lecturer in History, a post he was to hold until his departure from Cambridge in 1949. Much of his teaching in both supervisions and lectures was directed to the history of political thought. He quickly became known both for his mastery of an easy, conversational form of instruction and for a capacity to deliver carefully constructed formal lectures. It was one of the attractive features of the History faculty in Cambridge in those days (and this persisted until quite recently) that it was totally hospitable to members who were philosphers and moralists rather than conventionally defined professional historians. Earlier in this century philosophy at Cambridge was without a clearly defined and exclusive academic base, and so nobody minded if the subject was pursued by historians. Oakeshott exemplified this situation most vividly. His earliest articles were on religious matters and on Locke and Bentham. Then in 1933 his first book was published, *Experience and its Modes*, and this is a strictly philosophical treatise. Nobody unaware of the Cambridge scene could possibly have guessed that this austerely abstract treatment of human experience was written by someone who was, officially at least, an historian rather than a philospher.

*Experience and its Modes* is a remarkable book which, so it seems to me, retains its power to persuade rather more than some other parts of Oakeshott's writing. One reason for this is that it is a young man's achievement, presented with verve and self-confidence bordering on arrogance. Moreover, it is stylistically rather more attractive than some of the late works, being written in a flowing and relatively easy language, and showing no sign of anxiety about the author's capacity to say clearly what he wants to say. So sure is Oakeshott's touch in this first book of his that it is hard to believe, reading it nearly sixty years on, that he was not yet thirty-two when it appeared. His precocious philosophical assurance recalls Hume rather than Kant: like the former Oakeshott affirmed definite views early in life, but he also resembled the latter in that he was still struggling with his own ideas when already on the threshold of old age.

It is tempting to argue that *Experience and its Modes* sets the framework in which and out of which Oakeshott evolved later into a political philosopher. In some respects this is a correct view of the matter. The book sets out a philosophical position to which, in essentials, Oakeshott remained faithful for the rest of his life. It is also true that what he later had to say about politics and political philosophy remains congruent with the conclusions of *Experience and its Modes*. But without doubt it would be a serious mistake to imagine that this work of philosophy was seen by Oakeshott as an explicit prolegomenon to his later political writings. Like everything else in his life it was an experiment, a *ballon d'essai, ein Versuch*, undertaken for its own sake and dedicated strictly to the resolution of the particular questions which the author had in mind when he wrote it. What then does Oakeshott seek to do in *Experience and its Modes*?

His purpose was to examine the character of experience, to say something about what is involved in the philosophical understanding of it, and to present a view of philosophising as an intellectual activity. Right at the outset (p.7, *Experience and its Modes*) he asserts that philosophy is 'the effort in thought to begin at the beginning and to press to the end'. To philosophise (assuming that we actually get going) is always to enter on a critical engagement, a sustained and patient effort to tease out the postulates on which we talk about this or that aspect of experience. The aim is to recognise the limitations and the conditionality of what we commonly say about the world, and through the creative dismantling of our everyday categories of judgement eventually to achieve a more coherent account of experience.

With characteristic succinctness Oakeshott in 1985 summarised for the dust-jacket of a paperback edition of *Experience and its Modes* the aims of the work. It deals with 'Modality: human experience recognised as a variety of independent, self-consistent worlds of discourse, each the invention of human intelligence, but each also to be understood as abstract and an arrest in human experience'. The inquiry was pursued with reference to three modes of experience—history, science and practice. In essence what Oakeshott does is to establish what he regards as the only satisfactory terms in which to specify historical, scientific and practical experience: history is experience subject to the postulate of pastness; science is experience subject to the postulates of measurement and quantity; practical experience is experience subject to the postulates of willing and doing. To the understanding of each mode of experience there is an appropriate language, and to transfer the categories required by one mode of experience to another is to fall into categorial confusion or, more technically, to indulge in *ignoratio elenchi*. Oakeshott was to retain until the end of his life the essentials of this scheme of thought. True, he modified later some features of the terminology used in *Experience and its Modes*, and he qualified his account of the most familiar modes of experience by introducing aesthetic experience as a distinctive mode. But he remained convinced that though experience is in principle a whole, it is through distinctive varieties of experience that the experiencing subject becomes aware of his world. The task of philosophy is to elucidate the best way of talking sense both about these varieties of experience and about experience as a whole. In this way philosophy discharges a critical and therapeutic function: it adds nothing, but it can help us both to avoid confusion and to discern the lineaments of coherence in relation to experience as a whole and to its various distinctive modes.

*Experience and its Modes* made no great impact and it took over thirty years for a print-run of a thousand copies to sell. It appeared at a time when what soon came to be known as 'logical positivism' took off in British philosophy, becoming for several decades the dominant voice. It was easy for philosophers of that persuasion simply to ignore the book or to dismiss it as an exercise in a discredited idiom of Idealist philosophising. Moreover, we must not forget that not long after 1933 any way of thinking which appeared to owe debts to German philosophy became suspect, whilst at the same time there also emerged a preoccupation with critical empiricism in relation to both the natural and social worlds which was to lead in matters of social explanation to conclusions very different from Oakeshott's. Nevertheless, as more than one commentator has noted, Oakeshott's conception of philosophising was by no means as sharply at odds with what was recommended by practitioners of logical positivism, linguistic analysis, and common sense reasoning as has often been assumed. Like them Oakeshott attached more importance to philosophising as a method or mode of thought than to any conclusive utterances about life or reality which philosophers might make. He too wanted to achieve clarification in relation to our experience of the world around us, he too was profoundly impatient with muddled arguments. But doubtless there the resemblance ends. Compared with the majority of professional philosophers active in the years after the publication of *Language, Truth and Logic* (1936) Oakeshott was aiming high. His concern was how to clarify our understanding of experience as a whole, a large problem when compared with the preoccupation with tidying up linguistic muddles which soon came to dominate philosophical writing in Britain.

In the course of the thirties Oakeshott's interest in a philosophical understanding of 'politics' begins to emerge. In *Experience and its Modes* there are only cursory references to politics in the course of the analysis of practical experience where, indeed, he gives more space to religion as a type of practical experience. But he was already deeply engaged in a study of Hobbes, the first fruits of which were articles published in 1935 and 1937. Later this effort to grasp the thought of the man whom he regarded as England's greatest political philosopher was to culminate in the famous 'Introduction to *Leviathan*' (1946) and the essay, 'The Moral Life in the Writings of Thomas Hobbes', first published in *Rationalism in Politics* (1962). In the years before the Second World War Oakeshott was, however, already spreading his net beyond the history of political thought. He published in 1938 a remarkable essay, 'The Concept of philosophical jurisprudence', which prefigures his abiding concern with the nature and status of law as a specific framework for human relationships. In it he offered a stern criticism of all current jurisprudential theories and sought to set out what in his view were the proper points of departure for a philosophically adequate account of law. In 1939 came *The Social and Political Doctrines of Contemporary Europe*, a work untypical for Oakeshott and consisting of a collection of illustrative extracts for which he wrote an introductory commentary. If this seemed to indicate some edging towards an explicit preoccupation with contemporary 'goings-on', any such impression was firmly dispelled by the 1939 article in *Scrutiny* on 'The claims of politics'. Here he made no bones about his contempt for 'politics' seen as a bundle of remedies to be applied to the world in order to improve it. It called for some courage to write in such terms at *that* time. Perhaps too it called for some courage to publish in 1936 a book written jointly with a colleague, Guy Griffith, entitled *A Guide to the Classics or How to Pick a Derby Winner*. Though written with dry urbanity, this was a serious effort to 'offer a brief and businesslike account of the rational principles upon which we believe a winning selection may be based.' Fear of raised eyebrows did not deter Oakeshott from agreeing to a second edition of this light-hearted work in 1947.

The outbreak of war interrupted Oakeshott's academic career. He enlisted in the army in 1940 (though by then he was already thirty-eight) and after some time in the ranks was commissioned in Intelligence. There he served until 1945 in a unit called 'Phantom', the purpose of which was to collect, analyse and distribute information bearing on the effectiveness of artillery targetting. He appears to have adapted well to army life, even to have enjoyed it after a fashion. He formed friendships and experience of military life no doubt reinforced his profound respect for the diversities of human character and personality. Yet in his submission to the impositions of serving his country there was no enthusiasm at all for war itself. As he made plain in several passages in his post-war writings, war represents the very antithesis of an acceptable civil condition. It subjects those involved in it to the rigours of a common enterprise (winning) and necessarily excludes that freedom to live one's own life which he had come to regard as crucial to the definition of a civilised society. Whatever he took from Hegel, he had no time for that philosopher's grandiloquent comments on war and the virtues it may inspire.

After demobilisation Oakeshott returned to his teaching duties at Cambridge. By now a person of some seniority he became again a busy tutor and lecturer whose reputation was beginning to spread well beyond the confines of his college. That he steadily became more widely known was in part the result of his association with the newly founded *Cambridge Journal*, the general editorship of which he took over in 1947 and was to hold until the journal's demise in 1954. This gave him *inter alia* an outlet for several notable essays, including 'Rationalism in Politics', (November-December 1947) and 'Rational Conduct' (October 1950). But it also imposed a tremendous burden of work. After all, it was a monthly magazine running to ninety pages or so, it embraced an astonishingly wide spectrum of intellectual interests and concerns, and it carried a large number of book reviews. Though there was an editorial board, the work of editing fell almost entirely on Oakeshott. That he coped so successfully with this, that the journal attracted contributions from a dazzling constellation of scholars, and that he found time to write a substantial number of notable contributions himself is a tribute to Oakeshott's stamina and efficiency. But no doubt it was in part the burdens of editorship, combined with the demands of heavy teaching commitments, that led him to contemplate a move away from Cambridge in the hope of finding more time to devote to his own research and writing. Accordingly in 1949 he moved to Nuffield College, Oxford, a graduate college then in its infancy, which had the previous year elected him to an official fellowship.

The move to Oxford was to be no more than a brief interlude. Early in 1950 the chair of political science at the London School of Economics and Political Science became vacant on the death of Harold Laski. In September of that year the electors offered the succession to Oakeshott who agreed to come. Having left the comforts of Gonville and Caius for the rigours of Nuffield's temporary buildings on the Banbury Road and what must have been a shabby *pied à terre* in St Aldate's in order 'to follow up the research and writing I want to do' (letter to Henry Clay, Warden of Nuffield, November 1948), Oakeshott now went off to head what was probably the largest department of political science (or 'Government' as it was actually called) in the country. On the face of it the translation to the LSE was, for a man of Oakeshott's disposition and academic inclinations, puzzling. It meant acceptance of formal teaching duties again, it involved substantial administrative responsibility, and in some degree it was to thrust Oakeshott on to a public stage, something he had always disliked. But perhaps he suspected that the cunning of reason was at work in a modest way, and anyway his own approach to life required a cheerful response to the cards that fate dealt out. He must too have been somewhat flattered by the offer of election to the LSE chair, especially as he cannot have been insensitive to the irony implicit in the choice of himself to succeed Laski. This is reflected ever so gently in a letter he wrote to the Warden of Nuffield on 15 September 1950 telling him that if offered the chair, he would accept it. The reason he gave for this conclusion was that the students at the LSE 'have rather a raw deal and (that) I think they are worth while trying to help'. So at the end of 1950 Oakeshott's brief sojourn in Oxford was over and he exchanged the prospect of life as a full-time researcher for a renewed commitment to teaching. With hindsight it can be seen that he did the right thing: neither Oxford nor Nuffield could ever have offered an hospitable climate either for Oakeshott's style or for his ideas. The LSE was to provide opportunities not available in the older academies.

When Oakeshott arrived at the LSE the department he was to head had about a dozen members; when he left it had grown to nearly thirty. For fifteen years Oakeshott discharged the duties of head of department with skill and good humour. This administrative role was then separated from the academic duties of the chair of political science and devolved on one or other of the professors in it. By that time Oakeshott was not far off retirement, a threshold crossed at the beginning of 1969. His running of the department was economical in the calls it made on conventional bureaucratic resources: after all, here was a man who preferred to write letters in longhand. But he was no dilettante in the conduct of practical affairs. He had a strong sense of his own authority as head of the department, though showing a keen appreciation of what was required for the maintenance of amicable relations amongst his colleagues. He did, however, see the role of the head of a department in what would now widely be regarded as old-fashioned terms. Whoever holds such a position had in Oakeshott's understanding of the matter to be in the first place a scholar and a teacher, not an entrepreneur or a manager. He had no sympathy for empire-building, no desire to become deeply immersed in 'academic politics' as the game of bargaining inside universities is now called, and no real interest in acquiring positions of influence in external bodies which might be held to bolster the status of the departmental chairman within his own academic institution. Instead, he put his energies first into lecturing and the supervision of students: administration had to be attended to, but not at the expense of the primary responsibilities of the teacher.

The LSE gave to Oakeshott a stage which, in some elusive sense, he needed. It was then normal at the LSE for a senior professor to offer formal lectures for undergraduates, which were regarded as a major part of the instruction offered. Oakeshott's lectures on the history of political thought, delivered weekly as a rule to audiences of four hundred or so, became famous. They were not histrionic occasions, still less theatrical performances. But they did have the supreme merit of being exemplary: they showed in compelling language what efforts of thought were required of those who might hope to ascend to a modest plateau of understanding in relation to what is conventionally designated as 'politics'. Apart from lecturing Oakeshott also taught in smaller groups and was unfailingly generous in offering advice and guidance to individual students, both undergraduates and graduates. But he was not a directive supervisor, preferring always to leave the student free to explore a subject for himself. In his later years he must have despaired of the graduate research industry which has now become established with its emphasis on early definition of the research to be done as a precondition of 'higher output' and more rapid 'completion'. Another feature of Oakeshott's teaching life at the LSE was the seminar on the history of political thought which he gradually established on a permanent basis as a key element in the programme for a Master's degree in that subject. For at least a decade after retirement he remained the key figure in this seminar, and through the opportunities for conversation which it provided a serious interest in his ideas and arguments was ever more widely diffused. He had too a genuine interest in mature, part-time students and enjoyed in his earlier years at the LSE the evening classes provided for them.

Oakeshott was, however, neither preacher nor proselytizer. It is true that his great inaugural lecture, 'On Political Education', represented something in the nature of a *credo*, and thus could be regarded as akin to a manifesto or declaration of intent. In it he presented an account of tradition as the ground of political activity, gave a very clear statement of what the content of a political education should be, and rejected flatly all ideological thinking in politics. In words that were to become famous he asserted that in politics 'men sail a boundless and bottomless sea; there is neither harbour for shelter nor floor for anchorage, neither starting-place nor appointed destination. The enterprise is to keep afloat . . .' And those in his audience who found this a depressing doctrine were sharply reminded that this was so only for 'those who have lost their nerve'. But Oakeshott was temperamentally averse to the stridency of active persuasion and had no desire to gather a band of followers around him or to send missionaries out into the world. So he never tried to establish anything like an Oakeshottian orthodoxy at the LSE. He was content to be one voice—though no doubt a highly persuasive one—amongst several contributing to a conversation. If as a result some of those participating in the conversation came to understand the problems addressed in a manner Oakeshott appreciated, then so much the better: that was a bonus to be welcomed. But conversations were not to be transformed either into public meetings or into séances.

Not long after going to the LSE Oakeshott held in 1952–3 the Muirhead Lectureship at the University of Birmingham, a visiting appointment previously held by, amongst others, L. T. Hobhouse and J. S. Haldane. In 1958 he also spent some months as a visiting professor at Harvard. Generally, however, he eschewed external commitments of that kind. During his years at the LSE Oakeshott published little. Or, to put the matter more accurately, he did not write a great deal that was new. He did, however, see through in 1962 the publication of what is perhaps his most famous book, *Rationalism in Politics*. It is certainly his most dazzling and accessible work, and offers the most wide ranging introduction to his leading ideas about politics. *Rationalism in Politics and other essays* (to give it its correct title) consists of ten essays written over a period of fifteen years and seven of which had already appeared elsewhere. Two of them are directed explicitly to a critique of rationalistic thinking as applied to moral conduct and political life, but three more of them, those on 'Political Education' and 'On Being Conservative', which deal mainly with tradition as the necessary foundation of political life, and 'The Tower of Babel', which attacks the pursuit of abstract moral ideals as disruptive of a settled morality, also contribute to what is essentially the same argument. Of the remaining essays one deals with what is involved in writing history, another in the form of a book review illuminates the interconnection between a market economy and a liberal political order, and a third examines with subtlety and penetration Hobbes' conception of the moral life. Standing somewhat apart from the rest is the remarkable essay on aesthetic experience, 'The Voice of Poetry in the Conversation of Mankind', in which Oakeshott elegantly retracts an earlier remark about poetry by providing a careful account of a mode of experience which he believed he had failed to distinguish adequately when writing in 1933. Finally, there is the amusing and often sardonic essay on 'The Study of 'Politics' in a University'.

Certain themes which recur constantly in Oakeshott's thinking about politics, the philosophical understanding of this sphere of life, and the world of experience to which politics has to be related, dominate these essays. There is the attack on rationalistic constructions purporting to explain more or less scientifically what we are, how we got to our present position, and how we can engage in systematic improvement of our world. Such an approach, which Oakeshott traces back to Bacon, treats politics as an activity dependent on techniques. In Oakeshott's view all such thinking is ideological and at bottom inimical to human freedom: as he derisively remarks in a footnote, the Rationalist transforms everything into an abstraction, 'he can never get a square meal of experience'. There is the affirmation of existing practices and traditional forms of living together as the only possible basis both for a moral life favourable to individual self-development and for an acceptable mode of politics. There is persuasive deployment of the argument that all genuine politics as an activity is the 'politics of repair', 'the pursuit, not of a dream, or a general principle, but of an intimation'. There is an account of education in a university which identifies thinking critically for its own sake as the feature which distinguishes it from all other forms of education and 'training'. There is an urbane yet robust dismissal of positivist empiricism as the high road to some kind of systematic understanding of politics. And above all there is repeatedly the affirmation of forms of experience distinct from and owing nothing to politics which are valuable in themselves and need to be protected from the depredations of the philistines and *Banausen* who lurk in the political world.

The conception of politics that emerges most vividly from *Rationalism in Politics* is that of a sceptical conservative. True, there is much else in the work which properly considered qualifies and indeed demands amendment of this view of what Oakeshott was offering. But if during the 1960s and later he was by some erroneously typecast as an ingenious apologist for a vanishing world, and dismissed by others as a corrosive sceptic obstinately refusing to recognise the dawn of a new science of society, he hardly had grounds for complaint. He had explained with great care why he held all doctrines of progress and perfectibility to be both false and absurd, he had held up to ridicule many of the cherished shibboleths of the post-war epoch (including those of some of his academic colleagues), and he showed that he could do all this in a prose style of insinuating beauty which might well beguile the young and the unwary. At a time when Britain was moving towards the high-water mark of the Keynesian consensus such opinions were bound to be regarded by some as reactionary, by others as frivolous. By 1991 when a new and expanded edition of *Rationalism in Politics* was published in the USA by the Liberty Press some at least of Oakeshott's formerly unconventional opinions had secured a certain reluctant recognition.

Retirement, which was marked by the presentation to him of a notable *Festschrift* entitled *Politics and Experience*, must in some degree have been a release from bondage for Oakeshott. For many years after 1969 he continued to guide and animate the history of political thought seminar, and he retained a somewhat run-down room at the LSE. But freed from the diurnal duties of a professor he was able to return to writing. He put together his principal essays on Hobbes in a volume entitled *Hobbes on Civil Association* which came out in 1975. Meanwhile he was pressing on slowly, far more slowly than he had expected, towards completion of his most important work, *On Human Conduct*. This too was published in 1975 and consists of three long connected essays, the first on human conduct, the second on the civil condition, and the third on the character of a modern European state. In the preface Oakeshott records that the themes of which he writes have been with him nearly as long as he can remember. Then, after apologising for having taken so long to put his thoughts together, he concludes by confessing that 'when I look back upon the path my footprints make in the snow I wish that it might have been less rambling'. Even if there is artifice in this appeal to the reader, it is hard to resist the poetic beauty in which it is expressed.

*On Human Conduct* is a difficult book, written to some extent in a semi-technical language composed in part of Latin terms – *cives, civitas, lex, respublica, societas, universitas* and the like. But there are also complex and unusual conceptions presented in English, notably those of self-disclosure and self-enactment in human conduct. The denseness of the writing (at any rate in the first two essays, the third being easier to read) renders impossible a satisfactory summary of what Oakeshott contends for in this volume. As with most of his work, anyone who wants to understand it must get to grips with the original: there is no substitute for that. But if his argument is to be reduced to its essential elements, then it is as follows. Human beings are neither the objects of a process nor the components of a structure. They are intelligent agents who have to engage in transactions with each other in order to live. They are capable of understanding their lives both as revealing the terms of the moral practices in which they have grown up, and as demonstrating their own capacity for achieving fulfilment through fidelity to these practices. Above all human conduct is characterised by an ability to qualify actions adverbially, that is to say to do *this* or perhaps *that* in a certain way rather than simply to pursue ends such as a good salary, happiness or grace abounding. To theorise politics is to delineate the kind of state (or civil condition) appropriate to human beings capable of that kind of conduct.

The construction which emerges on this foundation is a spare rule of law state, what Oakeshott refers to as the civil condition or civil association. It rests upon a morality and is embodied concretely in the practices of civility appropriate to the society in which it is exemplified. (Practice is the concept which Oakeshott now prefers to tradition as allowing a more rigorous specification of the conditions of social life within which conduct *inter homines* takes place.) The law of such a state is general in form and appears to consist chiefly of prohibitions. There are offices of rule, notably those of deliberating the laws to be made, enforcing them, and adjudicating disputes arising from their application. In contrast to its long-standing competitor in the European political tradition, enterprise association, the civil condition prescribes no common purpose for those subject to it, and the authority of its laws rests entirely on the subjects' continued subscription to them. By virtue of that subscription the subjects are under an obligation to obey the law and can properly be punished if they do not. Yet the civil condition is very limited in its range. For the most part it prevents collisions between subjects in order that they can then safely get on with their own lives as they see fit. In the third essay Oakeshott attempts an historical outline of the emergence of this kind of state in modern Europe. This he does by presenting the two contrasting ideal types—civil association and enterprise association—as persistent themes which can be located at various points in the evolution of modern Europe and its states. In a rather loose way this essay might be regarded as presenting something like empirical backing for the two preceding theoretical discussions. But it is unlikely that this was Oakeshott's intention, and anyway his history is too lightly sketched in to be quite convincing. What we really have, therefore, is a continuation of the theoretical argument.

In *On Human Conduct* (as in many other parts of his writing) Oakeshott proceeds by constructing ideal types. This was his favoured method of presenting an argument, and one which can be regarded as a necessary consequence of his concern to expose the postulates of particular features of experience. It follows, of course, that it is irrelevant to ask how far we can actually show empirically (and that could only mean historically) that Oakeshott's ideal types are to be found in the world, past or present. They are not constructions derived by induction, they are constructs of thought achieved by reflecting critically on human experience. If we wish to escape from the higgeldy-piggeldy world of discrete facts—the slag-heap of innumerable happenings—then in Oakeshott's view the only way open to intelligent human beings is to consider the terms on which the muddle they face might be made coherent. This is, however, in his opinion by no means an arbitrary engagement. He was still enough of a philosophical Idealist to believe that the intelligent theorist can construct reality only in certain ways, and that he is capable of avoiding categorial confusion. The lessons of *Experience and its Modes* are thus re-affirmed in *On Human Conduct* and it is, incidentally, for that reason that we can properly regard *On Human Conduct* as presenting a political philosophy: it sought to show how a particular specification of politics was required and justified by a larger philosophical analysis of experience.

Both its style and the philosophical method employed contributed to the cool reception accorded to *On Human Conduct*. It was held by some to be remote and artificial, by others to be simply too clever and too paradoxical to be credible. Moreover, for those in or on the fringes of 'real' politics such a book was quite useless: after all, apart from warning against the New Jerusalem and a place called *Schlaraffenland* it offered no practical recommendations at all! Worse still, *On Human Conduct* appeared to dismiss such virtuous notions as basic human rights and social justice out of hand, and that at a time when they were at last coming into their own. But if disappointed by the reaction to his efforts to explain his understanding of politics as closely and as explicitly as he could, Oakeshott did not show it. And certainly he was not deterred from pressing on to a further elaboration of his position. This reached the public in 1983 (he was then approaching eighty-two) under the title *On History and other essays*. Once more he returned to questions which had preoccupied him for the best part of sixty years. What is the nature of historical knowledge? What is the minimum adequate specification of a rule of law? The book contains only one essay on the rule of law, though it is substantial in scale. In it Oakeshott provides a succinct, even terse re-statement of what he takes to be the minimal defining characteristics of the rule of law. Whilst in many respects he reiterates the arguments set out in the 1975 essay on the civil condition, he does in this later essay achieve a degree of completeness and compression in his treatment of the subject that testifies eloquently to the strength of his conviction that a rule of law, properly understood, is 'the most civilised and least burdensome conception of a state yet to be devised'. Equally impressive are the three essays on history which integrate in a compelling manner all the considerations which had over the years gone into his view of what is involved practically and theoretically in understanding the past. The lineage back to *Experience and its Modes* can easily be traced. Yet there is in this late work a far more comprehensive account of what history is and how we are to distinguish historical knowledge from other forms of knowledge than he had provided before. It is as if some of the philosophical baggage had been shed, thus enabling Oakeshott to focus sharply and intensely on a concept which is at one and the same time grossly misused and misunderstood, and yet crucial to the kind of self-understanding that has evolved in the West. The book concludes with another version of the fable of the Tower of Babel, an image to which Oakeshott often returned in his search for ways of illustrating the moral predicament of a world bewitched by the desire to 'Take the Waiting out of Wanting'.

After *On History and other essays* Oakeshott published no more on his own initiative. But he did bless a volume of essays on education which Professor Timothy Fuller edited and brought out in 1989 under the title *The Voice of Liberal Learning*. Most of the essays had appeared before in various places, but the book also contains some hitherto unpublished work. What is perhaps most valuable about it is that it brings together in convenient form most of the important statements about education and the character of a specifically liberal education that Oakeshott had written over many years. Yet there is an unavoidable sadness attaching to the volume: did it not appear just at a time when the very idea of a liberal education in Britain and elsewhere was in full retreat in the face of the advocates of education as a preparation for practical life and nothing more? By the end of the 1980s it did indeed appear that the cause of liberal education was about to be overwhelmed.

During the last twenty years or so of his life Michael Oakeshott lived chiefly at Acton, Langton Matravers, a village in a bleak situation on the Dorset coast not far from Swanage. It was only when approaching retirement that he purchased the cottages where he was to die on 19 December 1990 at the age of eighty-nine: up till then he had merely rented the various properties in which he had made his home. His hesitation about borrowing to buy property reflected some of those Victorian values in which he was brought up and to which he remained faithful throughout his life: a duty to pay as you go along and not to get into debt, frugality and rejection of ostentation in outward appearances, punctuality and regularity in working habits, courtesy and attention towards others, self-help and individual responsibility. Yet though there was this austere side to his character, he was at the same time a man of warm feelings with a gift for friendship. And to his many friends he showed unfailing kindness and generosity. He was too a man of unconventional dispositions, with much of the Bohemian and the romantic, even the eccentric, in him. It was in his relationships with women in particular that he was for most of his life an incurable romantic. He enjoyed many close attachments with the opposite sex, and nearly all of those who remember him from earlier years testify to the ease with which he was able to secure the company of engaging young ladies. No doubt it was his fascination with '*das Ewig-Weibliche*' that contributed to the difficulty he had in adapting to the ties of marriage. His first two marriages, one in early life and another some years later, ended in divorce; his third marriage came when he was just over sixty and endured until his death. But it is hard to write about Oakeshott's private life. He was an intensely private person who believed passionately in the individual's right to conduct as he saw fit that part of his life which was unconnected with public duties. Naturally, even in private life there were always obligations to be met, but it was for individuals to decide themselves what these were and how best to fulfil them.

Oakeshott was indifferent to, perhaps even contemptuous of the usual symbols of social recognition. He would accept no public honours and was extremely reluctant to take honorary doctorates, though eventually he yielded to the solicitations of friends and former students and did accept them from Durham (UK) and Colorado (USA) universities. He was also willing to become a Fellow of the British Academy in 1966. Yet whilst recognising the somewhat bizarre character of the British way with honours he could see its rationale: after all, as he is said to have remarked, honours should go to those who most enjoy them. Nor did he seek the company of the great and the good, still less was he ever on the lookout for a place on this or that committee of inquiry or council for sundry good works. To have courted favours in the world of public affairs would for Oakeshott have signified moral corruption as well as foolishness. Since he regarded politics as a highly ambiguous sphere of life and political science as a generally misconceived undertaking, he was only being consistent in steering clear of most entanglements in political life. This is one of the reasons why it is erroneous to link him at all closely with the Conservative revivalism of the Thatcher years. He sympathised with the Conservative party and no doubt approved of much that Mrs Thatcher set in motion, in particular her efforts to reduce the power of trade unions in the political life of the country. But in a profound sense Oakeshott was the antithesis of a party man: his vocation was to establish a philosophical understanding of politics. By definition that excludes both practical recommendation and dalliance with the world of affairs. Of all important British political philosophers since Hobbes he may well have been the most detached from current events and the actors on the political stage. Expressive of this detachment is the absence in his writings of virtually all explicit references to the great upheavals of his times: in this respect he was remarkably like Jane Austen in her novels. But for all his determination to eschew overt political engagement, he remained deeply committed to the traditional political forms and procedures of his own country. He had a strong feeling for England and it was chiefly from his reflections on the political experience and achievements of England that he drew the conclusion that the civil condition must rest on a slowly evolving practice of civility.

Oakeshott was an elusive and multi-layered thinker who resists straightforward categorization. He drew eclectically on many sources— philosophers and theologians, moralists and historians, poets, novelists and dramatists. But he cared little for the visible apparatus of scholarship and so provides few clues to the main influences on his thought (and some that he does offer are misleading too!). But three thinkers above all did inspire his own effort to understand experience and to construct a political philosophy: Montaigne, Hobbes and Hegel. About these three at least he is reasonably explicit. From Montaigne he derived the sense of life as *une aventure*, a moral exploration until death supervenes; from Hobbes comes much of what Oakeshott re-fashions as the rule of law and the civil condition; and from Hegel there comes both the Idealist philosophical heritage (or as much of it as Oakeshott chose to adopt) and an awareness that a genuine political order must rest on appropriate moral traditions in society.

The achievement of Michael Oakeshott was to transmute these pre-existing elements into a philosophical composition that is original, expressed wholly in his own style, coherent, and complete. There is an impressive consistency in his thinking from the philosophical foundations laid down in *Experience and its Modes* through the essays on more explicitly political themes of his middle years on to the chillier, almost magisterial conclusions of the works written in old age. His undertaking was and remained in the first instance to locate politics and political forms on a philosophically grounded map of experience: the project of establishing 'the connections, in principle and in detail, directly or mediately, between politics and eternity' which he attributed to Hobbes in his 'Introduction to *Leviathan*' was indeed what he pursued unremittingly himself. The outcome was a specification of politics as an activity and political association as a form of social order which is coherently related to a philosophical account of what we can know of experience and how we are to understand human conduct. And it is precisely because he adhered so rigorously to the effort to locate politics philosophically that he has so little to offer in the shape of specific recommendations. This does not mean that he had no views on what should be done in the world of affairs. On the contrary he often had strong private opinions on many matters. But in his public, academic capacity he just did not see himself as being in the business of telling people what to do.

Nevertheless, there is also much in Oakeshott's published work which at least indirectly has important practical implications. His critique of rationalism and ideology counts against all projects of total reform and, therefore, points to the *prima facie* benefits of a conservative position. The stress on tradition and established practices reinforces this conservative strand in Oakeshott's arguments. Yet he remains at the same time an unusual kind of liberal. For Oakeshott freedom was virtually the equivalent of intelligent human activity: the world is inhabited by individuals who can act intelligently and must do so if they are to survive. From this postulate Oakeshott derived both the impossibility of deterministic accounts of human conduct and social development and his conclusion that individuals should have as wide a scope as possible for deciding how to shape their lives. This leads to a very rigorous kind of liberalism, akin almost to a libertarian standpoint. Consistently with this position Oakeshott argued for something that looks rather like the minimal state, though he carefully steered clear of all dogmatic commitments purporting to define the exact scope and limits of government. But of one thing we can be sure. The kind of state Oakeshott was prepared to endorse had to be one which allowed its citizens a wide sphere of liberty in which they could then show that they were capable of intelligently shaping their own lives. Above all, the state which he recommended could not be a managerial or a planning state, it was not an enterprise association keen to thrust its common purposes on to citizens who might not want to take part in them.

Yet it seems to me that there is a still deeper motive inspiring Oakeshott's construction of the political realm. He believed that practical life is in some sense primary, in any event inescapable. As he remarks at the end of 'The Voice of Poetry in the Conversation of Mankind', 'there is no *vita contemplativa*; there are only moments of contemplative activity abstracted and rescued from the flow of curiosity and contrivance.' For most of the time we are caught up in practical life, and this entails willing, doing, seeking, trying, hopefully moving from one state of affairs to another which we then prefer. There is a restlessness about practical life which threatens to consume all else and to blunt our capacity to grasp other forms of experience. It is in this connection that we can best explain the close attention Oakeshott paid to history. Clearly he was as a philosopher (and no doubt as a somewhat dilettante historian) interested in what history is, the status of historical knowledge, and the proper philosophical context in which to grasp history as a mode of experience. But for him what was really striking was the contrast between historical and practical experience, and the constant danger that the latter will corrupt and consume the former. History is present knowledge which refers to a world that is dead and gone, it is knowledge for its own sake made possible by the human capacity to grasp 'pastness' as a category of experience. Thus the effort to isolate and specify historical knowledge in a rigorous way was at the same time an effort to keep practical life at bay and to hold back its incursions. The conclusions about history have, furthermore, a direct bearing on Oakeshott's account of politics. Just as he wished to save historical knowledge from those who would degrade it to 'the lessons of history', so he argued for a minimalist account of the civil condition in the hope that this would leave space for much else in life which he prized more highly than politics. Here we can see Oakeshott's affinity with Montaigne and Hume, and his lack of sympathy for an idealised view of the polis life *à la grecque*. It is the outlook of a humanist and sceptic who believes that an obsession with politics, apart from the risks of tyranny it brings, is bound to impoverish our lives. There are simply better things to be getting on with in life. Nevertheless, the kind of citizen who can accept a highly limited role for government and then get on with his own affairs, is in a minority. In one of his darkest essays, 'The Masses in Representative Democracy' (1957 in German, 1961 in English) Oakeshott depicts the anti-individual who prefers the comforts of benevolent despotism to the risks and rigours of a free society. If that harsh picture reflects what we can normally expect to encounter, the chances of keeping politics at bay and of sustaining Oakeshott's ideal of the civil condition are but modest.

Oakeshott will be remembered as a political philosopher, the most compelling and original British contributor to this rare genre in the twentieth century. But he will also be remembered as an essayist and as the protagonist of a liberal, humanist education. The essay was Oakeshott's preferred literary form, and in some measure all his work consists of essays, some more closely linked with each other than others. He took great pains over the composition of each essay, and the best of them reveal a remarkable unity of harmonious expression and carefully balanced structure which demonstrates his mastery of this art form. (He was equally a master of letter-writing and maintained an extensive correspondence). Moreover, Oakeshott had wit and irony at his command, qualities which he deployed skilfully to point up arguments and to enhance their persuasiveness. Surely many of his essays, especially those of his middle years, will survive simply as splendid examples of this literary form. About education he wrote sympathetically and persuasively on many occasions. In his concern to see each level of education contribute appropriately to an opening of the minds of those being taught, he was perhaps not so far away from many 'progressive' educationalists of quite different political persuasion who also stressed helping children and students to learn for themselves and in their own way. But Oakeshott totally rejected social engineering through education and was deeply critical of the modern obsession with training and the preparation for jobs. In his view all these errors of judgement could be traced back to a failure to draw the necessary distinctions in our thinking about education.

I have remarked several times that Oakeshott was a sceptic. His scepticism certainly extended to metaphysics, and probably to religion also. Notwithstanding his deep respect for Augustine as a thinker there is little reason to believe that he adhered to traditional Christian beliefs and there are only a few passages in his *oeuvre* in which religion is explicitly considered. Yet what he did write about this aspect of experience suggests that he attached great importance to it. In *On Human Conduct* there are some pages of haunting beauty in which Oakeshott characterises religious experience as 'a reconciliation to the unavoidable dissonances of a human condition'. In the same passage there is much else which evokes the transitoriness of human life and the inevitable frustration of so many of its hopes. Religion is a response to that awareness, a way of coming to terms with our mortality. The explicit references to religion by Oakeshott may be few and far between. But his whole work is pervaded by a sense of the mystery inherent in life and a perception of how difficult it is to find even modestly satisfactory words with which to express what needs to be said if experience is to be made intelligible. This is a feeling which we can detect in Hölderlin, a poet greatly admired by Oakeshott, and some have claimed to find it in much of Wittgenstein's writing too. Many of those who have been deeply sensitive to this sense of mystery in life have in their efforts to penetrate the veil of experience come to those margins of reflection where expression can be found only in mysticism. It may be that what created the deepest gulf between Oakeshott and so many of his contemporaries was precisely some unarticulated awareness of this undercurrent in his thinking. For a world addicted to rationalism and empiricism such a possibility was profoundly disturbing. No wonder that some dismissed him as a nostalgic reactionary, a Proust of political philosophy, whilst others simply passed him by uncomprehending. But the possibility remains that much of life is a mystery and that coming to terms with it is a hard matter. Oakeshott saw this possibility as a reality and took up the challenge implicit in it.

In the course of a long life Michael Oakeshott assumed, certainly without willing it, the character of a sage. Notwithstanding that most of his opinions and beliefs were persistently at odds with whatever happened to be the fashionable nostrums of the passing moment, he became for a considerable number of those closely concerned with the study of moral and political argument a source of inspiration. No doubt he would have protested against the ascription to him of such a position: was not his whole philosophical endeavour founded on the conviction that everyone must do his own thinking? Was there not in his writing so much awareness of the mystery and ambiguity of all experience that the very notion of a sage offering 'inspiration' would have struck him as mildly absurd, and more especially with himself in the guise of the sage? Nevertheless, he could not help exerting on others a certain fascination. He was able to use the English language with skill and distinction, commanding a full range of tones from elegaic sadness to dismissive contempt, from hilarious mockery to finely drawn semantic differentiation, from elegant simplicity to an almost tortured archaicism in the pursuit of exactness. Such stylistic gifts go some way towards explaining his impact even on those who never met him or heard him lecture. But for many the personality was compelling too. This was not because he ever sought to impose himself on others, still less to affirm his status as a scholar or his reputation as a philosopher. What was arresting about him as a man was his capacity to establish around himself a pool of stillness in the midst of which he would then engage in a conversation. For Oakeshott such occasions were in the first instance an opportunity to listen to others. Those who entered into conversation with him then nearly always came away with a mixture of awe and exhilaration prompted by the manner in which his penetrating intelligence was reflected back on to whatever features of the world they happened to be talking about. And above all the ideas he developed and the arguments he deployed in his published work are difficult and challenging. He offered no easy answers: there may be shortcomings and weaknesses in the arguments he presents and the conclusions he reaches. But he set out to scale a great peak. The intrepid endeavour to do so will continue for many years to come to command admiration and to serve as a compelling example of how to reason philosophically about politics. Through his writings he became a starting-point for others.

NEVIL JOHNSON
*Nuffield College, Oxford*

*Note.* I gratefully acknowledge my indebtedness to many of those who wrote or spoke about Michael Oakeshott at the time of his death and later. Dr Simon Oakeshott, Dr John Casey and Professor Kenneth Minogue were most helpful in providing information, and in particular I want to thank Dr Shirley Letwin for her perceptive advice and comments.

*Proceedings of the British Academy*, **80**, 425–431

# John Claude Trewinard Oates
# 1912–1990

FOR ALMOST FOUR DECADES students of 15th-century printed books have used the word 'Oates' to denote one of their most regularly cited references, *A Catalogue of the Fifteenth-Century Printed Books in the University Library Cambridge*, published in 1954. Its consistent use cannot be explained by the importance of this collection alone. 'Oates' is, along with other such conveniently short names like 'Hain', or more recently 'Goff' and 'Sack' (not to speak of acronyms like 'GW', 'BMC' and 'IGI') an infallible bibliographical guide to the material described, much improving on earlier and far less systematic methods of decription at this level. With its transparent layout and analysis of the items it set an example that was readily followed in many other catalogues. To the world at large the Cambridge catalogue of incunabula is John Oates's best-known work, but its particular value can be better appreciated if it is seen in the context of the other interests that were so clearly defined as central in its author's life and work.

John Claude Trewinard Oates was born in Gloucester on 24 June 1912. He was educated at the Crypt School in Gloucester and won in 1931 a scholarship to Trinity College, Cambridge, where he read classics. He graduated BA with first-class honours in 1935, and after a short interval which included some months spent in Germany intended as a preparation for a planned future in classical archaeology he was appointed as assistant under-librarian at the University Library, Cambridge. His obvious gift for scholarship had led his mentor at Trinity, A. S. F. Gow, to recommend him to the Librarian, A. F. Scholfield. The balance between scholarship and the organizational needs of the library were a first priority in Scholfield's librarianship, and striking this balance proved to be the main theme in John Oates's long career in the University Library. His career was interrupted

J. C. T. OATES

by war-time service but after his return he was promoted to the post of Under-Librarian in 1949. He became Deputy Librarian in 1975 and, just when he was on the point of retirement, was called upon to fulfil the function of Acting Librarian, following the sudden death of Eric Ceadel in 1979. A year later, after 45 years of service, he was at last free to complete the second of the major works of scholarship which he had undertaken, *Cambridge University Library: A History, from the Beginning to the Copyright Act of Queen Anne*, which was published in 1986. The catalogue of incunbalula of 1954 betrays the embryonic presence of the later book in the author's mind, in its extensive introduction containing a concise history of the collection, and even more in the annotation of each single item to explain its acquisition and whenever possible its earlier history. For this part of the collections Oates could claim to have achieved what more than thirty years later he would state as one of his aims for the history of the library as a whole 'a history which would tell [the reader] when, why, where, and in what manner every important manuscript or printed book had entered our collections and what scholarly use had been made of it since'.

In this respect, linking early ownership and the history of individual copies with the systematic bibliographical description of a collection, the catalogue is truly innovatory, and is an early sign of the direction the study of early printing was to take in decades to come: the history of the book-trade, of collecting and of libraries, and more recently, of reading and the spread of the printed book. One of the foundation stones for pursuing these new kinds of interest was laid by John Oates himself, but it also fell to him to complete an edifice for which the foundations had been laid by others. It cannot have been an easy inheritance. Some three generations before him the incunabula of the University Library had been the breeding ground for fundamental innovation in the study of this kind of material. Henry Bradshaw, University Librarian from 1867 to 1886, had outlined the principles of classification and description of incunabula in two short publications, developed and supported by contact and correspondence with other scholars. He took the collection at Cambridge (which he enriched considerably by acquisitions and gifts) as his point of departure and used it as his experimental material, thus almost incidentally beginning with a systematic catalogue of the collection. After Bradshaw's premature death in 1886 the torch was taken over by Robert Proctor and the classification of all 15th-century printing was accomplished on the collections of the British Museum and the Bodleian Library. A wealth of notes and unfinished materials remained in Cambridge, however, and Bradshaw's pupil and later successor F. Jenkinson (Librarian 1889–1923) displayed keen interest in incunabula, added many to the collection and produced several specialized studies. But the catalogue remained unfinished. This task proved ideally suited to John Oates, a young man, not yet distracted by the many obligations of office, unwilling to be lured by the many scholarly temptations offered by a large and wide-ranging collection.

Once the incunabula catalogue was completed, John Oates was free to follow his manifest inclination to accomplish the detailed and comprehensive study of the history of the University Library. That this took him over thirty years, in which time he brought the history not beyond the year 1710, is no sign of idleness. It goes without saying that his work was meticulous and of great integrity, but as it progressed his responsibilities in the Library grew, and he allowed his rapidly increasing experience to enrich his perception of the function of the collection and the institution.

A whole generation of scholars could follow his progress with the *History of the University Library* by a sequence of smaller publications which served as preliminary studies, several almost ready to be absorbed into the larger work.[1] In 1952 (the same year as his first Sandars lectures which appeared in print as the introduction to his catalogue of incunabula) he published with H. L. Pink the text of three 16th-century catalogues of the University Library. Several studies (in 1952, 1972 and 1974) were devoted to the development of legal deposit. A preliminary and abbreviated survey of the history of the Library 1400–1600 presented as a lecture to the Graduate Library School of the University of Chicago was published in *The Library Quarterly* in 1962. In 1974 a detailed analysis of the ineradicable misinformation published about the *Nachlass* of the Dutch orientalist Thomas Erpenius (which is in the University Library) was the subject of a lecture for the Bibliographical Society of Australia and New Zealand. The Sandars lectures for 1966, a study of Abraham Whelock 1593–1653, orientalist, Anglo-Saxonist, and University Librarian, became a chapter in the *History* of the Library.

Among Oates's short studies of English printing his excellent introduction to a facsimile edition of Caxton's *Vocabulary in French and English* (1964) deserves particular mention. He published a handful of articles about Sterne and his imitators among which *Shandyism and Sentiment, 1760–1800*, a commemorative lecture presented in 1968, stands out as a lucid and entertaining overview.

Meanwhile his disposition to share his knowledge of the collections

---

[1] A checklist of the published works compiled by D. E. Rhodes was added to a posthumous publication of a selection of his essays: J. C. T. Oates, *Studies in English Printing and Libraries*, London, 1991.

as well as of bibliographical discipline in its most recent developments exerted an inestimable influence on the large number of scholars who for part of their researches came to rely on the University Library. John Oates was generous in making his experience available to others, applauded and happily supported any new use made of the collections. A spectacular example is his understanding of the significance of the early records of the Cambridge University Press, which indirectly led to D. F. McKenzie's seminal analysis of these documents and their implications for our understanding of book production in the hand-press period. Such an instance gave him immense satisfaction and it is by no means isolated. I count myself among the very many scholars who have cause for lasting gratitude for a guiding hand and generous support on long and regular visits to Cambridge. The duties to the public of a rare-book librarian, as John Oates had now become, are not confined to visitors, and a substantial amount of time has to be given to correspondence. John Oates was in frequent epistolary contact with scholars on both sides of the Atlantic and in Europe. In such contacts he showed an excellent grasp of all current developments in historical bibliography which in his published work surfaces only occasionally. Although his correspondence was always carried out promptly, with great courtesy and understanding of the inquirer's needs and without wasting words, it offered occasionally scope for his remarkable talent for writing outrageously witty prose, a gift he used sparingly, as appropriate to a highly spiced ingredient. On very rare occasions, as in some book reviews, he allowed it to take over, to unforgettable effect but without real malice,[2] probably because he was fully aware that this could be devasting ammunition if used indiscriminately. The influence of Laurence Sterne to whom (with his imitators of the eighteenth century) he was devoted, is obvious, and, although he never descended into pastiche, a delightful hint of Sternianism pervades all Oates's prose. Let one example suffice, taken from the preface of his *History*, which also sums up his attitude to the allocation of priorities:

> . . . For a time my researches formed part of my official duties, and I made fair, if slow, progress, writing each chapter as the research upon it was completed. There are, I suspect, other and better ways of writing a book like this one. The tenor of my way began to change some fifteen years ago when subtle pressures began to be exerted upon me for the purpose of turning me into an administrator. These proved difficult to resist, the conversion being finally effected in the middle of a sentence now to be found on p. 367. It was almost a decade before I was able,

[2] The most delightful example must be the review of a revised edition of John Carter, *ABC for book collectors* which appeared in *The Library*, September 1962, pp. 272–3, 'by Z as dictated to J.C.T. Oates'.

after my retirement, to return to it and to carry on my work to its present
ending . . .

Juxtapose this to the end of a letter to William A. Jackson, written in
October 1956, which answers, with usual brisk efficiency a questionnaire
for STC and an expression of envy:

> . . . A life so tranquil indeed! When your letter arrived I was buried up to the
> neck in 13500 Christmas cards newly arrived from the press and was making
> arrangements for ULC to go into trade . . .

John Oates became an authoritative voice both in Cambridge and
in an international network of scholars in a wide-ranging variety of
bibliographical disciplines. Apart from the affection and gratitude of many
he received recognition of his gifts and achievements. He was Editor of *The
Library* from 1953 to 1960, during which years the journal flourished. His
strict standards of editing are preserved in the folk memory as nuggets of
editorial advice: that foot-notes should wherever possible be incorporated
into the text; that the time for research is *before* a paper is sent to press . . .
He served as President of the Bibliographical Society in 1970–2, and was
President of the Cambridge Bibliographical Society from 1977 to 1981. In
1964 he was one of the Founding Fellows of Darwin College, and he was
Reader in Historical Bibliography in the University of Cambridge from
1972. In 1976 he was elected Fellow of the British Academy.

The life and work of John Oates exemplifies that of the scholar-
librarian. In its traditions of librarianship this country has been blessed
with more than one of his kind in every generation, and has thus been
able to maintain (tenuously) a tradition that is constantly under threat
from professional demands partly of its own making. In the case of John
Oates there was never any question of giving the profession second place
by withdrawing into esoteric scholarship: the demands of the library and
assisting readers in using the collection to best advantage were his first
priorities. In later years his function as Reader in Historical Bibliography
gave a new dimension to the concept of this task, but even from this external
responsibility the library benefited directly, as testified by his didactic
disposition of reference material in the Munby Room. His successful efforts
to raise funds for the Munby Fellowship were yet another expression of
his intense support of scholarship centred on the University Library. Thus
the influence of a scholar dedicated to important collections can be seen
to pervade concentric circles: a close circle of friends in Cambridge to
whom he was 'Titus', and with whom he maintained an enduring exchange
of scholarly interests and encouragement. Immediately beyond this there
was a circle of younger colleagues and pupils, who greatly profited from
his teaching and the model he set, but, although friends, maintained some

respectful distance.[3] Somewhat more remote but perceptibly influenced over many years were the circles of the Bibliographical Society and colleagues in other British collections. And finally there was a very large circle of scholars, encompassing universities and libraries over half the world, who felt admiration and affection for him in about equal measure, and who acknowledged his guidance and advice in their many publications. That amid such rich diversity it remained possible for him to complete two major publications was not only due to his patience, tenacity, and sense of purpose, but above all to his systematic and sharp definition of what he wished to accomplish in these works. The world of bibliography and librarianship will remain deeply grateful to him.

LOTTE HELLINGA
*Fellow of the British Academy*

---

[3] Affectionate memorials were written by D.F. McKenzie in *Transaction of the Cambridge Bibliographical Society*, ix, 1990, pp. 401–8, and by D. J. McKitterick in *The Cambridge Review*, December 1990, pp. 188–90.

*Proceedings of the British Academy*, **80**, 433–452

# Hilary Seton Offler
# 1913–1991

H. S. OFFLER was born on 3 February 1913. His father, Horace Offler, was
manager, later general manager and secretary, of King's Acre Nurseries at
Hereford. This was a long-established and substantial firm, with a shop in
the city and from 120 to 200 men and boys on the pay-roll. The family lived
in the city and after attending a 'dame school' (his own phrase) Offler in
1923 entered Hereford High School for Boys, a school of some 250 pupils
with a small sixth form. In December 1928, two months before his sixteenth
birthday, he won a scholarship to Emmanuel College, Cambridge. Both
school and college were disconcerted at this achievement by one so young.
His headmaster, R. G. Ruscoe, who had written that he 'would certainly
be taken for a boy of 17 or 18 at least', explained that he had been put
in for the scholarship 'as a trial shot'; Edward Welbourne, history tutor at
Emmanuel, wrote that 'none of us knew . . . that he was so young—and
though I ought to have noticed it from his papers I did not feel conscious
of it in my talk with him'. It was agreed that the rules should be stretched
to allow Offler to spend a further year at school; 'the worst mistake,' wrote
Welbourne, advising him how to use this time, 'would be to know too much
history and too little else'.

His early success was due to sheer native talent. A near-contemporary
describes the school at this time as 'certainly no academic hot-house. . . .
It was a happy school and . . . not outstanding in really any other way'.
However, the history master, 'Araby' Heal, 'did really encourage us . . . ;
one always felt one could do a little bit better after that essay had come
back'. Offler himself deeply appreciated his school, looking for no more
from it than what it could offer. He wrote, long afterwards, that 'it was
a pretty rough world; but for the most part it was also tolerant and kindly.
. . . there was little attempt to frustrate the common ambition of us all,

H. S. OFFLER *(right)* with Professor Thacker

which was to turn into men as quickly as possible'. He had a special word for the woodwork master: 'On the whole the School understood craftsmanship far better than scholarship, and he was indeed a superb craftsman, teaching . . . —so gently, but quite inflexibly—the lesson that the only satisfactory way of doing any job was to do it in a proper fashion'. Among his schoolfellows, Offler

> had a reputation of being aloof, a very stern and efficient prefect, more feared by the juniors than Ruscoe himself. He must have had an enormous capacity for work. In the prefects' room . . . there were some large volumes of old history books . . . things like Lecky's *History of England*, and Offler had read them and annotated them from cover to cover.

According to another schoolfellow

> He was not just a 'swot', however. I remember a school cricket match at Wyeside when Offler was fielding at forward short-leg. A fast ball . . . was struck savagely in the direction of Offler, who turned to scan the boundary behind him, as did all the spectators. Offler, however, had caught the ball and transferred it to the pocket of his flannels with such speed that almost everyone around had been deceived.

Besides cricket, he played rugger, introduced in the school while he was there, and throughout his life he took keen interest in both games. Indeed, in all this there is much that those who knew him only in later life will recognize: a man who mostly seemed older than his years, stocky and sturdy, a strong personality, self-reliant and ready to accept the world as he found it, with a quick wit and mischievous sense of humour more often concealed than displayed, a prodigious and varied reader of history, a scholar whose work was marked by insistence on a craftsmanship little short of perfectionism. He became, however, sterner with himself than with other people and his aloofness cannot have lasted long, though he remained, in words he occasionally used of others, a very private person.[1]

In 1930 he went up to Emmanuel, aged seventeen. His undergraduate days were clouded by his parents' difficulties. The previous year Horace Offler had been ill and had had one leg amputated; during his unavoidably long absence from work the firm was less efficiently run and in May 1930 it collapsed, depriving him of both work and income. Offler's anxieties, long concealed, that he was adding to his father's financial burdens eventually

---

[1] This account of Offler's schooldays is drawn from the archives of Emmanuel College, Cambridge (henceforth ECA), tutorial file for Offler, letters of Ruscoe (14 Nov., 22 Dec. 1928), Welbourne (two of 18 Dec. 1928), Horace Offler (4 Mar. 1932); recorded recollections by Mr A. G. Gale; *Hereford High School for Boys. An Account of its first Fifty Years*, ed. R. G. Ruscoe (Hereford, 1962), pp.41–5; letter by Mr F. J. Handley in *Hereford Times*, 14 Feb. 1991.

produced short-lived physical symptoms of strain, whereupon Welbourne, now his tutor, went to much trouble to give practical help: he got the College to enhance the scholarship, corresponded with Horace Offler ('a most excellent and very courageous man, who has like Job, been persecuted by fate in a most alarming way'), and arranged for Offler to have a holiday in Paris under the aegis of an Emmanuel man who was in the diplomatic service. This was characteristic of Welbourne, who took a close and kindly interest in all his pupils; as he told Horace Offler, 'We are, as you may perhaps understand, more of a family and less of an institution than in appearance we may seem to be'.[2] Throughout Offler's Cambridge days, and later, Welbourne appears as his friend and guide. Offler, though very much his own man, seems to have had much in common with Welbourne in his wide reading and in his outlook on the world, and also later in the attention he paid to his pupils.[3] Welbourne, on the other hand, had little time for the technical mastery in dealing with historical sources that Offler made his own; whatever Welbourne's influence, Offler did not model himself on him.[4]

Welbourne soon saw Offler as a quite exceptional undergraduate. In June 1933 he wrote that he was 'not only the best historian who has been at this college for at least ten years, but is perhaps, the best I can fairly expect to meet as a pupil'. By then he had been placed in the first class in the first-year intercollegiate examination in history, and in Part I (starred for distinction) and Part II of the Historical Tripos. Early the previous year Welbourne had already envisaged his continuing at Cambridge on graduation, and he himself seems to have had no hesitation; his father wrote of 'his studious nature' and 'his great desire for a scholastic career', remarking that on completing Part II of the Tripos he 'had hardly reached Home ere he resumed his studies'. From his first year it was medieval history that had most attracted him. Welbourne consulted G. T. Lapsley and J. P. Whitney and all were agreed that he should take a fourth undergraduate year to work for Section III of Part II of the Theological Tripos, 'a Section entirely devoted to Church History, where the work is

---

[2] ECA, tutorial file for Offler, especially letters of Welbourne (26 Feb., 2, 5 Mar. 1932), Horace Offler (4 Mar., 15 Apr. 1932).

[3] They were alike too in typing their own letters, but Offler was much the better typist. In quotations, following editorial conventions of which Offler would approve, Welbourne's typing slips have been silently corrected. The correspondence between Welbourne and Offler from 1928 to 1945 in the ECA tutorial file is of more than simply personal interest in their comments on contemporary Cambridge, on European affairs before and during the war and on other matters.

[4] There are interesting memoirs of Welbourne in *Emmanuel College Magazine*, xlviii (1965-6), pp.6-12, and by D. Newsome, 'Two Emmanuel Historians', ibid., pp.21-34 (reprinted in *Emmanuel College Magazine: Quatercentenary Issue* [1984], pp.104-14).

so arranged as to facilitate candidature for the Lightfoot Scholarship, a university scholarship of some value and a good deal of distinction'. As Welbourne put it,

> so young a man as Mr Offler needs a year of undergraduate work, both to broaden his basis of knowledge, and to prevent the harm which would almost certainly be done to a man of the highest promise, by premature work on original sources.

His scholarship was renewed, and a year later he had not only been placed yet again in the first class but had won the Lightfoot Scholarship with work on the pontificate of Boniface VIII and had been elected to a research studentship at Emmanuel. In 1936 he was awarded a research fellowship, also at Emmanuel, which continued until 1940.[5]

Offler took part in few leisure activities at Cambridge. He walked, in and around Cambridge, he may have played some rugger in his first year and he certainly took a keen interest in the college's fortunes in athletics.[6] From his first year onwards he was a member of the college's Pococurante Club (named after the Venetian noble in *Candide*), an essay society of twelve members, to which he read papers 'In his inimitable fashion' on medieval and later topics; in one he used Antonio Magliabecchi, Florentine librarian and book-collector of the seventeenth century, 'as a stalking horse behind which to propound his own peculiar ideas about the necessity of a moratorium on the publication of books'.[7] According to Sir David Pitblado, his college contemporary and friend, 'Offler soon became a central figure in a loosely knit group brought together by mutual liking rather than common studies or political leanings (none of us, if I remember correctly, was a member of a political club, though we were well aware of the time in which we were living)'; though he had already developed the measured style of speech that was so weighty and authoritative when he was older, 'The rest of us were not overawed by his avuncular manner, but enjoyed the quality of his thought and wit'.[8] In his first long vacation he went with Pitblado on his first visit to Germany, walking in the Harz and the Thüringerwald and staying in youth hostels. On another holiday, in 1936, they stayed at a

---

[5] ECA, tutorial file for Offler, letters of Welbourne (10 June 1931, 2 Mar. 1932, 22 June 1933, 16 Jan. 1934), Horace Offler (24 June 1933).

[6] Memoir of Offler by Sir David Pitblado in *Emmanuel College Magazine*, lxxiii (1990–1), p.137; ECA, tutorial file for Offler, letter of Welbourne (30 Sept. 1943) mentions his playing rugger as an undergraduate but his name does not appear in the College Cup Competition teams listed in *Emmanuel College Magazine*.

[7] ECA, SOC 24/1,2 (minute books of the Pococurante Club); the quotations are from minutes respectively of 17 Oct. 1932 and 2 Nov. 1938 (the latter was written by Offler himself as secretary).

[8] Pitblado in *Emmanuel College Magazine*, lxxiii (1990–1), p.137.

country house on the Weser, where a baroness took foreign paying guests to improve their German; then they went to Berlin, full of preparations for the Olympic Games, with the Nazi Party much in evidence. 'My dear Pit,' declared Offler, 'I'm afraid we shall have to fight these people.' His realism and prescience are indisputable.[9]

By 1936, however, work as well as leisure was taking Offler to Germany. In April 1934 Welbourne had introduced him to C. W. Previté-Orton of St John's College, who supervised his research; the topic registered was 'Lewis of Bavaria'. Supervisor and subject were well chosen. After Previté-Orton's death in 1947 Offler referred to him as his 'master and friend', and Previté-Orton early remarked on Offler's 'fresh and original mind . . . following up clues and suggestions with remarkable skill and pertinacity'. This was in February 1936, when he reported that Offler

> seems to have produced an original and sound picture of Lewis, his reign, and Germany in his time. Out of a confused welter of events, persons, dynasties, feuds and political moves, he has made a coherent, purposeful history, and has changed an obscure farrago into an articulated and meaning development.

This much was achieved from printed sources. He now sought to revise and expand his work by research on manuscripts, and much of the following year was spent away from Cambridge: at Paris and Berlin in June and September 1936 for practice in palaeography and diplomatic, at the Public Record Office in the winter of 1936–7, at Marseilles, Avignon and Paris in March and April 1937 and at Munich, other places in Bavaria, Vienna and again Paris in the summer. His mastery of codicology and textual criticism is clear from his doctoral thesis, which includes detailed discussion and edited texts of documents he found on these travels; equally clear is his mastery of languages. Apparently he had already by 1934 taught himself German (only French was taught at his school), but by 1940 Welbourne described him as having 'a very intimate knowledge of Germany, good knowledge of German, some knowledge of French, some knowledge also of Italian, Spanish, Dutch and perhaps a little Czech, and an immense capacity for work'.

The products of this work were impressive, the more so as Offler did much tutorial work at Emmanuel throughout these years of research and in 1937–9 lectured for the Historical Faculty first on late-medieval German history, then on medieval European history in general. The dissertation which won him his research fellowship in 1936 dealt with Lewis's reign in general. His thesis, submitted in 1938 and accepted for a doctorate, was confined to 'The Emperor Lewis IV and the Curia from 1330 to 1347: Canon

---

[9] Ex inf. Sir David Pitblado.

Law and International Relationship in the first half of the Fourteenth Century'. Its aims were first to elucidate the negotiations between Lewis and the
papacy, reinterpreting the procurations, documents of authorisation for the
emperor's proctors at Avignon, and second to set these negotiations in the
wider picture of European politics. His first article, 'England and Germany
at the Beginning of the Hundred Years' War', was published in the *English
Historical Review* in October 1939; another, 'Kaiser Ludwig IV and die
Prokurationenfrage', was to have appeared at the same time in *Deutsches
Archiv für Geschichte des Mittelalters* and proofs were sent back in August,
'but,' he later wrote, 'what became of them I do not know; I imagine the
article was suppressed for patriotic reasons'. Meanwhile, however, work
on fourteenth-century politics led naturally to an interest in the writings
on political theory that either underlay or stemmed from them, and he
accepted an invitation to join J. G. Sikes and other Cambridge scholars in
editing the complete political works of William of Ockham. He collaborated
in searching for relevant manuscripts on the Continent, and in the first
volume, published by Manchester University Press in 1940, he edited
one tract himself, 'Consultatio de Causa Matrimoniali', and completed
the work of R. H. Snape on another, 'An Princeps . . . possit recipere
Bona Ecclesiarum'. These later works were in no way by-products of his
doctoral thesis, sections of it worked up for publication; rather, the thesis
was simply one, not especially important, stage in a longer programme of
intellectual exploration, which rapidly moved beyond it to further areas of
interest and discovery. In fact he never took the Ph.D. degree to which he
was entitled, seeing it perhaps as a mere bauble. 'Now you've got this out
of the way,' he long after told a younger colleague who had just achieved
a doctorate, 'go away and become a learned man—but it may take some
years.'[10]

   In Offler's case this process, which others might have supposed toler-
ably complete, was interrupted by war. His research fellowship expired in
June 1940 and, perhaps because of what he had seen of Nazi Germany, he
felt a strong personal commitment to fight. Welbourne tried to get him a
non-combatant post that would put his skills to best use: Offler 'is extremely
anxious to get into a combatant unit,' he wrote to the recruiting board,
'but I am anxious that his services should not be wasted'. Offler however,
'calling himself an author when teachers were a reserved occupation', cut
the ground from beneath his feet: 'Mr Offler made personal application

---

[10] These two paragraphs on Offler's work from 1934 to 1940 are drawn from papers in
the possession of Mrs B. E. Offler (henceforth Offler papers), application for Durham
readership; ECA, tutorial file for Offler, letters of Welbourne (27 Apr., 10 Oct. 1934, 15
July 1940), Previté-Orton (26 Feb. 1936); ECA, personal file for Offler, letter of Offler
(10 May 1938).

to this Office,' the secretary of the board replied, 'and requested that his calling up for service be expedited'. He joined up on 15 August. Medically he was below Class I because of poor eyesight—he already wore thick glasses—and this restricted the form of his active service.[11] He was placed in the Royal Artillery, in the 111th Heavy Anti-Aircraft Regiment (an attempt to transfer to the RAF was unsuccessful), and spent the following winter more or less uncomfortably in Scotland. In April 1941 he wrote as a Lance-Bombardier to Welbourne from Johnstone, Renfrewshire, where they were under canvas:

> We did our stuff reasonably competently in the Clyde blitz—that is to say we diverted the bombers from their industrial targets on to the tenements of Clydebank. There they killed some thousands, but the shipyards go on almost unaffected. But sometimes I wonder how long the men will fail to realise that this is the purpose of AA. gunnery—and how long I shall be able to refrain from telling them.[12]

For a time his battery was posted in Northern Ireland, but by October he was at Royal Artillery OCTU at Shrivenham. When commissioned he was posted to no.268 Battery of the 40th (Highland) Light Anti-Aircraft Regiment, in which he spent the rest of the war. It was part of the 51st (Highland) Division, heavily involved in the fighting from Egypt to Sicily and from Normandy to Germany, and much of his service was in the front line. He reached the Western Desert in September 1942, just before the battle of El Alamein. From March to August 1943 he was seconded to serve as liaison officer with a Free French flying column in Tunisia (1er Régiment de Marche de Spahis Marocains), which he described in a letter to Welbourne:

> They were Spahis, all ex-horsemen, and some had killed Germans and Italians in this war from horseback with pistol and sabre. Henceforward I shall always walk with my legs a little bowed. But they did teach me for the first time what is really meant by an eye for country and by and large were the most gallant collection of people I have ever met.[13]

What he did not tell Welbourne (or anyone else, perhaps even his own parents) was that he had been awarded the Croix de Guerre—for want of a new one General Leclerc took the cross from his own uniform and pinned it on Offler—and had been cited by Leclerc:

[11] ECA, tutorial file for Offler, letters of Welbourne (2 Feb., two of 15 July 1940, 30 Jan. 1941, 30 Sept. 1943), W. G. Brown (20 July 1940); Offler papers include notes, with precise dates, of his principal movements during his war service.
[12] ECA, tutorial file for Offler, letters of Offler (14 Jan. ['1940'], 5, 24 Feb., 18 Apr. 1941), Welbourne (30 Jan., 18 Feb. 1941).
[13] ECA, tutorial file for Offler, letters of Offler (20 Oct. 1941, 29 Aug. 1943).

A parfaitement assuré son service de liaison dans des conditions difficiles et souvent sous le feu violent de l'ennemi . . . . A rendu de réels services au Régiment et a été un bel exemple de courage, de sang-froid et de camaraderie au combat.[14]

When he rejoined his battery it was in Sicily; it returned to England in November, then sailed for Normandy immediately after the landings in June 1944. In August he wrote:

There is a most peculiar—and in some ways unhappy—difference between being with an Army which knows final victory is certain, and probably soon, and the old desert and even Sicilian days when we lived so much among uncertainties that they ceased to worry us . . . . This has been on the whole a much nastier war than the Mediterranean one—partly because we are always working at much closer quarters, because of the terrain . . .

Whether from events in Normandy or for other reasons, the war affected Offler deeply, and in later life he spoke little of his experiences. By May 1945 his unit was at Bremen. He was released from the army in June 1946.[15]

In his absence on war service attempts had been made to get him a post at Cambridge, but unsuccessfully. As Welbourne put it, 'he has left several of his contemporary rivals still adding to their academic accomplishments', and 'he will have gone to the War like so many other people to his cost'.[16] He was, however, appointed to a lectureship at Bristol University which he took up in October 1946; then, a year later, he was appointed Reader in Medieval History in the Durham Colleges of Durham University. In 1956 he was appointed Professor of Medieval History, the post he held until he retired, and he remained at Durham for the rest of his life. He married, in 1951, his colleague Betty Elfreda Jackson, and from 1952 onwards they lived in an attractively situated house in Old Elvet, in the centre of Durham. This patently happy marriage and their family life—they had two sons—were clearly of the greatest importance to Offler. He joined University College and became a prominent member of its Senior Common Room in Durham Castle. He was soon a keen supporter of the university's rugger club, though his own physical recreation was a daily walk in the outskirts of the city. There was a modestly convivial side to his life: he was a founder member of a college dining club and he enjoyed regular meetings with university and other friends in one or another of the city's pubs. For well over forty years his life was centred on Durham, a city that

[14] Ex inf. Mr R. Evans; Offler papers, copy of divisional order of 2 June 1943.
[15] ECA, tutorial file for Offler, letters of Offler (25 June, 29 Aug. 1944), Welbourne (12 May 1945).
[16] ECA, tutorial file for Offler, letters of E. M. W. Tillyard (21 Sept. 1943), Welbourne (30 Sept. 1943, two of 12 May 1945), Previté-Orton (15 May 1945).

strangely blends elements of the two other places most familiar to him, Hereford and Cambridge.

In the army Offler can have had little opportunity for systematic reading, though according to a fellow-officer 'even in the thick of it he had his nose in a book (or books)'.[17] The return to historical work must have been a severe challenge. He met it with an entirely new venture. The Swiss cultural organization Pro Helvetia had initiated the project of publishing, through Oxford University Press, *A Short History of Switzerland*, and Offler joined Edgar Bonjour of Basle and G. R. Potter in writing it. He was working on it at Bristol, when publication was expected in 1948; in the event it appeared in 1952. Offler's contribution, on the period from the Celtic settlement to the end of the fourteenth century, touched only in the last of its five chapters on his earlier work on fourteenth-century politics. Its hundred pages, readable and informative, are the longest piece of his own continuous prose that he ever published. To the end of his days he continued to work steadily on manuscripts and texts, to read, to ponder and to write, but he seems never to have recaptured the pace—or perhaps the intellectual excitement—of those years when at Cambridge and London, Paris and Munich, he was discovering for himself, from first-hand evidence, what was really going on between the imperial and papal courts in the mid-fourteenth century. The interruption and experiences of war may have contributed to this, and of course he was now acquiring new and time-consuming responsibilities, both academic and personal. But rather more it reflects the maturing of his views on the role of publication in historical work. He saw putting work into print as something not to be undertaken lightly, and he would warn younger colleagues against premature publication, in his generation more likely to be damaging to an academic career than it has since become. Publication should rather be the outcome not only of comprehensive research but of long, careful thought that was certain it had found the right answer—or as certain as possible. Already in 1937 he remarked cynically that 'Most historians would admit that to discover "Wie es eigentlich war" is beyond their usual attainment'.[18] He saw no point in writing a second time what had already been written once, or in writing anything at all unless one had something to say that was worth saying, and to publish something that was wrong would be to create error, a disservice to scholarship far worse than keeping silent. The historian should write primarily for other historians: 'historians' history—the only sort that matters', as he put it in 1958.[19] He saw the risk, however: 'If the

---

[17] Letter from Mr R. Evans to the author, 27 Jan. 1992.

[18] *English Historical Review* (henceforth *EHR*), lii (1937), p.323 (review of E. K. Winter, *Rudolph IV von Österreich*, vol.ii [1936]).

[19] H. S. Offler, *Medieval Historians of Durham* (Durham, 1958), p.5.

professionals are going to concentrate wholly on the puzzles,' he wrote in 1972, 'into what sort of hands will the writing of the narratives fall, and who, save a diminishing band of experts, will soon be interested even in the puzzles?'[20] *A Short History of Switzerland*, with no footnote references and the briefest of bibliographies, is the nearest he himself ever came to writing for a wide public, though later, in 1965, he also contributed a substantial and important section to *Europe in the Late Middle Ages*, edited by J. R. Hale, J. R. L. Highfield and Beryl Smalley.

After he left the army Offler never returned to Germany—indeed, after 1950 at the latest his only travel outside Britain, for work or for pleasure, was when he went to Trinity College, Dublin, as an external examiner. His research on manuscripts abroad was done through photocopies and microfilms. However, he soon resumed contact with German scholars and he published articles in the *Deutsches Archiv für Erforschung des Mittelalters* in 1951 and 1954.[21] The second of these, on the various political views at the court of Lewis the Bavarian in the autumn of 1331, examines the role of certain tracts in reflecting and forming opinion, and henceforward he worked not on the actual politics of the period but exclusively on the political writings these politics produced. 'I shall be most interested to see some up-to-date learning about Lewis the Bavarian and the Curia,' he wrote in 1983; 'It is many years since I have done much serious work on this subject—partly because of the way in which the edition of the *Constitutiones* for Lewis's reign has stuck at 1330; partly because I had little fresh to say about it.'[22] His paper to the Royal Historical Society in 1955, a general analysis of the aims and policies of popes and emperors from the 1320s to the 1340s, was the last he wrote simply on political events. In the words of Professor Jürgen Miethke it 'displays, in small compass, complete mastery of an intractable mass of detailed research, clear grasp, and reflection on the fundamental problems of the period and on historically acceptable solutions'.[23]

For the rest of Offler's life the core of his work in this field was the editing of William of Ockham's political works, continuing the project

---

[20] *EHR*, lxxxvii (1972), p.577 (review of R. W. Southern, *Medieval Humanism and Other Studies* [1970]).

[21] 'Über die Prokuratorien Ludwigs des Bayern für die römische Kurie', viii (1951), pp. 461–87; 'Meinungsverschiedenheiten am Hof Ludwigs des Bayern im Herbst 1331', xi (1954), pp. 191–206.

[22] Letter to J. Miethke, 29 Dec. 1983.

[23] 'Empire and Papacy: the Last Struggle', *Transactions of the Royal Historical Society*, 5th ser., vi (1956), pp.21–47; 'Sein Aufsatz über "The Last Struggle" zeigt in komprimierter Kürze die volle Beherrschung einer unübersichtlichen Detailforschung, klare Begriffe, Nachdenken über die Grundprobleme des Zeitalters, wie über historisch mögliche Lösungswege' (letter to the author, 7 Nov. 1991).

begun before the war under the leadership of J. G. Sikes. Sikes had died, tragically by suicide, in 1941 and had bequeathed all relevant material to Offler and R. F. Bennett, another of the first volume's editors, as his literary executors. Together they took over responsibility for the project. Offler himself edited volume three, containing the 'Tractatus contra Ioannem' and the 'Tractatus contra Benedictum' as well as the short 'Epistola ad Fratres Minores', and this was published in 1956. Volume two, however, presented a problem. It was to consist of the bulk of the long 'Opus Nonaginta Dierum', of which the first six chapters, edited by Bennett and Sikes, had formed the concluding section of volume one. Sikes had prepared the rest of the tract, and on his death it was at once set up in type; it needed, however, very substantial revision. Bennett began this, but in 1958 passed the work over to Offler: Manchester University Press, now having to pay the printer to keep the type standing, was pressing hard for its completion. It was published in 1963. Offler was conscious that Sikes, who had a 'nervous affliction of his hands, which made holding a pen a difficult and exhausting feat for him', had worked extremely hard to complete the text in the face of great personal and physical difficulties—he must, Offler commented to Bennett, 'have been very far from his proper self when he passed the copy for press (if he did so)'—and in the introduction, characteristically, wrote that

> those with experience in handling a work of this length will know that by far the heaviest labour comes at the first stage of establishing the text and verifying the references. That labour Sikes accomplished. If there is any credit to be had from editing a medieval author, let it go to the memory of a good scholar and a brave man. For the volume's deficiencies the responsibility is mine alone.

Those with such experience will in fact be more likely to agree with what C. R. Cheney wrote to him on its publication: 'your first pages of introduction are a model of modesty and generosity, and I hope that they will be widely recognized as such'. In the course of revision Offler had collated anew the three sources of the text and had reassessed their relative importance—in itself a major work. The problems, however, did not end with volume two. Stocks of volume one were exhausted and a reprint was mooted. In 1961 he wrote to Bennett:

> Nothing in the nature of a complete revision of the text can be envisaged (or needs to be): but simply the printing of a supplement correcting things (misprints, etc.) which are obviously wrong. What we all underestimated, I suspect, was the sheer mechanical difficulty Sikes found in communicating his intentions to the printers. Using vol. I over the years I have become more and more conscious of this, and so am unwilling that it should be reissued as a photographic reprint *tel quel* without an appendix of corrections.

He must have soon changed his mind; as he wrote to Cheney in 1972, 'Tinkering with that version would have been useless, particularly as there was a good deal of new ms. stuff to incorporate. So I have done the whole thing anew'. Offler's own annotated copy of the 1940 volume shows the scale of revision needed; in random samples of the sections that Sikes edited there are from forty to seventy notes per page. The revised edition of volume one was published in 1974, by which time he was well advanced with volume four. This he finished before his death, though it has yet to be published. With it he completed the work of editing Ockham's shorter political works, leaving for others only the Dialogus, 'the final towering massif'.[24]

Editing Ockham's political writings was unquestionably Offler's greatest work. Miethke describes his editions as 'models of the art of editing', a comment that, from one well versed in the German tradition of fine historical editing, would have given him especial pleasure.[25] His strength as an editor lay in his care and thoroughness and in his technical skills; he was a superb Latinist and textual critic, and every page of his editions shows the erudition with which he established correct readings and identified sources and parallels. He was discriminating in his references to other scholars' work and his accolade was never given lightly. Professor G. D. Knysh comments that 'I consider his terse "Knysh, *art. cit.*, pp.77–9" . . . to be one of the finest compliments I have ever received'.[26] Offler seems never to have questioned existing editorial conventions, and was in no doubt that an editor's job included standardizing spelling, capital letters and punctuation, to produce not only a text that reproduced the original writer's intention, but also a text easily intelligible to the modern reader. In a letter to Miethke in 1981 he remarked that 'Looking back after 50 years' activity in medieval history, more and more I incline to the view that much of the most genuine progress has occurred in the field of codicology. It would be a pity if it grew too far apart from the art of editing'. He then cited a recent edition, 'the codicology outstandingly good; the editing leaving much to be desired'.[27] Here, as in many other matters, he looked for improved performance within the existing framework rather than for reassessment of basic premises. In working on Ockham at Durham he

---

[24] ECA, tutorial file for Offler, letter of Offler (5 Feb. 1941); *Guillelmi de Ockham Opera Politica*, ed. J. G. Sikes et al. (in progress; Manchester, 1940– ), i (2nd edn), p.viii; ii, pp.ix–x; Offler papers, letters of Offler to Bennett (28 Dec. 1957, 2 Dec. 1961), Cheney (14 Nov. 1972), and of Cheney (20 May 1963). Offler's annotated set of the *Opera Politica* is in Durham University Library.

[25] 'Kabinettstücke der Editionskunst' (letter to the author, 7 Nov. 1991).

[26] The reference is in the forthcoming vol. iv of the *Opera Politica* (letter to the author, 7 Nov. 1991).

[27] Letter to Miethke, 19 Jan. 1981.

felt somewhat isolated; in 1972 he told Cheney, *à propos* financing the new edition of volume one, that

> since Jacob's death you are the only scholar in this country who has shown the slightest interest in this project (and abroad they are busy making their own books out of it—which is fair enough, and pleasing in its way, but not immediately helpful to me).

—a remark made without self-pity, a failing wholly alien to Offler, who once described it as 'perhaps intelligence's worst modern vice'.[28] He saw Ockham's political writings simply as a response to particular circumstances, having no significant connection with Ockham's philosophical or theological work; in this he differed from some other scholars. In 1982 he wrote to Professor A. S. McGrade:

> If pushed, I might be willing to admit that it was a loss to western thought that Ockham, by getting caught up in the imbroglio with John XXII and Michael of Cesena and Lewis of Bavaria, was diverted from the school study of theology and philosophy to the polemical activities which so preoccupied (wasted?) the last 25 years of his life.[29]

He thus viewed the texts he edited as historical documents, simply reflecting the events of their own time, rather than as works of political philosophy with wider application.

The work on Ockham produced not only the edited volumes but articles and notes on particular points arising from these and other contemporary texts. On the other hand, it was not only on Ockham that Offler employed his editorial talents. On moving to Durham, besides continuing the work he had already begun at Cambridge he embarked on an entirely new field of study: north-east England in the Middle Ages. He began with work on William of St Calais, Bishop of Durham 1080–96, writing one article on him for the *Transactions* of the local archaeological society and another, on 'The Tractate De Iniusta Vexacione Willelmi Episcopi Primi', in the *English Historical Review*; this discussed the content and date of this little work, showing that it cannot be safely used as a contemporary source of the events it describes and was probably 'a product of the period of brilliant literary activity at Durham in the second quarter of the twelfth century'.[30] Before long he had taken this interest a good

[28] Offler papers, letter to Cheney (14 Nov. 1972; 'Jacob' is, of course, E. F. Jacob); *Durham University Journal*, xl (1947–8), p.63 (review of F. M. Powicke, *Three Lectures* [1947]).

[29] Letter to McGrade, 7 May 1982.

[30] 'William of St. Calais, first Norman Bishop of Durham', *Transactions of the Architectural and Archaeological Society of Durham and Northumberland*, x, pt iii (1950), pp. 258–79; 'The Tractate De Iniusta Vexacione Willelmi Episcopi Primi', *EHR*, lxvi, pp.321–41 (quotation from p.341).

deal further. His inaugural lecture as professor, in 1958, on 'Medieval Historians of Durham', showed how familiar he had made himself not only with the medieval chronicles of the area but also with the works of later antiquaries; and from then on he published occasional articles on particular problems of the medieval north-east, showing still wider knowledge of local sources. He served as Secretary (and thus general editor) of the Surtees Society from 1950 to 1966 and as President from 1980 to 1987, and in 1971 he took as his subject for Durham's annual Cathedral Lecture 'Ranulf Flambard as Bishop of Durham (1099–1128)'.[31] All this was no mere *jeu d'esprit*. He had a profound belief in the importance of local history—and a clear sense of the distinction between local history and parochial antiquarianism.[32] Here, if anywhere, one might discover 'Wie es eigentlich war', and he once remarked in a review how 'Again and again . . . the ambitions of the synthesist shatter on the recalcitrance of the local facts'.[33] Very soon after Offler came to Durham he wrote, in reviewing Professor Barlow's *Durham Jurisdictional Peculiars*, that 'A prerequisite to progress is a diplomatic study of the whole corpus of Durham's twelfth century charters, based on a detailed comparative examination of all the originals'.[34] He may already have envisaged meeting this need. His edition of *Durham Episcopal Charters 1071–1152*, published by the Surtees Society in 1968, is the most important of his contributions to north-eastern history. It is an edition of a very different sort of document from Ockham's works but it is a no less impressive witness of Offler's editorial skills, not least in the way it treats problems of authenticity and in the thoroughness of the historical notes on each charter.

There can be few historians whose reviews are so well worth reading as a collection; Offler regarded reviewing as an important part of his work. It began in 1936, when his first review appeared in the *English Historical Review* (Previté-Orton was then its editor),[35] and from then until 1991 he published up to fifteen reviews every year, apart from the gap produced by the war. Besides the *English Historical Review*, where he appeared in nearly every volume, he reviewed particularly for the *Durham University Journal* and, from the 1960s, for *Erasmus* and the *Journal of Theological Studies*. In his reviews he put more of himself than in his other writings and

---

[31] Published in *Durham University Journal*, lxiv (1971–2), pp.14–25 (to which, in one copy in Durham University Library, an unknown annotator has appended 'In your usual tradition, Prof, punchy and sound'); also issued separately by the Dean and Chapter.

[32] Cf. Offler, *Medieval Historians*, p.13.

[33] *EHR*, xciii (1978), p.610 (review of *Die Burgen im deutschen Sprachraum*, ed. H. Patze [1976]).

[34] *Durham University Journal*, xlii (1949–50), p.125.

[35] *EHR*, li (1936), pp.520–3 (review of E. K. Winter, *Rudolph IV von Österreich*, vol.i [1934]).

their occasional asides and comments recall the brilliant choice of words, often epigrammatic, that made his conversation so memorable. Some tell us much about Offler the historian:

> Essays collected together provide a more concentrated distillation of the author's essence than do the chapters of a book; the reader can find himself in the plight of a thirsty man offered nothing more satisfying than repeated thimblefuls of *crème de menthe*.[36]

Others tell us more than he often revealed about Offler the man:

> But the Middle Ages give little comfort to the optimistic liberal reasoning that because persecution ought not to be successful, it never is. Is it indeed a misconception that belief can be enforced? . . . The horrid truth is that the medieval inquisition was very largely a successful institution.[37]

We get here a sudden glimpse of the young man who in 1940 asked that his call-up be expedited. But underlying all his reviewing was his belief that what was offered to the learned world in print should be definitive work of the highest standard. He was sometimes disappointed, and he criticized sternly what seemed to him any failing of judgment, accuracy or Latinity. He lost friends in this process—which was a pity: in his private correspondence with other historians he was just as uncompromising over any ideas or conclusions that he considered in the least slipshod, but his comments were always tempered with a wealth of positive advice and help. He put his own learning at the disposal of other scholars—whether well-established or beginners—with ready generosity. Some of his letters—notably, in latter years, his detailed technical correspondence with Knysh, McGrade and Miethke—are little less than learned articles, of what others would consider publishable quality.

This mixture of generous personal kindness and of uncompromising insistence on the highest standards informed all Offler's life in Durham. His teaching, perhaps especially attuned to the most able and to those who had most difficulties, was appreciated by all his pupils. One wrote, after his death, how his

> massive learning very imperfectly concealed a rich vein of humour. If we used to hang on his every word in tutorial, we eagerly looked forward to his brilliantly performed lectures and avidly collected fresh examples of the Offlerian *mot juste*. His clear and incisive judgements were constantly shot through with a spontaneous and biting wit. He was the first and

---

[36] *EHR*, lxxxvii (1972), p.576 (review of R. W. Southern, *Medieval Humanism and Other Studies* [1970]).

[37] *EHR*, lxxxiv (1969), p.575 (review of G. Leff, *Heresy in the Later Middle Ages* [1967]).

perhaps the only scholar I have encountered who made everything into an intellectual treat.[38]

'You and I,' he told one pupil, 'have something in common—we neither of us know how to spell sheriff but I look it up in the dictionary.'[39] From a lesser personality such a remark might soon be forgotten; Offler's magisterial utterance would be remembered for life. In his room was a copy of Lawrence Durrell's *Esprit de Corps* which he lent, as recommended reading, to those he suspected of overworking before examinations. His interest in those he taught was in no way assumed; he could recall long afterwards every detail of their performance in Finals. The story is told of a colleague driving him (he did not himself drive) to one address after another in the Durham outskirts in search of an errant pupil to whom he considered himself bound to deliver in person a note initiating formal proceedings on her shortcomings. Indeed, to all departmental administration he brought a conscientious thoroughness that secured the best by doing as much as possible himself; he disliked delegating work, even the typing of letters. For many years he and his fellow-professor of modern history personally interviewed all candidates for admission as undergraduates; other colleagues took no part in this chore. Throughout his career he himself always served as representative of history on the boards of studies of other departments. But besides himself shouldering much of his department's administrative work, he showed his generosity to his colleagues in many ways. They discovered only after many occasions that the annual examiners' lunch, assumed to be funded from some official source, was actually paid for on his initiative from professorial pockets. On the other hand he exercised strong personal control of the department and always knew what he wanted for it. It is well remembered in Durham how, when he was on research leave in 1966–7, the department in his absence voted to move from the Faculty of Arts to the Faculty of Social Sciences; breaking his leave, Offler insisted on speaking in Senate (of which he was not then a member), and single-handed secured the reversal of this decision. In Senate, indeed, he was not only a robust defender of his department's interests, but a strong and effective speaker on many matters. He had an instinct for timing his interventions and developed it to perfection; this, combined with his gift of language—he was a master of the telling phrase—and his weighty delivery, gave him unrivalled influence on its decisions.

He was indeed an awe-inspiring figure—as he must have been even when young. In 1941 when a Lance-Bombardier he wrote to Welbourne

---

[38] Letter from Dr J. C. Thewlis to Mrs Offler, 2 Feb. 1991.
[39] Letter from Mrs G. Cole to Mrs Offler, 10 Feb. 1991.

from Scotland 'as the comrade of men who living and working with me for the past 6 months persist in calling me Mr'.[40] In Durham there were few who addressed him as Seton, the forename he had used from childhood (it was the surname of the owner of King's Acre Nurseries), and he was probably always more at ease with the older masculine form of address by surname alone. This was at one with his rather old-fashioned way of life: neither the motor-car nor the television played any part in it, and he had a telephone at home only after his retirement, when it would not be a channel for the intrusion of business. But if he appeared conservative in his outlook and in his policy for the department this reflected pragmatism, not dogma: he always preferred the devil he knew. Certainly Offler was never dismissive of new approaches or techniques in historical work, though their value had to be proved and he scorned the merely pretentious. 'In its early years,' he wrote to Miethke in 1988, '*Annales* served a valuable function in widening horizons, but during the last few decades the pretensions of its school have become ridiculously exaggerated.'[41] He occasionally commented—whether justly or not—that no one in Durham would discuss history with him; and he seldom left Durham. He went each year to his wartime battery's reunion in Edinburgh, but conferences, seminars and other learned gatherings did not attract him. 'Do your utmost to frustrate any motions towards an Ockhamist "celebration" or "occasion",' he wrote to McGrade in 1983, '. . . I feel more and more doubtful about the value of such jamborees, except perhaps for the careers of the participants.'[42] However, he served on the Council of the Royal Historical Society from 1969 to 1972 and this, followed by his election to the Fellowship of the British Academy in 1974, brought him into wider fields of learned activity.

Offler retired from the university in 1978; his colleagues presented him with a printed bibliography of his historical writings, including reviews, an invaluable guide to his intellectual career.[43] He was given a room a few doors away from the history department in North Bailey, he lunched every week in University College and he continued to be a familiar figure in Durham, often to be seen, with stick and pipe, walking at deliberate pace through the streets or chatting to a colleague or other friend. For me, who now met him for the first time, the difficult task of succeeding Offler in the Chair of Medieval History was made infinitely easier by his extreme courtesy and correctness. In the years that followed there were many changes in the history department that he must have disagreed with, even disapproved of—among them, indeed, the department's transfer to

[40] ECA, tutorial file for Offler, letter of Offler (14 Jan. 1941 ['1940']).
[41] Letter to Miethke, 18 Feb. 1988.
[42] Letter to McGrade, 31 Mar. 1983.
[43] *A List of the Historical Writings 1936–1978 of Hilary Seton Offler* (Durham, 1978).

the Faculty of Social Sciences that he had so strenuously resisted. Whenever we met he never made the slightest reference to such matters. He continued to work and to publish on Ockham and related topics; a long article appeared in 1986 in the *Deutsches Archiv für Erforschung des Mittelalters* on the complicated question of the authorship of the tract 'Allegaciones de potestate imperiali', written in support of Lewis the Bavarian in 1338, and therewith on Ockham's part in the ferment of political views at this time.[44] In a note sending me an offprint of the shorter, but still weighty 'Notes on the Text of Marsilius of Padua's "Defensor Minor"', published in 1982, he remarked 'Not, I fear, what one could call a good read, though I am a little proud of the emendation at X.2.11'. He had reason to be:

> *Et rarius*: this interjection into a straightforward quotation of I Tim.1,20 is quite meaningless, though both Vasoli, p.134 and Quillet have managed to translate it. It is to be rejected as the intrusion of a corrupted gloss. Somewhere along the line of tradition to O the name *Alexander* in the scriptural quotation caught a scribe's eye; facetiously he added *et Darius*; after that, downhill all the way.[45]

In 1990 a further article discussed the origin of Ockham's political thought—'Rather sadly one has to admit that valiant efforts to show that Ockham's political and social ideas were determined by his philosophical positions seem to have run into a dead end'—and its effect on other thinkers down to the Council of Basle.[46] However, work continued too on the medieval north-east. An account of the complex politics behind an incident at Durham in 1318 appeared in *Archaeologia Aeliana* in 1988 as 'Murder on Framwellgate Bridge', the closest he ever came to what he would call a 'catchpenny title'. Work completed but still to be published includes not only the fourth volume of Ockham's political works but also an important article on the text of Boldon Book, the survey of the Bishop of Durham's estates made in 1183 or 1184.

Offler died suddenly on 24 January 1991 after four days' illness from which he was fully expected to recover. In a perceptive obituary Dr Margaret Harvey wrote that 'He was a proud man who would have hated to become helpless in old age'.[47] This is true; but we may be sure he would have met this with the same fortitude that he brought to all

---

[44] 'Zum Verfasser der "Allegaciones de potestate imperiali" (1338)', xlii (1986), pp.555–619.
[45] *Mittellateinisches Jahrbuch*, xvii (1982), p.215.
[46] 'The "Influence" of Ockham's Political Thinking: The First Century', in *Die Gegenwart Ockhams*, ed. W. Vossenkuhl and R. Schönberger (Weinheim, 1990), pp.338–65; the quotation is from p.345.
[47] *The Independent*, 31 Jan. 1991, p.29.

life's chances, still permitting himself the occasional flash of mischievous humour.

P. D. A. HARVEY
*University of Durham*

*Note.* I have had much help in compiling this memoir, not least from those who have kindly read it in draft, providing useful comments and suggestions. Above all I am grateful to Mrs B. E. Offler, who has generously and readily put at my disposal letters and other papers of her husband, as well as providing much other information; Mrs G. Cole and Dr J. C. Thewlis have kindly allowed me to quote extracts from their letters to her. Professor D. J. A. Matthew has made available to me the information he gathered on Offler's schooldays, and I am also much indebted to Mr A. G. Gale and Mr F. J. Handley for permission to make use of their recollections. The Master and Fellows of Emmanuel College, Cambridge, through their Archivist, Dr A. S. Bendall, very kindly gave me access to their records and permission to quote from them, and I am especially grateful too to Sir David Pitblado and Mr R. Evans, who gave me helpful information respectively on Offler's years at Cambridge and in the army. A particular word of thanks is due to the scholars who responded with much generosity to requests for copies of correspondence and for advice on Offler's contribution to a field of study of which I know little: Dr A. Black, Dr J. Coleman, Fr G. Gál, Professor J. Kilcullen, Professor G. D. Knysh, Dr R. Lambertini, Professor G. Leff, Professor A. S. McGrade, Dr A. E. McGrath, Professor J. Miethke, Professor J. Morrall and Professor B. Tierney. I have been able to draw directly on only a small part of the information and comments they sent me, but all has been of great assistance in building up a picture of Offler and his work. So many of Offler's friends and colleagues in Durham have provided information, suggestions and anecdotes that it is not possible for me to name them individually, but I am much indebted to them all and would particularly mention the help I have had from Professor W. R. Ward.

*Proceedings of the British Academy*, **80**, 453–472

# Otto Pächt
# 1902–1988

No scholar of his generation surpassed Otto Pächt in his knowledge of works of art in his chosen fields, the art of the Middle Ages, especially manuscript illumination, and the painting of the Netherlands in the fifteenth and early sixteenth centuries. None introduced more new material to scholarship, while at the same time recognising and clarifying its art historical significance.[1]

Pächt was born on 7 September 1902 of well-to-do Jewish parents, David and Josephine Pächt (née Freundlich). His father had textile interests with links to Manchester, a business which Pächt's brother was to continue. Pächt attended the Volkschule and Stadtgymnasium in Vienna XIII and began his studies in the History of Art and in Archaeology at the University in 1920 where Max Dvořák was Ordinarius. Dvořák's interests in fifteenth- and sixteenth-century Netherlandish art must have been a stimulus to Pächt to study a school of painting which was to preoccupy him throughout his career. His first publication in *Kunstchronik* for 1921–2 concerned problems of attribution to Ouwater and Bouts.

Dvořák's premature death in 1921, however, led Pächt to move to Berlin to attend Adolph Goldschmidt's lectures. Karl Swoboda, Dvořák's

© The British Academy 1993.

[1] Bibliographies of Pächt's writings can be found in *Kunsthistorische Forschungen Otto Pächt zu Ehren*, eds. A. Rosenauer, G. Weber, Salzburg, 1972, in O. Pächt, *Methodisches zur kunsthistorischen Praxis, ausgewählte Schriften*, eds. J. Oberhaidacher, A. Rosenauer, G. Schikola, 2nd edn. Munich, 1986, and in *Kunsthistoriker* as in note 6. In addition to the evaluations of Pächt's work by R. Preimesberger, A. Rosenauer, G. Weber, J. Mitchell, D. Bogner and M. Sitt printed in the latter see M. Sitt, 'Otto Pächt. Am Anfang war das Auge', *Kunsthistoriker in eigener Sache. Zehn autobiographische Skizzen*, ed. M. Sitt, mit einer Einleitung von H. Dilly, Berlin, 1990, pp. 25–61, and A. Rosenauer, forward to *Van Eyck. Die Begründer der altniederländischen Malerei*, Munich, 1989. I am most grateful to Charles Mitchell, the late Carl Nordenfalk, Michael Pächt, Artur Rosenauer and Jo Trapp for helpful comments and corrections to this memoir.

O. PÄCHT

assistant, asked Bruno Fürst, who became Pächt's lifelong friend, to 'take Pächt under his wing in Berlin', as Fürst later recalled with amusement. Pächt returned to Vienna the following year where Julius von Schlosser was now in charge of the Kunsthistorisches Institut, and took his doctorate in 1925 with a dissertation entitled 'Verhältnis von Bild und Vorwurf in der mittelalterlichen Entwicklung der Historiendarstellung'. He had also studied Archaeology with Emil Reisch and Emmanuel Löwy. Whether his interest in classical art led him to Riegl, or whether it was the other way round, in 1927 he published a new edition with notes of Riegl's *Spätrömische Kunstindustrie*. The main chronological poles of his work were thus already set from the late Antique to the Early Modern period, and his allegiance to the Vienna school of Art History and its founders. Wickhoff and Riegl, established.

In 1929 Pächt's first book *Oesterreichische Tafelmalerei der Gotik* appeared. This was followed by a long and closely argued article on Michael Pacher in the first issue of the *Kunstwissenschaftliche Forschungen*, 1931. This was a new theoretical art historical journal which he edited from its inception in 1931 to 1933 when it ceased publication due to lack of funding. In both book and article Pächt aimed to describe the debts to outside influences and also the specific characteristics of Austrian painting. This brought him to a conviction of the existence of national constants in art, which he never abandoned. Pächt had also contributed to the *Kritische Berichte zur Kunstgeschichtlichen Literatur,* which had been started in 1927 and was edited by Fürst, and initially Friedrich Antal, until 1938. He was thus already a prominent member of the 'Younger Viennese School'. as Meyer Schapiro called it in a lengthy review article of *Kunstwissenschaftliche Forschungen*, 2, 1933.[2] Hans Sedlmayr, slightly older than Pächt, was another prominent member of this group.[3] Schapiro described some of the main influences on their thought, especially Gestalt psychology, and drew attention to their strengths, 'the endeavour to forge a rigorous style criticism', and their weaknesses, 'unfounded theoretical claims'. 'We do not blame the authors for neglecting the social, economic, political and ideological factors, but rather for offering us as historical explanation a mysterious racial and animistic language in the name of a higher science of art'. Though Schapiro was in Vienna in the winter of

---

[2] *Art Bulletin*. 18 (1936). 260.

[3] Sedlmayr, born 1896, as is well known, made political compromises. He succeeded Schlosser in the Chair at Vienna from 1936 to 1945. In 1951 he was called to Munich. In a letter to Meyer Schapiro of 1 July 1952 Pächt wrote: 'What you wrote me last time about Sedlmayr's friendly gestures does not surprise me at all. There will be, if necessary, a third and a fourth volte face, but I am not interested in the psychology of chameleons'. Unlike Sedlmayr, but like Dvořák, Pächt never concerned himself with architecture.

1930–1, where he in particular sought out Emmanuel Löwy, he did not meet Pächt at that time. However, he initiated a correspondence via Fürst in 1934 and the letters in reply from Pächt, of which he has kindly given me copies, provide a fascinating account on two levels of Pächt's academic interest on the one hand and of the effects of the approaching Nazi threat on the other.

Pächt seldom spoke to me of his own past and was reticent on personal matters, so that I know little of his life at this time and the letters are consequently of special value.[4] The novelist, Robert Musil, was among his friends at this period, and Fürst and Pächt were among those who contributed to a small stipendium for him in these years. Pächt was instrumental in the publication in 1935 of Musil's *Nachlass zu Lebzeiten*.[5] Pächt kept in touch with Musil until his death in Geneva in 1942.[6] Another friend was Oskar Kokoschka, whom he probably met through Swoboda, and who later wrote a tribute to him in his *Festschrift*. A delicate water-colour of flowers by Kokoschka hung together with Old Master drawings and a Picasso etching in the house in Vienna in later years.

Pächt's Habilitationsschrift entitled 'Gestaltungsprinzipien der westlichen Malererei im 15. Jahrhunderts' was published in 1933 in *Kunstwissenscaftliche Forschungen*, 2, and he was appointed Privatdozent at Heidelberg University by August Grisebach. The Nazi prohibition on Jews holding jobs in Germany enforced in the same year prevented his ever taking up the post, however.[7] In the first letter to Schapiro dated 4 October 1934 and written from Vienna, that is only months after the assassination of the Austrian Chancellor Dollfuss in July, Pächt takes up the question of the national constants, evidently in response to Schapiro's critical comment. In this and three following letters of December 1934, February 1935 and June 1936, Pächt defended his views against Schapiro's criticisms which, though Schapiro's letters do not survive, can be reconstructed from the review mentioned and from a paper he published in 1936.[8] Pächt argued against Schapiro's charge that his views lent support to Nazi racialist theories, by pointing to the artists who like Gianbologna, though of foreign birth, took on the style of their adopted country. It could not be, therefore, a matter

---

[4] Fürst, who knew him so well, put nothing on paper unfortunately, though I remember him sketching a vignette of Pächt in a café in Vienna during the Spanish Civil War with his pockets stuffed with newspaper cuttings.

[5] H. Hickman, *Robert Musil and the Culture of Vienna*, 1984, pp. 168, 171.

[6] For a moving letter of encouragement from Musil written in July 1937 see 'Ein Brief Musils an Pächt', *Kunsthistoriker. Mitteilungen des Oesterreichischen Kunsthistorikerverbändes*, 5 (1988), 9–10.

[7] Saxl noted that this appointment at this juncture was a proof of Pächt's outstanding reputation.

[8] 'Race, nationality and art', *Art Front*, 2 (1936), 10–12.

of race. His observations, he says, are in any case based on empirical evidence, and a scholar must follow his conclusions, however unwelcome the consequences.

On another level the correspondence concerned the possibility of Pächt finding work, having been up to this point supported, evidently, by his father. He first visited England in December 1935, was there again at the end of 1936, also visiting his friend George Furlong (1898–1987, Director of the National Gallery of Ireland 1935–1950) in Dublin in March 1937. He returned briefly to Vienna in the summer of 1937 and finally settled in London in 1938. A letter of 2 April 1938 refers to the arrest of his father and another of 30 April canvasses the possibility of work in the United States.

In London Pächt had two points of reference. One was the Warburg Institute which had migrated from Hamburg in 1933. Correspondence with Fritz Saxl preserved in the Institute archive begins in March 1937.[9] He wrote to Schapiro on 3 December 1938 about a projected exhibition on 'Visual approaches to the classics' at the Warburg Institute and a letter of 30 January 1939 is written from the Institute. Already in the earlier letter, however, he mentioned that he had begun work on a projected catalogue of illuminated manuscripts in the British Museum. Pächt does not say where the original idea for this came from, perhaps it was Saxl's, but he mentions a stipendium for four months from the Society for the Protection of Learning and Science.[10] The correspondence with Schapiro suggests that he had already worked on illuminated manuscripts before coming to England, but the course of events now steered him towards a much closer involvement with them. A letter of 3 April 1937 mentions 'Warmald' already, that is Francis Wormald at that time in the Department of Manuscripts in the British Museum, who was to become his closest professional friend in England.[11] On 5 May 1939, the first of the letters to Schapiro in English, he wrote that he was reading available literature on manuscript illumination.[12]

[9] I am grateful to Miss A. C. Pollard, archivist at the Warburg Institute, for allowing me to go through the relevant files.

[10] This was set up by Lord Beveridge after a visit to Vienna in March 1933. See N. Baldwin, *The Society for the Protection of Science and Learning Archive*, Bodleian Library, Oxford, 1988. The archive also concerns material on the internment of refugees in 1940, to which Pächt among many others was subjected.

[11] He cannot have known him very well at this time, unless this is a misprint. For a memoir of Wormald by Julian Brown see *Proceedings of the British Academy*, 61 (1976 for 1975), 523–60.

[12] Pächt's first article in English concerns Bohemian early fifteenth-century illumination and appeared in the *Burlington Magazine* in 1938. He commented in a letter to Saxl in 1937 after a visit to see the Antwerp Bible, the subject of the article, that only three scholars had seen it this century! The Schapiros finally met Pächt briefly on a visit to London in the summer of 1939 and borrowed his flat during his absence.

'What a desert' is his comment, though a new book by Carl Nordenfalk on Canon Tables is a notable exception. Nordenfalk was to become another close friend, though they did not meet until after the War.[13]

On 11 January 1940 Pächt married Jeanne Michalopoulo whom he had met at the Courtauld Institute where she was working as Assistant Librarian. Their son, Michael, was born in October 1942. It was presumably due to the evacuation of the manuscripts from the British Museum at the start of the War that Wormald suggested that Pächt should catalogue instead the manuscripts of the Bodleian Library, Oxford. In Oxford, where he moved early in 1941, Pächt 'felt very much more at home, with its old buildings than I ever did in London, although the problems of housing and feeding are here much more difficult to solve'. Jeanne Pächt helped in the catalogue and slips printed in a format which Eric Millar had designed for the British Museum project were handwritten for every illuminated manuscript in the collection. Pächt wrote to Schapiro of his satisfaction with the project and his many discoveries, 'even in the field of English illumination'. A number of short publications resulted from this work during the War, for example of a pair of eleventh-century Psalters from Tegernsee, of a manuscript ascribed to the young Fouquet (now the artist is identified as the 'Jouvenel Master'), and of a manuscript illuminated by Holbein the Younger in England. But the main work, which involved not just ascription on stylistic grounds, but detailed research on texts, provenance via coats-of-arms, and the identification of comparative material, remained unpublished until I was engaged in 1962 by Dr Richard Hunt, Keeper of Western Manuscripts at the Bodleian Library, to prepare the slips for publication. The task was to update them and supply bibliography under Pächts supervision. I had started my Oxford D.Phil. under Pächt's supervision two years previously.

The three volumes of the catalogue, European other than Italian, Italian, and British, subsequently appeared in 1966, 1970 and 1973. The format, a very brief description of texts, type of illumination with a ranking, provenance and selected secondary literature, backed up with small illustrations for many of the entries, proved practical in that it enabled some three thousand three hundred manuscripts to be classified and thus made them accessible to interested scholars to examine further, even if much specific and necessary information could not be given.[14] Since Pächt left for Vienna in 1963 there was much correspondence involved in the revision, but we looked together, even if briefly, at every single manuscript during this time.

---

[13] At that time working in the Göteborg Museum of Art. Director of the Nationalmuseum in Stockholm (1959–69). For a memoir of Pächt by him see *Revue de l'art*, 1988, 82–3.

[14] Pächt may have had in mind the catalogues of illuminated manuscripts in Spanish collections by J. D. Bordona in 1933 as a model.

The Department of Western Manuscripts was an ideal place to do this work with its excellent reference collection on open shelves in Duke Humfrey and with the group of Oxford scholars interested in the manuscript book, Richard Hunt himself above all, Neil Ker and Albinia de la Mare for palaeographical problems, Graham Pollard for bindings, and many others such as A. B. Emden, Beryl Smalley, Malcolm Parkes, Roger Mynors, Richard Southern and later Bob Delaissé. There were many visiting scholars to be consulted too. I remember a visit by Winkler perhaps in 1963, and Pächt showing him the Italian Missal whose illumination he considered to be by Fouquet, a discovery reported to Schapiro already in December 1941.[15] Other visitors to Bodley included E. A. Lowe, André Grabar and Bernard Bischoff.

The Bodleian can today claim to be the best published major collection of illuminated manuscripts in the world for the use of Art Historians, its only rival being the Nationalbibliothek in Vienna of which more will be said later. The project of recording the manuscripts in colour microfilms initiated by Dr W. O. Hassall was also proceeding at the same time. Pächt had also surveyed the illuminated Byzantine manuscripts in Oxford in a small format Picture Book published in 1948.[16] His mapping of the Bodleian collections has in turn both served as an accessible reference point for succeeding catalogues in other libraries, and formed a basis of study for the next generation of students of book painting.[17]

The work enabled Pächt at the same time to lay the foundations of his knowledge of English medieval illumination, which already bore fruit in the article on the 'Giottesque episode in English art' published in the *Journal of the Warburg and Courtauld Institutes* in 1943.[18] This centred on evidence of knowledge of Italian Trecento art in England in the fourteenth century, such as the Crucifixion in the Gorleston Psalter in the British Museum and the classicizing figure blowing a trumpet in the Psalter of Robert of Ormesby in the Bodleian Library, as well as the complex problem of the sources of the Egerton Genesis with its transmission of early Christian iconographies. Pächt proposed a revised and more coherent chronology for early fourteenth-century English illumination in part based on the degree of its reception of Italian influence. But

---

[15] Ms. Canon. Liturg. 383. *Illuminated manuscripts in the Bodleian Library, 1, Oxford,* Oxford, 1966, no. 720. Winkler agreed, but the manuscript has still not been fully studied.

[16] The Bodleian Byzantine illuminated manuscripts have now been systematically catalogued by Irmgard Hutter.

[17] François Avril acknowledges their inspiration in his preface to the new series of catalogues of illuminated manuscripts at present being issued by the Bibliothèque Nationale, Paris.

[18] Pächt wrote to Saxl with a similar title for a lecture in August 1941.

this was subsidiary to the main purpose of the article which was to place works of English art in a context of European art and to analyse their specific stylistic characteristics, for instance the physical relations of miniatures, borders and initials in relation to the space construction of the scenes represented. The article was reprinted at the end of the War in 1945 with a series of other important pieces from the Journal in a collection significantly entitled 'England and the Mediterranean tradition'. A commitment to underlining the cultural relations historically existing between England and the Continent was clearly part of the Warburg Institute's policy under Saxl from the moment the War broke out.

Research on English medieval art also bore fruit in the collaborative monograph on the St Albans Psalter now in Hildesheim, published by the Warburg Institute in 1960. In this Francis Wormald wrote on the palaeographical and liturgical aspects, C. R. Dodwell discussed the style and iconography of the historiated initials to the Psalms, and Pächt dealt with the full-page miniatures. The Psalter had already been the subject of a monograph by Adolph Goldschmidt in 1895, who was, however, almost exclusively concerned with the historiated initials. Here again Pächt provided a wider European context not just in the matter of iconography, though this was the most sophisticated and detailed discussion of the iconography of an English manuscript to this date, but in wider aspects of the intersection of style and meaning.[19] Pächt demonstrated the debts both in style and iconography of the main artist, the 'Alexis Master', to Ottonian and especially Italo-Byzantine art, as well as to his native tradition of Anglo-Saxon art and even to Early Christian sources preserved in England. But he also demonstrated that the Alexis Master incorporated new imagery such as the Chalice included in the Agony in the Garden, an iconography to become standard in European Christian art from now on. Above all he revealed the achievement of the Alexis Master in forging a new form of sacred narrative.

At this period there was, in part due to Kurt Weitzmann's work, considerable interest in the nature and origins of Christian narrative art, and in its relations to late Antique and earlier Hellenistic narrative art. Also, partly due to the publications on the discovery of the Synagogue paintings at Dura Europos, the possibility of Jewish sources, whether monumental or in book illumination, for Early Christian art was widely

---

[19] For a review underlining this aspect see H. Swarzenski in *Kunstchronik*, March, 1963. Both Pächt and Wormald had been guests of the Institute for Advanced Study, Princeton, during their research for the book, and thus able to use the Index of Christian Art.

discussed. Pächt was also interested in this problem and a collaborative article written with Jeanne Pächt on 'An unknown cycle of illustrations of the Life of Joseph' appeared in *Cahiers Archéologiques* in 1954, whilst Pächt's contribution to the Festschrift for Swoboda in 1959 took up the same issues in relation to the Vienna Genesis. The nature and origin of 'continuous narrative' was a crucial topic here. As said earlier these concerns were already present in the 'Giottesque episode' article of 1943, and were informed by Pächt's earlier studies in Vienna of Late Antique art.

The nature of Christian narrative in English twelfth-century art was also handled in lectures published in 1962, *The Rise of Pictorial Narrative in twelfth-century England*. In the St Albans Psalter monograph Pächt had referred back to Emile Mâle's hypothesis of the influence of the incipient liturgical drama on art of the Romanesque period and had drawn attention to evidence of plays produced by Abbot Roger of St Albans for which Christina of Markyate, the probable commissioner of the Psalter, had provided vestments. This was also linked to the Peregrinus Plays with the three scenes of the Way to Emmaus included in the Psalter.

The question of the dating of the Psalter was of great philological importance since it contains the Chanson d'Alexis, one of the key early Anglo-Norman texts. Until then thought to be mid twelfth-century at earliest, since philologists had ignored Goldschmidt's book, Pächt was able to show that an early date based on the evidence of the obits in the calendar, was compatible with the stylistic evidence. Again this was not only a matter of compiling an oeuvre list for the Alexis master, but also of providing a coherent chronology of English twelfth-century illumination, largely new at that time, but which has formed the basis of all further discussion. It should also be noted that Pächt never wrote the book on English twelfth-century illumination which is referred to by T. S. R. Boase in the preface of his Oxford History of Art volume, *English art 1100–1216*, of 1953. Boase fully acknowledges the help given him by Pächt in his own book. Other studies on English twelfth-century art at this period were a discussion of an illustrated copy of Anselm's prayers, 1956, and the publication of the frescoes at Sigena as English work of the later artists of the Winchester Bible in 1961. Pächt had seen photos of these in the *Catalogo Monumental de España—Huesca*, Madrid, 1942, which reached Oxford shortly after the War. He thanks 'the late Professor Fritz Saxl' who, on being told of the discovery, 'with his usual keeness to promote research' had ordered photos of the paintings for the Warburg Institute.

In 1950 a short note published in the *Bodleian Library Record*

on the self-portrait by the monk Hugo 'Pictor' suggested a reading
of post-Conquest Norman art which acted as a balance to Wormald's
earlier stress on Anglo-Saxon continuity by emphasizing the progressive
elements in Norman art. In 1954 and 1955 Jean Porcher, Conservateur-
en-chef of the Cabinet des Manuscrits at the Bibliothèque Nationale
put on two exhibitions of French book painting, the first of manuscripts from the sixth to the twelfth, the second of manuscripts of the
thirteenth to the sixteenth centuries. Examples were drawn not only
from the Bibliothèque Nationale and other Paris libraries, but from
the French provincial libraries which are extraordinarily rich due to
the sequestration of monastic libraries after the French Revolution. The
exhibitions revealed an enormous amount of new, unpublished material.
Porcher became a close personal friend of Pächt, who in 1963 edited
with Carl Nordenfalk a Festchrift for him in the *Gazette des Beaux-
Arts* and like other scholars was intensely conscious of his debt to
Porcher who had opened up the collection and shared his knowledge with
such generosity. The group of scholars asked to contribute to Porcher's
Festschrift includes the majority of the leading authorities working on
manuscripts illumination at that time, Nordenfalk, Homburger, Mütherich,
Wormald, Swarzenski, Buchthal, Weitzmann, Delaissé, Meiss and Pächt
himself. It shows incidentally how comparatively few there were still at
this date.

Porcher's two exhibitions, together with that on Italian illumination
held at the Palazzo Venezia in Rome in 1950, and slightly earlier exhibitions in Bern and Munich, were milestones in the public appreciation
and the scholarly interest in Medieval and Renaissance book painting. And the work of this particular generation of scholars in teaching
and writing formed the foundation of the huge extension of interest
which has followed in more recent years in both Europe and North
America.

Pächt also contributed to this process in two much smaller but still
significant exhibitions, *Italian illuminated manuscripts from 1400–1550*
held at the Bodleian Library in 1948 and drawn from Oxford libraries
only, and, secondly, a selection of Flemish manuscripts of the fifteenth
and sixteenth centuries which was part of the Royal Academy of Arts
exhibition, *Flemish Art 1300–1700* in 1953. In the former he showed
that he had extended his competence to Italian illumination so well
represented in the Bodleian by the Canonici collection, but for which
there were then few signposts other than H.J. Hermann's catalogues of
the Vienna library holdings. Pächt's contribution to the Saxl Festschrift
of 1957 charted the origins of humanistic illumination in Italy, a subject
on which he had already lectured in 1954, and once again it has formed a

starting point for further research.[20] In the Royal Academy exhibition the manuscripts were drawn from Libraries all over the British Isles, London, Oxford, Cambridge, Glasgow, Edinburgh, Stonyhurst College, Holkham Hall, C. W. Dyson Perrins, as well as from the Bibliothèque Nationale, and the selection demonstrates the extraordinary extent to which Pächt had already familiarized himself with the contents of so many and diverse libraries.

No doubt Pächt was asked to make the selection in view of his short monograph, *The Master of Mary of Burgundy*, published in 1948. The fact that the eponymous manuscript is in the Nationalbibliothek in Vienna and that the Bodleian Library contains the Hours of Engelbert of Nassau as well as two other manuscripts illuminated by this Netherlandish illuminator working in the 1470s–80s was no doubt in part responsible for his writing the book. In the preface he emphasizes both the difficulties in the study of illumination in terms of access for the public, but also its importance. Of all his writings in English this perhaps gives the best idea of his methodological focus and his skill at describing an artist's style within the context of its time. Even if it builds on the work of scholars such as Friedrich Winkler and Hulin de Loo, the latter a scholar whose work Pächt especially admired, it contributed both new material and new arguments concerning the artist's identity, as well as a masterly analysis of the relation of miniature to the newly invented *trompe l'oeil* border and of the space construction involved. Pächt mentions that he had seen some of the manuscripts before the War, but that prevailing conditions made it impossible to see all of the material again.

In spite of the involvement with English twelfth-century art in the 1950s Pächt continued to be engaged in the problems of Northern fifteenth-century painting. In 1956 he published a manuscript in the Bodleian illuminated for Jean de Berry by his court painter, Jacquemart d'Hesdin, showing by stylistic analysis, to my mind convincingly, the impossibility that Jacquemart could be the painter of the Brussels Hours, as supposed by Meiss and others. He also suggested in 1956 that the Louvre leaf of Christ carrying the Cross, shown by Porcher in the 1955 exhibition, was part of the Grandes Heures of Jean de Berry and thus documented as by Jacquemart. This is generally accepted now.

In 1953 Panofsky's *Early Netherlandish Painting* was published and Pächt wrote a review article in two parts in the *Burlington Magazine* of 1956. While fully acknowledging the extraordinary scholarship, the

---

[20] Pächt had already contributed a section on Italian Humanism and England to the photographic exhibition held at the Warburg Institute in 1941, later published as F. Saxl, R. Wittkower, *British Art and the Mediterranean*, London, 1948.

scope and the achievement of Panofsky's book, Pächt expressed important methodological reservations, especially in the matter of Panofsky's
famous 'hidden symbolism', as well as a number of disagreements as to
interpretation and attribution. There was some criticism of the review at
the time, but it does not seem that Panofsky himself bore any resentment
and the two men continued to exchange offprints and correspondence.
Pächt particularly treasured a letter from Panofsky thanking him for the
offprint of his article on Riegl published in 1963, and he contributed to
Panofsky's Festschrift in 1961.

Other publications at this time discussed the interrelations of art
and artists north and south of the Alps, for example the article for
Panofsky on the Avignon Diptych, and that, written for Porcher, on
the relationship between the Limbourgs and Pisanello. Also bringing
together Italian and Northern evidence the article 'Early Italian nature
studies and the early calendar landscape' published in the *Journal of the
Warburg and Courtauld Institutes* of 1950, is perhaps the most widely read
of anything Pächt wrote, since it tackles the genesis of one of the major
genres of later European painting.[21] It does so in a ground-breaking way
typical of Pächt's scholarship, by introducing a whole range of new and
unpublished evidence, particularly in illuminated manuscripts, originating
both north and south of the Alps, and then analysing the changes in means
of representation of the natural world from the later Middle Ages to the
Early Modern period.

All this activity, for by no means all of his publications at this period
have been mentioned, was possible because Pächt had relatively few
other commitments. Oriel College, Oxford, had made Pächt a Fellow
and Lecturer in the History of Medieval Art in March 1945 due, as
he reports to Schapiro, to F. M. Powicke. Sir George Clark succeeded
Ross as Provost of Oriel in 1947 and Pächt retained great affection and
respect for him, always making a point of visiting him when he returned
to Oxford from Vienna. Pächt published a note in 1952 on the College
altarpiece, identifying it as a work of Bernard van Orley. He took British
citizenship in May 1947. Due to Clark he was made Senior Lecturer in the
History School in 1952 and Reader in 1962. He was not a particularly fluent
lecturer in English, nor did he make many concessions in subject matter to
any possible public taste, so neither lectures nor seminars were as widely
attended as they should have been. When he spoke on more 'popular'
topics, say Giotto or Dürer, as opposed to say European Romanesque
illumination, he reached larger audiences. Meanwhile the only other art
history provided in Oxford was study of Greek sculpture under the Literae

---

[21] Published in French translation *Le paysage dans l'art italien*, Paris, 1991.

Humaniores School, occasional series of lectures by such few scholars in the University as had any competence or interest, T. S. R. Boase, Walter Oakeshott, K. B. McFarlane for example, and the lectures of the annually appointed Slade Professors, who included Kenneth Clark, Ernst Gombrich, John Pope-Hennessy, George Zarnecki and Francis Watson in those years. Since no examinations were connected with any of these and no credit given for attendance, there was little incentive to undergraduates to come. Thus a majority of Pächt's audience were not students of the University but faithful attenders such as his friends Bruno Fürst or Emmy Wellesz, both resident in Oxford. Pächt had only had two graduate students in Oxford, John Beckwith who left to work in the Victoria and Albert Museum before completing his thesis, and myself. He did, however, help and encourage very many who sought his advice in these years and also later, for he was always generous in communicating his discoveries to those who needed and would benefit from them. Kathleen Morand in her book on Pucelle published in 1962 is one of many scholars to acknowledge his help.

In 1955, however, the University decided to fund a Chair in the History of Art and appointed Edgar Wind, who had come to England before the War with the Warburg Institute as a refugee scholar and then gone on to the United States. Pächt was disappointed to be passed over. He had no taste for or skill at University politics, nor for self-advertisement.[22] Wind on the other hand shone in learned discourse at College High Tables and was a brilliant lecturer who mesmerized his undergraduate audiences with his abstruse learning and his extraordinary eloquence. He was able to discuss artists with whose names at least they were familiar, Michelangelo, Reynolds, Picasso, and whose works they were led to believe were now being interpreted for them correctly for the first time. But for all its virtuoso skill, and it was a performance which filled the Oxford Playhouse twice a week, Wind's was a solo performance. Only when Wind was succeeded by Francis Haskell was any Art History other than classical admitted to the undergraduate curriculum in the form of options in the History School. Whether it would have been different if Pächt had been appointed may be doubted. Leading figures in the University like Maurice Bowra or John Sparrow might be impressed by Wind's deep classical learning, but the University as a whole were still sceptical of art history as an academic subject. Even much later Bob Delaissé, by that time a Fellow at All Souls, had to provide set texts ('Gobbets') for his examination papers, since, as he told me wryly, the History Faculty could not accept that works of art were themselves the original and primary documents for study. Pächt's eminence

---

[22] When invited to meet Bowra at this time in connection with the appointment he commented that Bowra spoke all evening without ever allowing him a word.

in his field was, however, recognized by his election to the British Academy in 1956. Later, in 1971, Oxford University conferred on him the Degree of D. Litt *honoris causa*.

In 1963 K. M. Swoboda retired from the Chair of Art History in Vienna University and Pächt was invited to return. A letter of 25 August 1962 to Schapiro sets out the pros and cons, time for research in Oxford, teaching with the prospect of good pupils in Vienna. Pächt chose the latter and thus at the age of sixty uprooted from Oxford, which was especially difficult for his wife whose circle of friends and ties were in England, and returned to take up a new and onerous post. He took his lectures very seriously and spent an enormous amount of time researching and preparing them, typing them out himself. He was stimulated and delighted by the response and they have become legendary. He was always a hard worker with an undeviating commitment to his work.[23] He remarked with evident approval how when he left work late in the evening, the students would still be there studying. At the same time Otto Demus returned to take up the Chair of Byzantine Art History and thus cordial relations existed between the two subject areas, very different from the days of Schlosser and Strygowski when Pächt had been a student.[24]

I think that Pächt never felt completely at home in England. I remember him reporting with astonishment the opinion of a fellow guest at High Table in Oxford that English weather was the best in the world! Was it a joke which he did not perceive? In any case he found the view incomprehensible, only possible in a country where Insularity can be considered a virtue. The early letters to Schapiro also make plain his sense of betrayal first by Britain and later by the United States at their failure to stem the Nazi threat in time. Perhaps subconsciously the resentment remained. The letters to Schapiro on the other hand show his attachment to France, for example a letter of 6 June 1940, which speaks with anguish of the collapse of France, the 'heart of civilization'. 'Since yesterday Nazi boots are trampling the Champs Elysées'. It was appropriate that he should be honoured by the French Government in 1982 with the Ordre National du Mérite and in 1984 made a Commandeur de l'Ordre des Arts et des Lettres.

Above all he returned to Vienna because he felt deeply that he belonged to and had a responsibility to uphold the Viennese tradition of art history. His deep knowledge and love of Vienna and its monuments as

---

[23] He used to quote with approval from Browning's 'Grammarian's Funeral', and he liked to refer to 'the scholar's lonely candle'. I do not know the origin of the quote.

[24] *Otto Pächt. Nachruf von Otto Demus* was published in the *Almanach der Oesterreichischen Akademie der Wissenschaften, 138. Jahrgang*, 1988, pp. 437–443.

well as of its great art collections, was evinced on conducted tours, and he delighted in sharing, as generous host, his enjoyment of Viennese cuisine. He remained a rather private man, preferring a small circle of friends and gaining his greatest pleasure from discussion of professional matters, from producing a photo, for instance, and challenging a response. The tragic illness and death from cancer of his wife in 1971 turned him even more in on himself, and in his last years he concentrated ever more exclusively on his work.

Inevitably publications fell off in the period immediately after his return to Vienna, but a significant initiative was the revival under a new and improved format of the catalogues of the illuminated manuscripts of the Vienna National Library. Pächt found that Hermann had left an unpublished volume on French illumination in manuscript form, and began by revising this with the help of an able research assistant, Dr Dagmar Thoss, whose work was funded by the Austrian Academy. This was published in 1974 and further volumes co-authored with Dr Thoss on later French illuminated manuscripts and printed books, and on Flemish manuscripts appeared in 1977 and 1983. Dr Ulrike Jenni who had been supervised by Pächt in her thesis on an early fifteenth-century patternbook in the Uffizi, collaborated on the latter volume and was co-author on a volume published in 1975 on the Dutch school. Pächt had been able to enlist the support of Herbert Hunger, President of the Austrian Academy, to which he had been elected as a Corresponding Fellow in 1965, becoming an Ordinary Fellow in 1967. It is good to know that the project to which Pächt devoted so much of his scholarly energies and on which he was working to the end, will continue.

The format devised for the catalogues was less bulky than that of Hermann but much fuller than the Bodleian catalogues, and has the advantage of making possible the inclusion of more codicological information as well as detailed descriptions of individual miniatures. The catalogues also set new standards in the deployment of philological evidence due to Dr Thoss' expertise, while Pächt used his by now unrivalled knowledge of manuscripts in collections world-wide to provide comparative material. The support of the staff of the Nationalbibliothek, especially Dr Otto Mazal and Dr Eva Irblich, of course proved crucial and this was also signalized by the holding of two exhibitions in the Library, one of French, the other of Netherlandish illuminated manuscripts in 1978 and 1987. Their catalogues, compiled by Dr Thoss, were dedicated to Pächt.

Pächt's retirement in 1972 was marked by a Festschrift for his seventieth birthday edited by Artur Rosenauer and Gerold Weber, who have both written about the charismatic effect of Pächt's teaching.[25] A second Festschrift was published in honour of 'the two Ottos', Demus and Pächt, born in the same year, as volume XXV of the *Wiener Jahrbuch für Kunstgeschichte*.

In retirement Pächt was able to return to his own researches and his publications, written once again in German, included two lengthy articles on René of Anjou published in 1973 and 1977, which brought together a wealth of new material based on many years interest in the problems of the identity of the artist of the Coeur manuscript in Vienna and of René's patronage of art. He also published in 1974 the attribution to Fouquet of the portrait in the Kunsthistorisches Museum of Gonella, court jester to the Gonzaga. This attribution once made seemed so obvious that it was incredible that it had remained so long a subject of conjecture with a constant harping in the literature on supposed links to Van Eyck.

A volume entitled *Methodisches zur Kunsthistorischen Praxis*, a mixture of earlier and unpublished papers, appeared in 1977. Pächt had seemed to abandon his early interest in the theoretical grounding of Art History after coming to England, though he published a short article on Riegl in a series on art historians in the *Burlington Magazine* of 1963. This emphasized Riegl's concept of the 'Kunstwollen' as grounded on empirical examination of the work of art and this belief in the possibility of unproblematized empirical evidence surfaces also clearly in the earlier letters to Schapiro, who indeed draws attention to it in his *Art Bulletin* review. Pächt's basic assumptions of the task and the methods of art history seem not to have changed and are enshrined in the paper which gives its name to the collection, a lecture given in Vienna in 1970/1. He remained committed to the analysis of stylistic development, using the term 'Strukturanalyse' of the 'Younger Viennese school'. He also remained sceptical of the cult of the individual artist if it implied that the genius could be an exception to rather than a fulfilment of the Kunstwollen, sceptical of the explanation of stylistic change by a social history of art, and sceptical of iconography as narrowly conceived by some of its practitioners. He writes about his view on iconography as a sterile study in itself if divorced from questions of style already in a letter to Schapiro of 1939, and his arguments are set down more fully in a paper of that time preserved among the letters to Saxl of 1937 at the Warburg Institute. A lecture given in Bonn in 1964 for the International Art Historians Congress on 'Künstlerische Originalität und ikonographische Erneuerung' argues that iconographical innovation is not

---

[25] See *Kunsthistoriker* (as in note. 6). Otto Demus (as in note 24) commented that: 'Seine Forscher- und Lehrtätigkeit machte Wien zu einem Mekka der Kunstgeschichte'. Theses written under Pächt reflect the width of his interests, ranging from Koichi Koshi's studies of the wall-paintings at Reichenau to Ursula Panhans–Bühler's work on Petrus Christus.

necessarily associated with great artists. It is a premise of his disagreement with Panofsky that artistic creation is unconscious, which he supports with a quote from Musil to the effect that the artist only knows what he wants to do when he has done it.

In the late writings there is in effect a return to the problem of the national constants, in that Pächt was arguing that the René Master's style was French not Netherlandish, therefore he could not be, as often thought (especially, ironically, by French scholars), Barthélémy d'Eyck. Similarly with the Gonella portrait he analysed a 'French' cubic space construction which he had already opposed to the 'Netherlandish' relationship of picture plane and represented space in his paper 'Gestaltungsprinzipien' of 1933. An article on 'la terre de Flandres' described the Netherlandish characteristics of landscape in fifteenth-century Flemish illumination, also seen as continuing in later Netherlandish painting.

Unlike Pächt's theory that the Coeur Master was René himself, the attribution of the Gonella has found general acceptance. Like an earlier stylistic perception of Pächt's, the dating of the Dresden Triptych by van Eyck, it was later confirmed by technical examination. In the former the date was discovered on removal of the frame, and in the latter infra-red reflectography revealed colour notes in French beneath the painting!

Other articles to appear in these years were also mainly concerned with problems of Northern fifteenth-century painting and typically dealt with works of art neglected or unknown which Pächt had unearthed in the Vienna collections, for example the drawing of a hoopoo by Marmion published in 1979, or with problems on which he had worked for many years, for example his last publication in the Festschrift for Carl Nordenfalk on the Salvator Mundi image in the Turin Hours. Pächt had continued to think about the Eyck problem, the relative contributions of Jan and Hubert. He would remark that only with a lifetime's experience could one hope to deal with the really difficult problems of Art History. In the event though he lectured on Early Netherlandish painting he did not himself publish his conclusions. Texts of nearly all his lectures exist, however, since he typed them out himself, and three series have been published, the *Buchmalerei des Mittelalters* with his imprimatur, and, posthumously, *Van Eyck. Die Begründer der altniederländischen Malerei* and *Rembrandt*, all issued by Prestel Verlag of Munich under the supervision of Michael Pächt, in whose skill as an editor and designer of books his father took great pride and pleasure.[26]

---

[26] Japanese and Spanish editions of *Methodisches* have appeared and an English edition is in preparation. *Buchmalerei* has been translated into English, Spanish and Italian. *Van Eyck* will appear in English shortly and another volume on Early Netherlandish Painting is in preparation.

All three books serve to introduce a general audience to a body of material and also by concrete example expound a methodology of visual analysis. In *Buchmalerei* this centres on the relation of image and decoration to the written text. The *Van Eyck*, in spite of the restricted title, is in fact a discussion of the shift in representation which occurs in the *ars nova* of the Netherlands from *c.* 1420. Whilst Jan's part in this is seen as crucial, Pächt is concerned to analyse the new representation by contrast to the work of predecessors and in relation to that of contemporaries, especially the Master of Flémalle. In this context the question of Jan or Hubert is subsumed within the broader analysis of representation as style and content with a consequential uncovering of distinguishing characteristics. As Artur Rosenauer points out in the Preface, Pächt was also much preoccupied with the recovery of lost compositions or designs by Jan, the 'Turin Master' and the 'Master of Flémalle', and it was his ability to see as it were the style beyond a style which enabled him to make such striking progress in this direction. The discussion of the vestments of the Order of the Golden Fleece is only one example. In the *Rembrandt* also Pächt's method is to analyse representation and narrative in the paintings. By considering them by genre he makes clear once again how form and content are inseparable and within a pictorial tradition shows the particularity of Rembrandt's vision.

Pächt's contribution to scholarship in his chosen area was perhaps foremost in classification and analysis of a notable range of new material. His knowledge of the whole history of manuscript illumination was greater than that of any contemporary or predecessor, and inevitably he thus played a key role in the enormous increase of interest in that particular medium of medieval art. He also saw its importance for the history of panel painting and the reconstruction of lost works by monumental artists. In the letter to Saxl from Vienna of 23 December 1937 after his visit to Antwerp, referred to earlier, he comments on the necessity of autopsy in investigating works of art. Even eminent art historians like Panofsky and de Tolnay, he says, have made mistakes by failing to see works in the original. Few scholars have travelled so widely or been so thorough and painstaking in their investigation of works of art at first hand.[27]

Though he had an extraordinary visual memory and perceptiveness, he was not only a connoisseur able to recognize a style or an artist. His perceptiveness was founded on a deep and broad historical and cultural knowledge. His writings included antiquarian and heraldic research,

---

[27] Pächt's fine library as well as his notes and collections of photographs were bequeathed to the Institut für Kunstgeschichte, Vienna University, where they are being catalogued with the help of the Getty Grant Program. They will be available to scholars who are also invited to contribute offprints, so that the collection remains a dynamic and growing one.

knowledge of written accounts of lost works of art in obscure texts and of early biographical sources, and philological investigations. An historical context is always an implicit foundation in his writings, and it is that which gives his work perspective and significance. In a letter to Schapiro in 1945 concerning his Bodleian Handlist he says: 'I have learned to see the work of art more closely connected with contemporary liturgy and general history. But I do not know whether I have made any progress worth mentioning in the methodological and theoretical sphere for which I once cared so much'. These historical interests are evident, for example, in *The St Albans Psalter* in his speculations on the artist's possible identity as Anketil, which conflicts with an earlier slogan of 'Kunstgeschichte ohne Namen', and in the long and complex chapter which discusses the text of the Chanson d'Alexis.

A further important aspect of Pacht's scholarship was his conviction of the scholar's responsibility to leave certain questions open, and not to claim to have solved all problems at once. At the end of his review of Baldass' book on Jan van Eyck he states his belief that by trying to do less, more will in the end be achieved.[28] His ability to see the larger questions, but to leave open those which he could not find a solution to is another reason why his writings have had such an impact and will continue to retain their relevance.

All the refugee scholars who came from the German to the English-speaking world before the War contributed immeasurably to cultural and academic life in their adopted countries.[29] Perhaps in no other subject in the humanities was this so evident as in Art History, which they transformed into a more professional and a more academic discipline. In Pächt's case in England this was by example as much as by direct teaching. He represented consciously a tradition of art history which though it is sometimes now decried as formalism, at its best interprets the work of art by 'considering style and meaning as inseparable'.[30] To read Pächt's description of the dedication picture of the Grandes Chroniques d'Hainaut in Vienna is to see it with new eyes and thus to understand it differently. That is why from the early interest in Gestalt psychology he placed such emphasis on seeing, on the eye's response. In a letter of 3 June 1939 he thanks Schapiro for an offprint and comments: 'I think it is the first "Strukturanalyse" of an high mediaeval work of art. Apart from that it seems to me to be a

[28] *Burlington Magazine*, 95 (1953), 253.

[29] For an account of their contribution in the United States see *The Intellectual Migration. Europe and America, 1930–1960*, eds. D. Fleming, B. Bailyn, Cambridge, Mass., 1969, especially the chapter by Colin Eisler, 'Kunstgeschichte American style: a study in migration'.

[30] The quote is from Margaret Iversen, 'Meyer Schapiro and the semiotics of visual art', *Block*, 1 (1979), 50.

completely new method of iconographical analysis which art history needs so badly'. And again in 1962 thanking Schapiro for his *Cézanne* he says: 'I always marvel at the richness of your descriptive vocabulary and the way the formal values of a particular painting are being related to a specific situation in the artist's development'. He is emphasizing the qualities he admired and himself exemplified in his own writings. I once said to him that I felt that either one could see a style or one could not, and that verbal description was otiose. But he disagreed strongly. Though he distrusted certain kinds of flowery and superficially brilliant language as applied to art, it is the struggle to describe in the right words the results of long and hard looking, which makes all his writings so rich and so fruitful.[31]

JONATHAN J. G. ALEXANDER
*Fellow of the British Academy*

*Note in proof.* P. Lasko, 'The impact of German-speaking refugees in Britain on the Fine Arts', in *Second Chance: Two Centuries of German-speaking Jews in the United Kingdom*, ed. W. E. Mosse (Tübingen, 1991), pp. 268–274, with its discussion of the contribution of refugee art historians in Britain, reached me at proof stage.

---

[31] Pächt discussed the problem of the verbal description of the work of art in one of his earliest writings, 'Das Ende der Abbildtheorie', *Kritische Berichte zur Kunstgeschichtlichen Literatur*, 3/4 (1930/31), 1–9.

*Proceedings of the British Academy*, **80**, 473–491

# Henry Habberley Price
# 1899–1984

HENRY HABBERLEY PRICE was born in August, 1899. He was a pupil at Winchester and a scholar of New College, Oxford. He obtained a First in Lit. Hum, in 1921. He was subsequently to become Fellow of Magdalen College, Oxford (1922–4), Assistant Lecturer in Philosophy at the University of Liverpool (1922–3), Fellow and Lecturer at Trinity College, Oxford (1924–35), Lecturer in Philosophy in the University of Oxford (1932–5), and then, from 1935, Wykeham Professor of Logic (at New College) in the University of Oxford. (It is said that a group of younger members of the Philosophy Faculty visited Sir David Ross, one of the selectors, to advocate his appointment.) He was elected to a Fellowship of the British Academy in 1943. While he was at Oxford he held visiting Professorships at Princeton and Los Angeles. He gave the Sarum Lectures (Oxford, 1970–1), the Boutwood Lectures (Cambridge, 1965) and the Gifford Lectures (Aberdeen, 1959–60). He was awarded an honorary D.Litt by the Universities of Dublin, St. Andrews and Wales. He was twice President of the Society for Psychical Research (1939–40 and 1960–1). He was the author of numerous and influential articles for learned journals. His books, most of which were and still are important, were *Perception*, *Hume's Theory of the External World*, *Thinking and Experience*, *Belief* and *Essays on the Philosophy of Religion*. He was a pilot in the R.A.F during the first world war (1917–19), and never lost an interest in flying. He was a founder member of the Oxford Flying Club. He was a keen painter, which interest was closely connected with his study of perception. He was an enthusiastic ornithologist, and possessed an enviable collection of replicas (I am glad to say) of owls, a bird which he was supposed to resemble. He was devotedly looked after by his sister for many years.

Henry Price was one of the kindest and most conscientious men I knew.

H. H. PRICE

*Ramsey & Muspratt*

It used to be said that the nastiest thing he could bring himself to say in criticism of another philosopher was 'There may be something in what you say', though I believe this is to do him an injustice. (I never knew whether he tended to overrate people, or was just too polite not to seem to overrate them. I suspect it was the latter.) It was said that if he received an unsolicited book from a publisher he felt under an obligation to pay for it. Once, realising that he had forgotten that he had undertaken to address a meeting of a student Philosophy society in Liverpool, he chartered a plane as the only way of getting there on time. His conscience, however, was mainly directed at himself, the only other persons he felt disapproval of being, I am told, drivers who slowed him down.

He was an excellent lecturer. During my time in Oxford, when many lecturers lost most or all of their classes before their courses were complete, his lectures were always well attended. I myself have never been to a course of lectures which I have found more interesting, more lucid, more considerately presented, or more enlightening. They were given with that apparent ease which can only be the product (though unfortunately it is not the invariable product) of much thought and the taking of endless pains. There was no nonsense about encouraging discussion, which took place in his informal instruction classes. As a teacher Price had the ability to make one feel that one's clumsiest remarks were novel and interesting. Indeed, I have always harboured the delusion, if it was one, that his enthusiasm for the subject was so great that he really did find one's remarks interesting. He had the gift of being able to devote his whole attention to one when he discussed anything.

Price was an extremely modest man. He possessed that very great and genuine humility, which sprang from a vision of the enormous extent of one's subject in comparison with one's own limited powers, which is lacked by those with little imagination. I suspect this, combined with the arrogance of some others, caused him to be sometimes underrated by those insufficiently discerning not to take at its face value humility in those more able than themselves. He always wrote with the same very great clarity with which he lectured, and, though sometimes I felt that his anxiety to be understood, especially at times when he was misunderstood, made him repeat himself unnecessarily, this was doubtless a fault on the right side. There was nothing superficial, pretentious, or slipshod about his work. If he did not thoroughly understand what he was saying, he did not say it. Philosophy would be a much more rewarding subject if other people did the same.

I would not have supposed that Price so much as understood the motive for spending time on getting oneself on, or of increasing the influence of oneself and the institution to which one belongs, had it not been for the

Machiavellian advice—too dreadful to relate—he gave me a long time ago, when I became head of a small department in a provincial university—an atmosphere which is not noted for producing saints. It could be, however, that he was *too* unworldly. He lacked the common touch. He could not fraternise with young men in pubs, to their benefit as well as his own, but instead went to bed with a cup of cocoa, a drink which he wrongly supposed to be a sedative. Nevertheless he was extremely hospitable, and frequently entertained quite boring students at high table at New College.

In politics he was an extreme individualist, and contrived to be conservative while at the same time disapproving of class-consciousness. He opposed the common market, and regarded religion as a socially binding force—a better reason, as I am sure he would have agreed, for persuading other people to be religious than for being religious oneself. He had a B.Sc. in Psychology, which helped him with his study of perception. He was an authority on the philosophies of Mahayana and Hinayana Buddhism.

Price's work was always constructive, and he seldom turned aside to enter into controversy, though the effects could be devastating on the very rare occasions when he did. One of the guiding lines of Price's work was to accept the empirical facts as he found them. This produced his acceptance of the sense-datum theory, of mental images and other introspectable phenomena, including an ostensible sense of the divine. He rejected theories which did not conform to the facts rather than, like most modern materialists, distorting the facts because they did not conform to the theories.

Price was one of the many victims of fashion in Philosophy. The uncertainty of Philosophers concerning the soundness of their methods seems to make them unusually susceptible to the proponents of false dawns. It is easy to forget that if the history of philosophy is the history of error—as to a distressingly large extent it is—one's own pet theories are unlikely to be sufficiently privileged to be immune to the fates which have befallen their predecessors. A flood of publications, and a high rate of obsolescence, which seems to vary inversely with the secure progress of the subject, makes it increasingly difficult to detect what is of permanent value. Price would not, like far too many British philosophers, have been carried away by a certain number of sometimes gimmicky doctrines from across the Atlantic. Nor would he have yielded to the temptation of thinking that technical virtuosity in the use of symbolism gives one the right to have accepted philosophical doctrines that cannot be put simply and lucidly into good plain prose.

Price's work contrived to be large in scale without sacrificing a most meticulous attention to detail. It was both sustained and intricate. Price had the gift of being able to say simply and clearly and briefly things which other philosophers struggled over many pages to express. Price's contribution to philosophy, especially to epistemology, was great, and deserves more recognition than it has received. I shall attempt in the following pages a brief exposition and defence of some of his views.


## Perception

Price's first book was *Perception*, published in 1932. This was one of the best books, if not the best book devoted exclusively to the Philosophy of Perception, that has ever been written. Whereas philosophers usually maunder on *ad nauseam* about whether there *are* material objects, Price, in *Perception*, explained how he thought not only how we knew that there were such things, but how we knew what were the shape, the size, position, and the colour and the causal properties of such objects. He explains such things as how we know we were seeing something square, and how a simultaneous unitary picture of an object was put together piecemeal by means of looking at it successively from different points of view, a process which he correctly said was one of syngnosis. (He eschewed the pretentious and inaccurate word 'synthesis'.) Quite incidentally and unassumingly (to take just one example) he gives what I suspect is a definitive solution to the question, which Kant makes such a hash of (for it has nothing to do with causality): How we do we know the difference between an objective succession (when the change in the appearance of things is due to the fact that the object is moving) and a subjective succession (when it is due to the fact that the observer is moving)?

It is most important to stress that what Price was doing in *Perception* was epistemology, not phenomenology. (One might call it phenomenological epistemology.) Most of Price's contemporaries, when they talk about perception discussed *words* like 'looks' and 'seems'. Price did not do this to nearly the same extent. He went straight to the phenomena, instead of approaching the phenomena indirectly *via* the words which it was customary to use to describe the phenomena. But he was not interested in the phenomena of perception just for their own sake. His interest was epistemological. He wanted to know what it was about the phenomena that made us say, for example, that we were walking in a straight line, that the object in front of us really was blue, or that it was impenetrable or soluble in water.

*Perception*, though it had a considerable reputation until the end of the second world war, lost its influence later. This was due to a number of factors. First of all, the sense-datum theory, according to which perceiving material objects was mediated by awareness of something other than a material object, viz. a sense-datum of that object (e.g., the yellow round shape or silver crescent which one sees when one perceives the moon), fell into undeserved disrepute. But all but the first couple of chapters of *Perception*, which defended the sense-datum theory, presupposed it. It was characteristic of the lack of historical perspective of the time that this theory, which in one form or another had been held by Locke and Berkeley (who called sense-data 'ideas') and Hume (who called them impressions), as well as by John Stuart Mill and G. E. Moore and Bertrand Russell (to mention only the major British empiricists) was, shortly after the war, supposed to have been conclusively refuted by a number of articles in learned journals.

Rejecting the sense-datum theory was partly motivated by reluctance to admit into one's ontology anything other than physical objects like electrons and combinations thereof (and perhaps also people, if people are more than complicated groups of physical objects.)

But the metaphysics of the aforementioned reluctance can be crude. Lucretius, the father of modern materialism, held that atoms and the void were the only things there were. He did not, however, attempt (as perhaps he ought to have attempted) to *reduce* the void to atoms). Sense-data, obviously, are neither. But the equator, for example, which certainly exists, is not a physical object, but one should not speak ill of it for that reason. Nor should one deny that there is such a thing for reasons such as that we cannot trip over it when we cross it. Dances, impulses, waves, tunes, novels, quadratic equations, plays, tunes, limited liability companies and bank balances, to name but a few, are similar. (Gilbert Ryle held that minds were the same.) It is obvious, too, that the existence of at least some of the large number of such abstract entities is not incompatible with the truth of materialism. Electrons can and do dance, and statements about impulses passing down lines of trucks are logically entailed by statements about the trucks, even though the impulse can move much faster than any of the trucks.

Before rejecting sense-data on the grounds that they were neither electrons nor composed of electrons, its opponents should have considered more carefully whether their existence, like the existence of impulses, was not compatible with materialism. They would be compatible with materialism if they were 'entities' like the equator, whose existence no sensible person supposes to entail the rejection of materialism. Materialism then, must be re-defined as not the view that everything is material, but as the view that every *substance* (in the sense of 'substance' which meant 'that which is capable of existing by itself', as cats can exist by themselves but grins can only exist on the faces of cats) is material. Lucretius could then have held (i) that atoms are the only substance, (ii) that the void, though it existed, was not a substance, and (iii) (which may be entailed by (i) and (ii)) that statements about the void could be reduced to statements about atoms.

Those who denied the sense-datum theory usually supposed that we were directly aware of the front surfaces of objects, rather than of sense-data. But *surfaces* are among those things that are not substances. Hence those philosophers who rejected the sense-datum theory on the grounds that what we were immediately aware of were not sense-data, but the front surfaces of material things, were inadvertently playing into the hands of the sense-datum theorists. For in that case our perception of material objects *was* mediated by something other than a material object, namely the *surface* of a material object. Hence our perceiving material objects (at least in those cases when the object, unlike the Northern Lights, *has* a surface) is mediated by our perceiving their surfaces, and to complain that we are prevented from perceiving material objects by an iron curtain of sense-data would be as sensible as to complain that we were prevented from perceiving material objects by an iron curtain constituted by their surfaces. If a philosopher were to be so naïve as to suppose that we can quite easily get behind the surface of an object—by cutting it open, let us suppose—he should remember that one then just sees the surfaces of other objects—half a loaf instead of a whole one, perhaps. An object is always hiding behind its surfaces, so to speak, from which it follows that we can never just 'read off' its properties. But this is just what the sense-datum philosophers maintained. There is no reason why a sense-datum theorist should maintain that sense-data are substances. Hume explicitly says they are. Berkeley held the monistic view that the only substances were minds.

Those who criticised the sense-datum theory assumed that if we are immediately aware of sense-data, then we are *not* immediately aware of the front surfaces of material objects. But, since sense-data are by definition only the immediate objects of perception, then, if the front surfaces of material objects are the immediate objects of perception, then we *are* aware of sense-data. If the coloured patches and trapezoid shapes beloved of the sense-datum theorists turn out to be the front surfaces of material objects, this does not mean that they do not exist. Rather, it means that they do. And even if sense-data were the front surfaces of material objects, this would not mean that the epistemological problems of the sense-datum theorists do not still arise, transposed into another key. There is still, for example, the Kantian problem of how we build a picture of an object having six (say) *simultaneously* existing and spatially related surfaces from having these surfaces presented to us one by one. Kant is obviously right in thinking that memory is one thing that is necessary.

There are as a matter of fact *two types* of rival to the sense-datum theory, the view that perception is direct, and views (discussed in Chapter II of *Perception*) according to which the characteristics that the sense-datum philosophers attributed to sense-data are the characteristics which the objects seen by means of their mediation look to have. An example of the latter is Whitehead's theory that objects possess their characteristics from a place. Hence, where the sense-datum theorists often (though not always or necessarily) held that seeing a penny from an angle involves seeing something which is elliptical, Whitehead held that what one saw was not elliptical, but only elliptical-from-a-point-of-view. The important thing is that neither the sense datum theory nor its alternatives held that perception was *direct*. Hence, though the sense-datum theory is certainly true as opposed to the view that perception is direct, it is only very problematically true in relation to certain other theories like Whitehead's. Here I think the truth is fairly evenly divided among them. Briefly, the sense-datum theory is true of some of the characteristics of material objects—their colour, perhaps—and its alternatives true of others—their shape. (Something can look elliptical without anything at all being elliptical.) Here, of course, if sense-data just are the front surfaces of material objects, they will have to have characteristics they do not seem to have, for the front surfaces of material objects can. There is no necessary connection between the view that our perception of objects is mediated, and the view that what are the immediate objects of perception must have the characteristics material objects seem to have. And from the point of view of doing philosophical phenomenology it does not matter a jot which view you accept. Of course, the fact that the sense-datum theory is *compatible* with the view that what we are directly aware of are the front surfaces of material objects does not mean that the sense-data *are* the front surfaces of material objects. Price, in Chapter II of *Perception* gives compelling reasons for thinking that this view is *not* true. For example, sometimes we are aware of two sense-data when there is only one surface, and other sense-data—those associated with mirror images—are not in the place where the surface of the object is.

I believe that another of the main reasons why the sense-datum theory is rejected is the belief that sense-data are private, and the belief that private objects cannot be talked about. If so, if there were any sense-data, it would be impossible to communicate the fact to others. The belief that private objects cannot be talked about is the result of two erroneous beliefs, (i) that a word has meaning only if it is governed by rules, and (ii) that private rules could not be checked. But in any case sense-data, defined as the immediate objects of perception, do not *have* to be private, though it may turn out that they are so. Part of the confusion on this subject is due to Ayer, who held that it was a matter of definition that sense-data were private. One might as well maintain that it was a matter of definition that swans are white. One can, of course, define the word 'swan' in such a way that what is not white is not a swan, but all that would follow from this is that, if this swan-like bird in Australia was not white, it would not properly be called a swan. It would not follow that it did not exist or that it was not white.

It was also a misunderstanding of Price's view to reject it on the grounds that material objects cannot be inferred entities, as its critics supposed the sense-datum theory implied. Philosophers like the late Professor J. L. Austin argued that though when we see the marks of a pig's feet outside what looks like a sty, we *infer* the existence of the pig, if we see a pig in a good light in an environment in which finding pigs is not surprising, we do not. This may well be so. Such philosophers, however were assuming an exhaustive disjunction between *inferring* and *immediate acquaintance*. And though Price thought—as any sensible philosopher must—that we were not immediately acquainted with material objects, he did *not* think that the ones we saw were inferred entities, as anyone who had read beyond the first couple of chapters of *Perception* before criticising it would have known. Two lengthy chapters are devoted to explaining how we *do* know facts about material objects. The first chapter is about what Price called *perceptual acceptance*, the second about *perceptual assurance*. Price repeatedly says that such processes, so far from being inferential, simulated immediate intuition, though they were not forms of it.

Though Price was accused of excessive conservatism, his approach is in fact less conservative than the arch-conservatism of the linguistic philosophy of his time, which makes it difficult—and, it then tended to be supposed, reprehensible—to improve upon the enshrined wisdom of generations of language users. Fortunately the two ways of doing philosophy are not incompatible, as Price (though not always the linguistic philosophers themselves) realised. But the epistemological phenomenalism is more fundamental than the verbalism, because the interest in the words is only derivative from interest in what the words are used to talk about.

If the sense-datum theory was so true, the question arises: How has philosophy got on for the last fifty years without it? Part of the answer is that it has not got on without it. Philosophers have evasively attempted to say some of the things that the sense-datum theorists said, but do not use the word 'sense-datum', but some equally ugly circumlocution instead. The other part of the answer is that the intellectual loss caused by the rejection of the sense-datum theory has been enormous. If one rejects the sense-datum theory, there will be a large amount of philosophy that one will be unlikely to appreciate. One example of this is the brilliant Leibnizian theory of perception (which I shall mention again later) put forward by Bertrand Russell in *Mysticism and Logic* and *Our Knowledge of the External World*, according to which material objects consist of vast and complicated systems of unsensed sense-data (which Russell called unsensed *sensibilia*) organised in a six-dimensional space. If one thinks there are no sense-data, one will be unlikely to give this theory the attention it deserves.

The most popular physicalist alternative to the sense-datum theory is the view that perceiving is believing. Physicalists think they have no difficulty in admitting that there is such a thing as belief, because they think belief is just goal-seeking behaviour. Even an anti-missile missile can and does seek goals. The view that perceiving is believing will not, however, survive a moment's unprejudiced examination. If I believe that I am seeing the moon, it is *because* of what I see (a crescent-shaped patch in the middle of my visual field, which may or may not be identical with the physical surface of the moon) that I believe that I am seeing the moon. *Examining* the moon from different points of view is *obviously* different from forming beliefs about the moon as a *result* of examining it.

## Hume's Theory of the External World

Price's second book, *Hume's Theory of the External World*, published in 1940, was one of the best books on Hume ever written. Part of the reason for this is (oddly) its length. Most people writing about Hume, or any other philosopher, tend to reduce his work to a fraction of the original length, a procedure which one would think could be adopted successfully only when writing about a philosopher who was extremely verbose (which Hume was not). Such writers seem to aim at giving a moderately accurate account of the work of a great philosopher for those who do not have time to read him for themselves. In contrast, Price's book spends 230 pages discussing some 22 pages in the original text. Partly as a result, it provides some extremely lucid and helpful exposition, careful discussion and lucid criticism, combined with attempts to find for Hume a way out of the difficulties which he faces (some, but not all, of which Hume was aware of himself), and alternative solutions to the problems that occupied him. This is the critical and constructive spirit in which a great philosopher ought to be read and written about.

Price's book contains, among other things, a most lucid exposition of Hume's account of what induces us to believe in the existence of an external world, i.e., the *constancy* and *coherence* of our impressions. We believe in the existence of such a world because we come across sequences of sense-data—the view can be presented without using the word 'sense-data'—such as the following: (Ai) blazing fire, dying embers, ashes; (Bii) blazing fire, dying embers, gap; (Biii) blazing fire, gap, ashes; (Biv) gap, dying embers, ashes; (Cv) blazing fire, gap, gap; (Cvi) gap, dying embers, gap; (Cvi) gap, gap, ashes; (Dvii) gap, gap, gap; which are what Price aptly christened 'gap-indifferent'.

(A *constant* sequence of impressions, e.g.: blazing fire, blazing fire, blazing fire, is, Price pointed out, just a limiting case of *coherence*. There is no need for us ever to have observed a complete sequence; we could get on perfectly well without (i) above.)

When this happens we involuntarily, for nature has not left it to our choice whether we believe in the existence of body or not, fill in the gap in any sequence with impressions like those in the gaps in the relatively gapless series. (I think Price and Hume should have stipulated that this gap filling is involuntary only in relatively simple cases. Detectives experience notorious difficulties in filling in the gaps of certain sequences from a knowledge of what is observed at these sequences' ends.) Knowledge of gap indifference is inductive, but involves a kind of induction that precedes and is presupposed by inductive knowledge of the behaviour of material objects.

Hume's view had the odd consequence (which Hume accepted, though perhaps he was not consistent about it) that, since there could not *be* any unobserved impressions (for their existence was dependent upon the state of sense-organs), and bodies were composed entirely of impressions, there could not *be* any bodies. That there are material objects is a false and unfounded delusion, but nevertheless a delusion that is so useful—one would say 'useful for good biological reasons' were it not that evolutionary biology could not be true if there were no (living) bodies for it to be about—that we cannot live without it.

Hume thought that there could be no unobserved impressions because he thought (probably rightly) that impressions could not exist without the sense-organs of observers. Price, under the influence of logical positivism, takes a more extreme view than this. He holds that it is meaningless even to talk about unobserved impressions, because the existence of unobserved impressions is unverifiable, and, according to logical positivism, sentences which express no verifiable statement must be meaningless.

This argument is an example of the modal shift fallacy. Price thought that the existence of unobserved impressions (or unsensed sensibilia) was unverifiable, because they were (by definition) unobserved. They are no more incapable of being observed, however, than bachelors are incapable of being married. A bachelor is by definition, just unmarried, not unmarriageable, and it is actually easier to marry men who are bachelors than men who are not. The modal shift fallacy alluded to above is (for example) the mistake of confusing the true statement that it is necessarily the case that if a man is a bachelor he is unmarried, with the false statement that, if a man is a bachelor, then, necessarily, he is unmarried. (It also involves a model shift to suppose that the existence of desert islands is unverifiable.)

In order to understand Price's two shots at replacing Hume's view of material objects (which would, if they could exist, be composed of unobserved impressions) with a theory that did square with the verification principle, it is best to start with Russell. According to Russell, material objects were vast systems of unsensed sensibilia, which existed in 'perspectives'. There were six dimensions in space, because three independent co-ordinates were needed to determine the position of a sensibile in its perspective (a visual field would be an example of a perspective) and three more to fix the position of this perspective in perspective space. The position of a perspective was the position of its point of view; it was rather as if one were given the task of ordering photographs of, say, a Normandy landing beach, and ordered them three dimensionally by the laws of perspective and (when necessary) the laws of governing the reflection and refraction of light.

If, however, you think that it is meaningless to talk about unsensed sensibilia, it seems to follow that it is also meaningless to talk about material objects. The first of the two ways out of this difficulty suggested by Price is to say that the world is *as if* I was sitting in my study, even though there are no unobserved impressions of my study. The second (the one suggested to Price by the work of F.P. Ramsey) is to say that material object sentences are in fact not statements but recipes. That this is a dagger that I see before me is not a statement, but a recipe saying 'Use the (concept of) dagger as a means of ordering your experiences, and of predicting what other experiences you will have'.

Neither of these theories are satisfactory (and I do not suppose that Price thought they were; he was just playing with them for the light they threw on Hume's difficulties.) The first looks circular. If it is meaningless to say that there are unobserved daggers, then it ought to be equally meaningless to say that one's experience goes on as if there were unobserved daggers. (If the expression 'slithy tove' is meaningless, one's experience cannot go on as if there were such things.) The second is unsatisfactory because the word 'dagger' occurs in the recipe for ordering one's experience. But, if the word 'dagger' is meaningless, then the principle 'Order your experiences on the principle that what you see is a constituent of a dagger' ought to be meaningless to.

## Thinking and Experience

Price's third book, *Thinking and Experience* (1953), is a sequel to *Perception* in that it deals with thinking *about* an object, which usually takes place when the object is not present to be perceived. Since the object is itself then absent, we have to make do with a substitute for it. Such substitutes, at least in humans, are usually words.

Many modern philosophers hold that thinking is symbol using, and that we understand a word (say the word 'cat'), if we can (i) combine it correctly with other words, and (ii) say some such thing as 'Pleased to meet you, O cat' when introduced to one. Price has a much more sophisticated and complex theory. Though he agrees that understanding a word does not involve the mind's passing from it to something (the universal: cathood, say) he does not agree that the only thing necessary to understanding a word is to abe able to combine it correctly with other words, and to apply it correctly to objects – to call a spade a 'spade', for example.

Price's account of thinking is nominalistic in that though he thinks that thinking involves awareness of substitutes for the object, it does not involve a passage of the mind from the substitute to anything other than the substitute. It is *not* nominalistic in that Price does not think that thinking involves the use of *words*. One can think with images, in actions, in gestures, in producing replicas (my having a concept of a boat can be manifested by my drawing one or making one or making a model of one), in non-verbal symbols, and in interpreting things that are a sign of them. (Taking smoke as a sign of fire is a rudimentary form of thinking, and animals are capable of it.)

And though Price's theory is dispositional – one understands a word if a certain set of hypothetical propositions are true of one – it is not wholly dispositional. Seeing or hearing a word 'sub-activates' the disposition; for example, one sees the word 'cat', which sub-activates one's disposition to recognise cats. It thus *may* avoid a difficulty for most dispositional theories – that I seem to know what I mean by a word without having to wait to see what I apply it to. The sub-activation of a concept is an introspectable phenomenon that can be detected immediately.

Words would be no use if they were not linked to reality. Words are linked to reality, according to Price, by the fact that some of them can be ostensively defined, and others defined in terms of these. Though many modern philosophers seem to think that one ostensively defines a word by showing someone an example of what it applies to, Price correctly points out that one needs numerous examples. (Ideally, in order to explain to someone who did not know what is meant by 'scrige', one would have to show them a collection of objects to which the characteristic of being scrige was the only one which was both *common* and *peculiar*.) The linkage of the word to the thing it symbolises, however, is not the application of a *rule*. There have to be rules about linkage, but linkage is not itself *defined* in terms of rules, but is a matter of association. Pavlov's rather revolting dogs were not obeying rules when they salivated at the sound of a bell, but the bell meant food to them all the same.

Price thought (correctly) that *one* of the ways in which understanding words, and therefore thinking, manifested itself was in producing appropriate imagery. E.g., mental images of cats were produced by the word 'cats', and an image of a map of London could be produced by the word 'London'—and would, indeed, help one find one's way about that over-populated entity. (The fact that the image structurally resembles a map, that itself structurally resembles what is mapped, seems to show that it is an entity of some sort.) Unfortunately Price does not adequately distinguish between using an image *as* a symbol, and using images to *cash* symbols; the symbols cashed by images may or may not themselves be images.

Gilbert Ryle, however, had in *The Concept of Mind* argued that it is a myth that there was a kind of cinema screen of images in one's head. (Fellows of the Royal Society, Galton discovered, were very deficient in mental imagery, and the same may be true of Fellows of the British Academy). Mental images may well not be in the category of substance (see above), but there certainly are such things. I have enjoyed having them all my life and only a prejudice in favour of the material can have made philosophers so reluctant to admit their existence.

A more modern view is that when I say I have a mental image, I am saying that something is going on in my head that resembles what is going in my head when I see the object imaged. Where Hume held that images were faint copies of impressions, modern materialists hold that, when I *have* the image, what is going on in my head is a faint copy (or something like it) of the neural activity which goes on there when I actually perceive the object imaged. (One wonders how they know this.) But this makes the existence of images a matter for speculation, whereas there they are, visibly gyrating in front of one's nose. In any case, it is the images, not our *having* them, that is suitable for cashing symbols. It is the image of a pillar box, for example, not our having it, that has some claim to be red. Proponents of the theory make a category mistake in applying epithets such as red to our *having* them. Many modern philosophers seem to suppose that dreams, and so on, are simply a matter of our having false beliefs. But though, when I dream, I do have false beliefs, or at least suspend true ones, the imagery that accompanies this is not a matter of having a belief, and the beliefs I have *about* my imagery – that it is or is not in colour, for example – may be true ones.

My impression is that mental images are becoming respectable again. Indeed, anything can be made compatible with materialism, provided one goes through the now unhelpful verbal ritual of saying that it is identical with happenings to neurons, (however unlikely this may seem to be the case). I shall say more about this in the next section. But the world is what it is, and contains what it contains, a fact which philosophers too frequently seem to forget.

I suspect that one thing that is wrong with present (or perhaps with all) philosophy is the failure of philosophers to use mental images to cash their thoughts in the absence of the things talked about. It is this that Berkeley recommended, and what is essential if contemporary philosophers are not to use their very high degree of logical subtlety and technical efficiency in symbol manipulation to talk nonsense without knowing it. It is perhaps to take philosophy too seriously to suppose that it is the philosophical view that there are no images that prevent people from doing this, but, to the extent that it does, it does a great deal of harm. I believe that Price would have agreed with what I have just been saying.

## Belief

Once upon a time the two main theories of belief in Anglo-Saxon philosophy were that belief was a species of feeling and that it was a disposition to act. According to the first, one believes a proposition (say the proposition that one can control the tides) if one experiences a feeling of confidence in its truth when one has this proposition before one's mind. According to the second, one believes a proposition if one would (*if* one had the opportunity) act in a way that would be successful in obtaining what one happened to want *if* this proposition were true. One believes that one can control the tides, for example if, *if* one *wanted* to impress one's courtiers, one would in their presence tell the tides to turn with a view to impressing them. On the other hand, one believes that one can *not* control the tides if one would tell the tides to turn if one wanted to embarrass one's courtiers. The popularity of the latter theory has doubtless been partly due to the fact that a behaviourist has little difficulty (superficially, at any rate) in accommodating overt action into his world view.

The latter theory has, I think, won hands down. Those who accept it, however, have tended to suppose that belief is manifested only in public actions, like addressing the tides. Price, though he agreed that belief was a disposition, thought that action was only *one* of the ways in which this disposition manifested itself. Price held what might be described as a multi-dimensional theory of belief (*Belief, 1969*). He argued, I think correctly, that, besides action, belief manifested itself in feelings of confidence, in such things as a feeling of surprise if what one believed turned out to be false, a disposition to give mental assent to the proposition one believed, and a disposition to rely on what one believed in one's internal thoughts. One could use a proposition one believed as a premise in one's private reasoning, for example, and believe other things in consequence. Hence Price's theory of belief was dispositional without being materialist.

One way in which modern materialists could try to accommodate what, according to Price, are the internal manifestations of belief, is by saying that such things were just happenings to neurons. What one wants is some reason for thinking that feelings are identical with material things, and this usually turns out to be that there is some empirically discoverable concomitance between feelings and brain activity, or causal dependence of the former upon the latter.

Concomitance or causal connection, of course, is one thing, identity quite another. One common objection to their being identical is that mental things have properties that the physical things do not. A thought (i.e. an act of thinking) for example, can be painful, but a brain event grey – or, if not this, a happening to something that is grey. And it is obvious that if two things are identical, it cannot be the case that one has a property that the other lacks.

One reply to this objection is to say that the things alleged to be identical have their properties not just simpliciter, but *qua* certain descriptions. Hence one and the same thing can possess an attribute under the description 'brain process', and some characteristic apparently incompatible with this under the description 'mental event'. Hence identical things do share all their properties. (i) The mental event has both the property of being, *qua* mental event, *not* coloured, but *qua* brain process coloured, and (ii) the brain event has the property of being *qua* brain process coloured and *qua* mental event colourless. (Strictly speaking, of course, it does not make sense to say that brain *processes* are grey, though they could be processes undergone by grey things.)

This line of defence works much better for some properties than it does for others. Marguerite Blakeney both worshipped the Scarlet Pimpernel and despised her husband, though her husband, unknown to her, *was* the Scarlet Pimpernel. Any apparent contradiction may easily be resolved by saying that one and the same person was both worshipped by Marguerite *qua* 'Scarlet Pimpernel' and despised by her *qua* 'Marguerite's spouse'.

But this only works well where 'intentional' characteristics are concerned, for it is these that are affected by the knowledge and the beliefs of the person having the intentions. Had it been held that Sir Percy Blakeney was six feet tall under the description 'Scarlet Pimpernel', but, under the description 'Marguerite's husband', only five foot nine, this defence would have been much less plausible. Yet this is what we are expected to believe of brain processes when we say that, *qua* description 'material' they are grey (or more accurately, happenings to grey things), but *qua* description 'mental' they are not.

I recently listened to an American philosopher of some eminence who claimed to have believed for most of his philosophical life that there were no such thing as beliefs, but now to believe that there are such things. When views such as these become current, one wonders if philosophy has advanced at all since Price wrote, or whether it is just that so much is written that it is impossible to keep up with it without losing the insights of the past (or, indeed, at all). In these circumstances it seems folly to put pressure on academics to produce even more.

## Psychical Research

Professor D. H. Armstrong once described Psychical Research as a black cloud hanging over physicalism. Price would have agreed, though he did not think of psychical research as a *black* cloud. Price's sympathetic attitude to psychical research, though much denigrated, was shared with philosophers as eminent as Henry Sidgwick and C. D. Broad.

Price's attitude, I think, stems partly from his study of Hume. Hume argued that there was no necessary connection between events, and that it was just a matter of empirical fact what events were connected with one another. Antecedently to observation, anything might be connected with anything else. Hence it was just a question of empirical fact whether or not there were such things as telepathy, clairvoyance, telekinesis, and veridical communications from people claiming to be trance mediums. (*Hume's* problem with spirits of the departed would have been not to show that there *could* be disembodied spirits, so much as to show that we were not all disembodied, or at any rate *non*-embodied spirits.)

However Price, unlike Hume, did not attach enough weight to the *antecedent* improbability of such events. My own view is that it is not known that paranormal phenomena do not occur. Given that this is not known, it is a good thing, I think, that some philosophers take psychical research seriously. There is no need for philosophers to indulge in field work themselves. But some modifications to the world view of modern physics is necessary if the alleged facts of psychical research are to be accepted. It is perhaps over-optimistic to suggest that some philosophers might try their hands at thinking out what kind of modification would be necessary, if the alleged facts of psychical research were to be accepted. This would at least be a training in what is not certainly misplaced ingenuity. If no such modifications are possible, this would be some reason for rejecting the facts that *some* psychical researchers think psychical research has uncovered. If predictions could be deduced from these theories, then so much the better.

Price's interest in psychical research went with an interest in abnormal psychology. One of the things that Price thought that abnormal psychology showed was that there was not necessarily a one to one correspondence between mind and body. Sally Beauchamp's body, it is said, had no less than four minds connected with it or inhabiting it. Materialistic philosophers do not pay enough attention to such facts, which I (but not always they) think would present as much difficulty for them if they were merely possible as they would if they were actual. A lover of the bizarre like Price would doubtless have been distressed, as I am myself, to read that some psychiatrists think that the phenomena sometimes explained by multiple personality is in fact the result of female patients having been so anxious to please male doctors interested in finding cases of it that they faked the symptoms. They must have been very good actresses (or acting for the benefit of very gullible doctors).

## Religion

Price's attitude to psychical research was partly due to his religion. For example, there is a close resemblance (though by no means an identity) between the Christian belief in the efficacy of petitionary prayer and the alleged phenomenon of telekinesis, and a close connection between trance mediumship and resurrection. Nevertheless, Broad supposed that the World Beyond was not so much like heaven as like a Welsh university, but the advent of academic assessment might have made him revise this opinion.

Two Eddington Memorial Lectures were delivered at about the same time, one by Price, the other by Richard Braithwaite. One might say that what the latter claims is that one has faith if one acts in such a way as to bring about good, and encourages oneself by telling oneself (but not believing) stories about the Father, Son and Holy Ghost (whose likeness to the English aristocracy Braithwaite was acute enough to discern). Since the Father, Son and Holy Ghost become on this view fictional entities, propositions about them would have to be false or neither true nor false. I sometimes suspect that, in trying to sell this theory to devout Christians, Braithwaite was indulging in an impish joke.

Price threw the weight of justifying God's existence on our having a sense of the divine. He valued psychical research partly because, if it could show that modern science (or at least modern physics) was false, it removed an obstacle in the way of supposing that there was a sense of the divine; our sense of it could hardly be the result of impulses from a timeless spaceless entity falling upon receptor organs connected with our brains. Whether or not Price thought there could still be a sense of the divine, even if psychical research was *not* true, I do not know.

To a large extent Price's attitude to religion was empirical. There were in the Old and New Testaments certain recipes, and one found out whether they were successful by acting upon them, and seeing whether they worked. Hence one would have oneself to cultivate a sense of the divine, as I am sure Price did, before one could assess claims made on behalf of it. Christ, it is reported in the New Testament, said 'Knock, and it shall be opened unto to you'. Price, like a true empiricist, knocked, and found that, for him, it was.

JONATHAN HARRISON

*Note.* I am indebted to Professor Timothy Smiley for reading the print-out of this obituary, and saving me from making a large number of minor mistakes and one or two major ones. I am also indebted to Sir Isaiah Berlin, Mrs Pamela Huby and Caroline Dalton, archivist at New College, for information about the deceased and some helpful advice.

*Proceedings of the British Academy*, **80**, 493–498

# Ernest Gordon Rupp
# 1910–1986

THROUGH FENLAND FOG AND FROST on a winter morning, a headstone inscription to 'GORDON RUPP, F.B.A., D.D.' as 'METHODIST PREACHER' suggests recognition of some nineteenth-century minister rather than a Cambridge don professing Church History in the third quarter of the twentieth century. Albeit bleak, the epitaph nevertheless has validity because it proclaims the enigma of a remarkable individual in striking yet succinct language.

It was an early exercise in polemic that brought the Reverend Gordon Rupp a certain notoriety. In itself this is hardly a singular circumstance. Yet how appropriate that Chislehurst's Methodist Minister should trouble to provide so effective a defence of Martin Luther at a time when anything remotely German was decidedly unfashionable. Although produced with due deference to standards dictated by war-time economy, Rupp's slim tract – *Martin Luther, Hitler's Cause- or Cure?* – successfully debunked the debunker. Indeed, an appendix entitled 'The Art of Select Quotation' proved so effective an antidote to the dangerous distortions of primary-source material in the pages of his adversary, that Rupp's reputation as a Reformation scholar was established almost overnight. After a brief spell at Wesley House, he gained a Tutorship at Richmond College, Surrey (1947); and from there, by invitation of the Master and Fellows of Trinity, he visited Cambridge again to deliver, as Birkbeck Lecturer, a considered course on Luther. Rarely has a guest lecturer been instrumental in revising accepted academic opinion, University circles buzzing with 'the Reformation according to Rupp' to such an extent that Herbert Butterfield was asked for an assessment of the current Birkbeck course in the columns of *The Cambridge Review*. The article made good reading, and remains of relevance. For when addressing himself to the place of humour in the

E. G. RUPP

*Methodist Recorder*

lecturer's art, the Professor of Modern History wrote that Rupp 'takes us through darker tunnels and thornier paths, into worlds well beyond the frontiers of wise-cracking'.

With the publication of his *Studies in the Making of the English Protestant Tradition* later that same year, followed by *Luther's Progress to the Diet of Worms* in 1951, it was no surprise to find Gordon Rupp appointed Lecturer in Divinity at Cambridge from Michaelmas 1952. This post he held for four years, treating historians and theologians to stimulating classroom expositions covering the whole range of Reformation Studies. Meanwhile, those preferring written analysis applauded the appearance of the Birkbeck course, now suitably extended for publication, and a major work of Luther Studies in English as *The Righteousness of God* (1953). In this place it is appropriate to emphasize the sheer englishness of the monograph, Rupp, with characteristic modesty, later informing a research student privileged with confidences *de temps en temps*, that his work merely introduced to Karl Holl those who would not, or could not, *Deutsch sprechen*.

In 1956 the University of Manchester instituted a new Chair in Ecclesiastical History, inviting Dr Rupp to become the first incumbent. By permission of the Methodist Conference he was able to accept the proffered post, not only filling it with distinction for twelve years, but also playing a wider role of increasing importance in such a significant Northern city. The appointment was a triumph, but if the eighteenth-century patronage of Norman Sykes had secured Rupp to be the first professor, the Cambridge upstart initially experienced such a hard time from an ambitious Senior Lecturer that, apart from the enjoyment work with the Free-Church Colleges brought him, Rupp found little comfort in work among the dark Satanic mills. Sykes's second *coup* thus helped his pupil almost more than the first, the creation of another Church History chair translating the troublesome Bishop Fraser Senior Lecturer, one Clifford Dugmore, to King's, London, in 1958. Gaining what he once described as 'a second wind', Rupp was at last able to get to grips with his real Manchester assignment, and quite apart from teaching Reformation Studies in the Department of History, became Dean of the Faculty of Theology (1961 & 1962), and, from 1966, held office as Public Orator to the University. That he also continued to work closely with the many Theological Colleges adorning Manchester in those days, explained the return to Cambridge of a man whose wide experience the Methodist Conference intended to use when he was appointed Principal of Wesley House (1967).

Shortly afterwards, the mantle of his mentor Norman Sykes fell upon him when the Electors chose Rupp as Dixie Professor of Ecclesiastical History in succession to Dr W. O. Chadwick. In fact, 1968 proved something of an *annus mirabilis*, for it was in June that Gordon Rupp was elected

President of Conference by a body of some six hundred Methodist Ministers and Laymen at the Central Hall, Westminster. After chairing the actual Conference session, a year of itinerant visitation of Methodist Districts throughout the length and breadth of the land followed, coupled of course with chairmanship of the Church's Central Committees. It was a demanding period requiring rare reserves of stamina and talent, but a time made altogether memorable by the President's revelations of wisdom and wit at new-style 'Teach-in' sessions designed to challenge and encourage the sect's faithful in the 'Good Old Cause'. On such occasions Gordon Rupp was evidently and effortlessly at home with all types of congregation—northern industrial 'ex-Primitive', London suburban, remote and rural, school and University. Possessed of consummate pastoral skills, as a preacher he could play on every kind of audience almost at will. In a trice sober men and women were thus led through helpless mirth at aspects of the human situation to an adoring meditation of the Christ Who inspired and confirmed them in the faith. Ten years on (1978) he would publish *The Sixty Plus & Other Sermons* and the briefest sampling of such homilies explains his pulpit approach and appeal. But in 1968 there were also sorrows to endure, for that year brought Rupp, just as much as Archbishop Michael Ramsey, considerable personal grief when the Church of England chose to ignore its leadership and reject the unity proposals for healing the schism with Methodism. Undaunted, however, Principal Rupp was well placed in Cambridge to achieve much in microcosm by encouraging dispirited students to play an active part building up a united theological college—to be known as the Cambridge Federation—based in Jesus Lane.

For some considerable time Dr Rupp had been in demand as a speaker at ecumenical conferences, and it was certainly appropriate that, in addition to the honorary doctorates and fellowships that now came his way, the ex-President of Conference should gain recognition as a Member of the Central Committee of the World Council of Churches. If colleagues in the Cambridge Faculties of History and Divinity sometimes bemoaned the absence of the Dixie Professor at academic boards, it was because his impish reserve invariably denied them any insight or reference to his world-wide involvement. The only complaint lesser mortals could reasonably make about Rupp was Samuel Johnson's critique of a Wesley so busy that he never found the time to 'fold his legs and have his talk out'. At Manchester Professor Rupp had done the work of two men; and *Alma Mater Cantab.* demanded even more of him. With the publication of *Patterns of Reformation* (1969), the Dixie afforded Reformation Studies another substantial work of scholarship, in particular bringing a much-needed balance and sanity to the historian's understanding of sixteenth-century religious radicalism. At Wesley House too, a College now transformed by the generous benefaction of the Rank Building and the enhanced community life thus symbolized, the counsel and vision of the Principal and his wife proved crucial in the implementation of the new training scheme for ordinands. Likewise, the higher reaches of ecumenical involvement continued to take their toll, so that if Professor Rupp was missed one Thursday because he was lecturing in the United States of America, absence the following week could be explained in terms of a visit to an Iron Curtain country. It might seem that he who once termed Erasmus 'the original flying Dutchman' was himself fast becoming something of a fleeting ecumenical vision. Yet in fact Cambridge, just as much as Manchester, gave full scope for the old priorities, regular evenings being set aside when Gordon and Marjorie attended their local church Bible class. As for retirement, Rupp had a Canterbury vision, for, a citizen of *Ave Mater Angliae*, Martin, only son of his marriage to Marjorie Edith (née Hibbard), was himself happily married with a family of three, with twins in the Cathedral Choir School. In Canterbury, too, was a little-used accession—the Weimar *Ausgabe* no less—in the Library of the University of Kent.

But the vision was never realized and Rupp's last years denied the man, like many a productive scholar, an Autumn of mellow fruitfulness. If his scholarly circle paid him tribute with a *Festschrift (Christian Spirituality*, edited by his pupil Peter Newman Brooks) as early as 1975, Rupp's death in 1986 prompted much comment on a man whose wider ministry touched a full spectrum of lesser mortals. On the whole, he was a man who wrote theological history—for many nowhere better than in his last 'big book', *Religion in England, 1688–1791*, a Clarendon Press study of a period in which, because of the origins of Methodism, he had regularly dabbled and held almost as dear as the Reformation itself. But reports of his unexpected death submitted Rupp to the widest social comment. Already known for his silence (or absence) at formal Faculty and College meetings in Cambridge, his reputation for participation elsewhere now became apparent. He had, it transpired, been acute as an observer for Methodism at Vatican II, and a leading Roman Catholic ecumenist noted that 'he spoke with such a sense of affection for the people he was talking to . . . yet we knew he could not attend a lot because of Marjorie's grave illness'. Nor was his comment uncritical, for the same witness found himself in shock when Rupp 'launched into a spell-binding exposition of the origins of controversy over the Eucharist; and throughout . . . the leading American Methodist sat in an armchair reading the *New York Times*!'

Like the two words engraved on that headstone in the Cambridge City Cemetery, such a spotlight reveals the man's commitment to the early principles of his sect. He had, after all, undergone ministerial training at Wesley House when men like Maldwyn Hughes and Newton Flew exerted powerful sway to mould the Christian witness of many. Such tutelage surely spawned both spoken and preached words, not to mention those Ruppian references to 'our hymns' or 'our doctrines'. For example, an early Epworth Press essay, *Protestant Catholicity* (1960), made it clear that albeit Protestant and reformed by commitment, Rupp was well aware that Protestantism and Catholicism meant much the same to their adherents. It was therefore liberalism he loathed, to make throughout his life a consistent and steadfast stand for orthodoxy, and to deplore contemporary emphases on a social gospel preached out of context for its own sake. As for 'Liberation theology', he once confided that such teaching could all be contained on the back of a postcard. For if Rupp wished to criticize, he invariably turned to satire, and the misused wealth of some American Methodists he readily lampooned as being far from the spirit of the founder.

No memoir can indicate the full dimensions of such a man, and if he wrote a lot, a book of the wit and wisdom of Gordon Rupp himself could make compelling reading. Although rarely worth the candle, so to state, archbishops, particularly of Canterbury, seem to command biographies. Despite the sensitive assessment of Gordon Wakefield and Ben Drewery in press and from pulpit therefore, in a century when the faith itself is under threat, Rupp is a far more significant subject for such treatment. Yet it is unlikely that such consideration will come his way, and what he once termed a 'Maitlandism' as he prepared to address the Downing Historical Society, should surely apply. The lines in question ran:

> Lives of great men all remind us
> As we o'er their pages turn
> That we often leave behind us
> Letters we had better burn.

P. N. BROOKS
*Robinson College, Cambridge*

*Note.* For re-used material in this essay, due acknowledgement goes to the S.C.M. Press for understanding and permission.

*Proceedings of the British Academy*, **80**, 499–508

# Jocelyn Mary Catherine Toynbee
# 1897–1985

JOCELYN TOYNBEE was, formally speaking, an art historian of the Roman imperial period. As such she played a significant role (in this country the leading role) in a movement which demonstrated the high quality that its artists could achieve. At the same time she firmly asserted, against some contemporaries in continental Europe, that continuity of Greek artistic traditions, increasingly integrated with those of Rome, was at its heart. Her fundamental interests, however, were the life and culture of the Roman Empire as an *oikoumene* and its evolution into the Christian world. The Empire was, for her, a *praeparatio evangelica*, although in practice she found it no less worthy of serious study in itself than for what it was to become. From its works of art she sought to read the conceptions of those who commissioned them as well as of those who made them; but came to recognise that there was much to be learnt also from the products of bungling craftsmen who would, in a mainly illiterate society, use much the same 'picture-language'. In consequence she gave time, very productively, to quite indifferent, even bad artefacts, working on them, as she did on the best art, *con amore*. The loving detail in which she examined objects was regularly noted by reviewers, together with the succinct and sometimes lightly humorous language in which she brought them vividly before the reader's mind. Equally helpful were the artistic parallels, the literary evidence, the context in political, social and cultural history which she sought to give them. But the detail was always disciplined and syntheses presented with marked lucidity were also characteristic features of her publications.

She cared for her subject in the conviction of its relevance to contemporary society, and was willing, therefore, to devote herself to teaching as well as to research; and she spoke and wrote frequently not only for academics

J. M. C. TOYNBEE

*B. Gaye*

but for a wider public too. She was ready to discuss with anyone interested, however young or untrained, giving generously of time and being entirely unprofessorial in her manner to them, drawing them into the search for understanding with her. Scholarship she believed to be an international undertaking and that was well illustrated by the correspondence in which she exchanged information with classical archaeologists throughout the world; but her links were especially close with Romano-British and with early Christian archaeologists. To both these groups her vigorous sympathy and her immense knowledge both of the monuments of the centre of the Empire and of those on other peripheries than the north west European—pagan and Christian alike – revealed a new dimension.

Much of her relevant family background was described in the obituary for her brother (Arnold Toynbee, Proc. Brit. Acad. 63 [1977] 441f.). She was the daughter of Harry Volpy Toynbee, a Secretary of the Charity Organisation Society, and of Sarah Edith Marshall Toynbee, a historian and teacher of history. Her childhood memories went back to a sight of Queen Victoria from a pram. What she said of her nursery days sounded typical for an Edwardian child; and she kept in touch with her school (Winchester High School, now St. Swithun's, Winchester) in a manner which certainly indicated that she had been happy there. Given that her father's health broke down when she was still very young, the influence of her mother was paramount at this stage. Edith Toynbee had been a student at Newnham College, and was placed (notionally) in the first class of the Cambridge Historical Tripos, along with a Newnham contemporary, on the first occasion when a woman achieved that distinction. She taught history before her marriage and for a time, but to a lesser extent, after it too, subsequently helped to organise the papers of Florence Nightingale and, later on, transcribed manuscripts in the Bodleian. Her patent love of historical study was communicated to her children, who, all three, Arnold, Jocelyn and Margaret, became professional historians. Her Newnham record adds that she had a great capacity for enjoyment, an appreciation of the amusing, a charm that won her many friends. In all this too Jocelyn Toynbee was recognisably Edith's daughter; for she took an evident delight in academic work, but also, at the proper time, in many other things, for instance in the company of friends, in young children, with whom she easily established a good rapport, in works of art of all periods, in beautiful country, in her animals (especially her cats), in light and colour (the purple jacket provided for her book *Death and Burial in the Roman World*, the elegant grey for Howard Scullard's book on elephants in the same series, gave her very real pleasure); she was a welcoming hostess, a good guest, a delightful travelling companion (although her indefatigability on a site could leave many in a state of exhaustion); and her sense of humour surfaced in her conversation on social occasions as well as in her writing and her lectures (but she felt quite strongly that it was not the first business of a lecturer to amuse).

In 1916 she went, like her mother, to Newnham, but, like her brother, chose Classics for her subject. She obtained first classes in both parts of the Classical Tripos, having taken the archaeological papers in Part II in 1919. There followed one year with a research award from the college, one as an assistant mistress in Classics at Cheltenham Ladies' College, and then an appointment to be tutor in Classics at St. Hugh's College, Oxford. That post she resigned in 1924 on a point of principle connected with the government of the college, but soon afterwards became a lecturer in the Classics Department of the University of Reading. In 1927 she returned to Cambridge as lecturer and director of studies in Classics at Newnham. In 1930 she was awarded the D.Phil. degree at Oxford, with a dissertation which became her first book (*The Hadrianic School*, 1934). From 1931 she was a lecturer in the Cambridge Classical Faculty and combined the University and College posts until her election to the Laurence Chair of Classical Archaeology in 1951. She held the Chair, in combination with a Professorial Fellowship at Newnham, until 1962 when, on completion of 42 years of teaching, she retired in order to have more time for research. She then became an Honorary Fellow of Newnham, but moved to live with her sister in what had been their mother's house in Oxford. There she was vigorously engaged for more than twenty years longer in research, in writing, in lecturing, in discussion with colleagues, in the supervision of graduate students.

In the years from 1919 to 1951 she had also received a number of research awards from Newnham and, in 1938, the Susette Taylor Travelling Fellowship of Lady Margaret Hall, Oxford. These enabled her to travel abroad in many vacations and occasionally for longer periods, and so to collect much new material for her articles and books while laying the foundations for her many friendships with foreign scholars. Her visits to Rome were especially dear to her and especially fruitful. They brought her, for one thing, into contact with Eugénie Strong, that grande dame of the contemporary archaeological and social life of Rome, whose appreciation of Roman imperial art was an encouragement and a stimulus to her. Mrs Strong's impact may be gauged in some degree from the obituary that she wrote of her (Antiquaries' Journal 33 [1943] 188–9) and, much later, from the dedication of her book *The Art of the Romans* ([1965] 14); and it should be noted that what she said of Mrs Strong's generosity in sharing knowledge and in drawing the beginner into discussion on apparently equal terms is what her own students and friends have said of her. At the same time these visits were of considerable importance to her deeply-felt religious life; and she became a convert to the Roman Catholic Church. That was a change that undoubtedly fostered her image of the Roman Empire as an *oikoumene* and, at the same time, quickened her interest in early Christian archaeology.

When she began her research the predominant sympathies of Classical art historians in this country were with Greek art. She chose a Roman subject, influenced in part, no doubt, by the more positive view of Roman art emerging in continental Europe (its most vigorous proponent for English-speakers being Mrs Strong) and by the work on Roman imperial coin-types undertaken by Harold Mattingly at the British Museum. It must have required courage to strike out into a field which her teachers regarded with something like contempt, to present it, in fact, as 'a chapter in the history of Greek art' (so the subtitle of *The Hadrianic School*). Unlike some contemporary protagonists for Roman art, she rejected for the imperial period any stress on Italic influences and any antithesis of Greek and Roman. She believed that the Greek tradition was an essential element in Roman art but one integrated into the Roman tradition and freely contributing to the visual expression of Roman concepts. Her choice of the Hadrianic period for her first work was made partly in reaction against those who saw in it no more than an artificial, barren and temporary attempt at revival of classical Greek art and partly because of her conviction that Hadrian himself brought to maturity an idea of the Roman empire as one world which was very notably expressed in the types of his 'province series' of coins. She focussed initially on the numismatic field, so that coin types were the subject of her earliest articles, and the main feature in *The Hadrianic School*; while the closely related medallion types formed the whole subject of her second book (*Roman Medallions*, 1944) as also of a projected third for which she began to collect material but which she never wrote. She had as a result a considerable reputation as a numismatist and was a Fellow and Medallist of the Royal Numismatic Society and a Medallist of the American Numismatic Society. Her concern was always essentially with coins as the media for visual messages and not as monetary units. She might nowadays be held to have been over confident that emperors played a leading part in the choice of types; but her powers of minute observation and her sense of the historical context of the issues that she studied gave her work a permanent value; and unlike many numismatists of her time she set the types in the context of similar or relevant representations in other artistic media. She was able to present them, therefore, as embodying not only the political and the cultural but also certain artistic principles of their period. The book became the standard treatment – and is still the major one available – of personifications in the art of the Roman imperial world.

But *The Hadrianic School* was not limited to a study of personifications in coin types. As a foil or contrast to the official art which they embodied she took also a number of contemporary examples of private art, choosing mainly sarcophagi and altars, in which, she held, the same artistic principles were illustrated in the service of individuals. It is apparent that everything that she had to say rested on extensive study of very many monuments of all kinds, sculpture in the round as well as relief, painting, mosaic, metal work, coins, gem-cutting etc.; and apart from her overall conclusions she made significant additions to the criteria which could be used for dating individual pieces and to the detail of their interpretation. Notably she included a discussion, sympathetic and sensible, of the substitution of inhumation for cremation as the normal method of burial in the second century AD.

The themes treated in these two books remained of importance to her all her life and recur in other books and in many articles. For her major conclusions she offered a series of complementary studies. In *Some Notes on Artists in the Roman World* (1951) she collected literary and epigraphic as well as some archaeological evidence to show that the majority of known artists in the Roman world were Greeks or Greek-speakers; and despite the discovery of new evidence the collection remains useful (but see below). In *Roman Portrait Busts* (1953), an exhibition catalogue, she presented a brief but comprehensive account of Roman portrait sculpture in which again she argued for a marriage of Greek and Roman traditions. In her British Academy Lecture, *The Ara Pacis Reconsidered* (1953) she treated in vivid detail one of the earliest of the great surviving historical reliefs of Rome in which Greek artistic traditions and Roman concepts were successfully combined. In her Charlton Lecture for King's College, Newcastle upon Tyne, *The Flavian Reliefs of the Palazzo della Cancelleria in Rome* (1957) she threw light on another work of the same general type which falls in the gap between the Ara Pacis and the period which had occupied her in *The Hadrianic School*.

But with the continuity of interest went also variety. When she returned to Italy after the interruption of the Second World War she found new stimuli, very especially in the excavations under the basilica of St. Peter's at Rome, and new archaeological friends, among them John Ward Perkins, by that time Director of the British School at Rome, to turn her mind in new directions. She began almost at once the joint work with Ward Perkins which was to make an account of the Vatican excavations available to the educated public, *The Shrine of St. Peter and the Vatican Excavations* (1956), a book still illuminating, although not now wholly up to date following recent systematisation of the material excavated. This and her participation in the first expedition which Ward Perkins and Kathleen Kenyon mounted in Tripolitania in 1948 gave her much closer experience of archaeological field work than hitherto and a sharper awareness of its potential importance in the interpretation of monuments. That awareness remained with her and informed the studies of Romano-British monuments which, with early Christian antiquities, became prominent themes in her subsequent work.

She had always taken an interest in Roman Britain (coins representing Britannia were the subject of her first articles) and lectured on it regularly in Cambridge. Her bibliography now shows an increasing number of articles on objects deriving from Romano-British contexts, and her programme included an increasing number of discussions, in person or by post, about newly excavated objects or puzzling ones already in museums. She began a book in which she planned to discuss the whole corpus of Roman works of art found in Britain and had completed a first draft when the Society for the Promotion of Roman Studies decided to celebrate its fiftieth anniversary in 1960 by an exhibition devoted to such objects. She put aside her draft, accepted heavy involvement in the undertaking and wrote the catalogue (*Art in Roman Britain,* 1962).

That book was, in itself, an important contribution to Romano-British studies, but also to those on the whole North-western group of provinces within which Britain was one element, and indeed to those of the whole Roman world. In it, taken with the resumed book *Art in Britain under the Romans* (1964), she made another step forward in the understanding of many individual pieces, but above all transformed our picture of Roman provincial society and culture in the west and of the complex interplay of central and local influences in art. She envisaged transmission of central concepts and traditions to the peripheries by a combination of the movement of actual works of art (in the equipment of Roman officials, for instance, in the cargoes of merchants, in the looting hands of marauding natives) and of travelling artists, probably supplied with pattern books, who might employ local men as apprentices, as well as the assistants whom they brought with them; she did not probe the psychology either of the transmitters or of the recipient peoples. She became at this period more conscious that locally born artists might play a part of their own in the artistic development of a province, and had she revised *Some Notes on Artists* . . . she would, surely, have given them a greater part in it; although, in the final resort, she would still—without doubt—have maintained that Greek artistic traditions and imperial Roman ideas were the fundamentals. Her current positions over a much wider area of Roman art were set out in a third book designed primarily for a less academic readership (*The Art of the Romans*, 1965). It is full of insights, comprises a remarkable combination of central Roman with provincial art, of public and official with private, and often modest, monuments; but rather much has been packed into the limited format of the series in which it was published, so that it is less satisfying to its readers.

During this period too the excavation of the London Mithraeum led her to a very thorough study of Mithraic monuments throughout the Roman Empire as a basis for her publications of the objects found there and she became an acknowledged authority in this field too. Her definitive publication of the sculptures found there was not finally published (through delays which were not of her causing) until after her death (*The Roman Art Treasures from the Temple of Mithras*, 1986). She followed with interest the more theoretical studies of those who subsequently began to treat the cult in the light of non-classical parallels, but did not herself participate in them.

Still more of an impulse came from the Christian finds of such sites as Lullingstone and Hinton St. Mary, and from her reaction to a series of articles published mainly in the *Jahrbücher für Antike und Christentum* which rejected the widely accepted Christian interpretation of a number of motifs used in late antique art. Her article *Christianity in Roman Britain* (1953) was both a thorough and a well-balanced survey of the Christian or possibly Christian monuments in the province but is now, inevitably, out of date in the light of new discoveries. Her reviews of the sceptics (in a series of volumes of *The Journal of Theological Studies* published in the sixties) were vigorous assertions of the existence of arguments against them. It is hardly surprising that her own Christian convictions are particularly apparent in her work on Christian monuments, leading her sometimes into very sensitive interpretations although sometimes, perhaps, into larger claims than can be sustained; but normally she gave the evidence against her view as well as her own arguments for it, and she maintained her independence of judgment in the academic field (she was, for instance, sharply critical of the Vatican's acceptance of the bones found beneath the high altar in the necropolis under St. Peter's as those of Peter himself). As with her work on pagan monuments her great achievement was in the detailed discussion of the objects she treated and the learning with which she set them in a context—the whole relevant artistic corpus of the Roman empire, pagan as well as Christian. In 1984 the value of this achievement was recognised by the award of the Frend Medal for Christian Archaeology by the Society of Antiquaries of London. It was the latest and probably the most treasured of her honours.

In retirement she continued to work on all these themes and picked up again some aspects of the monuments which she had previously treated as subsidiary. Thus in *Death and Burial in the Roman World* (1973) she focussed fully on funerary monuments and practices which had made a minor appearance in many earlier books. The result is a very thorough account of what survives and an invaluable basis for further work which would bring in the anthropological parallels on which she did not draw. *Animals in Roman Life and Art* (1973) was more of a parergon, the result of incidental although very sharp observations made over the years because of the pleasure which she herself took in animals; it is nicely dedicated to her cat Mithras, scourge of hapless visitors to her Oxford house. *Roman Historical Portraits* (1978) again picked up something treated earlier in a more summary way, but she had less to say in it that was new and it is perhaps the least effective of her books. She also devoted time and energy to the committee for the British volumes of the *Corpus Signorum Imperii Romani*, of which she was secretary from 1964 and chairman from 1967; those involved with her were very conscious that it was not for lack of effort on her part that the project moved slowly. Another 'cause' into which she threw herself wholeheartedly was the publication of the book *Roman Art* left in first draft by Professor Donald Strong at his sudden death in 1973; that entailed the laborious selection of the illustrations as well as the tidying up of the manuscript. She continued to write articles on specific items or groups of them, informatively and helpfully, well into the eighties (several appeared only after her death); and she never ceased to be interested in new finds and new ideas. In later years increasing deafness made it unprofitable for her to attend lectures, but she always maintained a capacity to communicate with one visitor or a few, and seized eagerly on journals brought to her by her sister and many friends in the nursing-home in which she spent her last years.

Many of her very considerable number of publications were produced against the background of a real commitment also to her College and to her Faculty as well as to a number of learned Societies, notably the Society of Antiquaries of London, the Society for the Promotion of Roman Studies (of which she was a Vice-President from 1946 and always a much valued advisor to the Editorial Committee), and the British School at Rome (for which she was Chairman of the Faculty of Archaeology, History and Letters from 1954 to 1958). She did not much care for administration, but saw that it was necessary (in moderation) and tackled what fell to her share very briskly, 'in order to save time for better things'; normally, indeed, she replied to letters by return of post. Not surprisingly she knew how to delegate. On committees she presented firm ideas succinctly and lucidly expressed, the more tellingly because she spoke without rancour and from a strong sense of humanity as well as of principle. With her colleagues she was co-operative and generous; it is hard to imagine a better predecessor to have, so determined not to look over her shoulder, so willing to support innovation (and even enjoy it), so sensitive with advice when it was needed. With students she had a rather special relationship. She taught with devotion. Indeed, although forbidden by the University regulations of the time to supervise undergraduates after she became a professor, she provided them with opportunities for meeting her which it was not easy to distinguish from supervisions. In Newnham she was one of a select number of dons whose proximity at the dinner table was welcomed by all for she had the faculty of stimulating the sophisticated (despite the somewhat austere and unfashionable first impression she made) as well as of encouraging the shy to converse. Moreover for many years it was her custom to offer in her room simple entertainment and serious discussion (often on religious issues) and the occasions are still remembered with pleasure by sceptical scientists as well as others who attended them.

She received many appropriate honours, becoming FSA in 1943, FBA in 1952, Hon.D.Litt. at Newcastle upon Tyne in 1967 and at Liverpool in 1968; as well as receiving the medals already noted for her work as a numismatist and as a Christian archaeologist.

Very shortly before her death she told a friend that she thought that she had completed all the research projects that she had had on hand; and indeed her papers showed that to be true. She was, of course, a child of her generation, some of whose ideas are no longer much in vogue. But what she did rested on a very sound basis of perceptive as well as of thorough scholarship and provided springboards from which others were already moving in new directions well before she died. It continues to have its effect on current scholarship.

J. M. REYNOLDS
*Fellow of the British Academy*

*Note.* I have received information and help from many friends, notably Professors R. M. Crook, S. S. Frere, R. M. Harrison, G. B. Waywell, J. J. Wilkes, Drs D. N. Ager, J. M. Huskinson, M. W. Stanier, S. M. Walker, R. J. A. Wilson.